AF269669

Errol Flynn

Errol Flynn

the
Illustrated Life Chronology

ROBERT FLORCZAK

LYONS PRESS
Guilford, Connecticut

LYONS
PRESS

An imprint of Globe Pequot, the trade division of The Rowman & Littlefield Publishing Group, Inc.
4501 Forbes Blvd., Ste. 200
Lanham, MD 20706
www.rowman.com

Distributed by NATIONAL BOOK NETWORK

British Library Cataloguing in Publication Information available

Library of Congress Cataloging-in-Publication Data available

ISBN 978-1-4930-4921-9 (hardcover: alk. paper)
ISBN 978-1-4930-4922-6 (e-book)

The paper used in this publication meets the minimum requirements of American National Standard for Information Sciences—Permanence of Paper for Printed Library Materials, ANSI/NISO Z39.48-1992.

Image Credits

(TL: top left, CL: center left, BL: bottom left, TR: top right, CR: center right, BR: bottom right, BC: bottom center)
All images in this book are from the collection of the author and are believed to be in the public domain except for those noted below:
Bonny Cother: 276BR. Josef, Fegerl: 22BL; 23BR; 45BR; 48TL; 54TL, BL; 58TL; 78BL; 191CR; 264TL, TR; 289BR; 290TL. Jose Luis Garcia, Garcia: 55 BR; 56BL; Volker Knies: 252TL. Library of Congress (Hollywood Starland Map): 31; Thomas, McNulty: 17TL; 19CR; 27BR. Joseph Musso: 63BR; 123TR; 191BR. Profiles In History: 34TC. Errol, Reichow: 304CL. Estate of Ron Shedlo: 278BL; 294BL; 299TR, TC; 301BR; 302BL, TR; 303TR, BR. Dr. Mary Leonide Sipski: 12CL, BC, BR; 13TR, CR, BR; 14TL, BL, BR. Photofest: 35BL; 39; 62BL; 301TL. Courtesy of Turner Entertainment Company, Warner Bros. Inc.: 28BL; 30TL; 32CL; 42BL; 100BL; 103BR; 104CL1, BL; 105 CL; 113 CR1, CR2, BR; 114 CL; 122 TL; 124 TR1, TR2; 131 TR; 136 TL; 148 TL; 165 TR; 167 TR; 170 TL2, CL2, BL2; 184 BL; 187 TR, CR; 193 CR1, CR2; 194 BL; 195 CL, TR, CR1, CR2, CR3, BR; 199 TR; 210 BL; 244 TR; 286 BL; 288 TR. Pete and Pam Weakland: 34CL.

The author regrets any unintentional oversight in properly crediting images and will be happy to apply the correct acknowledgments in future editions.

CONTENTS

Acknowledgments....6

Introduction......................7

The Why of Errol Flynn..........9

ChapterOne South Pacific Adventures, 1909-1933..11

ChapterTwo England, 1933-1934......................................24

ChapterThree Rising Star, 1935-1938......................................31

ChapterFour Star On High, 1939-1942......................................84

ChapterFive Troubled Waters, 1943-1948......................................142

ChapterSix Adrift, 1949-1953......................................206

ChapterSeven Falling Star, 1954-1959......................................259

Epilogue......................................310

Appendix I - The 1933 New Guinea Diary..........311

Appendix II - The 1937 Spanish Civil War Diary....313

Annotated Bibliography......................................316

Index......................................317

Acknowledgments

Though *Errol Flynn: The Illustrated Life Chronology* could have been completed in some manner by my hand alone, its present thoroughness would have been impossible without the help of a number of expert and generous souls.

First and foremost are **Inga Klein** in Germany and **Topper MacKay** in Las Vegas. Their keen knowledge of the subject, impressive collections, and generosity of time, materials, and effort toward the book have been incomparable. My utmost gratitude to them both.

The late and eminent Hollywood historian **Rudy Behlmer** looked over each and every one of the approximately 2,500 pages of the original manuscript as I produced them, made notes and corrections, and shared them over memorable lunches he made of peanut butter & jelly sandwiches and beer! Thanks to Rudy for the advice, the memorable anecdotes, and the Flynn film scores he would regularly and perfectly hum!

At the USC/Warner Bros. Archives, **Sandra Joy Aguilar, Jonathon Auxier**, and **Brett Service** tirelessly provided me with every scrap of paper on Flynn that the collection houses.

At the USC Cinematic Arts Library, **Ned Comstock**, who has probably been acknowledged in more books on Hollywood than any other archive librarian, garners another one here for his immeasurable assistance concerning Flynn's films at Universal, as well as Jack Warner's personal papers.

At the Margaret Herrick Library, **Stacey Behlmer** provided me with much personal material on Flynn in the library, including the papers of Ronnie Shedlo, Flynn's secretary/assistant in the actor's final three years of life.

My gratitude also to **Josef Fegerl** in Austria for the use of the photos he personally acquired from Flynn's close friend Dr. Hermann Erben; to **Kevin McAleer** for his immense help in editing the text of the essays, chapter introductions, and letters; to **Karen Figilis** for inviting me into her home in the Hollywood Hills where Flynn and his wife Lili Damita first lived; to **Dory** and **Isaac Soffer** for inviting me into their home in Beverly Hills where Flynn lived in the late 1930s and early 1940s; to **Connie Nelson**, who showed me through Flynn's beloved Mulholland house while Rick Nelson lived there; to **Errol Reichow**, who invited me to the house of his late father, Flynn's close friend Otto Reichow, where *Life* magazine photographed Flynn ten days before the actor died; to **Mike Fratatoni**, who personally toured me through the Los Angeles Hall of Justice where the infamous double rape trial took place; to **Terry Odem,** who first took me up to see Flynn's Mulholland house, lending her camera for me to take shots of the house, and making darkroom prints of those photos which are now included in this book; and to **Wallace Berry Jr.**, **Steven Bingen**, **Ron Fisher**, **Delvan Irwin**, **Gregory Maradei**, the late **Trudy McVicker**, **Tom McNulty**, **Joe Musso**, **Patti Marruchella O'Hara**, **Marc Wanamaker** and Bison Archives, and **Lynn Wilson** for enthusiastic support and encouragement along the way.

Lastly, a very special and heartfelt thank you to **Dr. Mary Leonide Sipski** who, while doing medical work in Adelaide, Australia, made several trips to Hobart, Tasmania especially for me. There she exhibited her pluck by knocking on the doors of Flynn's boyhood homes, getting herself invited in, and taking pictures in and around those premises, producing photographs the likes of which have never been seen in any other book on Errol Flynn. Some of the fruits of her photographic adventures are displayed in chapter 1.

Introduction

This book is not a biography in the strictest sense. There are already more than enough Errol Flynn monographs (at least thirty, as I write), some of them excellent, many not. This book is something very different: a day-by-day visual scrapbook of Flynn's life, presenting the events as they unfolded, through hundreds of photos, documents, and factual data, absent this author's personal editorializing. The reader is free then to absorb the book either page by page, or to casually leaf through, stopping at whichever spread might strike the eye and interest.

Errol Flynn: The Illustrated Life Chronology has been over ten years in the making, but in reality it has been decades. I first saw Flynn on the big screen on November 13, 1972, at the old TLA movie theater in Philadelphia *(left)*, a double feature of CAPTAIN BLOOD and THE ADVENTURES OF ROBIN HOOD. I was thoroughly captivated that night and soon after acquired my first of thousands of items about the star.

My deepening interest in the subject of Flynn was enhanced and aided by a move to Los Angeles in 1981. In a strange twist of fate, I moved into a house on Bella Vista, the estate of the late John Barrymore—the very actor whom *Flynn* had idolized! Along the way I was fortunate to be invited to tour the interiors of Flynn's three main Hollywood homes: his first home in the Hollywood hills, his next in Beverly Hills, and of course his beloved Mulholland Farm.

Over the years I also began searching out Flynn's footsteps in the many places in which he lived and worked—from the United States to Europe to Australia. In those varied locations I took photos, "then & now" shots that I lined up from the same vantage points as the vintage originals, in places often difficult to find or access. The beach in Laguna, California, for instance, where Flynn dueled with Basil Rathbone in CAPTAIN BLOOD, is sequestered within an almost unreachable cove, below a cliff of houses privately gated; I hiked for days through Bidwell Park in Chico, California—even back and forth *through* four miles of its stream—hunting for long-forgotten spots where the Sherwood Forest scenes from THE ADVENTURES OF ROBIN HOOD were filmed. Other locations were also sought out and visited: Bondi Beach in Sydney (where Flynn was first discovered); Schnebly Hill Vista in Sedona, Arizona (seen in VIRGINIA CITY); the beach at Newquay in Cornwall (seen in THE MASTER OF BALLANTRAE); the Italian alpine village of Courmayeur (used in WILLIAM TELL). Many of my photos from those travels are displayed throughout this book.

Gathering these acquisitions and experiences into a serious book was inevitable, so in 2009 I began researching everything available on Flynn in the Warner Bros./USC Archives, the 20th Century Fox Archives, the USC Cinematic Arts Library, and the Margaret Herrick Library, with an eye toward amassing the largest and most thorough collection of information on him thus far attempted. Meetings with people who had known Flynn or had in some way been connected with him further supplemented the research. The culmination of these forty-nine years of collecting, travels, and research is presented within these pages.

I would like to have included everything from the original 2,500-page finished manuscript, but a book of that size would have been hugely expensive and downright unwieldy. However, while the reduction to 320 pages was accomplished mainly through the omission of thousands of images, all of the researched and discovered information has been left intact, except for longer segments which have been edited of their superfluous passages. My hope is that, in moving through the book, the reader begins to get a real-time sense of what life was like day by day for

The Philadelphia Inquirer—
Nov. 13, 1972

a star of Flynn's magnitude, through the many photos, articles, correspondence, and even the decidedly non-glamorous business and legal affairs.

Regarding the images, I have tried to maintain a high standard. Very few images in this book are to be found in other books, and those that can be found are only included in this one because alternate images of a key event simply don't exist, or are not in the best presentable condition. A perfect case in point are the photos in chapter 1, few of which are new to the Flynn fan, but without which there would be nothing to present, considering how few photos exist from his earliest years. I have cleaned all images of as much blemish and imperfection as possible, and have tried to identify as many individuals in every photo as could be successfully discovered. The reader will notice that, since this book is about Flynn 's life and not a book only about his films, I have generally chosen candids during filming rather than stills from the respective film.

One of my other goals with this project was to correct the many errors I have seen over the years regarding the subject. It is dismaying how many books, articles, blogs, etc., perpetuate rumors, incorrect history, and mistaken photo information. With that in mind, if the reader should notice that I have committed errors of my own, please feel free to contact me with any corrections or suggested additions to the chronology at robertflorczak.com. It will be heartily welcome.

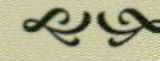

You, the Errol Flynn fan who reads this book, will no doubt discover that the data within have further clarified a number of events familiar to you, while thoroughly debunking a number of long-held but questionable legends. To you who may be new to the subject of Errol Flynn, I can only admit to my envy at your discovering for the first time this unique man—one of the most fascinating and colorful of the 20th century. Enjoy!

Robert Florczak
Pfalzdorf, Germany, 2021

A note about the text: There have been no changes made to original source material in terms of grammar, punctuation, or orthography. Where three ellipses appear, they represent the consolidating of the original source paragraphs; four ellipses represent the editing out of segments from the original text.

Above, Flynn in the Alabama Hills of Lone Pine, CA, in March of 1936 during the filming of THE CHARGE OF THE LIGHT BRIGADE, and below, the same spot today

What we have here is a life lived large. Too large, some will say, and there may be great truth to that, for few other famous lives in the 20th century were lived more grandly over so wide a world map in so brief a time. But the question is often asked, why the interest in *this* man? After all, wasn't Errol Flynn merely a popular movie star? One can begin to answer this question with a statement I once heard: "The more you know about Errol Flynn the more you want to know." In short, he is addictive.

Errol Flynn was indeed a popular movie star, one of the most popular of all time—but not "merely." He was also mariner, fortune hunter, globetrotter, epicure, pugilist, aesthete, athlete, inamorato, mercenary, savant, author, journalist. The usual introduction to him is generally by way of his films, and once his presence registers with the psyche, something kinetic begins to formulate within the viewer. Through his cinematic characterizations one senses a truth that goes beyond the big screen masquerading: "He was not acting," as Jack Warner eulogized him. "He was the personification of gallantry. The essence of bravery—the great adventurer." Consider then:

The films ~ One might have discovered them by accident on late-night television, or at a classic film revival house. There he is, in the title role of THE ADVENTURES OF ROBIN HOOD, exuding Technicolor sparks of equal parts laughter and gravitas; as a pirate in CAPTAIN BLOOD and THE SEA HAWK (*pictured here*), commanding sailing ships with cutlass and cunning; in CHARGE OF THE LIGHT BRIGADE, confidently leading whole companies of British lancers; in DODGE CITY dispatching outlaws on a Western Main Street; from there the curious viewer discovers his portrayals of the larger-than-life real characters of Lord Essex, General Custer, James J. Corbett. To be sure, no other screen star assumed so many heroic roles of this significance. So who was this man, and from what professional training did he draw inspiration for which to imbue these roles with such conviction? In fact, there was little training. His real life adventures were his classes in acting.

The adventures ~ Born and raised in Tasmania, the young Flynn early on developed an appetite for destinations afar. The sea, by proud admission his truest mistress, lured him via ramshackle yacht up the coast of Australia, across the treacherous Great Barrier Reef and Coral Sea, to primitive New Guinea, where he tried his hand as patrol officer, gold prospector, plantation overseer, carouser—all by the age of twenty-four. Later, as an already successful international film star living in the security of Hollywood affluence, he was drawn to the perilous front lines of the Spanish Civil War—against the wishes of his studio. He navigated his beloved yachts the world over, whether for pleasure, exploration, or deep sea studies with his marine biologist father. A burgeoning revolution enticed him to the jungles of Cuba to meet face to face with Fidel Castro and his band of guerrillas. That insatiable appetite for remote destinations lasted to the very final days of his life, even as his physical condition was noticeably deteriorating. And through to the end were the escapades—amorous in nature.

The escapades ~ From his earliest days dallying with schoolgirls, to involvements with wealthy cosmopolitan matrons, island exotics, Hollywood ingenues, prominent actresses, nocturnal professionals, royalty, and three wives, the allure of the female was one that Flynn could not resist. It brought him both deep gratification as well as profound legal woes. Stars like Clark Gable and Mickey Rooney may have married more times, but neither of them suffered the public indignation of a notorious double-statutory rape trial, whose daily episodes were front-page news, often above the day's WWII headlines. Aided by a thinly disguised relationship with a precocious teenager in his last two years, Flynn's swashbuckling image was inevitably entwined with feminine indulgence, both innocent and infamous.

Finally, no serious attempt at answering the "why" of Errol Flynn is complete without addressing the subject of the physical. Simply stated, his face and figure in their prime were near perfection. He has been variously described as "criminally good looking," like a "Greek god," and unlike other stars of the era, had no preference in his cinematographers because, as WB producer Henry Blanke noted, he was so "beautiful any camera made him look good." From an artist's perspective, the face was a study in classical balance, his features ideal and harmoniously arranged, of almost sculptural precision (*shown here in 1940*). His impressive physique could be found on the winning side of competitive tennis matches (he was one of the best players in Hollywood) as well as dazzling off the high diving board, and was not the product of weights and exercises in a gymnasium, but rather from years of the rigorous physical demands of sea sailing. Added to this was a most mellifluous voice, which in the later years was unfortunately coarsened through hard living. But beauty alone is not enough, else one be nothing more than a vacuous fashion model. With Flynn, the physical was augmented by a super-alive personality and irresistible charm. He was fully beautiful, while fully masculine.

Yet with all these tools—inherent or fashioned—Flynn had a self-destructive side that gave his biography an almost Shakespearean tragic arc: the first two-thirds of his fifty years saw him climb to the peaks of his aspirations, hover among them for a decade, and then spiral progressively downward into professional and personal defeat. Here, then, is a storybook character come to life, in all its dreams, triumphs, and disappointments. This, then, is the "why" of Errol Flynn.

1
SOUTH PACIFIC ADVENTURES
1909~1933

The Tasmania of 1909, having just been elevated from a penal settlement to an official Australian state only eight years earlier, was still shedding much of its rugged 19th-century way of life when Errol Flynn was born into its capital. Hobart was a growing port city (population then 39,000), with its many docks sending and receiving ships and cargo from all over the world. That, along with the expansive coastline around it, surely had an influence on the young Flynn, forming his life long love of the sea. But before tasting nautical freedom, he would have to endure years of being dismissed from one school after another, living from house to house, and moving from Hobart to Sydney to London and back again, with parents who couldn't seem to stay together for any settled length of time.

By 1930 the 21-year-old was already the owner of his first boat, and headed from Sydney to Port Moresby for the fortunes that promised to be discovered in the gold fields of New Guinea. Several other trips back and forth between the two countries, as well as attempts at various other careers proved unrewarding, but a serendipitous opportunity to star in a low-budget Australian film in Sydney for Charles Chauvel (not in Tahiti for a "Joel Swartz" as Flynn later claimed in his autobiography, *My Wicked, Wicked Ways*) planted a seed of interest that he would tap into at a later date. The film was made and forgotten by the fledgling actor, and he returned to the wilds of New Guinea yet again.

On his last trip to the island Flynn met Dr. Hermann Erben (renamed "Dr. Gerrit H. Koets" in *My Wicked, Wicked Ways*), an Austrian physician who would have a significant effect on Flynn's Weltanschauung. They decided to leave the South Pacific for Europe: Erben back to Austria and Flynn to England to now pursue the acting bug that had bitten him in Sydney. With a cache of diamonds purchased from a black-market seller, Flynn joined Erben on a ship to Hong Kong, never to return to the South Pacific.

A page in Captain Bligh's hand listing the names of the H.M.S. Bounty mutineers, including that of Edward Young (ninth line from the bottom), Errol Flynn's maternal ancestor; by pure coincidence, Flynn would portray Fletcher Christian in his very first film role

Errol's father, Professor Theodore Thomson Flynn

1909

Sat January 23
Prof. Theodore Thomson Flynn (b. October 11, 1883) and Lily Mary (later known as Marelle) Young (b. March 23, 1888) are married at St. John's Church of England, Balmain North, New South Wales, Australia; Marelle is a descendant of Midshipman Edward Young, one of the mutineers aboard the *H.M.S. Bounty* in 1789 *(top left)*.

March
Prof. Flynn accepts a position as lecturer in biology at the University of Tasmania.

Sun June 20
Errol Leslie Flynn is born at Queen Alexandra Private Hospital, formerly on Hampden Road at James Street in Battery Point, Hobart, Tasmania. *(Right, The Hobart Mercury, June 22, 1909)*

BIRTHS.

THOMSON FLYNN.—At the Alexandra Hospital, on June 20, the wife of T. Thomson Flynn, of Mildura, Warwick-st.: a son.

(Above left)"Mildura," Errol's first home at 52 Warwick Street in North Hobart; (above right) Errol, age five months, with his mother Marelle, probably taken at Mildura, and possibly the earliest photo of him

1911

Theodore Flynn is appointed Ralston Professor of Biology at the University of Tasmania; Professor Flynn leaves Hobart aboard the polar ship *Aurora*, participating in the Mawson Australian Antarctic Expedition which is researching off Macquarie Island.

1912-1913

Sometime during this period Flynn is a pupil in Miss Lola's Dancing Class, performing pantomimes at the Theatre Royal in Hobart.

1914

Lives at 10 Darcy Street until 1916 *(below left and next page top; below right, Errol's bedroom there as it appears today*

(Above left) Errol dressed as Robinson Crusoe in a backyard tent at the Darcy Street house with his dog Daisy; (above right) the same spot today

1916

July

Enters Franklin House School at Davey and Antill Streets (since demolished).

1917

June

Enters Hutchins Junior school; the family is living at Holebrook Place, now 296 Davey Street *(center right)*.

1918

Enrolls in the Albuera Street Model School.

September

Appears as a page in the entourage of Enid Lyons in the Queen Carnival charity pageant in Burnie, Tasmania *(bottom left)*.

Thu December 12

Attends Speech Night at Hutchins Junior High School.

1919

Moves to the Imperial Hotel on Collins Street in Hobart *(right)*.

Tue December 2

Errol's sister, Norah Rosemary Flynn (known as Rosemary) is born at Kirribilli Point, New South Wales.

With Enid Lyons, Errol on the right - September, 1918

Holebrook Place (now 296 Davey Street)

60 Duke Street, Sandy Bay

In London with his sister Rosemary - c.1921

10 Aberdeen Street, Glebe

1920

By the early 1920s the Flynn family is living at 60 Duke Street in the Sandy Bay area of Hobart *(left)*.

April

Enters the Friends School in North Hobart as a boarder *(below, Flynn's name on the second line of the school registry)*.

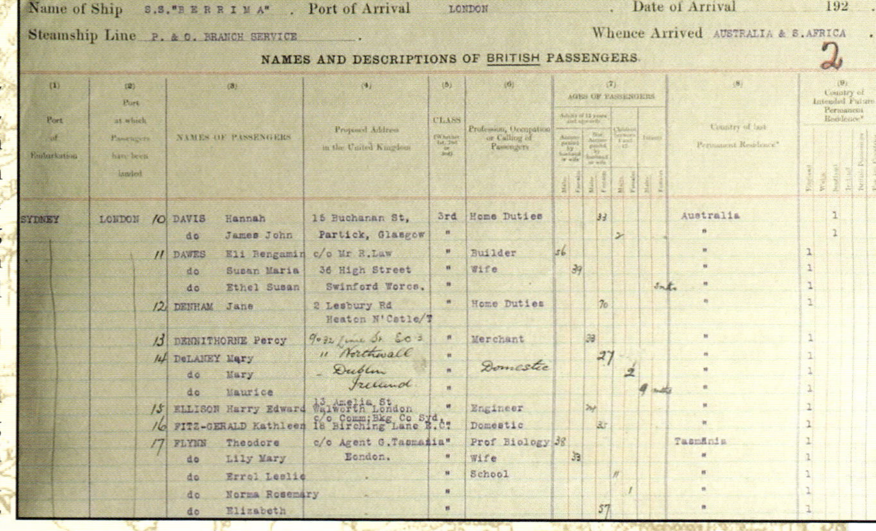

REGISTER BOOK.

No.	Name.	Where from.	Parent's Name.	Denomination.	Date of Admission.	Age last birthday.	Birthday.	Boarder or Day Scholar.	Class at Entry.	Class at Leaving.	Time at School.	Date of Leaving.	REMARKS.
1031	Ockenden, Percy O.	C. O. Ockenden, Cool Stores Moonah			20.2.	16.		D. O	VI				
2	Flynn, Errol L. T.	Prof. T. T. Flynn, Hazelmere, Douglas Rd. Hobart			20.2.	10.		B.	IVa				
3	Haddow, Alex.	Geo. Haddow, 8. Franklin St. N. Hobart			20.3.	9.		D. O	III	√h.	4yrs.	24. 4.	

Mon December 20

Leaves Friends School; at some point during this time moves to Sydney to join his mother and new sister; occasionally spends time at the home of his maternal grandmother, Edith Young Hammer, at 54 Carabella Street in Kirribilli.

1921

Sat May 28

Sails for England with his family, on the *S.S. Berrima (center right)*, stopping for a short time in South Africa, and finally settling in London. Sometime between 1921 and 1923 Flynn is in boarding school at South-West London College primary school (called Barnes), No. 99-101 Castelnau.

1923

Flynn later claimed to have been expelled from Barnes for cutting classes, and then enrolled in Colet Court Preparatory school of St. Paul's during his last year in England, 1923-24, though no independent evidence of this has been found.

The passenger manifest from the S.S. Berrima; Elizabeth (Betty) is Marelle's sister

Pressland House

1924

June

Returns to Hobart with his father after visiting his mother, sister, and Aunt Betty in the South of France.

Mon July 14

Enrolls in Hobart High School's second-year class; at this point is living with his father at 10 Aberdeen Street in Glebe, a suburb of Hobart *(bottom left)*; sometime later moves to Pressland House at 33 Melville Street *(bottom right)*.

1925

September

Ends school term twenty-ninth in a class of thirty; the quarterly exam record shows his grades to be (each out of a possible 100): English, 34; history, no grade; geography, 17; Latin, 9; French, 50; arithmetic, 10; algebra, 19; geometry, 6; physics, no grade; total, 160, and average, 22.9.

Mon November 2
Wins a tennis competition; *"Errol Flynn represented his Fernside Club and won another round."* The Hobart Mercury.

Wed November 25
Wins another tennis competition; *"The match between Flynn, the Fernside junior, and Turner, of Buckingham, was a fine contest, E. T. Flynn eventually winning in the third set. The tennis throughout was the best witnessed to date...."* The Hobart Mercury.

Mon November 30
Wins another tennis competition; *"Flynn commenced strongly, and by clean and forceful good length driving kept his opponent in the back court, quickly running to a lead of 4-1....a neck-and-neck struggle ensued until the score was four all. At that stage Flynn, by superior play, took the next two games, thereby gaining the rubber, and with it the title of B grade champion for the year."* The Hobart Mercury.

Wed December 16
Is "asked to leave" Hobart High School as a result of "contretemps" during the high school fair.

1926

March
Moves to Sydney; enters Sidney Church of England Grammar School (SCEGS); by August he is expelled for nocturnal "trysts" with a school domestic; for a time, according to his autobiography, he becomes homeless.

September
Begins working as a clerk in the general mail section of Dalgety & Co., Ltd., through a lead from his friend Ken Hunter-Kerr; gives his address as 28 Brighton Boulevard, Bondi, his paternal grandmother's home, though at times during this period he is living with Hunter-Kerr in the King's Cross section of Sydney

1927

Sun June 26
Transfers to Dalgety's Wharf and Stevedoring Department at Miller's Point.

Thu August 25
Boxes in the New South Wales Amateur Boxing Competition at the Sydney Auditorium; loses the bout—though controversially: *"In the heavyweight division, E. Flynn (11.10) beat F. Scarf (12.10) by a margin wide as the Sydney Heads....But both judges agreed for Scarf who did not land a decent blow owing to the other fellow's elusiveness. In the last round, the only hard blow by Flynn, a right swing, momentarily dazed his bigger and stronger, but infinitely less scientific opponent."* The Referee, 8/31.

September
Is fired from Dalgety's for stealing postage stamp money to buy a bicycle; moves back to Hobart; briefly attends University of Tasmania; late in the month leaves for Rabaul, New Guinea, aboard the *Montoro*; he never returns to Tasmania.

Sat October 1
Arrives in Rabaul, New Guinea; is soon thereafter assigned by the Australian government as a cadet and sent to an outpost in Kokopo; is dismissed after six weeks for lack of academic credentials; follows this with jobs as an assistant manager of the Kenabot Plantation south of Kokopo, as a mechanic at the Adams-Cooper Garage and Service Station in Rabaul, as manager of the Lemus Plantation near Kavieng, and as an air cargo clerk in Wau.

Below, with friends at Ken Hunter-Kerr's cottage in the King's Cross section of Sydney; Doddie Dog and Errol in the foreground, with (left to right) his future fiancée, Naomi Dibbs, her sister, Cecil Dibbs, Phyl McLauchlan (later Lady Collins), and third Dibbs sister, Miriam - 1927

Aboard the S.S. Montoro to New Guinea - September 1927

Left, government cadet Flynn (at far left) with a group of New Guinea natives in Kokopo - 1927

1928

It is here in Rabaul that he likely contracts the malaria that plagues him the rest of his life; he claims to have prospected for gold at Edie Creek where a gold strike had occurred in the early 1920s; becomes a native labor recruiter for several months on a schooner belonging to W. A. Money, owner of the Siassi Island Plantations near Umboi; befriends "Dusty" Miller, a fellow recruiter.

Summer

Claims to have traveled by rail to Queensland and worked in a bottling plant in Kyogle, but this is probably fiction.

1929

There is no independent documentation outside of Flynn's autobiography that places him in the Sepik River area, but if he was there it would probably have been sometime during this year; he claims to have shot a native in Edie Creek or Umboi, but the only record of this is a reference to it in a letter to his father (see May 24, 1932).

October

In Rabaul, probably staying at Chee's Jour Gnee [Guinea] Hotel, suffering from malaria and gonorrhea.

Tue October 22 to Wed October 30

Sails the *S.S. Montoro* for Sydney (probably with a loan of £100 from "Dusty" Miller—$9,197.28 in 2021 value and £400 he claims he won in a poker game the night before—$36,802 in 2021 value), arriving eight days later.

THE THIRTIES

1930

Earns income modeling suits for R. C. Hagon Ltd., 129 King Street, Sydney; meets Freddy McEvoy at Usher's Bar in Sydney, becoming close lifetime friends; at Neutral Bay he sees the yacht *Arop* (built of ironbark and kauri in 1881) and purchases it with £120 collected from his mother ($11,362 in 2021 value) and the possible help of relatives and friends; he later renames it *Sirocco (right)*.

The Sirocco *in Sydney harbor*

Sat February 15

With Ken Hunter-Kerr, Charlie Burt, Trelawney Adams, and Sydney's *Daily Pictorial* photographer, T. H. Arrowsmith, sails out of Neutral Bay on the *Sirocco* to test a new engine.

Mon February 17

"In Neutral Bay, just opposite Circular Quay, lies the 44-foot cutter Sirocco, which is being refitted by Errol Flynn, the 24-year-old [sic] *son of Professor T. Thompson Flynn, of the University of Tasmania....Flynn, junior, accompanied by two companions, will leave Sidney* [sic] *during next week in the Sirocco on a 2,400-mile voyage, most of it amid the tortuous Great Barrier Reef, to New Guinea, where he works a cocoa plantation. The adventurous young Tasmanian proposes to use the Sirocco in the establishment of a trading service between the islands that fringe the New Guinea coast."* The Advocate of Burnie, Tasmania; at some point, Rex Long-Innes joins the crew.

Tue February 25

Lars Halvorsen, from whose shop Flynn purchased the *Sirocco*, receives and deposits £11 from Flynn on a Bank of New South Wales check; on March 7th Halvorsen is informed by the bank that the check has bounced.

Mon March 10

Letter to Lars Halvorsen: *"With regard to my indebtedness* [for refitting and parts]*....I regret that at present I am unable to pay this balance...In consideration of you allowing me three months credit for payment....I undertake to remit the amount of the balance with interest....immediately on my arrival in New Guinea...."* Flynn pays the bill on April 24th.

Tue March 11

Leaves Sydney with Charlie Burt, H. F. Trelawney Adams, and Rex Long-Innes for the Great Barrier Reef and New Guinea; ports-of-call include Port Stephens and Tuncurry, from where Flynn writes the following letter to Lars Halvorsen *(next page, top left)*: *"....Would you be so kind as to send the spare parts of my engine on to Burns Philp & Co;*

Brisbane? There are various things among them which I need rather urgently so would be very grateful if you could oblige me in this matter...We have had very bad weather so far – nearly sank the first night out -- the Sirocco was half full of water & we're waiting now for it to fire up...." Continues on to Coff Harbor (suffering seasickness amid heavy seas), Ballina ("*Swimming, drinking, fishing, fighting, sailing and romancing girls were part of Flynn's daily menu.*" *The Rockhampton Morning Bulletin*), Brisbane, Bundaberg, Gladstone, The Narrows, and Port Alma.

Letter to Lars Halvorsen - Tue, March 11

Sun May 18

From the Narrows they sail on to Rockhampton, where Flynn loses a three-round boxing match to Bud Riley of the "Jimmy Sharman Troupe," a traveling boxing exhibition, but earns £5 ($473.36 in 2021 value); they then sail through the dangerous Great Barrier Reef; Flynn later wrote in his book *Beam Ends* that he romanced young Lucy Wilson, who desperately swam out to the *Sirocco* as it left port, unsuccessful in her attempt to get Flynn to stay; next they arrive at Bowen, Flynn with a serious bout of malaria.

Sun July 27

In Townsville, where he spends three days in the hospital battling his malaria; writes to his father: "....*We're leaving tomorrow morning at 2 A.M. direct to Cooktown, a couple of days there—out to Lizard Island for a day or so and then the piece d'résistance—Samarai or so—in the event of cyclone—Davy Jones' Locker…..I don't think I'll be able to return to Sydney for a long time because of Naomi* [Dibbs]. *I haven't got the moral courage to write her a straight letter telling her it's no go and in the meantime we're officially engaged in the papers…Of course it's hardly her fault either and although I didn't suggest the married state I just allowed things to drift that way. Now look at the mess! I've been in them before but never to this extent….*" Travels from Townsville to Hinchinbrook Island and on to Cairns where he takes a 26-hour rail journey inland to Mareeba with Long-Innes; Flynn claims the return trip took 36 hours.

Sun August 17

Writes to his father from Cooktown: "....*We're leaving for Lizard Island day after tomorrow and I will probably put in the night there cooking a goat and two fowls I 'captured' here—chased the confounded goat for about a mile before I cornered him. The fowls—both of them noble birds—died all unaware of approaching fate until plucked from their perch in the dead of night by the neck—one must live, a Communist tenet which I heartily support….one thing I've made my mind upon. When I've got a credit balance of several hundred I'm going to take myself to Cambridge to study History & Literature—I've been coming to the conclusion for a long time that the most vital thing in Life is to be able to understand something about it. God, what profundity, eh?....*" Sails on to Lizard Island; with natives helping to guide their way, the crew heads towards Port Moresby in late August or September, stopping on the way (according to Flynn) at the village of Tavai.

Wed December 10

Puts out to sea from Port Moresby with Long-Innes and a local barmaid, Anne Haywood.

Fri December 12

The *Sirocco* is wrecked at Taurama Point; Flynn reported to *The Sydney Morning Herald* (10/5/32) that the *Sirocco* was later "*repaired and is now destined to be a diving-tender, in the beche-de-mer industry.*"

1931

Wed January 7

Takes the commercial steamer *Morinda* back to Sydney with Rex Long-Innes, arriving on January 14th.

Clockwise from bottom: Charlie Burt, Trelawny Adams, Flynn, and Rex Long-Innes - 1930

OFF TO NEW GUINEA.

FOUR ADVENTURERS.

The Sirocco Calls In.

ONE TIME CRACK YACHT.

Long, narrow-waisted, black-hulled, with towering stick showing above the wharf decking, but bearing little signs of the buffeting she has received on her voyage, the Sirocco, late of Royal Sydney Yacht Club, now bound for New Guinea and the beche de mer and trochus shell, nine days up from Sydney, lies at the old town wharf.

Fifty years old, but as staunch as the day she slipped into the water for the first time at the Circular Quay slips, the Sirocco will know a different atmosphere now from the one she has been accustomed to so long. Her youthful crew know where they are going. First there is Captain Errol Flynn, late Cambridge undergrad, now planter on a lonely island 40 miles from mysterious Madang, the island of the "White Kanakas," where he dispenses high and low justice to his 40 odd natives and bears his share of the white man's burden.

"This is our navigator," said Captain Errol Flynn, from under his blankets when a "Bulletin" man stepped aboard. "You'll have to excuse me. Just a touch of malaria. But meet the crew."

Mr. T. Adams, another young Englishman, is the navigator. Close clipped moustache, accent, and physique brand him unmistakably the product of University. Mr. C. Burt, another member of the crew, is also an Englishman, and Australia is represented by Mr. Rex Long-Innes, son of Judge Long-Innes, who is going forth with the others to seek his fortune in the South Seas.

The Morning Bulletin *of Rockhampton, Queensland Wed, June 18, 1930*

LAUNCH WRECKED.

Near Port Moresby.

PORT MORESBY, Thursday.

It is feared that the launch Sirocco, which smashed on to the reef at Taurama Point this morning, will become a total wreck. Fortunately its three occupants reached shore in safety.

The launch is owned by Messrs. Errol Flynn and Rex Longines, and came to Port Moresby three months ago from Sydney. Last night she proceeded to Taurama Point, and left early this morning for Palli, with Miss Anne Haywood as a passenger. About 10 o'clock the oil pipe broke, putting the engine out of action, and anchor was dropped off Tavai. Flynn and Longines were working at the engine when the anchor carried away, and it was decided to return to Port Moresby with the aid of sails. A heavy sea was running when the launch rounded Taurama Point, and, unable to make headway, the craft crashed heavily on to the reef.

After many attempts to launch the dinghy, the party swam ashore, landing at Pari village, where the natives made a fire to dry their clothes. None of them is any the worse for the experience. The tide has since risen, but the launch remains fast on the reef, and little hope is held out for her salvage.

The Sydney Morning Herald - *Fri, December 12, 1930*

ENGAGEMENTS.

The Engagement is announced of Errol Thomson-Flynn, only son of Professor and Mrs. T. Thomson-Flynn, of Hobart, Tasmania, to Naomi Campbell-Dibbs, youngest daughter of Mr. and Mrs. R. Campbell-Dibbs, of Temora and Bowral, N.S.W.

The Sydney Morning Herald
Sat, January 24, 1931

Thu April 30

Returns to Port Moresby after buying a share in a tobacco plantation near the Rouna Falls on the Laloki River, with funds from backers like Dr. William Eric Giblin; Flynn eventually has a thatched house built on his Laloki Plantation.

Mon July 20

Writes a letter to The Sydney Bulletin about allowing Papuan tobacco to be sold in Australia without a tariff: *"Dear Bulletin: Papua is one of the natural homes of the tobacco plant, and, as Papua is part of the Commonwealth and is in receipt of a yearly subsidy of $40,000 from the Federal Government, the obvious market for its tobacco is Australia. But the market is closed by a prohibitive tariff…..It would be a nearsighted policy should the fact that the tobacco was grown by black labour prevent those responsible from assisting Papua in every way possible, when the country is being exclusively supported by the Australian taxpayer. And particularly when, as in this case, the assistance would not harmfully affect Australia, which is still and must be for years a large importer of the leaf. Yours. Errol Flynn (Papua)."*

According to *My Wicked, Wicked Ways*, it is about this time that Flynn romances a native girl named Tuperselai, but the name, at least, is probably fiction.

Tue August 4

A letter sent to his father c/o the Whitten Bros. in Port Moresby *(below left)*: *Dear Pater/ A swift line before the boat goes. I was hoping I might have heard from you by the last mail. By Jove Dad I do hope you'll manage to come up here as I suggested in my last letter to the University Club. I'm terribly anxious to see you before you buzz off to Belfast. My love & respect Dad Errol"*

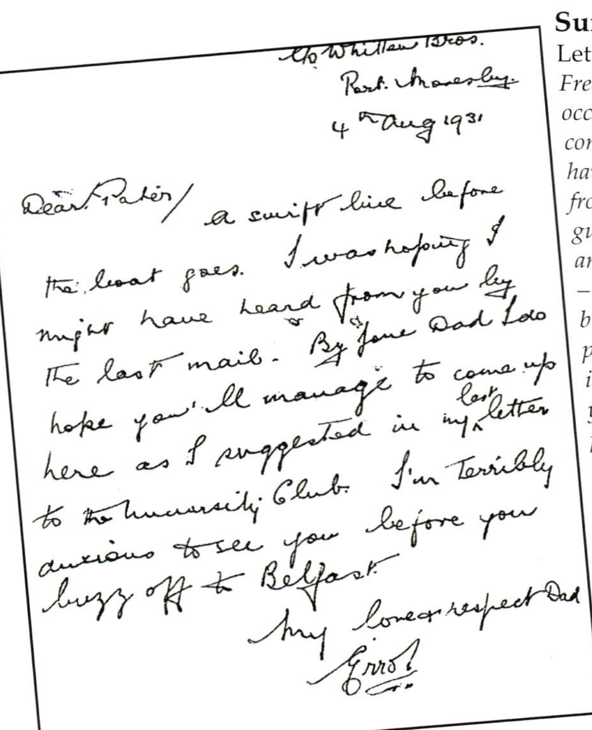

Sun October 4

Letter sent to his father from the Laloki Tobacco Plantation in Port Moresby: *Dear Dad / Your letter from Freemantle has just come to hand – quite the longest I've ever had from you although I seem to remember dimly, an occasion when you once wrote me 2 ½ pages….Thanks for your offer of the fare home to Belfast Dad – it's a quite comforting feeling which, God knows, I may avail myself of. That's one thing about tobacco – it's quick and one doesn't have to wait ten years as with coconuts to find out you're broke. Things look very promising at present and I'm going from daylight till dusk and very keen on the job – it's great to construct things and to watch a place grow under your guidance and management. Our place aroused widespread admiration with grudging remarks that we deserve to succeed anyway….The place certainly does look well now….long neat rows of seed beds with sliding slashes of cheesecloth shades – then the field itself on which the Govt. tractor is at present working running along the banks of the Laloki River….I'm building a curing barn at present according to the blueprints I had sent to me from America. It's just about turned me prematurely grey and I've had a helleva job making a furnace and patent fire ??? inside it out of concrete – the first one inside crumpled up when the blast of heat went through it – This one is allright though and should still be there in 200 years time barring earthquakes. It's a depressing thought to consider that at the end of that period of time I shall most probably not be here to enjoy the fruits of this labour….Cheerio Dad look after yourself – I'll write again next boat and I hope you'll answer….My love & respect. Errol"*

November

Joins Trelawney Adams (now skipper of the *Royal Endeavor* and *Ronald S.*) on an excursion to Kaparoko.

Wed December 2

Flynn's first article as "Laloki"about Papuan medicine men is published in *The Bulletin*: *"The result of the pourri-pourri séance in Port Moresby at which medicine men enjoying great prestige among the surrounding tribes failed to bring a dead dog back to life, should have been a moral victory for his Ex[cellency, the Governor of New Guinea]. But the pourri-pourri sorcerer is an astute opportunist. The chief pourri-pourri expert suddenly remembered that the medical officer, invited to satisfy himself that the dog was dead, had touched it with a stethoscope. That, of course, cleared up the mystery of the dog's refusal to come to life…."*

1932

Sat January 2

Is visited on his plantation by patrol officer Jack Hides, who reports favorably on Flynn's crop output.

Wed April 13

An article by Flynn is published in *The Bulletin* about the primitive New Guinea tribe, the Kuku-kukus.

May

Joins Trelawney Adams on an excursion to Kikori, staying at the Obamobu rubber plantation of Will Jefferson.

Tue May 24

Writes to his father from the Laloki Tobacco Plantation in Port Moresby *(center right)*:

"*No news yet about the tobacco sale – we should have it in about 3 weeks or so. I go to north Q'land* [Queensland] [by] *boat after next to engage upon a new and unusual enterprise – that of company floatation* [sic]....*If we get it floated I'll manage it for a year but no longer. Why only a year you ask? That's what I'm writing you about and it's going to be extremely difficult to explain and make you understand that I'm more earnest now than I've ever been before. I've acquired ambition....It seems to me, Dad, that I've arrived at the crucial point of my life, next month I'll be 23 and I realize I've reached the end of a rather prolonged adolescence. But if it's been slow it's been good and the consciousness of life I now have is perhaps all the more thorough on account of 4 ½ years in New Guinea. Two old friends of mine came over from Edie Creek the other day. One of them, Jack Ryan, is 50 years old and it was he who was mainly instrumental in having a charge of murder squashed against me in the other Territory when I shot a native there in 1929. The other fellow is the same age and he's going away for good on account of Blackwater* [severe malaria]. *He'll probably starve because he knows no country but New Guinea....It's always been my most cherished ambition, if I ever made the money here, to do something worth while. I intended to go to Cambridge and read for the Bar, knowing how well my natural advantage suited me for that profession and realizing I possess one really excellent advantage of an almost congenital knowledge of human nature which New Guinea has accentuated....*[W]*ould you put me through Cambridge? A big thing to ask, I know. 3 years at £300 is £900* [$90,980.85 in 2021 value], *and another year in the Inns of Court at something less — a bad investment, I must admit on the face of my performance to date. But I <u>know</u> I could get through it if you were prepared to take the risk and make the sacrifice. For God's sake, don't think I somehow expect you to educate me and give me a profession as a sort of paternal duty or obligation. I deliberately chose the bed I'm sweltering on at present, and unless you care to make the sacrifice I'm quite prepared to lie on it, unpleasant though it most decidedly will be....*"

Wed May 25

An article by Flynn is published in *The Bulletin* about a missionary in New Guinea.

Wed June 15

An article by Flynn is published in *The Bulletin* about the Motuan language.

Mon June 20

Flynn's 23rd birthday.

Wed July 20

An article by Flynn, "On New Guinea," is published in *The Bulletin*.

Late July

Returns to Sydney aboard the *M.V. Macdhui* (bombed by the Japanese and abandoned on 6/17/42).

Fri August 5

Arrives in Sydney.

Mon August 8

"*The Steamships Trading Co., Ltd., sued Mr. Errol Flynn for £74/2/7 for goods sold and delivered. Judgment was for plaintiffs for amount claimed and 11/6 costs, to be paid at the rate of £5 a month, commencing July 31.*" The Cairns Post.

Wed August 17

An article by Flynn is published in *The Bulletin* about a Papuan and his search for a *"pyblo"* (Bible) newspaper.

A Sunday in September

John Warwick, casting director for Cinesound Studios, spots Flynn on a beach near Bondi (Flynn is living with his grandmother in the area at this time) and suggests—through a phone call to Ken Hunter-Kerr—that Flynn audition for director Charles Chauval's upcoming film, IN THE WAKE OF THE BOUNTY; meets with the

Flynn's plantation house being built, he on the far right - 1932

The letter reproduced at center right reads:

Laloki Tobacco. Plan.
Port Moresby
Papua.
24th May 1932.

Dear Dad./ No news yet about the tobacco sale — we should have it in about 3 weeks or so. I got to nth Q'land the boat after next to engage upon a new and unusual enterprise — that of company floatation. I have a bundle of letters from big bugs here testifying unto my ... ability etc, both of which are ... stated to be excellent: a parcel of photografs, a folio full of facts and other pertinent papers which altogether make a pile about 2 ft high. What a charivture scene for me Dad! inviting hard headed business men both to lunch with me and to trust their hard won cash in my hands! Actually I, and other people here, think we stand a good chance of setting this place floated. We want £12000 of which £2500 is to go to Trelawny & self as vendors (half cash is the least All consider) Balance

On the Laloki plantation - 1932

MUTINY OF THE BOUNTY
Reconstructed for Films.

Mr. Charles Chauvel returned to Sydney on Saturday, after travelling 15,000 miles in little-known parts of the Pacific Ocean to make a film depicting the mutiny of the Bounty for Expeditionary Films, Ltd., an Australian company.

Every effort has been made to produce the film historically, and present a faithful picture of the wanderings of the mutineers before they reached Pitcairn Island, where they burned the Bounty, and Lieutenant Bligh's epic voyage of 4000 miles in an open boat to Batavia, after he had been cast adrift with 18 loyal members of his crew.

Mr. Chauvel followed the route of the Bounty and saw the remains of the ship lying in the clear water at Pitcairn Island. Native dances were filmed at Tahiti, where the mutineers stayed. Natives had to be specially chosen, as knowledge of primitive dances is rapidly dying out.

Members of the party had an unpleasant experience at Pitcairn Island. They were inspecting the coast in an open boat, when the engine failed, and they were blown out to sea. They managed to make repairs just before sunset, and make a dangerous return to the island through the surf, which is always heavy.

Mr. Chauvel said that his company believed that Australian history was too much neglected, and attempts would be made to fill in the gaps. Arrangements have been made for copies of the film to be prepared with Spanish and German comment.

The Sydney Morning Herald
Mon, August 29, 1932

Charles and Elsa Chauvel

Chauvels at the Long Bar of the Hotel Australia and gets the part of Fletcher Christian in the film.

September and October
Films his scenes for IN THE WAKE OF THE BOUNTY at Cinesound Studios, 65 Ebley Street, Bondi Junction.

Above left, Cinesound Studios in the early 20th century, and above right, the same building today

Wed October 5
Under the pen name Laloki, writes about the *Sirocco*, his final article for *The Bulletin*.

Sat October 22
"Errol Flynn, the tall good-looking lad who is engaged to Naomi Dibbs, has been selected by Charles Chauvel to play an important role in his talkie, 'The Mutiny On The Bounty', and I hear he photographs and records quite wonderfully. What a pity Naomi couldn't get a 'break', too, as I've heard she thinks she's another Garbo. Some of her creations certainly out-Hollywood Hollywood." *Smith's Weekly* newspaper.

November
Is living in a small, rented flat in the Kings Cross area of Sydney.

Right, as Fletcher Christian in a scene from
IN THE WAKE OF THE BOUNTY - *Fall 1932*

Fri November 4
"PAPUAN TOBACCO PLANTER BECOMES A TALKIE ARTIST." Headline from Port Moresby's *Papuan Courier*, reprinting the October 22nd article from *Smith's Weekly*.

November to December
In his autobiography, Flynn claims to have stolen the jewels of a society woman named Mrs. Madge Parks, whom he had slept with at this time, but this is probably a romanticized fiction replacing the truth of having later in New Guinea purchased illicit diamonds from a black-market seller named John Flato (see March 24, 1959); leaves Sydney and heads north to Townsville, booking passage to Port Moresby; he would never again return to Australia.

Sat December 30
Arrives back in Port Moresby via Townsville.

1933

Sun January 1 to Sun January 8
Sometime during this week he sells his portion of the Laloki Tobacco Plantation to a Miss Beatrice Grimshaw, as reported in the January 13th edition of Port Moresby's *Papuan Courier* (see February 17, 1933, printed article).

THE NEW GUINEA DIARY EXCERPTS*

Flynn keeps a diary, handwritten in pencil, that is discovered in August of 1935 in a trunk he left behind at the Hotel Salamaua in that city. The diary was fashioned from a school exercise book, cut in half to easily fit in his pocket.

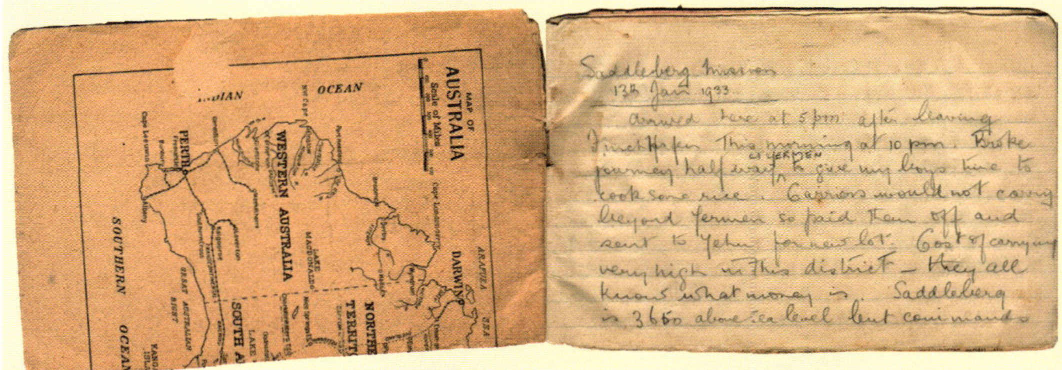

The inside cover and first page of the actual diary

Fri January 13

Written from Saddleberg [Sattelberg] Mission: *....Arrived here at 5 PM after leaving Finchafen [Finschhafen] this morning at 10 PM. Broke journey half way at Yermen to give my boys time to cook some rice. Carriers would not carry beyond Yermen so paid them off and sent to Yehu for new lot. Cost of carrying very high in this district--they all know what money is. Saddleberg is 3650 above sea level but commands wonderful outlook over the sea – I can see Umboi Island from here – it must be 80 miles away....Saddleberg Mission is the health resort for run-down and enervated missionaries. They're sent up here for a month every year to get the benefit of the excellent climate. I spotted a pretty girl when I came in today so I'll have to shave tonight. Three days' growth is no good even for a recruiter to wear....Long day's march tomorrow—hope to make the Hube country in four days from here. If the rain holds off may make it in three. If it doesn't I won't be able to cross the WARIA River, perhaps for a week. Thank God I brought 2 bottles of O.P. Rum and the Bible and will thus have both drink and something to read. Have often wanted to read the Bible -- I believe it's very entertaining & instructive....*

Sat January 14

....The paramount Luluai [territorial chief] of the District (Selembé) came up to see me this evening. We had a long discussion with WASANGE and TUTU MAN, the two TULTULs [native village interpreters] being present. The old man is a very distinct personality, quite a superior type. He has agreed to help me recruit, after no doubt making extensive inquiries about....

Sun January 15

Left Sattelberg after lunch at 2 P.M. and arrived at Fior [probably Fio] at 4:30. The track is about the best I have found inland and very beautiful besides. Crossed three mountain streams, each one dammed up at the crossing into crystal-clear pools. Bathed in the last one; first bath in three days. These pellucid pools were typical of New Guinea's specious beauty. They were fed by a sparkling stream flowing over bright limestone and fringed by capiac palms and coconuts. Several varieties of orchids were flowering among the surrounding undergrowth....As I lay there floating I noticed what I took to be innumerable black twigs attaching themselves one by one to my body, but took little notice of them. Then horrible thoughts occurred to me. I jumped up hurriedly and found my fears realized. I was covered in leeches who obviously hadn't had a square meal in months. Luckily I had matches with me so spent an hour burning them off....

Mon January 16

....There is a little stream running right through this village and the rest [of the] *house is situated a hundred yards or so from the village. Consequently I have no giant & irrepressible native pigs & dogs to annoy me. I thought at first I might get a little privacy too, but that is expecting too much. My every action has been keenly observed by at least 50 pairs of eyes ever since I arrived.....I hear there is trouble in Hube over a woman. Two villages are about to fight, so the talk goes. If it's right, things couldn't be better for me. Am bound to get recruits, probably from both villages if there's a fight as they'll want to get away to escape reprisals later.*

Tue January 17

First boy this morning—good stamp of native, too. He'll look well leading an axe about although he doesn't suspect it yet. He thinks he's going to be my cook. This is a very good omen—to get a boy from the chief's village means that I'll almost certainly get as many as I want from other villages....Big 'talk-talk' last night. The chief and his two tultuls came along and we discussed everything under the sun, including the late war, which appears to cause much amusement and astonishment. That all white men should indulge in extensive fighting among themselves after having given them, the black men, the very strictest injunctions against fighting, with prompt and severe punishment for disobedience, must, I suppose, appear to them somewhat paradoxical....

Wed January 18

Writes from Fio: *....Two more boys making three now. Excellent going....Three more boys today.*

Thu January 19

Continues the diary from Fio: *....The rush has set in properly. Tutuman came back with 7 boys which makes 13 and I'll have two more tomorrow....As all my boys come from the purlieus of this district all the old men of Fior decided to read me an address. It was rather amusing. The entire village gathered round me while I sat in the middle of the circle on a tucker box. One old grey beard then got to his feet and began to harangue me in forcible but quite incomprehensible terms as he spoke in his own language....I however nodded solemnly at each pause and later had his speech interpreted. He said in effect that Fior had given me all their young men and I must not sell any of them & when their time had finished must bring them back myself and then I would be given new boys to take their place. He then wound up by stating that although he was talking to me in strong words I must not think he was "cross"—and when I came would I bring him a dog? He then asked me, through the interpreter, if I would shake hands with him and I did.*

A fuller version of the diary appears in Appendix I on page 311

Fri January 20

Broke camp this morning having recruited 16 boys (with my 3 Aitapes makes 19) and proceeded.

His running diary ends here but contains other undated entries: ....*Marco Polo always recorded his surprise when he found no olives in the strange places he visited. The Chinese also betrayed astonishment when they learned the West had no bamboo--a lack which seemed to them incredible. So also of all the wonders of our modern civilisation nothing astounds News Guinea natives more than the fact that there are no coconuts growing in the lands whence we white men come....They cannot imagine a coconutless existence for to them the tree is the mainstay of life and supplies them with all their major necessities, food, clothing, house material, as well as countless other uses....*

Here Flynn offers a bold personal declaration, heavily lifted from Henry David Thoreau's "Walden" (inset): *I am going to China because I wish to live deliberately...New Guinea offers me, it is true, satisfaction for the tastes I have acquired which only leisure can satisfy + I am leaving economic security and I am leaving it deliberately. By going off to China with a paltry few pounds + no knowledge of what life has in store for me there I believe that I am going to front the essentials of life, to see if I can learn what it has to teach and above all not to discover, when I come to die, that I have not lived. We fritter our lives away in detail but I am not going to do this. I am going to live deeply, to acknowledge not one of the so called social forces which hold our lives in thrall + reduce us to economic dependency. The best part of life is spent in earning money in order to enjoy a questionable liberty during the least valuable part of it. To hell with money! Pursuit of it is not going to mould my life for me. I am going to live sturdily + Spartan-like; to drive life into a corner + reduce it to its lowest terms and if I find it mean, then I'll know its meanness, and if I find it sublime I shall know it by experience—and not make wistful conjectures about it conjured up by illustrated magazines...I refuse to accept the ideology of a business world which believes that man at hard labour is the noblest work of God. Leisure to use as I see fit... To learn what is worth one's while...*

Finally, a bit of philosophy: ....*Time, for example, just one hour of time is far more important than money for time is life. Whenever you waste your time over printed words that neither enlighten or amuse you, you are in a sense committing suicide. The value, the intrinsic value of our actions, emotions, thoughts, possessions, occupations, of the manner in which we are living: this is the first thing to be determined; for unless we are satisfied that any of these things have a true value, even if only relative, our lives are futile, and there is no more hopeless realisation than this.*

Sometime in late January or early February he stays at the Salamaua Hotel.

February

Briefly in New Britain.

Tue February 21

May have left Rabaul on the Eastern and Australian Steamship Company boat, the *Nankin,* although records show it sailed on to Manila and Hong Kong—the latter a location Flynn isn't known to have visited until May 7.

Wed March 15

IN THE WAKE OF THE BOUNTY begins opening around Australia, with a premiere at Sydney's Prince Edward Theater; Sydney's *Daily Telegraph* writes that Flynn's part is *"particularly well acted;"* "[Flynn's acting was] *completely adequate....."* The Sydney Mail; Smith's Weekly said that Flynn's performance was *"convincing and natural."*

Fri April 14

Meets Austrian Dr. Hermann Erben in Salamaua, New Guinea; sails for Vitu, a plantation on Garowe Island in the Bismarck Archipelago—in third class on the *S.S. Friderun.*

Sat April 15

Arrives in Vitu.

Mon April 17

Flynn and Erben travel to the Asalingi and Thiel Plantations *(bottom left)* in New Britain on board the schooner *Kokopo.*

Tue April 18

At Lassul Bay in New Britain.

Sat April 22

Leaves with Erben for Rabaul at 11am on the *Friderun*; acquires a passport—#A136412—in Rabaul.

At Thiel's plantation - Mon, April 17,
Flynn on the left (photo by Dr. Hermann Erben)

Miss Beatrice Grimshaw has purchased the property known as the Laloki Tobacco Plantation, about 15 miles from Port Moresby on the Sapphire Creek Road. Messrs. Flynn and Adams had one crop of tobacco therefrom, the samples being excellent, and the prices offered ranged from up to 3/6 per lb. But the "Dohore" feeling was in evidence and Mr. Flynn, who was in charge left rather much to the "boys" with the result that the crop, when it arrived in London, was mildewed. Miss Grimshaw hopes to induce her brother south and a very practical friend of his to take the venture on, and is having all preliminary arrangements made. She very considerately says, "I think it is much better at the present juncture to put capital into something in the Territory rather than outside the Territory." She has calculated as an investment just what she considers will be a necessary outlay to expend yearly in order that the venture may have some chance of success. One certainly wishes her that measure of success in that she has the courage to back her opinions of the country with solid cash instead of mere talk.

The Cairns Post
Fri, February 17

Sun April 23
With Erben, leaves Rabaul for Hong Kong on the *Tanda* (torpedoed and sunk by the Germans on 7/15/44).

Sun May 7
Arrives in Hong Kong.

Tue May 9
Sails with Erben at 4pm on the *D'Artagnan* for Saigon.

Fri May 12
Arrives in Saigon at Cape St. Jacques at 3pm.

Mon May 15
Sails for Singapore at 8am.

Wed May 17
Arrives in Singapore at 11am; sails at 9pm for Penang.

Fri May 19
Arrives in Penang, Malaysia; sails for Colombo, Ceylon (now Sri Lanka), at noon.

Tue May 23
Arrives late in Colombo at 7pm owing to a monsoon; writes to his father (though in his autobiography he claims the letter was written the previous March): *"Dear Pater: I am on a voyage of discovery....My heartfelt thank-you for cabling fifty pounds. Pal [Hermann Erben] and I were in a genuine spot when we reached Saigon. We promised the captain of the barkentine who took us from Shanghai that we would have money for him when your cable arrived, but alas, when the money came, we decided we could put it to better use than he...So we left him to find his own means of returning to China--doubtless a wiser voyager than when he set out with us. You won't believe it when I tell you that a Chinese laundry slip made it possible for us to get out of the Sino-Jap war and off the Asian continent....I think I am going to try to make a career of acting when I arrive in London. I feel that that is what I want to do and where I may make my fortune. Give my love to mother and to little Rosemary...Respectfully, your son, Errol."*

Wed May 24
Leaves by train for Talaimannar, in Colombo.

Thu May 25
Arrives in Talaimannar; ferries to Dnushkodi, India, and then to Madras at 11:16am.

Fri May 26
Arrives in Egmore, India, at 7:30, staying at the YMCA; dines at the Marina House; feverish but goes to the Rita brothel, spending 17 rupees.

Sat May 27
Still with fever, but dines at Besotto Hotel and visits the New World's Fair.

Sun May 28
Leaves at 11pm on the *S.S. Compiegne* for Pondicherry, India.

Mon May 29
Arrives in Pondicherry at 10am; punches a rickshaw driver.

Tue May 30
Sails for Colombo again at 7am.

Thu June 1
Arrives in Colombo; lunches at Mrs. Spittle's Snack Counter at the Hagenbeck Station; buys a monkey for his sister in England but doesn't pay for it.

Fri June 2
The monkey dies.

Fri June 9
Arrives in Djibouti.

Wed June 14
Arrives in Suez.

Tue June 20
Arrives in Marseilles at noon on his 24th birthday; travels with a Mr. Jesperson to Paris.

Right, the South China Morning Post Thu, May 4

JEWEL ROBBERY.

NEW GUINEA VISITOR VICTIM OF COUP.

DARING THEFT ON STEAMER TANDA.

$20,000 INVOLVED.

Over $20,000 is said to be involved in a daring jewellery robbery yesterday, the victim being Mr. Errol Flynn, a passenger aboard the steamer Tanda. The jewellery, which was enclosed in a small wallet, was extracted from the pocket of a discarded jacket when Mr. Flynn left the cabin for a few moments.

The Eastern and Australian liner Tanda arrived in Hongkong from Australian ports, via Rabaul and Manila, at noon yesterday. After tiffin aboard, Mr. Flynn, it is understood, went to his cabin, and began preparations for going ashore.

While dressing, he discarded the jacket containing the valuables, and left his cabin for a few moments.

Upon returning he discovered that the wallet had been extracted from the pocket of the jacket. Rushing to the doorway, Mr. Flynn immediately raised the alarm.

A search was at once instituted by the ship's officers, but there was no trace of the missing jewels or suspicious characters.

The water police were immediately informed, and within a few minutes were aboard the ship, which is berthed at the No. 1 Kowloon wharf.

Investigations were continued all through yesterday afternoon aboard the liner, members of the crew being interrogated by the police.

It is understood that Mr. Flynn has resided for some years in Rabaul, which is the main township in the Mandated Territory of New Guinea and at Edie Creek, where he is connected with large gold mining properties. Edie Creek, or Bulolo, has proved one of the richest goldfields in recent Australasian history.

Interviewed late last night, Mr. Flynn refused to make a statement, beyond confirming the fact that the robbery had taken place.

On the S.S. Compiegne - Thursday, June 15 (photo by Dr. Hermann Erben)

2

ENGLAND

1933~1934

In January of 1934 Errol Flynn wrote to his friend Dr. Hermann Erben that he was in the process of honing his acting technique with an eye toward "the big time in films." The seventeen months in England that represent this chapter of Flynn's life were spent pursuing that goal, probably the most focused and determined he'd ever been about any pursuit in his life. After auditioning for and being accepted into the Northampton Repertory Company in the English midlands, Flynn performed weekly in play after play, in both small and significant roles, making great leaps in ability by the time he began frequenting the offices of Warner Bros. Teddington Studios. After much prodding, studio head Irving Asher finally took notice of the handsome, charismatic young man who was regularly coming by looking for work. Asher met with Flynn and immediately gave him the lead role in a budget murder mystery, and signed him to a modest contract. Based upon this one performance alone, Asher then sent a copy of the film to Hollywood, urging Jack Warner to watch it and consider bringing this new prospect to the home studio.

While all this good luck was brewing for Flynn, he had also been setting his sights on a French film actress in whom he had been interested since he was a teenager. His posthumous autobiography, as well as the many publicity stories about him over the years, all perpetuated a narrative of Flynn and Lili Damita first meeting on the ocean liner that brought them both to America at the end of 1934. They had, in fact, met earlier in Paris and London and later admitted to those encounters in at least one interview (see November, page 40).

That letter to Dr. Erben that Flynn wrote outlining his long-term plan also included the goal of going to Los Angeles "in about a year from now." In the end it didn't take that long. The Flynn good fortune saw him off to America in but nine short months.

June

Sees Lili Damita (born Liliane Marie Madeleine Carré in France on July 10, 1904) at a party in Paris and has himself introduced to the French actress with whom he has long been infatuated *(right)*.

July

Arrives in London, staying at the Berkeley Hotel; visits family in Belfast where his father is professor of biology at Queen's University; rooms at the Portland Residential Hotel (now gone) in Finsbury Park; appears as a dance extra in the film I ADORE YOU (now lost); may also have been an extra in the play "Once In a Lifetime" at the Queen's Theatre, Shaftsbury Avenue; orders a series of portraits taken by "Sasha" (Alexander Stewart) at the photographer's London studio *(below left)* and continues to use them in various promotion fliers—often with an inflated résumé *(below right)*.

Lili Damita

Left, a portrait from the Sasha studio, and above, a promotional ad - Summer 1933

Wed July 5

Writes a letter to Hermann Erben *(center right)*: "Dear Doc / Expect letter from me in three or four days time with an idea for making money using your photos for a lecture tour—my father thinks he can arrange it with some folk who have cash—really good money. Send the photos as soon as possible. Hope you're okay? Regards Errol Flynn."

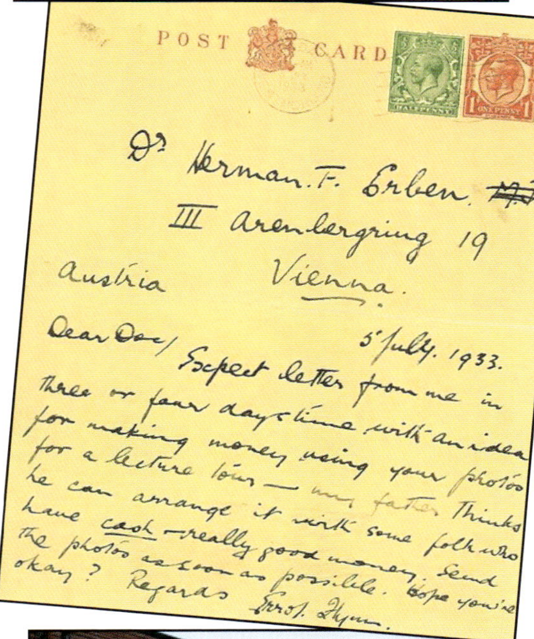

Autumn

Drives to Northampton; is hired by its repertory company at £6 a week (about $621.83 in 2021 value), soon reduced to £3; first home, with his girlfriend (probably fellow thespian Freda Jackson), is the top floor of 13 Hazelwood Road *(bottom right, left side)*.

Tue August 22

Letter to Hermann Erben from Seaford, England, regarding, among other subjects, the quality of sex to be had in this coastal town: *".....It's absolutely phenomenal! My poor old penis is hanging by a mere thread!....I have done a couple of small parts in pictures...but it will be some time...before a decent chance comes my way....All the men I've met so far are either quaers or such damned hypocrites that I couldn't be bothered talking to them. The women I do not care to talk to but am prepared to poke...."*

Thu August 31

"....The historical passages [in IN THE WAKE OF THE BOUNTY] *have been excellently done. In these scenes, Mayne Lynton as Bligh, and Errol Flynn as Fletcher Christian, act convincingly and naturally. They supply a proof that Australia has actors capable of vitalising any of the great Australian historical dramas that have still to be made...."* The Cairns Post.

Mon September 11

Is defeated in a singles tennis match at Eastbourne.

Fri September 22

Letter to Hermann Erben from the Portland Residential Hotel in London: *"....Sorry haven't written you before this thanking you for the photos. Truth is I've been in the midst of charming love affairs which I'm sure you'll aprec. takes*

13 Hazelwood Road, Northampton

Playbill for Flynn's first stage performance - December 1933

40/50 Guildhall Road, Northampton

precedence over any of the more mundane of human activities...."

November
I ADORE YOU opens.

Mon December 18 to Sat December 23
Stage debut as Edward Wales in *The Thirteenth Chair (top left)*.

Wed December 27 to Sat December 30
Plays the part of Prince Donzil in *Jack and the Beanstalk*.

1934

January
IN THE WAKE OF THE BOUNTY opens in Hobart at the Avalon Theatre on a bill with *The Crime of the Century*, starring Jean Hersholt and Stu Erwin, and at the Strand opposite *Blondie Johnson* with Joan Blondell (his future co-star); it received no press concerning its hometown star and screened for only six days.

Mon January 1 to Sat January 6
Plays the part of Geoffrey Wedderburn in *Sweet Lavender*.

Sat January 6
Letter to Hermann Erben: *"I've taken to the stage myself and have been playing for the last month - an experience which is proving invaluable for technique and will help later if I ever make the big time in films. I plan to go to Los Angeles in about a year from now...."*

Mon January 8 to Sat January 13
Plays the part of Marcovitch in *Bulldog Drummond*.

Fri January 12
"ERROL FLYNN~FILM STAR AND SPORTSMAN Writing of Repertory matters makes me wonder how many playgoers know that the newest member of the company, Mr. Errol Flynn, who plays the part of Marcovitch in this week's play, Bulldog Drummond, was a film actor....He had a large following of fans in Australia, for he took the hero part in at least six important Australian pictures....And that is not all about this versatile personality. Amateur boxing and swimming have both claimed his attention. Mr. Flynn reached the finals of the amateur boxing championship of Australia, and he was among those chosen to compete in swimming contests at the Olympic Games....Despite his experience in films, he prefers the stage to the screen, and at the moment is most interested in repertory." From "My Friday Diary" by "Alys" in the *Northampton Chronicle and Echo*; Flynn himself undoubtedly provided these exaggerated claims.

Mon January 15 to Sat January 20
Plays the part of Nils Kogstrad in *A Doll's House*; Flynn *"…made a splendid villain..."* The Chronicle and Echo

Mon January 22 to Sat January 27
Plays the part of Mike Feeney in *On the Spot*.

Mon January 29 to Sat February 3
Plays the part of the 2nd bystander in *Pygmalion*.

February
Drives to London sometime this month to see Lili Damita, who is appearing in *Here's How* at the Saville Theatre on Shaftesbury Avenue; he reintroduces himself backstage.

February/March
Moves to 40/50 Guildhall Road *(bottom left)*.

Mon February 5 to Sat February 10
Plays the part of Charabanc Driver in *The Crime At Blossoms*.

Sat February 10
Around 2:30am, alerts a doctor at the Salon de Danse in Franklin Gardens (which he had just left) of a road accident.

Mon February 12 to Sat February 17
Plays the role of Joe Varwell in *Yellow Sands (right)*; "Easily his best piece of acting with the Company," wrote Aubrey

As Joe Varwell in Yellow Sands *(Flynn on the right) - February 1933*

Dyas of Flynn in *Adventure In Repertory* after witnessing his performance; *The Chronicle and Echo* critic found Flynn *"always convincing…"*

Mon February 19 to Sat February 24
Plays the role of Mr. Cornthwaite in *The Grain of Mustard Seed*.

Mon February 26 to Sat March 3
Plays the part of Thomas Hayden in *Seven Keys to Baldpate Inn*.

March
At the Northampton Banks Ball.

Mon March 5 to Sat March 10
Plays the parts of Ludovico and the 1st Senator in *Othello (top right)*.

Wed March 7
Is in the Borough Police Court pleading guilty to charges of no car tax, insurance, front lights, or tail light on his red 1925 Swallow sports car; Mayor/Councilor Edward Allitt fines Flynn £3.50 ($362.76 in 2021 value). Sometime later he buys a dark green 1931 MG Midget, license plate #GY 6929.

Mon March 12 to Sat March 17
Plays the part of Trump in *The Green Bay Tree*.

Sat March 17
An article called "Why I Became An Actor" by Errol Flynn appears in the *Northampton and County Independent*.

Mon March 19 to Sat March 24
Plays the part of Geoffrey Sands in *The Fake*; *"That clever young actor, Errol Flynn, came into the limelight again last night. As Geoffrey Sands, who murders Stanton's son-in-law in the cause of justice, he was always splendid…..such splendid acting deserved a larger audience."* The Chronicle Echo.

Mon March 26 to Sat April 7
Plays the part of George Smerdon in *The Farmer's Wife*.

Mon April 9 to Sat April 14
Plays the part of John Williams in *The Wind and the Rain*.

Mon April 16 to Sat April 21
Plays the part of a reporter in *Sheppey*.

Mon April 23 to Sat April 28
Plays the part of Jan in *The Soul of Nicholas Snyders*.

Mon April 30 to Sat May 5
Plays the part of Rev. Anthony Anderson in *The Devil's Disciple*.

Fri May 4
Takes part in the jubilee celebration of the Northampton Opera House, performing there in *By Candle Light* for such distinguished guests as the Mayor and Mayoress and members of the Town Council.

Mon May 14 to Sat May 19
Plays the part of Tom Smith in *Conflict* (the author of the play, Miles Malleson, later played a part in the 1955 Flynn film KING'S RHAPSODY).

Thu May 24 to Sat May 26
Plays the part of Dr. Davy Adair in *Paddy the Next Best Thing*.

Mon May 28 to Sat June 2
Plays the part of James Everett in *9:45*, his last performance in Northampton.

Tue May 29
Letter to Cyril L. Phillips Esq. at Sir Barry Jackson's offices at 3 Clifford St. New Bond St. London (bottom right): *Dear Mr. Phillips/ Do you want me at the Old Vic for Monday's rehearsals? If essential I can be there, but an extra day or so would be valuable time (removing effects soon). Kindest regards, Errol Flynn."*

June
In London, daily attending the Old Vic for a week or more.

Background photo: The Royal Theatre & Opera House, home of the Northampton Repertory

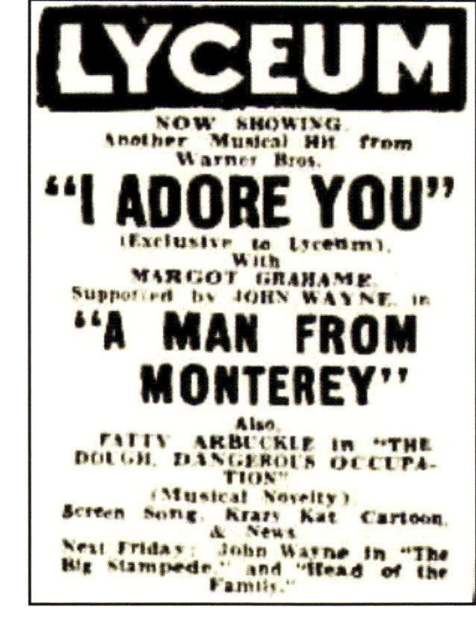

MONDAY, MARCH 5th, 1934, for Six Days.
6.30 p.m. —— and —— 8.50 p.m.

NORTHAMPTON REPERTORY PLAYERS Ltd.

Present—

THE TRAGEDY OF

OTHELLO,
THE MOOR OF VENICE

By WILLIAM SHAKESPEARE.

CHARACTERS:

Roderigo, a Venetian Gentleman	DONALD GORDON.
Iago	OSWALD DALE ROBERTS.
Brabantio, a Senator	JOHN STOBART.
Brabantio's Household	A. NEVILLE MEIER.
	ELIZABETH INGLIS.
	ZILLAH GREY.
Othello	G. N. HOLME.
Cassio	PETER ROSSER.
Duke of Venice	JULIAN CLAY.
First Senator	KENNETH GRINLING.
Second Senator	ERROL FLYNN.
Desdemona	FREDERICK TUCKLEY.
Montano	FREDA JACKSON.
Emilia	HAROLD CHANDLER.
Bianca	DOROTHY GALBRAITH.
Lodovic	SHEILA MILLAR.
Gratiano	ERROL FLYNN.
First Gentleman	JOHN STOBART.
Second Gentleman	A. NEVILLE MEIER.
Soldier	G. N. HOLME.
Soldier on Guard	A. NEVILLE MEIER.
Nubian Slave	F. SCRIMSHAW.
Serving Man	PETER YOUNG.
Trumpeter	F. TUCKLEY.
	W. J. CLARK.

Silverware by Messrs. Knight & Son, Mercers' Row.
China by Miss E. J. Adams, The China Gift Shop, Abington Street.

Playbill from Flynn's Shakespeare role - March

The Courier Mail *of Brisbane, Australia -
Fri April 27*

38 Worcester Road, Malvern (on the left)

With fellow actor Richard Caldicot at a Malvern garden party

October 19th/1934.

Mr. Irving Asher,
Warner Bros. First National Productions, Ltd.,
Teddington, Middlesex.

Dear Mr. Asher,

My signature at the bottom of this letter signifies my acceptance of an option to be taken by you on my services, said option to be exercised not later than ten days after the completion of my present engagement in your film now known as "MURDER AT MONTE CARLO". This option is for an agreement for my services as an artiste for a period of seven years divided into six-months optional periods, the option to be on your part, each six months period to be 24 out of 26 weeks. The other two weeks can be at your discretion without salary. It is understood that the terms of this agreement will be as follow:-

The first period of 24 weeks out of 26 weeks at a salary of £15. per week when not working and £20. per week when working.

The following two periods of 24 weeks out of 26 weeks each at a salary of £15. per week when not working and £25. per week when working.

The following two periods of 24 weeks out of 26 weeks each at a salary of £25. per week when not working and £35. per week when working.

The following period of 24 weeks out of 26 weeks at a salary of £25. per week when not working and £50. per week when working.

:2:

The following period of 24 weeks out of 26 weeks at a salary of £40. per week when not working and £200 per week when working.

The following period of 24 weeks out of 26 weeks at a salary of £50. per week when not working and £250. per week when working.

It is understood that each period of 24 weeks out of 26 weeks carries with it a guarantee of at least six weeks at the working salary in each case whether I work or not.

It is understood that the terms of this Agreement will be embodied in the usual Artiste's Agreement to be drawn up in the near future, and I thoroughly understand that this letter is binding.

I acknowledge the receipt of the sum of £1. (One Pound) as consideration for giving you this option.

ACCEPTED....(signed) ERROL FLYNN.

WITNESSED....   "   F.R. ROYCE.

Flynn's first Warner Bros. contract

July

Moves to Malvern for six weeks, sharing rooms with Richard Caldicot and Geoffrey Toone at "Branksome," 38 Worcester Road *(top left)*; appears in the Malvern Festival in the part of a Roman soldier in *A Man's House* (George Bernard Shaw is in attendance on opening night).

Tue July 24

The Tragical History of Dr. Faustus opens at Malvern, Flynn in the parts of Pride and a Knight.

Wed July 25

The Marvellous History of Saint Bernard opens at Malvern, with Flynn playing the parts of Envy and Servant to Miolans.

Thu July 26

Plays the part of Commandant Lanigan in *The Moon and Yellow River* until Tuesday, August 14th; a critic from *The Malvern News* wrote: "*The portrayal of Commandant Lanigan, who shoots down his comrade of earlier days, just as the German (Tausch) has described Ireland as a country where all is talk and 'nothing ever happens' was another strong feature. Mr. Errol Flynn had this part."*

Sat July 28

Mutiny opens at Malvern, Flynn playing the part of Corporal Martin until Thursday, August 16th.

Summer

Begins a relationship with Marjorie Bickham from Ledbury, England, who was evidently not as ardent about it as was Flynn. Some excerpts from his letters to her: "*Do you think you might snatch a brief moment from the hilarious mad whirl of pleasure at Sark* [Island] *to drop me a line?" "They're playing a tune now we know but can't think of the name of it and I know it so well - we danced it together or at least you did and I trampled you underfoot and I couldn't get you to look at me and I didn't like to ask you to go into the garden with me, and when we did go I wanted like the very devil to kiss you but for the life of me couldn't think how to set about it - very puzzling indeed that, for it's a sorry admission that I'm not normally at a loss in such matters." "I left Malvern thinking of you – drove to the middle of England with you still along and reached the border and you were still most insistently present, and devil* [not] *another thought in my mind but you! Is that right? Is it just? If you could hear my mind working at the moment you'd pause and wonder what it was all about. Because there's the most extraordinary confusion there just now."* From the Caledonian Hotel in Edinburgh he writes: "*…funny how you can't be candid—or sincere in a letter. I can't anyway. There's so much I'd like to say to you…Perhaps I could if I knew for certain you wanted to hear it. I'm going to bed—I know I shall think of you until I go to sleep. 'Night—Margy."* From Leeds he promises: "*…I'll ring you up at the Forum Club in the morning – if you're out or anything I'll leave a message and ring again. Gosh I'm keen to see you! Au revoir a bientot –Errol."*

Marjorie Bickham

Mon August 20 to Sun August 26

Performs with the Malvern cast in *A Man's House* at the King's Theatre in Glasgow.

Sat September 8 to Sat September 22

Performs in *A Man's House* at the New Theatre in London's West End (now the Noel Coward Theatre).

Fall

In London, works as an extra at Teddington Studios; is said to have played a bit in the film MIMI, seen by Douglas Fairbanks Jr., who then, along with Warner Bros. First National Britain's managing director, Irving Asher, recommends Flynn to Warner Bros. in Hollywood.

October

Makes weekly visits to the offices of Warner Bros. Teddington in Middlesex until a secretary, Mrs. Boyd, recommends to her boss, studio head Irving Asher, that he interview Flynn as a potential actor; telegram from Irving Asher to WB Hollywood: SIGNED TODAY SEVEN YEARS' OPTIONAL CONTRACT BEST PICTURE BET WE HAVE EVER SEEN. HE TWENTY FIVE IRISH LOOKS CROSS BETWEEN CHARLES FARRELL AND GEORGE BRENT SAME TYPE AND BUILD EXCELLENT ACTOR CHAMPION BOXER SWIMMER GUARANTEE HE REAL FIND.

Note from Flynn concerning an unpaid bill for clothing items: "*Thursday Messrs. MacCormack's Agency Northampton Dear Sirs/If you would care to wait about a week longer I will be able to pay your account in full. The only reason it has not been settled previously is inability, not disinclination. Yrs etc. Errol Flynn"*

Plays the part of newspaper reporter Dyter in the WB First National film MURDER AT MONTE CARLO.

Flynn's later self-assessment of his work in the film: *"The Cameraman didn't pay much attention to me. My jaw sagged, I had a face two feet long and looked exactly like a horse."*

Fri October 19

Signs his first film contract, a modest deal with Warner Bros. First National Productions for £20 per week ($2,072.82 in 2021 value); the contract is renewed on October 29th; WB First National London managing director Irving Asher to Jack Warner: *"I have sent you under separate cover some film of Flynn which I think will show you what he is like. This is the first time he has ever played a part in a picture and this is a quickie where he has had no direction to speak of. He has absolutely no make-up of any kind on, and I think you will agree with me that for a first picture he certainly shows promise. (He does not have to talk as English as he does in this stuff) He is a level–headed, intelligent fellow and you can do anything with him. For god's sake – if you don't like him send him back to us, as we can use him to fine advantage here...The picture I cabled you that I could have rented him for was a B.I.P. picture 'Abdul Hamid', which is being made on a big scale, and they wanted him to play the part which was originally intended Charles Farrell would play. The reason I cabled you is they offered me £125. a week, which is $625 [$12,960.78 in 2021 value], on a five-week guarantee – and as we pay him $75. a week [$1,480 in 2021 value] I though it was pretty good profit...I am attaching hereto details of the contract, and am sending a few stills, which is all I have at the moment. I have no portraits of him. I am buying him a few clothes – as a matter of fact quite a few – about $1,0000's worth [$19,733 in 2021 value], as he has just been an extra man and has no tails, tuxedo, suits, shoes, or anything, and I feel he can get better things cheaper here, and if you decide to you can take it out of his salary from time to time later, but I think it is ridiculous to have him arrive there without some sort of wardrobe...I am also attaching a few notes of interest on the boy, his past experience, etc."*

Tue November 6

Completes work on MURDER AT MONTE CARLO.

Wed November 7

Answers one of his first fan letters to a Miss Norfolk in Northampton: *"Thanks very much for your letter + your good wishes which I thought very nice of you indeed...I am leaving for Hollywood in a week but until I get there I'm not quite sure what I'll be doing...I hope 'Murder At Monte Carlo' goes up to Northampton--it's a good comedy with quite a few thrills + we finished it yesterday...Again, thank you for your letter. Yours sincerely Errol Flynn"* Flynn's address at this point is 28 St. Petersburg Place, London W2.

Wed November 14

Leaves Plymouth, England, for the United States aboard the ocean liner S.S. Paris; on board, he reacquaints himself with Lili Damita.

Tue November 20

Arrives in New York.

Wed November 21

Irving Asher to Jack Warner: *"By the time you receive this letter you will have seen Errol Flynn [in photo and film], and I hope you will feel that it was worth while sending him."*

Fri November 23

"Errol Flynn, the Irish actor, signed by Warner Brothers studio, is scheduled to arrive here today. He has had a varied career as a gold prospector and a diver for pearls in the South Seas. He has been a popular idol in London." Edwin Schallert, The Los Angeles Times.

Sat November 24

"Errol Flynn, Irish actor just signed to a long-term ticket by Warners, once was a gold prospector in the wilds of New Guinea." Read Kendall, The Los Angeles Times.

Tue November 27

Signs a contract with Warner Bros. for 26 weeks (6 weeks idle) at $150 per week ($2,960 in 2021 value), effective November 26th; all notices were ordered to be sent to Flynn at the Knickerbocker Hotel in Hollywood; WB legal counsel Roy Obringer to Jack Warner: *"Please be advised that the standard form contract with Errol Flynn has been signed...Flynn, however, states that while our London and New York offices provided his transportation expenses to Hollywood, it was necessary for him to expend an additional $30.00 [$592 in 2021 value], and he would appreciate if he could be reimbursed in this amount. Will you please okay this memo, and I will reimburse him in the above amount."*

Flynn with Georgie Harris and Eve Gray in a still from MURDER AT MONTE CARLO

1	2	3	4	5	6	7	8	9	10	11	12	13	14	15
No. on List	Head-Tax Status	Family name / Given name	Age Yrs.	Mos.	Sex / Married or single	Calling or occupation	Able to — Read / other language / Write	Nationality (Country of which citizen or subject)	Race or people	Place of birth Country / City or town	Immigration Visa, etc.	Issued Place / Date	Data concerning verifications of landings	*Last permanent residence Country / City or town
1		de LIMA — Josette Georgette	31		F / M	Designer	Yes / French-Engl. / Yes	FRANCE	French	France / Montbeliard	RP. IOOOI33 IOOI473	Washington 3/28/34		U.S.A. / N.Y.C.
2		SIMON — André	57		M / M	Lecturer				Paris	N.I. 4217 T.V.	London 11/8/34		England / London
3		" — Edith	56		F / M	None			English	England / Grantham	1213			"
4		VOTION — Jack W.	34		M / M	Director		BELGIUM	French	Belgium / Antwerp	RP. 688078 093360 (Extens.12/28/33 & 7/24/34)	Washington 2/13/33		U.S.A. / Beverly Hills
5		DAINTY — Ruth Pauline	25		F / S	Journalist	English	GR.BRITAIN	English	England / London	N.I. 3316 T.V.	London 11/13/34		England / London
6		FAIRLESS — Margaret	23		F / S	Independant				Portland	QIV. 200	London 11/8/34		
7	TEMP. STAY	FLYNN — Errol Thomson	25		M / S	Actor	French-Engl.			Tasmania / Hobart	N.I. 3276 T.V.		VI. 355/	
8		JORDAN — Thomas	60		M / M	Merchant	English			Canada / Acton	NO VISA			Canada / Montreal
9	TRANSIT	HAYWARD — Charles Louis	25		M / S	Actor				Transvaal / Johannesburg	N.I. 3208 T.V.	London 11/6/34		England / London

Above, the passenger manifest from the S.S. Paris; actor Louis Hayward is listed at the bottom

Arriving in Los Angeles - Tue, November 23

At the premiere of Flirtation Walk -
Sat, December 1

Sat December 1
Attends the premiere of *Flirtation Walk (top right)*.

Mon December 10
Jack Warner to Irving Asher: *"I saw Errol Flynn in person as well as the film and I certainly think he looks great. We are making a flock of tests with him and he definitely will make good unless I miss my guess. It was very fine of you to send him to us."*

Tue December 11
"Errol Flynn, new Irish star at Warners, got a ticket five minutes after he bought a car, driving on the left-hand side of the street." Read Kendall, *The Los Angeles Times*.

Sat December 29
WB head studio counsel, Roy Obringer to Mr. F. R. Royce, Warner Bros. Teddington Studios in the U.K: *"I have questioned Mr. Flynn with respect to this wardrobe expense [£123, approximately $12,751.66 in 2021 value], whether or not this money was advanced to him in order to complete his wardrobe prior to arriving in the states with the intention that we would deduct the same from his contract salary, or whether it was an outright expense to be born by us and form part of the contract agreement...Mr. Flynn seems to be somewhat hazy as to his understanding with Mr. Asher, or whoever made the arrangements. Normally, if advances of this nature were made here at the studio for an artist's wardrobe, and which incidentally I might add is very seldom done, it is generally with the understanding that we would be repaid by deductions from his salary. If this is true in connection with the advance made Flynn, I would appreciate you advising me in order that I may make arrangements with him to arrange for these deductions."*

Flynn's revised Warner Bros. contract

The first official Hollywood portrait for Warner Bros.

A promotional shoot for Gold Diggers of 1935
(Flynn was not in the film)

3

RISING STAR

1935~1938

Between January of 1935 and the start of the following year, Errol Flynn went from unknown to world acclaim on the basis of a single film. Up until that film, the Hollywood fledgling had been given only six minutes of screen time in two B movies before Warner Bros. gambled on placing him in the lead role of their biggest budgeted film of the year, CAPTAIN BLOOD. And their gamble paid off: the film and its star were an international smash. From that position of unquestionable success and new found popularity, Flynn never really looked back, becoming Warners' main adventure star for the next seventeen years and single-handedly reviving a genre of film that he all but dominated: the swashbuckler. During the four-year period of this chapter, he made six adventure films, including the title role in THE ADVENTURES OF ROBIN HOOD, a role he seemed almost predestined to play and which would forever seal his reputation in film history.

In the personal sphere, Errol's sizzling affair with Lili Damita culminated in a combustible marriage, and his growing riches afforded him the ability to acquire boats, the most notable of which was the 75-foot ketch *Sirocco*. He also moved a number of times in this period, once sharing a house with David Niven during one of the regular fallings-out Flynn had with Lili. With him at all times, seemingly more so even than his wife, was his beloved schnauzer Arno. The two could be found together on the Warner Bros. soundstages, on locations, and even—portentously—at sea.

All the success Flynn had longed for from his earliest days was now realized in these years, and the success was such that he felt secure enough to skip out of the country in early 1937 in search of adventure—dangerous adventure—near the front lines of the Spanish Civil War. Along with him on this trip was his old friend Dr. Hermann Erben, whose own involvement in the escapade fanned the flames of suspicion for years to come as to his true motivations. Warner Bros. was naturally indignant that their highly bankable star would do something so risky and delinquent, but Flynn took it all in stride and returned home with his usual insouciant smile.

Other than the continuing friction in his marriage, little in the way of gray skies clouded his days. Those clouds would appear soon enough in the following years, just as he stood at the pinnacle of personal and professional gratification. But for now, Errol Flynn held the world in the palm of his hand, and in these years enjoyed himself to the hilt.

1935

At the Los Angeles Tennis Club - Winter 1935

February 19, 1935

Mr. Irving Asher
Warner Bros. First National Productions, Ltd.
Teddington Studios
Teddington, Middlesex
ENGLAND

Dear Irving:

I am attaching herewith a copy of a letter which I sent to Mr. F. R. Royce under date of December 29, 1934, and to date I have received no reply.

Naturally the expense of Hunter is not contested, but in connection with ERROL FLYNN, we treated the advances made to him of 123 pounds for wardrobe as purely a loan and to be paid back to us by deduction from his salary. Our interpretation of this is borne out by the fact that we received from our New York office a charge against Flynn to be collected by us here.

Flynn, however, takes the attitude that this was a charitable move on our part, believing that the purchase of his wardrobe was to be absorbed by the studio and were he to pay for it himself, he would not have got such high priced wardrobe. Personally, I believe that Flynn is acting very stupidly to his own advantage and is trying to get away with having us pay six or seven hundred dollars for wardrobe which is not our normal practice.

Will you, therefore, give me the definite understanding you had with Flynn as to whether or not this was a gift to him or purely an advance to be deducted from his salary, in order that we may be governed accordingly.

Yours very truly,

R. J. OBRINGER

With Lili at the Hotel del Coronado Tennis Club
Mon, March 25

Mon January 21

A tentative cast list for THE CASE OF THE CURIOUS BRIDE on this date shows George Meeker in the role of Gregory Moxley; Jack Warner to producer Hal Wallis: *"I overheard a typical Mike Curtiz-Harry Joe Brown squawk about not wanting to use Errol Flynn in Case Of The Curious Bride. I hope that they did not change you because I want him used in this picture, first because I think it is a shame to let people like Curtiz and Harry Brown to even think of opposing an order from you or myself and, secondly, when we bring a man all the way from England he is at least entitled to a chance and somehow or another we haven't given him one. I want to make sure he is in the picture. Let me hear from you on this the next time we see each other."*

Tue January 22

Final casting now includes Flynn in the role of Moxley.

Mon January 28

With Lili at the Trocadero; Marlene Dietrich is also in attendance.

Wed February 6

"Errol Flynn, Irish leading man from the London stage, will play in 'The Case of the Curious Bride.'" Edwin Schallert in *The Los Angeles Times*.

Sat February 16

Attends a cocktail party with Lili at the home of William Haines.

Wed February 20

First day of shooting on a Hollywood picture, THE CASE OF THE CURIOUS BRIDE, working from 5:45-6:15pm with Margaret Lindsay on a scene in Moxley's (Flynn) apartment, and completing it in one take.

Thu February 21

More work on THE CASE OF THE CURIOUS BRIDE.

Tue February 26

Finishes work on THE CASE OF THE CURIOUS BRIDE; total screen time is about one minute; his salary for the film is $900 (about $17,495 in 2021 value).

March

Moves with Lili Damita into the Garden of Allah Hotel (now gone).

Sun March 24

At Guy Rennie's King's Club on Sunset Blvd.

Mon March 25

With Lili at the Hotel del Coronado Beach and Tennis Club *(bottom left)*.

With Margaret Lindsay filming
THE CASE OF THE CURIOUS BRIDE -
Wed, February 20

Wed March 27

Jack Warner to Hal Wallis: *"I just saw all the tests on Captain Blood and first, Jean Muir looks magnificent and we want to give her very serious consideration. Likewise, Errol Flynn was great in his bits of the test. Anita Louise looks magnificent likewise in her tests. You and I want to have a good chat before we decide who plays these important parts in Captain Blood."*
Edwin Schallert in *The Los Angeles Times* reports: *"Curtiz to Guide 'Captain Blood' There are some indications that 'Captain Blood' will soon be under way. First of all, Robert Donat will be returning to Hollywood April 10 and also Michael Curtiz, who did such an excellent job in directing 'Black Fury,' has been assigned to guide this feature. Furthermore, Errol Flynn, the English picture actor, who took part in productions at the Warner studio abroad, will assume the role of the pirate leader in this swashbuckling tale."*

Thu March 28

Roy Obringer to studio treasurer, Cy Wilder: *"At the present you have an accounts receivable for certain wardrobe purchased for Errol Flynn by the London studio. I have taken this matter up with Irving Asher, who made the arrangement with Flynn, and he states that the wardrobe is to be paid for by the studio on account of the low figure for which he was able to get Flynn to contract for. Therefore, the charge should be wiped off the books, and I presume charged to picture overhead."*

Spring

Moves with Lili to 8946 Appian Way in the Hollywood Hills *(top right)* though continues to use the Knickerbocker Hotel mailing address as a cover, presumably because he and Lili are not married; their telephone number is GR-0031.

Thu April 4

THE CASE OF THE CURIOUS BRIDE opens at the Strand in New York.

Mon April 8

Screen tests are made available to be seen in WB Projection Room #5; they include those of Anita Louise, Olivia de Havilland, Jean Muir, and Bette Davis for the part of Arabella; Basil Rathbone and Louis Calhern for the part of Levasseur; and Paul Hurst, Tom Moore, and Errol Flynn for the part of Hagthorpe (which eventually went to Guy Kibbee).

Mon April 22

Hal Wallis to assistant director Dick Maybery: *"Are we using Errol Flynn for the part of the boy in 'Not On Your Life'* [early title for DON'T BET ON BLONDES] *who takes* [Dolores] *Del Rio to the night club--where the gangsters come around his table? Let me know if he is set for the part."*

Mon May 6

Begins work on DON'T BET ON BLONDES, filming the nightclub scene; Flynn's contract is extended another twenty-six weeks.

Sat May 11

Finishes work on DON'T BET ON BLONDES filming at Lakeside Country Club across from the WB Studios from 2:15 to 2:30pm *(center right)*; total screen time in the film is about five minutes.

With Claire Dodd filming DON'T BET ON BLONDES *at the Lakeside Country Club - Sat, May 11*

With Lili at the Santa Barbara Biltmore - Wed, May 22

Friday May 24

"Lily Damita Shrugs Off Rumor Of Her Betrothal-'Oh my, dear me!' With a shrug of her shapely shoulders, Lily Damita started out in this wise yesterday when told Hollywood was reporting her betrothal to Errol Flynn, young Irish actor, because they had been seen together in the gardens of the Santa Barbara Biltmore...And then she went on: 'Life she is some beautiful kettles of fish when a girl cannot go to see tennis matches with a man without marrying him. We went to see the tennis matches-and we heard them say, "Forty, love," but there is no romance. We are just good friends.'" The Los Angeles Times.

Sun May 26

Beats studio art director Walter Ledgerwood in singles tennis, 6–3 and 6–4, at the Los Angeles Tennis Club.

Thu May 30

Loses a tennis match to WB talent scout Solly Baiano at the Los Angeles Tennis Club.

Sun June 2

At a costume party thrown by the Countess di Frasso.

Wed June 5

Hal Wallis to director Mervyn LeRoy: *"I would like to have a couple of very good tests made on Thursday of George Brent and Errol Flynn for the part of Captain Blood in the picture of that name. As you know, Curtiz is shooting the picture and I will appreciate it if you will arrange to shoot these."*

Thu June 6

Films another screen test for the title role of CAPTAIN BLOOD.

Tue June 11

With Lili at the King's Club in Hollywood.

Sun June 16

Errol and Lili attend Carole Lombard's party on the Ocean Park amusement pier at Venice Beach, CA *(right);* also in attendance are Marlene Dietrich, Claudette Colbert, Bruce Cabot, Zeppo Marx, and many others.

With Marlene Dietrich, Carole Lombard, and Lili at Venice Beach - Sun, June 16

8946 Appian Way in the Hollywood Hills, Errol and Lili's first home; he can be seen standing on the veranda

LILY DAMITA WED IN YUMA

Bride of Flynn, Irish Athlete; Lilian Bond Betrothed to New York Broker

---

"I nevair knew a wedding she could be so tres grande! She was heavenly!"

Lily Damita, French film actress, so exulted yesterday as she became the bride at Yuma of Errol Flynn, Dublin actor and one-time boxer, who found his way to Hollywood via the 1928 Olympic Games.

MISS BOND TO WED

And while Lily was going into ecstacies over the nuptials, another film actress named Lilian was announcing her engagement to one of la Damita's erstwhile devoted swains—Sidney Smith, New York stock broker and big game hunter.

By telephone from San Francisco, where she is appearing on the stage in "Accent on Youth," Miss Bond said she will marry Smith soon, "possibly within a short time after the close of the play Saturday night."

TRIP MAID BY AIR

The marriage of Miss Damita and Flynn was the fortieth ceremony in which film couples were united by Justice E. A. Freeman, famed as "the marrying judge," according to dispatches from the Gretna Green of Arizona. Bud Ernst, airplane pilot, flew the pair to Yuma.

Until shortly before the take-off from here a double marriage had been in the offing, Ernst having planned to take Lyda Roberti, blonde actress, as his bride.

LYDIA'S PLANS UPSET

But Miss Roberti at the last moment was called on location, and Ernst participated only as best man.

"Flynn was about as nervous as any man I've ever seen," Judge Freeman said, according to the dispatches.

"Everything was all right until he couldn't find the ring. He searched every pocket and at last realized it was stuck on his thumb."

Both the principals gave their ages as 26 years.

NAME GIVEN BY EX-KING

Miss Damita signed the license with her true name, Lillian Madellene Carre. The name "Damita" was the benediction of Alfonso, deposed King of Spain. It means "Little Lady."

Above, the old Gretna Green Wedding Chapel, 744 W. 1st St., Yuma, AZ, and below, the same location today

Wed June 19

Marries Lili Damita at the Gretna Green Wedding Chapel in Yuma, Arizona *(photos this page)*, Judge Earl A. Freeman officiating; the couple, along with Bud Ernst, were piloted there by Ted Brown; Ernst was enlisted by Freeman as *"bridesmaid,"* while the judge's clerk, J. G. Livingstone, stood in as best man.

Thu June 20

Flynn's 26th birthday; *"Lili Damita and Errol Flynn's honeymoon house atop Lookout Mountain was the 'location' for high revelry…when they entertained at a formal dinner, not only to celebrate their marriage on the previous day, but Errol's birthday as well."* The *Los Angeles Times* (6/24); Hal Wallis to production manager William Koenig, producer Harry Joe Brown, and director Michael Curtiz: *"We are going to make another series of tests with Errol Flynn for the part of 'Captain Blood'….the test should be made Tuesday, June 25th. Between now and that time, I would like Harry Joe Brown and Koenig to get together and really lay out these tests properly. Have a wig fixed properly for Flynn, even if we have to make one; get some good clothes for him without all these spangles and gold braids on them. In other words, dress him pretty much as he will be dressed in the picture. Also, between now and the end of the week, Harry Joe should get Flynn in and lay out the scenes which Flynn will be required to do. There should be two or three scenes of different types so that we can test Flynn exhaustively, and definitely decide if he can do the part…(1) There should be one scene between 'Blood' and 'Levasseur' with somebody to play 'Levasseur's part also…(2) There should be a scene between 'Blood' and his men…(3) A scene between 'Blood' and the girl…In other words, pick out material that will give Flynn the opportunity to get over every emotion. We want Jean Muir to work with him in the test…When making the tests, Mike Curtiz should move the people around, instead of just parking Flynn in front of the camera and shooting a close-up. He should actually play the scene…Please let's not have any slip-up on this series of tests, as the result of them will determine whether or not Flynn is to do the part, and let's have everything right; have Flynn up in his scenes and really do this thing correctly so that we won't have a lot of excuses next week as to why we did not do this or why we did not do that…I am leaving this entirely in the hands of Koenig, Brown and Curtiz and the tests should definitely be made Tuesday, as I want to see them Wednesday, before I leave. We have ample time now to prepare them properly."*

Tue June 25

More screen tests for CAPTAIN BLOOD; Hal Wallis to cameraman, Ted McCord: *"Mike Curtiz is making a lot of tests today of Errol Flynn on 'Captain Blood'. See that these are rushed through, so that we can get them back by noon Wednesday, and as soon as they come in have somebody start cutting them, playing most of the action favoring the boy. We want to see these after lunch."*

Wed June 26

Wallis assistant Walter McEwan to William Koenig, Harry Joe Brown, and costumer Dwight Franklin: *"This is a written reminder about the meeting in Projection Room 5 at 8 PM this evening with Mr. Wallis on 'Captain Blood'."* Dolores Del Rio hosts a party in her Santa Monica home (757 Klingman Avenue) for the newly-wed Flynns.

Thu June 27

Hal Wallis to Harry Joe Brown, William Koenig, and Michael Curtiz: *"Before we get set definitely with Errol Flynn for the part of 'Captain Blood', we are going to test Ian Hunter for this part. Will you please get busy immediately and make this test of Ian Hunter."*

Thu July 4

DON'T BET ON BLONDES opens at the Warner Downtown Theater.

Errol Flynn has finally been chosen to play the male lead in Warner's "Captain Blood." The young Irish actor recently married Lily Damita. Olivia De Havilland has been assigned to play the feminine lead in this Rafael Sabatini's adventure classic which Michael Curtis will direct.

The Film Daily - *Tue, July 9*

Mon July 8

Jack Warner to Irving Asher: *".....We have placed Errol Flynn in the big role of CAPTAIN BLOOD and am sure Flynn will come through with flying colors. His tests are marvelous. If he has anything at all on the ball he will surely come out in this picture and go to great heights. If he hasn't it will be one of those things, but we will do all in our power to put Flynn over in grand style."*

Sat July 13

Attends a banquet with Lili at the Trocadero in Hollywood.

Fri July 19

In Santa Barbara with Lili.

Summer

MURDER AT MONTE CARLO opens in Britain and Australia; *".....Errol Flynn contributes a high pressure portrayal."* The British Kinematograph Weekly.

Sat July 20

With Lili to Club New Yorker in Hollywood.

Tue July 23

Irving Asher to Jack Warner: *"Am terribly anxious to know how Flynn gets along with CAPTAIN BLOOD....."*

Tue July 30

Hal Wallis to Harry Joe Brown: *"Am just looking at the tests of Errol Flynn and the wigs. The #1 wig is the one we want to use—the first take on the reel. The*

Above, with Lili on the front porch of their Hollywood Hills house after Errol has been given the lead role in CAPTAIN BLOOD, *and below, the same spot today*

Looking over costumes for CAPTAIN BLOOD in the WB wardrobe department - July, 1935

#2 wig, that is, after he gets to Port Royal and the sugar cane, is too greasy; there is too much grease on the hair. The cut of it is about right but it is too greasy—it takes too many high-lights.

August

Flynn's South Seas diary is found among his possessions in New Guinea by Salamaua Hotel owners, Mr. and Mrs. Allen Inness.

Wed August 7

First day of shooting on CAPTAIN BLOOD (11am–6:45pm), filming scenes in Dr. Blood's home with Jesse Ralph and Ross Alexander *(next page top left)*; all production photos by Mickey Marigold; Jack Warner to Irving Asher: *"We started shooting with Flynn on CAPTAIN BLOOD...We have had a tough*

With Olivia de Havilland during a CAPTAIN BLOOD *promotional shoot behind the WB administration building - July, 1935*

With Jessie Ralph; the very first still taken on Flynn's first day of filming CAPTAIN BLOOD *- Wed, August 7*

With Olivia de Havilland (their first scene together), Lionel Atwill, Harry Cording, and Ross Alexander - Tue, August 13

break on this as he had a high fever on Monday and Tuesday and could not shoot any sooner. I know Flynn is on the way to success and feel sure he will make it as he seems to be a very sensible chap." Hal Wallis to William Koenig: *"Be sure that Errol Flynn does not wear the chain around his neck at any time during the picture."*

Thu August 8

Filming in Blood's house and street scenes; Hal Wallis to Michael Curtiz: *"As discussed with you, I think the first day's dailies—on the whole—are good. Flynn looks all right and the action was good. The only difficulty was that it was hard to understand him, principally, I think, because of his cold, and secondly, because the photography was so dark that you couldn't see him, and then with the voice being muffled by the cold, it was almost impossible to make out what he was saying. We may have to go back and do some close-ups...In any event, be sure and pick up a closeup of him at the door, when the old lady asks him if he will be back for breakfast, and let him speak his line and close the door and exit, as on this we will probably lap dissolve."*

Fri August 9 and Sat August 10

Filming the Taunton Hall scenes and (on 8/10) in the Baynes farmhouse.

Sun August 11

MURDER AT MONTE CARLO opens at the Deansgate Theatre in Manchester, England.

Mon August 12 through Sat August 17

Filming in the stockade and cane field; on August 13 Olivia de Havilland films her very first scene ever with Flynn *(bottom left)*; Hal Wallis to Michael Curtiz (8/13): *"I think Flynn is doing very well, except that in the court-room I thought you played him down a little too much.... Particularly those speeches where he talks about having been in prison for three months and a little later on, where he says 'Very well then', and where he tells the Judge that he is a doctor and tells the Judge about his own condition. It seems to me you could have gotten a little more fire in him...let his eyes light up a little, get a little more fire in his eyes in scenes of this kind. He plays a little too much in monotone. These repressed scenes are good, but they should be varied a little. Also, in the scene with Captain Hobart, in the farmhouse, he was very good in it, but if he had gotten a little more sparkle in his eyes, I think it would have been better. Watch this from now on, and see if you can't help him a little. Let him put a little more guts in the stuff...I know he can do this, it is just a matter of direction. There is a test here that was made of Flynn in England, where he played a great scene, with a lot of guts and a lot of fire, and I wish you would look at it to prove to yourself that he can do these things; so, in your direction, give him a little more of this action and let him have a little more fire."*

Mon August 19

Filming in the slaves' huts and Taunton Castle (Viennese Street on the backlot).

Tue August 20 and Wed August 21

Filming in the Governor's house and stockade; Hal Wallis to Michael Curtiz (8/21): *"The last dailies look nice. The scene with Errol Flynn and the group around him looks good. Flynn was very good in this stuff. He is sincere and convincing. Get him to smile once in a while, when the opportunity presents itself—especially in the scenes coming up with the girl—let him smile whenever possible, and in the scenes with the two doctors, and whenever you get the chance, because he has a nice personality and it will relieve that seriousness and that monotone that we are worried about."*

"Around his neck," so this cannery's Press department informs me, "Flynn wears a thin gold chain, given him by a dying missionary in the tropical interior of New Guinea.... There is an ugly scar on his shin-bone, the mark of a poisoned arrow...." Mr. Flynn's adventures in polar, Papua, and the number of beautiful scars he can show for them, are not recorded. Still, it gives you an idea.

Strangely enough, I believe at least half of the Flynn publicity saga. He is the kind of man who couldn't have helped having adventures. There is nothing movie-starish about him.

The U.K. Daily Express
Thu, February 13, 1936

Visiting Lili who is filming The Frisco Kid *on a neighboring soundstage - Thu, August 15*

Thu August 22 and Fri August 23
Filming at Port Royal on the Vitagraph backlot at Prospect and Talmadge Avenues in Hollywood; on 8/23 the company is released between 1:35 and 3pm to attend the Will Rogers Memorial ceremony.

Sat August 24
Filming the slave market and in the Governor's Judgment Hall.

Mon August 26
Filming in the Governor's bedroom and living room.

Tue August 27
Filming in the Governor's Judgment Hall and living room.

Wed August 28
Filming in the office of Dr. Bronson and Dr. Whacker.

Thu August 29
Filming in the Port Royal slave market and the cane field.

Fri August 30
Continues filming in the Port Royal slave market and Governor's living room; associate producer, Gordon Hollingshead: *"Waited for sun till 9:30 AM. Bothered with planes all day. 4 of the set ups were retakes."*

Sat August 31 and Mon September 1
Filming at Port Royal on the Vitagraph backlot and in the ship's hold.

Tue September 3
Continues filming at Port Royal (the slapping sequence with Col. Bishop) and in the ship's hold.

Wed September 4
Filming the stockade watchtower and the ship's hold.

Thu September 5 and Fri September 6
Filming outside the Governor's mansion with Olivia de Havilland.

Mon September 9
Filming at Port Royal on the Vitagraph backlot with de Havilland; Hal Wallis to Michael Curtiz: *"The dailies in the garden, between Blood and the girl—generally—were good, except for a little spot here and there in the scenes which we can cut around. I think the stuff plays very nicely...However, I don't know why you didn't get a close-up of Errol Flynn in the big scene with the girl, where he finally calls and says 'Lord Willoughby, she loves me!' You picked his close-up about half-way through the dialogue scene, and he wasn't very good in his close-up.... he was biting his lip through the early part of it. I want you to go back and do this whole thing over—do his close-up over, that is—and do it over from the beginning of the dialogue. Why do you take a dialogue scene of this kind, between a girl and a boy, and play the girl all the way through in a close-up, and you don't play the boy all the way through. Why did you leave out the stuff where she says 'What are you going to do now?' and he says 'Stay here', and all of that, which is the most charming part of the scene. Why didn't you shoot a close-up of him? Are you sore at this boy, or something, or what is it?..He plays the scene at the carriage very well. The scene where he says he's going to depend on the Governor's scout to help him out and all of that. He plays that very nicely, and if you will work with the boy a little, and give him a little confidence, I know he can be twice as good as he is now, but the fellow looks like he is scared to death every time he goes into a scene....I don't know what the hell is the matter. When he has confidence and gets into a scene, he plays it charmingly."*

Tue September 10
Home with the flu (or a recurrence of malaria); does not work.

Wed September 11
Filming on the deck of the *Cinco Llagas*.

Thu September 12
Filming on the *Cinco Llagas*, on Bishop's ship, and at Governor Steed's carriage.

Fri September 13 and Sat September 14
More filming on the *Cinco Llagas*.

Mid September
Is given a gift of a schnauzer puppy from producer Robert Lord; Flynn names it Arno and it becomes his inseparable companion for the next six years.

With Olivia de Havilland during wardrobe tests

On the Vitagraph backlot

Above, with Basil Rathbone at Three Arch Bay in Laguna Beach, CA - September; below, the same spot today

Mon September 16 through Wed September 18

Filming the beach scenes of Virgen Magra at Three Arch Bay in Laguna Beach, CA, with Basil Rathbone and Olivia de Havilland; inter-office memo from producer Gordon Hollingshead: *"Company called at 6:00 AM to be shooting at 8:00 AM."* Bad light between 9:45am and 4pm on 9/17; delays from a two-hour cloud cover and planes flying by on 9/18; Flynn is mentioned in the press as part of the cast in the upcoming Warner Bros. production CHARGE OF THE LIGHT BRIGADE.

Thu September 19

Continues filming the beach scenes at Three Arch Bay; bad light from 10:25am to 4:05pm; company dismissed at 4:30.

Fri September 20

Inter-office memo from Gordon Hollingshead: *"From 7:30 to 10:30 company lined up set keys and rehearsed. Sun broke though at 8:45 for about ten minutes. At 10:30 the company was ordered to report to F.N. Stage 18 [First National on the WB lot] to shoot at 3:00 PM [scenes in the Tortuga private room]. Arrived at FN at 12 noon."*

Sat September 21

Continues filming in the Tortuga private room, and also principal room.

Mon September 23

Filming on Levasseur's (Rathbone) ship (process shots), in the Tortuga private room, and on the *Cinco Llagas*.

Tue September 24 through Thu September 26

Filming on the beach at Three Arch Bay in Laguna; Gordon Hollingshead: *"Were unable to shoot because of high fog till 12:00 when sun broke through."* From 8 to 10:30am on 9/25, shots were made with artificial light; the sun broke through at 12:15; on 9/26 shots were made under artificial light from 8 to 10:20am, Flynn filming with Basil Rathbone only.

Fri September 27

Filming on the *Cinco Llagas*.

Sat September 28

Filming exteriors on the *Cinco Llagas* and on the *Arabella*.

Mon September 30

Continues filming on the *Arabella*; Hal Wallis to Michael Curtiz: *"I have talked to you about four thousand times, until I am blue in the face, about the wardrobe in this picture. I also sat up here with you one night, and with everything else connected with the company, and we discussed each costume in detail, and also discussed the fact that when the men get to be pirates that we would not have 'Blood' dressed up...Yet tonight, in the dailies, in the division of the spoil[s] sequence, here is Captain Blood with a nice velvet coat, with lace cuffs out of the bottom, with a nice lace stock collar, and just dressed exactly opposite to what I asked you to do...I distinctly remember telling you, I don't know how many times, that I did not want you to use lace collars or cuffs on Errol Flynn. What in the hell is the matter with you, and why do you insist on crossing me on everything that I ask you not to do? What do I have to do to get you to do things my way? I want the man to look like a pirate, not a molly-coddle. You have him standing up here dealing with a lot of hard-boiled characters, and you've got him dressed up like a God damned faggot...When you get this note I want you to stop shooting and come up and see me, and I want to find out once and for all why it is that you insist on doing things that I tell you not to do. For my own satisfaction, I want to hear you tell it to me, because I can't for the life of me figure out why you do things that are so obviously wrong, after you have been told not to do them time and time over again...You get one good day's dailies, and then you go all to hell again, and do everything ass backwards...From now on, and I don't want any argument about this, and any reason why you couldn't do it, from now on I want to okay Errol Flynn in every costume that he wears, in every sequence that he goes into---from now on! If you have to stop shooting, you send him up to my office and let me see him in the clothes he's going to wear, because I certainly can't trust you with it any more...I suppose that when he goes into the battle with the pirates (the French) at the finish, you'll probably be having him wear a high silk hat and spats...When the man divided the spoils you should have had him in a shirt with the collar open at the throat, and no coat on at all. Let him look a little swash-buckling, for Christ sakes! Don't always have him dressed up like a pansy! I don't know how many times we've talked this over…I hope that by the time we get into the last week of shooting this picture, that everybody will be organized and get things right. It's about time."*

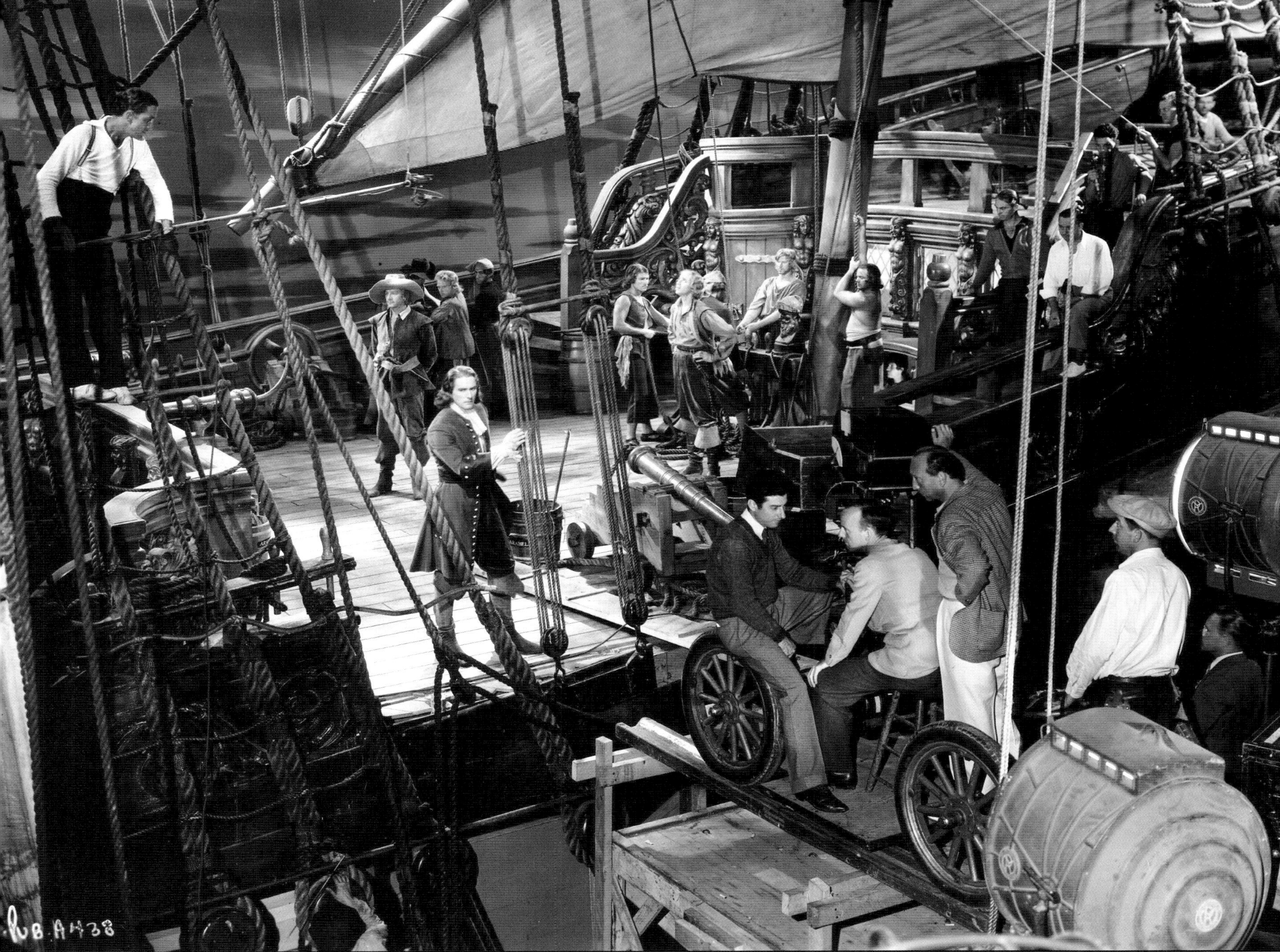

Filming on the Arabella; *in the hat behind Flynn is Robert Barrat; at center right looking up is Ross Alexander; director Michael Curtiz is in jacket on the right, standing behind the camera*

Tue October 1 through Sat October 5, and Mon October 7
Continues filming on the *Arabella* with de Havilland and (on 10/5) on the stern of the *Cinco Llagas.*

Tue October 8
Filming in Blood's cabin with de Havilland.

Wed October 9
Filming in Blood's and Arabella's (de Havilland) cabins (a chair *"squeaked"* at 10am), in the corridors, and outside Blood's cabin.

Thu October 10
Filming with de Havilland on the *Arabella.*

Fri October 11
Filming the crow's nest and Port Royal at night on the WB backlot.

With Olivia de Havilland in Palm Canyon, CA - Mon, October 28

Sat October 12
Filming in Arabella's cabin on the merchant ship and on the Port Royal streets of the Vitagraph backlot.

Monday October 14
Filming on the *Arabella* and at Port Royal on the Vitagraph backlot (delayed by rain from 7 to 8pm and 9:50 to 10:20pm).

Wed October 16 and Thu October 17
Filming retakes on the *Cinco Llagas*.

Fri October 18 and Sat October 19
Filming on the *Arabella* and (on 10/19) on the second French ship.

Mon October 21 through Fri October 25
Continues filming on the *Arabella*, in the French boat (on 10/22); from 11am to 12:25pm (on 10/23) filming second unit process shots of the English port and on the *Arabella* with Robert Barrat; inter-office memo from Gordon Hollingshead (10/23): *"Delay in starting due to director's [Jean Negulesco] tardiness."* Continues filming on the *Arabella*, in the rowboat, and in English village with de Havilland and Robert Barrat (on 10/25).

Mon October 28
Filming the romantic scenes with de Havilland at Palm Canyon, CA; the cast and crew have trouble with flies while filming!

November
In an article about Errol and Lili in this month's issue of *Hollywood Magazine* the couple acknowledge that they had met in Europe on several occasions before their mutual sea voyage to America in November of 1934.

Sat November 2
Remains with Lili in Palm Springs at the El Matador Hotel after filming the CAPTAIN BLOOD love sequences.

Mon November 11
Filming retakes with de Havilland on the bridle path at the WB Ranch to match up with scenes from Palm Canyon (several takes are interrupted by tractor noise!); also filming added Virgen Magra scenes.

Tue November 12
Filming on the *Cinco Llagas* and on the *Arabella*.

Wed November 13
Completes work on CAPTAIN BLOOD, filming on the *Cinco Llagas*, only with Barrat; salary for the film is $2,132.07 ($41,444 in 2021 value).

Fri November 22
Performing scenes from CAPTAIN BLOOD with Olivia de Havilland on the CBS radio program *Hollywood Hotel*.

Wed November 27
With Lili at a Thanksgiving eve party hosted by the Countess di Frasso.

Above, in the living room of the Hollywood Hills house - Autumn 1935; below, the same room today

Thu December 12
Roy Obringer to a Mr. Booth in the payroll department: *"Errol Flynn is leaving for New York tonight to be there in connection with the preview of Captain Blood. Mr. Warner has okayed an advance of 2 weeks contract salary...As Flynn is leaving the studio to prepare for the trip in about an hour, is it possible to have this check at this time."*

Sat December 14
Hal Wallis to Harry Joe Brown: *"Would you please look over material on 'The Sea Hawk', which we own, and let me know what you think of it as a possible follow-up on 'Captain Blood' for a big sea picture on next year's program."*

Mon December 16
Arrives in New York with Lili, staying at the Ritz Towers at Park Ave. and 57th St.

Wed December 18
Telegram from story editor Jacob Wilk to Roy Obringer: ERROL FLYNN CONTRACTS ARRIVED STOP FLYNN WANTS ARRANGEMENT BY WHICH HE GETS FIFTY PERCENT OF ANY SUMS WE RECEIVE BEYOND WHAT WE PAY HIM FOR LOANING HIS SERVICES TO ANY OTHER PRODUCER STOP WIRING THIS INFORMATION TO JACK FOR HIS DECISION. *"Robert Montgomery and Errol Flynn will lead the gallop in Warner's 'Charge of the Light Brigade.'"* Paul Holt in the *Daily Express*.

Fri December 20
Telegram from Roy Obringer to Jacob Wilk: REFERENCE ERROL FLYNN STRONGLY RECOMMEND NO CONCESSION BE GRANTED AS WE NEED FULL CARRYING CHARGE ALLOWED ON LOAN OUTS TO MAKE UP FOR HAVING TO CARRY FLYNN BETWEEN PICTURES.

Wed December 25
CAPTAIN BLOOD premieres in New York at the Strand.

Thu December 26
Performs scenes from CAPTAIN BLOOD with Olivia de Havilland on the *Standard Brands Rudy Vallee* (radio) *Show*.

Fri December 27
Flies back to Hollywood with Lili; signs a new contract commencing on January 2, 1936, guaranteeing 52 weeks at $750.00 per week ($14,579 in 2021 value), 12 weeks off without pay; he was given a $750 bonus upon signing.

Sat December 28
Associate producer Robert Lord to Hal Wallis: *"Dear Hal: I am the worst possible judge of material like this [GREEN LIGHT]....The script made a profound impression on me: I became so angry and disgusted with it that I began kicking it around my office. But it will make money. Which is one of the reasons why our civilization is crumbling; why the future of the white races has past [sic]; why the world of the future belongs to the Japs!"*

Tue December 31
CAPTAIN BLOOD opens in Hollywood and across the United States.

1936

Thu January 2
MURDER AT MONTE CARLO is still being screened, currently at His Majesty's Theatre in Flynn's hometown of Hobart, Tasmania.

Wed January 8
Is interviewed by Frederick Shields on the Jack Joy program at 7:30pm over KFWB radio.

Sun January 12
PIRATE PARTY ON CATALINA ISLAND opens at the Paramount Theater in Provo, UT.

Tue January 14
With Lili, Bud Ernst, and Lida Roberti (Mrs. Ernst) at Frank Sebastian's Cotton Club in Culver City.

Tue January 21
Is admitted to Cedars of Lebanon Hospital with appendicitis. *"An examination made by Dr. Harley Gunderson revealed an operation was not immediately necessary. Flynn, however, declared he would rather undergo the operation at once rather than be bothered by the offending appendix. 'I want to play in a picture entitled The Charge of the Light Brigade in April,' Flynn declared, 'So let's have the operation, and I'll be fit by that time.'"* The Los Angeles Examiner

Wed January 22
Has an appendectomy and is reported by *The Los Angeles Examiner* to be *"resting comfortably."*

'ANOTHER MATINEE IDOL is on the way', warns *M. P. Daily* after seeing Warners' dashing Errol Flynn as 'Captain Blood.' Photo shows new star Flynn and wife Lili Damita arriving in N. Y. for Strand's Xmas Day premiere of film already hailed by critics as 'big time show...in heavy money division.'†

The Film Daily - *Fri, December 20*

LILY DAMITA
HUSBAND TO
FACE KNIFE

Errol Flynn. Film Actor, Stricken Suddenly and Taken to Hospital

Stricken suddenly yesterday, Errol Flynn, motion picture actor, was removed to the Cedars of Lebanon Hospital where he will undergo an appendectomy at 7:30 a.m. today. Flynn is the husband of Lily Damita, French screen actress.

Dr. Harley Gunderson will perform the operation. Fortunately Flynn is not working in a picture at present and is not scheduled to begin his new Warner Brothers production, "The Charge of the Light Brigade," until six weeks hence.

(left) The Los Angeles Times - *Wed January 22, 1936*

At Cedars of Lebanon Hospital - Mon, January 27, 1936

With Lili at the Academy Awards ceremony in the Biltmore Hotel; Jack Warner on the left, director Max Reinhardt on the right - Thu, March 5

APPLICATION TO EXTEND TIME OF TEMPORARY STAY

U. S. DEPARTMENT OF LABOR
IMMIGRATION SERVICE

Test copy of Application for Extension of Stay - March 1936

Sat February 1

Returns home from the hospital.

Tue February 25

Attends the "Adieu" party for businesswoman and philanthropist Joan Whitney Payson at the home of actor Michael Bartlett.

Sun March 1

Attends a gathering at the Los Feliz home of Ouida and Basil Rathbone along with over one hundred screen and society luminaries.

Thu March 5

Attends the Academy Awards ceremony held at the Biltmore Bowl of the Biltmore Hotel *(top left)*.

Fri March 6

Hal Wallis to Michael Curtiz: *"Next time you make a test of Errol Flynn in his costume* [for CHARGE OF THE LIGHT BRIGADE], *which I understand will be Saturday morning, have him darken his moustache down a little with a pencil, and let's see what effect we get. The moustache is a little too vague in the test we have."* Harry Joe Brown to Hal Wallis: *"I am very anxious to read the story Errol Flynn left with you* ["The White Rajah"]. *He told me about it last night. If you have too much to read over the week-end, will you let me have it?"*

Sat March 7

Wardrobe test of fatigues for CHARGE OF THE LIGHT BRIGADE.

Tue March 10

More wardrobe tests; Jack Warner to Hal Wallis: *"I am looking at the new tests of Errol Flynn with his mustache darkened and he looks very good. As far as I am concerned, I think it would be a good idea to leave the mustache on. It gives him a little more punch in this particular role. What do you think?...I am now looking at the helmet with the sash on, and Flynn looks excellent. The mustache certainly looks good; I am sure the mustache is the thing for this picture."*

Thu March 12

Roy Obringer to legal counsel Stuart H. Aarons in the Warner Bros. New York office: *"…I was under the impression that Mr. Flynn was in the United States under a quota number and did not become aware of the fact that he was here on temporary visa until today when Mr. Flynn came into my office much concerned over the fact, advising me that due to his recent illness which has existed for a period of approximately 3 months, and involved hospitalization, and that as a result of his worries and illness, he had quite forgotten to take steps to extend his stay…As you undoubtedly know, Mr. Flynn is under a long term contract with us and appeared in our recent picture, 'Captain Blood', and is scheduled to go into our picture, 'The Charge Of The Light Brigade', which is to be one of our outstanding 1936 productions, and it is vitally important that his stay in the United States be cared for so as to in no way interfere with this production or the contract in general…I would appreciate your giving this your immediate attention and advising me what results you have in this matter."*

Mon March 16

Writes a letter to the registrar of births in Hobart, Tasmania, requesting a copy of his birth certificate for immigration purposes; telegram from Stuart H. Aarons to Roy Obringer: FILING APPLICATION FOR EXTENSION OF STAY TODAY STOP YEAR EXTENSION LOOKS HOPELESS STOP WIRE WHETHER LIGHT BRIGADE IS IN PRODUCTION OR IF NOT WHEN PRODUCTION WILL COMMENCE STOP SUGGEST THAT YOU IMMEDIATELY START ON SETTING UP QUOTA NUMBERS FOR FLYNN STOP IF IMMIGRATION OFFICERS QUESTION FLYNN ADVISE THEM THAT HE HAS FILED HIS APPLICATION FOR EXTENSION OF TEMPORARY STAY STOP DON'T LET ON THAT HE IS SETTING UP QUOTA NUMBERS AS THIS WOULD KILL HIS APPLICATION FOR TEMPORARY STAY STOP SIMILARLY IN SETTING UP QUOTA NUMBERS DON'T LET ON THAT HE IS APPLYING FOR EXTENSION OF STAY.

Tue March 17

With Lili at Café La Maze in Hollywood.

Fri March 20

More wardrobe tests for CHARGE OF THE LIGHT BRIGADE.

Sun March 22

Attends a farewell tennis luncheon with Lili at the home of Dolores del Rio and husband Cedric Gibbons, who are about to leave for Europe; later attends a supper event with Lili at Café La Maze; still later attends a party for New York banker Jules Bache at the home of Basil Rathbone.

Thu March 26
Flynn and his writing partner William A. Ulman present Warner Bros. with a treatment for their film concept, "The White Rajah," based on the life of adventurer James Brooke; Flynn goes so far as to have himself photographed in appropriate period costume; the studio pays them $13,000 for the rights ($245,374 in 2021 value).

Sun March 29
Leaves at 6:30pm from Burbank's Southern Pacific Depot for Lone Pine, CA.

Mon March 30
Arrives in Lone Pine at 6am; filming begins with the dust storm (ultimately not used), and the horse-buying scenes; unit manager, Frank Mattison: *"Weather very bad—rained, and cloudy throughout day."*

WESTERN UNION

BAE101 13DLY PAID=1035A EDT APR 1 36 KA0 98

MR ROY OBRINGER=

NO FONE HOLLYWOOD CAL

HAYS OFFICE ADVISES THAT IMMIGRATION BUREAU GIVES FLYNN THIRTY DAYS TO LEAVE COUNTRY OTHERWISE WARRANT WILL ISSUE FOR HIS DEPORTATION AT END OF THIRTY DAYS= HE SHOULD GO TO MEXICALI AND THEN RETURN UNDER QUOTA= IMMIGRATION OFFICE WANTED TO ISSUE WARRANT FOR FLYNN'S DEPORTATION IMMEDIATELY BUT HAYS OFFICE GOT THIRTY DAYS EXTENSION=

STUART AARONS= WARNER BROS NYC

Tue March 31
Continues filming the horse-buying scene.

Wed April 1
Filming Jowett's and Sir Humphrey's companies; inter-office memo from unit manager Frank Mattison: *"Big fire destroyed restaurant where company eats. Also garage where some company equipment kept. All equipment saved despite company moved from [The Dow] hotel with wardrobe. Fire under control at 2:45am. Company called at 5:00AM. Will work as per schedule."*

Thu April 2
Filming on the road and more horse-buying scenes.

Fri April 3
Continues filming horse-buying scenes and the battle with the Arabs.

Sat April 4
Filming the horse-buying scenes and falcon hunt; leaves Lone Pine at 8pm.

With David Niven and Patric Knowles in Lone Pine, CA - March

Above, in the Alabama Hills of Lone Pine, CA - March; below, the same spot today

Sat April 5
Returns to Burbank at 4:55am.

Mon April 6 and Tue April 7
At Warner Brothers in Burbank resumes shooting THE CHARGE OF THE LIGHT BRIGADE with scenes in Surat Khan's (C. Henry Gordon) tent.

Wed April 8
Filming of the leopard hunt in Lake Sherwood, CA, and in Geoffrey Vickers' (Flynn) quarters.

Thu April 9
Filming in Surat Khan's tent at Lasky Mesa (in Calabasas), CA; many blown lines by the cast.

Fri April 10 and Sat April 11
Filming of the first scenes in the Chukoti garrison at Lasky Mesa.

Mon April 13
Filming in Vickers' quarters in Calcutta, the leopard hunt close-ups at Lasky Mesa, and process shots of the hunt in the Warner Bros. train shed on the backlot.

Tue April 14 and Wed April 15
Filming the Russian battery at Lasky Mesa (delayed 40 minutes by fog on 4/14) and Khan's battle sequence.

Thu April 16
Filming in the Chukoti Commander's office.

With C. Henry Gordon at Lasky Mesa in Calabasas, CA - April

Above, with Olivia de Havilland at Lake Sherwood, CA - Mon, May 11;
below, the same location today

Fri April 17
Filming the Russian batteries and Chukoti Garrison at Lasky Mesa.

Sat April 18
Fog at Lasky Mesa prevents shooting; company leaves at 12:15pm for the studio and films in Colonel Macefield's office; attends the premiere tennis and cocktail party at The Westside Tennis Club; with partner Jinx Falkenberg is defeated by Eddie Burns and Peggy Stratford, and later with partner Frank Shields is defeated by Eddie Burns and Henry Culley.

Sun April 19
With Lili at the Mayfair Club's garden party in Beverly Hills.

Mon April 20
Filming retakes in Khan's tent.

Tue April 21
Filming in Col. Macefield's (Henry Stephenson) office.

Wed April 22
Filming in Col. Macefield's orderly room and office.

Thu April 23 to Sat April 25
Filming of ballroom sequence at the studio.

Sat April 25
With Marlene Dietrich, Dolores del Rio, and Lili at Café La Maze.

Mon April 27
Continues filming the ballroom sequence.

Tue April 28
Filming in Col. Macefield's office and orderly room.

Wed April 29 and Thu April 30
Filming at Chukoti Garrison at Lasky Mesa and (on 4/30) in Khan's tent at Lasky Mesa.

Fri May 1 and Sat May 2
Filming in the staff office and the council room; (on 5/2) attends the birthday party of William Randolph Hearst in Santa Monica.

Mon May 4
Filming with de Havilland at the Chukoti Garrison at Lasky Mesa.

Tue May 5 and Wed May 6
Home; does not work.

Thu May 7 to Sat May 9
In Mexicali to correct his immigration status.

Mon May 11 and Tue May 12
Filming the river attack at Chukoti and Lohara at Lake Sherwood, CA, with de Havilland.

Wed May 13
Filming in the farmhouse at Lasky Mesa.

Fri May 15 and Sat May 16
Filming in the Chukoti compound and the Lohara guns at Lasky Mesa.

Mon May 18
Filming in and outside Col. Campbell's (Donald Crisp) Calcutta home.

Tue May 19 through Thu May 21
Filming in the barracks.

Fri May 22
Filming outside the barracks and in the Chukoti compound at Lasky Mesa.

Sat May 23
Filming pickup shots at Chukoti.

Sun May 24
Writes a $527.50 check ($9,957 in 2021 value) to A. Poole as down payment on 8.5 acres of property in

the Hollywood Hills, eventually totaling $9,500 ($179,312 in 2021 value) and ultimately the location of his Mulholland Drive house.

Mon May 25
Filming the horse-buying sequence at Iverson Ranch in Chatsworth, CA.

Tue May 26
Filming in Geoffrey's (Flynn) Calcutta quarters, and in the wooded glade on the WB backlot with de Havilland and Patric Knowles; the press announces Flynn will star in a story of his own authorship, *The White Rajah*, based on the life of Sir James Brooke.

Wed May 27
Filming outside the farmhouse and lancers' encampment at the WB Calabasas Ranch.

Thu May 28
Filming the horse-buying sequence at Iverson Ranch in Chatsworth, CA.

Fri May 29
With Ruth Waterbury (of *Photoplay* magazine), Gene Raymond, and Jeanette MacDonald (Mrs. Raymond) at a party given by Frances Marion at the home of director Harry Lachman; the *Los Angeles Times* announces that Olivia de Havilland will co-star with Flynn in the filming of his story, "The White Rajah," with Michael Curtiz probably directing *(costume suggestion, top right)*.

Sat May 30
"Without encountering serious opposition from Errol Flynn, the wild-haired Irish star of films, Solly Baiano, the defending champion….won his way into the third round of the eleventh annual Motion Picture Tennis Association championship at the Los Angeles Tennis Club. After receiving a default from Ralph Bellamy in the initial round, the Italian violinist, a ranking doubles star in championship play, eliminated Flynn from further competition by scores of 6–1, 6–4." The Los Angeles Times

Thu June 4 through Mon June 8
The main charge at Lasky Mesa is filmed without the cast.

Wed June 10
"Errol Flynn, Warner's new he-man, will do a remake of the famous 'Sea Hawk.'" The Daily Express.

Fri June 12
Attends French actress Ketti Gallian's huge supper event at the Trocadero with Lili and over 200 guests; telegram from Flynn's agent Minna Wallis to Jack Warner: MARY PICKFORD WOULD LIKE ARROL [sic] FLYNN FOR BROADCAST JUNE TWENTY FIRST WILL MENTION WARNER BROTHERS LIGHT BRIGADE ANY WAY YOU DESIRE MAY WE PLEASE HAVE YOUR OK AS THEY MUST ADVISE NEW YORK BY THREE O CLOCK OUR TIME

Wed June 17
Filming the leopard hunt (with retakes) at the WB Calabasas Ranch; in Col. Macefield's office and in the barracks (both with added scenes) at the WB studio.

Sat June 20
Flynn's 27th birthday; with Lili at the Westside Tennis Club.

Sun June 21
On the radio program *Parties at Pickfair* with Mary Pickford *(bottom right)*.

Thu June 25
Filming unfinished Lone Pine pickup shots at Chatsworth with Patric Knowles.

Fri June 26
Filming on the battlefield at Lasky Mesa with Nigel Bruce, G. P. Huntley, and Walter Holbrook.

Sat June 27
Continues filming on the battlefield at Lasky Mesa, finishing the charge sequence; producer Henry Blanke to Hal Wallis: *"[Screenwriter Sheridan] Gibney has now a copy of this….script* [GREEN LIGHT] *and will add to same the points Flynn has brought up and criticized."* Hal Wallis to production manager Tenny Wright: *"Errol Flynn is now definitely set for GREEN LIGHT and is anxious to get started as quickly as possible, as we promised to give him a vacation on completion of GREEN LIGHT."*

A test costume for the never-filmed version of Flynn's self-scripted The White Rajah

With Mary Pickford at Pickfair - Sun, June 21

From an Elmer Fryer portrait session - Summer 1936

Mon June 29
Filming outside the Chukoti Garrison, the Dragoons, the Huzzars, and lancer encampment at Lasky Mesa.

Tue June 30
Final day of filming at Lasky Mesa with pickup shots and falls, and inside the fort.

Wed July 1
Completes filming of THE CHARGE OF THE LIGHT BRIGADE with scenes on a Balaklava street (on the WB back lot with Knowles and de Havilland), and river scenes at Lake Sherwood with de Havilland and C. Henry Gordon; salary for the film is $10,253 ($193,525 in 2021 value).

Sat July 4
At the Vancouver, British Columbia, Cricket Club.

Mon July 13
Begins filming GREEN LIGHT (the daily production notes for this film are missing); Hal Wallis to Henry Blanke: *"I happened to drop in on the Borzage set and saw Flynn in his first outfit. His clothes, generally, look good but he should get some new shoes for the next change and have his hair trimmed up a little in the back. It looks a little scraggly and the suede shoes he was wearing did not look very good to the eye, although they may photograph better."*

Tue July 14
Henry Blanke to Hal Wallis: *"I took Errol Flynn to see the dailies with me. Had a nice talk with him and he absolutely agrees with you. He also believes that the shirt is lousy and makes him look like an actor and not like a doctor--which he is supposed to portray. He will switch the shirt in the next sequence and will start to wear home-spuns and tweeds."* Jack Warner to Hal Wallis: *"I saw the dailies on 'Green Light', and I agree with what you said about Flynn's collar. Be sure that he wears a collar like everyone else does, and not like Warren William. We'll get by with his hair-cut in the one reverse shot, but it's also a Warren William haircut. I know you've taken care of this already...I'm very happy the way Flynn is speaking. We don't want him to use any 'shawnts' or 'cawnts'---speaking just like he is will be swell. The scenes are good."*

Wed July 15
Sends a telegram to his friend Dr. Hermann Erben in New York.

Sat July 18
Filming with Spring Byington in the hospital room, and retakes with Margaret Lindsey.

Mon July 20
Signs a letter agreement with Warners giving him 12 consecutive weeks' vacation with pay after completing GREEN LIGHT.

Tue July 21
Filming the operation scene.

Wed July 22
Continues filming the operation scene with Flynn as Dr. Paige exclaiming, *"You cut the cord too short!"*

Sat July 25
Attends a party at the Santa Monica home of Dolores del Rio and Cedric Gibbons.

Sat August 1
Attends a going-away party for Marion Davies, who would be leaving on a trip to Europe; also in attendance are William Powell, Norma Shearer, Kay Francis, and Jack Warner.

Mon August 3
Filming in Dr. Paige's (Flynn) apartment.

Tue August 4
Hal Wallis to Roy Obringer: *"On the completion of 'Another Dawn', we will give him his twelve weeks vacation, so will you please keep track of this."*

Wed August 5 or Thu August 6
Filming the first "perspiration" scene.

Fri August 7
Filming in a car with Anita Louise.

Sun August 9
Flynn's article "I'd Rather Play Tennis" appears in *Screen & Radio Weekly*.

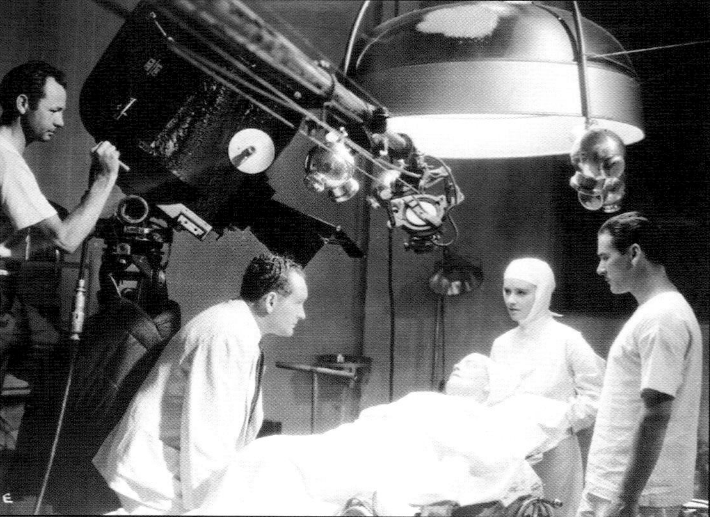

With director Frank Borzage (under the camera), Spring Byington (on the operating table), and Margaret Lindsay - Tue, July 21

Mon August 10
Attends a party hosted by director George Cukor at a French cafe in Hollywood.

Tue August 18
The press announces Flynn will travel to Borneo to photograph background scenes for his own film, *The White Rajah*.

Wed August 19
Telegram from Flynn to Dr. Hermann Erben: JUST ABOUT TO SIGN NEW DEAL WITH WARNER BROTHERS... TRIP POSTPONED INDEFINITELY….Casting director Max Arnow to Hal Wallis: *"….our best bet for the role of Miles Hendon* [in THE PRINCE AND THE PAUPER] *would be George Brent or Patric Knowles. The way the part is written it is not sufficient in size to warrant putting in Errol Flynn or Fredric March."*

Thu August 20 or Fri August 21
Filming the scene where the old patient dies.

Mon August 24 through Wed August 26
Filming in the field station with Walter Abel and (on 8/25) in the farmhouse.

Thu August 27
Filming the scene at the breakfast table in the field station looking for the missing tick.

Fri August 28
Continues filming in the field station.

Sat August 29
With Anita Louise filming in the park and process shots in the car as it comes into the park.

Thu September 3
Completes work on GREEN LIGHT.

Fri September 4
Unit manager Robert Fellows to Tenny Wright: *"The following may be none of this department's business-but I feel you should know that Errol Flynn from all indications is leading up to being a very difficult man to handle...He is never on time-it's almost impossible to get him out of his chair and in front of the camera—his first remark in the AM is usually, 'What do I say here?'—etc—it's difficult to put on paper exactly the attitude he has—and it's most difficult to prove...From chance remarks dropped his attitude in general, coupled with his own knowledge of his value—and from my previous experience in seeing such conditions develop before, I know that unless someone has a serious talk with him and explains what he is expected to do for the studio and then tries to get him to come clean with his complaints—the studio is going to have another Cagney on its hands...Sorry to bring this up, but I feel to ignore it will only make the problem more difficult."*

Tue September 8
Tenny Wright to Hal Wallis: *"Inclosed* [sic] *you will find a note that was sent to me by Bob Fellows* [see previous post]. *Thought you might like to read it as this is something I believe for you to handle rather than me. Thank you."*

Thu September 10
Harry Joe Brown to Hal Wallis: *"Dear Hal: After seeing 'Last Of The Mohicans', then 'Charge Of The Light Brigade' and other pictures that look like big money-getters, and are, I bring to your attention again 'The Sea Hawk'…..After seeing 'Light Brigade', I was very happy to see the great improvement in Flynn's work. He looked great to me in the picture, and he certainly should be 'tops' of all his type."* Hal Wallis to Harry Joe Brown: *"We have not forgotten 'The Sea Hawk', and it's only because Flynn has been so tied up that we have put it aside---that and the fact that only a comparative short time has elapsed since 'Captain Blood'...However, I figure on going into 'The Sea Hawk' very soon after the first of the year."*

No Date
Story department head Walter McEwen to Hal Wallis: *"Mr. Wallis: Spoke to Errol Flynn as per your instructions. Apparently his reason for asking the starting date of Another Dawn is his hope that he will have a little time between it and Green Light, as he is very tired. He asked me to relay this to you."*
After completing GREEN LIGHT, Errol flies with Lili to the Klamath River in northern California for salmon fishing while living in a car trailer; salary for the film is $10,377 ($195,865 in 2021 value).

Fri September 11
Appears in the release of the documentary short SCREEN SNAPSHOTS.

Mon September 14
Makeup and wardrobe tests with Ian Hunter for ANOTHER DAWN; Hal Wallis to director of publicity Charles

At Providencia Ranch in Burbank - Thu, August 27

With Anita Louise

At the Los Angeles Tennis Club -
Wed, September 23
(photo by Dr. Hermann Erben)

Einfeld: *"Are you sure you want to bill Anita Louise as big as Errol Flynn? Flynn, of course, should be a very big star after 'Light Brigade' and I wonder if you want to give the girl as much prominence."*

Wed September 16 and Sat September 19

More makeup and wardrobe tests for ANOTHER DAWN; Hal Wallis to Harry Joe Brown (on 9/16): *"I saw the test of Ian Hunter and Errol Flynn, and I don't like Hunter with a mustache. It may be that by experimenting they can get one that looks better, but unless they can improve it we will have him without a mustache. He looks phoney this way. Also, I hope Errol Flynn shaves his mustache off for the test, as I asked him to do. I don't care whether or not the English Army Officers wear mustaches. We have our problem to get over in this picture, and that is that Flynn must look much younger than Hunter, and if we have to do it by taking their mustaches off, we are going to do it—regardless of technicality. 99% of the people who see the picture don't know that the British Army Officers wear mustaches, and for that 99% we're going to make the picture...There is no doubt about it, Flynn without the mustache looks much younger. My own opinion would be to use both Flynn and Hunter without mustaches, as I think Flynn looks so much younger without his, and that the difference in the ages will be sufficient."*

Sun September 20

Participates in the Pacific Southwest Tennis Tournament at the Los Angeles Tennis Club; he loses.

Mon September 21

Hal Wallis to makeup artist Perc Westmore: *"For Another Dawn, Ian Hunter....will not wear a mustache. Flynn will wear a small mustache."* At the Los Angeles Tennis Club with Lili for the Pacific Southwest Tennis Championships.

Tue September 22

Films retakes for GREEN LIGHT; Dr. Hermann Erben visits Flynn, their first time together since June of 1933.

Wed September 23

With Erben and Lili to Los Angeles Tennis Club in the afternoon *(top left)*; Hal Wallis to William Dieterle, director of ANOTHER DAWN: *"I have just seen the new tests of Ian Hunter with the mustaches, and I feel definitely that we now have the right combination in test #3. That is, with mustache #3. Let us definitely use this on him...."*

Thu September 24

Dines with Lili and Erben at the Westside Tennis Club.

Fri September 25

Films first scenes on ANOTHER DAWN: in Col. Wister's (Ian Hunter) office and the Colonel's bedroom with Ian Hunter and Herbert Mundin; visit from Erben on the set, then out together for lunch.

Sat September 26

Filming night scene on Wister's veranda, and in the office with Kay Francis, Hunter, and Mundin; attends the Pacific Southwest Tennis Tournaments with Lili at the Los Angeles Tennis Club.

Mon September 28

Filming at the army post at Lasky Mesa with Kay Francis.

Tue September 29 and Wed September 30

Continues filming at army post with Francis, Hunter, and Mundin; dinner with Erben (on 9/29).

Thu October 1

Continues filming at army post, and hillside and canyon at Lasky Mesa with Francis, Hunter, and Mundin.

Fri October 2

Filming exterior and interior of Metropolitan Airport (now Van Nuys Airport), and in Wister's office with Hunter and Mundin.

Sat October 3

Filming in Roark's (Flynn) bedroom.

Mon October 5

Filming the army post, cricket match, and night airplane scene at Lasky Mesa; Hal Wallis to editorial supervisor Harold McCord: *"Who is cutting 'Another Dawn'? I want him to be right up on the cutting of this picture, as there are already some retakes that I know of, and Flynn is going away right after the*

With Kay Francis, Ian Hunter, and Frieda Inescourt - Fri, October 23

picture finishes, and will be gone three months."

Tue October 6
The Oakland Tribune reports that Flynn plans to sail for Borneo via Japan around November 15 to begin filming *"atmosphere shots"* for his self-written (with William A. Ulman) film, *The White Rajah*.

Fri October 9
Performing scenes from CHARGE OF THE LIGHT BRIGADE with Olivia de Havilland on the CBS radio program *Hollywood Hotel*.

Sat October 10
Filming in the living room at the post, and on Wister's veranda.

Mon October 12
Filming in Julia's bedroom and at Lakeside Country Club; production note: *"Waiting for Mr. Flynn until 1:50."*

Wed October 14
Filming in the wireless room, barracks hospital, and in Julia's (Kay Francis) bedroom.

Thu October 15
Filming in Wister's office.

Fri October 16
Filming in Mutessarif's garden with Kay Francis.

Sat October 17
Continues filming in Mutessarif's garden with Francis, and in Wister's office; Hal Wallis to Harry Joe Brown: *"Be sure that we shoot the ending of 'Another Dawn' with both finishes. That is, so that Hunter goes out in the plane and gets killed, and also that Flynn does and shoot all necessary connecting shots and individual scenes necessary, so that we can cut the picture either way."*

Mon October 19
Filming interior and exterior of Roark's rooms.

Tue October 20
Filming in Wister's office and an "alternate ending"; living room and "alternate ending"; veranda and "alternate ending"; in Julia's room; THE CHARGE OF THE LIGHT BRIGADE opens at the Warner Hollywood Theater.

Wed October 21
Filming in Wister's office and living room; on the veranda and retakes; in Roark's room and retakes.

Thu October 22
Filming process shots of touring car and roadster.

Fri October 23 and Sat October 24
Filming the exterior of the native station at Dikut in the WB train shed (*previous page, bottom left*); appears on the *Screen Guide* radio program over NBC (10/23).

Tue October 27
Filming on the exterior tower at Lasky Mesa, a process shot of plane, and a retake of the Dikut exterior .

Wed October 28
Filming in Roark's living room; sprains his ankle slightly.

Thu October 29
Leaves South Pasadena train station at 8am en route to Yuma, AZ, arriving at 3pm.

Fri October 30
Unit Manager Al Alleborn: *"Working on shot scene in which Mr. Flynn does not appear, allowing him to rest and doctor his ankle which was slightly sprained Wednesday night."*

Sat October 31
Filming in interior of ruined outpost and exterior of Achaben's (George Regas) tent, with the Colorado River in the background; these scenes were not used in the finished film.

November
Flynn's autobiographical novel *Beam Ends* appears in a condensed version in *Cosmopolitan* magazine.

Sun November 1
Filming in the Algodones Dunes (Imperial Sand Dunes) and desert in California, just west of Yuma.

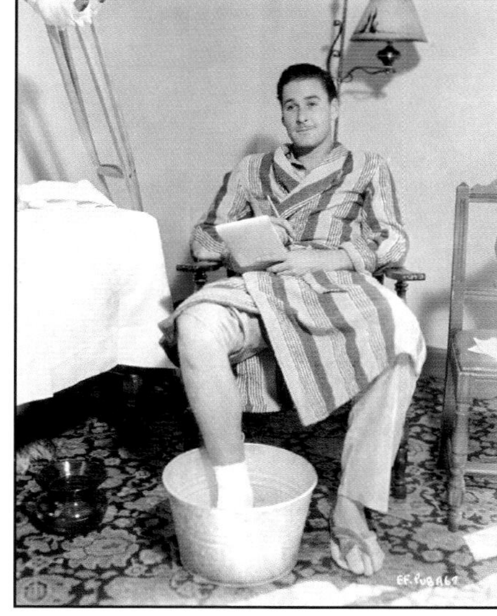

Soaking his sprained ankle in Yuma, AZ - Fri, October 30

Above, still with a sprained ankle, outside Yuma, AZ - Sat, October 31

With Clyde Cook in the Algodones Dunes, CA - November

With Kay Francis - November

*With Lili at Café La Maze in Hollywood -
Sat, November 14*

Mon November 2 through Fri November 6

Continues filming in the desert and dunes; Al Alleborn (11/3): *"Unable to shoot because of wind blowing. Extra camera had to be sent back to hotel to be cleaned because of sand."* Leaves Yuma at 7pm on 11/6, arriving in Los Angeles the next morning at 6am.

Mon November 9

Filming in Grace Roark's (Frieda Inescort) living room, and in Achaben's tent (scene not used).

Tue November 10

Continues filming in Grace's living room, and in Julia's bedroom; an inter-office memo from production manager Tenny Wright relates an incident from this day, reporting how he contacted Jack Warner about Flynn's agent, Myron Selznick, ordering Flynn to wait in his (Flynn's) dressing room and not come out for filming (presumably over a contract dispute); Flynn eventually did come out and Warner dealt with Selznick harshly in a phone conversation.

Wed November 11

Continues filming in Grace's living room; filming in Grace's hallway and outside Grace's home.

Thu November 12

Filming outside the post tower, in Grace's living room, outside Grace's house, and in Grace's hallway.

Mon November 16

"With a party of friends at Café La Maze, Hollywood, screen actor Errol Flynn was having a gay time the other eve [probably the previous Friday or Saturday night], *when in walked his wife, cinema actress Lili Damita. They posed for this exclusive picture* [bottom left], *she turned her back on him, he watched her ruefully. A few minutes later she left in tears. Their supposed matrimonial difficulties have been film colony gossip for some months—and her tearful leave-taking makes a trip to divorce court expectable for the two."* International News, Los Angeles Bureau. *"HOLLYWOOD—It is reported that Errol Flynn and Lily Damita have decided on a trial marriage separation to begin on Wednesday* [November 18th]. *Flynn will visit New York, Tahiti, and Borneo, while Damita probably will appear in a Broadway play. After the trial period the couple will decide whether to obtain a divorce."* The Melbourne Argus.

Tue November 17

At a dinner party in honor of English socialite Lady Castlerosse, hosted by Paulette Goddard at the actress's home.

Sat November 21

Filming a retake of a tent exterior for ANOTHER DAWN.

Thu November 26

"Errol Flynn and Lili Damita have forgotten that trial separation business and are sailing together soon for Europe." The Daily Express.

Sat November 28

In the release of the documentary short SCREEN SNAPSHOTS; Warner Bros. advances Flynn $2,325 ($43,884 in 2021 value).

Tue December 1

Leaves with Lili for New York.

Fri December 4

Agrees to postpone his 12-week vacation in lieu of $25,000 ($471,873 in 2021 value) to do THE PRINCE AND THE PAUPER.

Wed December 16

Signs a new contract guaranteeing $2,250 per week ($42,469 in 2021 value), effective February 15, 1937.

Fri December 18

Arrives in London with Lili, on their way to spend Christmas with his parents in Belfast.

Tue December 22

Hal Wallis to Tenny Wright: *"…we want to test Flynn without a mustache or a beard, then with a mustache only and, thirdly, with a mustache and a beard similar to the type we had on Ian Hunter in his tests."*

Thu December 24

Hal Wallis to makeup man Perc Westmore: *"We are going to play Flynn with his own hair, without any pieces, and without a moustache or a beard, and we will use makeup the same as used in 'Another Dawn'."*

Errol Flynn, Lily Damita Try Married Life Again

Hollywood, Cal., Nov. 25.—[Special.] —Errol Flynn, movie actor, and Lily Damita, French actress, decided to-day to try married life again. They called off lawyers who were to file a divorce complaint and bought two tickets for New York. They will embark on a second honeymoon of several months in Europe. The couple have separated several times.

The Chicago Tribune
Wed, November 25

Mon December 28

Begins work on THE PRINCE AND THE PAUPER, filming in Canty's hovel with Elspeth Dudgeon; Robert Lord to Hal Wallis: *"Dear Hal: I agree with you that our dog is not a very good actor. He is a fine physical type but lacks ability, somewhat like Lili Damita."*

1937

Mon January 4

Filming in Hendon's (Flynn) room *(top right)* with Bobby Mauch (pronounced Mowk, as in cow); Hal Wallis to Robert Lord: *"I am afraid we are going to have a close shave now on finishing Errol Flynn in the six week period which, as you know, is part of the agreement under which we brought him back, and I would rather not stop for retakes of any kind until the end of the picture…"*

Wed January 6

Continues filming in Hendon's room with Bobby Mauch; Hal Wallis to director William Keighley: *"I agree with you that the dailies with Flynn could have been much better. There is no spontaneity in the stuff. Possibly, now that Flynn has been spoken to, we'll get a little more sparkle in the stuff."*

Fri January 8 and Sat January 9

Filming in the throne room; Hal Wallis to William Keighley (on 1/9): *"Dear Bill: Both Mr. Warner and I have been quite worried about Errol Flynn in the sequence in Hendon's flat—both as to the action, which did not seem to have the flare that he has shown in previous pictures, and as to the photography. He looked thin and drawn, and also not well photographed….I know that we are trying for sketchy lighting on all of these scenes, but I would rather forgo some of this and have Flynn well photographed, and don't have the room so dark."*

Sun January 10 and Mon January 11

Filming on the studio backlot at the church on Dijon Street and (on 1/11) in the alley on Dijon, and outside Westminster Abbey.

Tue January 12

Filming in Hendon's room with Bobby Mauch.

Fri January 15

Dining with Lili at the Hollywood Brown Derby.

Mon January 18

Ill; does not work; Tenny Wright to Hal Wallis: *"Errol Flynn was taken sick on Saturday, but at that time expected to be able to work on Tuesday. In checking with him this morning, we find that Flynn is running a temperature and doesn't expect to work until Thursday morning…Have notified Obringer to send Dr. Conn to his residence in order to give us his report."* Obringer to Warner, Wallis, Wright, and Lord: *"I have just talked to Dr. Conn, who visited Errol Flynn this morning. He says that Flynn very definitely has an attack of the flu, with a high temperature and severe congestion in his bronchial tubes. Dr. Conn said that he would make an effort to get Flynn on his feet as soon as possible, but…..if he would attempt to get into a varied temperature, it might very easily be fatal by developing into pneumonia."*

Tue January 19 to Fri January 22

Ill; does not work.

Sat January 23

Appears in the film short *Breakdowns of 1937*, released on this day; Harry Joe Brown to Hal Wallis: *"Dear Hal: I understand Erroll [sic] Flynn is to return to the studio, ready for work Monday. We will immediately make arrangements with The Prince and The Pauper company, so we can shoot a new finish; or have you any more information as to when Kay Francis will return."*

Mon January 25

Ill; does not work.

Tue January 26

Filming in the Running Fox Inn, Flynn's first scene ever with Alan Hale; they would go on to do eleven more films together.

Wed January 27 and Thu January 28

Filming inside and outside the Running Fox Inn with Hale; Jack Warner to Hal Wallis (1/27): *"Dear Hal: I have okayed Flynn and de Havilland going on the Lux Hour [radio show], February*

With Bobby Mauch - Mon, January 4, 1937

Errol Flynn And Wife To Part Again

Abbe Children Writing Book 'Around Hollywood in 11 Days'; Bette Davis Still Ill

BY SHEILAH GRAHAM.

Hollywood, Jan. 11.—The Errol Flynns have again decided to call it a day on their marriage, and will separate permanently just as soon as Errol finishes his role in "The Prince and the Pauper"—if not before.

The Hartford Courant
Tue, January 12

Rehearsing with fencing master Fred Cavens

As Miles Hendon in THE PRINCE AND THE PAUPER (photo by John Ellis)

22nd. We are writing all copy and will get some great plugs on 'Light Brigade', 'Green Light', and 'Call It A Day'...There was another reason for my doing this as this broadcast does not go on until February 22nd which means Flynn will have to stay here or be back at that time giving us the opportunity to make retakes when [Kay] *Francis returns. Confidentially, this was the most important reason for allowing them to go on the Lux program."* Hal Wallis to Tenny Wright (1/28): *"I talked to Errol Flynn and he expressed his willingness to stay here until* [Kay] *Francis returns February 12th, to make the retake on 'Another Dawn'. Consequently we will wait until that time to make over the scene on the tower with Francis and Flynn and Dieterle directing."* Signs a new contract (1/28), including provisions for THE ADVENTURES OF ROBIN HOOD.

Fri January 29
Filming in the woods with Hale and Barton MacLane, and process shots on horseback; performs scenes from GREEN LIGHT with Anita Louise on the CBS radio program *Hollywood Hotel*.

Sat January 30
Continues filming in the woods, and process shots on horseback.

February
Beam Ends is published by Cassell and Co. *(top right)*; makes a deal with Hearst newspapers to cover the Spanish Civil War as a journalist.

Mon February 1
Filming outside Hendon's room on Dijon Street on the backlot, and in the thieves' booth with Bobby Mauch.

Tue February 2
Filming in the woods with Bobby Mauch and Alan Hale.

Wed February 3
Filming outside the tavern on Dijon Street on the backlot, and outside the palace gates.

Thu February 4
Filming in the woods and in the tavern.

Fri February 5
Filming in Hendon's room and in the woods; Hal Wallis to Roy Obringer: *"Just a reminder to tell Errol Flynn to stay around town until we decide on the retake of 'Another Dawn'."* Handwritten in ink on the previous note and signed RJO (Roy J. Obringer): *"Talked to Flynn on this today. They will not finish until tomorrow and of course we will have to pay when he works. He will await official notice from us on retakes."*

Sat February 6
Continues filming in the woods; completes work on THE PRINCE AND THE PAUPER with retakes at the tower with Hale and the Mauch twins; salary for the film is $29,800 ($554,438 in 2021 value); Robert Lord to Hal Wallis: *"The two close shots and the two close ups of this sequence, which you will see in today's dailies, are better than the stuff in yesterday's dailies. Nevertheless, Mr. Flynn's performance in these scenes is far more inspiring."*

Sun February 7
Performing scenes from THE PRINCE AND THE PAUPER with Billy and Bobby Mauch on the CBS radio program *Hollywood Hotel*.

Fri February 12
GREEN LIGHT opens at the Strand in New York City.

Sat February 13
Completes work on ANOTHER DAWN with a retake on the tower with Kay Francis; salary for the film is $13,377 ($248,883 in 2021 value).

Mon February 15
Signs a new contract guaranteeing $800 per week ($14,884 in 2021 value) for fifty-two weeks.

Tue February 16
Attends the Fred Perry-Ellsworth Vines tennis match at the Pan-Pacific Auditorium in Hollywood.

Wed February 17
In court with Dr. Hermann Erben and someone Erben refers to as the *"chinkgirl."*

Flynn's first book

With Bobby and Billy Mauch

With Phyllis Barry

Above left, aboard the Queen Mary *(photo by Dr. Hermann Erben) - Thu, February 25; above right, the same spot today*

At the funeral for the victims of the Clichy riots in Paris (photo by Dr. Hermann Erben) Sun, March 21

Thu February 18

Erben is an overnight guest at Flynn's home.

Mon February 22

Radio performance of "Captain Blood" for the *Lux Radio Theatre* at CBS affiliate, KNX, Los Angeles.

Tue February 23

Arrives at Newark Airport and checks into the Hotel St. Moritz in New York.

Wed February 24

Leaves for England at 10am with Erben on the *Queen Mary*; stays in room M38 (since renumbered as M012).

Thu February 25

Spends the day on board with Erben *(top left)*.

Mon March 1

Lands and debarks at Cherbourg.

Tue March 2

Meets up with Lili at the Paris train station.

Thu March 4

Flies from Paris at 9:00pm to Croydon Airport, south of London.

Fri March 5

With Erben and actor Frank Lawton to the musical *Swing Along* at the Gaiety Theatre in London.

Sat March 6

At the U.S. Consulate in London; authorizes William Best to oversee business issues concerning his Mulholland properties; purchases Rhodesian Ridgeback dogs from Olive, Lady Baillie of Leeds.

Mon March 8

Flies to Belfast to visit his father who is the Chair of Zoology at Queen's University.

Sat March 13

Beam Ends is reviewed in *The Saturday Review*.

Wed March 17

Flies out of Belfast for London.

Thu March 18

Is reunited with Lili at the train station in London; they go on to Paris, staying at the Plaza Athenee.

Sat March 20

With Lili and Erben in Paris; according to Erben, he (Erben) had a *"big quarrel"* with Lili.

Sun March 21

Attends funeral with Lili and Erben for the victims of the Clichy political riots *(bottom left)*.

Mon March 22

Obtains visa for Spain.

Tue March 23

Lunches at the hotel with Erben.

Wed March 24

With Lili in Paris.

Thu March 25

At the Spanish Embassy for a reception given for the U.S. Medical Unit.

Fri March 26

Travels with Erben by train to Port Bou, Spain, and then on to Barcelona; Erben borrows 850 pesetas (about $28).

Lili and Errol with eccentric Paris photographer Willy Michel - third week of March, 1937

THE SPANISH CIVIL WAR DIARY (excerpts)*

"So! On train at last. Very nearly boarded the wrong one going in the opp direction due to the usual last minute frenzied rush always necessary when Damita is along. A lone photographer at station - don't know what paper - who made a number of pictures of self and Damita - then infuriated that lady by asking in French, "And what is the lady's name?" Erben left last night (25') after having been refused all visas by U.S. consul…I am to meet him in Perpignon tomorrow (27) and see if he has his papers - any sort of papers. I only hope he has not got to try to dive across border. Two men killed day before yesterday - shot as they crawled out of river near Cerbere. I know he'll get in - somehow....

Sat March 27

Flynn's Spanish Civil War diary continues: *Just arrived Perpignon....Beautiful spring day warm sunshine, country beautiful. How can people fight a war in this lovely weather? Four hours train journey from here the most savage cruel fratricidal war is being waged….Erben is over! How, when or why I don't know. When, yes. He crossed last night at 8 p.m. so his note said. Naturally he couldn't say more....The train is stopped. Plane has been heard. All lights out - there weren't any before to speak of - all the bulbs had been painted with blue so that one can hardly see across the compartment. The stink is something! We are crowded with young Loyalists - all armed and with the oddest assortment of uniforms. Some have everyday suits, revolver, and just the cap of a uniform. Train stands absolutely still for at least an hour after the plane has been heard. No smoking allowed and it's cold. More soldiers, all kids, get in at every station. We are like sardines and smell like bad ones...Two hours late getting to Barcelona. Fernandez, Warner's man, greets me although how he could see me I don't know - the station is almost pitch dark....Afterwards go to Shanghai Rest, meet many people. Have to give short speech and am cheered when I finish up with clenched-fist Communist salute and the word "salute" - almost my only Spanish one. Great reception! Erben reminded me afterwards I said "God bless you all" - heresy here naturally as religion has been abolished. Lucky they didn't understand...We ride around in a horse cab. No taxis after 8 p.m. and then only for a certain distance. This is to conserve gasoline - which is going to win or lose this war. There is a great shortage....There are no private autos in Catalonia or Red Spain. All have been commandeered for the use of govt. officials and the military. All fly flags of one sort or another. If I am ever allowed to write what I know & think back in America then the Propaganda Ministry will have made a bargain in supplying me with car….A regular army*

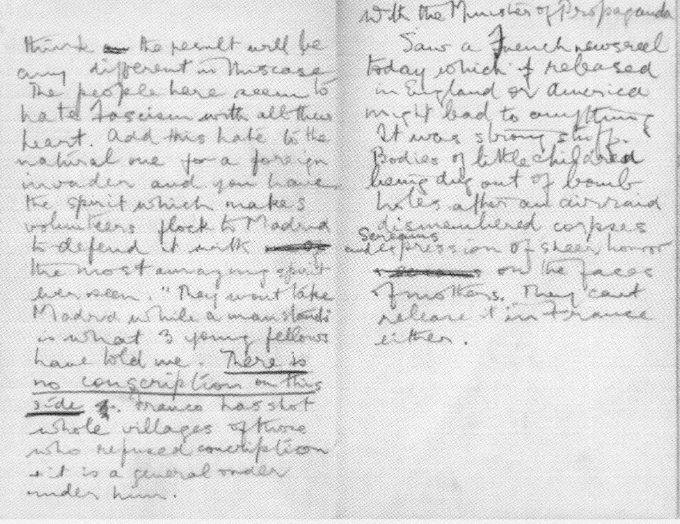

Two pages from the actual diary - Sat, March 27

machine gun nest was place[d] in a tunnel sweeping a street. Anarchists had to pass this street. [Francisco] Ascaso said, "I'll fix that gun for you." He ran around the corner, clasped the gun to his entrails and died riddled. The gun was silenced long enough for his friends to shoot the gunners....Another priest…Fat, fifty, not very popular. But the people don't dislike him quite enough to shoot him. So they decide to make him walk on top of a narrow ancient Roman aqueduct - certain that he'll fall & kill himself. Like a tightrope walker the fat old priest carefully picked his sweating way across. The crowd sees he might get across to their great surprise. Some want to shoot him before he gets across. But some latent sporting instinct makes others stop them. He makes the walk & escapes...Bishop of Siguenza (where the battle is now raging) was with a handful of fascists in the town defending the cathedral. Finally the Bishop was captured with 10 fascists and all of them lined up against a wall for execution. The machine gun and rifles trained on them "Fire!" & of the 11 men only the Bishop falls. The other 10 absolutely unharmed. This shows the traditional hatred of the people for the priests. Every gun was trained on the Bishop. The firing squad did not stop laughing for hours - this being a joke which appeals greatly to the Spanish. Then someone suddenly remembered the other 10. "Come on don't let's keep them waiting, boys." Again the sporting instinct. The soldiers so grateful for the good laugh they let the other 10 off with prison. American Hospital at Teracon. 14 wounded brought in Jarama...Dr. Byrne (American) states emphatically that now the majority of wounds are explosive bullets. Most terrible wounds. Shattered faces. One English doctor was shot in the penis by stray bullet 2 klms behind Jarama front - went through scrotum. Another American boy - completely blinded. He told me, talking of America, he once saw the Califor hills & Golden Gate. Gave a faint terribly sad smile as said so. Am absolutely sick at the dishes of blood & puss everywhere. One little boy of about 6 leg amputated below knee after his town was bombed 3 weeks ago. They are dressing his stump. He is crying "Madre! Madre! Madre!" Erben took picture. Horrible… *A fuller version of the diary appears in Appendix II, page 313.

Sun March 28

Visits the office of the propaganda minister in Barcelona and, along with Erben, signs the guest book *(bottom right)*; beneath their signatures is also that of journalist George Seldes.

Mon March 29

At Warner Bros. First National Barcelona for a press visit.

Tue March 30

Visits the royal palace in Barcelona.

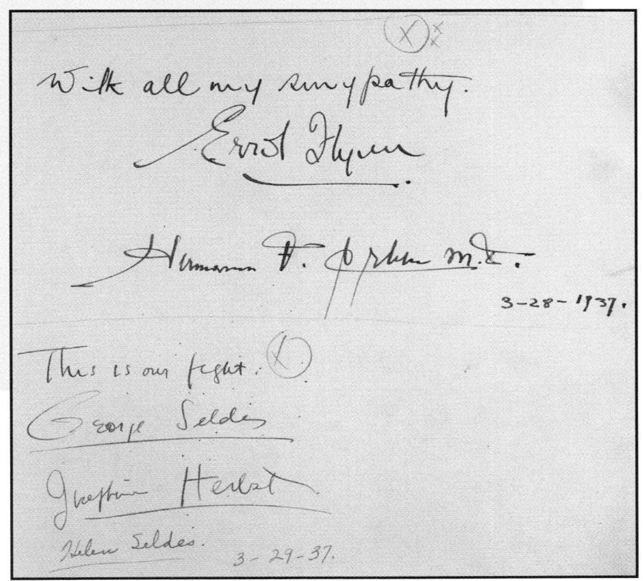

The signatures of Flynn, Erben, and foreign correspondent George Seldes from the guest book in the office of the Commissioner of Catalan Propaganda - Sun, March 28

Wed March 31
Leaves with Erben by car for Valencia, arriving at 7pm.

Thu April 1
Flynn's diary continues: *having food with the International Brigade - writing this on a long table of French food spirits - no one wears same uniform as another - hardly two types of headgear similar - many berets....The pathetic result of piety of the peasants was that the money they gave or was coerced into giving was used by the Church to buy arms for the fascists to use against them...Millions of pesetas - tens of millions lying in the coffers of the priests and nuns. Little of it spent in hospitals and for the poor. The poor when sick were told they must pay for some more candles to be lit for them, not spend a penny for a doctor. No wonder there was a reaction....Most desperate poverty along Madrid road - as bad as Ireland - but these are not the people who are fighting - they are all working the fields young & old, men & women...El Pedernoso...Here stands the windmill at which Don Quixote tilted - Erben took a picture of it - 140 kilometers from here is the Madrid front line...We are staying the night at Quinta del Oro - outside supposedly forming section of Madrid front. I can hear desultory shells in distance...This little hostel is full of soldiers. One is being taken into Valencia hospital, having been hit by dum-dum bullet. He scorns the idea that this side uses them too. Food terrible. No lights in town - the fascist planes come over every night. Am writing this by ancient lamp of oil in which floats a wick. Am still being told by young Spaniards that don't give a damn about politics - they are fighting for their country against an invader. And with what a spirit!....Am sure Don Quixote stayed in this inn - it's so old. Rat holes in room corners - walls all crumbling away. Over one large wall hole - to hide it doubtless - is a very modern 3 ft. x 2 ft. mirror - wonder how got here...New platoon has just arrived from Madrid - all Russians I think. Great big cheerful fellows & very hungry. They are bringing in their wounded for hot macaroni. proceeding up to Madrid front tomorrow at 6 a.m. - have to pass very close fascist lines...Had a minor war of my own tonight for possession of my bed. Six Russians wanted it finally won out by getting into it in middle of argument. Am sure 100 men have slept in it - very dirty.*

Fri April 2
Hal Wallis: *"There will be a preview at Warner's Hollywood Theatre Monday night, April 5th, at approximately 8:25 P.M., of our picture…'The Prince And The Pauper'."* Arrives in Madrid with Erben; takes a nighttime stroll; attempts by Warner Bros. to cable Flynn in Paris are unsuccessful, with no reply from either *"Flynn or his wife."* WB is concerned about the casting of Flynn's next picture.

Flynn's diary concludes: *Madrid Front Line...We drive up to Madrid front lines (Barra de Arguelles) with 100 metres. Here city is a shambles. Tall houses absolutely demolished, the debris of which form the graves of hundreds of people. Here the guns cannon & machine are hard at - the echoes reverberating through the deserted streets. We are silent knowing we are walking over the bodies of many. Walking through am missed narrowly by some falling debris. Some beautiful furniture being used in guard bivouacs. As we pass down what was once the Rosales, a great wide plaza with the rifle & machine guns right in my ears suddenly sound of piano comes from one great house. Go in - a soldier is playing a beautiful grand piano - the roof is off over his head - shell holes - he is quite alone playing to himself. This is weird - he is accompanied by the whine of shells. Can see the fascist trenches from over a park, one half mile or less away.... Suddenly right across street shot is fired in front our hotel. We slink into doorway after seeing the flash. Can't see a soul moving. Finally cross street to where it came from - not a soul in sight. Meal terrible tonight - not only do we have iced water in the hot water tap but the fried fish was also ice cold for dinner. So was the coffee.*

Sent Damita a telegram tonight. Finished up with "need bath terribly also a romp." The sensor [sic] *was most suspicious. I tried to explain "romp" was the word to play. Very rightly didn't believe me. Made me cut it out. Don't know if he allowed the former or not about the bath.*

Sat April 3
At the Guadalajara front visiting soldiers with Erben *(below left)*; decides to leave and packs until 2am.

Below left, visiting soldiers at the Guadalajara front - Sat, April 3; below right, the same location today

Sun April 4

Leaves Madrid at 6am.

Mon April 5

Press reports Flynn has been killed *(top right)*; evening preview of THE PRINCE AND THE PAUPER at Warner's Hollywood Theater.

Tue April 6

Press corrects erroneous report of Flynn's death; Jack Warner alerts the WB Paris office to be sure that Flynn knows he needs to be back at the studio by April 16th: "ALREADY POSTPONED PICTURE ACCOUNT HIS DELAY....INADVISABLE FLYNN PARTICIPATE THIS HIGHLY DANGEROUS POLITICAL SITUATION BECAUSE OF CERTAIN OFFENSE TO COUNTRIES SYMPATHISING WITH ONE SIDE OR OTHER....THIS SITUATION DYNAMITE... HIS COMPLETE FUTURE IN JEOPARDY...."

Wed April 7

Hal Wallis to Tenny Wright:*"Errol Flynn arrives in New York April 16th and is flying to the coast so that he will be here Saturday, April 17th. This means he will start the picture* [THE PERFECT SPECIMEN] *on the 19th."*

Fri April 9

At the 400 Club in London with Lili, celebrating his return from Spain.

Mon April 12

Under advice from his doctor, Flynn is not able to sail on the *Bremen*, but on the *Queen Mary* on April 14th.

Tue April 13

Telegram from Hal Wallis to Jacob Wilk: ON FLYNN'S ARRIVAL INSTRUCT HIM RETURN TO COAST BY RAIL STOP DON'T WANT HIM FLY.

Wed April 14

Returns to the United States on the ocean liner *Queen Mary (center right)*.

Thu April 15

Telegram from Roy Obringer to story editor Jacob Wilk: WE ARE UNDER NO OBLIGATION TO FURNISH FLYNN TRANSPORTATION AS HE IS ON VACATION ON HIS OWN STOP....MEET HIM AT BOAT AND DISCREETLY ADVISE WE VERY ANXIOUS HIS RETURN ACCOUNT OF HOLDING UP PICTURE STOP IF FLYNN THEN STATES HE INTENDS TO FLY YOU THEN ADVISE HIM COME VIA TWENTIETH CENTURY AND CHIEF STOP IF FLYNN INDICATES HE LEAVING BY TRAIN SAY NOTHING STOP THIS IMPORTANT FROM ANGLE WE INTEND SUSPEND CONTRACT FROM APRIL TWELFTH TO DATE HE REPORTS TO STUDIO BUT IF WE EXERCISE CONTROL OVER HIM IN NEW YORK BY DIRECTING MEANS OF TRAVEL THIS MEANS WE WOULD HAVE TO PUT HIM ON PAYROLL NEW YORK

Wed April 21

While in Chicago Flynn denies he has any affiliation with *"the reds,"* after reports are published that he is a central figure in the anti-communist crusade being waged by the Knights of Columbus.

Sat April 24

Flynn's article, *A Night On The Town*, appears in *Collier's* magazine.

Sun April 25

Attends a bon voyage party at the home of Dolores del Rio for Ann and Jack Warner, who were leaving on a cruise to Europe; David Niven, Gary Cooper, and Marlene Dietrich also attended.

Mon April 26

Meets Lili at the Pasadena train station on her return from Europe; with him are his Rhodesian ridgeback dogs, Stella and Billy, the first line of their breed in the United States.

Sat May 1

Attends with David Niven the birthday/costume party of William Randolph Hearst in Santa Monica; he and Niven dress up as a "shovel brigade" in blue and white striped sweatshirts and tight pants.

Wed May 5

THE PRINCE AND THE PAUPER premieres at the Strand in in New York City.

Friday May 7

Radio performance of "The Prince and the Pauper" on the CBS program *Hollywood Hotel*; appearing with Flynn are Louella Parsons and Bobby and Billy Mauch *(bottom right)*.

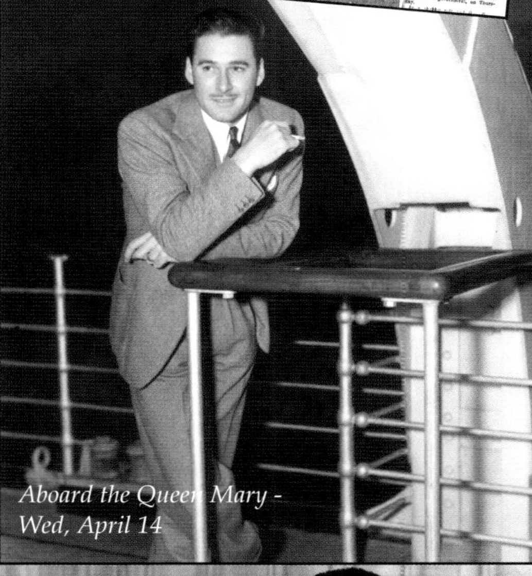

*Aboard the Queen Mary -
Wed, April 14*

*Radio performance of "The Prince and the Pauper"
with Billy and Bobby Mauch and Louella Parsons -
Fri, May 7*

Dancing with Olivia de Havilland at the Coronation Ball - Wed, May 12

With Kay Francis, director Delmer Daves, and Humphrey Bogart at the 17th annual Screen Snapshots event - June 1937

At the radio performance of Secret Agent *with Frances Farmer, Nathalie Bucknall, and Cecil B. DeMille - Mon, June 7*

Sat May 8

THE PRINCE AND THE PAUPER opens nationwide.

Wed May 12

King George V Coronation Ball at the Ambassador Hotel with David Niven and Olivia de Havilland *(top left)*; at around this time Flynn and Niven begin sharing a beach house at 18904 Pacific Coast Highway in Malibu.

Sat May 15

Begins work on PERFECT SPECIMEN, filming scenes outside the Wickstead mansion.

Sun May 16

In a tennis match at the Westside Country Club in Cheviot Hills *(top right)*.

Mon May 17

Ill, does not work.

Tue May 18 and Wed May 19

Filming in the interior and exterior of Hooker's garage on Canadian Street on the backlot.

Thu May 20 and Fri May 21

Filming inside the Wickstead mansion and (on 5/19) in the dining room.

Tue May 25

Filming in grandma Wickstead's office with Edward Everett Horton and May Robson.

Thu May 27 through Sat May 29

Filming in the Wickstead living room, his first scenes with Joan Blondell.

June

With Kay Francis, director Delmer Daves, and Humphrey Bogart at the 17th annual Screen Snapshots event, sometime this month *(center left)*.

Tue June 1

Filming on the Wickstead grounds at upper Busch Gardens in Pasadena.

Wed June 2

Filming in the Wickstead living room.

Thu June 3

Filming on the Wickstead grounds at Busch Gardens, and in Grattan's (Edward Everett Horton) room.

Fri June 4, Sat June 5, and Mon June 7

Bad weather prevents filming at Busch Gardens (6/4); filming in Gerald's (Flynn) room, and upstairs in the Shaw Hotel; on 6/7 does a radio performance of "British Agent" at CBS affiliate, KNX, Los Angeles, for the *Lux Radio Theatre (bottom left)*.

Tue June 8

Filming on the Wickstead grounds at Busch Gardens.

Wed June 9

Filming upstairs at the Shaw Hotel, and on the sleeping porch.

Thu June 10 and Fri June 11

Filming on the Wickstead grounds at Busch Gardens with Blondell alone (on 6/10) and (on 6/11) with Blondell and Dick Foran.

Sat June 12

Filming in the Wickstead mansion, and in Hooker's garage.

Sun June 13

Attends a surprise birthday party for Basil Rathbone at Rathbone's home.

Mon June 14

Filming in Mona's (Joan Blondell) hotel.

Tue June 15

Continues filming in Mona's hotel, in Gerald's room, and outside the Shaw Hotel.

At the Westsdide Country Club - Sun, May 16

Wed June 16
Filming in the Shaw home.

Thu June 17
Filming outside the Wickstead mansion at Flintridge, CA.

Fri June 18 and Sat June 19
Filming outside the Carter home in Laurel Canyon with Blondell and Harry Davenport *(top right);* ANOTHER DAWN opens on 6/18 at Radio City Music Hall in New York City (Kay Francis has top billing).

Sun June 20
Flynn's 28th birthday; his Rhodesian ridgebacks, are entered in the Pasadena Summer Kennel Shoe competition.

Mon June 21
Filming on a country road at Sherwood Forest, CA, with Blondell, Allen Jenkins, and Dennie Moore.

Tue June 22
Filming in the Shaw home.

Wed June 23
Filming outside Hooker's garage; process shots in a truck and in Gerald's car.

Thu June 24
Filming outside the Waldorf Hotel on the backlot.

Wed June 30
Filming in Mona's car; process shots inside a bus and in Gerald's car.

July
Article by Flynn, "What Really Happened to Me in Spain," appears in this month's *Photoplay* magazine; sometime this month Flynn works out with professional boxing trainer Mushy Callahan in preparation for the boxing scenes in PERFECT SPECIMEN.

Thu July 1
Process shots inside Gerald's car with Blondell; Bob Fellows: *"Mr. Flynn was 35 minutes late returning from lunch."*

Fri July 2
More process shots inside Gerald's car with Blondell; inter-office memo from Bob Fellows: *"Mr. Flynn was 30 minutes late in getting ready for shooting in AM."*

Sat July 3
More process shots inside Gerald's car with Blondell; filming the chase sequence.

Tue July 6 and Wed July 7
Filming on a country road at Sherwood Forest, and the truck fight.

Wed July 7
Attends a party given by director, Edmund Goulding, and Michael Brooke (the Earl of Warwick) at Brooke's Foothill Road home in Beverly Hills.

Thu July 8 through Sat July 10
Filming the boxing match on soundstage 14; attends the dinner-dance opening of the Beverly Hills Tennis Club on 6/10.

Sun July 11
The Chicago Tribune reports that Flynn suffered a broken rib from a punch by Jack Roper in the fight scene being filmed on 7/10, though no indication of this exists in the daily production notes.

Mon July 12
Process shot of the car chase; filming outside a small tower alone with Blondell.

Tue July 13
Filming inside the hotel, and outside at Providencia Ranch.

Wed July 14
Continues filming the boxing match.

With Joan Blondell and Harry Davenport in Laurel Canyon - Fri, June 18

With WB physical trainer Lewis Hoppe; note the tape measure including Flynn's arm in the chest measurement

On his yacht
the Cheerio II (later called the Bachelor) with
his skipper - July 1937

Tue July 20

Inter-office memo from Hal Wallis: *"Flynn has left"*; Walter McEwen to editor, Terry Morse: *"Dear Terry, Flynn is away on vacation, so we will not get that retake with him until he returns. Mr. Wallis has been fully apprised of the situation so that when he sees the picture assembled he will know what's wrong."*

Sat July 24

The Columbia Broadcasting Co. requests that Flynn portray the lead of Orlando in their radio production of Shakespeare's *As You Like It;* Jack Warner turns down the request on August 12th.

Sat July 25

Arrives at the Coronado Yacht Club on his boat the *Cheerio II* with plans to water ski and fish for marlin.

Wed July 28

"Somewhere off the Mexican coast, Errol Flynn, of the movies, and Ernest Hemingway, the author, are catching big ones and swapping stories about their adventure in Spain. In an apparent effort to shun publicity, the pair made a quiet departure from here to Flynn's yacht with only two members of the crew to keep them company on their fishing trip. There is a possibility that Hemingway also may be acting as literary adviser to the star, as Flynn confided to friends that he expected to devote part of the cruise to working on the first draft of a new book. Its subject, Hollywood hears, is Spain." Harrison Carroll in *The Los Angeles Evening Herald Express.*

August

Flynn's article, "Young Man About Town," appears in this month's issue of *Photoplay* magazine.

Sun August 1

Returns from his fishing trip in Mexico.

Mon August 9

Tenny Wright to Jack Warner: *"Errol Flynn's four week vacation will be up Thursday, August 12. That is, he can start back to work, if we need him, on August 13. Of course, we may make tests at this time, which I will check on later. Also, kindly have a talk with Mr. Flynn and tell him to be on time for his call and not come in to the studio at the last moment. He can not [do his] make up at home as this is Technicolor, and he must be on time. Also, he is not to be dissipating around and come in to the studio with bags under his eyes, as this is a very expensive picture and we do not want to be waiting around for our leading man, with a lot of extra people and other expensive actors. Kindly have this talk with him, as you suggested, and get him straightened out before we go into production."* Tenny Wright to unit manager Al Alleborn and assistant director Lee Katz: *"Kindly let me know at anytime that Flynn does not report at the studio at the time of any call you may give him. Do not keep this a secret; I want a written note any time he is late or does not show up, as this picture is too big for us to wait around for an actor. Be sure you follow this out to the letter."*

Mon August 16

Reports to WB at 10:30am for wardrobe (the baron noble and Robin's band costumes), make-up, mustache, and wig tests for THE ADVENTURES OF ROBIN HOOD.

Wed August 18 through Fri August 20

Archery and broadsword rehearsal at WB; meets Howard Hill, who will become a close, life-long friend; completes work on PERFECT SPECIMEN (8/19) with retakes of the rear of Hooker's garage and in the Wickstead dining room; salary for the film is $22,750 ($423,270 in 2021 value).

Sat August 21

With Lili on Catalina Island for a tennis match in which he doubles with Hungarian screen star Irén Biller.

Mon August 23 through Fri August 27

Continues archery and broadsword rehearsal, with Bud Ernst standing in as Little John on 8/26.

September

Flynn's article, "Hollywood Women, Heaven Preserve Them!" appears in this month's *Photoplay* magazine.

Thu September 2, Fri September 3, and Wed September 8

Continues archery and broadsword rehearsal; Hal Wallis to William Keighley, Henry Blanke, and Tenny Wright (on 9/8): *"Errol Flynn asked me if he could go over and do some fishing at Catalina and always be within two hours' call*

During broadsword rehearsals for
The Adventures of Robin Hood - *August*

Above, with Lili in the foyer of the Beverly Hills house - Summer; below, the same spot today

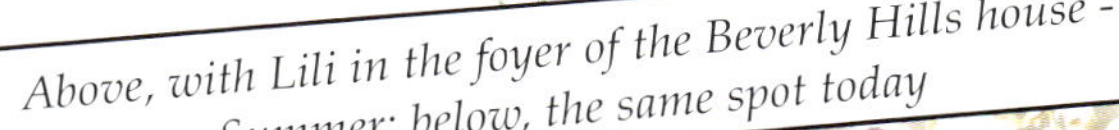

With Lili in their bedroom in the Beverly Hills house, and below, the same room today

The Flynn home at 601 North Linden Drive, Beverly Hills, CA

of the studio. I told him this depends entirely on you gentlemen and whether or not he was needed for wardrobe, fencing lesson, or for any other preparations on the picture. Keep in mind, however, that we are aiming for a starting date on this picture between September 20th and 27th, and let us get all of his make-up, wardrobe, hair, and everything else set...Last time

From the Scotty Welbourne photo session at the Beverly Hills house - Summer 1937

Costume test - Tue, September 15

Above with tennis pro Donald Budge, Jinx Falkenburg, and agent Victor Orsatti at the Westside Tennis Club - Mon, September 20

With Basil Rathbone during costume tests for the canceled jousting scene

we looked at the hair tests, it was agreed that we were going to make another wig—a sort of an in between of two on the early test that we were partial to. So far I have not seen anything further in the way of a wig test of Flynn. As I understand it, Westmore was to make a new wig, which certainly should be ready by this time. Let me know about this, as I have not yet seen the final make-up of Flynn as to his hair and beard as it will be in the picture, and I don't want to let this go until the last minute." Tenny Wright to Hal Wallis: "I do not think it is a good idea to let Flynn go to Catalina except on Saturday afternoon and Sunday as he cannot be here on two hours' notice because when we want him he would be out on the boat, so I think the best thing to do is to allow him Saturday afternoon and Sunday, not during the week when we most likely be needing him for wardrobe tests, fencing lessons, etc."

Labor Day Weekend, Sat September 4 through Mon September 6
Sails to Ensenada, Mexico ,with Lili, Dolores del Rio, and Cedric Gibbons.

Thu September 9
Tenny Wright to Hal Wallis: "Would it be all right if we tested the new wig for Errol Flynn in black and white instead of Technicolor as it is very expensive to call in a Technicolor camera for one day if we only have a wig to test, and still I would like to show the test to you as we have the wig ready now." Wallis to Wright: "I want the new wig for Errol Flynn tested in Technicolor. You don't necessarily have to call a crew in for this one test…"

Wed September 15
Tests for wardrobe (the Nottingham Hall and forest scenes), make-up, mustache, wig, etc. *(top left)*; a jousting match was originally to be the opening scene in the film *(costume tests bottom left)* until canceled by Hal Wallis on October 7th; attends the party to honor the visiting players of the Pacific Southwest Tennis Championships at the Westside Tennis Club in Beverly Hills.

Sun September 19
Attends the Southwest Pacific Coast Tennis Championships at the Westside Tennis Club in Beverly Hills.

Mon September 20
Plays in a charity match at the Westside Tennis Club in Beverly Hills.

Tue September 21
Wardrobe tests for Robin's shirt.

Fri September 24
THE PERFECT SPECIMEN previews at the Warner Hollywood Theater; telegram to Flynn from WB assistant treasurer P. A. Chase: AS YOU KNOW IT HAS BEEN NECESSARY FOR YOU TO TAKE CERTAIN FENCING LESSONS IN ORDER THAT YOU MAY BE FAMILIAR WITH THE ART OF FENCING IN CONNECTION WITH THE ROLE YOU ARE TO PORTRAY IN OUR PHOTOPLAY ENTITLED ADVENTURES OF ROBIN HOOD STOP IN ORDER THEREFORE THAT YOU MAY RECEIVE ADEQUATE FENCING LESSONS FOR YOUR SAID ROLE IN SAID PHOTOPLAY IT WILL BE NECESSARY FOR YOU TO REPORT TO THE FENCING MASTER WHO HAS BEEN HERETOFORE INSTRUCTING YOU AT OUR STUDIO AT BURBANK CALIFORNIA AT NINE THIRTY A.M. SATURDAY SEPTEMBER TWENTY FIFTH 1937 AND CONTINUE THEREAFTER WITH SUCH FURTHER FENCING INSTRUCTIONS AND/OR OTHER PREPARATIONS NECESSARY FOR THE ROLE YOU ARE ABOUT TO PORTRAY IN THE ABOVE PHOTOPLAY.

Sat September 25
With Alan Hale, continues archery and broadsword rehearsal; leaves for Chico, CA, at 6:15pm.

Sun September 26
Arrives in Chico at 9:30am for location filming of THE ADVENTURES OF ROBIN HOOD; principal cast members stay at the Richardson Springs Hotel.

Mon September 27
Al Alleborn to Hal Wallis (written on 10/1/37;): "Keighley company called 8:45 AM, finished 4:00 PM. Company did not shoot today due to cloudy weather and lack of sunshine. Started and worked Errol Flynn, Alan Hale, Patric Knowles. Rehearsed Eugene Pallette. Company rehearsed at Ext. Woods—Bridge and Stream in Bidwell Park, Chico location. Picture 1 day behind schedule." Tenny Wright to Henry Blanke: "For your information, the company arrived on location at 9:30 AM yesterday morning, Sunday…..Today the company was up at 6:00 AM and on the location at 8:20, including Errol Flynn; however, the weather has been foggy and he (director, Keighley) was unable to shoot anything this morning but at the time this note is being written (2pm), he has changed his set-up and is now going into close-ups."

Tue September 28
First shots of THE ADVENTURES OF ROBIN HOOD are filmed with scenes of Robin and Will Scarlett (Patric Knowles) walking through the forest toward the log bridge; first shot at 11:15; at one point in the filming, Will's lute hits a tree and breaks, necessitating a delay in shooting until the instrument can be repaired; begins filming

the duel on the log bridge with Little John *(top right)*.

Wed September 29
Continues filming on the log bridge over Big Chico Creek.

Thu September 30
Alan Hale ill, unable to work until 2:30pm; continues filming on the log bridge.

Fri October 1
Cloudy and rainy; no shooting; telegram from Hal Wallis to a Mr. Berkowitz: JL WARNER AUTHORIZED ONE RADIO APPEARANCE FOR ERROL FLYNN…..OKAY FOR THEM USE FLYNN PICTURES IN ADS ANNOUNCING RADIO BROADCAST BUT NOT IN CONNECTION WITH ANY SALE OR ENDORSEMENT OF [Rogers] SILVERWEAR STOP ALSO SHOULD GET PLUG IN ADVERTISING OF FURTHCOMING [sic] FLYNN PICTURE PERFECT SPECIMEN.

Sat October 2
Still cloudy and rainy; no shooting.

Sun October 3
Continues filming the log bridge scene.

Mon October 4
Filming on horseback with Knowles and Much the Miller's son (Herbert Mundin) being chased by mounted Norman knights.

Tue October 5
Filming on the log bridge, with Robin falling into the stream—Flynn requesting heaters to warm the chilly water!—and in the glade with Hale, Knowles, and Mundin (who is filmed shooting the deer); stream noise was diminished with sandbags and strips of burlap.

Wed October 6
Filming the meeting of and duel with Friar Tuck at Five Mile Pool *(center right and below right)* until the generator breaks down; one take is ruined by the sound of a train whistle four miles away (*"The Sherwood Special,"* Keighley joked).

Thu October 7
Hal Wallis cancels the jousting tournament and christening of the Merry Men scenes; a new generator arrives for the Friar Tuck duel.

Sun October 10
Completes filming of the Friar Tuck duel.

The same location today as on the right

Top, with Alan Hale and Patric Knowles in Bidwell Park - Tue September 28; Above, filming Robin meeting Friar Tuck (director William Keighley at center in the light jacket) - Wed, October 6; and left, the scene itself with Eugene Palette

Richardson Springs.
Chico. Cal
24th Oct.

Dear Hal/ First let me thank you again

Bidwell Park, CA – Thu, October 21

Mon October 11
Filming of scenes in Robin Hood's camp with King Richard (Ian Hunter).

Tue October 12
Filming scenes of archery practice, and Tuck and King Richard exchanging punches, but the scenes are never used; Basil Rathbone arrives in Chico.

Wed October 13
Rain; cast rehearses in the morning and are free the rest of the day; Flynn and Howard Hill go pheasant hunting with shotguns—illegally out of season—are found out, arrested, and fined $25 each.

Thu October 14 and Fri October 15
Rain; no filming.

Sat October 16 to Mon October 18
Continues filming in Robin's camp with an injured Much being carried into camp.

Mon October 18
Telegram from Flynn to Hal Wallis: PERMISSION WAS GIVEN ME BY JACK [Warner] OVER PHONE TO DO COUPLE QUOTE RADIO SHOWS UNQUOTE STOP CANNOT UNDERSTAND WHY THIS IS NOW REFUTED AND AM MUCH EMBARRASSED BY HAVING CANCEL ONE AT THE LAST MOMENT.

Tue October 19
More filming with Little John at the log bridge; telegram from Hal Wallis: DEAR ERROL REFERENCE YOUR WIRE RE TWO RADIO BROADCASTS STOP MY DEFINITE ADVICE FROM JL [Warner] TO EFFECT HE ONLY OKAYED ONE PROGRAM WHICH WE HAVE GRANTED YOU RIGHT TO DO THIS BEING LUX PROGRAM IN DECEMBER STOP HOWEVER IN CONNECTION WITH SECOND PROGRAM WHICH WE UNDERSTAND IS SILVER THEATRE ON NOVEMBER FOURTEENTH WILL GRANT YOU PERMISSION MAKE THIS APPEARANCE YOUR CONDITIONS FIRST THAT YOU AVAILABLE IN HOLLYWOOD AND YOUR APPEARANCE ON PROGRAM IN NO WAY INTERFERES YOUR WORK IN PRESENT PICTURE AND SECOND SPONSORS SUBMIT SCRIPT TO US FOR OUR APPROVAL…..SO AS TO PROTECT BOTH YOU AND OURSELVES FRANKLY HAVE HAD BAD REPORTS ON STAR MATERIAL USED BY OTHER PERSONALITIES THIS PROGRAM AND WE REALLY LOOKING AFTER YOUR INTERESTS BY MAKING THIS CONDITION…..

Wed October 20
Filming with King Richard in the forest and camp.

Thu October 21
Continues filming the meeting of King Richard and his men, Robin dropping down from a tree *(top left)*.

Fri October 22
Olivia de Havilland arrives; filming of the forest banquet scene begins; telegram from Hal Wallis to Al Alleborn: JUST LEARNED THAT FLYNN AND KNOWLES ARE DOING SOME FLYING UP THERE FROM LOCAL AIRPORT IN RENTED PLANE STOP ABSOLUTELY INSIST THAT FLYNN KNOWLES AND ALL OTHER MEMBERS OF COMPANY STOP THIS IMMEDIATELY STOP WE ARE INVESTING CLOSE TO TWO MILLION DOLLARS IN PRODUCTION AND THESE FOOLHARDY STUNTS MUST BE STOPPED.

Sat October 23
Filming with Sir Guy (Basil Rathbone) and Marian (Olivia de Havilland) riding through the forest, and in Robin's camp; THE PERFECT SPECIMEN opens.

Sun October 24
Filming with Sir Guy and his men in rags at Robin's camp; handwritten letter from Flynn in Chico to Hal Wallis *(bottom left)*: *Dear Hal/ First let me thank you again for fixing things re the radio deals. I was pretty sure you yourself probably didn't know any of the facts until the last minute and then straightened it out for me. Now one other, minor, but to me very important squawk. My wig—I loathe the bloody thing. With the hat on it's fine, and the alteration I want to suggest does not affect any of the stuff we've shot so far—the part that's wrong is hidden by the hat. The center part in the wig is my chief complaint. I would like an almost unnoticeable part on either side so that one side or the other could sweep back like this [sketch] off the forehead. The fringes would then, when the hat is removed, not look like fingers but just as few locks of loose hair carelessly falling over the brow. My drawing of course is helpless but I've explained to the make up here who*

say they will write to the studio and explain it. The point is, I haven't had my hat off yet and when I do, the new wig would match. Would you ask them to make me one like that described & send it up so we can get it right before we come down? I'm quite certain you will think it an improvement Hal. If you don't – nothing has been lost. I hate this present one so much I shudder every time I see the Goddamn thing – and I've had nothing but comments from people, when they see it with the hat off, about the stupid looking fringe & centre part. So there must be something to it. I feel like one of the oldest inhabitants of Chico now – we all do. And we're all very sick of it but consoling ourselves with the report or rather rumour that you like the stuff [dailies] down there. Is it so? All the best Hal & kindest personal regards. Errol."

Filming the banquet sequence in Bidwell Park, Flynn standing on the table, director William Keighly seated at bottom right, cinematographer Tony Gaudio standing to his left - October

With Olivia de Havilland - Mon, October 25

Mon October 25

Filming of Robin and Marian at the banquet table *(center right)*; telegram from Hal Wallis: DEAR ERROL-HAVE HAD REPORTS ABOUT YOUR JOYRIDING IN PLANES UP THERE AND REQUESTED ALLEBORN TO ASK YOU PLEASE DISCONTINUE DOING SO STOP IN SPITE OF THIS UNDERSTAND YOU ARE CONTINUING FLYING STOP HAVE ALWAYS TRIED TO BE COOPERATIVE AND ACCEDE TO VARIOUS REQUESTS FROM YOU FROM TIME TO TIME STOP AM ASKING YOU NOW TO PLEASE CUT OUT THIS FLYING AT LEAST UNTIL PICTURE IS FINISHED.

Tue October 26

Filming of Robin releasing Sir Guy's knights.

Wed October 27

More filming in Robin's camp.

Thu October 28

Filming of Robin showing the injured Saxons to Marian.

Fri October 29

Filming with Will rescuing Much, and with Marian.

Sat October 30

Windy and rainy; no filming; rehearsing the fight sequence.

Sun October 31

Filming of the fight between Robin's men and Sir Guy's knights; the caravan is filmed by second unit director B. Reeves "Breezy" Eason.

Mon November 1

Continues filming the fight in Sherwood Forest.

Tue November 2

Filming of confrontation between Robin and Sir Guy; former heavyweight champion Max Baer visits the set.

Thu November 4

Filming of more forest fight scenes; after filming, flies with Knowles to an air show in Willows, 30 miles southwest of Chico; upon return they lose their way in the darkness and are guided to a safe landing by Billy Miller of the Chico Airport who lined the runway with the headlights of parked cars (the airport had no runway lights at the time).

Fri November 5

Filming of Robin swinging from vine to rock (*"Welcome to Sherwood, m'Lady!"*); between scenes, the city of Chico dedicated a plaque on the site of Robin Hood's glade; a farewell dance for *"All Members Of Warner Bros. Troupe On Location In Bidwell Park"* is held at the Chico High School Gymnasium.

Sat November 6

Ill, but no shooting because of cloudiness.

Sun November 7

Filming in the forest; goes flying yet again with Patric Knowles.

With Lili - Fri, November 5

With Olivia de Havilland - Mon, November 8

Filming the archery tournament at Lower Busch Gardens in Pasadena, CA - November

Mon November 8

Filming of Robin's oath (claims of Hooker Oak as the location appear to be incorrect per the author's research in the area); filming of Robin and Marian when she begins to "understand" him *(top left)*; completes filming at the Chico location and leaves at 8pm; production is nine days behind schedule; Tenny Wright to Hal Wallis: *"For your information, both Flynn and Knowles went up in a plane again yesterday. Also, Flynn is coming in to talk to you about getting some time off. For your information, there is no time for this as he must start rehearsals for his duel at the end of the picture, and I would not suggest letting him go away. This is too big a picture to have him out in a boat at sea, or some other place….When Flynn puts the pressure on you to get away, kindly do not let him do it. I know you will agree with me on this, but I am giving this information to you so you can be prepared for a visit from Flynn."*

Tue November 9

Arrives in Burbank at 11:30am.

Thu November 11

A Jack Paper to Tenny Wright: *"Errol Flynn was given a call last night to report for rehearsal today, Thursday, at 11:00AM. In the meantime, Mr. Warner's office wired him to be in their office at 12:30 P.M. Flynn wired a reply to Warner's office. Flynn did not show up for rehearsal at 11 this morning and after many attempts at checking, the information was that he had left his home at 11 to go to the studio. He finally showed up here arriving at the gate at 12:35 P.M. His agent, whom I contacted, was here before that time and said that he talked to Flynn at 9 this morning and was told by Flynn that he was going to be here for rehearsals at 11:00 A.M."*

Fri November 12

Archery rehearsal; Hal Wallis to Roy Obringer: *"Be sure to keep in touch with the 'Robin Hood' company on Errol Flynn, so that we can give him his two weeks' notice two weeks before the end of his work on the picture. My intention, of course, is to have Flynn's vacation start within a day or two after he finishes the picture."* Roy Obringer to Mr. Ralph Lewis of Freston & Files, Bank of America: *"Mr. J.L. Warner, despite my advise [sic] to him that our consent to a withdrawal of these [trust] funds in amount of $22,500 [$418,619 in 2021 value] by Flynn for purpose of lifting a mortgage on his home would practically wipe out the trust fund and leave us over the well-known barrel in the event Flynn should act up after the withdrawal, at least insofar as the trust fund is concerned, for the possible recovery of any damages growing out of litigation resulting in our favor, has okayed our making arrangements whereby this Monday could be paid over to Flynn...Therefore, it occurs to me that the trust fund agreement will have to be amended to care for this withdrawal."*

Sat November 13

Signs a modification and partial revocation of his trust agreement.

Mon November 15

WB head of publicity Mort Blumenstock to Charles Einfeld: *"Dear Charlie: Will you please have Ed Selzer or somebody talk to Errol Flynn and tell him to call off the dogs in regard to the advertisement which appeared in Time Magazine September 20th on page 34. As explained to Ed Selzer….I obliged the insurance company, who, by the way, do considerable business with Warner Bros. with permission to use a photograph of Errol Flynn and Basil Rathbone [from CAPTAIN BLOOD]. I did it mainly, however, out of respect for N.W. Ayer & Son of Philadelphia [the said insurance company], looking forward to the time when I might have to ask them for a favor...I don't know why the time of so many people must be wasted in order to satisfy some lousy 10% agent that he is earning his keep."*

Wed November 17 and Thu November 18

Continues archery rehearsal.

Fri November 19

Filming of the archery tournament at Lower Busch Gardens.

Sat November 20

Filming in Nottingham Castle on a WB soundstage.

Mon November 22 and Wed November 23

More filming of the archery tournament at Lower Busch Gardens; screenwriter, Norman Reilly Raine to Henry Blanke (11/23): *"Dear Henry: Here are the changes [Robin's wig] which Mr. Flynn calculates will make him happy. Since they are unimportant and will make him very, very happy, we might as well let him have them."* Roy Obringer to Sig Marcus of the Myron Selznick Agency (11/23): *"I have an agreement which modifies the Trust Agreement under the Flynn contract, whereby Flynn can now be paid $22,500. This was arranged between Flynn, Noll Gurney [Flynn's agent], and J.L. Warner about a week ago, and it appears that Flynn asked for this money when Mr. Warner asked Flynn to please stop flying airplanes of questionable safety while he was in our present picture...."*

Wed November 24

Rehearsing the duel; in a fact-finding legal deposition for WB, makeup artist Ward Hamilton claims that Flynn told him privately during a makeup session for THE ADVENTURES OF ROBIN HOOD that he (Flynn) was *"disappointed in his relations with Warner Bros., that he felt he was entitled to more compensation, that he intended to get more compensation by hook or crook, and that the only method of securing more compensation was to get [WB] 'over a barrel.'* He went on to add that *"should he, Flynn, make any complaints relative to his beard, wig, and/or make-up, that he was doing so for the purpose of stalling in the aforesaid picture, and that....[Hamilton] should know what he meant thereby and cooperate with the said Flynn so that the suspicion of the officers of the aforesaid corporation would not be aroused...."*

Fri November 26

Completion of filming of the archery tournament at Lower Busch Gardens.

Sat November 27 and Mon November 29

Filming in Marian's apartment; sprains thumb (11/29).

Tue November 30

Rehearsing the duel; complains of sore thumb; Keighley directs his final scene: Sir Guy discovering Marian and her letter to Robin; Roy Obringer to Jack Warner: *"It is my understanding that Flynn will not be needed for rehearsals prior to the day of broadcast [of the Lux Radio Program], and that he will not have to leave the studio until around 3:30PM on the day of the broadcast [12/6]. Flynn may give you a different story and try to get out earlier on December 6, but Mr. Wolf of the Selznick Agency, who is handling this deal for Flynn, advised me Flynn need not leave the studio prior to 3:30 or 4:00PM";* attends a dinner party in honor of operatic singer Richard Tauber and Tauber's wife Diana Napier, given by Edmund Goulding and Michael Brooke (the Earl of Warwick) at Goulding's home.

December

In a legal statement made this month WB Teddington producer Irving Asher recalls that during the month of October 1934, his secretary, a Mrs. Boyd, advised him of *"the continued visits of one individual, subsequently known....as Errol Flynn, for the purposes of seeking employment in....motion pictures...."* Asher claims he (Asher) was probably too busy to take note of Flynn at the time until after Flynn had made a number of weekly visits and Mrs. Boyd insisted that *"in her opinion the said Flynn had motion picture possibilities...."* Asher finally did take note and cast Flynn in MURDER AT MONTE CARLO.

Wed December 1 and Thu December 2

Director, Michael Curtiz, replaces William Keighley; filming in the castle banquet hall; de Havilland is ill and does not work (12/2).

Sat December 4

Filming Robin's escape from the castle; unit manager Al Alleborn to Tenny Wright: *"Should you get any requisitions from the Prop Dept. for tables to be lighter in weight than those now on the set for Mr. Flynn to handle, please disregard these as I have turned them down. The ones that we have in the set are light and a boy 14 years old could throw them over. I see no reason for going to any expense to make lighter tables for Mr. Flynn."* Attends a dinner and dance party thrown by the Basil Rathbones at their Los Feliz home.

Sun December 5 and Mon December 6

Continues filming in the banquet hall; radio performance of "These Three" with Barbara Stanwyck for the Lux Radio Theatre at CBS affiliate, KNX, Los Angeles (12/6, *center right*).

Tue December 7 and Wed December 8

Continues filming in the castle interior; Roy Obringer to attorney Ralph Lewis (12/8): *"You are undoubtedly familiar with the cat-and-dog fight that is being conducted at the present time between certain radio producers and so-called air scandal mongers, such as Jimmie Fidler, and*

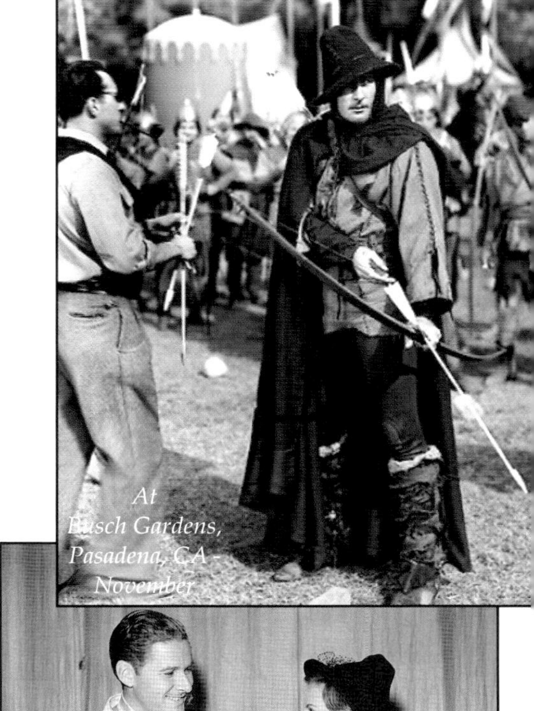

At Busch Gardens, Pasadena, CA - November

With Barbara Stanwyck at KNX Radio studio, Los Angeles - Mon, December 6

Filming in the banquet hall - December

As Robin of Locksley in THE ADVENTURES OF ROBIN HOOD (photo by Homer van Pelt)

others...I am enclosing herewith a letter which Errol Flynn proposes to employ in a system of boycotting the product of the sponsor by appealing to his fans, and starting up some sort of chain letter propaganda of complaining to the sponsors of the attacks made by Fidler, and with a threat to not purchase the sponsor's product.....will you please peruse this and give me your reaction from a legal standpoint...."

Fri December 10
Rehearsing the final duel; Roy Obringer to Flynn: *"Dear Errol:.....the series of letters which you propose may not only bring a definite reaction from the sponsors of the individual as to your interference with their business and trade, but may tip over into some technical violation of the Federal Postal Laws.....you undoubtedly have read in the trade papers where the Agents Guild proposes certain legislation to be passed covering this...Therefore, although I can hardly blame you for your frame of mind, it may be best to wait and see how far future activities of these broadcasts are curbed.....before you take any different steps."*

Sat December 11
Filming of King Richard's entrance into the castle.

Mon December 13 and Tue December 14
More filming in the castle.

Wed December 15
Filming of Robin's lead-up to hanging on Dijon Street on the backlot.

Thu December 16 through Sat December 18
Filming of Robin's hanging *(top right)*; (on 12/16) signs a new contract guaranteeing $2,750 per week ($51,165 in 2021 value).

Mon December 20
Filming the castle fight in the Great Hall *(center right)*, and Prince John's (Claude Rains) banishment.

Tue December 21
Filming in Prince John's room, and the Great Hall.

Wed December 22 and Thu December 23
Continues filming in the Great Hall.

Fri December 24 and Mon December 27
Filming in the castle's outer hall, and (on 12/24) the close-up of a dead Sir Guy.

Tue December 28 and Wed December 29
Continues filming in the castle's outer hall, and (on 12/28) in Marian's apartment; (on 12/29) the University of Alabama football team, who will be playing in the upcoming Rose Bowl game on January 1st, visits the set *(bottom right)*.

Thu December 30 and Fri December 31
Continues filming in the castle's outer hall and in the dungeon cell; Al Alleborn to Tenny Wright (12/30): *"Mr. Errol Flynn advised me today that owing to the fact that he is called ready to work at 8:30 AM and 9:00 AM in the morning on this heavy work of fighting and dueling, which is taking place in the Castle and Dungeon, he will not be able to work after 5:00 PM in the afternoon and advised me that starting today, December 30th, 1937, he will expect to be dismissed at 5:00 PM because he feels he will not be able to continue any longer in a days work than 5:00 PM."*

1938

January
Flynn's article, "Hollywood's Not-So-Ancient Mariners," appears in this month's *Photoplay* magazine.

Mon January 3
Filming in Dijon Street on the backlot.

Tue January 4
Filming the royal box on Dijon Street.

Wed January 5
Filming in Lake Sherwood, CA, with Hale, Pallette, Knowles, and Mundin; attends a cocktail party given by Mary Astor at her home; David Niven and Herbert Marshall were also in attendance.

Thu January 6
Does not work.

With Nick De Ruiz - December

With Basil Rathbone - Mon, December 20

With the University of Alabama football team, Basil Rathbone (in costume), and Michael Curtiz (holding the ball) - Wed, December 29

With Olivia de Havilland at the Warner Bros. Calabasas Ranch, filming an ending that was not used - Wed, January 12

With Patric Knowles at the Warner Bros. Calabasas Ranch, filming Robin's entrance in the movie - Fri, January 14

Left, with Olivia de Havilland, filming their final scene in THE ADVENTURES OF ROBIN HOOD - Fri, January 14

Fri January 7
Filming retakes and additional material in Marian's apartment; a second unit at Lake Sherwood films the scenes of Robin's men jumping Sir Guy's caravan.

Sat January 8
Filming retakes with de Havilland and Knowles at Lake Sherwood.

Mon January 10 and Tue January 11
Filming and completion of the archery tournament at Midwick Country Club in Alhambra, CA; with Lili (on 1/11) at the Los Angeles Tennis Club for the match between Ellsworth Vines and Fred Perry.

Wed January 12
Filming castle exteriors, the tag, and at the Nottingham gate with Knowles, and with de Havilland at the WB Ranch (though ultimately not used); process forest shots are filmed.

Thu January 13
Filming in Dijon Street on the backlot, in Marian's apartment on the soundstage, and a process shot of Robin escaping on horseback.

Fri January 14
Completes work on THE ADVENTURES OF ROBIN HOOD with the filming of Robin and Will jumping their horses over a log at the WB Calabasas Ranch; later that day he films his climb up the ivy-covered wall to Marian's apartment; salary for the film is $30,625. ($569,787 in 2021 value).

Mon January 17
Hal Wallis to Roy Obringer: *"For your information, we gave Errol Flynn permission to go east on Saturday with the understanding that he is subject to return at our request...I couldn't reach him Saturday, but told Lili Damita to advise him that we would probably want him back here next Thursday or Friday and that if it was possible for us to permit him to stay in the east a little longer we would so advise her or him within the next couple of days."*

Sat January 22
Flies to Newark Airport.

Mon January 24
Travels to Boston where he purchases a 75′ ketch from John G. Alden for $17,500 ($316,548 in 2021 value); built in 1929, the vessel was originally named *Karenita*, then changed to *Avenir* in 1930. In 1933 it became the *Simoon*, the *Watchettein* in 1933, and returned to its original name *Karenita* in 1936. Ignoring superstition, Flynn rechristens it the *Sirocco* after his boat from the 1930 Great Barrier Reef voyage.

Wed January 26
Returns to Hollywood.

Mon January 31
Radio performance of "Green Light" for the *Lux Radio Theatre* at CBS affiliate, KNX, Los Angeles.

Tue February 1
Attends the Henry Armstrong–Chalky Wright prize fight with Lili at the Olympic Auditorium in Los Angeles.

Fri February 4
Begins work on FOUR'S A CROWD with scenes in the City Room; Roy Obringer to Sig Marcus of the Selznick Agency: *"Recently when Errol Flynn was on location in Chico in connection with our picture 'Adventures of Robinhood' [sic] he had Mrs. Flynn visit him and as a result we were billed by the Richardson Mineral Springs Hotel for board and lodging incurred by Mrs. Flynn in the amount of $131.17 [$2,372.66 in 2021 value]...I am sure you will recognize this as a bill Flynn should pay....and I would appreciate your cooperation in having him send us a check to cover the same."*

Sat February 5
Filming in the City Room and the upper corridor of the Butler Pierce (Joseph Crehan) home.

Tue February 8
Filming in Buckley's (Patric Knowles) office.

Wed February 9
Filming in the corridor, and interior and exterior of Buckley's office.

Thu February 10
Filming in the City Room; Hal Wallis to Michael Curtiz: *"Will you please stop Flynn from saying 'Old Chap, Old Fellow, and Old Boy' every two or three lines of his speech. It is getting annoying; probably affect the audience the same way. Let's cut out all this English business in this picture. We are supposed to be telling the story of a couple of fast-talking, bright American men. So let's cut out all of this 'Old Chap' and 'Old Boy' stuff. If it is in the script, take them out before you shoot the scene."*

Sat February 12
Filming in the exercise room, steam room, Buckley's bedroom, Lorri's limo, and Dillingwell's office.

Mon February 14
Flynn, Olivia de Havilland, Patric Knowles, and Rosalind Russell all out ill; company does not work.

Tue February 15
Filming in Landsford's office.

Wed February 16
Filming in Dillingwell's home; title of of the current film, *All Rights Reserved*, changed to FOUR'S A CROWD due to potential copyright infringement.

Thu February 17
Filming on the Dillingwell patio.

Fri February 18
Filming in the interior and exterior of Dillingwell's home (Flynn is 25 minutes late returning from lunch).

Sat February 19 and Mon February 21
Filming on the Dillingwell estate.

Tue February 22
Filming the miniature trains on the Dillingwell estate; Flynn is 25 minutes late from lunch because of posing for publicity stills.

Wed February 23 and Thu February 24
Filming in the clinic, and (on 2/23) the interior of the Dillingwell home; Hal Wallis to Michael Curtiz (2/24): *"One thing that bothered me quite a bit in this day's dailies is Flynn's outfit. He certainly is a bad dresser. That light coat and the dark trousers looked very bad, and that pancake hat that he wore, and to top it all that light-colored, button-down-*

Portrait taken at the Boston Globe studio - January

At the KNX Radio studio in Los Angeles with Cecil B. DeMille, J. E."Dinty" Boyle (radio editor of the N.Y. Journal-American), Olivia de Havilland, and C. Aubrey Smith - Mon, January 31

Background photo (left)—the Karenita, later to be christened the Sirocco by Flynn

With Olivia de Havilland (bottom left) and Rosalind Russell (center left) filming their 3-way telephone conversation; Flynn is at top center, and standing below him in fedora is director Michael Curtiz

With Olivia de Havilland - Sat, February 28

With Lili and dolls in the likenesses of Warner Baxter, Lewis Stone, W. C. Fields, Adolph Menjou, and Fredric March - March

the-front sweater or vest that he wore under the coat he looks awful in that outfit. You will have to watch him more closely on his clothes, because he is one of those careless dressers, which is all right when he can wear a scarf around his neck and a shirt open at the throat, and that kind of stuff, but when he puts on business clothes, watch him. Don't let him wear a sweater of that kind—button-down-the-front sweater, and be careful of the hats he wears. Keep him out of hats as much as you can during the picture, and when he does have to wear them, at least you don't have much more stuff in this particular outfit, and for the balance of the picture, please watch his clothes carefully. He looks awful in this makeup [clothing]."*

Fri February 25
Filming in the clinic and on the exterior of the Dillingwell estate.

Sat February 26
Filming on the exterior of the Dillingwell estate and in Lorri's (Olivia de Havilland) bedroom.

Mon February 28
Filming in Lorri's bedroom.

March
With Lili at a party at the Bel Air home of businessman, Jay Paley *(bottom left)*.

Tue March 1
Filming in Lorri's bedroom, in the kitchen, and in the Dillingwell home; C. W. Cannon, c/o Bank of America, to Warner Bros.: *"Gentlemen: In accordance with the request of Mr. Errol Flynn, under date of March 1, which was approved by you, we have paid to him $2,951.84 [$53,394.28 in 2021 value], being twenty-five percent of the deposits held in your account with him, February 15, 1938. There now remains on hand in this account $8,855.53 [$160,183.01 in 2021 value]."*

Wed March 2
Roy Obringer to Ralph Lewis: *".....Flynn, of course, is rather a difficult person to deal with, and he would take every advantage that may be given him; therefore, if, technically, there would be any possible out on account of this soundtrack proposition [for THE ADVENTURES OF ROBIN HOOD] as distinguished from added scenes, retakes, or changes, I would not want Flynn to put us over a barrel by not paying him this one day's pay.....I know you have expressed your opinion that Flynn is not entitled to this additional compensation, but if we should eventually get into difficulties with Flynn, I think it best that our files reflect the fact that we have given this proposition due consideration and that the procedure we adopted in paying or not paying him was justified."*

Thu March 3
Filming in Jean's (Rosalind Russell) apartment and in Landsford's (Flynn) office.

Fri March 4
Filming in Landsford's office.

Sat March 5
Filming at the exterior of the Dillingwell Building, the exterior of the Justice of the Peace office (on Midvale St. on the backlot), and in the Dillingwell home.

Mon March 7 through Wed March 9
Filming in Landsford's office and (on 3/9) in the filing room.

Thu March 10
Filming in the Jamaica Room.

Fri March 11
Flynn's yacht, the *Sirocco*, is reported to be grounded on a mud bank in Boston while being prepared for delivery to Florida; Flynn is scheduled to pick up the *Sirocco* in Miami.

Sat March 12
Filming a retake of the barber scene.

Mon March 14
Filming on the exterior of the Dillingwell estate at Upper Busch Gardens and the interior of Landsford's office.

Tue March 15
Filming at the exterior of the Justice of the Peace; records a retake of dialogue for THE ADVENTURES OF ROBIN HOOD, probably the dubbed line at the castle gate, *"Here I am. Stand by!"*

Wed March 16

Filming at the exterior of the Dillingwell estate at Upper Busch Gardens.

Thu March 17

Filming process shots of the two taxi cabs, the exterior of a building under construction (on Brownstone St. on the backlot), process shots in the elevator, and the interior of the guest room.

Fri March 18

Filming on the exterior of the Dillingwell estate with Olivia de Havilland (actually the pool of the Lakeside Country Club), the main title shots (on New York St. on the backlot), and the exterior of Jean's apartment; Hal Wallis to Roy Obringer and a Mr. Levinson: *"Neither of you told me the outcome of the Errol Flynn situation relative to the making of the sound track for 'Robin Hood' the other day. I would like to know if Flynn agreed to do this without compensation and if he signed the letter. If there is any stalling around on this, this memo will be Obringer['s] authorization to pay him a day's salary for the work he did and to see that he gets it next Wednesday."*

With Michael Curtiz, Olivia de Havilland, Rosalind Russell, and Patric Knowles - Fri, March 18

Sat March 19

Retakes at the exterior of the Justice of the Peace Office, process shot in the taxi cab, and in the clinic.

Mon March 21

Filming in the Justice of the Peace office, process shots in Flynn's cab, and the exterior of both cabs (on New York St. on the backlot).

Tue March 22

Filming in Jenkins' (Hugh Herbert) home.

Wed March 23

Filming in the Justice of the Peace office and retakes in Landsford's office; Ralph Lewis to Roy Obringer: *"I am quite positively of the opinion that Flynn is not entitled to any extra pay for these services* [soundtrack retakes for THE ADVENTURES OF ROBIN HOOD]*.....it may be that Flynn will in person demand a check. In the file I note an authorization to pay him if Flynn attempts to make trouble.....There is no doubt in my mind, if you attempt to deliver a check to him, he will take it and you will never get it back, since you will not go to the extent of bringing suit or otherwise irritate the artist.....If you must continually yield to his demands no matter how unreasonable, in order to keep him happy, then that is a different proposition entirely, but personally I should hesitate, were I an official of the company....."*

Thu March 24

Completes work on FOUR'S A CROWD, filming retakes in Landsford's office and in Buckley's office, interior of the Dillingwell house, and a wild track for the lower hall; salary for the picture is $36,375 ($657,968 in 2021 value); Tenny Wright to Hal Wallis: *"Mike Curtiz and* [associate producer] *David Lewis feel that the process shot in the tag of the picture where Flynn and Knowles, Rosalind Russell and Olivia de Havilland are riding away from the Justice of the Peace's home is bad. At least that portion of it which involves Flynn and Miss Russell and they feel that another shot to cover this should be made with Flynn and Miss Russell...We could not get this shot ready before 6:30 PM yesterday and Flynn definitely refused to work after 6:00 PM and walked out on us.....[Miss Russell] agree'd to an appointment with the Unit Manager, to be here on the lot at 2:00 PM this afternoon.....Would you kindly look at this film, or perhaps you have already seen it, and let me know right away whether we want this shot retaken."* Phone call message from Warner Bros. Studios: *"Mr. Warner WHILE YOU WERE OUT Mr. Errol Flynn Called Up AND HE SAID Please Call Cr. 8666... Called 7.20 AM 3/25/38...Signed J. L. Warner - did not call back."*

Fri March 25

Flies to Miami, stopping over in Atlanta along the way; meets up with Lili in Miami and the two are guests later at a dinner dance at Southwood, the Palm Beach villa of Jell-O heiress, Mrs. Woodward Vietor.

Sat March 26

Roy Obringer to Ralph Lewis: *"Knowing Flynn as I do, and in view of the fact that he contemplates a cruise off Florida and through the Canal, and particularly due to the frame of mind in which Flynn left for his vacation, as evidenced by his blue memo to J. L. attached to the file, arising out of our failure to grant him a radio broadcast last Saturday, I am extremely doubtful if Flynn will return April 22, 1938* [to begin work on THE SISTERS]*."*

Sun March 27

With Lili in Miami, overseeing the preparations of the *Sirocco* for their voyage upon it to the Caribbean; outfitting and repairs are done by the Fogal Boatyard.

With Lili in Miami on his newly purchased yacht Sirocco - Late March

Tue March 29

Sails the *Sirocco* for the first time. Roy Obringer to Sig Marcus: *"Mr. Al Alborn [Alleborn], Unit Manager of the company when approached by Mr. Richardson [of the Richardson Springs Hotel outside Chico, CA] for this bill [Lili Damita's $131.17 board and lodging balance, $2,372.66 in 2021 value], apparently paid the same out of his own pocket, and he is the one who will stand the loss in the event that Flynn does not repay it. This expense had nothing to do with Flynn's location expenses.....but as I understand it, it was the expenses of Mrs. Flynn who was visiting at the location site.....I note the [extra] charge on the enclosed bill of $8.71, which leaves me with some doubt as to the propriety of this being a personal charge against Flynn, inasmuch as it apparently had something to do with a publicity tie-up [tie-in], but it is possible that Flynn took the arrow home with him instead of returning it to our Property Dept."*

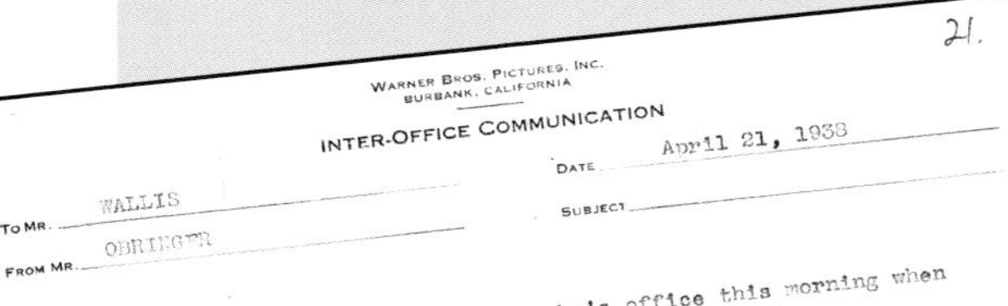

WARNER BROS. PICTURES, INC.
BURBANK, CALIFORNIA

INTER-OFFICE COMMUNICATION

DATE April 21, 1938

TO MR. WALLIS

FROM MR. OBRINGER

SUBJECT

Noll Gurney was in Blanke's office this morning when he received the following message from his office:

"CAN PROVE CONCLUSIVELY NERVOUS DISORDER DANGEROUS MY HEALTH BEGIN WORK STOP AM ADVISED TAKE LENGTHY VOYAGE PLEASE ASK SIX MONTHS' SUSPENSION REGARDS FLYNN."

I could say a lot about this wire, but the point at hand is, what can we do. Obviously Flynn does not intend to report back. He has based his failure to report back on illness, which would preclude our holding him responsible for damages for delay of the picture. We do have a right under the contract, if his absence is based upon physical incapacity, to examine his physical condition. This involves a problem of first getting a competent doctor to examine him, and second, the doctor being able to contact him. A nervous disorder is hard to diagnose, especially when the patient wants it to be so. I don't believe that you will want to agree to any suspension of 6 months.

I am having a conference with Herb Preston and Ralph Lewis this afternoon on this entire situation so that we can determine what can be done, and I will advise you upon my return.

Gurney and Blanke came into my office, and I advised Gurney that I would not discuss the wire until I had talked to you, which I will do immediately upon my return from Preston & Files.

R. J. OBRINGER

April

This month's *Photoplay* magazine publishes Flynn's article, "The Seamy Side of Hollywood."

Mon April 4

Sneak preview of THE ADVENTURES OF ROBIN HOOD in Pomona.

Mon April 11

Sneak preview of THE ADVENTURES OF ROBIN HOOD at the Warner Bros. downtown theater in Los Angeles.

Wed April 20

Sails to the Bahamas with Lili, Arno, and a crew of three (crew chief, cook, and crewman); on this day is somewhere between Miami and Bermuda; Roy Obringer to Hal Wallis: *"I have been unsuccessful all day in trying to get [Flynn's agent Noll] Gurney on the phone or anyone at the Selznick [Agency] office who can give me any dope on Flynn.....[Flynn's business manager William] Best stated he expects to hear from Flynn by tomorrow or Friday and that he believes Flynn is somewhere between Bermuda and Miami but exactly where he does not know and he doesn't know exactly when Flynn could get back to Hollywood."*

Thu April 21

Telegram from Frank Mattison to WB director of publicity Robert Taplinger: FROM THINGS OVERHEARD AM SURE TROUBLE BREWING BETWEEN FLYNN STUDIO STOP DONT THINK FLYNN HAS ANY INTENTION RETURNING UNTIL OBTAINS CONCESSIONS WHATEVER THEY ARE STOP THINK HE PLANS DISAPPEARING ACT; Warner Bros. to Flynn: *"We have been advised today by your local representative that your physical condition is such as to preclude you from rendering your services under your contract with us. We are entitled, of course, under our contract with you, to have you examined by a physician of our choice, and to that end this letter will serve to introduce our representative and agent Mr. William Guthrie, who has full authority to arrange with a physician to whom we request you to submit to a physical examination, as you have agreed to under your contract with us."*

Tue April 26

Telegram to Jack Warner from Hal Wallis aboard the *S.S. Lurline*: ROBIN [HOOD] REVIEWS TERRIFIC STOP SHOULD DEFINITELY DO WILLIAM TELL; Roy Obringer to Flynn: *".....please be advised that we hereby exercise the right in said contract [of 12/16/36] granted to us to refuse to pay you any compensation with and including April 22, 1938 and until you resume your duties for us under said contract."* Telegram from Mattison to Taplinger: NO TRANSPORTATION UNTIL FRIDAY UNLESS PRIVATE PLANE CALLS STOP NEED EXPENSES FLYNN DEPARTING HAVANA TOMORROW.

Wed April 27

Another telegram from Wallis to Warner from the Lurline, regarding the positive film review from columnist, Jimmie Fidler: FIDLER FIVE BELLS ROBINHOOD

Fri April 29

The short, FOR AULD LANG SYNE is released; Errol and Lili appear as themselves.

Sun May 1

Back in Miami for storm repairs on the *Sirocco*.

Tue May 3

Photographed by *Life* magazine aboard the *Sirocco* in Miami.

Wed May 4

THE ADVENTURES OF ROBIN HOOD premieres in Chico, CA.

With Lili on the Sirocco *somewhere off the coast of Florida - Spring 1938*

Thu May 12
THE ADVENTURES OF ROBIN HOOD opens at Radio City Music Hall in New York and nationwide.

Fri May 13
Telegram to Flynn from WB thru Noll Gurney at the Selznick Agency: AFTER TALKS WITH JL WARNER WALLIS HAVE ARRANGED AS FOLLOWS IF YOU RETURN AND RESUME SERVICES UNDER EXISTING CONTRACT STARTING JUNE FIRST THIRTY EIGHT AND FULLY COMPLETE SERVICES NEXT PICTURE ASSIGNMENT WARNER BROS WILL WAIVE ALL DAMAGE CLAIMS ACCOUNT YOUR FAILURE TO RETURN STUDIO APRIL TWENTY SECOND NINETEEN THIRTY EIGHT STOP ALSO PRIOR YOUR START NEXT PICTURE ASSIGNMENT FREE TO TALK TO JL WARNER STOP WARNER BROS DOES NOT HOWEVER WAIVE ANY OTHER CONTRACT RIGHTS NOR IS YOUR RETURN CONDITIONED ON ANY EXPRESS OR IMPLIED PROMISES TO YOU OR AGENTS OTHER THAN WITH RESPECT TO DAMAGES ABOVE SET FORTH.

Sat May 14
Arrives with Lili in Cuba.

Sun May 22
"Michael Curtiz is preparing for the Warner remake of 'The Dawn Patrol', which will star Errol Flynn." The Motion Picture Daily.

Mon May 23
Is the cover story in this week's issue of *Life* magazine *(center right)*.

Thu June 2
Leaves Havana with Lili for Los Angeles.

Fri June 3
Arrives back in Hollywood.

Mon June 6 and Tue June 7
Wardrobe tests for THE SISTERS; unit director Al Alleborn to production manager Tenny Wright (6/6): *"Mr. Flynn is to come in this morning for final fittings on his wardrobe and I will keep you advised as to whether he shows or not."* Flynn's haircut is *"a little too close to the head for that period,"* according to unit manager, Al Alleborn (6/7).

Wed June 8
Competes in the Film Players Tennis Tournament.

Fri June 10
Begins work on THE SISTERS, filming in the Elliot kitchen, living room, and dining room.

Mon June 13
Filming in the interior of Elliot Drug Store, and the upper corridor and living room.

Tue June 14
"Errol Flynn in bed with a sprained back, received from too much exuberance on the West Side tennis court." Louella O. Parsons in *The Los Angeles Examiner.*

Wed June 15
Filming in the interior of Elliot Drug Store, the upper corridor and living room, the interior of Grace's (Jane Bryan) bedroom, and the exterior of the Silver Bow (on Canadian St. on the backlot).

Thu June 16
Flynn tests for *"character changes for the latter portion of the picture,"* reports Al Alleborn.

Fri June 17
Filming in the interior of the Silver Bow ballroom.

Sat June 18
Filming in the Medlin apartment.

Mon June 20
Flynn's 29th birthday; filming in the the Silver Bow ballroom.

Tue June 21 and Wed June 22
Filming in the the Silver Bow ballroom and (on 6/21) the interior of the Knivel living room; Flynn released to grow a beard for several days.

Tue June 28
Jack Warner to head of publicity Robert Taplinger and to advertising and publicity man Charles Einfeld:

ERROL FLYNN'S FISTS RESTORE PEACE IN CUBAN FREE-FOR-ALL

HAVANA. May 17. (U.P.)—Errol Flynn, star of adventure films, today convinced Cubans that he is just as effective in throwing punches in real life as on the screen.

Flynn and a party of friends were at the Eden Concert night club early today when one of the actor's group and a man from another table began to quarrel. Almost immediately a free-for-all fight broke out with chairs and bottles flying through the air. Flynn then intervened and restored order by throwing two or three rights at his nearest assailants.

One unidentified American received a broken nose and a cut eye, but Flynn and the others were unhurt.

Lili Damita, Flynn's wife, told friends she thought the fight was "all so funny."

The Los Angeles Times

With Bette Davis

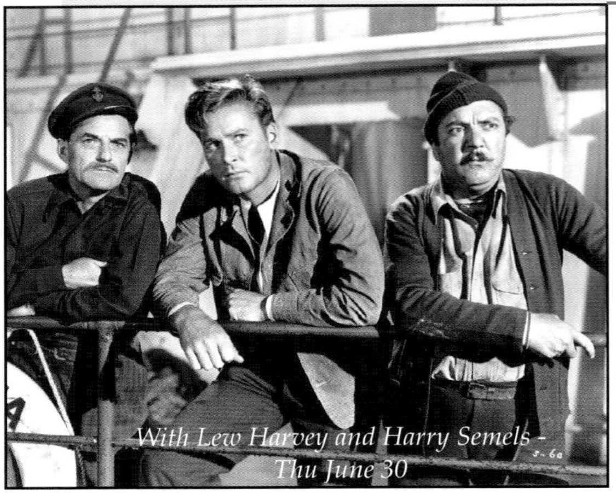

With Lew Harvey and Harry Semels - Thu June 30

At the Hotel del Coronado - Sun, July 3

With Arno during filming of THE SISTERS - Summer 1938

"Thursday, Friday, and Saturday of last week there were many visitors on 'The Sisters' set. It seems that everyone who comes through the studio goes right over to the Bette Davis and Errol Flynn set...This is the story, and it is costing a fortune as Flynn is nervous and blowing his lines, requiring 19 takes and various other things which I don't want to put into writing. You will have to divert everyone from this set, with the exception of the very, very important newspaper people."

Wed June 29
Filming in the waterfront saloon and in the second water-front saloon.

Thu June 30
Filming in Louise's (Bette Davis) office, in Benson's (Ian Hunter) office, process shots in Knivel's (Dick Foran) cab, and on the deck of the *Peralta (top left)*; with Lili at Sebastian's Cubanola Club in Hollywood.

Fri July 1
Filming in the captain's quarters of the *Peralta*, on the *Peralta's* deck, on the San Francisco pier in the Little Dock Restaurant (on the backlot), and in the wireless room.

Sat July 2
Filming in the news office corridor, in the editor's office, and outside the Silver Bow (at Providencia Ranch).

Sun July 3
"Jack Tidball nudged Errol Flynn out of the twenty-third annual championships here [Coronado, CA] today, but the shock of getting the better of Robin Hood was too much for the ex-national collegiate titlist and he was bowled out of the tournament unexpectedly, but spectacularly, by Ben Dey...The appearance of the handsome Flynn brought out a capacity crowd and he amply repaid their interest by staging a terrific duel of powerful services with the brilliant but erratic Tidball, the screen star finally losing, 7-5, 9-7. Tidball proved to be Flynn's nemesis later in the day. With [Jack] Kramer as his partner he eliminated Flynn and young Bob Carrothers, 6-4, 9-11, 6-1, in a quarter-final doubles match." Bill Henry in *The Los Angeles Times (center left)*.

Mon July 4
At the Hotel del Coronado in San Diego.

Thu July 7
With Lili on the *Sirocco* in Catalina.

Mon July 11
Filming in the corridor of Medlin's (Flynn) apartment, inside Medlin's apartment, and on the Silver Bow ballroom balcony.

Tue July 12 and Fri July 15
Filming in Medlin's apartment; a preview for FOUR'S A CROWD is held at Warners Hollywood Theatre at 8:20pm (on 7/12).

Sat July 16 and Mon July 18
Filming in Medlin's kitchen and living room; Flynn threatens to quit cast of THE SISTERS if the producers choose to give the film a happy ending (7/18); Erskine Johnson in *The Los Angeles Times* reports (on 7/18) that Flynn visits the Mermaid Club alone in Hollywood (now the Rainbow at 9015 Sunset Blvd., West Hollywood).

Tue July 19
Filming outside and inside Elliot's Drug Store.

Thu July 21 and Fri July 22
Filming in Medlin's apartment, in Benson's private office, and in Louise's office.

Sat July 23
Filming in Medlin's apartment, outside a San Francisco window (on Brownstone St. on the backlot), and on the train station platform (at the train shed on the backlot).

Mon July 25 and Tue July 26
Filming in Medlin's apartment and (on 7/26) in the hospital.

Wed July 27
Filming in the hospital and on the upper balcony.

Thu July 28
Filming in the ballroom, on the upper balcony, and on a San Francisco street (the sequence after the earthquake is filmed without cast on this day).

Fri July 29 and Sat July 30
Filming in the San Francisco fight arena and (on 7/30) outside Elliot's Drug Store.

Mon August 1
Filming in the Silver Bow, the upper balcony, in Medlin's apartment, and outside the lake saloon.

Tue August 2
Filming on the upper balcony, process shot on the deck of the *Peralta*, in Medlin's corridor, and in the Pullman car.

Wed August 3
Attends the Tribute to Irving Berlin held at 20th Century Fox.

Thu August 4
FOUR'S A CROWD premieres in New York.

Sat August 6
"Screen actor, Errol Flynn, like aviator Douglas Corrigan, apparently got his directions mixed, but his friends declared there was no mistake in his arriving in Nevada, a state where people quickly settle their marital differences. Flynn left Hollywood to sail down the Mexican coast and some hours later turned up in Reno (top right)*, where according to his wife, Lili Damita, he is 'resting.'"* The Associated Press; returns to Hollywood from Reno.

Wed August 10 and Thu August 11
Begins work on THE DAWN PATROL, filming in the farmhouse mess hall and barroom; *"Errol Flynn flew into town yesterday from his jaunt to Cal-Neva Lodge and Reno. His yacht, the Sirocco, docked a few hours earlier at San Pedro. It ran into a storm after leaving Cape San Lucas, lost its mainsail and had to seek shelter until the wind blew itself out. Then, 100 miles south of Ensenada, it ran out of fuel and had to make a long tack out to sea to reach the Mexican port. The overhaul will cost the actor a pretty penny."* Harrison Carroll in *The Los Angeles Evening Herald Express* (8/10). FOUR'S A CROWD opens at Radio City Music Hall in New York City.

Fri August 12
Filming in Brand's (Basil Rathbone) office (Flynn had to change makeup three times); attends the Tailwaggers Foundation Fundraiser with Lili at the Beverly Hills Hotel *(center right)*.

Sat August 13
Filming in Brand's office; released at 12:30 for photo session with Bette Davis for THE SISTERS, by which time Flynn had grown a mustache for THE DAWN PATROL.

Mon August 15
Filming in the mess hall and barroom, and in Brand's office.

Tue August 16
Filming outside the farmhouse, at the hangar, and at the planes, all at the WB Calabasas Ranch.

Wed August 17
Filming in the farmhouse, mess hall, and barroom; signs a new contract that guarantees $4,500 per week ($81,398 in 2021 value—paid on Wednesdays); letter to Warners from Flynn: *"Gentlemen: I hereby revoke any and all prior authorization for Mr. William Best to secure any salary checks which may become due and payable to me and/or transact any other business on my behalf with your company; and I hereby authorize Mr. Vernon Wood and/ or his associates Mr. C. J. Wood and Mr. Heinz[e] to pick up all salary checks due and payable to me...."*

Thu August 18 through Sat August 20, and Mon August 22
Filming in the farmhouse, mess hall, barroom, and (on 8/22) filming an added scene for THE SISTERS on the upper balcony, in Louise's (Bette Davis) bedroom, and in a bedroom in Oakland.

Tue August 23 through Thu August 25
Filming in the farmhouse, mess hall, and barroom, and (on 8/25) in Brand's office; also on 8/25, Flynn is offered the lead in the popular Woodbury radio series, until recently starring Tyrone Power; though he is excited by the prospect of $3,500 per each of the thirteen weeks of the scheduled season, Warner turns down the offer.

Fri August 26
Filming at the hangars and farmhouse; Roy Obringer to Ralph Lewis: *"Attached hereto you will please find the new Errol Flynn agreement dated August 17, 1938. Of course this agreement, like all Flynn's agreements, was made under pressure....."*

Sat August 27 and Mon August 29 through Wed August 31
Filming at the hangars and farmhouse, and (on 8/30) in Courtney's (Flynn) and Hollister's (Peter Willes) offices.

In Reno, NV - Sun, August 7

With Barbara Stanwyck, Gary Cooper, Lili, Rocky (Mrs. Gary) Cooper, and Robert Taylor at the Beverly Hills Hotel - Fri, August 12

With David Niven - August 1938

With David Niven and Michael Brooke (on the ground), Basil Rathbone, director Edmund Goulding, Donald Crisp, Peter Willes, and Melville Cooper at the Warner Bros. Calabasas Ranch - Summer 1938

With Basil Rathbone and David Niven

With Hermann Erben and Arno in the backyard of the Beverly Hills house - Sun, September 18

Thu September 1
Filming outside the farmhouse, the wrecked plane, fuselage, and Scott's (Niven) plane; Flynn's agent Noll Gurney to Jack Warner: *"Dear Jack: Errol asked me to have a talk with you about* [DODGE CITY] *whenever convenient to you. He seems a little dubious about his ability to play a part that is essentially American—or accented as he puts it—but Bob Lord is so enthusiastic about Errol for this part, and I know you are too, that I feel if we have a talk together it will give Errol some confidence."*

Fri September 2
Filming in Courtney's office, and outside the farmhouse and hangars; attends a boxing match for the opening of the new Hollywood Legion Stadium, a building he announces as *"Per-fect."*

Sat September 3
Filming in Courtney's office; sails to Mexico on the *Sirocco* with Howard Hill.

Tue September 6 and Wed September 7
Filming in the farmhouse, mess hall, and barroom.

Thu September 8
Filming in the farmhouse and Courtney's office; sends a telegram to Dr. Hermann Erben in Libertad, El Salvador; Erben had purchased four parrots for Flynn the day before in Leon.

Fri September 9
Filming in the farmhouse; inter-office memo from unit manager, Bob Ross: *"There were delays yesterday afternoon* [9/8] *due to long scenes with Mr. Flynn over the telephone with a great deal of dialogue, and it was quite a job for him to memorize it."*

Sat September 10
Filming in the farmhouse and Scott's (David Niven) room.

Sun September 11
Publicizing for Warner Bros. as a guest on the NBC radio show *The Chase and Sanborn Hour.*

Mon September 12
Filming in the farmhouse and Scott's room.

Tue September 13
Filming in the farmhouse, barroom, and in Scott's and Courtney's rooms.

Wed September 14
Filming a process shot on the motorcycle, in the farmhouse, and outside the hangar at night.

Thu September 15
Filming a process shot (alone) in Courtney's plane.

Fri September 16
Filming in the farmhouse, barroom, mess hall, in Scott's and Courtney's rooms, and a process shot of Scott's plane with Courtney on the wing; appears in the release of the documentary short *Screen Snapshots.*

Sat September 17
Filming process shots in Scott's, Courtney's, and Donnie's (Morton Lowry) plane.

Sun September 18
Completes filming THE DAWN PATROL with scenes in the barroom and a process shot in Courtney's plane; salary for the picture is $36,055 ($652,180 in 2021 value); at a party at Warner Bros. Studios with Lili, Dr. Hermann Erben, Dolores del Rio, Norma Shearer, Bette Davis, Ramon Navarro, Gary Cooper, and others; *"If monkeys have blue asses, I can have blue tits!"* remarked Lili who was admired at the party for her tight-fitting blue dress.

Mon September 19
In Cedars of Lebanon Hospital in Beverly Hills for undulant fever; dinner with Erben, an aviator, a Mrs. Oakie (possibly Jack Oakie's wife), and the actress Venita Varden.

Tue September 20
Has mustache shaved and completes work on THE SISTERS, filming one final scene with Bette Davis in the Silver Bow ballroom; salary for the picture is $36,055 ($652,180 in 2021 value); Bette Davis' salary is $30,000 ($542,654 in 2021 value); with Erben and director Edmund Goulding, at the Trocadero.

Wed September 21

At the dentist; has a quarrel with Lili, according to Erben's diary; with Erben, director Edmund Goulding, and David Niven; later with Erben and Goulding to San Pedro, seeing Erben off on the *S.S. Matsonia* for San Francisco; the next day, Lili leaves for a European vacation.

Fri September 23

At home, ill with flu.

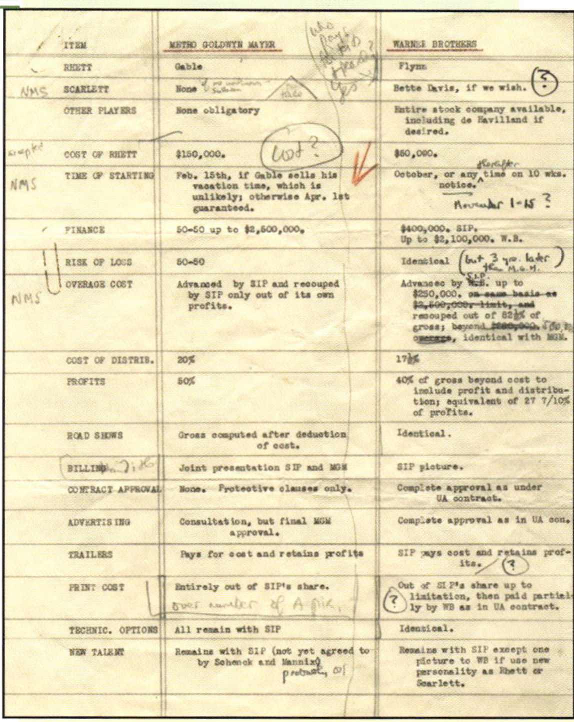

ITEM	METRO GOLDWYN MAYER	WARNER BROTHERS
RHETT	Gable	Flynn
SCARLETT	None	Bette Davis, if we wish.
OTHER PLAYERS	None obligatory	Entire stock company available, including de Havilland if desired.
COST OF RHETT	$150,000.	$80,000.
TIME OF STARTING	Feb. 15th, if Gable sells his vacation time, which is unlikely; otherwise Apr. 1st guaranteed.	October, or any time on 10 wks. notice.
FINANCE	50-50 up to $2,500,000.	$400,000. SIP, Up to $2,100,000. W.B.
RISK OF LOSS	50-50	Identical
OVERAGE COST	Advanced by SIP and recouped by SIP only out of its own profits.	Advanced by WB. up to $250,000. on same basis as $2,500,000. limit, and recouped out of 82½% of gross; beyond overage, identical with MGM.
COST OF DISTRIB.	20%	17½%
PROFITS	50%	40% of gross beyond cost to include profit and distribution; equivalent of 27 7/10% of profits.
ROAD SHOWS	Gross computed after deduction of cost.	Identical.
BILLING	Joint presentation SIP and MGM	SIP picture.
CONTRACT APPROVAL	None. Protective clauses only.	Complete approval as under UA contract.
ADVERTISING	Consultation, but final MGM approval.	Complete approval as in UA con.
TRAILERS	Pays for cost and retains profits	SIP pays cost and retains profits.
PRINT COST	Entirely out of SIP's share.	Out of SIP's share up to limitation, then paid partially by WB as in UA contract.
TECHNIC. OPTIONS	All remain with SIP	Identical.
NEW TALENT	Remains with SIP (not yet agreed to by Schenck and Mannix)	Remains with SIP except one picture to WB if use new personality as Rhett or Scarlett.

The MGM list of cast considerations for Gone With The Wind *from about this time*

Sun September 25

Letter from Dr. Thomas Hearn to Hal Wallis: *"I am attending Mr. Errol now....His upper respiratory infection was no doubt acquired due to his lowered resistance from excessive work during the last few months at the studio....my advice to Mr. Flynn, would be to take a four or five week vacation following his recovery...."*

Tue September 27

After his temperature has risen to 103.5, Flynn enters Good Samaritan Hospital with pneumonia.

Wed September 28

Lili returns from New York to nurse Errol after canceling her trip to Europe; *"Errol Flynn, star of the films 'Robin Hood' and 'Captain Blood,' was rushed to Good Samaritan Hospital in Hollywood today...The influenza he contracted on a fishing trip recently took a sudden turn for the worse. His temperature rose to 103.5, and it was feared that pneumonia might develop. His wife, glamorous Lili Damita, postponed a trip to Europe in order to remain with him."* The Daily Express.

October

Sails to the Channel Islands, CA, early in the month.

ERROL FLYNN IS SERIOUSLY SICK

HOLLYWOOD, Sept. 26—(AP)— Film star Errol Flynn, seriously ill with an infection of the upper respiratory organs, had a fever of 102.2 degrees early today, Dr. T. M. Hearn reported.

The physician said Flynn's case was complicated by the probable recurrence of malaria which he contracted five years ago when prospecting for gold in New Guinea.

Flynn was stricken early last week.

The Vicksburg, MS Evening Post
Mon, September 26

Fri October 7

Flies to Palm Springs to continue recuperating, staying at the home of director Edmund Goulding; Lili joins him two days later.

Fri October 14

THE SISTERS opens nationwide.

Mon October 26

Arrives in Hawaii.

Flynn claims to have studied surfboarding on this trip with Duke Kahanamoku, world-renowned surfer and early proponent of the sport.

Tue November 1

Hal Wallis to Michael Curtiz and associate producer Robert Lord: *"When you go on location, be sure to take an assortment of hats, shirts, and scarfs [sic] along, as it is possible that Flynn will get off the boat in San Francisco on November 9th and will come directly to the location from there....I would use Bruce Cabot with the moustache provided that Flynn doesn't wear a moustache. If Flynn wears one, I would not have one on Cabot....All in all, I think a lousy job has been done on the men's wardrobe for this picture."* Flynn ultimately wore the mustache.

The passenger manifest of the S.S. Lurline - Fri, November 4

Fri November 4

Departs Hawaii on the *Lurline* (bottom left); while aboard he wires Robert Taplinger (on 11/5) specifically requesting Frank Heacock as publicist for DODGE CITY.

Wed November 9

Arrives in San Francisco from Hawaii.

Thu November 10

Begins filming DODGE CITY, 27 miles northeast of Modesto, CA, staying at the Covell Hotel.

Fri November 11

Out with a sprained ankle; does not work.

Outside Modesto, CA - November, 1938

With Olivia de Havilland - Tue, November 22

Sat November 12 through Mon November 14
Filming at the cattle pens, on the plains, and near Little River in Modesto.

Tue November 15 and Thu November 17
Filming at the stockyards and near Little River, and (on 11/17) near Little River; Hal Wallis to Tenny Wright (11/17): *"Last night I found out that Flynn arrived the morning of the 9th, was met by [location manager, Joe] Berry and then for some reason or other Barry [sic] left him and picked him up again that night, and in the meantime Flynn did some fool thing or other and showed up on location with a sprained ankle. Consequently, the whole first day Mike was handicapped by having to shoot close-ups because Flynn couldn't get his boots on, and the entire second day Mike had to shoot around him, making odd shots and long shots, while Flynn stayed in bed and had his ankle treated…..Don't you think that I know what I was talking about when I asked you to have a man meet Flynn at the boat and take him right to location, or do you think that I just sit up here and think these things up for my health or because I like to?"*

Fri November 18
Filming at the stockyards and the country hillside.

Sat November 19
Filming the driving in of the Golden Spike.

Sun November 20
Filming on the plains and at the Spearville Station at sunrise.

Tue November 22
Filming on a secluded side road and the hillside love scene with Olivia de Havilland *(top left)*.

Wed November 23
Filming the buffalo, and the rear of the railroad tender; inter-office memo from unit manager Frank Mattison: *"We did everything to the railroad including tearing up the main line."*

Fri November 25, Sat November 26, and Tue November 29
Filming in the Irving home at WB Studios, and (on 11/29) in the Drover Hotel and the Dodge City Star news office.

Thu December 1
Filming in the Dodge City Star and a process shot in the passenger coach.

Fri December 2
Filming outside the Drover Hotel at the WB Calabasas Ranch.

Sat December 3
Filming in the printer's shop.

Mon December 5
Filming in the news office and a process shot outside the stagecoach.

Tue December 6 and Wed December 7
Filming on a Dodge City street at the WB Calabasas Ranch.

Thu December 8
Filming Flynn on the runaway horse outside the jail at the WB Calabasas Ranch; Frank Mattison to Tenny Wright: *"Have arranged to excuse Flynn for him to have his dental work attended to."*

Fri December 9
Filming on a Dodge City street; Frank Mattison to Tenny Wright: *"Will dismiss Mr. Flynn this afternoon…so that he can go to the dentist tomorrow morning and he will not work all day tomorrow, Saturday."*

Sat December 10
Dentist appointment; does not work.

Sun December 11
In a fistfight with Irish polo player, Aidan Roark, at a Hollywood cocktail party *(next page, top left)*.

With Alan Hale (to his right) outside Modesto, CA - November, 1938

The Washington Post - *Mon, December 12*

Mon December 12

Returns to his dentist to check on his teeth owing to the fist fight the night before; no damage was discovered except for a small cut on the upper lip; at a preview for THE DAWN PATROL at the Warners Hollywood theater *(top right)*.

Tue December 13

Filming in the Pure Prairie League office and in the barber shop.

Wed December 14

Filming in the barber-shop.

Thu December 15

Filming in the jail and in the barbershop; Lili returns from Europe on the *Queen Mary*.

Fri December 16 and Sat December 17

Filming in the jail.

Tue December 20

Fills out a Declaration of Intent towards becoming a U.S. citizen.

Thu December 22

THE DAWN PATROL opens nationwide.

Sat December 24

Hal Wallis' secretary Paul Nathan to Robert Taplinger: *"Dear Bob— As you probably know, at the sneak of 'Dawn Patrol' we passed out reaction cards—the first time we've ever done this. Well, they were really great—almost every one a real rave, and majority of cards said they were happy to see a picture with an all-male cast, and Flynn and Niven both got raves."*

Mon December 26

Attends the opening of Earl Carroll's Sunset Boulevard nightclub with Lili *(bottom right)*.

Tue December 27

Faces the loss of the *Sirocco* due to excessive tonnage and length limitations imposed by the Federal Government on alien-owned craft.

Thu December 29

Filming on a Dodge City street at the WB Calabasas Ranch and a process shot on the locomotive engine.

Fri December 30 and Sat December 31

Filming on a Dodge City street at the WB Calabasas Ranch; spends the New Year's weekend with Lili at the San Bernardino mountain retreat of Myron Selznick. Other guests included Joan Bennett, Paulette Goddard, Vivien Leigh, Myrna Loy, Kay Francis.

With Bruce Cabot at the Warner Hollywood Theater - Mon, December 12

With Ann (Mrs. Jack) Warner, Lili, Marlene Dietrich, and Jack Warner at the Earl Carroll Theater - Mon, December 26

From a George Hurrell portrait session ~ late 1938

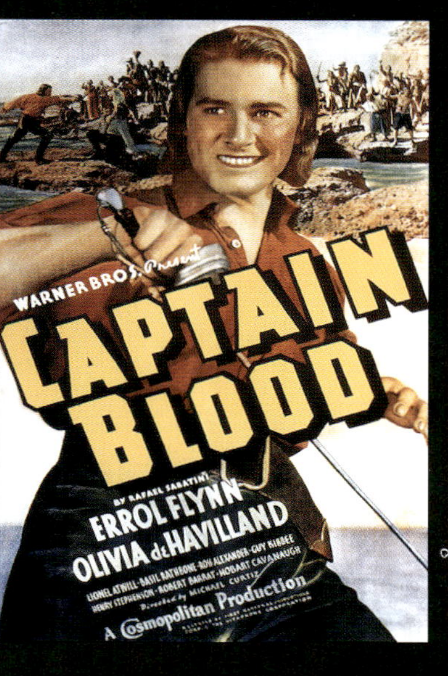

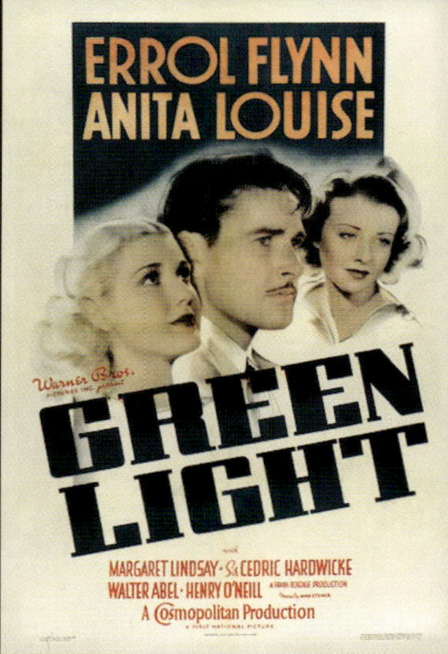

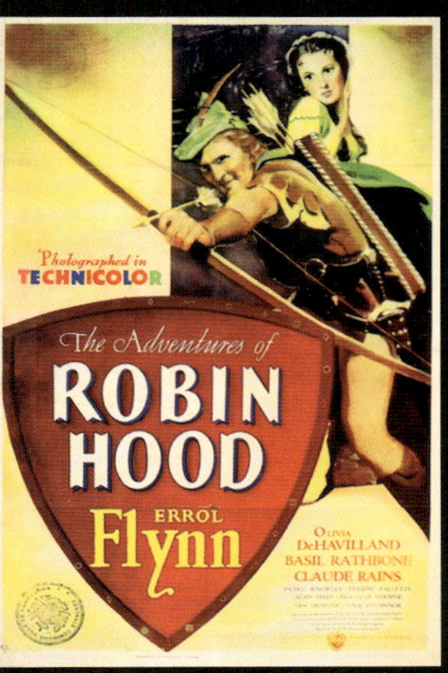

The films of 1935~1938

By the end of this period, Errol Flynn had added another ten adventure and period-costume classics to the annals of film history, including his first forays into the field of Westerns, a field about which he was initially unsure but which proved as popular and bankable as any other of his outings. Among these ten were two hugely successful biographical portrayals, that of military legend Gen. George Armstrong Custer and boxing great James J. Corbett.

He continued with his love of the sea, sailing the *Sirocco* up and down the coasts of California and Mexico, while the ups and downs of his volatile marriage to Lili also continued. There was initial hopefulness on their home front when Lili gave him his first child—a son they named Sean—but the glow of home and hearth was short-lived, and they parted for good soon after Sean's birth, finally divorcing the following year.

But all was far from gloomy for Flynn at this point. It is safe to say that the short period between March and October of 1942 represented the most perfect days of his life: he was no longer married, he had moved into his sprawling new home above Mulholland Drive in the Hollywood Hills, he completed one of his personal favorite films (GENTLE-MAN JIM) and was earning the current equivalent of $117,580 per week. He was rich, famous, and free. His star had risen and looked to remain aloft.

Yet those four idyllic months were bookended by both good and bad events: on one end was the freedom Flynn won through the March 31st divorce from Lili, while on the other end was the night of October 11th when two policemen from the Los Angeles Juvenile Control Division showed up at his door announcing that a charge of statutory rape had been made against him. The year ended with his perfect world coming apart. His star was wavering.

1939

Mon January 2
Radio performance of "The Perfect Specimen" with Joan Blondell for *the Lux Radio Theatre* at CBS affiliate, KNX, Los Angeles.

Tue January 3
Warners announces Flynn will star in *Cyrano de Bergerac*.

Wed January 4
Filming in Surrett's (Bruce Cabot) office.

Thu January 5
Filming in Surrett's office and in the baggage car; unit manager, Frank Mattison: *"They [the company] did not finish this set, however, owing to Mr. Flynn and Mr. Cabot not knowing their lines and being compelled to learn the lines on Technicolor film, Mr. Curtiz was thoroughly disgusted and told both of the gentlemen so, but there was nothing to do but stop and come back again this morning* [the 6th] *when we can* [re]*shoot scene 250 and complete this set."*

Fri January 6
Filming in the baggage car.

Sat January 7
Filming in the end car.

Mon January 9
Filming in the train, an alternate tag, and in the baggage car.

Tue January 10
Attends the Baby Arizmendi vs. Henry Armstrong prize fight at Olympic Stadium in Los Angeles.

Wed January 11
Filming in the coach and in the baggage car; unit manager, Frank Mattison: *"For your information, Saul Gorss had his hands severely burned last night* [the 11th] *in the fire scene on stage 19. It appears that the crew put too much gasoline in the set. The flames were so high they went up to the ceiling and turned on the sprinkler system and ruined some electrical equipment. All of the crew and the actors were able to get out of the scene except Saul Gorss."* Attends the Ellsworth Vines vs. Fred Perry tennis match at the Beverly Hills Tennis Club.

Thu January 12
Filming in the upper floor of the Irving house and a process shot on the train.

Fri January 13
Filming a process shot between the second car and baggage car; attends a Friday the 13th party on Stage 16 given by Warner Bros. comptroller, Cy Wilder.

Sat January 14
Filming outside the baggage car.

Sun January 15
Plays in a match with Cedric Gibbons at the Beverly Hills Tennis Club *(center right)*.

Wed January 18
Completes work on DODGE CITY with a retake in the upper floor of the Irving home; salary for the picture is $41,300 ($768,398 in 2021 value).

Fri January 20
Is advanced $13,500 ($251,171 in 2021 value) by WB to *"take care of certain personal tax matters prior to* [his] *departure from this country on a proposed vacation trip."*

Fri January 20 to Monday January 23
On a boating trip to Catalina with Lili and Arno; goes hunting for wild boar with Howard Hill on Santa Cruz Island, CA.

Sat January 21
"Warner Brothers are shooting this year 'The Life of the First Rajah of Sarawak.' Synopsis has been prepared by the ranee, and probably Errol Flynn will be leading man." The Daily Express.

With Victor Jory, Douglas Fowley, Bruce Cabot, Robert Homans, and Alan Hale - January 1939

With Cedric Gibbons at the Beverly Hills Tennis Club - Sun, January 15

With Arno and Lili on the Sirocco - the weekend of January 20

With President Roosevelt in Ft. Myer, VA - Thu, January 26

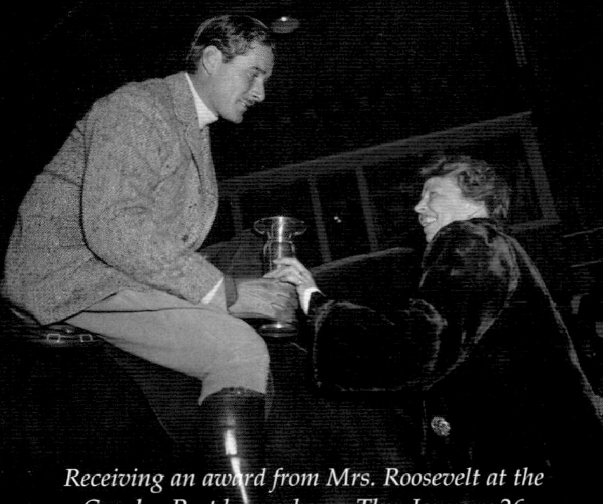

Receiving an award from Mrs. Roosevelt at the Cavalry Post horse show - Thu, January 26

In Mexico, the Sirocco in the background - Early March

Wed January 25

Arrives in Arlington, VA.

Thu January 26

Visits the president and Mrs. Roosevelt in the Presidential Box at the Cavalry Post horse show in Fort Myer, VA *(top left)*; he later rides the president's entry, Badger, in the race …and wins one of the division awards *(center left)*.

Fri January 27

Drives out with Bruce Cabot to Mrs. John Hay Whitney's Virginia estate, Llangollen, to ride horses.

Sat January 28

A luncheon to honor Flynn is given by socialite and columnist Jack Vietor in Washington.

Sun January 29

Is the guest of President and Mrs. Roosevelt for a 7:45pm dinner at the White House; later, James Roosevelt Jr. joins them at the National Theater to see the play, *Outward Bound*.

Mon January 30

Is a guest of President and Mrs. Franklin Roosevelt at the president's birthday ball at New York's Waldorf Astoria Hotel.

Tue January 31

With Lili at El Morocco in New York.

February

Invests in properties on Huntington Drive in South Pasadena, apartments on Selma Avenue in Hollywood, and land on Sunset Plaza Drive in (now) West Hollywood.

Fri February 3

Errol and Lili are guests for a few days at Llangolen, the Virginia home of socialite Elizabeth "Liz" Whitney and her husband, former ambassador and publisher, John "Jock" Whitney.

Mon February 6

While staying at the estate of John Hay Whitney, receives a telegram from his business manager, Vernon Wood, that Arno misses him; Flynn responds and requests Arno be flown out to him.

Tue February 7

Arno arrives from Los Angeles.

Wed February 8

Attends the opening of a Washington, D.C., club with Lili, Liz Whitney Tippett, and Harry Hopkins.

Fri February 10

With Lili and Arno in Miami.

Sat February 18

Warner Bros. announces Flynn will play the lead in a production of Jack London's *Burning Daylight*. At some point around this time, Arno is sent back to Los Angeles.

Tue February 21

At Mardi Gras in New Orleans.

March

Appears in the WB short BREAKDOWNS OF 1939.

Wed March 8

With Lili in Brownsville, Texas.

Thu March 9

Flies with Lili to Mexico City on their way to Mazatlan, where they will begin a fishing trip with Howard Hill and photographer Al Wetzel.

Mon March 13

Telegram from Flynn to Noll Gurney: AM DUE BACK NINETEENTH STOP CANT MAKE CONNECTION BEFORE THAT STOP WIRE PAN AMERICAN AIRWAYS MAZATLAN.

Wed March 15

Telegram from Robert Taplinger to Flynn: [Vernon] WOOD SAYS BEST RATE FIVE PASSENGER PLANE FIVE HUNDRED FIFTY DOLLARS ROUNDTRIP. REGULAR PAN AMERICAN SERVICE FROM MAZATLAN EIGHTY

THREE DOLLARS TO HERE. THIS FAR MORE ECONOMICAL BUT IF YOU WANT PRIVATE PLANE WIRE WOOD AUTHORIZATION. OBRINGER ADVISES SATISFACTORY YOU LEAVE NOT LATER THAN MONDAY MARCH TWENTIETH. DO YOU WANT PHOTOGRAPHER BEFOREHAND. ADVISE. Hal Wallis to Roy Obringer: *"…..Are we going to let Flynn appear on one of these [radio] broadcasts even though it is after the expiration of his eight weeks vacation. Personally, with all the grief you have with Flynn and the plan of having him go to Dodge City [on the promotional junket], I believe it would be wisest to let him appear on the program."* Obringer to Wallis: *"Errol Flynn telephoned Taplinger from some place in Mexico near Mazatlan and wanted Taplinger to send a still man down there to make some pictures."*

In Mexico - Early March

Wed March 22
Weather prevents the Flynns' flight home.

Thu March 23
Arrives home from Mazatlan.

Sat March 25
"Mary Agnes Butterfield, 21, five-and-10 clerk in Dodge City, Kan., who won a contest sponsored by the local Chamber of Commerce and will have Errol Flynn, movie star, as her week-end guest when he appears in her town for the premiere of his latest movie." The Lawrence (KS) Journal-World.

Mon March 27
"Mary Agnes Butterfield of Dodge City, Kas., was the happiest girl in the city when she drew the name of Errol Flynn, movie star, in a lottery to select local hosts and hostesses for some thirty movie actors who are coming to the small southwestern Kansas community for a movie premiere. Then her 11-year-old brother, Joe, got the measles, and the Butterfield home was quarantined. So she sold her ticket to Miss June Brody, 22-year-old waitress, and Flynn will spend a week-end at the Brody home…." Acme Photo Agency; the lottery was actually a Warner Bros. publicity stunt and Flynn never visited the Brodys.

THE "DODGE CITY" JUNKET

Thu March 30
Leaves Los Angeles for San Bernardino, CA, at 9pm on the Warner Bros. DODGE CITY Junket; leaves San Bernardino for Barstow, CA, at 10:50pm.

With Bud Ernst in Union Station, Los Angeles

With Olivia de Havilland, who will shortly leave the junket in Pasadena

With Jack Warner in Albuquerque, NM - Fri, March 31

Fri March 31

Leaves Barstow for Needles, CA, at 1:05am; moves on through Seligman and Winslow, AZ, then on through Gallup and Albuquerque, NM; leaves Albuquerque for La Junta, CO, at 7pm.

In Albuquerque with (front row, l-r): Leon Turrou, Hoot Gibson, Buck Jones, Lee Lyles, Guinn "Big Boy" Williams, Humphrey Bogart, Jean Parker, and Frances Robinson; (back row, l-r): Frank McHugh, Chief Santa Fe, Maxie Rosenbloom, Priscilla Lane, John Garfield, Jack Warner, Rosemary Lane, and Wayne Morris

Sat April 1

Leaves La Junta, CO, traveling through Syracuse, KS, arriving in Dodge City, KS, at 9am; DODGE CITY premieres this night in three Dodge City theaters.

The Dodge City crowds greeting the junket

With Mayo Methot, Claire Windsor, Frank McHugh, Lola Lane, Priscilla Lane, and Jean Parker; on the ground are Humphrey Bogart and John Garfield

In the parade through the streets of Dodge City

Standing in as best man at McCarty Stadium (with maid of honor Ann Sheridan) for the wedding of Byran Carpenter and Gladys Bell

The national radio broadcast over NBC

The premiere at the Dodge Theater

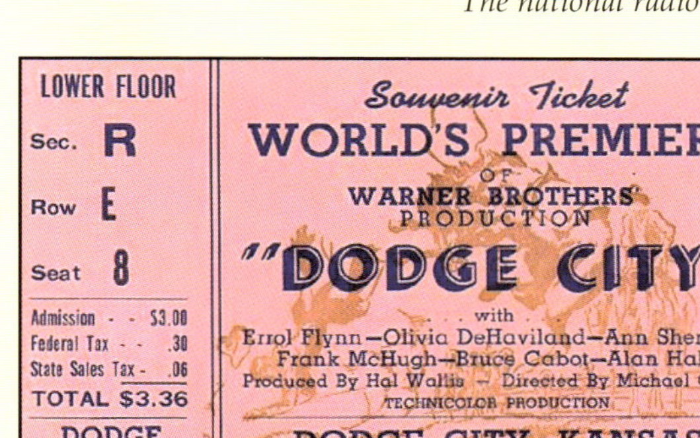

Souvenir ticket from the Dodge Theater premiere

The sidewalk plaque now in front of the Dodge Theater, commemorating the 1939 premiere

Tue April 4

Hal Wallis to Tenny Wright: *"Now that Flynn is back from his 'Dodge City' trip, be sure that he is kept available at all times for testing on the picture, makeup, wardrobe, etc. He is on salary and I don't want you or any of your assistants on the picture or anyone to give him permission to go away for extended week-ends, or for jaunts on his boat, or anything of the kind. We have a lot of preparatory work on this picture, and Flynn must be available for it, as we will probably have to start the picture without [Bette] Davis and work with Flynn for a week or so, and all of his stuff must be in readiness."*

Wed April 5

DODGE CITY opens in Los Angeles; flies to Mexico for a few days' rest, Lili to Palm Springs; Hal Wallis to Tenny Wright: *"In planning your sets for 'The Knight And The Lady', please plan these on stages where they can be saved after this production as we will be able to use practically every set again for 'The Sea Hawk' and this will save us a fortune."*

Tue April 11

Flies to Asunción Bay on the coast of Baja California to rescue Roy Hays, a sailor on the *Sirocco* who has suffered a burst appendix; the victim is flown to a hospital in San Diego, the plane piloted by Flynn's friend Bud Ernst.

With Olivia de Havilland at the DODGE CITY premiere in Modesto, CA - Sun, April 23

Wed April 12
Flies with the stricken Roy Hays back to Los Angeles from San Diego *(top right)*.

Sat April 15
Attends a charity given by Ouida (Mrs. Basil) Rathbone at the Rathbones' Bel Air home.

Sun April 23
A special premiere of DODGE CITY is held at the Orpheum Theater in Modesto, CA, attended by Flynn, de Havilland, Hale, Curtiz, and other principal cast and crew *(top left)*; a Western atmosphere was created on the premises for the party.

Mon May 1 and Tue May 2
Costume test for THE PRIVATE LIVES OF ELIZABETH AND ESSEX *(below left)*.

Tue May 9
Helmet tests.

Thu May 11
Begins filming THE PRIVATE LIVES OF ELIZABETH AND ESSEX with Donald Crisp in Essex's room and bed chamber.

Fri May 12, Sat May 13, and Mon May 15
Filming in the foggy Irish bog on a WB soundstage; attends Basil Rathbone's charity banquet (5/12); Hal Wallis to Michael Curtiz (5/15): *"In the Flynn close-ups, there were one or two shots where on the left side of his mouth a tooth seemed to be missing. Be sure that this is checked upon immediately and that Flynn gets this fixed before we make any more close-ups—as it looked very bad."*

Tue May 16 and Wed May 17
Filming in Essex's tent and the Irish bog.

Thu May 18
Filming in the cell.

Fri May 19
Filming the falcon hunt at Triunfo Canyon; inter-office memo from unit manager Frank Mattison: *"Mr. Flynn had considerable difficulty with his lines as you will notice that the OK'd takes were numbers 5 or 6."*

Sat May 20
Filming the entrance at White Hall Palace gate with large crowds.

Sun May 21
Serves as master of ceremonies in a radio appearance on *Variety Review* for the Gulf Screen Guild Theater, CBS.

Mon May 22
Filming in Ye Virgin Queen Tavern, the boat, White Hall, and yard.

Tue May 23
Filming in the Tower courtyard at 30 Acres on the WB backlot, and the prison corridor with John Sutton and Collin Kenny.

Wed May 24
Filming in the long hall to the Presence Chamber (Bette Davis and Olivia de Havilland begin filming).

Thu May 25 and Fri May 26
Filming in the throne room; inter-office memo from unit manager, Frank Mattison (5/26): *"If Flynn knows his lines today we should finish this Council Chamber scene by tomorrow."*

Sat May 27 and Mon May 29
Filming in the Council Chamber.

Wed May 31
Filming on the balcony and retakes in Essex's room and the tent; Frank Mattison: *"There are still two set-ups to be made in the tent but Mr. Flynn would not stay after 6:00 PM as he has a big scene to do today [6/1] with Bette Davis."*

Thu June 1
Filming in the Council Chamber and throne room; attends the horse races at Hollywood Park.

Costume test for the role of Lord Essex - Mon, May 1

The Los Angeles Times
Wed, April 12

Fri June 2, Sat June 3, Mon June 5, and Tue June 6

Filming in the throne room, and alone there with Bette Davis on 6/6; inter-office memo from Frank Mattison (6/7): *"Yesterday [6/6], what should have been a very excellent day, turned out to be a very poor one. Miss Davis was compelled to stop work at 5:00 PM, as she and Flynn had been working all day in a very difficult scene."*

Thu June 8 and Fri June 9

Filming in the throne room corridor and (on 6/8) outside the window.

Sat June 10

Filming a pick-up shot in the throne room, the queen's corridor, and retakes in the tent; memo from Frank Mattison: *"When we were discussing Monday and Tuesday's work with Miss Bette Davis, she flatly informed us that she positively would not and will not jump directly to the big love scene with Errol Flynn and then to the Tower scene with Mr. Flynn..."*

Sun June 11

Competes in the Film Players Tennis Tournament at the Los Angeles Tennis Club, losing his match to Stanley Briggs; Jack Warner also plays—and loses.

Tue June 13

"Errol Flynn gets the old Valentino role in 'Blood and Sand.'" The Daily Express; it never transpires.

Fri June 16 and Sat June 17

Ill; does not work; Frank Mattison to Tenny Wright [6/17]: *"Confidentially, this show is now 3 days ahead of schedule, and if Flynn knows his lines we should be able to make up even more time between now and the end of the picture.....I am going to call Mr. Flynn's house about noon today and will let you know what I can of his illness as we absolutely must have him for work on Monday."*

Mon June 19

Filming in the Tower room; inter-office memo from Frank Mattison: *"At 3:00 PM Pete Hungate, electrician, fell from catwalk to floor. Injuries undetermined. Was taken to hospital. Company resumed work at 3:25"*; Flynn claims to have been involved in an auto accident this evening.

Tue June 20

Flynn's thirtieth birthday; Frank Mattison to Tenny Wright: *"Mr. Flynn's man, Max, phoned me this morning at 9:15 AM, informing me that Errol had been in an accident with Mrs. Flynn, and that he had a cut on his head and a cut over his eye, and that the doctor was there at the time...In accordance with the instructions of Mr. [Tenny] Wright I went out to Mr. Flynn's home at 601 Linden Drive, taking [assistant director] Mr. Sherry Shourds along. We were ushered to Mr. Flynn's bed and met Dr. Frank Nolan there, who informed us the cuts were quite deep and that there were two of them, one narrowly missing the eye, and the other on his head. These had been stitched up, and he informed us it would probably be Monday of next week before Mr. Flynn would be able to appear with the scar healed...Mr. Flynn informed us that he and Mrs. Flynn were in Mrs. Flynn's car and turned off Sunset Boulevard at the street west of Sunset Towers [Olive Drive], and going down the hill a truck pulled past them, and he swerved to the right to avoid hitting the truck, and hit a wall, which caused both himself and Mrs. Flynn to bump against the windshield, which injured them as above stated. He says outside of the cuts he feels very well and regrets exceedingly that this had to happen."* From Jack Warner's office to Obringer (who was asked to call Mr. Warner at home at CR5-6152): *"Mr. Warner wants you to call Noll Gurney and put a terrific fright into him about Flynn, as this is liable to mean very big legal entanglements and ensuing damages and plenty of money if Flynn is not in condition by Monday. Also, that Warners are going to be very careful, in the future, about putting him in any pictures over a certain cost, and Mr. Warner is thoroughly disgusted. In addition, the District Attorney's Office has been asked to make an investigation on this."*

With Bette Davis, director of photography Sol Polito (seated, center), and director Michael Curtiz (in dark jacket)

Commercial tie-in ad for Chesterfield cigarettes

With Bette Davis in THE PRIVATE LIVES OF ELIZABETH AND ESSEX (photo by George Hurrell)

Rumor Spiked by Errol Flynn

Reports Injured Star and Wife Weren't Hurt in Auto Crash Blasted

Hollywood rumors that Errol Flynn's face was so badly disfigured in a recent accident that he would be unable to appear before the cameras in months were dissipated when the star returned to work yesterday at Warner Bros. studio.

At the same time Flynn took time out to deny reports that have swept through the film colony that he suffered his injuries in another manner than an automobile accident.

CALLS RUMORS SILLY

"These rumors that I was not hurt in an automobile accident, but in some other way, are annoying as well as silly," he remarked. "Just say for me that I am all right and that I will not be scarred."

Flynn reported he was injured on the night of June 21 when he and his wife, Lily Damita, left the apartment of Peggy Fears and A. C. Blumenthal, where they were guests at a party given in honor of their fourth wedding anniversary.

CAR HITS WALL

He said he lost control of his car turning a corner near the apartment house and struck a wall. He and Miss Damita, he said, were thrown against the windshield.

The actor received a cut requiring six stitches over his left eye and another on his forehead. He went immediately to Dr. Frank Nolan, who sutured his wounds and kept him under ice packs until a plastic surgeon could be called in to treat him. Studio officials had feared there would be a costly delay on his current picture pending Flynn's return, but the treatment proved successful.

MAKE-UP HIDES CUTS

The cuts were noticeable to the plain eye yesterday but after a visit to the make-up department they were covered in such a manner as to escape camera detection. He is co-starring in a picture with Bette Davis, "The Lady and the Knight" in Technicolor.

Flynn said that his wife was up and around yesterday for the first time since the accident. She received a discolored eye and slight facial cuts but otherwise was not hurt.

The Los Angeles Times
Wed, June 28

Wed June 21
Appears at an event displaying the injuries from the recent "auto accident."

Thu June 22
Takes a few days off (probably to allow his laceration to heal) and goes sailing with Howard Hill.

Tue June 27
Filming in the Tower.

Wed June 28
Filming alone with Bette Davis in the Tower; inter-office memo from Frank Mattison: *"It seems Mr. Curtiz can make fast time until he gets with Errol Flynn, and then we slow down to a walk."*

Thu June 29 and Fri June 30
Filming in the Tower with Davis and de Havilland *(top right)*, and (on 6/30) in the Privy Chamber; inter-office memo from Frank Mattison (6/30): *"The retake of Mr. Flynn and Mr. Hale will be quite expensive, as it will cost around $400* [$7,442 in 2021 value] *for rigging, building platform, re-dressing the set, costumes, etc."*

Sat July 1
Filming alone with Bette Davis in the Privy Chamber; inter-office memo from Frank Mattison: *"I remember instructions from J. L. Warner that we were to work one hour extra Saturday night, but both Miss Davis and Mr. Flynn refused to work after 6:05PM."*

Mon July 3
Filming alone with Davis; Frank Mattison to Tenny Wright: *"Mr. Flynn did not arrive in the Studio until 9:20A.M., and was on the stage at 9:38…..We lost considerable time because of Mr. Flynn's continual blowing up of his lines. We made 20 TBD* [to be determined] *takes, all on account of Flynn. Mr. Curtiz dismissed him at 5:00PM as it was absolutely impossible to accomplish any more than he had already done."*

Wed July 5
Filming in the Privy Chamber with Davis and Donald Crisp; inter-office memo from Frank Mattison: *"Mr. Flynn was 35 minutes late into the studio in the morning."*

Thu July 6
Filming in the Privy Chamber and retakes of the bog scene with Alan Hale; completes filming of THE PRIVATE LIVES OF ELIZABETH AND ESSEX; salary for this picture is $41,300. ($768,398 in 2021 value).

Fri July 7
With Bette Davis in the George Hurrell studio shooting color stills for advertising.

Fri July 14
Jack Warner to Roy Obringer: *"Noll Gurney has been bothering me about permitting Flynn's salary to run at $4500 for next year. We definitely will not change this salary to other than the contractual figures."*

Sun July 16
Flynn's father, mother, and sister arrive in Los Angeles for a visit.

Mon July 17
With his family at the Trocadero *(bottom right)*.

With Olivia de Havilland - Thu, June 29

With his mother Marelle, sister Rosemary, Lili, and father Theodore, at the Trocadero in Hollywood - Tue, July 17

*With Rosemary, Lili, Theo, and Marelle in Catalina -
Thu, July 20*

*With Desi Arnaz (far right) at La Conga in New York -
Sat, August 5*

Thu July 20
On Catalina Island with his family *(top left)*, staying at the Eagle's Nest Lodge.

Mon July 24
Returns to the mainland with his family.

Fri July 28
With Noll Gurney to Jack Warner's office at 3:30pm.

Mon July 31
Hal Wallis to all departments: *"The final and definite title for the picture heretofore known as 'Elizabeth And Essex' ('The Knight And The Lady') will be…..'The Private Lives Of Elizabeth And Essex.'"*

Tue August 1
"Hollywood says Errol Flynn is coming to London to star in 'Captain Hornblower,' but London says he isn't. I guess it's a private fight." The Daily Express.

Wed August 2
Performs in an adaptation of the Cary Grant–Katherine Hepburn hit *"Holiday,"* on KNX radio, along with Betty Winkler and Elliot Lewis.

Thu August 3
Requests no publicity on his New York arrival on Friday.

Fri August 4
Arrives in New York with his sister Rosemary, staying at the Waldorf Astoria.

Sat August 5
At La Conga nightclub *(center left)*.

Mon August 7
At the Romanian House Restaurant at the World's Fair.

Fri August 25
Wires Hal Wallis asking about his next picture (THE SEA HAWK); he has been laid off from September 2nd to September 30th.

Tue August 29
Warners turns down Flynn's request of stopping payments to the Selznick Agency.

Sat September 9
Telegram from Flynn to Warner: DEAR JACK: WILL REPORT SEPTEMBER 30TH AS REQUIRED. ADVISE IF YOU NEED ME BEFORE. RECALLING YOU ASSURED ME DEFINITELY DEHAVILLAND [SIC] WOULD NOT BE CAST OPPOSITE. WOULD LIKE TO KNOW WHO IS. PLEASE AIR MAIL SCRIPT HERE TILL TUESDAY. THANKS FOR WIRE. BEST, ERROL. Flies to Washington, D.C., with his sister Rosemary to be with their mother Marelle, who has had a mild heart attack.

Fri September 15
Marelle recovers and flies with Theodore, Rosemary, Errol, and Lili to Newark Metropolitan Airport.

Sat September 16
Sees his family off from Port Washington, NY (Manhassat Isle Airport), as they fly to Southampton, England, at 7:30am on Pan Am Clipper Boeing 314; flies back to Los Angeles from New York with Lili.

Sat September 23
In a tennis tournament at the Los Angeles Tennis Club.

Wed September 27
Premiere of THE PRIVATE LIVES OF ELIZABETH AND ESSEX at the Warner Beverly Hills Theatre *(bottom left)*; tickets are $3.30 downstairs, $2.20, mezzanine, and $1.65 balcony ($61.40, $40.93, and $30.70 in 2021 value).

Thu September 28
Hal Wallis to Michael Curtiz: *"Errol Flynn will be back on salary on September 30th, and is subject to call from that day on for tests, wardrobe, etc."*

Fri October 13
Sound and photo tests for VIRGINIA CITY at WB studios; Warner Bros. announces Olivia de Havilland will replace Brenda Marshall in THE SEA HAWK; this does not transpire.

Tue October 17
Sound and photo tests with Randolph Scott.

Sat October 21
Wardrobe test (George Reeves assisting); inter-office memo from Frank Mattison: *"Mr. Flynn talked with me Saturday* [10/21] *about using his horse in the picture and he would rather have us pay him $35 a day* [$651.18 in 2021 value] *flat for his horse and his hostler than to make separate checks to his hostler direct. Mr. Flynn says he pays this man by the month and taking care of his horse is part of his work."*

Sun October 22
Attends the National Professional singles championship matches at the Beverly Hills Tennis Club.

Wed October 25
Associate producer Robert Fellows to Hal Wallis: *"Flynn likes the script but would like to change his name from Patrick to Michael* [it is eventually changed to Kerry]. *I don't think it's important one way or the other."* Roy Obringer to Hal Wallis: *"Errol Flynn has asked that we advance him $4,000* [$74,421 in 2021 value] *to take care of some emergency real estate transaction he is in. As you know, we tie up a certain portion of his weekly salary in trust. We could advance him this $4,000 and deduct it at the rate of $1,000 or $500 per week from this portion of his salary check which is payable to him. Will you please let me know on this, as Flynn is calling me around 12:00."*

Thu October 26
Hal Wallis to Roy Obringer: *"Errol Flynn, according to Taplinger, has consented to make a shot* [an appearance] *with Louella Parsons which she will use as a trailer in connection with the act which she is taking out on the picture circuit for several weeks...This shot is supposed to be made tomorrow. Will you please prepare a letter for Flynn to sign whatever kind of waiver is necessary as I will not release the film unless you have this kind of a letter. Let me know when you get it signed."*

Wed November 1
Begins filming VIRGINIA CITY with the tunnel and kitchen scenes; inter-office memo from unit manager Frank Mattison: *"Company was held up 2¼ hours, waiting on a beard makeup for Errol Flynn. It appears Perc Westmore had to do this beard personally, as the first beard was unsatisfactory."* Telegram from Jack Warner to Hal Wallis and Roy Obringer: INFORM FLYNN DEFINITELY IMPOSSIBLE LEND HIS NAME TO ANYTHING BUT PICTURE AS TIME SERIOUS ENOUGH RIGHT NOW WITHOUT HAVING FLYNNS NAME USED ANYTHING ELSE BUT OUR PICTURES.

Thu November 2
Filming in the tunnel and kitchen; leaves Pasadena at 7pm for Flagstaff, AZ.

Fri November 3
Arrives in Flagstaff at 8am.

Sat November 4
Begins filming in Tuba City, AZ.

Sun November 5
Sandstorm (*"Weather: VERY CLOUDY"* production note).

Mon November 6 through Wed November 8
Filming at the Mormon outpost.

Thu November 9
Filming the stagecoach scene in Sedona, AZ, with Humphrey Bogart.

Fri November 10
Filming at Shallow Creek and the mountain stream with Miriam Hopkins.

Sat November 11
Filming outside the stagecoach station at Schnebly Hill Vista in Sedona (*center right*); THE PRIVATE LIVES OF ELIZABETH AND ESSEX opens.

Sun November 12
Filming at the mountain stream.

Mon November 13
Filming in Cabby's grove and the "Nevada Hills."

Tue November 14
Filming the decoy wagon.

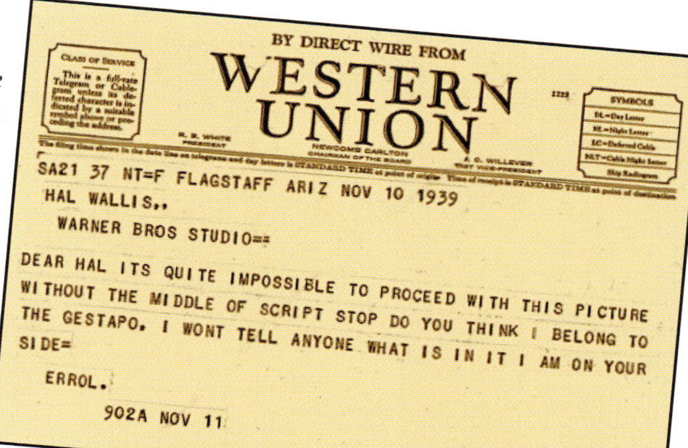

BY DIRECT WIRE FROM

WESTERN UNION

Above, with Miriam Hopkins in Sedona, AZ - November; below, the same location today

Mr. W. Ward Marsh
The Plain Dealer
Cleveland, Ohio

Dear Mr. Marsh:

Sunday, a day of rest for most of the country, but not for the majority of us up here in Northern Arizona on location with Warner Bros., "Virginia City" troupe. Location companies, you know, work Sundays and holidays. I'm more fortunate than Miriam Hopkins, Humphrey Bogart, Randolph Scott, Alan Hale, Frank McHugh, Big Boy Williams, Moroni Olsen, John Litel, Director Mike Curtiz and the rest of the troupe, for I got the day off. They didn't.

This letter is a sort of penance for the privilege of getting a holiday. I thought I'd make good use of the time by writing an account of what has been happening to us in this little town whose population is numerically less than one half its 6900 feet altitude.

We've been here for three weeks and it will probably be another fortnight before our work is completed. The company of two hundred undoubtedly is spread out over more landscape than any other location company ever has been. "Hoppy" -- that's our pet name for Miriam Hopkins -- Randy Scott and "Bogey" -- that's Humphrey Bogart -- are living fifty-five miles from the Flagstaff headquarters, at the Indian trading post of Cameron, which hangs on the canyon wall over the Little Colorado. It's in the heart of the Navajo country and a few mud hogans, looking like huge upside-down salad bowls squat right under their windows.

When the company is at work on the reservation, the Navajos appear shortly before lunch. They arrive on horseback, in trucks and afoot, but the squaws and the children always are afoot. They come to get the leftovers of the company's lunch. On the first day in the desert only a few Indians arrived. Shy, they remained at a distance and the lunches were carried to them by members of the cast and crew. Sandwiches were eaten without removing the paper wrappings. None knew how to open the bottles of milk, until one clever buck thrust his thumb through the top and received a milk shower bath. None of the Navajos admit they understand English until a camera is pointed at them. Then they demand "twenty-five cents".

Things happen once in a while that are not on the production schedule. Like two days ago when, returning to the trading post after a hard day in the saddle in front of the cameras, Randy Scott and I found a disabled car on Highway 89 and discovered in it, of all things, seven of Billy Rose's Aquacade nymphs on the way to the coast. The girls had a flat.

Cordially,

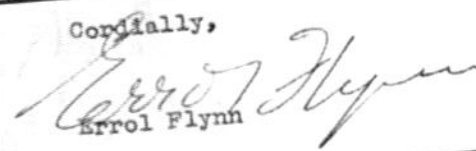

Errol Flynn

Flynn's letter to The Cleveland Plain Dealer
Sun, November 19

With actress Helen Gilbert and Howard Hughes at the Beverly Hilton Hotel - Sat, December 23

Wed November 15
Filming in the desolate country, the "Nevada Hills," and in the canyon with Scott, Hopkins, and Bogart.

Fri November 17
Filming in the canyon, the prairie road, and at the crest of a hill.

Sat November 18
Filming with the 2nd unit and Randolph Scott alone at the Mormon station, and in Rocky Canyon and Batton Hill; appears at the La Cuesta Dance at Northern Arizona State Teachers College (now Northern Arizona University) in Flagstaff, judging contestants for the queen of the college and crowning the winner; Charles Einfeld reporting from the college to publicity man Frank Heacock: *"Queen affair Big success. Errol chose Alice Moore Statuesque brunette from final field of twelve. Much Art* [publicity]. *Hutch* [publicist] *covered wires* [media]."

Sun November 19
Filming the Rocky Hill battle and with the 2nd unit at the Mormon station; writes a letter to Cleveland newspaper *The Plain Dealer*, mailed on 11/22 (*center left*).

Mon November 20 through Wed November 22
Filming the Rocky Hill battle; leaves Flagstaff at 7:30pm on 11/22.

Thu November 23 (Thanksgiving Day)
Arrives in Pasadena at 8am.

Fri November 24
Filming in Drewry's (Douglass Dumbrille) garrison office at the studio.

Mon November 27 and Tue November 28
Filming in Dr. Cameron's (Moroni Olsen) office, and (on 11/28) in Hooker's headquarters.

Wed November 29
Filming in Hooker's headquarters.

Thu November 30 through Sat December 2
Filming in the blacksmith's shop, and (on 12/2) in the Southern hideout.

Mon December 4
Filming in the street at the WB Calabasas Ranch and in and behind Cameron's house.

Tue December 5
Filming process shots in the covered wagon, in the Libby Prison, and in the blacksmith's shop.

Wed December 6 and Thu December 7
Filming process shots atop the stagecoach with the 2nd unit, and (on 12/7) in Julia's (Miriam Hopkins) room.

Fri December 8
Filming in Rocky Canyon on the WB soundstage.

Sat December 9
Filming in the gold camp and in the Mormon station.

Sun December 10
Warners announce Flynn will star in *Out Of Gas*; it never transpires.

Mon December 11 and Tue December 12
Filming battle scenes on the soundstage, and (on 12/12) wagon train process shots; leaves for Victorville, CA.

Thu December 14
Filming the river crossing at Victorville; leaves Victorville afterward.

Fri December 15
Filming in the Mormon station, in Julia's room, and in the bank.

Sat December 16
Filming battle scenes and at the Mormon station.

Mon December 18
Filming process shots of stopping the runaway stagecoach horses, battle scenes in Rocky Canyon, and the wagon camp; attends the Javanese Ballet led by Devi Dja at the Philharmonic Auditorium.

Tue December 19 through Sat December 23
Filming in the Sazarec Saloon, and (on 12/21) a process shot near Mormon station with the 2nd unit; at a charity Christmas party hosted by the Motion Picture Guild at the Beverly Hilton Hotel (12/23 *previous page, bottom left*).

Tue December 26
Filming process shots in and out of the stagecoach.

Wed December 27
Filming process shots in the stagecoach, and on the Virginia City Street at the WB Calabasas Ranch; Frank Mattison to Tenny Wright: *"Regarding the starting date on 'The Sea Hawk,' I was talking about this picture with Errol Flynn and he informed me 'off the record' that he was going to insist on 3 weeks vacation between the finish of 'Virginia City' and the start of 'The Sea Hawk'! This is for your information only."*

Thu December 28
Filming a process shot outside the stagecoach and the court martial scene.

Fri December 29
Filming on a cliff on a soundstage, and on the Virginia City street at the WB Calabasas Ranch at night; it is reported in the Santa Rosa Press Democrat that Warners is reading Flynn's original script, *Illegal Passage*, whose characters are based on his friends.

Sat December 30
Filming in the swamp and cemetery at 30 Acres on the backlot *(top right)*.

1940

THE FORTIES

Tue January 2
Filming battle scenes for VIRGINIA CITY.

Wed January 3
Filming Flynn's horse sliding down the cliff at the wooded mountains at 30 Acres on the backlot, a process shot of the stagecoach, and in the saloon.

Fri January 5
Roy Obringer to Jack Warner: *"I talked with Errol Flynn this morning, and, in order to feel him out as to when he expected to report for 'The Sea Hawk', I asked him if he had the Kate Smith broadcast set. Flynn advised me that the broadcast was going to interfere with our needing him at the studio to prepare for wardrobe, make-up, etc., on 'The Sea Hawk' in no event later than the 18th...Flynn stated that he was at the present time working with the writers on the script, that he was working with Westmore on the make-up, and that he was getting his wardrobe lined up, and that he did not intend to leave until next Wednesday, the 10th, and would have everything ready relative to 'The Sea Hawk' before he left; also that he intended to fly back after the broadcast, and he assured me that he would be here by the 20th...For your information.....I have checked with Westmore, who states that he had Flynn all day yesterday, that he has all of his measurements, sample of his hair, etc., and that as far as the make-up is concerned, Flynn can go to work the day he returns, as he will have everything lined up... Also, I checked with Burns in the Wardrobe, and he advised that he naturally has all of Flynn's measurements, etc., and that Flynn and Curtiz are supposed to go into the Wardrobe today to select styles, etc., and Burns states that he will be ready with Flynn's wardrobe."*

Mon January 8
Bob Fellows to Tenny Wright: *"Dear Tenny: I understand that Flynn wants to leave town on Wednesday and if we are to get the tag for 'Virginia City' he should stay for a day or two longer. As you know we have to shoot this on the ranch. It might be possible to grab this tag upon Flynn's return, before he starts 'The Sea Hawk', but naturally, it would be better to get it before he leaves.....Curtiz and I will be glad to talk to Flynn if you think we should, but I thought you might want to take this up with Mr. Warner first."* Roy Obringer to Jack Warner: *"Just to remind you: You want to talk to Flynn today to make sure he will be back the 20th. As you know, he intends to do the Kate Smith broadcast on the 19th and assured me he would fly back here the 20th. I understand he is taking care of his wardrobe and make-up before he leaves."*

Wed January 10
Completes work on VIRGINIA CITY, filming scenes on the Virginia City street, the side yard of a house, in the gold camp, and in the saloon; salary for the picture is $50,000 ($930,264 in 2021 value).

Fri January 12
Flies to New York *(bottom right)*.

Tue January 16
Telegram to Roy Obringer: MATERIAL UNSUITABLE KATE SMITH PROGRAM SO WOULD LIKE TO CHANGE TO

With Guinn "Big Boy" Williams and Alan Hale at WB 30 Acres on the backlot - Sat, December 30

In his dressing room with Arno in a Robin Hood hat

Arriving in New York - Fri, January 12, 1940

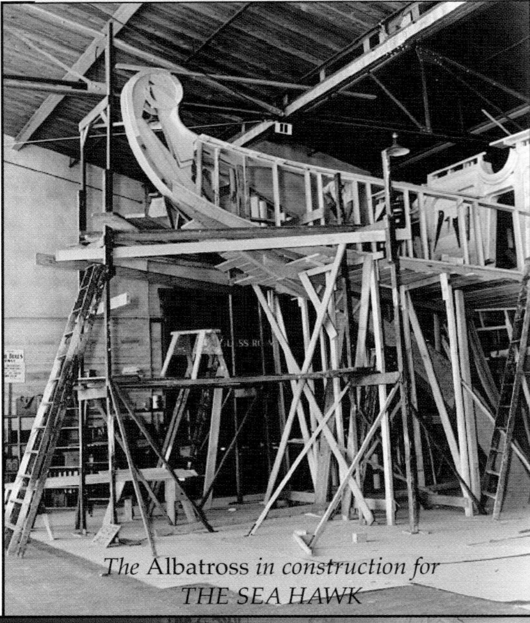

The Albatross *in construction for* THE SEA HAWK

With Flora Robson and Michael Curtiz - February 1940

With Brenda Marshall - Wed, February 7

LUX IN MARCH. WILL YOU PLEASE WIRE ME OKAY

Wed January 17
Charles Einfeld to Roy Obringer: *"Flynn says he will positively report on January 22 and will not break his promise to Jack Warner even if he has to walk back. Thanks you for permission to appear on Lux program instead of Kate Smith. Says Lux program will probably be March 23 which will be good for us because it will tie in with current releases of 'Virginia City.' There was no argument on Flynn's part about anything and he said to be sure to tell you 'I am gentleman of my word and will stick to it about returning on 22nd'."*

Fri January 19
Returns to Hollywood.

Sun January 21
With Lili at the Palm Springs Racquet Club.

Wed January 24
Wardrobe tests for THE SEA HAWK.
A 165' long ship, the *Albatross* (top left**)**, and another 135' long ship, will be floated in a 12' deep tank in the huge soundstage 21, specially built for THE SEA HAWK; they will be worked and swayed by hidden hydraulics. The cost of the completed *Albatross* is $59,500, and $45,000 for the Spanish ship ($1,107,015 and $837,238, respectively, in 2021 value)

Fri January 26 and Sat January 27
Makeup tests for THE SEA HAWK, and (on 1/27) wardrobe tests.

Sun January 28
Participates in a tournament at the Westside Tennis Club.

Wed January 31
Flynn is home with foot injuries (possibly from the tennis tournament on 1/28); does not work; Tenny Wright to Hal Wallis: *"Flynn's man called up this morning and said Flynn would not come in until the doctor arrived at 9:00 a.m. I immediately called Mattison and sent him out to Flynn's house...Our doctor arrived at 9:00 a.m., and suggested that Flynn stay in bed again today, but thought it would be all right for him to be in tomorrow.....Blanke is familiar with the situation, and he was in my office when Mattison called me from Flynn's bedside. We also talked to Flynn, who said he felt sure he would be in tomorrow morning, and was sorry that he said last night he would be in this morning, as he was weaker than he thought he was."*

Thu February 1
Filming interior scenes in the Spanish council room and in the queen's private chamber; Flynn begins work on the film, reporting to the studio with a bruised heel and two blistered toes, and seeks help from the First Aid Department; Hal Wallis to Tenny Wright: *"Did Flynn show up today, and are we set with him now so that we can start tomorrow and really get a day's work?"*

Fri February 2
Continues filming interior scenes in the Spanish council room and in the queen's (Flora Robson) private chamber; Hal Wallis to Michael Curtiz: *"I noticed in the scene with Flynn where the monkey jumps on his arm that you are starting to ad-lib the script again. The added lines about a lot of monkeys already living in the palace and the pulling the tail line are ad-lib cracks put in on the set and have a tendency to make the scene phoney because they are colloquialisms and take the whole thing out of character.....Are you going to keep harassing me all through this picture or are you going to shoot the script?"*

Sat February 3
Filming interior scenes in the Spanish council room, the queen's private chamber, and the ambassador's chamber.

Mon February 5
Hal Wallis to Henry Blanke, commenting on dailies: *"I wish Flynn had referred to Robson at least two or three times in the dialogue as 'Your Majesty' or 'Your Highness', as it is written in the script, instead of calling her Madam all of the time. It gets a little monotonous, and at the same time it seems to lack the dignity and respect."*

Wed February 7
Filming in the palace rose garden on Dijon Street on the WB back lot (*bottom left*).

Not Permanent Actor Says of Separation

By Louella O. Parsons
Motion Picture Editor International News Service

Errol Flynn, whose marital life is just as hectic as the gay adventure stories he brings to the screen, has moved into the Sunset Towers. His actress wife, flashing-eyed Lili Damita, remains in the palatial Beverly Hills family home. The news that Lili and Errol were living apart was received with surprise by their friends, for no one had an inkling that he had moved out of his home.

The Los Angeles Times
Sat, February 10

Fri February 9 and Sat February 10

Filming in the throne room; Warners announces (on 2/10) that Flynn will next star in a Tahitian-themed film, *Out of Gas,* followed by *Capt. Horatio Hornblower, Simon Bolivar,* and *White Rajah,* the latter film of Flynn's scripting; none of these were ever made.

Mon February 12

Continues filming in the throne room.

Tue February 13

Filming the queen's knighting of Thorpe (Flynn) on the WB soundstage *(top right)*; inter-office memo from Frank Mattison: *"All depts. on the lot deserve a vote of thanks for their co-op. in getting this big set underway this morning."*

Wed February 14

Filming in the throne room and with the queen at the end of the great duel *(center right).*

Thu February 15

Filming in Maria's apartment; a party is held at Pier 21 in the WB shipyard where the two large sailing ships are presented in a ceremony for studio guests and the press; speeches are made by Flynn and Curtiz, after which Bette Davis leads guests aboard the *Madre de Dios;* the press reports that the ship carries 1,500 yards of canvas, pneumatic hoists under the hull that sway the ship as if on waves, all in a 12-foot-deep studio "ocean" 270 feet long by 160 feet wide by 85 feet high; the *Madre de Dios* and its sister ship took 375 workers 11 weeks to build.

Fri February 16 and Sat February 17

Filming in the palace corridor (2/16), Wolfingham's (Henry Daniell) apartment, and the dueling sequence; Louella Parsons suggests in her column (2/17) that *"Warners would clean up putting Lili Damita and Errol Flynn in a domestic comedy based on their own tangles as soon as they start speaking again...."*

Tue February 20

Filming in the chart master's shop on the WB back lot (Dijon Street); Frank Mattison to Tenny Wright: *"Last night (Monday) at 10:30 Errol Flynn called me at home and wanted to know if it would be possible for him to come in at 11:00 o'clock instead of 9:00, so I re-juggled the schedule accordingly so that we could shoot the second sequence first without Flynn. He has just called again at 9:20 saying that it would be impossible for him to get in by 10:30 this morning. After I talked to him, however, he said that he would be able to make it by 1:00 o'clock, but I am to call him again at 11:00. We only need him for about three hours on the Dijon Street to complete the retakes and the sequence in which he appears there, so we are trying our damndest to get him in."* Inter-office memo from Frank Mattison: *"Mr. [Henry] Daniell is absolutely helpless and his close-ups in the duel will be mostly from the elbows up."* Inter-office memo from Frank Mattison: *"The casting office and everyone connected with the picture were duly warned of Mr. Daniell's inability to fence long before the picture started, and we knew of him being taken out of a part of 'Romeo & Juliet' because he could not handle a sword."* Films a trailer for VIRGINIA CITY with Humphrey Bogart, Jack Warner, Ann Sheridan, and Nevada governor Edward Carville; leaves the studio early with 100° fever.

Wed February 21 and Thu February 22

Ill; does not work (Lili calls in to the studio for Errol on 2/21); Frank Mattison to Tenny Wright (2/22): *"This morning when I called Mr. Flynn's home, I was informed he had a very restless night and the doctor said he should stay home today on account of the weather and Mr. Flynn being very ill."*

Fri February 23

Roy Obringer to Tenny Wright: *"Errol Flynn has been given permission to appear on the Lux Theatre Of The Air next Monday, March 4th, and he is to be allowed to leave the studio early on the day of the broadcast, but not earlier than 4:30PM."* Director Raoul Walsh in a letter to Hal Wallis concerning Flynn's upcoming film, FOOTSTEPS IN THE DARK: *"The story is an ordinary murder mystery that has been done a great number of times in small budget pictures.... There is nothing I could do with this story to make it interesting. It is just a lot of people talking and the plot is pretty dull."*

Sat February 24

Filming in palace corridor, the rose garden, and the chart shop interior; Flynn and director, Curtiz, both very *"weak from illness."* Roy Obringer to comptroller Cy Wilder: *"In accordance with my former instructions to you, you have, since the week ending September 30, 1939, been deducting from checks that become due and payable to Errol Flynn*

Filming the Queen's knighting of Geoffrey Thorpe - Tue, February 13

With Flora Robson, Una O'Connor, and Brenda Marshall - Wed, February 14

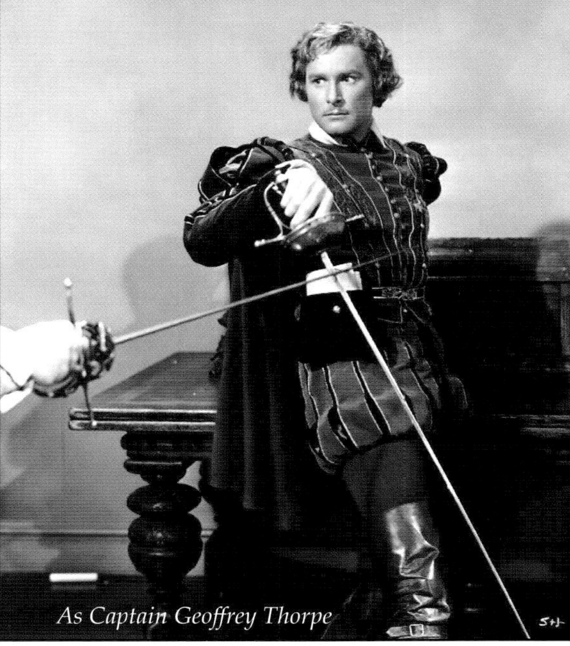

As Captain Geoffrey Thorpe

With Jack Warner and Louella Parsons (center) at the Academy Awards in the Ambassador Hotel - Thu, February 29

the sum of $1,000 per week and paying it over to the Bank of America....Flynn wants to raise a fund of $43,000 [$800,027 in 2021 value]. The $23,166.67 trust fund he will now get, plus the 19 normal trust fund deductions which we will forego, will total almost $43,000, although it may be that we will also pay to Flynn the $1,000 trust fund deduction on the 20th week...."

Mon February 26

Ill, does not work; signs an agreement with Warner Bros. to loan him the $43,000; is named in an F.B.I. investigation of the "White Slave Traffic Act" for possible involvement with certain men and women in question; it was later determined he was unaware of the illegal activities of the men to whom he had lent his car.

Tue February 27

Ill; does not work.

Wed February 28

Filming in Thorpe's cabin, the throne room, and more of the duel; leaves early at 5:30pm with complaints of being *"pooped out."*

Thu February 29

Filming in Thorpe's cabin; attends the 12th annual Academy Awards ceremonies at the Ambassador Hotel *(top left)*.

Fri March 1 and Sat March 2

Filming in the throne room, and (on 3/2) in the corridor and in Wolfingham's study.

Mon March 4

Radio performance of "Trade Winds" with Joan Bennett for the Lux Radio Theatre at CBS affiliate, KNX, Los Angeles.

Tue March 5

Filming on the Spanish ships.

Wed March 6

Filming in Thorpe's and Maria's (Brenda Marshall) cabin.

Thu March 7

Hal Wallis to Michael Curtiz: *"....Flynn particularly has no drive in his performance and in his delivery of lines. I don't know whether or not he knows his lines, but if he doesn't, we had better stop the picture until he learns them, because the stuff as it is is not good...We are putting a fortune into this picture, as everyone knows, and if the actors are not prepared to do their scenes properly, then I am not going to start any more pictures of this kind with Flynn, or with anyone else, who won't cooperate...I want you to have a talk with Flynn and tell him of my complaint, and that I expect him to do better."...'I do not (not 'don't') drink with thieves and pirates'* [admonition to Brenda Marshall on how to properly phrase the line]."

Fri March 8

Filming in the vestibule and cabin of the Spanish ship.

Mon March 11

Filming in the interior of the coach, the cabin of the *Madre de Dios*, and the exterior of the Dover port on Bonnyfeather Street on the backlot.

Tue March 12

Filming on the *Albatross* and Spanish ships.

Wed March 13 and Thu March 14

Filming on the exterior of the Albatross, and (on 3/14) on the Dover port on Bonnyfeather Street on the backlot, and on the exterior of the chart shop; memo from Hal Wallis to Tenny Wright (on 3/14, *bottom left*):
"For the past few days, I have been getting a lot of reports via the grapevine about Errol Flynn. Also, Mike [Curtiz] has told me he loses hours every day on account of Flynn and is days behind because of him, that he doesn't know his lines, etc."

WARNER BROS. PICTURES, INC.
BURBANK, CALIFORNIA

INTER-OFFICE COMMUNICATION

DATE March 14, 1940

WRIGHT

WALLIS

SUBJECT "THE SEA HAWK"

For the past few days, I have been getting a lot of reports via the grapevine about ERROL FLYNN. Also, Mike has told me he loses hours every day on account of Flynn and is days behind because of him, that he doesn't know his lines, etc.

I also understand that Flynn is late on the set practically every day, that he was called to work the other afternoon at 4:30, and at 9:00 o'clock said he was cold and that he was going home and proceeded to leave before the set was finished.

I also understand that the other day he was given a 2:30 call, and at 2:00 o'clock he called up to find out how far along Mike was, and when told he was needed, said he would be right down, and of course, he got there an hour late or something of the kind.

Do you know about these things? Do your assistants or Unit Managers tell you what is going on, and if you do, why don't you do something about it? If you can't do anything about it, why don't you at least let me in on it so that I can? Why do you as Studio Manager tolerate a condition of this kind? Do you let the actors come and go as they please and disregard calls, and go home when they like without saying or doing anything about it?

I want you to answer this, and I want a full report on the situation and answers to the above questions. After I get your letter, I want a meeting with you, Mattison, and Jack Sullivan.

HAL WALLIS

Sat March 16

At 8:30am a crowd of over 10,000 in Reno is waiting for the stars, where a radio broadcast over NBC is hosted by Art Linkletter; at 10:30 is a horseback parade through town, after which the entourage travels on to Virginia City, NV, for various festivities, including a stop at Schnitzer's Beer Garden; at 6pm the junket travels back to Reno for the world premiere of VIRGINIA CITY, with a nationwide radio broadcast of the event hosted by Ken Murray.

Sun March 17

The junket leaves Reno at noon and stops for recreation at the Sugar Bowl Ski Resort in Norden, CA; after several hours of fun in the snow the train travels back to Los Angeles.

With Rosemary Lane (in blue vest) and William "Hopalong Cassidy" Boyd (on the right) in Reno - Sat, March 16

Mon March 18

Filming on the exterior of the Spanish ship and the *Albatross*, and at the London Gate on Dijon Street on the backlot; Hal Wallis to Michael Curtiz: *"The last day or two with Flynn are so much better than it has been for some time, and I hope it continues this way."*

Tue March 19

Filming in the coach; Hal Wallis to Michael Curtiz: *"There's another thing in the dailies that bothered, and that bothered me the other day in a similar scene—I noticed when the sailors cheer for any reason, that a great many of them use a clenched fist in what is really the Communist salute. This is very noticeable, and I don't understand why you allow the people to do it."*

Wed March 20

Filming on the *Albatross* and Spanish ship.

Thu March 21

Filming in the *Albatross* rowboat.

Fri March 22 and Sat March 23

Filming in the galley of the Spanish ship, and (on 3/23) the palace gate on the back lot (Dijon Street); VIRGINIA CITY opens (on 3/23) and Flynn attends the premiere at the Warner Theater in downtown Los Angeles.

With Harry Cording, Charles Irwin, and Alan Hale - March

With Alan Hale, David Bruce, J. M. Kerrigan, Julien Mitchell, and Charles Irwin - Thu, March 21

With Mary Astor and Frances Robinson in Norden, CA - Sun, March 17

With Alan Hale, Claude Rains, Brenda Marshall, and Una O'Connor - March

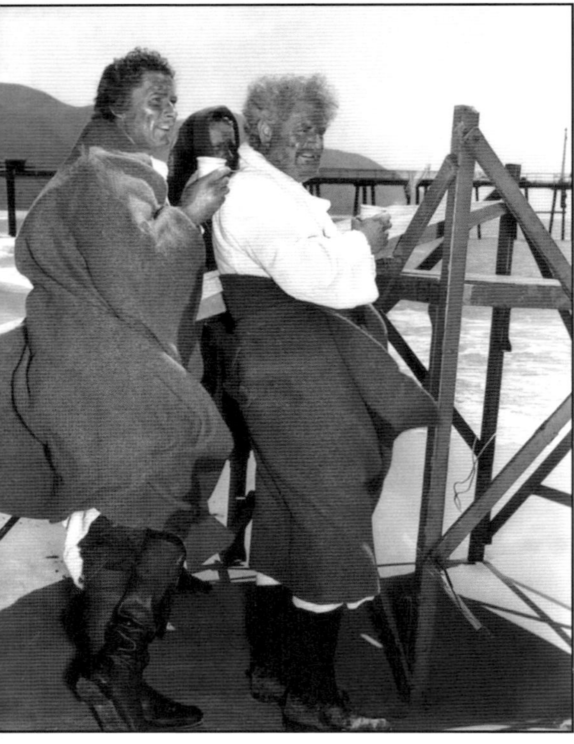

With Alan Hale at Point Mugu, CA - Mon, April 15

Mon March 25
Calls in sick.

Tue March 26 and Wed March 27
Filming in the galley of the Spanish ship.

Thu March 28
Frank Mattison to Tenny Wright: *"Errol Flynn will have to rehearse today from 12:00 Noon until 2:00P.M. on his Kraft Music Hall program, and he will have to leave this afternoon again at 5:00 o'clock. We have arranged our shooting schedule accordingly"*; filming in the Spanish galley, at the palace gate, and in the interior of the coach; guest stars in a comedy sketch with Bing Crosby, Mary Martin, Brenda Marshall, and Victor Borge on Bing's NBC radio show, *Kraft Music Hall.*

Fri March 29
Filming the exterior and interior of the captain's quarters.

Sat March 30
Filming on the main deck of the *Albatross.*

Mon April 1
Filming on the exterior of the *Albatross.*

Tue April 2
Filming in the palace corridor, and dueling close-ups; with Lili at Ciro's nightclub.

Wed April 3
Filming on the exterior of the *Madre de Dios.*

Thu April 4
Filming scenes in the Panama jungle at 30 Acres on the backlot.

Fri April 5
Filming on the *Madre de Dios* and the ship galley; Frank Mattison to Tenny Wright: *"I had some complaint yesterday from Ellis Erwin* [sic]; *the cast included both an Ellis Irving and a Charles Irwin] who with Julian Mitchell and Clifford Brooke, complained that they should be furnished with rubber stockings to work in the swamps, as Mike had them in the water up to their knees yesterday. You will remember we made no provisions for rubber underwear except for Flynn and Hale. I understand these rubber stockings can be purchased for about $4.00 a pair* [$74.42 in 2021 value], *and we should get them for our principals."*

Sat April 6 and Mon April 8
Filming jungle scenes at 30 Acres, and (on 4/8) with the mule train at 30 Acres.

Tue April 9 through Fri April 12
Filming jungle scenes at 30 Acres, and (on 4/11) the bridge blowing up, and the battle.

Sat April 13
Filming jungle scenes at 30 Acres and the Dover dock on Bonnyfeather Street on the backlot.

Mon April 15
Filming of jungle scenes and the beach (*"heavy winds"*) at Point Mugu, CA; Flynn offers to come in to the WB Studio later that day on his own time to pose for promotional stills.

Tue April 16
Filming more jungle scenes at 30 Acres.

Wed April 17
Filming of the tribunal inquiry and the exterior of the palace courtyard; the Los Angeles Census report for this day has Errol and Lili living at 601 N. Linden in Beverly Hills (value of the home at $25,000–$465,132 in 2021 value) with their 34-year-old Dutch maid, Sophie.

Thu April 18
Filming on the exterior of the *Albatross* and the *Madre de Dios.*

Fri April 19
Completes filming of THE SEA HAWK with scenes in the coach.

Thu April 25
Sails on the *Sirocco* to Catalina Island for a few days.

Fri April 26

"Errol Flynn almost didn't get away on his yachting race to Guadalupe, Mexico. Just as he was about to leave, a friend asked him facetiously, 'are you going to look for mermaids?' In the same spirit, Errol replied, 'I'm taking some with me.'" Sheilah Graham in *The Hartford Courant.*

Sat April 27

Enters his four Rhodesian ridgebacks in the Beverly Hills Hotel dog show *(center right).*

Mon April 29

Hal Wallis to Jack Warner: *"Errol Flynn called. Said he has to go to court in the [Myron] Selznick case on Wednesday, as you know, and as part of his testimony he wants to say that previous to his last deal, sometime last July, Noll Gurney tried a number of times thru me and thru Obringer to see you... Flynn wants to know if he can say this and if he does can I remember such occasions."*

Wed May 1

In court for the case against his former agent, Myron Selznick, for failure to pay commissions.

With Arno at the Sirocco, berthed in Wilmington, CA

The Pirates' Den souvenir card

Fri May 3

Opening night in Hollywood of the Pirates' Den, a club/restaurant co-owned by Bob Hope, Bing Crosby, Errol Flynn, Johnny Weismuller, Fred MacMurray, Rudy Valee, and others *(left).*

Tue May 7

Sails to San Diego.

Wed May 8

Continues sailing south for an extended vacation.

Thu May 9

Jack Warner to Hal Wallis: *"Will you please arrange to run the picture* [THE SEA HAWK] *at my house tonight at 8:30?"*

Wed May 15

Hal Wallis to Roy Obringer: *"On his trip to South America, Flynn is to make personal appearances and other appearances as requested by Warner Bros. representatives in the cities he visits...For these services we are to pay him one thousand per week for five weeks. Flynn is paying all of his expenses while on the trip. Payments to commence on May 18th...This has nothing whatsoever to do with his present contract and establishes no precedent."*

Late May

In Miami with Lili, staying at the American Hotel.

Sat May 18

Letter to Hal Wallis: *"....I'm so glad you agree that I should do this picture next* [*Jupiter Laughs*], *and, quite apart from the play, I'm sure that it will make a hell of a picture, with the nice spiritual quality it seems to have, but I do hope that you can work it out for me to do the play as well even if only for eight weeks...."* Wallis ultimately made the film as *Shining Victory* with James Stephenson and Geraldine Fitzgerald.

Wed May 29

Returns with Lili to Hollywood.

Sat June 1

Leaves with WB publicist Johnny Meyers and a film crew on a tour of Central and South America, sponsored by Warner Bros.; while on this trip, agrees to the $1,000 per week ($18,605 in 2021 value) compensation in his contract.

Sun June 2 through Wed June 5

Flies from Miami to Port-of-Spain, Trinidad, staying at the Macqueripe Hotel and fishing (on 6/4) with Johnny Meyer on an outing arranged by hotel manager, Dan McInerny.

Thu June 6

Arrives in Rio de Janeiro, Brazil, and is mobbed by fans *(next page, top left)*; stays in a five-room suite at the Copacabana Palace Hotel (at $8 a night, $148.84 in 2021 value).

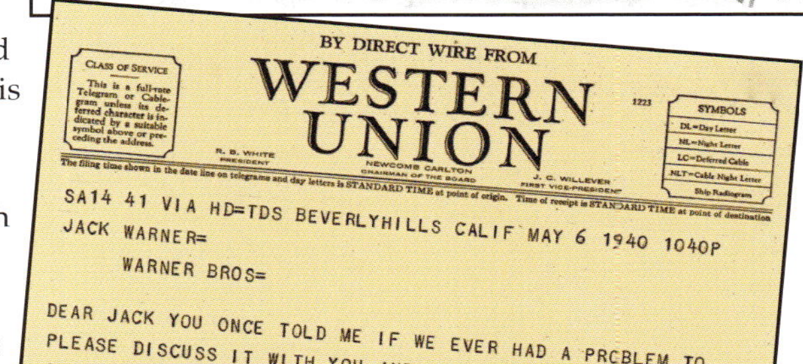
At the Beverly Hills Hotel dog show - Sat, April 27

Arriving in Rio de Janiero - Thu, June 6

Flynn fans in Rio hoping to see him

Tue June 11

Flies to Montevideo, Uruguay; the press reports that Flynn and Olivia de Havilland will star in *The Constant Nymph*; it is eventually made with Charles Boyer and Joan Fontaine.

Fri June 14

Flies to Buenos Aires.

Mon June 17

Jack Warner to Roy Obringer: *"If Errol Flynn doesn't appear on the date he is due back, we will suspend him. He should appear here on June 22nd."*

Wed June 19

Attends an Arturo Toscanini concert at El Teatro Colon; the concert featured performances of Mozart's The *Magic Flute*, Brahms' *Symphony No. 1*, Franck's *Les Éolides*, Respighi's *The Fountains of Rome*, and movements from Wagner's *Parsival* and *Die Meistersinger*; Flynn then flies to Valparaiso, Chile; telegram from a Mr. Novak to Jack Warner: FLYNN SENSATIONAL SUCCESS WITH ADDRESSES ALONG FLIGHT ON PAN AMERICANISM ESPECIALLY RIO AND BUENOS AIRES STOP FLYNN VISITING RANCH WANTS TO KNOW STARTING DATE AND NEXT PICTURE CAN MAKE TWENTY FOURTH BUT WILL MEAN MISSING ALL OF COAST COUNTRIES. Telegram from Jack Warner to Mr. Novak: INFORM FLYNN MUST ARRIVE AT STUDIO JULY FIRST STOP DELIGHTED FLYNNS SUCCESSFUL TRIP STOP HAVE FLYNN PERSONALLY CABLE ME IMMEDIATELY AUTHORIZATION HE GAVE AT LEAST ONE THOUSAND DOLLARS TO REDCROSS STOP ALSO CONFIRMATION HE BE STUDIOS JULY FIRST AS PREPARING VERY BIG PICTURE STARTING FEW DAYS AFTER HIS ARRIVAL.

Thu June 20

Flynn's 31st birthday.

Sat June 22

Flies to Santiago, Chile, as a guest of British ambassador Sir Charles Bentinck.

Mon June 24

THE SEA HAWK previews in Huntington Park, CA, commencing a series of road show openings of the film; Steve Trilling to Hal Wallis: *"For your information: John Wayne was in this morning and read the 'Santa Fe Trail' script. He was not keen about the part—did not feel it gave him enough opportunity to characterize it—that it was merely a straight part that just carried thru as a foil for Jeb Stuart* [Errol Flynn]...*Michael Curtiz and Bob Fellows spoke to him at length about what they were going to do to make the part important, etc. Wayne promised to think it over and let us know tomorrow...I will advise you as soon as we hear from him but from his conversation with me, and later with Curtiz and Fellows, I am dubious of a favorable answer."* Telegram from Jack Warner to Flynn in Santiago, Chile: DELIGHTED SUCCESS PERSONAL APPEARANCES STOP YOU KNOW THERES WAR GOING ON AND MILLIONS PEOPLE NEED SUCCOR STOP ASKED YOU GIVE THOUSAND FOR RED CROSS STOP CABLE IMMEDIATELY THIS OKAY STOP DEFINITELY STARTING YOUR NEXT PICTURE JULY EIGHTH STOP YOU POSITIVELY BE HERE JULY FIRST.

Wed June 26

Steve Trilling to Hal Wallis: *"John Wayne advised me late yesterday that he just could not change his views regarding the part of 'Custer' in 'Santa Fe Trail'—as expressed to us Monday. He understood, of course, that it was a temporary script.....Under the circumstances I am afraid we will have to forget about him—unless we can afford to wait till the new script comes out and go after him at that time."* Telegram from Jack Warner to Flynn: YOUR NEXT PICTURE COSTING HUGE SUM STOP YOU MUST BE STUDIO NO LATER THAN JULY FIFTH STOP PICTURE STARTS JULY EIGHTH STOP NEED LEAST THREE DAYS WARDROBE PREPARATION.

Thu June 27

Flies to Lima, Peru; tour is rescheduled, canceling trips to Quito, Ecuador; Bogotá, Colombia; and Panama City, Panama.

Mon July 1

Flies to Mexico City.

Wed July 3

Telegram from Jack Warner to WB publicity man J. G. Mullen in Mexico City: READ LOCAL PAPERS ERROL

Meeting fans in Buenos Aires

FLYNN ILL STOP WIRE STRAIGHT HIS CONDITION. Telegram from J. G. Mullen to Jack Warner: FLYNN ARRIVED MEXICO WITH FEVER AND HAS BEEN IN BED UNDER DOCTORS CARE EVER SINCE STOP HE FLIES BACK TO BURBANK FRIDAY MORNING STOP AM ADVISING YOU SO THAT YOU CAN MAKE YOUR PLANS ACCORDINGLY BECAUSE I AM SURE HE WILL NEED A FEW DAYS REST BEFORE ATTEMPTING ANY ASSIGNMENTS.

Thu July 4
THE SEA HAWK is previewed at a theater in Pomona, CA.

Fri July 5
Arrives back in Los Angeles; telegram from J. G. Mullen to Jack Warner: FLYNN LEFT ON THIS MORNINGS PLANE STOP HIS FEVER GOT WORSE EVERY DAY STOP YESTERDAY IT WAS ONE HUNDRED AND THREE STOP DOCTORS HERE WERE UNABLE TO DIAGNOSE HIS CASE.

Sat July 6
Telegram from J. G. Mullen to Jack Warner: I PERSONALLY TALKED WITH DOCTOR TWICE STOP HE WAS NOT SURE WHETHER IT WAS A RECURRENCE OF AN OLD MALARIA ATTACK OR A FORM OF FLU STOP DOCTOR FEELS SURE FLYNN WILL BE OK AFTER A FEW DAYS REST STOP HIS TEMPERATURE VARIED CONSIDERABLE [sic] REACHING ONE HUNDRED THREE YESTERDAY STOP THIS MORNING BEFORE LEAVING HE LOOKED SOMEWHAT BETTER.

Sun July 7
Preview of THE SEA HAWK at the Warner Hollywood Theater at 8:25pm.

Mon July 8
"Dear Errol: Attached is the first portion of the script [SANTA FE TRAIL]. I expect to have practically all of the balance by the end of the week. Hope you are feeling better and will look forward to seeing you as soon as you can get in. Kindest regards. Sincerely, Hal Wallis."

Mon July 15
Begins filming SANTA FE TRAIL with scenes of the West Point cavalry drill grounds on Gopher Flats at Providencia Ranch, and in Robert E. Lee's (Moroni Olsen) office *(top right)*; an article in the *Panama City Herald* quotes Flynn as saying that after his recent travels through South America he fears it may be too late for the United States to prevent the Nazis from taking over Brazil and Argentina.

Tue July 16
More filming of scenes of the West Point cavalry drill grounds on Gopher Flats at Providencia Ranch.

With Moroni Olsen (in the foreground), Frank Wilcox, David Bruce, George Haywood, Ronald Reagan, William Lundigan, and William Marshall - Mon, July 15

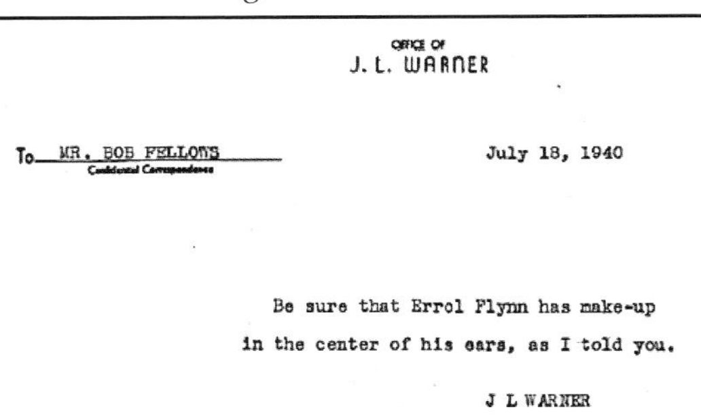

Wed July 17 and Thu July 18
Filming the West Point graduation at Lower Busch Gardens; Olivia de Havilland's first scenes *(bottom right)*; THE SEA HAWK previews at the Warner Hollywood Theater at 8:25pm (7/17).

Fri July 19
Filming in the barracks and barber shop.

Sat July 20
Filming in the barbershop and a process shot in the train shed.

Mon July 22 through Wed July 24
Filming process shots in the train.

Thu July 25
Filming process shots on a treadmill in the West Point corridor, in the barber shop, and at the stables at Providencia Ranch.

Sat July 27 and Mon July 29
Filming in the freight yards at the WB Calabasas Ranch.

Tue July 30 and Wed July 31
Filming John Brown's (Raymond Massey) wagons at Lasky Mesa.

Thu August 1
Filming guns being taken down from John Brown's wagons at Lasky Mesa.

With Olivia de Havilland at Lower Busch Gardens - Wed, July 17

With Ronald Reagan at Lasky Mesa - Tue, August 6

Fri August 2
Filming in Maj. Sumner's office, the corridor, and hospital ward.

Tue August 6
Filming on the trail at Lasky Mesa *(top left)* and in John Brown's camp.

Thu August 8 and Fri August 9
Filming in Fort Leavenworth at the WB Calabasas Ranch; THE SEA HAWK premieres at the Strand in New York City on 8/9.

Sat August 10
Filming the campfire at Sky Valley Ranch near Chatsworth, CA.

Mon August 12
Filming in Shubel Morgan's house and retakes in Maj. Sumner's office.

Wed August 14
Filming in Shubel Morgan's (Russel Simpson) barn.

Thu August 15
Filming outside Shubel Morgan's barn at the WB Calabasas Ranch.

Fri August 16
Roy Obringer to Tenny Wright: *"Last night I talked to Errol Flynn about reporting for work today at the W-B Ranch at 3:00PM, telling him we needed him to complete a sequence where he drags the kid from under the wrecked wagon to match up shots made by the 2nd unit. We need these shots to finish Gene Reynolds* [the kid] *in the picture. I told him we also may need him tonight outside the barn in scenes after the fire. Mr. Flynn informed me he positively would not work both day and night, and insists he will go home at 6:00 o'clock tonight...."* Frank Mattison to Tenny Wright: *"With reference to the copy of the memo sent you by Mr. Mattison relative to Flynn's not desiring to do day and night work and that he proposes to leave the studio at 6 o'clock tonight....If Flynn refuses to stay on and do the night work, he would be in default under his contract. For such default, you might be able to terminate the contract, or you could sue him for damages, but I feel quite certain we would not want to pursue the former course, and hauling Flynn into court and suing him for damages may prove a little awkward. The only thing that we can do, assuming we want to keep the contract with Flynn, would be possibly to report his conduct to the Screen Actors Guild, but heretofore in reporting such infractions to the Guild, the Guild insisted that their decision in any such complaints would be final, which, of course, we would not accept, because we are liable sometime in the future to find ourselves in a position where we do not want to make an issue of a situation and would rather have the court decide than the Guild."* Filming the wagon crash at the WB Calabasas Ranch and the Shubel Morgan barn at night.

Mon August 19
Filming in John Brown's Maryland hangout, and the Shubel Morgan barn at night at the WB Calabasas Ranch.

Thu August 22 through Sat August 24
Filming in the arsenal.

Mon August 26
Filming outside the arsenal at the WB Ranch; Frank Mattison: *"....Mr. Flynn informed me this morning that he would refuse to do the scene at the hanging of John Brown the way it is now written."*

Tue August 27
Filming the Delaware crossing and Maryland camp at the WB Calabasas Ranch.

Wed August 28
Filming John Brown's hanging at Lasky Mesa *(bottom left)*; Frank Mattison to Tenny Wright: *"Up to the time of my leaving the location, about 1:00 o'clock today, everything had seemed to go all right and there had been no further complaints from Flynn."*

Thu August 29
Filming in the arsenal and a process shot of the hilltop.

Fri August 30
Filming in the Washington, D.C., ballroom.

With William Lundigan, Henry O'Neill, Ronald Reagan, Olivia de Havilland, and William Marshall at Lasky Mesa - Wed, August 28

Sat August 31
Filming close-ups at the Virginia hanging and process shots of the wedding sequence.

Tue September 3
Filming in the Washington, D.C., ballroom; Bob Fellows to Hal Wallis: *"Regarding the Lee speech of which Flynn was supposed to speak part of the dialogue, Mike, after discussing it with Flynn, felt that it was out of character for Flynn to express the viewpoint contained in the lines and therefore talked Flynn out of saying them...As you remember, Flynn's objection to the scene was not that he had too little to say but that [Raymond] Massey had entirely too much to say."*

Wed September 4 and Thu September 5
Filming in the Washington, D.C., ballroom, retakes of the hanging process shots (on 9/4) and (on 9/5) retakes in the Beecher and Morgan homes.

Fri September 6
Filming outside the arsenal, Palmyra Street, and barber shop at the WB Calabasas Ranch.

Sat September 7
Filming the barbecue sequence at the WB Calabasas Ranch.

Sun September 8
Flynn refuses to shoot retakes; Frank Mattison to Tenny Wright: *"Inasmuch as Flynn refused to take a call for the retakes this afternoon….we have ordered a double to take his place in the foreground of the shot so that the retake can be made today."*

Mon September 9
Filming outside the arsenal and the barbecue at the WB Calabasas Ranch.

Tue September 10
Filming in the barracks corner; Frank Mattison to Tenny Wright: *"….we did not finish because Mr. Flynn insisted upon leaving at 3:15 in the morning. We will have at least 3 hours work there when we return."* Tenny Wright to Bob Fellows: *"I want you to immediately sit down and give me a full report on how Errol Flynn has behaved during this picture, his cooperation to calls, etc., and if he held you up at any time. I want this report on my desk no later than 6:00 PM tonight, as Mr. Warner wishes this. Needless to say, do not say anything about this note or this report. If you do not understand, come in and I will explain."* Bob Fellows to Tenny Wright: *"Dear Tenny: In answer to your note regarding Flynn's attitude in "Santa Fe Trail." I can only tell you that his behavior during the latter half of this picture, when he apparently for the first time read the script, has been one of continual complaint about his part...He precludes [sic] every statement with the fact that he is trying to do his best and then launches into a tirade against this picture and all the outdoor pictures he has ever been in...He has refused, as you know, to accept a late afternoon call and work on into the night....his attitude has been that of the typical star."*

Wed September 11
Filming process shots in the train and outside the barn; Hal Wallis to Bob Fellows: *"...the retakes of de Havilland's closeup in the scene with Flynn [are] not good. I want them done over again. This time we will have Mike direct them, and I want Flynn there working with de Havilland, instead of Henry O'Neill or a stooge talking to her. How can you expect to get any feeling into the scene? The girl is supposed to be playing a scene with a man that she's in love with, and you have Henry O'Neill reading the lines off-stage. De Havilland is very phoney in the scenes…"*

Thu September 12
Filming outside the arsenal and Fort Leavenworth at night at the WB Calabasas Ranch; Frank Mattison to Tenny Wright: *"About 11:30 last night, Mr. Flynn's man, Max, called my home and told me Mr. Flynn was quite ill and that the doctor was there, and then he had the doctor talk to me who explained that Mr. Flynn was suffering a severe case of nerves and he did not think he would be able to work either Thursday or Friday. I told him that it would be possible for us to work today (Thursday) without him, but it was almost imperative that we have Flynn out at the Ranch tonight, Thursday, so that we could finish up a big set which was left there on account of Mr. Flynn, and he said he did not know about this but that it would be better to consult with Flynn tomorrow (Thursday)...The rest you know and the result of our visit to Flynn's home at 12:00 Noon today, Thursday."* Tenny Wright to Roy Obringer: *"Dear Roy:—I know you received a copy of Mattison's note to me regarding Flynn. Will you kindly step into this and do as suggested, and have Flynn's agent straighten out the gentleman so we can get afternoon and night work out of him. Kindly let me hear from you regarding this."*

Sat September 14
Filming pickup shots of the West Point drill grounds at Providencia Ranch and retakes in the Halliday

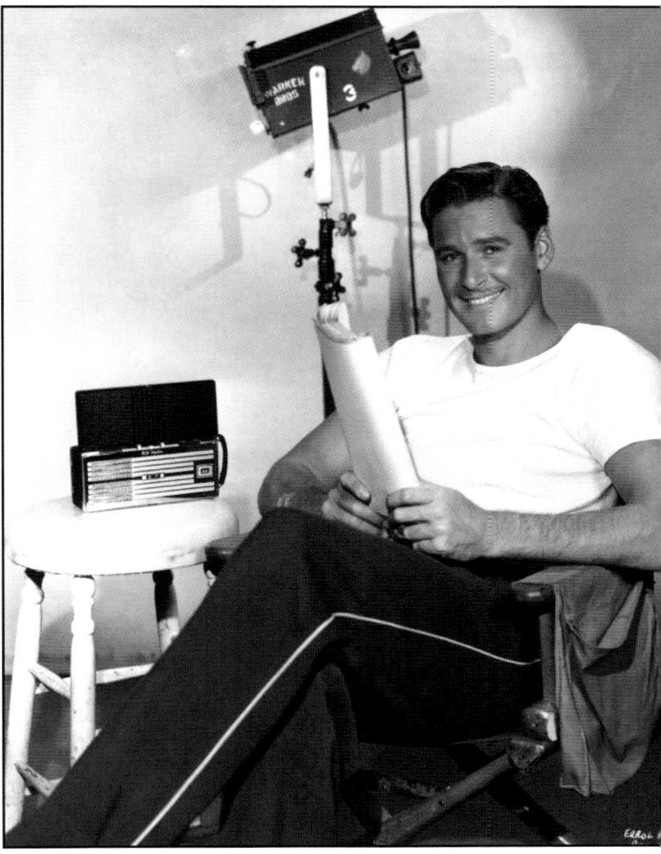

Errol Flynn Sues Publishers and Author for $2,000,000

Film Actor Charges His Reputation and Career Damaged by Reference to Him in Madrid Novel

BY JIMMIE FIDLER

Errol Flynn, dashing hero of many a thrilling screen story, believes that his reputation and professional career have been damaged to the extent of $2,000,-000 and he set that figure for his claim yesterday in a suit he filed in the United States District Court.

The defendants in the action are the New York publishing house of Harcourt, Brace & Co., Constancia de la Mora and the printing company of Quinn & Boden of New Jersey.

The basis of the action, filed by Attorney Joseph J. Cummins of the firm of Cummins & Cummins, revolves about the printing and distribution of a book titled, "In Place of Splendor, the Autobiography of a Spanish Woman."

The complaint quotes excerpts from the book, authored by Constancia de la Mora, relating a certain incident that took place prior to 1939 when he visited Spain and was wounded on the Madrid front during the revolution.

Flynn asserts in the suit that the narrative "is false and untrue in each and every respect and has no truth in fact whatever."

He said that the narrative as set forth in the novel would be understood as charging "that the plaintiff would stoop to any and all sorts of means for the purpose of obtaining publicity."

Furthermore, he claims that the book received wide circulation in Hollywood, Beverly Hills and elsewhere, and that "the statements and charges are false, malicious and untrue and unprivileged, and brought plaintiff into public scandal, hatred, ridicule and disgrace, thereby greatly injuring him and his good name and reputation."

He demands $1,000,000 compensatory damages and $1,000,000 punitive damages.

The Los Angeles Times - Thu, September 5

Advertising RCA's new portable radio

Right and below at the Los Angeles Tennis Club - Sun, September 15

With Flora Robson and Brenda Marshall re-christening the Albatross *from* THE SEA HAWK *- Thu, September 26*

freight yards at the WB Calabasas Ranch.

Sun September 15

Frank Mattison to Tenny Wright: *"The Haskin [second] unit was called Friday for 9:00 AM, but owing to Mr. Flynn's delayed appearance they did not get their first shot until 10:20 AM, but they worked through all night last night finishing at 4:45 AM this morning."* Plays at the Los Angeles Tennis Club for the Pacific Southwest Tennis Championships, losing a doubles match with Robert Peacock to Robert Carrothers and Douglas Woodbury *(top and center left)*.

Mon September 16

Filming special effects shots in and around the Shubel barn; Hal Wallis to Jack Warner: *"Flynn will finish [SANTA FE TRAIL] tomorrow. I would suggest that you have Bill Schaefer [Warner's executive secretary] make a definite appointment with Flynn for sometime tomorrow, at which time we should put the question to him pointblank as to whether or not he is going to do 'Footsteps In The Dark'. There is no use beating around the bush with him. We may as well know our position now so that we may be guided accordingly. There is no use in building sets or starting to cast and hold everything in abeyance wondering if Flynn is going to report."*

Tue September 17

Finishes SANTA FE TRAIL, filming scenes outside the arsenal at the WB Calabasas Ranch, and process shots in the barn; salary for this film is $66,667 ($1,240,359 in 2021 value).

Fri September 20

Inter-office memo from Jack Warner to Hal Wallis: *"Here is my plan of action on Flynn if we don't straighten him up definitely to do 'Footsteps In The Dark', directed by Lloyd Bacon, picture to start September 30th: We will arrange to give him a call on Monday, September 23rd, and if he doesn't show up…..we will immediately suspend him. You and I are not going to waste our time with Flynn or anyone else."* Robert Lord to Hal Wallis: *"P.S. Flynn and de Havilland are to be here Saturday morning to make color stills for the big Hearst break we have."*

Sat September 21

In a promotional photo session for SANTA FE TRAIL with Olivia de Havilland at WB Studios.

Tue September 24

Robert Lord to Hal Wallis: *"Miss de Havilland would be excellent in the part [in FOOTSTEPS IN THE DARK] if the star of the picture were not so terribly opposed to her—and she to the star."* Jack Warner to Ralph Lewis: *"Errol Flynn will start his next picture, Footsteps In The Dark, on October 14, 1940. Therefore, do not remove him from the payroll."*

Thu September 26

Re-christens the SEA HAWK ship for the benefit of Brenda Marshall, who could not be there for the original event; Flora Robson, who played Queen Elizabeth in the film, also attends *(bottom left)*.

Fri September 27

An attachment is placed on the *Sirocco* because of an outstanding lawsuit of $47,000 against Flynn's manager, Walter Heinze ($874,448 in 2021 value).

Mon September 30

Jack Warner to Hal Wallis: *"I think it would be a good idea for you to hold a meeting with Flynn in your office so you can straighten him up, for if he goes into [Robert] Lord and Lord says 'No', we will have to start all over again...I know you are better equipped to do this and as there are not many changes you can get through with him in a few minutes, so it is worth this effort. Jack."*

Wed October 2

Note to various studio executives from Flynn's assistant, Johnny Meyer: *"I have received: a. shooting script of Footsteps, etc. b. wardrobe plot c. letter to Mr. Flynn which I will deliver to Mr. Flynn in Honolulu."* Flynn is currently staying at the Royal Hawaiian Hotel.

Thu October 17

Arrives in San Francisco on a flight from Honolulu and lands at San Pedro the next day *(right)*.

PASSENGER LIST

40364 Sheet No. 2.

"CALIFORNIA CLIPPER" ARRIVED SAN FRANCISCO, CAL. OCTOBER 18, 1940.

HONOLULU, T. H. , on October 17 19 40

(Place of embarkation)

NO 18602

	NAME		AGE	SEX	Married or Single	NATIONALITY	DESTINATION	Number Pieces of Baggage
1	FLYNN, ERROL	Beverly Hills, Cal 601 No. Linden Dr	30	M	M	British	LOS ANGELES	3
2	NADLER, HENRY	1372 Bdwy, NYK	55	M	M	American	LOS ANGELES	4
3	NADLER, FLORENCE	"	50	F	M	American	LOS ANGELES	—
4	ROBINSON, EARL H.	4040 Rigali, LOS	37	M	S	American	LOS ANGELES	5
5	OLAZABAL, VICTORIA DE	680 N. Palm Dr, LOS	36	F	M	American	LOS ANGELES	—

With Brenda Marshall

October 22, 1940

TO: Warner Brothers Pictures, Inc.

For Hire of Stallion "Onyx" on

"Santa Fe Trail"

21 days at $25.00 per day . . . . . $ 525.00

Errol Flynn

Please forward check to:

W. O. Heinze
8511 Sunset Boulevard
Hollywood, California

Sat October 19

Begins work on FOOTSTEPS IN THE DARK, filming in the corridor of Warren's (Flynn) office.

Sun October 20

Guests on the NBC radio show, *Chase And Sanborn Program*.

Mon October 21

Filming in the corridor of Warren's office and in Warren's bedroom.

Tue October 22 through Fri October 25

Filming in Warren's bedroom and (on 10/23) in his boudoir.

Sat October 26

Filming in Fissue's apartment; sails with Dr. Hermann Erben on the *Sirocco* in heavy rain to Emerald Bay in Catalina.

Sun October 27

Hunting quail on Catalina with Lili, Erben, Bud and Mrs. Ernst, and *Sirocco* skipper William Keil; returns to San Pedro; Erben stays at Flynn's home.

Mon October 28

Filming in the breakfast room of Warren's home; Erben spends the day on the set.

Tue October 29

Filming in the breakfast room of Warren's home; in court with Cummings & Cummings (and Dr. Hermann Erben) for action against the Selznick company.

Wed October 30

Filming in the breakfast room of Warren's home; Erben spends the day on the set; at 1:30 pm, Flynn and Brenda Marshall release two carrier pigeons—"Miss San Francisco" and "Miss Pacific"—carrying a message from Los Angeles mayor Fletcher Bowron to San Francisco mayor Angelo Rossi declaring Freedom of the Press Week; with Erben, and later with business manager Walter Heinze to discuss plans for the Mulholland house.

Thu October 31

Filming in the breakfast room and entrance of Warren's home; with Lili and Erben at Cobina Wright's Halloween party at Ciro's; according to Erben's diary, he gives Flynn doses of hyoscine and phanadorm; salary now $6,000 per week ($111,632 in 2021 value).

Fri November 1

Filming in the living room.

Sat November 2

Filming in the entrance and living room; with Lili, Guinn "Big Boy" Williams, and Lupe Velez to Brandeis Ranch in Chatsworth, CA.

Mon November 4

Filming in the entrance and living room; with Johnny Meyers and Erben to look at Chilean actress Gloria Lynch's apartment, possibly renting it for her.

Tue November 5

Filming in the entrance and living room; with Gloria Lynch and Erben (covering for Errol by posing as her date) for dinner at a Hungarian restaurant.

Wed November 6

Filming in the Warren home and the Warren car; Lili is angry over finding out about Gloria Lynch.

Thu November 7

Filming on the backlot in the cottage (Midvale Street), in the alley (Tenement Street), and in Warren's car; Erben, Edmund Goulding,

With Olivia de Havilland and Jinx, the official mascot of the SANTA FE TRAIL junket, the film opening in that city on Friday the 13th

With Brenda Marshall releasing carrier pigeons Miss San Francisco and Miss Pacific, with Arno looking on - Wed, October 30

With Alan Hale, William Frawley, and Lee Patrick - November

With Lee Patrick - November

With Ralph Bellamy

and Gloria Lynch visit Flynn's dressing room.

Fri November 8
Filming in the Gaiety Theatre on the Vitagraph lot.

Sat November 9
Riding at his Mulholland property; drives with Lynch and Johnny Meyer to Palm Springs at 2pm.

Mon November 11 and Tue November 12
Filming in Fissue's (Noel Madison) apartment.

Wed November 13
Continues filming in Fissue's apartment, in Warren's bedroom, and in Mason's office; with Erben after work.

Thu November 14
Continues filming in Mason's (Alan Hale) office.

Fri November 15
Continues filming in Mason's office, a process shot in Warren's car, and in the cottage living room.

Sat November 16
Continues filming in the cottage, police station (on Brownstone Street on the backlot), and in the garage (on Tenement Street); sends a cable to his sister Rosemary in Belfast congratulating her on her engagement to James Elliot.

Mon November 18
Filming in the Warren home, garage, bus terminal, and Dorchester Arms Hotel on Brownstone Street.

Tue November 19
Filming in Blondie's (Lee Patrick) apartment.

Wed November 20
Continues filming in Blondie's apartment; Robert Lord to Hal Wallis: *"Dear Hal: I just saw the dailies with Flynn playing the Texan and want to attack before you attack...I know you are going to hate this part of the story; but in its context, I think audiences will laugh at it. Flynn tried his level best; Lloyd tried his level best—everybody did their best. I would suggest retaking it, but I honestly don't think that Flynn can ever do it any better...He does an Irish dialect as badly as the Texas dialect—and the idea of the Irish dialect is not half as funny as that of the Texas...In conclusion, I think that we can get by with this episode as it is now, but I don't think you will ever like it."* (Flynn's coach for the Texas dialect was his groom at Mulholland, Walter Hill.)

Fri November 22
Continues filming in Blondie's apartment.

Sat November 23
Continues filming in Blondie's apartment and Mrs. Belgarde's (Sarah Edwards) apartment.

Sun November 24
In the Screen Guide Radio performance of *Allergic to Ladies*.

Mon November 25
Ill; does not work.

Tue November 26
Filming at a taxi stand (on NY Street), and the Dorchester Arms Hotel, both on the backlot; at a party at John Decker's home at 419 N. Bundy in Brentwood, CA, to celebrate John Barrymore's divorce decree.

Wed November 27
Filming in the hallway of Blondie's apartment and in Davis' (Ralph Bellamy) office.

Thu November 28 and Fri November 29
Continues filming in Davis' office.

Sat November 30
Filming in the café.

Mon December 2
Filming in Davis' office, Mason's office, a process shot in Davis' car, in Blondie's hallway, in the F.B.I. office, a process shot in Warren's car, and on the exterior of the Warren home; *"Errol Flynn is going to be made honorary member of the New Mexico State Mounted Police."* Jimmie Fidler in the *Los Angeles Times*.

Tue December 3

Completes work on FOOTSTEPS IN THE DARK, filming in the cabin cruiser and coroner's office.

Thu December 5

Guests on Bing Crosby's NBC radio show *Kraft Music Hour* with Mary Martin and Victor Borge; Flynn sings "The Wagon Song"; leaves in the evening for a personal appearance at a Christmas charity dinner in Cleveland, returning on Wednesday the 11th on a TWA Stratoliner (along with Franklin Roosevelt Jr.) from Chicago.

Thu December 12

Leaves Pasadena at noon on a special train to promote SANTA FE TRAIL, along with Olivia de Havilland, Rita Hayworth, and many other stars, WB executives, and journalists; stops on this day include Barstow and Needles, CA.

The crowds in Pasadena seeing the junket off

With Peggy Diggin, Johnny Weismuller, Olivia de Havilland, Charlie Ruggles, Jean Parker, and Martha O'Driscoll at the Pasadena station

With WB publicity chief, Charles Einfeld. and Rudy Vallee on the junket train

Fri December 13

The SANTA FE TRAIL junket train arrives in Albuquerque, NM, at noon where Flynn temporarily loses his dog, Arno; Arno is later found and sent along to Santa Fe, NM where the junket arrives at 3pm; another junket with celebrities (including Raymond Massey, who co-starred in the film) and press also arrives from New York; over 10,000 fans are at the station to greet the stars; at 5:30 in Fort Marey Park a 40-foot-tall effigy called Tio Coco is set alight by Flynn *(bottom left and center)*, opening the Santa Fe Trail Days ceremonies. Dinner at La Fonda *(bottom right)* follows

at 7:00 with the governor of New Mexico, John E. Miles, Senator Carl Hatch, and Santa Fe mayor Alfredo Ortiz in attendance; the day is topped off with a Gran Baile costume ball at the La Fonda Terrace.

Sat December 14
Olivia de Havilland is flown back to Los Angeles, where she undergoes an emergency appendectomy; Flynn and the entourage travel to the lodge at Hyde State Park in the Sangre de Cristo mountains for an afternoon of skiing *(center left)*; Indian ceremonies at the St. Francis Auditorium follow *(below center)*, Flynn being made an honorary Pueblo Indian brave, after which there is dinner and the highly anticipated screening of SANTA FE TRAIL in three separate theaters; the evening ends with a vaudeville-styled show at Seth Hall, which is emceed by Rudy Vallee, Flynn joining in on saxophone *(below right)*.

Skiing at Hyde State Park

At the Indian ceremonial dance at St. Francis Auditorium

With Wayne Morris and Rudy Vallee

Mon December 16
Arrives back in Pasadena at 8am.

Tue December 17
The *Sirocco* sets out for Hawaii from Los Angeles with a seven-man crew skippered by William Keil; Flynn is not aboard.

Thu December 19
With Bruce Cabot and Joan Blondell at the opening of Romanoff's restaurant in Beverly Hills *(bottom left)*.

Fri December 20
Premiere of SANTA FE TRAIL in New York.

Mon December 23
The F.B.I. reports surveilling Flynn on six different dates (Oct. 17th, 28th, 30th, and 31st, Nov. 4th, and Dec. 3rd, 1940).

Thu December 26
Appears at Mayor Kelley's Christmas show in Chicago.

Fri December 27
Returns to Hollywood; the Coast Guard is asked to look for the overdue *Sirocco* which was to have arrived in Los Angeles by this point in time.

Sat December 28
SANTA FE TRAIL opens nationwide; the Sirocco finally arrives back in Los Angeles after battling sea storms on its unsuccessful attempt to sail to Hawaii, having left the coast on December 17.

Tue December 31
Flies to Honolulu.

With Bruce Cabot and Joan Blondell at Romanoff's - Thu, December 19

1941

Wed January 1

Arrives in Honolulu, staying at the Royal Hawaiian Hotel in Waikiki; Sheriff Duke Kahanamoku and his Olympic swimmer brother, Sam, meet Flynn at the airport and take him to the Pineapple Bowl football game.

Fri January 3

Moves from the Royal Hawaiian to a private cottage in Honolulu.

Mon January 13

Flies to the big island of Hawaii for sightseeing, where he is met by his new host, Senator Francis I. Brown.

Tue January 14

Flies with Senator Brown to the island of Maui for sightseeing.

Wed January 15

Flynn and the senator are house guests of a Mrs. G. R. Carter, later in the day attending a cocktail party at the home of Mr. and Mrs. Albert Waterhouse.

Thu January 16

Flynn and the senator are guests at a cocktail party hosted by ranchers Mr. and Mrs. Harold F. Rice, and later for a dinner party at the home of Mr. and Mrs. L. A. Baldwin.

Fri January 17

Flynn and the senator travel to Kona, staying at the senator's estate.

Tue January 21

Tours the Kohala Coast in the northwest area of Kona.

Wed January 22

Goes spear fishing in Kapaau.

Fri January 24

Returns to Honolulu with Senator Brown.

Mon January 27

The Chicago Tribune announces that Lili is expecting a child in May.

Tue January 28

Flies back to Kona with Senator Brown, staying at the Kona Inn.

Wed January 29

Attends a cocktail party hosted by Mr. and Mrs. Marshall Henshaw and Mr. and Mrs. Ernest Parker at the home of financier Charles Boettcher at Kalama Beach.

Thu January 30

Attends the President's Ball at the Kona Inn.

Sat February 1

Goes deep sea fishing off the coast of Kona, reeling in a 165-pound blue marlin.

Wed February 5

Returns to Honolulu.

Sat February 8

In business discussions for the purchasing of ranch property on the big island of Hawaii.

Wed February 12

Puts a $10,000 deposit down toward the $225,000 [$4,156,500 in 2021 value] purchase of the 16,000-acre Huehue Ranch in north Kona, stating that he'd *"rather live on the island of Hawaii than any place in the world."*

Thu February 13

Meets with the Stillman family, the owners of the Kona property, to close the sale.

Fri February 14

Departs Honolulu for California on the *S.S. Lurline* out of Pearl Harbor.

*Above, fishing in Hawaii -
February 1, 1941*

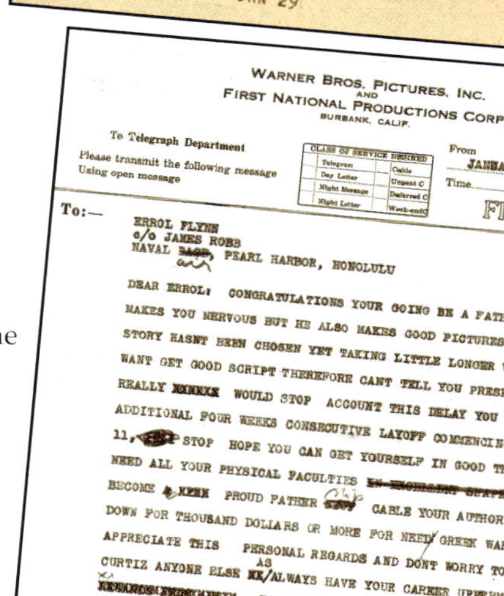

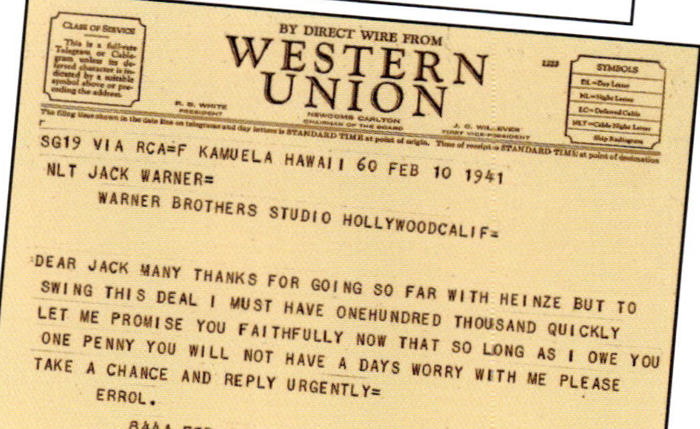

$250,000 Hawaiian Ranch Purchased by Errol Flynn

HONOLULU, Feb. 13 (AP). -The Star Bulletin said today that Errol Flynn, Hollywood movie actor, had bought the large Huehue ranch on Hawaii Island for approximately $250,000.

The Chicago Tribune
Fri, February 14

With Zsa Zsa Gabor at the Mocambo - Tue, February 25

The passenger manifest for the S.S. Lurline - Fri, February 14

Wed February 19

Arrives in San Francisco from Honolulu, flying the next day to Union Air Terminal in Los Angeles; Roy Obringer to producer Ed Selzer: *"Errol Flynn has agreed to contribute $500 [$9,237 in 2021 value] to the Greek Relief Fund. Will you please follow through on this."*

Tue February 25

At the Mocambo *(top left)*.

Wed February 26

Hal Wallis to Robert Lord: *"Please be sure and send a script to Flynn immediately so that if he has anything to say about his part we will know how to proceed....This script should be sent to Flynn through Obringer office inasmuch as Flynn is not yet on salary and Obringer will send it to him with the proper kind of letter."*

Thu February 27

FOOTSTEPS IN THE DARK opens at the Warner Downtown Los Angeles and Hollywood Theaters.

March

Hedda Hopper awards Flynn "stingiest" star in Hollywood in this month's *Photoplay* magazine.

Fri March 14

Technicolor test for DIVE BOMBER, 11am-3:35pm; Robert Lord to Hal Wallis: *"When the blue pages come flooding out, stop and consider the number of agencies and persons who will undoubtedly want changes made: 1....Mike Curtiz who, in my experience, scarcely misses a day without wanting something rewritten. Most of his changes are trivial—but they have to be rewritten. 2....The Hays office which always objects to several lines, business of drinking, etc...5....Flynn—who does not like his part; has already been after me to take things away from Joe [Fred MacMurray's role] and give them to him. Most of his changes cannot be made without wrecking the story completely.....I am going to have trouble with him for weeks...."* Location man Bill Guthrie to Tenny Wright: *"I may be talking out of turn here, but for your information I have definite instructions from the Navy Department that no dogs or pets of any kind used in the picture will be allowed on the San Diego location at the Naval Base. My reason for putting out this warning is that, as you know, heretofore Flynn has always taken his dog with him. This dog will definitely not be allowed on the location at any time. I also understand that Flynn has a bodyguard, or valet, or whatever you want to call it. This man is not on Warner Bros. payroll, and will definitely not be allowed to come on location. These are definite instructions that Comdr. [Seth] Warner, our liaison Officer, brought me this morning. He said that due to the fact that the Navy is working under war time restrictions, we must be very definite about this."*

Sat March 15

"No [personal] cameras are allowed on location." General Info (military orders).

Wed March 19

Leaves for the San Diego location, staying at the Hotel del Coronado.

Thu March 20 through Sat March 22

Begins filming DIVE BOMBER on the flying field of the North Island Navy Base, and (on 3/22) in Joe's office.

Mon March 24

Filming in Art Lyon's (Robert Armstrong) hangar, and on the flying field.

Tue March 25

Filming in the bachelors' quarters entrance and the School of Aviation Medicine.

Wed March 26

Filming on the flying field and in the squadron hangar.

Thu March 27 and Fri March 28

Filming in a field near the hangar, and (on 3/28) in the flying boat hangar, at the sea wall, and at the crossroads.

Sat March 29

Filming in Art Lyon's hangar and on the flying field.

Mon March 31 through Sat April 5

Filming on the landing field (doubling for Honolulu), at the wreck (on 4/1 and 4/3), and in the hangar (on 4/5).

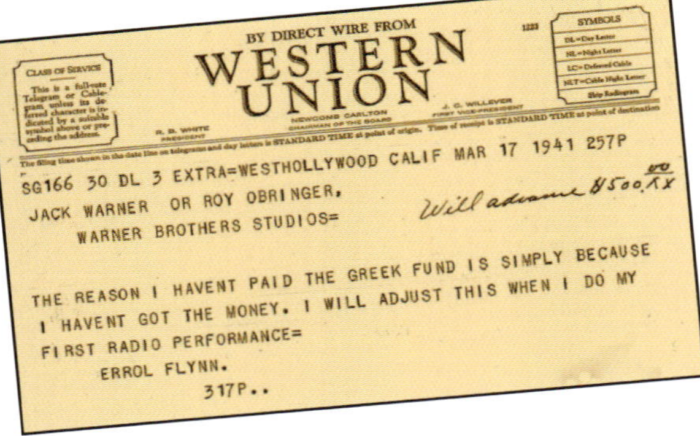

At North Island Navy Base in San Diego, CA - March

Mon April 7 and Tue April 8
Filming on the aircraft carrier *U.S.S. Enterprise*, and (on 4/8) hosts a party on the *Sirocco* "for all the biggies in the Navy."

Thu April 10
Filming on the airfield and at the lighthouse at Point Loma *(top right)*.

Fri April 11 and Sat April 12
Ill; does not work.

Mon April 14
Back at the WB studios filming in the hall and dispensary, the X-Ray room, operating room corridor, and washroom.

Tue April 15
Filming in the flight surgeon's office and in the ambulance.

Wed April 16 and Thu April 17
Filming in the ready room, and (on 4/17) in the ambulance, the operating room corridor, and washroom.

Fri April 18
Filming in the medical classroom, the dispensary, and washroom.

Sat April 19 through Tue April 22
Filming in the exam room *(bottom right)*.

Wed April 23
Filming in the research lab and animal room; hosts a party in honor of Doris Duke at the Garden House of the Beverly Hills Hotel.

Thu April 24 through Sat April 26
Filming in the low-pressure chamber; showed up late at 2pm on 4/25 because of illness; first-aid man called in to spray his throat.

Sun April 27
Is among 350 guests at the Mack Sennett Bathing Party held at the Sand and Pool Club of the Beverly Hills Hotel, with Milton Berle emceeing.

Mon April 28
Continues filming in the low-pressure chamber.

Tue April 29
Filming in the research lab and Lance's (Ralph Bellamy) office; Roy Obringer to Flynn: *"I checked with Mr. Warner last night relative to your radio program. He apparently checked with the Production Dept. to see where you stood on the finish of 'Dive Bomber,' and advised me that it would be okay for you to figure on the radio program June 5th or the regular weekly program following May 26th, as he stated there was a very definite possibility that you would be in 'Dive Bomber' on the 26th....He also stated that this okay was given upon the condition that you donate $1,000 [$18,473 in 2021 value] or at least $500 to the Greek relief benefits for its war stricken people, and in this connection he reminded me of your wire of March 17th wherein you advised him that you would pay your $500 pledge to the Greek War Relief Fund from your first radio performance....Why not, Errol, arrange your program for a week following May 26th and give $500 to the Greeks and have it all set and over with."*

Wed April 30
Continues filming in the research lab and Lance's office (12 takes due to Flynn blowing his lines); Warner Bros. purchases the title "Dive Bomber" for $250 [$4,618 in 2021 value] from pulp author, L. Ron Hubbard, who had written a story with that name for the magazine *Five Novels Monthly*, published in the July 1937 issue.

Thu May 1
Filming process shots in the test plane; filming in the research lab, exam room, animal lab, classroom, and ow-pressure chamber; Roy Obringer to Flynn: *"So that there will be no misunderstanding reference your radio program which, per my memo to you, Mr. Warner approved upon the basis that you would move it to the week following May 26th and upon the further condition that you donate $1,000 or at least $500 to the Greek War Relief Fund, Mr. Warner is inquiring today as to whether you have committed yourself to comply with the above two conditions, as I am afraid he will not approve of your radio program in the event you do not. I suggest that you get this straightened out."*

Above, at Point Loma, CA - Thu, April 10; below, the same spot today

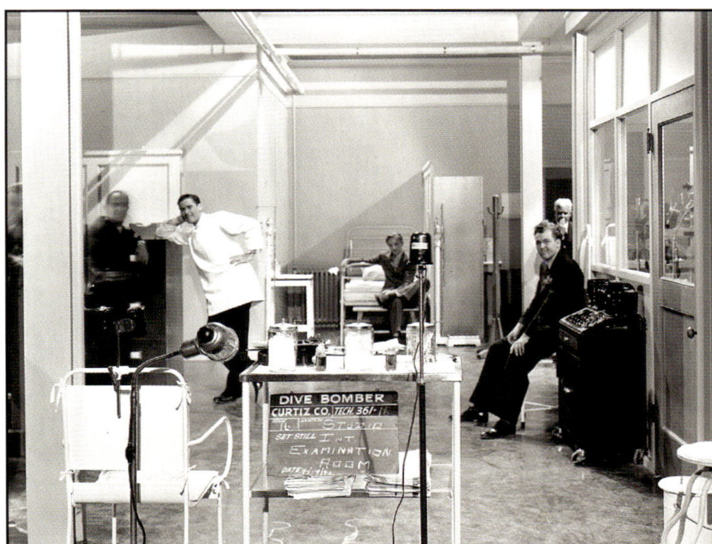

With Allen Jenkins (out of focus on the left) - Sat, April 19

As Lieutenant Doug Lee

Fri May 2
Filming process shots in the plane (Vincent Sherman temporarily directing), and with the second unit in the isolation ward corridor (worked with Sherman until 6:05pm, then complaining of illness).

Sat May 3
Ill; does not work; Roy Obringer to Flynn: *"With respect to your charity situation, in view of the comments contained in your letter, Mr. Warner is not concerning himself further with this angle."* From the WB legal department to Flynn's manager Walter Heinze: *"As you know we have extensions to May 15, 1941 for the filing of the Flynn Federal and State Income Tax Returns. Accordingly, we shall need the following amounts to meet the first installments due on that date: Federal–$12,168.56 State–$3,107.52 [$224,794 and $57,406 in 2021 value]. Unfortunately, Flynn's tax reserve account has been entirely depleted, due primarily to his extensive layoff, and secondly, because of his expenses on the Hawaiian trip."*

Mon May 5
Filming in Lyon's hangar and the workshop (Flynn blows many lines).

Tue May 6
First day of work for Alexis Smith; filming in the bar (scene needed to be broken up into shorter segments because of Flynn and MacMurray blowing their lines) and the bachelors' quarters.

Wed May 7
Continues filming in the bar and bachelors' quarters.

Thu May 8
Filming at Providencia Ranch, in Joe's (Fred MacMurray) office, and Art Lyon's workshop.

Fri May 9 and Sat May 10
Filming process shots in the radio control tower.

Mon May 12
Filming in the officers' living room.

Tue May 13
Continues filming in the officers' living room, filming in the bar, and process shots in the bomber; filming with the second unit at the crash site in Palos Verdes *(center left)*; Roy Obringer to Jack Warner: *"Wally Heinze was in today and stated that Errol Flynn...would need $15,000 [$277,100 in 2021 value] to pay his Federal and State Tax. He stated that Flynn is short of money on account of losing approximately $10,000 on the ranch deal in Hawaii, which he got out of, and having to put up his own money to build on his investment in Pasadena,*

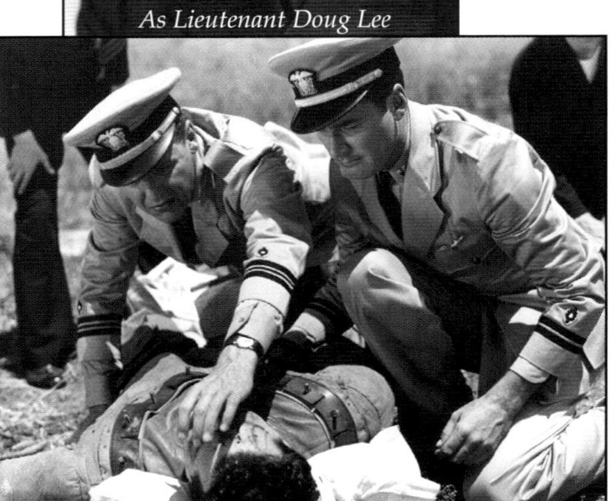

With Ralph Bellamy and Fred MacMurray - Tue, May 13

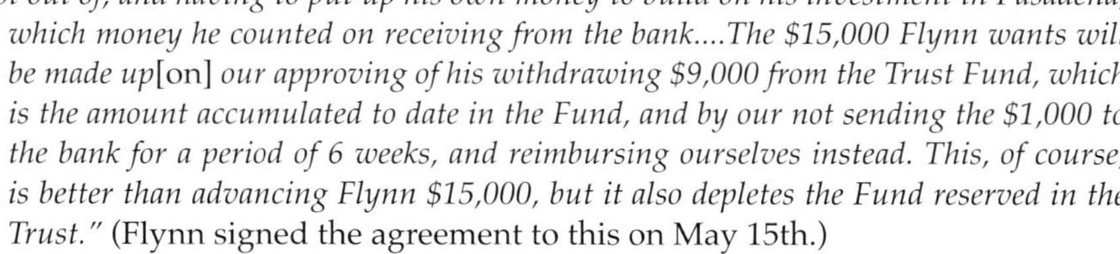

which money he counted on receiving from the bank....The $15,000 Flynn wants will be made up[on] our approving of his withdrawing $9,000 from the Trust Fund, which is the amount accumulated to date in the Fund, and by our not sending the $1,000 to the bank for a period of 6 weeks, and reimbursing ourselves instead. This, of course, is better than advancing Flynn $15,000, but it also depletes the Fund reserved in the Trust." (Flynn signed the agreement to this on May 15th.)

Wed May 14
Filming at the crossroads in Palos Verdes, process shots in the bomber, and in the training plane.

Thu May 15 and Fri May 16
Filming in the hotel dining room *(bottom left)*, and (on 5/16) in the pressure ship.

Sat May 17
Filming process shots in the pressure cabin .

Mon May 19
Filming in the training plane, the pressure ship, the torpedo lab (all process shots), and the research lab.

Tue May 20
Filming at the Providencia Ranch crossroads, and process shots in the RAF cockpit and trainer.

Wed May 21
The winners of the Warner Bros. photo contest pose with Flynn at the studio.

With Alexis Smith, Ann Doran, and Fred MacMurray - Thu, May 15

Thu May 22
Tenny Wright to Jack Warner and Hal Wallis: *"For your information, we were to test Errol Flynn today at two o'clock for his role in 'They Died With Their Boots On.'....At about twelve o'clock today, Mr. Blum, apparently Flynn's agent, called Jack Sullivan, the assistant to the picture, and notified him that Flynn would not be in today* [to] *make the tests, until he had a talk with Mr. J. L. Warner."*

Fri May 23
Filming in Art Lyon's office and the low-pressure chamber; wardrobe and makeup tests for THEY DIED WITH THEIR BOOTS ON.

Mon May 26
Filming process shots outside the pressure cabin plane, and filming in the training plane; radio performance of "Virginia City" for the Lux Radio Theatre at CBS affiliate, KNX Los Angeles.

Tue May 27
Filming process shots in the training plane; Robert Fellows to makeup men, Perc Westmore and Lou Burns: *"Confirming our conversation regarding the first series of tests of Flynn as 'Custer', in the first change when 'Custer' is a student at West Point, we will eliminate the mustache....Secondly, the chin piece was placed in the wrong position. It should be a little higher and on the next test this will be corrected. Wallis feels that the chin piece is too small and we will test with a larger chin piece....The mustache with the last change was too stiff and this will be corrected in the next series of tests...."*

Wed May 28
Filming process shots on the carrier deck; Tenny Wright to assistant director, Eric Stacy: *"Do not make any tests of Errol Flynn until he has finished in 'Dive Bomber' unless you can make them without shaving off his mustache."*

Thu May 29
Filming process shots in the pressure plane at the L.A. Icehouse.

Sat May 31
Son, Sean Leslie, is born to Lili in Los Angeles; filming process shots in the high-hat bomber and test plane.

Mon June 2
Filming process shots in the fighter plane, and filming in the pressure cabin.

Tue June 3
Finishes work on DIVE BOMBER with a process shot in the pressure cabin plane; salary for the picture is $68,857 ($1,272,018 in 2021 value); makes costume tests for THEY DIED WITH THEIR BOOTS ON.

Wed June 4
Attends a party at the Florentine Gardens; Robert Fellows to Hal Wallis: *"Flynn finished yesterday, Tuesday, June 3rd, in 'Dive Bomber', and he made costume tests in the afternoon for 'They Died With Their Boots On.'....He told me he would report for work Monday morning, June 23rd, but he insisted he was tired, etc. He is quite anxious about all phases in this picture and very enthusiastic. He wants to come in on Monday and make a test with the girl who is to play his sister* [a part later scrapped]. *He would like us to test Diana Dill* [the future Mrs. Kirk Douglas], *a new contract player here for the part of his sister. I am lining up this test for Monday afternoon and we will also test the remainder of Flynn's wardrobe."*

Sun June 8
Plays in the first round of the 16th Annual Motion Picture Tennis Tournament at the Westside Tennis Club, winning by default; further rounds are played there in the coming weeks.

Tue June 10
Tenny Wright to Hal Wallis: *"For your information, we have finished photographing Flynn in all of his changes for* [THEY DIED WITH THEIR BOOTS ON]....*Thought perhaps you might wish to let him go away for a few days unless you have some further plans for him, or changes you may wish to make in his wardrobe or makeup."*

Sat June 14
At the Brown Derby with Bud Ernst and Gwynne Pickford (Mrs. Ernst).

Sun June 15
Defeats Frank Losee in the second round of the Annual Motion Picture Tennis Tournament.

Tue June 17
Hal Wallis to Tenny Wright: *"'They Died With Their Boots On' will start shooting Wednesday, June 25th....Will you please prepare for that date and notify Flynn through the regular channels."* Tenny Wright to Frank Mattison: *"Will start Wednesday, June 25th; be sure and give Flynn his call for this date this week and get everything ready on the show. After you have called him, see me."*

With Fred MacMurray - May

At this point Flynn is living at 1709 Tropical Avenue in Beverly Hills while his Mulholland house is being built

Wed June 18
Attends a Father's Day party at Bill Jordan's Bar of Music in Miami.

Fri June 20
Flynn's 32nd birthday.

Sat June 22
Defeats Oleg Cassini and Gilbert Roland in the quarter finals of the Motion Picture Tennis Tournament,

Mon June 23
Robert Fellows to Hal Wallis: *"Flynn called me at home last night and wanted to know when we are going to start the picture....I told him his call was to be ready Wednesday morning to shoot the exterior West Point and he told me he got the same call from the Production Department through his man....He asked me to tell you and Mr. Warner that it was very unfair for the studio to expect him to start another tough picture just after he finished one. That he was coming into the studio today to see you and Mr. Warner and that he is leaving tomorrow night for New York. He said that he will report to the studio a week from tomorrow, July 1st to be prepared to start on Wednesday, July 2nd."*

Tue June 24
Tenny Wright to all departments: *"This is to inform you that 'They Died With Their Boots On' will start shooting as of Wednesday, July 2nd. Kindly make preparations for this date."*

Thu June 26
In Dallas for a fund raiser in support of the British War Relief.

Sun June 29
Loses to Lloyd Hanson in the finals of the Motion Picture Tennis Tournament at the Westside Tennis Club.

Mon June 30
Has wardrobe and makeup tests with Olivia de Havilland *(top left)*.

Tue July 1
Reports to the studio to have his hair dyed dark blond.

Wed July 2
Begins filming THEY DIED WITH THEIR BOOTS ON with the scene in Taipe's (Stanley Ridges) quarters at West Point; Flynn late because of hair being prepared.

Thu July 3
More filming in Taipe's quarters; wire from Jack Warner to Flynn: YOUR VERY COMPLICATED WIRE REFERENCE THE USO DRIVE AND SEEING ME IS RATHER AMUSING. WHAT IS THERE TO SEE ME ABOUT. YOU WERE ASKED TO CONTRIBUTE TO THE USO AND IF YOU DON'T WANT TO GIVE BY YOUR OWN FREE WILL AND GOODNESS OF HEART IT IS NEEDLESS TO BOTHER WALLY HEINZE OR EVEN WESTERN UNION TELEGRAPH COMPANY. PLEASE STOP ANNOYING YOURSELF ON SUCH MATTERS. ALL YOU HAVE TO DO IS THE SAME AS EVERYONE ELSE WHO HAS GIVEN JUST SIGN A BLANK X FOR X DOLLARS AND GIVE. ALL THIS NONSENSE ABOUT MAKING TRADES IS SOMETHING I AM NOT INTERESTED IN SO PLEASE SEND AN IMPORTANT AMOUNT OF MONEY FOR THE BOYS WHO, I HOPE IT DOESN'T COME TO PASS BUT YOU CAN NEVER TELL, ARE MAKING IT POSSIBLE TO GET THREE SQUARES FOR YOU AND MYSELF ON THAT OLD ROUND TABLE. THE FIRST DAILIES ON BOOTS REALLY HAD A KICK IN THEM. HAPPY FOURTH OF JULY TO YOU LILI AND SEAN.

Sat July 5
Finishes filming in Taipe's quarters; filming the Washington, D.C., scenes.

Mon July 7
Filming of Custer (Flynn) arriving at West Point at Lower Busch Gardens in Pasadena, CA *(bottom left)*; a permit is given Flynn to begin construction of his home on Mulholland Highway in the Hollywood Hills.

Tue July 8
Filming of the parade ground at Lower Busch Gardens in Pasadena, CA; Jack Warner to Flynn: *"I returned from my first voyage on the South Wind* [Warner's yacht] *and I am very sorry you weren't at White's Landing* [in Catalina] *on the*

Celebrating Olivia de Havilland's birthday (a day early) with a birthday cake - Mon, June 30

With Joe Sawyer at Lower Busch Gardens - Mon, July 7

With Olivia de Havilland at Lower Busch Gardens - Wed, July 9

Fourth on Sunday. It was really lovely over there, and I hope to see you this Sunday if you are coming over. When I returned this morning I thought sure I would find your U.S.O. Contribution, but inasmuch as your wire of the 3rd stated that you and Wally Heinze wanted to come in and see me to discuss the amount, I will be very happy to do this. You know I am always glad to see you, and if you will phone my secretary I will be glad to make a date suitable to your convenience."

Wed July 9

Continues filming on the parade grounds; first scenes with de Havilland *(top left)*.

Thu July 10

Continues filming on the parade grounds *(right)*; Hal Wallis to Jack Warner: *"Eddie Goulding told me this morning that Flynn had dropped in to see him last night, and they discussed the Constant Nymph. Goulding asked Flynn when he would finish this picture* [THEY DIED WITH THEIR BOOTS ON], *and Flynn thought the latter part of September, afterwhich, Flynn said, he was going to have a four week vacation. This is for your information, in the event we do decide to put 'Nymph' into production following 'Boots.'"* Hal Wallis to director, Raoul Walsh: *"In tonight's dailies, I don't think the action was very good where Flynn grabs hold of Kennedy, and pushes him over. It was too slow, and the whole thing failed to have a kick, because of the time taken by Flynn to step out of line, reach over and grab Kennedy, shake him and push him over. There was so much time elapsed that the Sergeant or Major Taipe, or someone could have stopped him or called out an order or something, instead of just standing around waiting for the conclusion of the action. I think it would have been much better had Flynn just reached out and socked Kennedy with his fist, after Kennedy spoke his line. In that way, it would have happened very quickly, before anyone could do anything about it and the action on the screen would have been better."*

Fri July 11 and Sat July 12

Filming of the railroad station on WB Stage 7 and (on 7/12) in the Commandant's office.

Sun July 13

Flynn's beloved dog Arno is lost at sea, having fallen overboard from the *Sirocco*.

With Joe Sawyer and Arthur Kennedy at Lower Busch Gardens - Thu, July 10

Waiting to film the hospital scene - Fri, July 18

Mon July 14

Filming of the porch scene at the Sheridan home.

Tue July 15

Continues filming in the Commandant's office and in the West Point classroom.

Wed July 16

Filming scenes at Sullivan's place.

Thu July 17

Continues filming at Sullivan's place and the wedding scene in Bacon's garden.

Fri July 18

Continues filming at Sullivan's place and the hospital scene *(bottom left)*.

Sat July 19

Filming in the Bacon home.

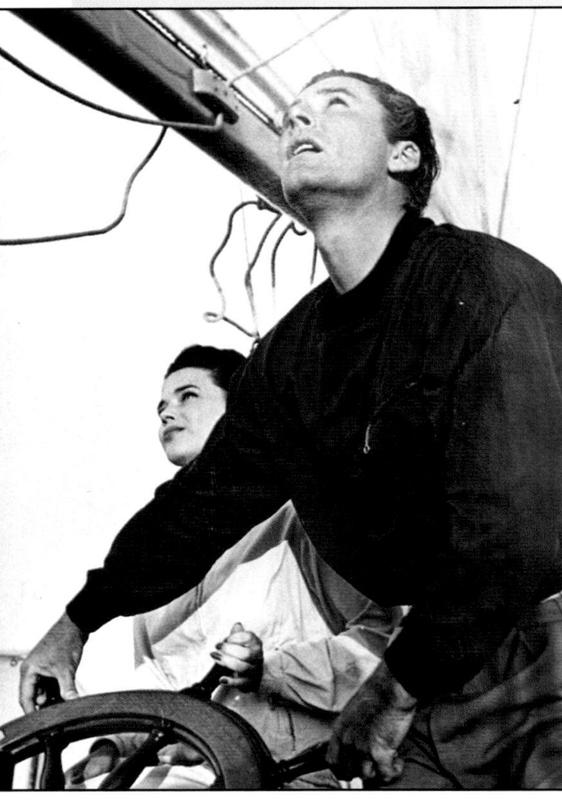

*Above, manning the wheel with
Peggy LaRue Satterlee,
and below, up on the mast of the* Sirocco -
Sun, August 3, Catalina, CA

Sun July 20

At the Coral Casino of the Santa Barbara Biltmore, entertaining guests (including Doris Duke Cromwell) with his skill off the 30-foot diving platform.

Mon July 21

Filming in the Bacon home in the kitchen, dining room, and hallway.

Tue July 22

Filming retakes at Lower Busch Gardens in Pasadena, CA; more filming in the Bacon home.

Wed July 23 and Thu July 24

Continues filming in the Bacon home and (on 7/24) the restaurant scene in Washington, D.C., with Sydney Greenstreet.

Sat July 26

Filming in the General's office, Scott's (Sydney Greenstreet) office, and the farmhouse.

Mon July 28

Filming in the War Department and on the backlot on Dijon and Bonnyfeather Streets.

Tue July 29

Filming at the farmhouse and in the Bacon home drawing room.

Wed July 30

Filming the battle scenes of Hilltop and the bridge at the WB Calabasas Ranch; riding extra, John "Jack "Budlong, falls off his horse and onto his sword, sustaining a fatal wound; dies on 8/5.

Thu July 31

Continues filming the Hilltop battle scenes and at the farmhouse.

Fri August 1

Continues filming the Hilltop battle scene and Civil War sequence; after many ups and downs in their marriage, Lili, along with two-month-old Sean, leaves Flynn for good.

Sat August 2

Sails the *Sirocco* from San Pedro harbor to Catalina island for a *Life* magazine photo layout by photographer, Peter Stackpole; along for the trip is 15-year-old Peggy LaRue Satterlee *(top left)*; parties at the Hawaiian Hut in Fourth of July Cove.

Sun August 3

Is photographed swimming, skin-diving, spearfishing, and climbing the *Sirocco* mast *(bottom left)* by Stackpole; dines again at Fourth of July Cove; returns to San Pedro at 10:30pm.

Mon August 4

Calls for an ambulance because of sickness (hoarse voice); rests in hospital and decides against working.

Tue August 5

Columnist Harrison Carroll announces that Flynn has been given a gift of a seven-month-old boxer dog from his friend and double, Jim Fleming; Frank Mattison to Tenny Wright: *"....owing to the hoarseness of Errol Flynn's voice, he was sent to Dr. Turnbull who examined his sinus, but I believe we can have him back in a day or two."*

Wed August 6

Ill; does not work; Frank Mattison to Tenny Wright: *"I talked with Mr. Walsh this morning and it appears he has talked to Dr. Turnbull, the doctor who has charge of Errol Flynn in the hospital, and from what Walsh tells me they expect Flynn to be able to come back to work on tomorrow, Thursday, about noon...."*

Thu August 7 to Fri August 18

Ill; does not work.

Fri August 8

Tenny Wright to Frank Mattison: *"We just heard from our own Doctor that Errol Flynn will not be out of the Hospital until either Monday or Tuesday, and our Doctor advises that he should not come back to work for at least another couple*

Film Extra Killed in War Scene
Heir to Millions of Budlong

Jack Budlong, film extra player, who died Tuesday of injuries received on a motion-picture set, yesterday was disclosed as the heir to the multimillion-dollar fortune of the late Milton John Budlong, automobile pioneer, who died July 7, last.

The 30-year-old player was impaled on an old-time Civil War saber when he was thrown from his horse during filming of the Battle of Gettysburg scene for a forthcoming motion picture at a ranch at Calabasas on July 30.

Listed by the Coroner's office as "Jack" Budlong, it was learned yesterday he is the John Budlong, son of Mrs. Margaret Budlong of Beverly Hills and the late car magnate, who lived at Newport, N.Y.

Last September he was married to Verne Rogers, daughter of Mrs. James Whitlock of Richmond, Va., at La Cruces, N.M. He lived at 10703 Ashton Ave., West Los Angeles.

The Los Angeles Times - Thu, August 7

of days after that, so the best I can tell at this time we may get Flynn about Thursday, so we will have to scare up something [else] to do—long shots, etc.—maybe with Indians or perhaps with the Troop under march—to keep the company going." Jack Warner to Tenny Wright: *"I received the following message from Dr. Bluechel about Errol Flynn: 'Mr. Flynn is definitely improved, his temperature being normal today. However, he will probably have to remain in the hospital until Monday or Tuesday of next week, and he should not return to work immediately after leaving the hospital—probably not before the end of the week.'"* Ralph Lewis, reporting at the inquest into the death of stuntman John "Jack" Budlong, testified that Budlong was portraying a 1st sergeant or lieutenant leading Union soldiers towards a bridge when he was thrown from his horse. He first arose on his own and walked to a fence. *"When given first aid was fully conscious and did not appear to believe he had been badly hurt.....the sabre had gone through the back at a point just below the shoulder blade and about an inch and a half from the spine, and the point of it had come out below the eighth rib on the left side in front— only about half an inch of the sabre had come clear through. It apparently ticked the lung cavity, gone through the diaphragm, and had also punctured the transverse colon."*

Tue August 12
DIVE BOMBER is given a triple-theater premiere in San Diego; Flynn does not attend.

Wed August 13
The Los Angeles family court is told that Flynn needs $14,595 for monthly living costs ($269,618 in 2021 value)—the court disagrees; with concern over the potential lawsuit relating to the death of cavalry extra, Jack Budlong, Jack Warner writes to Tenny Wright: *"Tomorrow by 2:30 we must decide if we are going to continue 'They Died With Their Boots On.'"*

Mon August 18
Returns to the studio to film scenes in the committee room in Washington, D.C., and the triumphal return of Custer to Monroe *(above right)*.

Filming Custer's homecoming - Mon, August 18

Tue August 19
Filming scenes in the Custer home; Frank Mattison to Tenny Wright: *"Mr. Flynn was at work yesterday [8/18], as you know, but he told me he was very weak, but he felt that a couple of days inside and he would be much better. I spoke to him about going out to the Ranch but he said to let him stay in at least until he got his strength back enough so that he could go out to the Ranch on the Exterior."*

Wed August 20
Filming in the Bacon home study; Flynn goes to the doctor's office.

Thu August 21
Filming continues in the Bacon home, and the Custer bedroom on Stage 16; Frank Mattison to Tenny Wright: *"It was necessary for Mr. Flynn to go to the Doctor's office yesterday [8/20] noon again, and he was gone for about 1 ½ hours."* DIVE BOMBER opens.

Fri August 22
Finishes filming in Custer's bedroom, the departure scene with de Havilland *(bottom right)*.

Sat August 23
Filming in the Bacon home dining room; films retakes of scenes in the committee room.

Filming at Iverson Ranch in Chatsworth, CA - Mon, August 25

Filming the departure scene with Olivia de Havilland - Fri, August 22

CUMMINS & CUMMINS

```
                        ERROL FLYNN

        EQUITIES IN REAL AND PERSONAL PROPERTY AS PER AUDIT

               BY HASKINS & SELLS, C.P.A., dated 9/9/41


REAL PROPERTY:                                      $  2,402.62
                                                      30,820.32
    601 No. Linden Drive Beverly Hills                 4,000.00
    Mulholland Highway Property                       51,792.94
    Utah Farm Acreage                                    400.00
    La Nola Apartments                                            $89,415.88
    Sunset Lot


PERSONAL PROPERTY:                                    13,300.00
                                                      17,483.85
    Boat "Sirocco"                                     6,900.95
    Cash Value of Insurance                            7,083.31
    Automobile, Jewelry & Personal Effects            3,000.00
    Investment in Crude Oils, Ltd.                     5,700.00
       "        "   Flynn-Hill Productions                       $53,468.11
       "        "   Listed Securities
                                                                $142,883.99
```

Above, with G. P. Huntley and Charlie Grapewin at Lasky Mesa, CA - September; below, the same location today

Mon August 25
Filming the wagon train at Iverson Ranch in Chatsworth, CA (*previous page, bottom left*).

Tue August 26
Filming the Fort Lincoln scenes and Custer's home at the WB Calabasas Ranch.

Wed August 27
Filming the hoot owl sequence in the Bacon home garden on WB Stage 12; Raoul Walsh to Robert Fellows: *"I had to let Flynn go to the doctor at 4 o'clock so got very few scenes with him."*

Thu August 28 and Fri Aug 29
Continues filming the Fort Lincoln scenes (an unbilled Eleanor Parker worked on this day).

Sat August 30
Filming in the Bacon house study and balcony.

Tue September 2
Filming at Fort Lincoln at the WB Calabasas Ranch, and wagon train scenes at Iverson Ranch in Chatsworth; Flynn has been leaving early for several days for doctor visits.

Wed September 3 and Thu September 4
Filming at Iverson mountain pass and (on 9/3) at the river bank.

Fri September 5 and Sat September 6
Filming of the canteen scenes on WB Stage16.

Mon September 8
Filming the fight scene in the canteen.

Tue September 9
Filming the pow-wow and battle scenes at Lasky Mesa, CA; more filming of the Fort Lincoln scenes, and in the company office on WB Stage 16.

Wed September 10
Is given an advance by Warner Bros. of $24,000 ($443,360 in 2021 value) to cover tax payments on September 15; continues filming the Fort Lincoln, canteen, and Custer home scenes at the WB Calabasas Ranch; Hal Wallis to Raoul Walsh: *"We should retake the shot of where Flynn is strangling Taipe. Flynn's voice was much too melodramatic, and the action also was overdone. The way he had his face screwed up, I'm afraid he is going to get a laugh. You will have to tone it down, and watch it."*

Thu September 11
Filming the Battle of Little Big Horn at Lasky Mesa, CA.

Fri September 12 and Sat September 13
Ill; does not work.

Sun September 14
On his yacht, the *Sirocco*.

Mon September 15
Filming at the farmhouse, Fort Lincoln, and the jail interior at the WB Calabasas Ranch; Frank Mattison to Tenny Wright: *"I talked with Flynn late Saturday before he left the Hospital for his boat and he promised me faithfully that he would be at the Ranch this morning at 9:00AM."*

Tue September 16
Filming in Custer's tent on WB Stage 7; Flynn is scheduled to see a medical specialist in New York and on this day requests permission to do the Kate Smith program on October 10th while there; he also asks permission to be on the Silver Theater program in Hollywood on November 30th.

Wed September 17
Filming the wagon train night encampment and Fort Lincoln interior; the Superior Court finally reaches a judgment in favor of Myron Selznick for $15,000 ($277,100 in 2021 value), representing 10% back commission.

Thu September 18
Flynn visits his doctor at 4pm.

Fri September 19
Filming at Fort Lincoln at the WB Calabasas Ranch; Frank Mattison to Tenny Wright: *"Last night when*

[2nd asst. director] Claude Archer talked to Max (Flynn's man), Max said that Mr. Warner had sent word to Flynn that he wanted to see him this morning, Friday."

Sat September 20

Filming the Battle of Bull Run at the WB Calabasas Ranch; at the Mocambo nightclub with Bruce Cabot, where he engages in a fight with columnist Jimmie Fidler, who had written negatively about the loss of Flynn's dog, Arno; later at the Scheherazade Restaurant he demonstrates the infamous "slap" he gave Fidler and exhibits the bloody ear he received from a fork stab by Fidler's wife.

Mon September 22

Filming at the Bacon home balcony and study, the interior of the covered wagon, the Custer home porch, and the railroad carriage; this day would be the very last in which Errol Flynn and Olivia de Havilland ever filmed scenes together; unfortunately, no stills are taken this day.

Tue September 23

Filming in Sullivan's place, at West Point, and in the canteen.

Wed September 24

Frank Mattison to Tenny Wright: *"We still do not know at this time, 6:30AM, whether Mr. Flynn has to appear in the Beverly Hills Court today or not* [for the Jimmie Fidler brawl]*....if he has to go to Court today, it means we will have to go back to the Ranch again tomorrow to clean up the Civil War stuff...."* Filming the battle of Hanover and at the farmhouse at the WB Calabasas Ranch.

Thu September 25

Filming close-ups of Custer's last stand and death at Lasky Mesa; Frank Mattison to Tenny Wright: *"We did not get to shoot the Int. Senate Committee room as Flynn complained of being sick and went directly home from location. He also phoned Russ Saunders from his home at 6:00 o'clock* [in the morning] *informing him that he did not feel well and that he would not be out to work this morning, but would be there at 1:00PM unless he had a decided change for the worse."*

Fri September 26

Continues filming of Custer's last stand; Frank Mattison to Tenny Wright: *"Flynn did not arrive at the location until 2:00PM* [this] *afternoon and consequently we had a very slim day so far as results were concerned."* At Ciro's for the going-away party given by Hal Roach for Ben Lyon and Bebe Daniels, who were leaving for Britain to aid in the war effort.

Sat September 27 and Mon September 29

Continues filming of Custer's last stand.

Tue September 30

Completes THEY DIED WITH THEIR BOOTS ON with scenes at Lasky Mesa, and West Point; at a hearing earlier in the day before Justice Cecil D. Holland in the Beverly Hills Court, the battery complaint against Flynn by columnist Jimmie Fidler is dropped, with Flynn assuring the court he *"will not punch Fidler any more."*

October

At this point, Flynn has been living at the home of Bruce Cabot, awaiting completion of the house on Mulholland Drive in the Hollywood Hills.

Travels to Mexico, then flies to the Bahamas, Nassau, Cuernavaca, and back to Mexico City.

Wed October 1

Meets with Lili's lawyers, Loeb and Loeb, concerning property settlements and support payments: is forced to give up all household furniture from 601 N. Linden, his Cadillac, one-half interest in Crude Oil Inc., half of all shares of Flynn and Thomson Inc., some of his South Pasadena property, pay $1,500 per month alimony, $100 a month for Sean's education ($27,710 and $1,847, respectively, in 2021 value), and the income tax on the alimony.

Thu October 2

Leaves for New York, commencing four weeks' vacation without pay.

Fri October 3

Arrives in New York with Buster Wiles, staying at the Ritz Hotel.

Sat October 4

Flies to Chicago with Buster Wiles; while there they visit friends in Madison, WI.

With Charlie Grapewin at Lasky Mesa, CA - Thu, September 25

Flynn, Fidler Fight in Film Night Club

Wife of Columnist Enters Melee, Injuring Actor After He Knocks Down Her Husband

"The Star-Spangled Banner" saved the day in a bout between Errol Flynn, motion-picture star, and Jimmie Fidler, cinema columnist, and his wife Bobbe, which took place early yesterday morning in a night club on the Sunset Strip.

Right at the moment when it looked as if the fight might grow into a real fisticuffs, someone ordered the playing of the National Anthem, everybody stood at attention, and the adversaries in the battle were never permitted to resume their cafe joust.

The encounter between Flynn and Fidler had its setting at the Mocambo Cafe, and Flynn, who was at one time on the Olympic Games boxing team from England, became involved in what was practically a battle royal because Bobbe Fidler, Jimmie's wife, also entered the fray.

HOLLYWOOD SENSATION

Varying accounts were given of what occurred by the principals in the combat, which lasted scarcely more than a minute, and various alleged eyewitnesses among the night club attaches and others.

The event caused a sensation in Hollywood, coming as it did following Fidler's appearance as a witness before the Senate subcommittee which has been investigating the film industry because of asserted warmongering.

WIFE JOINS FIGHT

"Fidler told one too many lies about the motion picture business," declared Flynn, right after the clash. "That's why I went up to his table and told him what I thought about him. I put my left fist up against his chin and gave him a slap with my right hand on the side of the head. I said, 'You're not worth a fist.'

"Then his wife became angered and I tried to hold her to one side, still gripping Fidler, but finally she jabbed at me with a fork, which would have stuck me in the eye had I not turned my head. Instead it pierced my ear.

"I must say that I admire Mrs. Fidler, God bless her. She has the courage to try to defend her husband — much more courage than he himself has."

Jimmie Fidler

Errol Flynn

The Los Angeles Times
Mon, September 22

Mon October 6

Flies back to New York with Buster Wiles.

Wed October 8

Flynn has committed to do the Kate Smith radio show without the approval of Warner Bros. *(top right).*

Thu October 9

Telegram from Roy Obringer to Charles Einfeld: MR. WALLIS LAST NIGHT GAVE WALLY HEINZE FLYNN'S BUSINESS MANAGER OUR APPROVAL FLYNN APPEAR SMITH PROGRAM TENTH SUBJECT TO CONDITION THAT FLYNN SUBMIT RADIO SCRIPT TO EINFELD FOR HIS APPROVAL TO THE END NOTHING IN SCRIPT OBJECTIONABLE OR DETRIMENTAL TO OUR AND FLYNN'S INTERESTS [Flynn was staying at the Sunset Towers in New York]. Telegram from Flynn to Hal Wallis: THANKS HAL THAT WAS VERY NICE OF YOU.

Fri October 10

Appears on Kate Smith's radio program.

Fri November 7

Lili sues for divorce.

Wed November 12

Performs in a comedy skit on the NBC radio program, *The Eddie Cantor Show.*

Sun November 16

Visits the Ruptured and Crippled Children's Hospital *(top left);* "Errol Flynn, star of 'They Died With Their Boots On', presents the boots he wore in the film to little Michael Rockman, age three and a half, at the Ruptured & Crippled Children's Hospital in New York. Flynn enlisted in the campaign against Infantile Paralysis which will begin with the President's Birthday Party January 30th." Photoplay magazine.

Mon November 17

Radio performance of "They Died With Their Boots On" for the Cavalcade of America, radio network; after the show, is presented with the Young America National Weekly's Popularity Award by the magazine's publisher, Stuart Scheftel; wire from publicity director Robert Taplinger to Roy Obringer: PLEASE AIR MAIL TO ME RELEASE TO BE SIGNED BY FLYNN WHICH STATES THAT IN RETURN FOR STUDIO PERMISSION FOR HIM TO APPEAR ON SILVER THEATER PROGRAM DECEMBER 7 HE WILL ACCEPT NEW YORK MIRROR AWARD ON STAGE OF STRAND THEATRE AND PARTICIPATE IN INDIAN INDUCTION CEREMONIES IN CENTRAL PARK MONDAY DECEMBER 1 AND COOPERATE ANY OTHER PUBLICITY ENDEAVORS AT HIS DISCRETION.

Wed November 19

THEY DIED WITH THEIR BOOTS ON opens at the Strand in New York City.

Mon November 24

In New York's Central Park for initiation into the Sioux Indian tribe *(bottom left);* his given Indian name is O-Han-Zee.

Thu November 27

Is a guest with sportscaster Ted Husing on Jack White's radio show; "Errol Flynn, WB star who won the local Sunday Mirror Magazine's Motion Picture Medal of Merit, will be presented with the award by pic critic Lee Mortimer on the Strand's stage this evening at 6:30 o'clock, and Harry Hershfield will act as master of ceremonies." The Film Daily.

Fri November 28

Returns to California with Buster Wiles; his new Packard car is awaiting him.

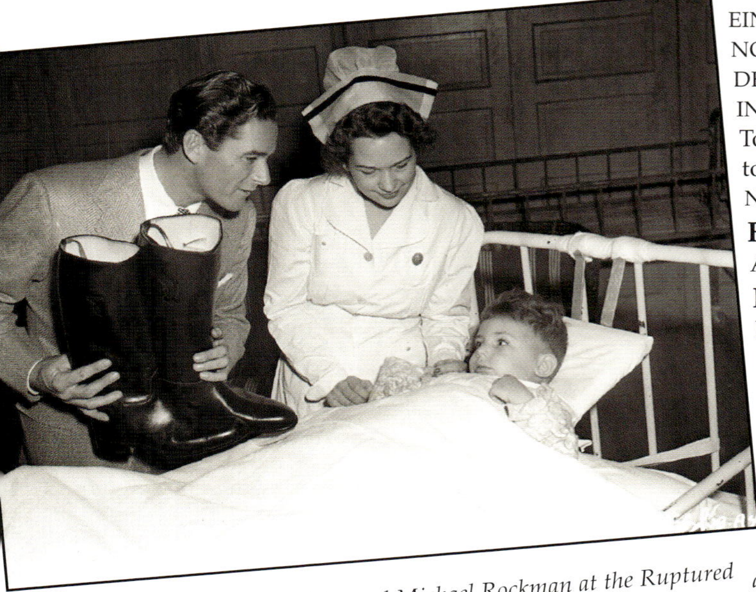

With nurse Marie Franklin and Michael Rockman at the Ruptured and Crippled Children's Hospital in New York City - Sun, November 16

Being initiated into the Sioux tribe in New York's Central Park - Mon, November 24

The two Western Union telegrams shown at top right read:

CLASS OF SERVICE — This is a full-rate Telegram or Cablegram unless its deferred character is indicated by a suitable symbol above or preceding the address.

BY DIRECT WIRE FROM WESTERN UNION

SF152 15 COLLECT HOTSPRINGS ARK OCT 8 1941 720P

HAL WALLIS

WARNER BROS STUDIO

FLYNN PHONING FRANTICALLY REFUSED TALK TO HIM BE POSITIVE HE RESTRAINED FROM RADIO APPEARANCES.

JACK WARNER.

BY DIRECT WIRE FROM WESTERN UNION

WG-5. NEWYORK NY OCT 9 1941

EINFELD TO WALLIS----UNDERSTAND FULLY ABOUT FLYNN. NO ONE WILL CONTACT HIM ALTHO FLYNN TELEPHONED BLUMENSTOCK LAST NIGHT AND WANTED TO KNOW WHY HE WAS BEING HELD OFF KATE SMITH PROGRAM. BLUMENSTOCK EXPLAINED THAT FLYNN HAD MADE THESE ARRANGEMENTS WITHOUT STUDIOS PERMISSION AND THAT FLYNN WAS UNAUTHORIZED TO DO SO. FLYNNS LAST WORD WAS HE WAS GETTING IN TOUCH WITH JL AT HOT SPRINGS.

Sun December 7
Performs in the NBC radio comedy, "For Richer, For Richer" *(top right),* which is preempted due to the bombing of Pearl Harbor on that day.

Wed December 10
Attends a party at the Rain Room of the Beverly Hills Tropics.

Thu December 11
It is reported to Flynn's accountant/managers, Heinze and Blum, that Flynn's illness on THEY DIED WITH THEIR BOOTS ON is not a result of anything in the filming environment and therefore not compensable.

Fri December 19
Performing with Flora Robson in "The Lady Vanishes" on the *Phillip Morris Playhouse* radio program.

Sat December 20
Attends the engagement party for Ava Gardner and Mickey Rooney at the Beverly Hills Tropics.

Sun December 28
Attends the wedding of Gloria Vanderbilt to Pasquale di Cicco in Santa Barbara and serves as an usher; the best man was Bruce Cabot.

At the NBC Radio studio with director Conrad Nagel - Sun, December 7

1942

Thu January 1
THEY DIED WITH THEIR BOOTS ON opens.

Fri January 2
Hal Wallis to Roy Obringer: *"Flynn was here Wednesday. I gave him a treatment to read and asked him to come in this morning to have a talk about the story and he promised to do so....I wish you would notify his agent or Wally Heinz that Flynn is on salary, that we are preparing a picture, and he is subject to call. I don't want him running off to Catalina and getting stuck and stalling me three or four days at a time when we have to start a picture in about ten days. We need him for wardrobe and a lot of other things, including German lessons which I spoke to him about, and I want you to tell Flynn's agent and his business manager that I want to see him Monday morning at 11:00 o'clock, and we want him available at all times after that to actively prepare this picture."*

Tue January 6
On or about this date Flynn finally moves into his new house (which he calls Mulholland Farm) in the Hollywood Hills; his live-ins are butler Alex Pavlenko, grounds keeper Mr. George, and secretary, 18-year-old Mary Ann Hyde; his phone number is CR1-8232.

Fri January 9
The Odessa American News (TX) reports that Flynn is down to his original pair of Rhodesian ridgeback dogs.

The New Jersey Record - *Tue, January 6*

Tue January 13
Hal Wallis to Tenny Wright: *"Be sure that Errol Flynn is given a definite call to be in the studio at 10: o'clock every morning to spend a couple of hours on his German and to spend the rest of the time with* [director, Raoul] *Walsh getting his wardrobe set, and all other preparations made for the picture."* Attends a party at Ching How restaurant in North Hollywood (owned by noted cinematographer, James Wong Howe); Cary Grant is also in attendance.

Thu January 15
Paul Nathan to Jack Warner and Hal Wallis: *"You can bet your bottom dollar Flynn won't be here on Monday...He had a wire from Mr. Warner to be at the meeting Monday and you know that he knows what it is about. I told him that for business reasons it was imperative that he be here Monday. He laughed and said, 'I'll probably see you a week from today,' and hung up. I told all of the above to Obringer tonight."*

Fri January 16
Flynn is skiing at Sugar Bowl Ski Resort near Norden, CA.

Flynn's house on Mulholland Drive in the Hollywood Hills, and below, the circular "casino" - photos taken by the author on Sat, April 11, 1981

Sun January 18

Telegram from Flynn to Hal Wallis: AM IN BED WITH SEVERE COLD SINUS IF DUBIOUS CALL DR VERNON AT SUGAR BOWL OUT OF TRUCKEE CALIF; Flynn's contract is temporarily suspended while he ails.

Thu January 22

Roy Obringer to Wally Heinze: *"At the present time there is a charge on our books for personal telephone calls made by Mr. Errol Flynn in the amount of thirty dollars and ninety-five cents ($30.95) [$520.11 in 2021 value] and which, despite numerous billings has not been paid….I would greatly appreciate your cooperation if you would arrange to have Mr. Flynn send me his check in the above amount, made payable to Warner Bros. Pictures, Inc. so that this matter will be taken care of before our next audit, which is due in about two weeks."*

Sat January 24

Makes a recording at the request of Gen. William Donovan through the Hollywood Victory Committee *"to be utilized for short wave broadcasts to Australia, and as a specific request was made to hold the matter confidential and secret"* (memo Steve Trilling to Roy Obringer); sees Dr. Carl Bretthauer, who reports that Flynn is *"suffering from a cold with some involvement of the sinuses. He also has a mild cough,"* and advises that *"Mr. Flynn should be able to begin his work on Wednesday January 28."*

Mon January 26

Memo from Jack Warner to Roy Obringer: *"Be sure that Errol Flynn is not paid for the three or four days he did not show up last week."*

Mon February 2

Visits his doctor for an Army X-Ray; is disqualified from Selective Service by reason of *"tuberculosis, pulmonary, chronic reinfection (adult), type in the right apex,"* signed by Joseph P. Szukalski, Major M.C., examining physician; begins filming DESPERATE JOURNEY in the hall outside the lounge, in Forbes' (Flynn) quarters, the officers' mess lounge, the switchboard, Coswick's (Charles Irwin) office, and the bomber command.

Tue February 3

Filming in the English operations office; inter-office memo from unit manager, Eric Stacy: *"For your information and for the record, Flynn had a call for medical examination at the Draft Board today, Tuesday, which was changed with the cooperation of Frank Mattison and was completed yesterday, Monday. Mr. Flynn told me today that he was told to go to the Army X-Ray Division today, Tuesday, but in order not to be away from the company went to his own doctor yesterday, Monday, and obtained this X-Ray. He expects to be reimbursed for this expense. His theory is that he should be paid for this rather than go on the company's time and get it made by the Army and thus hold up shooting on the picture."*

Wed February 4

Filming in Forbes' quarters and hall (retake), the mess lounge, a process shot in the RAF truck, the bomber airport, and a process shot in a bomber.

Thu February 5

Filming in the bomber; inter-office memo from Eric Stacy: *"As you know, Flynn is leaving at 11:45 today to return for some X-Ray photographs, and the company will continue shooting without him; he is expected back in the middle of the afternoon."* At a party given by Barbara Hutton at her home for Bugsy Siegel, who has been released from jail on this day.

Fri February 6 and Sat February 7

Continues filming in the bomber (process and straight shots).

Sun February 8

Appears opposite Lana Turner on the Gulf Screen Guild Theatre radio program in an adaptation of "Mr. & Mrs. Smith."

Mon February 9

Letter from Flynn to Hal Wallis, sometime before this day's scene was filmed: *"Dear Hal / Since we had not come to it as yet I haven't mentioned to you the very bad feeling I get from leaving Kennedy dead in the bomber while I talk cheerfully to Reagan and jokingly to the C.O. in England over the short wave. It is, to say the least, callous and I don't think the audience will forget for one moment the corpse flying with us in the back seat while we ignore him. Can he be wounded – or killed outside the plane?...Please let me know...Regards Errol."* Filming in the crashed plane *(next page, top right)* and a process shot in the cockpit.

Tue February 10

Continues filming in the crashed plane and a cockpit (a process shot); Hal Wallis to Raoul Walsh: *"The only other*

On the set of DESPERATE JOURNEY - February

shot that I think needs retaking is Flynn's close up after the bomber is hit and he goes into a crash landing. He seems much too casual about it all and while I would not want him to be overly excited, at the same time there should be a little animation in the reading of his lines as he tells the men to stand by for crash landing, etc. Otherwise the whole scene will seem casual to the audience."

Wed February 11

Filming in the wooded hillside and a retake close-up in the bomber (a process shot).

Thu February 12

Filming in the starboard and port side of the blisters (the clear, dome-like protrusions) and bomber cockpit; Tenny Wright to Hal Wallis: *"Errol Flynn....was given his call by the Unit Manager and the Assistant and he refused to accept the call....I contacted Flynn myself and this is what he said: That on account of his physical condition his Doctor did not wish him to work on any exteriors at night for the next few weeks. I asked him what his physical condition was and he said he would bring a letter from his Doctor...."* Hal Wallis to Tenny Wright: *"We should have a meeting immediately about the Errol Flynn night-work situation."*

Fri February 13

Filming in a bomber cockpit (a process shot) and in the clearing; inter-office memo from Eric Stacy: *"Flynn delayed the company 1/2 hour today, Friday, in reporting to work."* Production Code Administration to Jack Warner: *"In scene 207, the cries of 'Feur' must be deleted, since their sound so closely resembles the English translation 'Fire,' which word is on the Association list of banned words, by reason of possible public panic."*

Sat February 14

Filming in the bomb bay, the starboard and port blister, and on the wooded hillside.

Mon February 16 through Wed February 18

Filming at the bridge in Piru, CA *(center right),* and (on 2/18) at the river.

Thu February 19

Filming inside and outside the bomb bay, outside the bomber, under the bridge, and in the rear of the blisters.

Fri February 20

Filming under the bridge at the studio.

Sat February 21

Filming retakes under the bridge; inter-office memo from Eric Stacy: *"For the record, Flynn went home on Saturday at 4:00 PM suffering from sinus trouble, which has been bothering him for several days. Understand from his man that he has been taking care of this at home and has not been going out, etc."*

Mon February 23

Continues filming retakes under the bridge.

Tue February 24

Roy Obringer to Jack Warner: *"Dr. Brettnauer examined Flynn this morning, found that he had no fever and that his pulse was down, but that Flynn looked exceptionally tired and worn.....he felt Flynn's tired condition was due to his being undernourished and suggested to Flynn that he build up his diet to give him more strength."* Inter-office memo from Eric Stacy: *"For the record, Flynn went home at 4:40 last night suffering from sinus trouble and as already known, he could not appear today, Tuesday, for work."* Roy Obringer to multiple recipients: *"As of today J.L. Warner okayed paying Flynn the four days we deducted from his salary on commencement of his services in his present picture 'Desperate Journey.' The four days will be paid Flynn, however, upon the completion of his services in the picture and only upon the condition that he does not give us any trouble of any nature whatsoever during the picture, and if he does, the promise is off. This will be oral and nothing in writing."*

Wed February 25

Ill; does not work.

Thu February 26

Continues filming retakes on the bridge, and in Baumeister's (Raymond Massey) office (the Dutch road chase is filmed today at Point Mugu with the second unit but without Flynn).

With Alan Hale, Patrick O'Moore, and Arthur Kennedy, and in the foreground, Ronald Reagan and Ronald Sinclair - Mon, February 9

In Piru, CA. Flynn can be seen just to the left of the sign; to his left are Ronald Reagan, Alan Hale, and Arthur Kennedy - Mon, February 16; below, the same location today

With Ronald Reagan, Alan Hale, Ronald Sinclair, and Arthur Kennedy - Sat, February 28

As Flight Lt. Terrence Forbes, at Sherwood Forest in Lake Sherwood, CA - March

Fri February 27

Continues filming in Baumeister's office; inter-office memo from Eric Stacy: *"Flynn had a late call today, Friday, because they are doing the scene with Reagan and Baumeister (the double-talk scene). This is the scene that Flynn wanted to do himself, and I understand that the fact they wouldn't give him this scene to do in place of Reagan might be the cause of his not reporting for work the other day [2/24-25]."*

Sat February 28

Filming in the peat bog *(top left)*.

Mon March 2

Continues filming in the peat bog; inter-office memo from Eric Stacy: *"Want to report that Reagan is continually late on this production. He is always 5 to 15 minutes tardy every morning. He has been told about it but nothing seems to happen, and for your information when Flynn does work he is always on time. Must say this in his favor."*

Tue March 3

Continues filming in the peat bog, the brook, and hill; memo from Eric Stacy to Tenny Wright: *"…at approximately 4:15 Flynn had to leave to go to the doctor on account of his sinus trouble…Mr. Flynn reported sick again today, Wednesday, and telephoned you to say he was suffering from his sinuses; his face was swollen and had to go to the doctor to get relief, and would not be able to appear before lunchtime… understand Flynn has just called Wallis and told him that he is under a lamp and is feeling better, and is very 'sorry' he is holding up the company."*

Wed March 4

Filming in the private car of the hospital train (in the WB train shed); inter-office memo from Eric Stacey: *"At 10:AM Flynn called me from home where he is in bed and said he cannot report for work at all today, Thurs., and added that he should not have come in yesterday since it has made his cold worse today. He hopes to be able to come in tomorrow, Friday."*

Thu March 5 and Fri March 6

Ill; does not work.

Sat March 7

Filming in the salon car and side track.

Mon March 9

Filming on the Dutch road and woods at Sherwood Forest in Lake Sherwood, CA.

Tue March 10

Filming in the woods and clearing; inter-office memo from Eric Stacy: *"There was a great amount of discussion about this scene—both Errol Flynn and Reagan criticized the scene and made fun of it, and wanted to change it."*

Wed March 11

Filming in the railroad coach.

Thu March 12

Filming in the woods and on the highway; filming retakes in Baumeister's office, in the bomber, and the river drop.

Fri March 13 and Sat March 14

Filming in Dr. Mather's office reception room, and (on 3/14) the hallway and office.

Mon March 16

Filming in the camouflaged hangar at Sherwood Forest; inter-office memo from Eric Stacy: *"Mr. Flynn reported that he would not work after 5:00 o'clock any day he is called to work at the location at 9:00 AM since his time, he figures, starts at 8:00 when called to leave the studio…Also for the record, the Flynn situation is being handled by the Attorney and his agent, and at the moment we have no ruling as to whether he will remain after 5:00PM."*

Tue March 17

Continues filming in the hangar; Tenny Wright to Roy Obringer: *"This is a report of the conversation which occurred March 17, 1942, on location at Sherwood Forest, Walsh Company, between T.C. Wright and Errol Flynn…Mr. Wright asked Mr. Flynn if he had told the Company that if he had an 8:00 o'clock call in the morning at the studio that he would not work beyond 5:00 P.M. at night. Mr. Flynn replied to Mr. Wright, 'Yes, that is exactly what I told him'. Mr. Wright told Mr. Flynn that there was nothing in his contract which said that he had the right to quit at 5:00. Mr. Flynn replied, 'Then it becomes a legal matter. What are you going to do now – sue me?'...Mr. Wright tried to explain to Mr. Flynn that we were on location and that he didn't think it any hardship for Flynn to continue working as long as the light was good – until 6:00 o'clock. Flynn replied that he would not work beyond 8 hours of working time, that he was a sick man, and if he didn't believe so to look up the army record. Also, that lots of time before 5:00 o'clock he was very tired but he would keep going until 5:00 but not beyond, unless we gave him a later starting call, which, of course, is not good business...Also, he said that nobody did him any favors, including Mr. Wright or the Company. Mr. Wright drew to his attention that Mr. Wright had agreed to give him 4 days salary when he was on suspension if he would cooperate. Mr. Flynn said, 'If you think you are doing me a favor giving me that 4 days salary, as far as I am concerned, you can stick it, as if that is the reason you want to give me that little money and have me work later, I can not do it.'...Mr. Wright then asked him again if he would work until around 6:00, and Flynn said, 'No, and you can repeat for me, "I will not work beyond 5:00 on an 8:00 o'clock call at the studio."'*

Wed March 18
Continues filming in the hangar, in the wooded ruins, in the clearing, and in the blister.

Thu March 19
Continues filming in the camouflaged hangar, the bomber, and in the fuselage and cockpit.

Fri March 20 and Sat March 21
Filming in Dr. Mather's home, and (on 3/20) in the reception room and private office.

Sun March 22
At the Brown Derby for dinner with Shirley Cowan, bridesmaid for Gloria Vanderbilt at the recent wedding on the 28th of the previous December (*right*).

Mon March 23
Filming on the muddy country road.

Tue March 24
Filming at the front door and dining room of Dr. Brahm's (Felix Basch) home.

Wed March 25
Ill; does not work; inter-office memo from Eric Stacey: *"Today, Wednesday, Errol Flynn's man called up at 8:15AM and announted [sic] that Flynn was too sick to report to work, and the company, after checking with Wallis regarding any possible scenes, has been dismissed. Flynn's doctor [Dr. Lee Siegel] and he tells [sic] me that Flynn is suffering from sinus, sub-normal temperature, and a chest cold, but the Doctor tells me that Flynn should be able to work tomorrow, Thursday."*

Thu March 26 and Fri March 27
Ill; does not work; inter-office memo from Eric Stacey: *"Today, Thursday, Flynn was again unable to report for work after receiving a message last night, Wednesday, at approximately 9:00 PM from the Doctor who called into the studio and said he had given Flynn a sedative and that he (Flynn) had to stay in bed all day today, Thursday."* Inter-office memo from Eric Stacy (3/27): *"Company called--dismissed, unable to shoot due to Mr. Flynn's illness."*

Sat March 28
Eric Stacey to Tenny Wright: *"Following is a report of what went on regarding Errol Flynn's non-appearance to work today, Saturday: At 8:00AM, Claude Archer, 2nd Assistant, telephoned Errol Flynn's house to see if everything is all right....Errol Flynn answered the telephone when Claude Archer called and said that he had got up and was preparing to come to work in all good faith, but had felt so sick and weak that he was compelled to go back to bed again; Claude Archer then telephoned me and I in turn got in touch with Dr. Siegel (CR. 6-7574) and asked him whether or not he knew of any reason why Flynn could not have appeared today, Saturday. Dr. Siegel talked at great length to me and told me that.... the original sinus trouble was cured and that Flynn was having trouble with his chest, and in course of the conversation told me also that Flynn had undoubtedly taken sleeping pills in order to get a night's rest and had taken too many, which was the reason that he was so loggy this morning. The doctor also mentioned that an average person can need only take one sleeping pill—Flynn had to take three pills....Dr. Siegel mentioned in his talk to me that Flynn has a condition in his chest sufficiently serious to prevent him from being eligible to join the army but did not mention what it was, but left me to gather my own conclusions. It would appear to me that maybe Flynn had been in pain and taken more sleeping pills than he should. It is my personal opinion (if you want it) that Mr. Flynn is not taking as good care of himself as he should, and*

With Shirley Cowan at the Brown Derby, doing his Charlie Chaplin routine - Sun, March 22

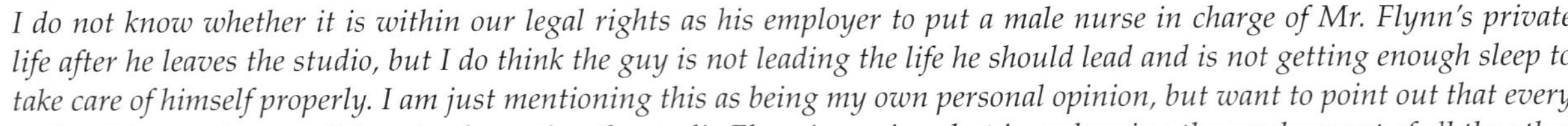

I do not know whether it is within our legal rights as his employer to put a male nurse in charge of Mr. Flynn's private life after he leaves the studio, but I do think the guy is not leading the life he should lead and is not getting enough sleep to take care of himself properly. I am just mentioning this as being my own personal opinion, but want to point out that every day this man is away it is not only costing the studio Flynn's services, but is prolonging the employment of all the other actors concerned and running our costs up very highly." Roy Obringer to Jack Warner: *"Dr. Brettauer [Bretthauer] examined Errol Flynn at 11:30 this morning."* Dr. Bretthauer's report on Errol Flynn: *"Flynn's condition shows that he hasn't been getting much sleep. Flynn states that he goes to bed early, but doesn't sleep. Flynn's blood pressure is up.... There is a little tenderness over the left cheek bone from his sinus....Dr. Bretthauer told Flynn that he would have to slow up and that he should eat a better breakfast and lunch and try to rest some (while working) during his lunch time...Flynn has a heart murmur which causes him to tire more easily...."*

Mon March 30 and Tue March 31

Filming in Dr. Mather's (Albert Bassermann) home and Dr. Brahms' home, and (on 3/31) in the kitchen and dining room; also on 3/31 Lili obtains a divorce from Flynn, whom she charged with "paying more attention to his yachts than me"; she is to receive alimony payments of $1,500 a month ($25,207 in 2021 value).

April

Sometime during this month Flynn applies to the Navy Dept. for an I.D. card to enable him to enter the restricted area in L.A. Harbor when using his boat; it is also probably during this month that John Barrymore stays at Flynn's Mulholland house, as related in Flynn's autobiography, *My Wicked, Wicked Ways*.

Wed April 1

Filming in Dr. Brahms' attic, on the rooftops, and on the steep roof.

Thu April 2

Continues filming on the rooftops, the dormered attic, the flat roof *(top left)*, in the brush, and in the cockpit of the Hudson.

Fri April 3

Filming on the backlot on Munster Street and in the alley, and a process shot in the bomber cockpit; inter-office memo from Eric Stacy: *"Flynn was considerably indisposed, had his Doctor on the set and had a temperature."*

Sat April 4

Continues filming on Munster Street, on the rooftops, in the bomber, the vestibule, and a process shot in Forbes' car *(bottom left)*.

Mon April 6

Continues filming the process shot in Forbes' car; inter-office memo from Eric Stacy: *"Mr. Flynn reported late this morning (9:30) and still has quite a bad cold."*

Tue April 7

Continues filming the process shot in Forbes' car.

Wed April 8

Filming in the wine cellar.

Thu April 9

Filming at the viaduct, in Baumeister's office, at the railroad, and at the grave.

Fri April 10

Night filming in the alley, in Dr. Mather's home, in Berlin Street (Brownstone Street on the backlot); a conference was held with Jack Warner, Jules Stein, Lew Wasserman of MCA Universal, Charles Einfeld, and Roy Obringer to discuss a new deal for Flynn, commencing on August 18, 1942, to pay him $85,000 [$1,428,406 in 2021 value] each for three pictures a year. At the completion of the third picture, Flynn could produce his own under Warner Bros.

Sat April 11

Continues night filming in the alley and at the factory gate.

Mon April 13

Night filming at the factory's buttressed wall.

Tue April 14

Filming in the apothecary, storeroom, at the crossroads, and at the factory wall.

With Nancy Coleman - Thu, April 2

Filming a process shot with Arthur Kennedy and Ronald Reagan - Sat, April 4

Wed April 15

At a gala at the Hollywood Palladium to support Marion Davies' War Work Hospital.

Thu April 16

Arrives 80 minutes late because of the gala the night before; filming retakes in the bomber and on the rooftops.

Fri April 17

Completes work on DESPERATE JOURNEY filming close-ups at the hay wagon from 7pm to 2:15am.

Thu April 30

Wardrobe and makeup tests for GENTLEMAN JIM; a wig for the front of his hair is part of his makeup.

May

Trains for GENTLEMAN JIM with boxing coach Mushy Callahan.

Mon May 4

At Baltimore's Johns Hopkins Hospital for three days of tests; he is advised to *"avoid strenuous physical activity."*

Fri May 8 and Sat May 9

Travels to Washington, D.C., to visit Secretary of War Henry L. Stimson in hopes of receiving some role in the war effort.

Tue May 12

Arrives back in Los Angeles; signs a new contract wherein *"The Producer agrees to pay the Artist as compensation for all services required of Artist in connection with each motion picture produced hereunder the sum of Ninety Thousand Dollars ($90,000), payable in installments (of $6,000)* [$1,512,430 and $100,829, respectively, in 2021 value]….*said installments to be due and payable on Wednesday of each week…."* Frank Mattison to Tenny Wright: *"I have just phoned Errol Flynn's home and talked to his man. He informs me that Flynn has not arrived as yet and he has received no word of his expected arrival today, Tuesday, May 12th…I believe we should give him the benefit of the doubt and I will check his home late this afternoon with the prospect that he may arrive on a late plane today."*

Wed May 20

Begins work on GENTLEMAN JIM, filming at the Comstock Bank on New York Street on the backlot with Alexis Smith, Alan Hale, and Jack Carson; inter-office memo from unit manager, Frank Mattison: *"Company got off to a good start…and everyone is in high spirits."*

Thu May 21

Continues filming in the Comstock Bank, and in the bank president's office.

Fri May 22

Filming in the Corbett dining room.

Sat May 23

Continues filming in the Corbett dining room, and in back yard.

Mon May 25

Filming in the Corbett home, the back and front porch; inter-office memo from Frank Mattison: *"Mr. Flynn worked out in the morning and was on the set at 10:00 o'clock. We will know if this is going to work out better in a day or two…Tuesday…is the first fight of Flynns* [sic]*, but it is to be a short & sweet one."*

Tue May 26

Filming in the Corbett home and stable.

Wed May 27

Filming in the Olympic Club card room and outside hall.

Thu May 28

Filming in the Club lounge, the Corbett stable, dining room, and outside the house.

Fri May 29

Filming in the Olympic Club gym and door outside; John Barrymore, Flynn's Hollywood idol, dies at age 60.

Mon June 1

Continues filming in the Olympic Club gym.

Tue June 2

Filming on the Olympic Club terrace with Alexis Smith; attends the Barrymore funeral with Buster Wiles at Calvary Mausoleum in Los Angeles.

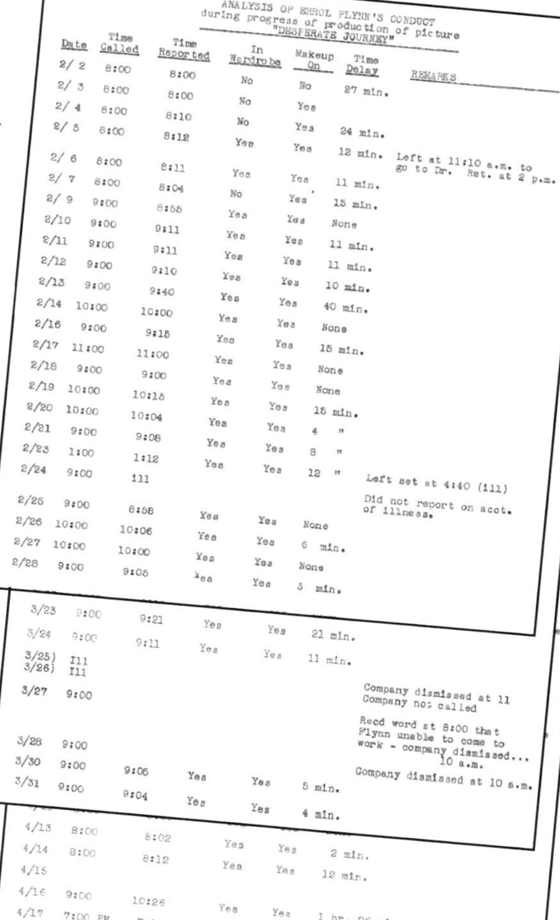

ANALYSIS OF ERROL FLYNN'S CONDUCT
during progress of production of picture
"DESPERATE JOURNEY"

Date	Time Called	Time Reported	In Wardrobe	Makeup On	Time Delay	REMARKS
2/2	8:00	8:00	No	No	27 min.	
2/3	8:00	8:00	No	Yes		
2/4	8:00	8:10	No	Yes	24 min.	
2/5	8:00	8:12	Yes	Yes	12 min.	Left at 11:10 a.m. to go to Dr. Ret. at 2 p.m.
2/6	8:00	8:11	Yes	Yes	11 min.	
2/7	8:00	8:04	No	Yes	15 min.	
2/9	9:00	8:55	Yes	Yes	None	
2/10	9:00	9:11	Yes	Yes	11 min.	
2/11	9:00	9:11	Yes	Yes	11 min.	
2/12	9:00	9:10	Yes	Yes	10 min.	
2/13	9:00	9:40	Yes	Yes	40 min.	
2/14	10:00	10:00	Yes	Yes	None	
2/16	9:00	9:15	Yes	Yes	15 min.	
2/17	11:00	11:00	Yes	Yes	None	
2/18	9:00	9:00	Yes	Yes	None	
2/19	10:00	10:15	Yes	Yes	15 min.	
2/20	10:00	10:04	Yes	Yes	4 "	
2/21	9:00	9:08	Yes	Yes	8 "	
2/23	1:00	1:12	Yes	Yes	12 "	
2/24	9:00	111				Left set at 4:40 (111)
2/25	9:00	8:58	Yes	Yes	None	Did not report on acct. of illness.
2/26	10:00	10:06	Yes	Yes	None	
2/27	10:00	10:00	Yes	Yes	6 min.	
2/28	9:00	9:05	Yes	Yes	None	
			Yes	Yes	5 min.	
3/23	9:00	9:21	Yes	Yes	21 min.	
3/24	9:00	9:11	Yes	Yes	11 min.	
3/25)	Ill					
3/26)	Ill					
3/27	9:00					Company dismissed at 11. Company not called
3/28	9:00					Recd word at 8:00 that Flynn unable to come to work - company dismissed... 10 a.m.
3/30	9:00	9:06	Yes	Yes	5 min.	Company dismissed at 10 a.m.
3/31	9:00	9:04	Yes	Yes	4 min.	
4/13	8:00	8:02	Yes	Yes	2 min.	
4/14	8:00	8:12	Yes	Yes	12 min.	
4/15			Yes	Yes		
4/16	9:00	10:26	Yes	Yes	1 hr. 26 min.	
4/17	7:00 PM	7:00	Yes	Yes		

Flynn's daily "conduct report" for
DESPERATE JOURNEY

With Pat Flaherty - Tue, May 26

With Alexis Smith - June

Wed June 3 through Fri June 5
Continues filming on the terrace, and (on 6/3) the Corbett vs. Jack Burke (Art Foster) fight, and (on 6/5) in the foyer of the Olympic Club (Freddie Steele is Flynn's boxing double).

Sat June 6
Filming in the jail cell on Brownstone Street on the backlot, outside the Olympic Club on New York Street on the backlot, outside the bank, and in the Olympic Club gym.

Mon June 8 and Tue June 9
Filming in the Olympic Club ballroom and bar.

Wed June 10
Filming in the open lot fighting ring.

Thu June 11
Filming the warehouse fight; attends the Navy Relief Ball at the Cocoanut Grove with his secretary Mary Ann Hyde.

Fri June 12
Filming in the Salt Lake City hotel room.

Sat June 13
Filming in the theater lobby and in the alley.

Sun June 14
With actress Faith Domergue at the Mocambo.

Mon June 15
Filming on the barge *(bottom left)* and the Corbett vs. Joe Choynski (Sammy Stein) fight.

Tue June 16 through Thu June 18
Continues filming the Corbett vs. Choynski fight and (on 6/18) under the wharf.

Fri June 19
Filming on Market Street on New York Street on the backlot and in the Olympic Club gym.

Sat June 20
Flynn's 33rd birthday; filming in the hotel lobby and New York theater; a birthday party is thrown at the Mulholland house with guests including the Jack Warners, Ava Gardner, Cedric Gibbons, Patric Knowles, Mike Romanoff, Mickey Rooney, Arthur Kennedy, Merle Oberon, Eleanor Parker, Tyrone Power, Charlie Chaplin, the Raoul Walshes, Cary Grant, and others.

Mon June 22
Flynn (and Smith) ill; calls the studio at about 7am and does not work; calls Lou Baum at 10pm; F.B.I. director, J. Edgar Hoover, drafts a letter to his Los Angeles Special Agent in Charge to *"discreetly"* look into Flynn's health records with regard to the actor's military deferment.

Tue June 23
Filming in the New York theater boxes.

Wed June 24
Before the day's work, is at the Los Angeles Federal Building for a citizenship interview; continues filming in the New York theater, including the John L. Sullivan (Ward Bond) sequence.

Thu June 25
Continues filming the Sullivan theater sequence and

Boxing Sammy Stein, with Joseph Crehan officiating;
a ship built for THE SEA HAWK is on the right - Mon, June 15

The F.B.I. report on Flynn - Fri, July 3

Mon June 29

Ill; shooting canceled; because of Flynn's illness, Warner Bros. must pay 63 extras at the rate of $10.50 per day [$176.45 in 2021 value], and bit woman Clara Blandick a rate of $200 per day [$3,361 in 2021 value]; William Davidson as "Donovan" is to receive $150 per day [$2,521 in 2021 value], and Jean Del Val as "Renaud," $100 per day [$1,680 in 2021 value]; Roy Obringer to Jack Warner: *"A doctor called after examining Flynn and advised that Flynn has a very bad throat condition and that his neck is sore and painful from the throat inflammation, but that his sinus condition, while still present, is secondary to the throat ailment., He stated that Flynn had no fever, and that he should be able to work by Wednesday at the latest, and Flynn indicated he might come in tomorrow but that he would call Tenny Wright this afternoon on this...."*

Tue June 30

Ill; shooting canceled.

Wed July 1

Filming in the railroad coach, outside the train, and in the hotel room and lobby.

Thu July 2

Continues filming in the hotel room, the Olympic Club terrace, Sullivan's dressing room, and hall.

Fri July 3

Filming inside and outside the Corbett home.

Mon July 6

Filming at the training camp at the Lucky Baldwin Ranch in Arcadia, CA (now the L.A. County Arboretum); exercising scenes and a scene with Flynn and other cast members in vintage, striped bathing suits are not used; F.B.I. agent, R. B. Hood reports back to J. Edgar Hoover on the reasons for Flynn's military deferment,

on the New York street; leaves the set at 12:15 because of illness, and calls Lou Baum at 9:30pm to update him.

Fri June 26

Ill; does not work; Lou Baum to Tenny Wright: *"....Errol Flynn called up early last Monday morning to advise us that he was not feeling well and would definitely not come to work any earlier than 1:00 o'clock on Tuesday..... Flynn advised me Tuesday afternoon that he had to appear on Wednesday morning at the Federal Building for an interview regarding his citizenship papers. He showed up Wednesday afternoon at 2:00 o'clock....Flynn made his appearance at 9:00 o'clock Thursday morning, and by 12:15 when we had finished this sequence he advised me that he was too sick to continue, and insisted on leaving the studio immediately...I spoke to Flynn last night, Thursday, about 9:30PM, and he advised me that he definitely was too sick to appear on the set this morning, Friday."*

Sat June 27

Filming in the New York hotel lobby, outside the theater, and on the New York street.

Above, sparring with Art Foster at the Los Angeles County Arboretum - Mon, July 6; below, the same spot today

With Bruce Cabot on the New Orleans hotel set; Cabot is on a neighboring stage filming *Desert Song* - Thu, July 9

With Joseph Crehan and Ward Bond - Tue, July 14

With Alexis Smith - July

citing the actor's disqualification due to *"tuberculosis, pulmonary, chronic reinfection (adult), type in the right apex."*

Tue July 7

Continues filming at the training camp and lake at the Lucky Baldwin Ranch.

Wed July 8

Filming in Sullivan's and Corbett's dressing rooms.

Thu July 9 through Sat July 11

Filming in the New Orleans hotel room *(top left)* and (on 7/10 and 11) on the hotel balcony.

Mon July 13 and Tue July 14

Filming the Corbett vs. Sullivan fight *(center left)*.

Wed July 15

Ill and in the hospital; company did not work; inter-office memo from Frank Mattison: *"As you know, Mr. Errol Flynn reported & collapsed in the Makeup Dept. with the result that the company was dismissed as of 10:45 AM."*

Thu July 16

Ill and in the hospital; company did not work; Frank Mattison to Tenny Wright: *"Early yesterday morning, July 15th, about 8:45AM, Mr. Errol Flynn appeared at the Makeup Dept. in his usual good spirits in company with Buster Wiles. He was joined a few minutes later with Mushy Callahan and Hamilton [Bud Westmore] the Makeup man. Mr. Dennis Morgan came in about 8:50AM and had a few remarks with Errol, and all of a sudden Errol Flynn rose up in his chair and started to walk away from it only to collapse into the hands of Ward Bond and Dennis Morgan. With aid of Mushy Callahan they got him back on the chair. Mr. Flynn was turning pale – had a sort of palpitation, with the result they rushed to the phone and called the first aid department. Mr. Paul McWilliams appeared and ordered by telephone the nearest doctor whom he could reach—Dr. Crosby of Burbank. Dr. Crosby arrived about 9:15AM and with Paul McWilliams made a hurried examination of Mr. Flynn. Mr. Raoul Walsh put in a call for his own doctor, Dr. Chapman, who arrived about 9:50AM. Dr. Chapman examined Mr. Errol Flynn and came out and spoke to Mr. Walsh and myself stating that the man was suffering from exhaustion. He stated, however, that the heart was strong and that he thought there was no ailment concerned with the heart. He did state, however, that Mr. Flynn would have to go and rest immediately; suggested that he go to the hospital—suggesting the Good Samaritan [where he was admitted]....Mr. Walsh and myself questioned him concerning the condition of Mr. Flynn and he stated that Mr. Flynn would be able to work on next Monday, July 20th. He did state, however, that it would be impossible for him to do any strenuous fighting, etc., for possibly two weeks. He described the case as utter exhaustion...."* Frank Mattison to Tenny Wright: *"....[Dr. Chapman] says that Mr. Flynn's lungs are, as you know, spotted....however, there is nothing wrong with Mr. Flynn that cannot be corrected by proper diet and the proper hours of sleep....less alcoholic beverages and more proper living...."*

Fri July 17

Ill and in the hospital; company does not work; Frank Mattison to Tenny Wright: *"....Mr. Errol Flynn telephoned me at 12:05PM today, Friday, and informed me he was feeling much better and was going home this afternoon, and that he expected to probably go on the boat tomorrow, Saturday and Sunday. He said he was feeling very well and that he would be on the set ready to work next Monday morning, July 20th...."*

Sat July 18

Ill; company does not work.

Mon July 20

Filming on the patio and balcony of the New Orleans Hotel; attends a Victory Committee fund-raiser at the Mocambo with actress June Millard; Roy Obringer to Tenny Wright: *".... You will recall that Flynn was sick during 'They Died With Their Boots On' and ran up a large doctor and nurse bill at the Good Samaritan Hospital, and tried to pass it on as a studio expense. I rejected each one of these bills as Flynn's sinus trouble was not held by our insurance company as a compensation case....I understand that Flynn's present illness is due to a heart condition, etc. Flynn will undoubtedly claim that the fight scenes, etc. brought on his exhaustion, and therefore try to tie up his sickness and his expenses in connection therewith to his work in the picture. I, therefore, do not feel that Buster Wiles or Flynn should be encouraged in the thought that the company will stand his medical expenses unless our insurance doctors hold it to be a compensable case, and I seriously doubt that they will."*

Tue July 21
Frank Mattison to Tenny Wright: *"….I have received in this morning's mail, Tuesday, July 21st, two bills for nurses for Errol Flynn while he was in the hospital on July 15th to July 17th…..I assure you that I did not tell anyone that we were to pay these bills or that they even were to be sent to me. It was an expedient measure of Mr. Buster Wiles to get Mr. Flynn out of the hospital without paying these bills* [$18 for nurse Mary Hohman, and $12 for nurse Elizabeth Clark].*"*

Thu July 23
Finishes filming GENTLEMAN JIM with a montage of the interior of the fight ring (the Kilrain and Miller fights).

Fri July 31
Sound and photograph tests for EDGE OF DARKNESS *(top right)*.

Mon August 3
Flies to Mexico City, checking in to the Hotel Reforma.

Fri August 14
Becomes a U.S. citizen; his naturalization number is 89452.

Tue August 18
Receives a threat from Warner Bros. via telegram that his $7,000 a week salary ($117,633 in 2021 value) will be docked if he doesn't return to work on Thursday the 20th of August.

Wed August 19
Telegram from Roy Obringer to Flynn: THIS WIRE WILL SERVE AS A REMINDER AND CONFIRMATION OF STEVE TRILLING'S TELEPHONE COMMUNICATION WITH YOUR AGENT AS OF YESTERDAY AND TODAY THAT WE SHALL EXPECT YOU TO RETURN TO LOS ANGELES TOMORROW, THURSDAY, IN ORDER THAT YOU WILL BE ABLE AND READY TO REPORT TO THE STUDIO AT NINE O'CLOCK A.M. FRIDAY. AUGUST 21ST, 1942, TO COMMENCE YOUR SERVICES FOR US IN YOUR NEXT PICTURE.

Fri August 21
Flies back to Hollywood.

Fri August 28
Leaves for Monterey, CA, on the Southern Pacific Railroad.

Sat August 29
Arrives in Monterey, staying at the Hotel Del Monte.

Sun August 30
Begins work on EDGE OF DARKNESS, filming in the tree shelter in the cliff above the sea.

Mon August 31
Continues filming in the tree shelter, and in the woods.

Tue September 1 and Wed September 2
No shooting because of fog.

Thu September 3
Filming in the woods and in the shack; is interviewed for an article in the *Washington Post* (for 9/27).

Fri September 4
Continues filming in the shack.

Sat September 5, Tue September 8, and Wed September 9
Filming in the woods and (on 9/8 and 9) in the clearing.

Thu September 10
Filming on the Monterey pier; inter-office memo from Lou Baum: *"Several minor delays during the day due to boats in scene which can not be controlled."*

Fri September 11 and Sat September 12
Continues filming on the pier.

Mon September 14
Filming at the barbed wire emplacement and cliff; leaves for Los Angeles in the evening; a contract is signed between Warner Bros. and Flynn's Thomson Productions for Flynn to produce his own films.

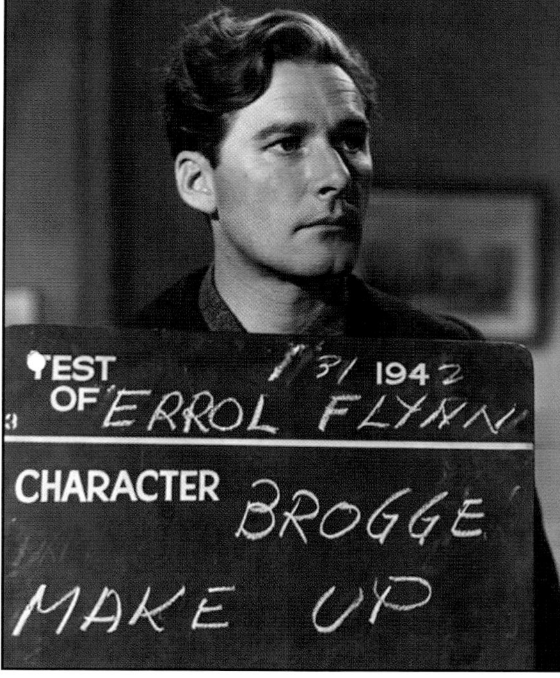

Makeup test for the role of Gunnar Brogge - Fri, July 31

With Ann Sheridan in Monterey, CA - August

Tue September 15

Arrives in Los Angeles; Flynn's attorney, Robert Ford, requests that a new contract be entered into that would reimburse Flynn for medical bills totaling $1,589 ($26,703 in 2021 value); the request is denied.

Thu September 17

Filming in the Torgerson home and (on 9/17 and 18) in Brogge's (Flynn) shack.

Sat September 19, and Mon September 21 through Wed September 23

Filming in the church.

Mon September 21

DESPERATE JOURNEY has its first showing at the State Theater in Harrisburg, PA.

Thu September 24

Filming in Osterholm's (Art Smith) cellar.

Fri September 25

Continues filming in Osterholm's cellar.

Sat September 26

Supposedly ill (*top left*); does not work; plays a tennis match later in the day with Bill Tilden at the home of Freddie McEvoy, Bruce Cabot, and Stephen Raphael on 321 St. Pierre Road in Bel Air, CA; meets Betty Hansen there, who later in the year accuses him of statutory rape during the early hours of Sunday, September 27; in an interview published on this day in the *Washington Post*, Flynn tells writer Robert Myers that *"when I left Tasmania—I was only two years old!"* and that *"I have never in my life said I was a member of the* [1928 Olympic Games boxing] *team. The truth is, I tried out for it and failed to make it."*

Mon September 28

Ill; does not work.

Tue September 29 and Wed September 30

Filming in Brogge's shack, and (on 9/30) outside the hotel and on its porch.

Thu October 1

Filming in Malken's (Roman Bohnen) store on Norwegian Street on the WB backlot.

Tue October 6 and Wed October 7

Filming in the Stensdgard home, and (on 10/7) in the tree shelter.

Thu October 8

Filming on the cliffs.

Fri October 9

Ill; does not work.

Sat October 10

Filming in the woods and in the Osterholm cellar.

Sun October 11

Late in the evening Flynn is brought to Juvenile Hall by Police Lieutenant R. W. Bolling and Sergeant Edward Walker of the Los Angeles Juvenile Control Division on charges of statutory rape of Betty Hansen (born September 21, 1925); she was found to have Flynn's private telephone number in her possession; Flynn is met at the hall by his attorney Robert Ford, and released on his own recognizance; there are no charges filed and no bail posted.

Mon October 12

Is called before the grand jury along with Freddie McEvoy, Roland Dell, Eddie White, Buster Wiles, Betty Hansen, Lynne Boyer, and Chi-Chi Toupes; the jury decides not to indict Flynn; continues filming in Osterholm's cellar.

Tue October 13

Continues filming in Osterholm's cellar, in the ship's cabin, the cannery balcony, and Stensgard's (Walter Huston) home.

Wed October 14

Continues filming in Osterholm's cellar, and in the church.

Thu October 15

Filming inside and outside the church, and in Stensgard's home; Jack Warner to Henry Blanke: *"Dear*

On location studying his script for
EDGE OF DARKNESS

A sick note—from the same day of the tennis match/house party in Bel Air - Sat, September 26

The reproduced document reads:

WARNER BROS. PICTURES, INC.
BURBANK, CALIFORNIA

INTER-OFFICE COMMUNICATION

DATE SEPTEMBER 26, 1942

TO MR. T. C. WRIGHT

SUBJECT "EDGE OF DARKNESS"

FROM MR. LOU BAUM

COPY SENT BY T. C. WRIGHT 9/26/42 - HM

Mr. Errol Flynn's butler called the Operating Office this morning about 8:00 AM to advise us that Flynn was ill in bed with a cold. I checked his home this morning at 10:30 AM, and talked to Buster Wiles, who also confirmed this, he said Mr. Flynn was going to remain in bed until he had broken this cold.

I will check him tomorrow, as well as Monday, and will be guided by the information received then as to how we will go.

LOU BAUM

LB;rb

Betty Hansen with policewoman Dorothy Pulas - Fri, October 16

Armand Knapp, Morris "Morrie" Black and Joseph Geraldi - Fri, October 16

Henry—I definitely want a great big schmaltz love scene between Flynn and Sheridan." Betty Hansen appears before the grand jury with Agnes "Chi-Chi" Toupes and Lynne Boyer, who were said also to have been at the party where the rape of Hansen was alleged to have taken place.

Fri October 16

Filming in Osterholm's cellar; appears at a hearing before Municipal Judge Oda Faulconer in Los Angeles Court and is formally charged with two counts of statutory rape; pleads innocent; is arraigned, fingerprinted, and released on $1,000 bail ($16,805 in 2021 value).

Sat October 17, Mon October 19, and Tue October 20

Continues filming in Osterholm's cellar.

Wed October 21

Filming inside and outside the butcher shop, in Malken's store, in the tailor shop, and outside the doorway; Flynn is accused of a second rape, that of Peggy LaRue Satterlee (born February 7, 1926) on the *Sirocco* in August of 1941.

Thu October 22

Filming in the town square on Norwegian Street on the WB backlot.

Fri October 23

Does not work; meets with his newly added attorney Jerry Giesler and is informed the two rape charges will be combined; three young men—Armand Knapp, 18, Morris "Morrie" Black, 22, and Joseph Geraldi, 20 *(bottom left)*—are charged with raping Betty Hansen and appear in court; attends the boxing matches at the Hollywood Legion Stadium with Buster Wiles.

Sat October 24

Does not work; a $62,500 damage suit ($1,050,298 in 2021 value) is brought against him and co-defendant Jim Fleming concerning an altercation at the Mulholland house with Flynn's former butler Eric Gosta; the occasion was Flynn's June 20th birthday party of this year.

Mon October 26

Filming a process shot of the town square, in Osterholm's cellar, and the hotel lobby; Judge Byron J. Walters dismisses the rape charges against the three young men.

Tue October 27

Continues filming in the hotel lobby.

Wed October 28

Does not work; meets with his attorneys; GENTLEMAN JIM has its first showing at the Strand Theater in Hartford, CT (it had an earlier sneak preview there on 8/31).

Thu October 29 through Sat October 31

Filming in the town square.

Mon November 2

Does not work; a statement is written claiming Flynn's total salary for 1941 was $199,250 ($3,348,351 in 2021 value), and from December 31, 1941, to October 27, 1942, was $257,000 ($4,318,827 in 2021 value); preliminary hearing before Municipal Judge Walters, with Jerry Giesler representing Flynn; Betty Hansen makes accusations in court; Flynn is charged with three counts of statutory rape.

Errol Flynn Accused of Attack on Girl, 17, at Bel-Air Party

Charge Pressed After Grand Jury Fails to Return Indictment

Dashing, debonair Errol Flynn, actor, yesterday was accused in a District Attorney's complaint of criminally assaulting a 17-year-old girl during a gay Bel-Air dinner party last Sept. 27.

Named in the same complaint were three film studio employees—Armand Knapp, 18; Morrie Black, 22, and Joseph Geraldi, 20. All are charged with mistreating pretty Betty Hansen, a Lincoln (Neb.) girl who came to Hollywood seeking glamour.

FOUR ARRAIGNED

Flynn and the others were arraigned late yesterday before Municipal Judge Oda Faulconer, released under $1000 bail each and ordered to appear for preliminary hearing next Friday.

Miss Hansen appeared last Thursday before the county grand jury with Agnes Touper, brunette beauty known as "Chi-Chi," and Lynne Boyer, blond singer, who assertedly were at the house party with her.

'EVIDENCE IGNORED'

The jury failed to press charges against Flynn and his codefendants. Dist. Atty. John F. Dockweiler, in issuing the complaint at the insistence of police juvenile officers, commented:

"The grand jury apparently ignored the evidence in the case."

Miss Hansen, taken into custody by juvenile officers Oct. 9 when she was reported missing from the home of her sister, Mrs. Patricia Marsden, told the grand jury she accompanied Knapp to the home of Fred McEvoy, British sportsman. She was promised an introduction to Flynn and told the swashbuckling actor might be able to obtain film work for her, the witness said.

'DID LITTLE DANCE'

At the luxurious estate the guests played for a while in the swimming pool, then had dinner, according to testimony. Miss Toupes said she later "did a little dance" and recalled that she did not see Flynn or Miss Hansen in the room at the time.

SURRENDERS—Errol Flynn lights cigarette after surrender on charge of attacking 17-year-old girl at a party.

Henderson Hints Coast to Get More Gasoline

Special Attention Paid to Special Needs of West, O.P.A. Head Tells Senate Group

Presaging a possible increase in the amount of gasoline to be allotted western motorists, O.P.A. Director Leon Henderson yesterday told a Senate appropriation subcommittee in Washington that the people of the West will find "that special attention has been paid their special needs" when nation-wide gasoline rationing goes into effect Nov. 22.

This was in answer to an ever-increasing clamor by Pacific

Paul Barksdale d'Orr, State rationer, yesterday announced that all experts in gasoline, tire and automobile rationing are scheduled to attend a three-day conference in San Francisco next Thursday, Friday and Saturday for detailed instructions.

The experts will be given their printed instructions from Washington, and then other experts who have attended conferences

The Los Angeles Times - Fri, October 17

SECOND GIRL ACCUSES FLYNN

Los Angeles.—A second charge of assault, involving a 17-year-old girl, was filed yesterday against Actor Errol Flynn.

Juvenile Officer Lieutenant R. W. Bowling signed a complaint charging the swashbuckling film idol attack Peggy Larue Satterlee, 17, Aug. 3, 1941, during a week-end trip to Catalina Island on the actor's yacht.

Flynn is scheduled to appear for preliminary hearing Friday on a charge of attacking Betty Hansen, 17, movie-struck Lincoln (Neb.) girl, at a party the night of Sept. 27.

Deputy District Attorney Thomas W. Cochran said the actor's lawyers plan to surrender him on the new charge.

The Chester (PA) Times - Thu, October 22

With his attorneys Jerry Giesler and Robert Ford; behind them are defendant Peggy LaRue Satterlee and prosecutor Thomas Cochran (above Ford) - Wed, November 4

With Roman Bohnen and Ann Sheridan at the WB Calabasas Ranch - November

Tue November 3

Filming a tag in the woods of Elysian Park in Los Angeles.

Wed November 4

Does not work; in court with Peggy LaRue Satterlee on the stand *(top left);* she claims Flynn had nicknames for her: J.B., which stood for jail bait, and SQQ, which stood for San Quentin Quail; the examining physician, Dr. Etta Gray, who had examined Satterlee two days after the alleged August 3, 1941, incident, also takes the stand.

Thu November 5

Does not work; in court; Satterlee is again on the stand being cross-examined by Giesler about details of the alleged incident; Peter Stackpole, the *Life* magazine photographer who was along on the same Sirocco trip to Catalina Island as Satterlee, is also called.

Fri November 6

Does not work; Judge Walters orders a trial be held on November 23rd on three counts of statutory rape.

Fri November 13

Filming in the clearing in the woods, on the hotel balcony, and in the woods, all at the WB Calabasas Ranch; receives an anonymous letter demanding $10,000 in bribery ($168,048 in 2021 value): *"Dear Mr. Flynn If you value your life and career send ten thousand dollars in cash wrapped in a small package addressed to Jack Gelstrom —Ottos Malt Shop 383 EST. Your phone will be tapped and you will be followed so make no attempt to call police A hint—this concerns Betty Hansen and Peggy Satterlee Have it there by Nov. 18th or something will happen."*

Sat November 14

Filming inside and outside the wire outpost, in the woods, and in the machine gun nest, all at the WB Calabasas Ranch.

Mon November 16

Filming in the machine gun nest, the clearing in the woods, and on the hotel porch and doorway, all at the WB Ranch.

Tue November 17

Continues filming in the clearing in the woods and in the machine gun nest at the WB Calabasas Ranch; J. Edgar Hoover advises his Los Angeles agent to investigate the lead they have on Flynn's extortionist (see 11/13), warning to *"Take precautions to avoid premature publicity...."*

Wed November 18

Filming in the church, in the belfry, and in the trench in the square (Norwegian Street on the WB backlot).

Thu November 19

Filming in Koenig's (Helmut Dantine) office, the wagon, and a process shot in the woods; a Los Angeles F.B.I. agent reports having discovered and apprehended Flynn's extortionist, who turns out to be a 13-year-old boy, Billy Seamster, a Flynn fan from San Bernardino; because of Seamster's age he is not prosecuted.

Fri November 20

Filming on the hotel roof, in the square, in Koenig's office, and in the hotel lobby; the Los Angeles district attorney's office files a formal complaint against Flynn, charging him with three counts of statutory rape; the Los Angeles Times reports beneath its main headline: "EXTORTION NOTE TO ERROL FLYNN BRINGS ARREST."

LAST MINUTE NEWS

U. S. CASUALTIES IN AFRICA TOTAL 1910

Washington, (INS)—The War Department announced today that the American casualties, both Army and Navy, in the landing operations in North Africa totaled 1910. U. S. Army casualties were estimated at 1600, including 350 killed. American Navy casualties totaled 310, of which ten were reported killed.

ERROL FLYNN PLEADS NOT GUILTY

Hollywood, (UP)—Film star Errol Flynn, appearing as jaunty as in his heroic movie roles, pleaded innocent today to triple charges of statutory rape upon two teen age girls. Superior Judge Edward R. Brand set Jan. 11 as date for his trial.

ANTI-POLL TAX BILL KILLED

Washington, (INS)—The Senate today rejected a motion to limit debate on the Anti-Poll Tax Bill in order to break a filibuster, and thus in effect killed the bill for the duration of the present session of Congress.

GERMANY'S LUFTWAFFE STRETCHED TO LIMIT

New York, (INS) — Germany's Luftwaffe is now "fully stretched" and its effectiveness has been greatly diminished, Air Commodore H. N. Thornton, British Air Attache in Washington, declared today.

The Chester (PA) Times - *Mon, November 23*

With Walter Huston (on the left) on the WB backlot - November

Sat November 21

Finishes EDGE OF DARKNESS, filming in the woods and machine gun nest at the WB Calabasas Ranch; attends an enlistment party for Bruce Cabot at the Mocambo.

Mon November 23

Roy Obringer to Jack Warner: "…[Lew] *Wasserman advised that Flynn is arranging with his local draft board to be away from the city for two weeks in order that he can take a rest, and his trial does not come up until January 11, 1943. Flynn is now asking if he can have….two weeks' salary* [to] *also use it to meet some other personal expenses."* With Jerry Giesler and Robert Ford representing him, is arraigned before Deputy District Attorney Arthur Veitch; Flynn simply states his name and enters a plea of *"Not Guilty as charged in the information,"* and is released on $1,000 bail ($16,805 in 2021 value).

Tue November 24

Leaves for Mexico City with Freddie McEvoy, staying at the Ritz Hotel; there Flynn meets 18-year-old Blanca Rosa Welter, a name she—not Flynn, as has been claimed—changed to Linda Christian in 1943; she later married Tyrone Power in 1949.

Wed November 25

It is reported that Flynn received 17 write-in votes for governor of California by Los Angeles County voters in the November 3rd election.

Thu November 26

Flynn, Freddie, Blanca, and two of her chaperones fly to Acapulco, staying at the Hotel Riviere.

Thu December 3

Flynn and McEvoy return to Hollywood for the weekend.

Mon December 7

Flynn returns to Mexico City, meeting up again with Blanca and her family.

Sun December 13

At the bullfights in Mexico City with Rosa to see the famous toreador, Manolete.

Mon December 14

Returns to Hollywood.

Fri December 25

Spends Christmas with Lili and Sean.

Wed December 30

Rehearsing the song "That's What You Jolly Well Get" for the film THANK YOUR LUCKY STARS with pianist Moe Jerome and choreographer LeRoy Prinz from 2 to 3pm.

Thu December 31

Continues rehearsing "That's What You Jolly Well Get."

During rehearsals for
THANK YOUR LUCKY STARS

From a George Hurrell portrait session ~ Summer,1939

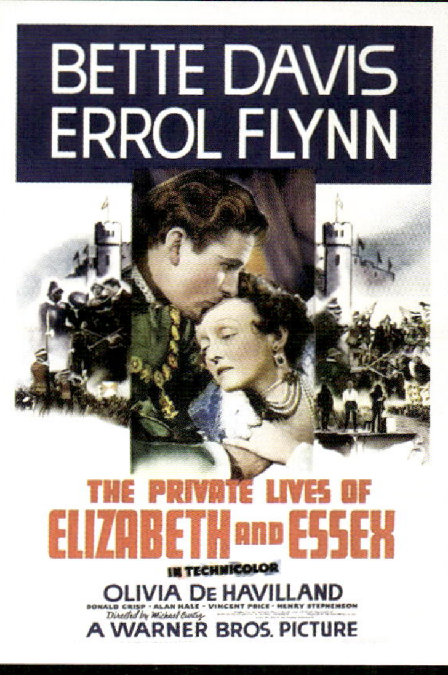

The films of 1939~1942

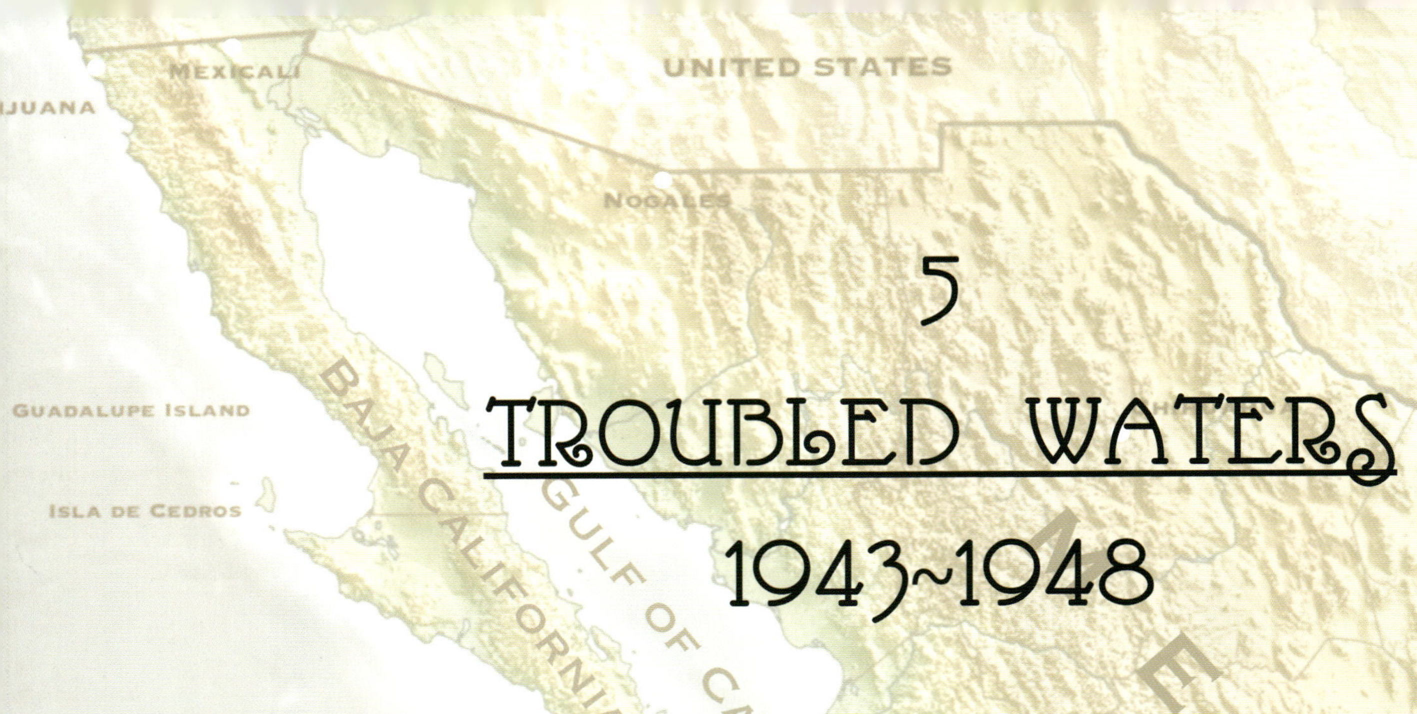

5

TROUBLED WATERS

1943~1948

One could make the case that Errol Flynn's life was divided into two distinct segments: the breathtaking ascent to 1943 and the spiraling decline from that climacteric year. Though he was acquitted of the charges, the double statutory-rape trial of 1943 served to gradually darken his heretofore blithe image.

While the public gradually accustomed itself to this transformation from cinematic hero to sexual hedonist, Flynn's career and private life still provided ample opportunities through which he could find gratification. The mid-1940s brought him a second (this time amenable) wife, two precious daughters, the sailing vessel of his dreams, and several respectable films. He also discovered Jamaica, an island that seemed to fit his dream of the perfect paradise.

UNCERTAIN GLORY, the first of three films made by Flynn's own production company, offered him the opportunity to play an anti-hero and give, for the first time, an unusually shaded characterization. Despite the embarrassment which OBJECTIVE, BURMA! caused him when Warners pulled it from circulation in the U.K. after British critics skewered it—and Flynn—for appearing to give America sole credit for the successful Burma campaign in WWII, he would later write that it was "one of the few pictures of which I am proud." At the end of this period, Flynn starred in ADVENTURES OF DON JUAN, portraying the infamous title character in a way that seemed to mirror Flynn's own world-weariness and distaste for his reputation as a womanizer. The rape trial, which became international news that sometimes eclipsed the war headlines, had spawned the phrase "in like Flynn," and what began as a sly bit of humor was now becoming the totality of Flynn's public persona.

1943

Sat January 2, Mon January 4, and Tue January 5
Continues rehearsing "That's What You Jolly Well Get," with Art Foster, Monte Blue, Fred Kelsey, and assistant dance directors Jack and Bob Crosby.

Sun January 3
Blanca Rosa Welter (Linda Christian) begins living at Flynn's Mulholland house for the next five weeks; Flynn's friend Buster Wiles has also been living there since October.

Wed January 6
Prerecording the song "That's What You Jolly Well Get" on WB stage 9 from 9:30am to 1:20pm; rehearses from 2:20 to 5:30pm; inter-office memo from Frank Mattison: *"I'm afraid it's going to take from now to Saturday night to complete this number."*

Thu January 7
Filming "That's What You Jolly Well Get," directed by David Butler.

Fri January 8
Inter-office memo from Frank Mattison: *"Today...Mr. Flynn will not be in until 10:00 AM, and will have to leave at 1:00 PM...I will do my best to get Flynn to stay until 1:30 PM if he will...however, I know he will have to go this afternoon—on account of the conversation we had last night."* Filming from 10am to 1pm.

Sat January 9
Inter-office memo from Frank Mattison: *"Yesterday...this unit was called for at 9:00 AM, but due to Mr. Flynn's inability to get in before 10:00 AM—we did not get our first shot until 10:30 AM, and stopped shooting at 1:00 PM."* Finishes shooting his song for THANK YOUR LUCKY STARS.

With Ted Billings, Charles Irwin (back to the camera), Will Stanton, Art Foster, Freddie McEvoy, and unidentified

Among the daily throng of spectators outside the courtroom - Wed, January 20; below, the same location today

THE TRIAL

Mon January 11
Flynn is in court at the Los Angeles Hall of Justice during jury selection; presiding is Judge Leslie E. Still, prosecuting district attorney is Thomas W. Cochran, along with prosecutor John Hopkins and bailiff Fred Moxom; a temporary jury includes Charles Boyd, Homer Jacobsmeyer, Ruby Anderson (foreman), Nellie Minear, and Warren Curtis.

Tue January 12
Flynn is at the courthouse during continued jury selection, which on this day is completed with the addition of Mildred Leahy, Teresa Wood, Georgette Welch, Jennie Larson, Lena Morgan, Lorene Boehm, Elaine Forbes, and Mrs. A. Chalfont, the alternate juror.

Wed January 13
After two alternate witnesses are sworn in, the trial begins; opening prosecution statements are made by Deputy District Attorney Thomas Cochran; defense statements are made by Jerry Giesler and Robert E. Ford.

Thu January 14
With 150 spectators waiting outside the courtroom, the first witness is Patricia Marsden, Betty Hansen's sister, followed by Lt. R. W. Bolling of the L.A.P.D. Juvenile Division, who testified about his photos of the room where the rape had allegedly taken place; finally, Betty Hansen takes the stand for the rest of the day and is led weeping from the courtroom after her testimony.

Fri January 15
Betty Hansen is cross-examined by Jerry Giesler, as are singer Lynne Boyer and dancer Agnes "Chi Chi" Toupes, guests at the Bel Air party who are called as witnesses for the prosecution; also taking the stand on this day are Peter Stackpole, photographer on the *Sirocco* cruise, Peggy Satterlee's mother Florence, sister Mickey June, and police department physician Etta Gray; Lynne Boyer testifies to having heard voices from behind a locked door on the night Betty Hansen charges Flynn had sex with her; Miss Boyer claims not to be able to identify the voices but that one could have been Flynn; after testifying she breaks down in the arms of attorney John Hopkins and threatens to jump out of the courtroom window when reporters try to take her picture; when two jurors are found to be prejudiced Judge Sill halts the trial until Monday.

Sun January 17
At the West Side Tennis Club for lunch with Blanca Rosa Welter.

Peggy LaRue Satterlee (1/11/43)

Flynn's attorneys Robert Ford and Jerry Giesler (1/21/43)

Prosecutor, Thomas Cochran (11/2/42)

Betty Hansen (1/14/43)

Prosecutor, John Hopkins (1/28/43)

Dr. Etta Gray

Judge Leslie E. Still

Captain Owen Cathcart-Jones

Mon January 18

Mrs. Alice F. Chalfont replaces juror Elaine Forbes; Lynne Boyer completes her testimony.

Tue January 19

Flynn's arresting officer Lt. R. W. Bolling takes the stand to testify about the arrest at Flynn's home; Sergeant Edward Walker of L.A.P.D. is next on the stand to verify Bolling's testimony; Peggy LaRue Satterlee then takes the stand for the first time; the day ends with Jerry Giesler cross-examining her.

Wed January 20

Jerry Giesler continues his cross-examination of Peggy Satterlee, questioning her on her relationship with Canadian captain Owen Cathcart-Jones; Virginia Morgan is called to the stand to discuss the camping trip to Lake Arrowhead that Satterlee took the previous year with Cathcart-Jones, Morgan having been Satterlee's chaperone on the trip; Satterlee is called back to the stand, during which time it is brought out that she had an abortion—illegal at the time—about fourteen months after her trip on the *Sirocco*; the day ends with Peter Stackpole on the stand, the *Life* magazine photographer who had been on the *Sirocco* taking photos for the magazine during the fateful voyage of August, 1941.

Thu January 21

Peggy Satterlee is again cross-examined by Jerry Giesler; next is Peggy's mother Florence, who testifies about her daughter's relationship with Cathcart-Jones, and about taking her to be examined by county juvenile physician Dr. Etta Gray after the voyage; Peggy's sister Mickey June next takes the stand, relating how it was through her that her sister met Flynn, the actor referring to both as SQQ—"San Quentin Quail," implying their beautiful but underage status that could send a man to San Quentin Prison for having relations with them; finally, Dr. Gray takes the stand to testify about the medical exam she gave Satterlee the day after the voyage, and how in her professional opinion Satterlee had been sexually molested—and a virgin before that.

Fri January 22

Dr. Gray's testimony continues; obstetrician Dr. Henry Rooney is next on the stand to corroborate Dr. Gray's testimony; police photographer J. W. Maurer then presents drawings of the *Sirocco*'s floor plan, which are displayed on the courtroom chalkboard; rounding out the day, Captain Cathcart-Jones gives an accounting of Satterlee visiting a morgue where the 16-year-old accuser of Flynn *"played hide and seek among the corpses"*; with that, the state rested its case; at the end of the session, Flynn posed with the *Sirocco* drawings for reporters and photographers.

Mon January 25

After hopeful audience members had begun lining up at 4:15am, the trial convenes with *Sirocco* crew member Corporal Hubert L. Oliver testifying that all seemed quiet on the night in question, and that all portholes had been closed prior to setting sail—contradicting Satterlee's claim that Flynn enticed her to look at the moon through the porthole in her room; theater owner Jay M. Sutton then testified that he gave Satterlee a job in September of 1940 on the basis of believing her claim to be 18 at the time; next, police woman Mrs. Mary Ross relates Betty Hansen's admission at Juvenile Hall that she had *"undressed herself in the bedroom"* at the McEvoy-Cabot party and that she and Flynn had been intimate on *"a large bed,"* stories that were inconsistent with her testimony in court; Miss Helga Brabon, McEvoy's and Cabot's caretaker, then takes the stand to describe how the bedroom door that Hansen claimed Flynn supposedly locked, had been broken for some time; this was followed with

Lynne Boyer (1/15/43)

Jean Longworth (1/27/43)

Elaine Patterson (1/13/43)

The bedroom at 321 St. Pierre Road in Bel Air

testimony from apartment house manager Mrs. Addie E. Odell concerning a week's rent in the previous October paid by a man named M. Black for Betty Hansen; soda-fountain waitress Mona Mervyn tells the jury that Betty Hansen, who had worked alongside her, informed her that Flynn told her he would *"get her work in the movies"*; the day ended with carhop Elaine Patterson, a member of the party aboard the *Sirocco* during the weekend in question, who claims not to have heard any disturbances or yelling during the time Satterlee claims to have been seduced by Flynn, and states that Satterlee was happy and told her she had *"a very nice trip"* when they all left the yacht.

Tue January 26

Peter Stackpole -
Wed, 1/20/43

Prof. C. M. Cleminshaw

Elaine Patterson begins the day back on the stand for cross-examination from Cochran and Hopkins; then Freddie McEvoy, the host of the Bel Air party, testifies that the day in question started with matches with tennis pro Bill Tilden from 2 to 6:30pm, followed by dinner at 8:30, after which Flynn left at about 10:15; he claims that Hansen had not been invited to the party but had crashed it; Joe and Sophie Jebbink, McEvoy's butler and maid, next testify that all the beds in the house appeared *"untouched"* after Flynn left; director Raoul Walsh takes the stand and relates how he had been invited on the *Sirocco* cruise but had to turn it down due to a previous engagement; 18-year-old showgirl Jean Longworth then testifies that Satterlee told her, *"My mother took me to court to claim Flynn had mistreated me, but I didn't want to, because it wasn't true"*; next to take the stand is Private Martin E. Ross, a Hollywood bellboy, who relates that Hansen was a frequent overnight visitor to his hotel, calling herself Bunnie Baker, aged 25, and who, on one occasion, was banned by Ross from the hotel; Flynn's close friend Bud (now Army Lieutenant) Ernst is the next witness, testifying that he was at the Bel Air party and observed Hansen first sitting on the arm of Flynn's chair and then sliding down to share the chair with him; finally, Hansen's boss Philip N. Hanly testifies that she had quit her job on the day of the party, claiming that she was going to a party to *"meet Errol Flynn and get into pictures"*; Agnes "Chi-Chi" Toupes and Buster Wiles, who both had been prospective witnesses, were never ultimately called to the stand.

Wed January 27

Jean Longworth returns to the witness stand; prosecuting attorney Cochran accuses her of prejudice against Satterlee and calls for her impeachment, which is denied; an affidavit written by *Sirocco* skipper Hayward Kingsley (now on active military duty) is next read to the court, in which he claims he *"did not see or hear anything on board the yacht while he was aboard"*; Flynn's attorney Robert Ford next takes the stand to relate his conversations with Hansen and Longworth at Juvenile Hall the previous October and November; Flynn poses for pictures for the press during the noon recess *(bottom right)*, and then takes the stand himself for the first time; he is questioned by Giesler, and testifies to calling Peggy Satterlee the day after the cruise to inquire why she had called the D.A.'s office; *"you'll find out,"* he was told by Satterlee.

Thu January 28

Flynn takes the stand again to testify about Hansen, taking questions from Giesler and then cross-examination by Hopkins, which also includes questions about the Satterlee case; Giesler returns to question Flynn and recommends that the jury be taken to Balboa to visit the *Sirocco*.

Fri January 29

Meets Patricia Harvey, a 20-year-old fan who has hitchhiked from New Jersey to attend the trial; Mickey June Satterlee (in long pigtails with pink bows) starts the day with questioning from Cochran; this is followed by McEvoy housekeeper Stella Green, who testifies that she never tested the lock on *"the Blue Room bedroom door,*

Posing for photographers before testifying for the
first time - Wed, January 27

Attorneys Jerry Giesler (L) and Thomas Cochran examining the door lock from the Bel Air house bedroom - Fri, January 29

nor ever tried to lock it"; police chemist Sgt. Leland P. Jones then testifies to having gone to the Bel Air home on the previous Wednesday (1/27) to examine the bedroom door (which has now been brought into the courtroom, along with metal filings discovered on the floor beneath it; *top left*); L.A.P.D. Lt. Robert W. Bolling is recalled to testify about comments made by Flynn at the hearing in November; next on the stand is district attorney investigator Joe McClure, who had interviewed Jean Longworth and found her comments about Satterlee to be biased and prejudiced against the defendant; Professor C. M. Cleminshaw of the Griffith Park Observatory then testifies to the position of the moon over Catalina on the weekend of August 1, 1941, demonstrating that Satterlee's claim of Flynn showing her the moon through her room's porthole would not have been possible, as the moon was on the other side of the *Sirocco* from the position in which it was moored; next on the stand is Mrs. Elizabeth Cathcart-Jones, whose separation from Captain Cathcart-Jones made it a distinct possibility that the Satterlee sisters could have been occupying his apartment; photographer Stackpole is recalled to identify photos of his showing Satterlee aboard the *Sirocco* on the weekend in question; H. W. Douglas of the U.S. Weather Bureau testifies for the prosecution about weather conditions and wind direction during the *Sirocco*'s return to Balboa on August 3rd; Flynn had claimed the winds were strong enough to require him to be at the wheel the entire distance, but Douglas' answer (*"Sorry. I don't know. Our instruments are on land, not at sea."*) does nothing to discredit Flynn; the day ends with Judge Still announcing there will be no jury trip to the Sirocco.

Sat January 30
Flynn and Raoul Walsh escort Blanca Rosa Welter (Linda Christian) to Warner Bros. Studios for a screen test.

Mon February 1
Cochran and Giesler revisit in detail the bedroom door from the Bel Air estate; aiding in the examination are locksmiths C. D. Pope and Lloyd Eads, and Leonard V. Moss, the manager the Bel Air property; after the noon recess, Giesler again questions his partner Robert Ford, after which the defense rests.

Tue February 2
With neither Betty Hansen nor Peggy LaRue Satterlee in the courtroom, day-long closing arguments are made by Deputy District Attorney Thomas Cochran, beginning with, *"Flynn is the glamour man of all glamour men"*; Judge Still then calls a recess until the following day at 1:00pm to honor the funeral of District Attorney John F. Dockweiler, who had died of pneumonia the previous Sunday; it was Dockweiler who had decided to circumvent the conclusion of the grand jury in favor of trying Flynn.

Wed February 3
Jerry Giesler begins his closing arguments in defense of Flynn at 1:00pm and speaks for the rest of the day.

Thu February 4
Giesler continues his final arguments, referencing a *"Mr. X,"* the unidentified character involved with Satterlee's abortion; near the day's end, Hopkins begins his final rebuttal, in some cases name-calling the defense witnesses to the point of Judge Still demanding that he cease; Blanca moves out of Mulholland on this day.

Flynn shaking the hand of jury foreman Ruby Anderson after his acquittal (2/6); next to her are jurors Mildred Leahy and Teresa Wood; behind are jurors Lena Morgan, Jennie Larson, and Lorene Boehm

Fri February 5
John Hopkins and Robert Ford make their final statements; the jury is given their instructions by Judge Still and retires to the jury room at 11:21am to begin deliberations on the three counts against Flynn; at 9:54pm, after seven hours and no verdict, the jury is ordered locked up for the night; at this point, Peggy LaRue Satterlee is free to go home with her parents to Applegate, CA, while Betty Hansen remains in custody in Juvenile Hall.

Sat February 6
At 11:19am, after thirteen hours of deliberation, the jury of nine women and three men bring in a verdict acquitting Flynn of all charges; he and Giesler shake the hands of each jury member and then leave the courthouse.

The logo of one of several national support organizations for Flynn

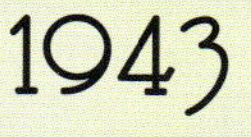

Wed February 10

Los Angeles Herald–Express journalist Agnes Underwood hosts a spaghetti dinner for Flynn at her Los Angeles home, attended by other journalists, along with Flynn's attorney Robert Ford and friend Buster Wiles *(top right)*.

Mon February 15

EDGE OF DARKNESS is previewed at the Warner Beverly Hills Theater, with Jack Warner there to gauge audience response.

Tue February 16

Wire from Jack Warner to Mort Blumenstock: TO: MAJOR BERNHARD KALMENSON KALMINE SCHNEIDER BLUMENSTOCK SCHLESS HUMMEL— HAD FIRST PREVIEW LAST NIGHT EDGE OF DARKNESS AT OUR BEVERLY HILLS THEATRE WHICH IS TOUGHEST AUDIENCE WE EVER PREVIEWED BEFORE. NEVER HEARD SUCH APPLAUSE AT END OF PICTURE. IT'S BIG IN SCOPE AND A TREMENDOUS PRODUCTION. FLYNN SHERIDAN HUSTON BALANCE OF CAST PHENOMENAL [sic]. THIS IS ONE OF THE TOP PICTURES IN YEARS TO COME.

Sun February 21

Through his friend Buster Wiles, Flynn invites Nora Eddington *(top left)* to the Mulholland house for lunch; during the trial he had seen her working at the courthouse cigarette stand *(center and bottom right)*; Wiles chauffeurs her and her friend Marda up to the house.

March

Flies to Mexico for a two-week vacation.

Mon March 15

A loan of $40,000 is made to Flynn ($616,507 in 2021 value), with $4,000 being deducted weekly from his paycheck.

Tue March 16

The F.B.I. bugs a telephone conversation between Flynn and his friend Freddie McEvoy wherein Flynn mentions posting a $500 bond to have an arrest warrant withdrawn on McEvoy for receiving a radio transmitter in Acapulco for the *Sirocco*.

Fri March 19

Along with Dennis Morgan, Nancy Coleman, Hedda Hopper, Faye Emerson, Julie Bishop, and a planeload of other stars and journalists, Flynn leaves for Mexico on the American Red Cross Drive, sponsored by Warner Bros. *(bottom left)*.

Sat March 20

Visits the floating gardens of Xochimillo, and at night attends the premiere of *Yankee Doodle Dandy* along with Bette Davis, Alexis Smith, Ann Sheridan, Edgar Bergen and Charlie McCarthy, political dignitaries, and others.

Sun March 21

At the newly opened Hippódromo de las Américas racetrack, and later with Freddie McEvoy to the bullfights at Toreo de la Condesa.

Wed March 31

An F.B.I. report characterizes Flynn as a *"highly-sexed individual…of low moral character, with absolutely no regard for women with whom he has been associated with in pictures."* It goes on to claim he *"has had an affair with every woman who has ever worked on the Warner Bros. lot from 'from grandmothers on down."* A handwritten line on each page stating, *"Info does not pertain to Errol Flynn"* calls the report into question.

Nora Eddington

Being "bibbed" by Agnes Underwood during the tribute dinner for Flynn at her home - Wed, February 10

Above, the cigarette stand (on right) in the lobby of the Hall of Justice, and below, the same spot today

Leaving for Mexico on the American Red Cross Drive with (clockwise from bottom left) Juanita Stark, Nancy Coleman, Dennis Morgan, Hedda Hopper, Faye Emerson, Lynn Baggett, and Julie Bishop - Fri, March 19

On the set of
NORTHERN PURSUIT

April 23, 1943

MULHOLLAND FARM

Letter to Nora: *"Don't forget what I told you—only get the best, or it's not worth getting. Thank you for last night; and I hope you have a lousy time tonight! And now I have something to look forward to tomorrow night Goodmorning!"*

Mon April 5
Comes down with sinus trouble at the Acapulco Flamingo Hotel.

Tue April 6
Telegram from Jack Warner to Flynn: THANKS YOUR CABLE BUT CANNOT CONSENT YOU POSTPONE REPORTING TO STUDIO UNTIL APRIL THIRTEENTH…,..REGRET EXCEEDINGLY LEARN ABOUT YOUR SINUS BUT FEEL SURE LOS ANGELES CLIMATE MUCH MORE BENEFICIAL. THEREFORE CABLE ME YOU ON WAY AS IMPERATIVE YOU BE AVAILABLE NOT LATER THIS FRIDAY FOR [NORTHERN PURSUIT] PREPARATION, ETC…."

Fri April 9
EDGE OF DARKNESS premieres in New York.

Tue April 13
Returns to Los Angeles from Mexico.

Mon April 19
Begins work on NORTHERN PURSUIT, filming in McBain's (Alec Craig) store and Steve's (Flynn) cabin.

Tue April 20 and Wed April 21
Continues filming in Steve's cabin and (on 4/21) in the inspector's office, and the outer office; memo from NORTHERN PURSUIT's director, Raoul Walsh, to Jack Warner (4/21): *"Dear Col: Just a few lines that might make you feel very happy. Errol is very enthusiastic about the script and he worked until 6:48 last night… This looks like a record day."*

Thu April 22
Continues filming in the inspector's office; Flynn's attorney Robert E. Ford in a note to Steve Trilling: *"….In accordance with the agreement between you and Thomson Productions, Inc., we hereby submit as our choice of a story for our next production 'Cortez', which is the life of Cortez, an outstanding figure in the history of Mexico….We have done considerable research on the life of Cortez and are firmly convinced that a vehicle based on his life is ideally suited for Errol Flynn….Mr. Flynn is personally well acquainted with the life of Cortez and suitable locations for the filming of his life and he will be happy to discuss the story with your representatives at your convenience."* EDGE OF DARKNESS begins opening in cities across the United States, on this day in Los Angeles.

Fri April 23
Filming in McBain's store and the street outside, and at the Bear Lake Hotel (on Canadian Street on the WB backlot).

Sat April 24
Filming in the recruiting office; inter-office memo from Lou Baum: *"Mr. Flynn ordered hash for his luncheon (yesterday) and it made him sick to his stomach; he was ailing all Friday afternoon. (Today) he again ordered hash to definitely confirm the fact that it didn't agree with him. This time it 'knocked him out cold'. Mr. Flynn could not continue and the company, as usual being the fall guy, had to fold up at 3:30 PM at which time Flynn turned as gray as a sidewalk. At your earliest convenience you might add to what I have already told Flynn—to permanently stay away from hash until the picture is over."*

Mon April 26
Filming in the barber shop and the Royal Canadian Mounted Police Headquarters.

Tue April 27
Filming in the hotel lobby and dining room; Warner Bros., through Roy Obringer, turns down Flynn's request to film *Cortez* in favor of UNCERTAIN GLORY.

Thu April 29
Flynn's attorney Robert E. Ford informs the Los Angeles Office of the F.B.I. that his client has received an extortion letter (mailed to the old North Linden house in Beverly Hills) postmarked 4/23/43 from a Robert Street of Quincy, MA. The letter, with the word *"Beware"* written on the envelope flap, reads: "MR. FLYNN!!! IF YOU KNOW WHAT IS GOOD FOR YOU YOU WILL PAY ATTENTION TO THEM GIRLS YOU RAPED. I KNOW YOU DID IT. YOU CAN NOT FOOL ME. SO YOU BETTER FORK OVER SOME DOE [sic]. PUT YOUR ANSWER IN THE BOSTON DAILY RECORD. PUT IT NEAR [Walter] WINCHELL COLLUMN [sic] AND JUST SAY ANY THING BUT GIVE A HINT YOU RECEIVED THIS AND IN A WEEK IF YOU DON'T WANT TROUBLE. GET WHAT I MEAN CHUM. BE HEARING FROM YOU DON'T FORGET A WEEK FROM TODAY THAT WILL BE APRIL 29 DEADLINE AND THEN I WILL SEND YOUR INSTRUCTIONS ON WHERE AND WHEN TO LEAVE THE MONE[y] AND HOW MUCH. DO NOT

WORREY [sic] IT WILL NOT BE OVER 15,000 [$231,190 in 2021 value] FOR THAT'S ALL I NEED TO SKIP TOWN." *(top right)*

Sat May 1
Filming in the internment camp and mess hall, the kitchen, storeroom, Steve's cabin, and retakes in the RCMP Headquarters.

Mon May 3
Filming in the jailhouse office, the jail cell, train, and snow bank (the train shed on the WB backlot).

Tue May 4
Filming in and outside the Royal Hotel, in the King Edward Hotel, and in the courtroom.

Wed May 5
Continues filming in the courtroom, the depot, the parcel and check room, ticket window, and gate to the train (on Tenement Street on the WB backlot).

Thu May 6
Filming in the RCMP Post, the internment camp, and Pullman car.

Fri May 7
Filming outside the courthouse on New York Street on the WB backlot, in the Pullman washroom, and in the small station.

Mon May 10
Filming in Steve's cabin, and the rendezvous.

Tue May 11
Continues filming the rendezvous, in Steve's hotel room, and in the Winnipeg RCMP office.

Wed May 12 through Sat May 15
Filming in Dagor's (Bernard Nedell) cabin.

Mon May 17
Ill; does not work; Tenny Wright to Steve Trilling: *"As you know Errol Flynn did not report for work today, claiming he had a headache. Now I understand from Lou Baum, who talked to Flynn personally, that he has to go to the hospital on account of his throat being in bad shape, which he claims is from the artificial snow we are using on Stage 7...."*

Tue May 18
Ill; does not work; Tenny Wright to Steve Trilling, Roy Obringer, and Raoul Walsh: *"At 11:50 this morning Lou Baum talked to Dr. Stevens, who had just returned from the hospital having seen Mr. Flynn. He advises that Flynn's condition is not bad, and that he will try to have him ready for work by next Thursday, and if not then, definitely by Friday."* Roy Obringer to Steve Trilling: *"Our Dr. Brettnauer reported today that Flynn's illness is in fact due to a recurrence of his sinus trouble but Flynn, of course, contends that it is due to a throat condition on account of the artificial snow. Flynn's doctor is not disputing this with Flynn, as he feels that no benefits will be derived by reminding Flynn that it is his sinuses. However, Flynn's doctor states that Flynn will not be able to get out of the hospital until Wednesday or Thursday and, therefore, may not be able to return to work until Thursday or possibly Friday."*

Wed May 19 and Thu May 20
Ill; does not work.

Fri May 21
Filming a process shot in Keller's (Helmut Dantine) truck, and outside Dagor's cabin *(bottom right)*; in the release of the documentary short *Business At War*.

Sat May 22
Filming in Dagor's cabin.

Sun May 23
Dinner at Chasen's with Nora.

Mon May 24 and Tue May 25
Continues filming in and (on 5/25) outside Dagor's cabin.

Wed May 26 and Thu May 27
Filming in the MP Post and on the road.

The extortion letter sent to Flynn - fourth week of April

With Julie Bishop, Gene Lockhart, and Helmut Dantine - Fri, May 21

With a crew member on the WB soundstage - Wed, June 2

Being presented the portrait of him done by his artist friend, John Decker (center), during the filming of NORTHERN PURSUIT; the film's director, Raoul Walsh, is on the right; the painting would hang in Flynn's Mulholland home; below, the photo from which the portrait was painted

Fri May 28

Ill; company is closed down early; Lou Baum to Roy Obringer: *"Errol Flynn called up this morning to advise that he was not feeling well. As soon as I got the word, I called him at home, and he reported to me that he was running a fever of 102 and he had a call in for the doctor to come and see him...I have just finished talking to Dr. Hearn….and he advises that as yet he has not had a chance to see Flynn but will do so sometime this morning, and I will contact him after he has been there and give you his report."* *Film Daily* reports that Warner Bros. has cast Flynn as John James Audubon in a film called *Singing In The Wilderness*; Flynn does not star in the film.

Sat May 29

I'll; does not work; Lou Baum to Tenny Wright: *"Just got through talking to Dr. Hearn, the attending physician to Mr. Flynn, and he advised me that he has definitely instructed Errol Flynn to stay in bed today due to his feverish condition. However he feels that Flynn should be ready for work on Tuesday morning."*

Tue June 1 and Wed June 2

Filming on the trail and in the lean-to.

Thu June 3 through Sat June 5

Continues filming in the lean-to and (on 6/4 and 5) on the trail.

Mon June 7 and Tue June 8

Continues filming on the trail.

Wed June 9

Ill; company dismissed; Lou Baum to Roy Obringer: *"Please note that when we contacted Errol Flynn this morning at about 10:00 o'clock to inquire as to whether he would appear for his 10:30 call he advised us that he simply could not make it; he was feeling too bad. The arrangements now stand that we are to contact him tomorrow morning at 8:00 to see whether he will be with us tomorrow."*

Thu June 10

Ill; does not work.

Fri June 11 and Sat June 12, and Mon June 14 through Wed June 16

Filming in and (on 6/11) outside the cave.

Thu June 17

Filming outside the mine and on the trail; memo from Jack Warner to all departments: *"The picture formerly titled 'To The Last Man' will definitely be called 'Northern Pursuit.'"*

Fri June 18

Continues filming on the trail and in the lean-to.

Sat June 19

Filming a process shot of the approach to the avalanche and trail.

Sun June 20

Flynn's 34th birthday.

Mon June 21

Filming outside the mine shaft.

Tue June 22 through Thu June 24

Continues filming outside the mine shaft (on 6/22), inside the mine shaft, in Keller's room, and (on 6/23 and 24) in Steve's room.

Fri June 25

Filming outside the mine and bomber, and a montage in the mine.

Sat June 26

Filming in and outside the mine shaft and on the trail.

Mon June 28 and Tue June 29

Filming in the bomber and (on 6/29) on the trail, and more mine montage.

Wed June 30

Filming outside the mine.

July

Sometime this month Flynn purchases *The Man Is At Sea*, *(top right)* an 1899 painting by Vincent Van Gogh; it was acquired from Cesar Diorio of New York City for $48,000 ($739,808 in 2021 value).

Thu July 1

Filming retakes in the King Edward Hotel, outside the Royal George Hotel, in Steve's hotel room, and in the cheap hotel room.

Fri July 2

Filming in the furnished room, the street corner on New York Street on the WB backlot, the train vestibule, and the office.

Sat July 3

Filming a process shot in the bomber and more mine montage.

Tue July 6

Filming a lake montage.

Wed July 7

Filming more mine montage.

Thu July 8

Filming a process shot of the trek and parachute, and inside the bomber.

Wed July 14

Finishes work on NORTHERN PURSUIT filming a tag in the Bear Lake Hotel.

Sat July 17

Travels with Buster Wiles to Mare Island Navy Yard in Vallejo, CA, to visit Dudley "Mush" Morton, the skipper of the *U.S.S. Wahoo* submarine; they take practice runs and dives off the San Francisco coast (the *Wahoo* and all hands are lost in a sinking on October 11).

Mon July 19

Travels back to Los Angeles.

Fri July 23

Flies with Raoul Walsh to Mexico City, according to an F.B.I. report investigating Flynn on the White Slave Act concerning Nora.

Mon July 26

Travels to Acapulco, staying at the Hotel La Riviera, room 7; his 22-foot motorized fishing boat, the *Little Sirocco*, had been shipped in December and is moored at the Acapulco Yacht Club; spends the next two weeks fishing, swimming, and water skiing.

Thu August 5

The F.B.I. closes the extortion case of April 29th, apprehending a married couple who are described as "screwballs"; no charges are filed.

Mon August 9

The I.R.S. files a lien against Flynn for $22,454 ($346,076 in 2021 value) in additional taxes due to an accounting error; Nora travels to Acapulco to meet up with Flynn.

Fri August 13

Notifies his business manager Albert Blum to inform the press there was no recent marriage to Nora.

Sat August 14

Is taken ill while in Mexico and enters a hospital; Warners announces he will star as artist John James Audubon (he never makes the film); the *Sirocco* is sold for $20,000 ($308,253 in 2021 value) to Fred Muller, a Hollywood gas station owner.

Wed August 18

Nora leaves Mexico; Errol travels to Mexico City two days later.

Sun August 22

Leaves Mexico City for Los Angeles, arriving on the 23rd.

Flynn's Van Gogh, The Man Is At Sea, *which hung in his Mulholland home*

At the Mocambo in Hollywood around this time

Thu August 26
Begins filming UNCERTAIN GLORY, the first film made by his own newly-formed company, Thomson Productions (the daily production notes for this film are missing).

Filming UNCERTAIN GLORY on a WB soundstage

With Paul Lukas

With Jean Sullivan at Melrose Ranch in Escondido, CA

Fri September 10
"Warners are rushing production of 'Uncertain Glory' starring Errol Flynn, in a story of the invasion of France by the United Nations, and 'Passage To Marseilles' also with a background in France, to again keep pace with anticipated world news events." Film Daily.

Mon September 20
A lien is filed against Flynn for $121,858 ($1,878,156 in 2021 value) in unpaid taxes for 1942.

Thu September 23
THANK YOUR LUCKY STARS opens at the Fox in Spokane, WA.

October
"Errol Flynn has never spoken of his divorce from Lili Damita or mentioned his small son, Sean....The loss of his son, [friends] say, is the one thing in Flynn's life that has ever touched him deeply....There is no doubt that Errol feels keenly the fact that he has no hand or share in his son's life." From this month's issue of *Photoplay* magazine; sometime late this month Flynn purchases the 1902 Paul Gauguin painting, *Famille Tahitienne (bottom left)*.

Flynn's Gauguin, Familie Tahitienne, (1902), which hung in his Mulholland home

Thu October 14
Flynn is sued by Shirley Evans Hassau, asserting that he is the father of her two-year-old daughter, Marilyn *(bottom right)*; in the suit it is asked that Flynn be made to pay $1,750 monthly child support ($26,972 in 2021 value) as well as $17,000 in further costs ($262,015 in 2021 value); Flynn denies the charges through his attorney, Robert Ford.

Sun October 17
In court to defend against paternity suit brought by Miss Hassau.

Fri October 22
Completes principal filming of UNCERTAIN GLORY; a preliminary

Shirley Evans Hassau and daughter Marilyn

hearing takes place in Superior Court concerning the Hassau paternity case.

Mon October 25

Filming retakes for UNCERTAIN GLORY.

Tue October 26

An official denial of paternity by Flynn via affidavit is entered in the Hassau paternity case.

Thu October 28

The Hassau paternity case is delayed until 1944.

Wed November 10

NORTHERN PURSUIT opens natiionwide.

Fri November 12

Filming retakes for UNCERTAIN GLORY.

Mon November 15

Requests to be absent from work for eight weeks commencing November 24th so as to be able to go on the USO Camp Shows tour.

Wed November 24

Leaves from Seattle, WA, on the USO Victory Tour of Alaska, arriving on this day at Fort Richardson in Anchorage; in the entourage are actress Martha O'Driscoll, singer-guitarist Jimmie Dodd and his wife, singer Ruth Carrell, and magician Harry Mendoza.

In the study of his Mulholland home - November

Flynn Turns Woes Into Gags on Tour

HEADQUARTERS. Alaskan Department, Nov. 30 (UP)—Actor Errol Flynn has arrived in the Alaskan theater with other entertainers for a tour of military installations on the mainland of the territory and in the Aleutian Islands.

In his opening perfomance before a large audience of American troops, the swashbuckling star made frequent gag references to his legal entanglements involving 'teen-age girls and a pending paternity suit filed by blond Shirley Evans Hassau.

"I like this cold climate," Flynn said. "It was getting plenty hot for me in Hollywood and I'm not kidding you. You should have seen the crowd at the airport when I left. Hundreds of people—all my lawyers."

With Flynn on the tour are Singer Martha O'Driscoll, Magician Henry Mendoza, Guitarist Jimmy Door and Singer Ruth Carroll.

The Pittsburgh Press
Tue, November 30

December

Written to Nora: *"Hello my pet / Am flying along at 10,000 feet somewhere – can't say where – in the frozen north, slightly amazed that from this height one can't see Tokyo. The country is fantastic! Ice, snow, sleet, a driving rain and occasionally a weird glimpse [sic] on white mountain caps of sun. Show's a great success – thank God. All big army and navy shots delighted, and not hesitating to tell us it's far and away the best show (including Bob Hope's) to come here. One feels good about this naturally. It's packed full of laughs and the boys seem to love it. Terribly hard though – am knocked out already thru no sleep and continual rush – hope we can finish. Must stop now – we're running into bad weather all of a sudden and I can't write. Miss you and love and love you. That thing and many kisses – Errol."*

Sat December 4

Flies with the tour to the naval station on the island of Dutch Harbor, AK.

Tue December 7

Is given a tour of a submarine docked at the base.

Thu December 9

Flies to the Army airfield at Amchitka Island, AK; is gifted a blue fox that he names Tundra Lil.

Fri December 10

The troop celebrates Ruth Carrell's birthday.

Mon December 13

Written to Nora: *"ALASKA Somewhere in the Aleutian Area [A.P.O. 980] Dec. 13, 1943...Hello Youngin / Well, we've just cleaned up this particular place – not allowed to say where – and are off again tomorrow morning, I think by plane, one never knows until the last minute. Seems amazing to think one has only been gone three weeks – it seems*

With Harry Mendoza, Ruth Carrell, Martha O'Driscoll, and Jimmie Dodd at Dutch Harbor, AK - December

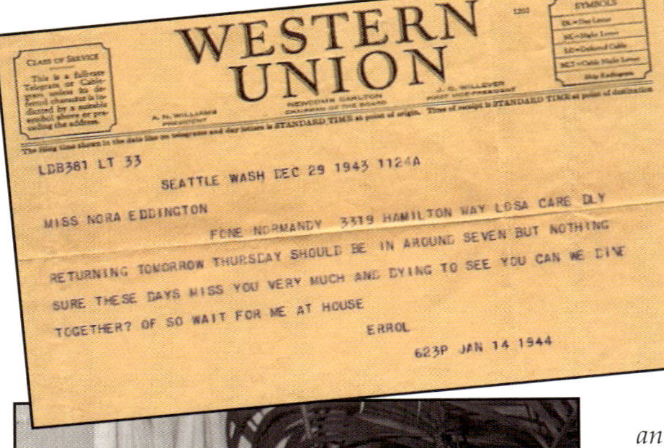

With Nora at a party at Warner Bros. Studios for Army, Navy, and Industrial Leaders - Sat, January 15

Performing a radio adaptation of GENTLEMAN JIM with Alexis Smith and Ward Bond at the Lady Esther Guild Theater in Hollywood - Mon, February 14

like a lifetime. One can have no conception how it must feel for the poor devils who've been here 2 or 3 years – I'm continually astounded how they can endure it. Was hoping to hear from you – what happened?...I must make this short as to find five minutes to oneself up here is as rare as snow in the Mojave. Just wanted you to know I was thinking of you with much sentiment and already dying to get back. My God – this country really makes one appreciate all the things one takes so easily for granted at home...Please call Buster and say we all wish he had been along on the trip – the crap games are out of this world – no one can spend any money and it's sort of been piling up for a few years... Much thought! Errol"

Tue December 14
Flies to the Naval Air Station, Adak, AK.

Sat December 18
Flies to the Alexai Point Army Airfield at Attu, AK; the island had only been recaptured from the Japanese on May 30th; letter from producer Jerry Wald to Jack Warner: "....When you get around to reading 'Don Juan,' I wish you'd keep it in mind as a vehicle for Errol Flynn. The combination of Flynn in 'The Adventures of Don Juan' can't help but be an outstanding box-office film. Flynn was always at his best when he was in costume and had a sword in his hand (No gag intended.)....The thing I wish to stress in this note is that Flynn needs a vehicle of this kind and I believe this is a good one for him...."

Thu December 23
Flies to Fairbanks, AK, visiting Big Delta Army Airfield and Ladd Field.

Sat December 25
Christmas is celebrated in Fairbanks, the entertainers exchanging gifts bought at the base PX.

Tue December 28
Leaves Fairbanks for Seattle, WA.

Wed December 29
On a stopover in Seattle at the end of the USO tour.

Thu December 30
Arrives back in Los Angeles and is met at the airport by Nora and his artist friend John Decker.

1944

Tue January 4
Poses with the blue fox (Tundra Lil) brought back from the USO tour of Alaska.

Wed January 12
Wire from Jack Warner to Flynn: DEAR ERROL: WE ARE HAVING A PREVIEW OF YOUR PICTURE UNCERTAIN GLORY TOMORROW NIGHT THURSDAY. BE AT OUR STUDIO PRIVATE DINING ROOM AT SIX THIRTY TOMORROW EVENING SO YOU CAN ATTEND THIS PREVIEW. WIRE ME IMMEDIATE REPLY.

Thu January 13
Attends a private screening of UNCERTAIN GLORY at the WB Studios.

Sat January 15
Blowout party at Warner Bros. for Army, Navy, and Industrial Leaders *(center left)*.

Mon January 17
Begins a tour for the Treasury Department's 4th War Loan Bond Drive, the first week spent in Louisiana; stays with Buster Wiles at the Roosevelt Hotel in New Orleans and performs two shows daily at the Municipal Auditorium; others on the tour include Victor Mature and Billy De Wolfe.

Sun January 23
Travels through Louisiana with the War Bonds Drive, going to Birmingham and Mobile, AL, on the 24th.

Thu January 27
Final stop on the War Loan Bond Tour is Missouri; in St. Louis he stays at the Chase Hotel with Buster Wiles; also on this leg of the tour are Gene Tierney and Anthony Quinn.

Mon February 7
Returns to Hollywood.

Mon February 14
Performs a radio play of *Gentleman Jim* with Alexis Smith and Ward Bond on the *Lady Esther Screen Guild Theater* for CBS *(bottom left)*.

March

Sometime this month Flynn acquires another schnauzer which he names Moody.

Fri March 3

At the Mocambo *(top right)*.

Sat March 18

On or about this date Flynn pays all expenses (including future rent and utilities) for an apartment/art gallery for his artist friend John Decker at 1215 Alta Loma Road in (now) West Hollywood.

Thu April 6

Roy Obringer to Flynn: *"I am advised by the Accounting Department that there stands on the company books an Accounts Receivable from you in the amount of $132.91 [$1,989.63 in 2021 value] due to personal telephone calls made by you and charged to your account. This charge has long been unpaid and it is our desire to remove this account from our books by having payment made by you therefor. Would you therefore, kindly forward your check made payable to Warner Bros. Pictures, Inc., in the above amount, to M.E.L. De Patie, auditor of this company."*

Fri April 7

UNCERTAIN GLORY premieres at the Strand in New York City.

Sat April 8

Attends a birthday party for Sonja Henie at her home; in the latter hours of the party Flynn gets into a brawl with Sonja's husband Dan Topping.

Wed April 19

Wardrobe and makeup test for OBJECTIVE, BURMA!.

Sat April 22

UNCERTAIN GLORY opens nation wide.

Sun April 23

With Freddie McEvoy at the Mocambo when an altercation at a nearby table results in a patron crushing a raw egg on Flynn's head.

Mon May 1 to Sat May 6

Filming begins on OBJECTIVE, BURMA! at the "Lucky" Baldwin Ranch in Arcadia, CA (now known as the Los Angeles County Arboretum).

Mon May 8 and Tue May 9

Filming jungle scenes at Whittier Park, CA. Flynn is staying at the Eaton Hotel in Pasadena, CA, until the 17th.

Wed May 10

Ill; does not work; Frank Mattison to Tenny Wright: *"For your information, I tried to get Errol Flynn twice yesterday afternoon and four times last night, but was unable to reach him at anytime. The first time a woman informed me he would not be back until after dinner and when I called after dinner the phone was off the hook."*

Sat May 13

Ill; does not work; Frank Mattison to Tenny Wright: *"As I told you early this morning, Mr. Flynn was ill last night and the doctor arrived late; when I called this morning he said he would not be able to come out today. However, we have a good day's work to do without him, and we will have him again on Monday. With good luck we will finish this location [Whittier Park] on Tuesday night."*

Wed May 17

Continues filming jungle scenes at Whittier Park; Frank Mattison to Tenny Wright: *"Yesterday we had some little discussion; Mr. Flynn objected to our shooting too far out of continuity. Our reason for jumping out of continuity was because we wanted to stay at each location and finish it up or stay there as long as we could before moving all the equipment on account of gasoline and tires. Mr. Flynn complained to Jerry Wald and no doubt you will hear about it today."*

Thu May 18

Does not work; attends the opening of the Decker-Flynn Gallery *(center right)* with Nora; fifty canvases are exhibited, including Flynn's Manet painting, *Marguerite de Conflans Wearing a Hood.*

Bottom right, the back and front of the gallery's opening program

With actress Peggy Maley and producer Bill Girard at the Mocambo - Fri, March 3

With Richard Erdman, Frank Tang, and George Tyne at the Los Angeles County Arboretum - First week of May

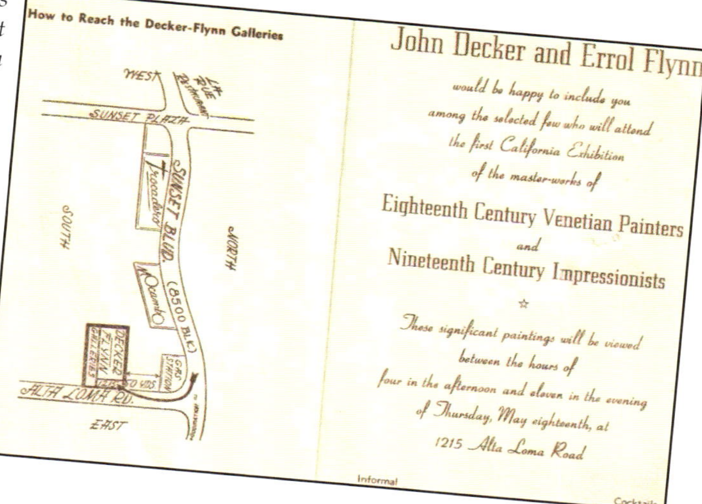

With Frank Tang, William Prince, and Henry Hull at Whittier Park, CA - May

Filming in the transport plane - Fri, June 2

On a lunch break with George Tobias (front) and Henry Hull (rear right)

Fri May 19, Sat May 20, and Mon May 22
Continues filming jungle scenes at Whittier Park.

Tue May 23
Films the supply drop at Whittier Park.

Wed May 24 and Thu May 25
Filming at Whittier Park; on 5/25 he threatens to walk off the set because of noisy planes overhead.

Fri May 26 and Sat May 27
Continues filming at Whittier Park; Frank Mattison to Tenny Wright (5/26): *"We are losing a great deal of time on account of airplanes overhead and Mr. Walsh is very worried about going to the airport at Metropolitan [now Van Nuys Airport] where he is afraid we will be held up even further. Yesterday it was so bad Mr. Flynn was real peeved and threaten [sic] to walk out and leave the scene undone on account of airplanes."*

Tue May 30
No work; Memorial Day.

Wed May 31
Is on set but doesn't work because of inclement weather.

Fri June 2 and Sat June 3
Films inside the transport plane on Stage 14 *(center left)*.

Sun June 4
The film company leaves from the WB studio at 6pm to travel to Palm Springs, CA, arriving at 10pm; the cast stays at the Del Tahquitz and Palm Springs Hotels.

Mon June 5 and Tue June 6
Films the India airport scenes at Palm Springs, CA.

Wed June 7 to Wed June 14
Filming continues at Whittier Park with jungle and abandoned airstrip scenes.

Sun June 18
Attends the wedding of Alexis Smith and Craig Stevens at the Church of the Recessional at Forest Lawn in Glendale; announces to the studio that he is refusing to work because of problems he has with the script.

Mon June 19
Filming in the Burmese village at the Los Angeles County Arboretum but refuses to work; Frank Mattison to Tenny Wright: *"As you know, Mr. Errol Flynn has refused to come out to work today. I had Mr. Jerry Wald on the phone last night and again this morning and it is up to him to straighten it out... As you know, Mr. Flynn says he has been waiting for changes to come through and the Saturday script is apparently unchanged from the previous script. Mr. Flynn has told me that he is still walking through the picture and not a damn thing has happened since the picture started where anything other than routine dialogue and walking has been photographed...This is in Jerry Wald's lap and I just hung up the phone, telling him that we could take about 9 setups without Mr. Errol Flynn."*

Tue June 20 to Thu June 22
Continues filming in the Burmese village; Flynn's 35th birthday (6/20).

Fri June 23
Filming at the Metropolitan Airport.

Sat June 24
Filming the Burmese village and Japanese soldiers at the Los Angeles County Arboretum.

Mon June 26
Develops pleurisy, which advances into back and bladder problems; does not work for two weeks.

Wed June 28
Frank Mattison to Tenny Wright: *"As you know, Mr. Errol Flynn was at home suffering with a bad back. Last night he called Charlie about 6:00 o'clock and informed him that the doctor has forbidden him to come in to work today, Wednesday, on account of a bad bladder, but assured him that he would be in tomorrow, Thursday."*

Wed July 5
At the Decker-Flynn Gallery; also in attendance are John Decker, Gene Fowler, and Erich von Stroheim.

Sat July 8
Frank Mattison to Tenny Wright: *"As a matter of record, Mr. Errol Flynn will have to have either today, Saturday, or Monday off on account of a visit to a doctor, requiring two days of examinations. We are calling for him for today, Saturday, so that we can finish the Santa Anita location* [the Los Angeles Arboretum]. *We can work Monday without him on the location at Whittier."*

Mon July 10
Has barium testing; results are negative vis. cancer.

Tue July 11
Ill, does not work (*"awfully sick,"* according to Frank Mattison).

Wed July 12
Returns to work at Whittier Park.

Thu July 13
Continues filming at Whittier Park; Flynn and Walsh are angry over the loss of work from rainy weather; Frank Mattison to Tenny Wright: *"Today, Thursday, this company is continuing on the EXT. of the jungle location at Whittier. We are working with Mr. Errol Flynn; he was there yesterday and seems to be in good spirits and good health."*

Fri July 14 and Sat July 15
Continues filming at Whittier Park; Frank Mattison to Tenny Wright: *"Mr. Walsh and Mr. Flynn were both foaming about the loss of time* [the day before] *on account of inclement weather, but there is nothing we can do about it."*

Mon July 17
Continues filming at Whittier Park; 55 minutes late for work; Frank Mattison to Tenny Wright: *"Just as a matter of record, after we took the trouble to get the wind machines there and fill the chutes partly, the Major* [Charles S. Galbreath], *our Technical Advisor, said this would be an improper landing so they abandoned the idea and had the chutes flat on the ground. I wish they would send the Major home; we would get this picture done quicker and better. He knows nothing about how the stuff has to be cut and at times interferes with the work. Also, please check with the Still Dept. and you will find that he is stopping all stills that shoot below Flynn's knees because he says the boys do not have the proper shoes. I think this should be checked on as he is holding up many stills and condemning them."*

Tue July 18 to Sat July 22
Filming at the Japanese radar station at the WB Calabasas Ranch.

Mon July 24
Finishes work at the WB Calabasas Ranch with filming of the blowing up of the radar station.

Tue July 25
Filming in the jungle and lake at the Los Angeles County Arboretum.

Thu July 27
Filming at Metropolitan Airport.

Fri July 28
Continues filming at the Los Angeles County Arboretum.

Sat July 29
Filming at Whittier Park.

Sun July 30
In a command radio performance over the Armed Forces Radio System before 400 WAVES, with Cass Daley, Dick Haymes, June Allyson, Sterling Holloway, and Linda Darnell, and hosted by Barbara Stanwyck (*bottom right*); in one routine, Flynn sings while in a shower.

Mon July 31 and Tue August 1
Continues filming in the jungle at Whittier Park; on 8/1 two workers die in a fall while dismantling a steel tower between 4 and 4:30pm.

"Capt. Nelson" on a lunch break

With Cass Daley, Dick Haymes, June Allyson Sterling Holloway, Barbara Stanwyck, and Linda Darnell at a performance for the Armed Forces Radio System (AFRS) - Sun, July 30

With Moody and the "dressing room" at Providencia Ranch, CA - August

On the hilltop over Providencia Ranch - August

Wed August 2 through Fri August 4

One hour late for work; continues filming in the jungle and in the clearing at Whittier Park.

Sat August 5

Bedridden; does not work.

Mon August 7 to Thu August 10

Filming at Providencia Ranch (now Forest Lawn Cemetery) in Burbank, CA.

Fri August 11

Sinus problems; does not work; Frank Mattison to Tenny Wright: *"At 6:45 AM today Mr. Errol Flynn phoned me to say that his sinus trouble had swollen his face and it would be necessary for him to go down and have his head cleaned out."*

Sat August 12

Flynn's letter to Tenny Wright, complaining about the dressing rooms: *"....locations are never comfortable particularly the sort we have had on 'Objective Burma.'...My dressing room, as we laughingly call it, had certain novel features. I counted as many as ten holes in the canvas sides through which I found some children examining me in the act of robing and disrobing....[the floor] consisted of a thin strip of moth-eaten matting....the rest was solid cow-dung. This undoubtedly explains the fascination the room held for ten million assorted insects....I cannot adequately describe the general filth....my dressing room had been changed over night and....I was now dressing in one that I had myself used the previous day as a toilet (in company with two or three hundred gentlemen)....the day before yesterday....my dressing room had completely disappeared....A hue and cry was raised to find my clothes. Several gentlemen at last located them by the side of the road....plugging my hand into my pocket I discovered that I had been ratted for all the money that was in my pockets. No, pardon me, the sum of 78¢ was left. But the $62.00 green was on its way to Glendale or elsewhere....One can stand anything for a few days but we have been on this picture four months with everyday outside....Without wishing to draw envious comparisons between my own plight and that of others consider Miss Bette Davis....Nature is on her side too. If, reluctant to enter the nauseating precincts of the canvas structure marked 'WOMEN', she seeks fragrant solace of the California shrubbery, there is little chance of her acquiring a dose of Poison Oak upon those hanging appendages with which Nature has endowed the male of the species."*

Sun August 13

Competes in a tournament at the Westside Tennis Club.

Mon August 14

Filming at Gopher Flats in Providencia Ranch, and at the water basin (scenes filmed are of the men coming down the hill at the end of the picture and watching the parachutists descending).

Tue August 15

Continues working in the jungle and hilltop at Providencia Ranch.

Wed August 16

Filming a new tag at Providencia Ranch.

Thu August 17

Filming at field headquarters at Providencia Ranch; Warner Bros. recommends *Cheyenne* to Thomson Productions as their second film; Thomson never produces it.

Fri August 18 and Sat August 19

Filming continues at Providencia Ranch with the foxhole scenes.

Sun August 20

Competes at the Westside Tennis Club for the championship of the Motion Picture Tennis Tournament, teaming up with Paul Lukas against Lowell Gilmore and Bill Self.

Mon August 21

Filming night sequences (with Jim Fleming and Buster Wiles) at the WB Calabasas Ranch from 6:00pm to 1:15am.

Tue August 22 to Thu August 24

Filming on the hilltop at the WB Calabasas Ranch.

Fri August 25

Filming with a double on Mulholland Drive.

Sat August 26

Filming on the hilltop at Providencia Ranch and sky process shots with James Brown on a WB soundstage; Frank Mattison to Tenny Wright: *"For your information, Mr. Errol Flynn told me confidentially he expected to be back perhaps September 18th or possibly a day or two before. I believe he went to Mexico."*

Mon August 28
Flies to Mexico to be with Nora, he staying at the Hotel Reforma, she—very pregnant—staying in a nearby apartment; during this trip they sign documents to legalize a proxy wedding in Cuernavaca.

Wed September 6
Steve Trilling to Jack Warner: *"Dear Colonel: [Lew] Wasserman contacted Flynn by telephone—Flynn has space guaranteed via airplane Saturday, the 16th, which will bring him into L.A. Saturday night or Sunday morning...He is going up to Mexico City over the weekend to try to move the date up to Wednesday or Thursday, the 14th, which would have him report back to the studio on Friday, the 15th, but questioned if they would be able to accommodate him. Therefore he asked if our Location Department would try from this end..."*

Sat September 16
Returns to Los Angeles; the proxy wedding had probably taken place earlier this day, according to Nora's book, *Errol and Me.*

Sun September 17
"The Decker-Flynn Gallery, after a brief, glamorous and expensive career, is closed. Errol Flynn gave the property to Painter John Decker, the latter stated last week. It is now his home and studio." The Los Angeles Times.

Mon September 18
Handwritten notes by Steve Trilling about ADVENTURES OF DON JUAN: *"$2,500,000- Budget [$37,424,425 in 2021 value] / Seriousness Try + keep this on schedule / Technicolor must make it good and Flynn look good / Make up [on] time – not in making up in car / ready [to] shoot at 9:50 AM, stay here till thru / not [off] to lunch 4:00 or 5:00 / lay off parties except Sat nite even then / Flynn on trial and probation."*

Tue September 19
Inter-office memo from unit manager Frank Mattison: *"Mr. Flynn is coming in today, Tuesday, for a test of wardrobe and to rehearse with the guitar player."*

Wed September 20
Rehearsing his song for SAN ANTONIO; inter-office memo from Frank Mattison: *"There were various discussions in the Music Dept. relative the stuff that Mr. Flynn is to do in his guitar playing and this has been straightened out."*

Thu September 21
Begins filming SAN ANTONIO with scenes at the Peon Adobe.

Fri September 22
Rehearsing dance sequence; continues filming in the Peon Adobe *(top right).*

Sat September 23
Inter-office memo from Frank Mattison: *"Mr. Flynn re-hearsed this number (Put Your Little Foot Out) with the dancer yesterday afternoon at 4:00 PM and both Flynn and Miss Alexis Smith will be in today, Saturday, at 11:00 AM on this number. We are having them rehearse now as there will be no available time after today should this picture start on Monday."*

Mon September 25 and Tue September 26
Filming in the Peon Adobe; telegram to Nora ("Wilson") in Mexico (9/25): REALIZE YOU ARE TERRIBLY BUSY THEREFORE IMPOSSIBLE WRITE A POSTCARD WOULD BE WELCOME....PLEASE SEND ME WHITE GOAT SKIN RUG SIX BY FOUR....MISS YOU LOVE."

Wed September 27
Rehearsing the varsovienne dance with Alexis Smith.

Thu September 28
Ill; does not work.

Tue October 3
Filming at Cotulla Station.

Wed October 4
Letter from Flynn's accountant Al Blum to the WB Accounting Dept.: *"....Mr. Flynn has requested that I ascertain from you how much of the enclosed [telephone] bill represents long distance calls and how much represents local charges."*

Thu October 5
WB cashier, R.V. Watson to Al Blum: *"....According to the Chief Operator…..the majority of the [telephone] calls*

With Eva Puig and John Litel - Fri, September 22

On a call during filming of SAN ANTONIO

With Xavier Cugat at Ciro's nightclub - Sat, October 7

have been local calls; Mr. Flynn has made few long distance calls and has refused to accept any calls with reversed charges."

Fri October 6

Filming in Roy Stuart's (Paul Kelly) office and Clay's (Flynn) hotel room.

Sat October 7

Continues filming in Clay's hotel room; inter-office memo from Frank Mattison: *"I want to call your attention to Saturday's work of 4 1/2 pages where Mr. Errol Flynn did most of the dialogue. He knew the lines perfectly with the result that we cleaned up 4 1/2 pages in rapid time, but we had better not slap him on the back for it because it may never happen again."* At Ciro's night club *(top left)* with Bruce Cabot.

Sun October 8

Telegram from Jack Warner to Roy Obringer: ASCERTAIN WHAT ERROL FLYNN OWES COMPANY FOR TELEPHONE CALLS EVERYTHING ELSE AND INFORM [Flynn's agent Lew] WASSERMAN WE WANT THIS MONEY PAID AS WE MADE GOOD ON OUR PROMISE AND HE SHOULD MAKE GOOD ON HIS

Mon October 9 and Tue October 10

Filming in Cotulla Station and (on 10/10) a process shot on a horse.

Fri October 13

Filming on the plaza (WB Calabasas Ranch); inter-office memo from Frank Mattison: *"Would like also to call your attention to the fact that we are using up days on which Errol Flynn does not appear and if anything happens to him in the way of illness we will be 'screwed' proper."*

Sun October 15

While attending a party at Bruce Cabot's home at 9419 Sunset Boulevard, Flynn's gray coupe is stolen from in front of the house *(right)*.

Mon October 16 through Fri October 20

Continues filming on the plaza.

Sat October 22

Writes a letter to Nora, who is living at 94 Nueve Quarto Lerma, Apt. 5, in Mexico City: *"Honechile!...I can hardly believe the evidence of my eyes! Two letters from you – in two months! I am speechless! Where did you get all that ink? Yesterday Margie [Nora's step-mother] brought your uncle out to location – an extremely nice guy by the way and I think he enjoyed watching us all cavort before the camera...Picture's going quite well – we're almost on schedule so I'm as certain as it's possible to be I'll be finished before Xmas. Maybe possible to spend it with you – sure hope so, pet. Are you watching your food, teeth, weight and tits? Be careful of all these things and just don't kiss them off casually as is your habit – particularly the food. Your letter sounded happy, honey, for which I am heartily thankful and am proud of you for not getting in poor spirits – that's also mighty important too. Any museums you've seen? Or galleries, or other things of interest. Hope you dig up some funny places you can take me to when I arrive. Yes – I'm working like a dog. Don't laugh – doing the book [presumably Showdown] over from beginning to end. Stubborn – that's me. I want it to be good....Love, your Errol...WRITE!"*

Mon October 23 and Tue October 24

Continues filming on the plaza.

Wed October 25

Filming in the Colonel's office at the WB Calabasas Ranch.

Thu October 26 and Fri October 27

Filming in the plaza at night at the WB Calabasas Ranch.

Sat October 28

Filming at the Alamo at the WB Calabasas Ranch.

Mon October 30

Filming in the Colonel's headquarters.

Errol Flynn's Coupe Stolen

Film Actor Errol Flynn was minus a gray coupe yesterday, he reported to the Hollywood Sheriff's substation. The actor said the car was stolen while it was parked in front of 9419 Sunset Blvd., Beverly Hills, early yesterday.

The Los Angeles Times
Mon, October 16

With John Litel and Robert Shayne at the WB Calabasas Ranch - October

Tue October 31

Filming in the plaza.

Fri November 3

Filming in Jeanne's room.

Mon November 6

Filming in the plaza.

Tue November 7

Filming in the Cotulla cantina and on the hotel patio.

Wed November 8 and Thu November 9

Ill; does not work; inter-office memo from Frank Mattison (11/9): *"Mr. Errol Flynn, incidentally, has also been ailing and sick with the same flu as the rest of* [the cast] *and will be required to go to the doctor today at 12:00 noon and at 3:00 PM."*

Above, at Hollywood Park Racetrack - Fri, November 10; and below, with Alexis Smith

Fri November 10

Filming in Stuart's office; at the Special War Charities Event at Hollywood Park racetrack with Bruce Cabot and Lorraine Dora *(top right)*.

Mon November 13

Completes filming of OBJECTIVE, BURMA! with a scene on the exterior of a glider; filming in the Bella Union, and working with the second unit company; telegram from Roy Obringer to Jack Warner:…DAMITA OBTAINED COURT ORDER CALLING FOR FLYNN'S COURT APPEARANCE NOVEMBER 29TH TO SHOW CAUSE WHY HE NOT HELD IN CONTEMPT OF COURT FOR FAILURE TO PAY APPROXIMATELY TWELVE THOUSAND DOLLARS INCOME TAX [$179,637 in 2021 value] ON DAMITA'S ALIMONY PAYMENTS WHICH HE AGREED [to in] PROPERTY SETTLEMENT. FLYNN THEREFORE VERY NERVOUS AND ASKING OUR HELP TWO WEEKS PAYMENTS NEXT PICTURE. THOMSON FINAL DATE ADVISE US RE FRONTIERSMAN FRIDAY NOVEMBER 17TH. HOWEVER TOMORROW 14TH FINAL DATE FOR THOMSON SUBMIT ONE OR TWO STORIES AND IF THEY FAIL SUBMIT OR IF THEY DO SUBMIT AND WE REJECT THEIR STORIES WE THEN IN POSITION AFTER NOVEMBER 17TH TO DESIGNATE EITHER CHEYENNE OR FRONTIERSMAN. ALL PAPERS CARRYING FLYNN COURT ACTION WHICH FEEL SURE HE CAN AVOID IF MAKES PAYMENT PRIOR 29TH. PLEASE ADVISE.

Tue November 14

Continues filming at the Bella Union; telegram from Jack Warner to Roy Obringer: RE ERROL FLYNN DOES HE MEAN HE HASN'T TWELVE THOUSAND TO PAY DAMITA. THIS REALLY COMICAL. WILL NOT ADVANCE ANY MONEY TO HIM UNTIL WE SET DON JUAN WITH FLOREY DIRECTING AND THE FRONTIERSMAN TO BE THOMSON PICTURES. IF HE CONSENTS TO FLOREY AND THE FRONTIERSMAN IN WRITING, ADVANCE HIM THESE TWELVE.

Wed November 15

Ill; does not work; inter-office memo from Frank Mattison: *"Today, Wednesday, we are continuing on the* [musical] *number and whatever we can shoot in the set without Mr. Flynn. Mr. Flynn phoned a short while ago that he would be unable to come into the studio today. This is the first time on the picture that we have been held up or delayed on his account but we can do very little without him after today; in fact, if he cannot come in tomorrow, Thursday, I do not know of anything we can do."*

Thu November 16 and Fri November 17

Filming in the Bella Union; inter-office memo from Frank Mattison (11/17): *"In accordance with instructions from Steve Trilling Mr. Errol Flynn will appear at the studio tomorrow, Saturday, and we will be ready for him promptly at 9:00'clock. He will leave the studio at 10:30 and we expect him back at 2:00 PM from the War Bond Parade. Mr. Trilling suggested that I go along with him to see that we*

Errol Flynn Faces Charge of Contempt

Los Angeles, Nov. 10.—(AP.)—A contempt of court citation was issued today against film star Errol Flynn on the complaint of his former wife, Lily Damita, that he had failed to keep an alleged agreement to reimburse her for income taxes on alimony he paid her.

She receives $1500 monthly from the film hero, and said she had paid $11,336 taxes on it in 1942 and 1943. She alleged he had refused to reimburse her although he had deducted the payments from his own taxes. A hearing date on the contempt citation was set for November 29.

The Hartford Courant
Fri, November 10

With Alexis Smith

Errol Must Pay Ex-Wife's Taxes

Los Angeles, Nov. 30—(P)—Actor Errol Flynn has agreed to pay his former wife, Lili Damita, $11,336 as reimbursement of income tax she paid on alimony received from him during 1942 and 1943.

His alimony payments approximate $18,000 a year.

A superior court commissioner ordered Flynn also to pay a $1,000 fee to Miss Damita's attorney. The commissioner said a contempt of court citation against Flynn would be dismissed as soon as the money is paid.

The St. Petersburg Evening Independent
Thu, November 30

get him back to the studio. I understand that the sheriff's car will take him down there, but I will arrange to have one of our own cars there to pick him up and bring him back."

Sat November 18

Marches in Los Angeles in the 6th annual War Bond Cavalcade of the West Parade from 10:30am to 2:30pm; continues filming in the Bella Union.

Mon November 20 through Wed November 22

Continues filming in the Bella Union.

Sat November 25

Filming in the Alamo at the WB Calabasas Ranch.

Mon November 27

Ill; does not work; inter-office memo from Frank Mattison: *"Mr. Errol Flynn will not be in today on account of catching cold on Saturday. I was informed of this by telephone at 7:55 this morning."*

Tue November 28

Ill; does not work; inter-office memo from Frank Mattison:*"....Mr. Errol Flynn was in bed yesterday (so he said when I called him at 5:00 o'clock) and he informed me that he was running a temperature. The doctor, he said, had advised him to stay in bed for at least another day. This coincided with what the butler, Alex, told me in the morning. He said that Mr. Flynn had had the doctor and the doctor recommended that he stay in bed for a couple of days........If we cannot have the projector head (for process shots) tomorrow, Wednesday, we will be unable to work without Mr. Errol Flynn."* Steve Trilling to Jack Warner: *"Errol Flynn will probably be hauled into court on the Damita case—he has renewed his request now to pick up a couple of weeks salary to make settlement and avoid the embarrassment and publicity that will ensue... Do you want to reconsider in light of his agreeing to be a good boy on 'Don Juan' and accept* [director Robert] *Florey?"*

Wed November 29

Continues filming in the Bella Union; Flynn's attorney Bernard M. Silbert represents him in court, where it is determined Flynn will pay the $11,336 of taxes ($169,697 in 2021 value) on the 1942 and 1943 alimony payments to Lili in installments, along with her attorney's bill of $1,000 ($14,970 in 2021 value).

Thu November 30

Continues filming in the Bella Union.

Fri December 1, Sat December 2, Mon December 4, and Tue December 5

Continues filming in the Bella Union and (on 12/2 and 5) a process shot in the stagecoach.

Wed December 6 and Thu December 7

Continues filming in the Bella Union (on 12/6), and in Jeanne's (Alexis Smith) dressing room; attends a party for the president's son, Col. James Roosevelt, and wife (12/7).

Fri December 8

Is 40 minutes late to the set; continues filming in Jeanne's dressing room.

Sat December 9

Inter-office memo from Frank Mattison (mis-dated 12/8): *"His (Flynn's) condition yesterday was no secret but he attributed it to his presence at the party for Col. Roosevelt and his bride. I can truthfully state that he was so sick late in the afternoon that it was impossible for him to work."* Both Flynn and Smith are a half hour late; continues filming in Jeanne's dressing room.

Mon December 11

Filming in Legare's (Victor Francen) office and in the Bella Union.

Tue December 12 and Wed December 13

Filming on the Bella Union patio and (on 12/13) a process shot on the horse treadmill.

Thu December 14

Filming in the Alamo, and on Laredo Road (at Lasky Mesa).

Fri December 15

Filming on the Bella Union patio, and a process shot on the horse treadmill.

Sat December 16

Filming a process shot in the stagecoach and at the river bed; inter-office memo from Frank Mattison: *"We did not return to Stage 4 for the process inasmuch as Flynn was full of dirt and everyone was underfoot. Mr. Flynn said he was willing to work but it would take one hour and a quarter at least for him to get his clothes changed, a shower bath, and a rub-down….[Director David] Butler gave him a work-over in the mud in the fight stuff."*

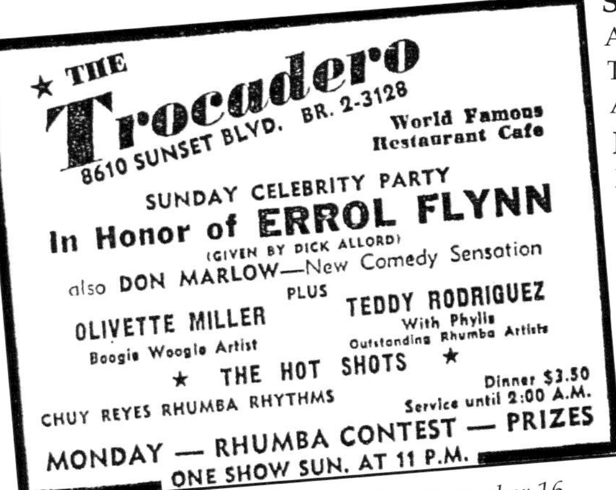

The Los Angeles Times-*Sat, December 16*

Sun December 17
Actor Richard Allord throws a dinner party at the Trocadero night club in honor of Flynn *(top left)*; Allord had a role in 1943's NORTHERN PURSUIT.

Mon December 18
Filming a process shot in the stagecoach *(top right)*.

Tue December 19
Ill; does not work.

Wed December 20
Continues filming a process shot in the stagecoach.

Tue December 26
With Eddie Jackson, Bert Wheeler, Jimmy Durante, Jack Benny, and Earl Carroll at the Earl Carroll Theater, celebrating its sixth anniversary.

Wed December 27
Inter-office memo from Tenny Wright to Jack Warner: "….

With Alexis Smith and Florence Bates - Mon, December 18

Errol Flynn called me up and again asked me why he hadn't been notified officially that he was to do 'DON JUAN'. I told him he had been….he didn't think [Robert] Florey was the right director, and you never heard such a routine of other things he wanted to take up….He went into a routine about who was to be his fencing instructor. I told him I was trying to get Fred Cavens. He told me he thought Cavens was old fashioned….he wanted to get the French champion, [Aldo] Nadi, and I said I would never employ Nadi, as I didn't think he was any good and….he is an arrogant son-of-a-bitch and caused a lot of trouble at Paramount….Whether Flynn is trying to get out of the picture I don't know, but he asked when we were going to start shooting, and when I told him between January 15th and February 1st, he said, 'Well I won't be here that soon, so don't get any ideas like that'…. let's get this set once and for all, because I am looking for a lot of trouble from Mr. Flynn if we don't…." Written to Nora with the date "End of Month": *"Hello!…Just thinking of you – nice things. And hoping! If it's a man, with your permission, his name will be 'Held.'…Okay? Errol…P.S. And if it's a dame you name the unmentionable beast. Okay?"*

Thu December 28
At Ciro's with John Decker; *"Errol Flynn is due in New York next week from the Coast, to confer with publishers, interested in bringing out his new novel, 'The Longbow' [presumably an early title for his novel, Showdown]."* The Film Daily.

1945

Sometime before their daughter Deirdre is born, Flynn writes to Nora in Mexico: *"Hello darling…Gosh, I wish you were here tonight! A wind blows outside, whistling around the place in a very lonely manner – There's something forlorn about a wind about a house – I hope you're happy, my darling; and well - as your letter sounded…Held. I can't remember where I heard Held. I think I knew a small boy when I was a small boy and liked his name. But it's a name – and it's Irish and it's unusual. And I think for all those reasons it's a good name for a young man to have. I like it – don't you? Please like it – if you don't we'll think of something else. Now if it's a dame how about Diedre? You pronounce it Deardre. And of course I wasn't serious when I uttered dire threats about what I'd do if it was a girl – it doesn't matter at all. In fact I think [it] might be rather nice – particularly since I remember how much you thought you'd like a dame… Margie [Nora's step-mother] was supposed to talk to you tonight, and your money, I told her, was on the way – the extra dough. I'll send you more as soon as Warner's give me some. But on all accounts – if you are short, or need one thing, wire me right away….Please, please be extra careful about yourself now – you seem to have no concern for your well-being at all and it's so important that our baby is strong + healthy, isn't it. Huh? Watch those colds! Or I'll clip you!…I can't wait to see you! And I love you – very much!!! Errol…And don't ever feel lonely, because as your time gets shorter my heart goes out to you – closer, with more respect, and deeper feeling for you --- Yes."*

Filming outside the Alamo at the WB Calabasas Ranch - Mon, January 8

Tue January 2
For his air raid work in the U.K., Errol's father Professor Theodore Flynn is made a member of the Order of the British Empire (OBE) by King George VI.

Mon January 8
Finishes SAN ANTONIO filming outside the Alamo at night at the WB Calabasas Ranch.

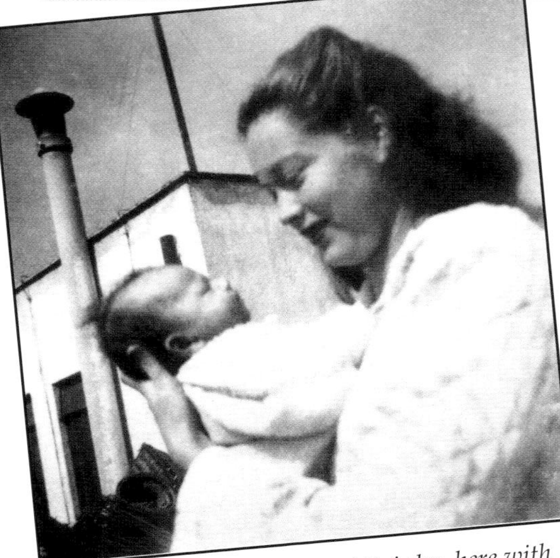

One of the earliest photos of Deirdre, here with mother Nora in Mexico City - January

At New York's Thirteenth Regiment Armory with tennis pro Bill Tilden, warming up for their upcoming charity match - Tue, February 13

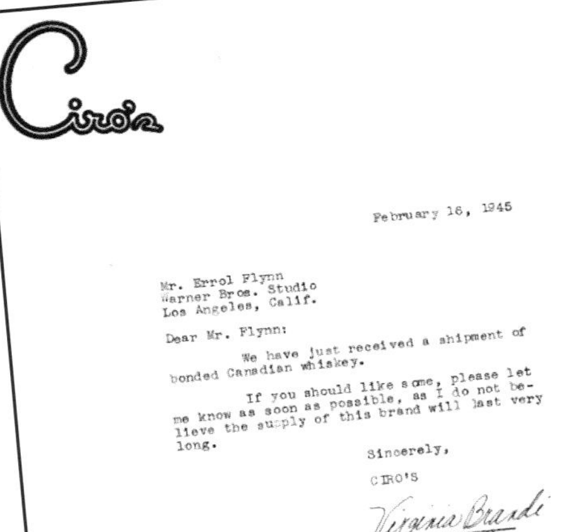

Ciro's

February 16, 1945

Mr. Errol Flynn
Warner Bros. Studio
Los Angeles, Calif.

Dear Mr. Flynn:

We have just received a shipment of bonded Canadian whiskey.

If you should like some, please let me know as soon as possible, as I do not believe the supply of this brand will last very long.

Sincerely,

CIRO'S

Virginia Brandi
Virginia Brandi
Retail Liquor Dept.

Tue January 9
Flies to Mexico City to be with Nora for the impending birth of their child; stays at the Hotel Ritz.

Wed January 10
Flynn's daughter Deirdre is born at the British-American Hospital in Mexico City; the baby weighs 9lbs.-8ozs., and is registered (on January 19th) with the Mexico Federal District Vital Statistics Bureau as the daughter of Nora Eddington and cinema actor "Leslie Flynn."

Sat January 13
Letter sent from the Hotel Ritz in Mexico City to his accountant Albert Blum: *"Dear Al/ I meant to mention this to you before leaving but forgot; there is a great wastage of food in the house, particularly when I am gone. Would you please arrange some sort of budgeting arrangement? The boy who has been living there, Jack Stroll, should be gone by now. George has a habit of disappearing when I am gone – do you think you could find me someone, anyone, to replace him?... The trouble with the wastage is I think Marie forgets to cancel the standing orders...."*

Sun January 14
Flies to Acapulco with Freddie McEvoy.

Fri January 26
Special premiere of OBJECTIVE, BURMA! at the Strand Theater in New York; Jerry Wald to Jack Warner: *"In the early days when we were getting 'BURMA' ready for production, there were times when Brother Flynn refused to become part of the entire project and I know that it was you, injecting your confidence into the production, that succeeded in selling Flynn into making the picture. Flynn, too, should be grateful because I sincerely feel that it will do more good for him than anything he has done on the screen...I have received innumerable calls from friends of mine of the press, who commented mainly on how good Flynn was in the picture and how surprised they were that he was capable of turning in such a legitimate, honest performance."*

Wed January 31
Rumors of Flynn's marriage and daughter appear in the press.

Fri February 2
Arrives at La Guardia Airport in New York with Freddie McEvoy and stays at the Waldorf Towers.

Sat February 3
Admits publicly to marriage with Nora.

Sun February 4
Telegram from Jack Warner to Flynn c/o Freddie McEvoy at the Waldorf Towers in New York: HAVE BEEN INFORMED BY LOCAL NEWSPAPERS YOU REPUDIATING STATEMENT YOU GAVE AUTHORITY YESTERDAY TO WARNER BROTHERS HOME OFFICE AND STUDIO PUBLIC RELATIONS DEPARTMENT TO RELEASE [from his contract]. IMPOSSIBLE TO REACH YOU ON PHONE. YOU CANNOT REPUDIATE YOUR STATEMENT OF YESTERDAY. CAN'T UNDERSTAND WHY YOU DOING THIS. EXPLAIN IMMEDIATELY STRAIGHT WIRE TO ME AT 1801 ANGELO DRIVE, BEVERLY HILLS, SO THERE WILL NOT BE ANY FURTHER MISUNDERSTANDING.

Tue February 6
Telegram to Jack Warner: I RECEIVED YOUR PERSONAL WIRE AND I SHALL COME AND SEE YOU WITH IT UPON MY RETURN INSTRUCTIONS FOR WHICH I AM AWAITING.

Tue February 13
Warms up with tennis pro Bill Tilden in preparation for a charity match on Saturday the 17th *(center left)*.

Wed February 14
Cable from Mort Blumenstock to Charles Einfeld: FLYNN WANTS TO DO BERLE SHOW FEBRUARY 21 SAYS HE HAS RIGHT TO SIGN HIMSELF TO THREE SHOWS WITHOUT CONSULTING BUT HE WANTS TO PLAY BALL WITH US. TOLD HIM THAT WOULD ASK YOU IF OK. PLEASE ADVISE IMMEDIATELY. WE WILL SEE SCRIPT.

Fri February 16
OBJECTIVE, BURMA! opens.

Sat February 17
Competes with tennis great Bill Tilden in a match against John Noghady and Vincent Richards for the Grossinger Canteen-by-Mail charity event held at the Thirteenth Regiment Armory at 33rd and Park Avenue in New York City; each team wins one set, with no rubber match played; Flynn's racket is auctioned off and sold to Harry Grossinger for $800 ($11,707 in 2021 value).

Tue February 20

Wire from Jack Warner to Flynn: AS YOU ARE WAITING MY INSTRUCTIONS TO RETURN TO THE STUDIO PER YOUR TELEGRAM OF FEBRUARY SIXTH PLEASE RETURN AT ONCE AS WE ARE PREPARING TO START THE ADVENTURES OF DON JUAN, RAOUL WALSH DIRECTING. WIRE STRAIGHT WHEN YOU LEAVING AS WE STARTING ALL PREPARATIONS FOR PRODUCTION.

Wed February 21

Guests on Milton Berle's *Let Yourself Go* program at 10:30pm on WABC radio from Radio City Music Hall.

Thu February 22

Telegram from Flynn to Jack Warner: I HAVE MADE ARRANGEMENTS TO RETURN VIA FLORIDA INASMUCH AS YOU HAVE RECONSIDERED YOUR SELECTION OF DIRECTORS, DOES THIS MEAN SCRIPT CHANGES.

Fri February 23

Telegram from Jack Warner to Flynn: ....WALSH AND WRITER POLISHING SCRIPT AND WILL BE ALL SET BY NEXT THURSDAY LATEST....WE URGENTLY NEED YOU FOR ALLOVER PREPARATION OF PICTURE AND AS WE GOING TO HUGE EXPENSE GET SETS CONSTRUCTED CAST COMMITTED AND ALL OTHER PREPARATIONS AM DEPENDING ON YOUR ARRIVAL MARCH FIRST.

Tue March 6

Note from Steve Trilling to Lou Espinosa: *"Please send the following telegram—straight—Errol Flynn...141 17th. Street, NE...Atlanta, Georgia...Winston Lowell, branch manager at Dallas exchange arranging transportation for you Wednesday. Please wire him at 508 Park avenue, Dallas advising when you arrive so he can meet you at airport. See you soon. Regards."*

Wed March 7

Telegram from Flynn to Jack Warner: I CANNOT GET OUT OF DALLAS AND WOULD LIKE TO VERY MUCH.

Thu March 8

Telegram from J. W. Loewe to WB publicist Irving Yergin: ERROLL [sic] FLYNN ARRIVING AMERICAN AIRLINES 3:03 PM.

Mon March 19

Tenny Wright to Jack Warner, Steve Trilling, and Roy Obringer: *"Received a phone-call from Errol Flynn, saying that he had gone to his dentist, and the dentist sent him to his doctor, and the doctor said he had undulant fever and for him to go home and rest, and that he would be unable to come in for fittings today. I asked whether he would be in tomorrow, and was told it all depends on his condition...I am bringing this to your attention because from what I understand, this fever comes from drinking raw milk, and if he actually has it, he may be up and down for weeks, or even months."*

Tue March 20

Steve Trilling to Tenny Wright: *"Lew Wasserman phoned me about 7:30 last night that he had talked to Errol Flynn and the undulant fever is something he has been afflicted with for the last year, so it is nothing new and nothing to be concerned about....Flynn will be in at 11:00 today, Tuesday, for fittings and preparations on 'Don Juan.'...Here's hoping he's up and never down for weeks, or even months."*

Wed March 21

At Warner Bros. Studios for costume fittings for ADVENTURES OF DON JUAN; Nora arrives at Burbank airport from Mexico with daughter Deirdre (*center right*) and moves into a house at 9250 Cordell Drive in (now) West Hollywood.

Fri March 23

In a script conference with Raoul Walsh and Jerry Wald; at the Brown Derby and Ciro's with Nora on their first public appearance together as a married couple (*bottom right*).

Mon March 26

Flynn's letter to producer Jerry Wald: *"Although at this date the studio hasn't given me any starting date for DON JUAN to go before the cameras I am worried about the script. We agreed....[it] lacked certain vital qualities which you thought could be remedied. So far out of our discussions has come thirty four pages of a new (and much better) treatment. But even these thirty four pages we decided could be improved - as clearly outlined in our conference of this 23rd. March, with [Raoul] Walsh....I am now getting concerned about the rest of the script...."*

Thu March 29

Jimmy Starr in the *Evening Herald* reports that after Flynn finishes *The Adventures of Don Juan*, he will *"don a natty [B-29] flier's uniform for 'Target Japan,'"* to be directed by Raoul Walsh; the film is never made.

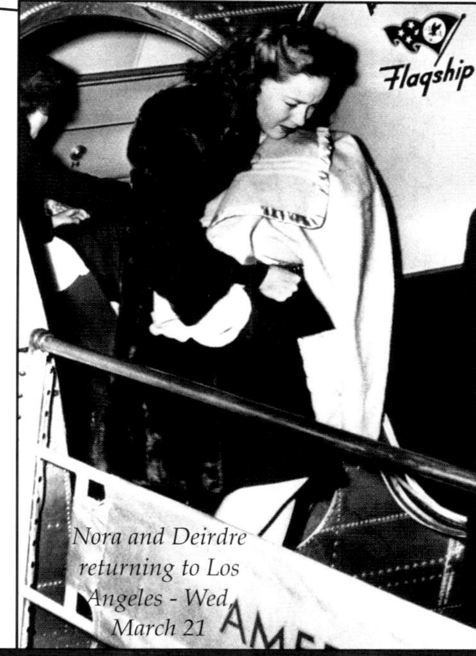

Nora and Deirdre returning to Los Angeles - Wed. March 21

With Nora at Ciro's - Fri, March 23

Mon April 2

Begins fencing rehearsals with fencing master Fred Cavens for ADVENTURES OF DON JUAN; at this point, Raoul Walsh is still listed as director.

Sat April 7

Al Alleborn to Steve Trilling: *"Errol Flynn has been in one day this week, which was Monday, April 2nd, for his fencing rehearsals. He has been ill because of the fever he has and has been going to the doctor for shots. His right arm was considerably swollen after his rehearsing on Monday and, quoting him, he is ' still suffering from it, but continuing with shots as prescribed by the doctor.'...He is up on his first duel and knows it well and is now ready to go into the next duel. He has promised to be in Monday, April 9th."*

Mon April 9

Continues fencing rehearsals; Al Alleborn to Tenny Wright: *"Wish to call to your attention the fact that he (Flynn) is looking bad and seems to be weak and tires very quickly. He is continuing with his shots at the doctor's and it seems that everytime he takes a shot his arm swells up and he suffers bad results."*

Tue April 10

Al Alleborn to Tenny Wright: *"Today, Tuesday, Errol Flynn did not come in to rehearse. We called him on the telephone and he said he was too ill from rehearsing yesterday, Monday, and would not be in, but will come in tomorrow, Wednesday for wardrobe fittings."*

Wed April 11, Fri April 13, Mon April 16, and Tue April 17

Continues fencing rehearsals; Al Alleborn to Tenny Wright (on 4/16): *"Company did not work Saturday, 4-14-45, Proclaimed day of National Mourning for President Roosevelt."*

Wed April 18

More wardrobe tests for ADVENTURES OF DON JUAN; a check written to Nora on this day indicates she is now living at 3319 Hamilton Way in Hollywood.

Flynn's party at Mulholland to introduce Nora, here presenting a fencing demonstration; standing to the right of Flynn is Gary Cooper, seated next to him his wife Rocky, and seated on the ground next to her, Helmut Dantine - Sun, April 22

Sun April 22

Flynn throws a party at the Mulholland house to introduce Nora to his Hollywood friends; in attendance are the Gary Coopers, Helmut Dantine, John Decker, the Mark Hellingers, Peter Lawford, Ida Lupino, and others; a fencing exhibition is held for the guests at poolside *(top left)*.

Mon April 23

Al Alleborn to Tenny Wright: *"Flynn did not report to work on Saturday for rehearsals on this picture."* Al Alleborn to Tenny Wright: *"This is to advise you that Errol Flynn did not report for fencing rehearsals on [ADVENTURES OF DON JUAN] again today."*

Tue April 24, Thu April 26, and Fri April 27

More wardrobe tests.

Sun April 29

Is in a fistfight with John Huston at a party at David O. Selznick's house *(bottom right)*.

Mon April 30

Does not show up for fencing rehearsal, probably as a result of the previous night's fist fight.

May

Note by Flynn to a Miss Lowe: *"1/ Please call Mr. Blum to say I can't meet him tomorrow. 2/ If Mrs. Flynn calls, please have George get me info instantly. 3/ Otherwise Mr. Raoul Walsh will call about going to races—please call him at 10:15 (at Warners) to say I cannot go with him to track but ~~would~~ will be dining with him."*

Tue May 1

Al Alleborn to Tenny Wright: *"For your information, Errol Flynn did not again show up for rehearsals on Monday and today, Tuesday.*

Errol Flynn Introduces Bride to Hollywood

Hollywood, April 23, (Ⓟ)—Errol Flynn has formally introduced his 20-year-old bride, the former Nora Eddington, to Hollywood.

The Flynns had a reception at his Mulholland Drive home yesterday. Invited were the Gary Coopers, the David Butlers, Gene Fowler, Fred Astaire, Mary Pickford, Ida Lupino, the David O. Selznicks, Sir Charles Mendl, Helmut Dantine, Bruce Cabot and scores of others.

Nora, who recently said she intended to sue for divorce, declined to say whether she had changed her mind. She previously had said that if she obtained the divorce she expected Flynn to provide for their infant daughter, born in Mexico, but that she wanted nothing for herself and planned to seek a job.

The Harrisburg Telegraph
Mon, April 23

Errol Flynn Reported in Fist Fight With Former Director

Errol Flynn, whose fights off and on the screen have become almost a legend, and Maj. John Huston, former director and son of Actor Walter Huston, reportedly swung fists at each other early yesterday at a party at a Beverly Hills home.

Neither was available for comment on the "fight" and comments from guests who asked that their identities not be disclosed varied. One said "it was a honey" while another remarked "there wasn't much to it." No one knew of any cause.

Huston was said to have required medical treatment for injuries to his face while Flynn was declared to have emerged unscathed. Here again reports varied and a close friend of Huston's denied he had any injuries.

The home of David O. Selznick was said to have been the "battle" zone but Selznick also was "not at home."

Flynn's wife, the former Nora Eddington, was reported to have accompanied him to the party.

The Los Angeles Times
Mon, April 30

I think this is due to the conditions you are familiar with and have no doubt read about."

Sun May 6

Attends a Russian Easter party at Romanoff's hosted by Reginald Gardiner in honor of Gardiner's Russian wife, Nadia Petrova; also in attendance are Danny Kaye, Paulette Goddard, Gene Tierney, Oleg Cassini, and others.

Mon May 7

Fencing rehearsals at his Mulholland home with Fred Cavens; the short subject, *Peeks At Hollywood*, in which Flynn appears is released.

Wed May 9

THE ADVENTURES OF DON JUAN is indefinitely put on hold because of an industry-wide strike between two AFL union locals over studio set designers.

Sat May 19

Attends a party for artist friend John Decker at the Beverly Hills home of Capt. and Mrs. Edward Hillman.

Thu May 24

As of this date, Flynn is showing a willingness to do the film *Frontiersman*; it never comes to fruition.

Thu May 31

In a letter to Warner Bros., Flynn accuses the company of secretly wanting only to extend time under the existing agreement, and not to do *Frontiersman* whose starting date, like ADVENTURES OF DON JUAN, was postponed.

Sun June 17

Attends a party at the home of director Eddie Sutherland in honor of Ben Lyon and Bebe Daniels visiting Hollywood after 10 years in Europe.

Wed June 20

With Nora at a party for his 36th birthday thrown at Bruce Cabot's house *(bottom left)*.

Thu June 21

Flynn sends a letter to Olivia de Havilland on Thompson Productions letterhead *(bottom right)*.

Wed June 27

Arrives in San Francisco with Bruce Cabot.

Thu June 28

In a tennis match with Bruce Cabot for the War Bond Sport Show at the Civic Auditorium.

Fri June 29

In an afternoon and evening tennis match with Bruce Cabot for the War Bond Sport Show.

Tue July 3

Leaves San Francisco by train for Hollywood.

Wed July 4

In a charity cricket match for the Commando Benevolent Fund hosted by C. Aubrey Smith; among the players are Basil Rathbone, Nigel Bruce, Arthur Treacher, Ronald Colman, and Alan Mowbray.

Thu July 5

Production manager Don Page to Tenny Wright: *"…I gave Mr. Flynn a call for wardrobe tests at 1:00PM Monday afternoon and he informed me that, although he was flat on his back, he would do everything possible to be here [next] Monday for these tests."*

With Nora at his 36th birthday party thrown at Bruce Cabot's house - Wed, June 20

Fri July 6

Accused by police of speeding and *"sassing"* an officer; Flynn's attorney appears in court in his stead.

Sat July 7

Two tailors from the WB wardrobe department visit Flynn at his home to take measurements for new suits to

Notes re ERROL FLYNN

Our Picture, OBJECTIVE BURMA, is now playing in theatres. It cost $1,600,000.   In it we tried to show him as a war hero, doing something for democracy.

We have $2,200,000 in SAN ANTONIO which does not include cost of prints, advertising and distribution.

We are preparing to spend $1,800,000 in the making of DON JUAN, and Flynn has to get himself involved in another public fight.

Have received hundreds of letters from men, women and children all over the country saying they were disgusted with his conduct and actions.

The same type of publicity due to his actions forced us to release GENTLEMAN JIM prematurely at a loss of $500,000 to $750,000 in domestic income alone.

Am going to suggest that since he is 4F and cannot join the army he should go as a Red Cross worker and give up pictures until the war is over. We are not going to make pictures where we are always at the mercy of a man who will get into a public brawl at the drop of a hat. Regardless of whether he is forced into fights, he just cannot afford public scandal and disfavor.

Flynn is asking for $270,000. Even if we have to settle with him for that sum he cannot keep the money because of the taxes.

Jack Warner's notes concerning the Flynn/Huston scuffle

THOMSON PRODUCTIONS, Inc.

222 EQUITABLE BUILDING
6253 HOLLYWOOD BLVD
HOLLYWOOD, CALIF.
GRanite 6161

Miss Olivia de Haviland
Bel Air.   June 21st. 1945

Dear Livvy,

Many thanks for your note and the enclosure (My God, it was longer than Gone With The Wind!).

I didn't know you were back or I would have tried to reach you before this as I wanted very much to talk to you about an idea for a picture. Having a pretty fair notion just how you feel about the lovely Bros. Warner I know this is taking a long shot in hoping to interest you but anyway here goes. The picture is at present called Never Say Goodbye, concerns two divorced people and a very original treatment about their daughter of about six who of course brings them together with the blessings of the Hays Office. My main reason in hoping to interest you is because I know how the goodly public, or at least quite a sprinkling of it, would like to see us together once more (in this connection I've tested out a number of exhibitors) Thomson Prods. is a partner with Warners, so I could guarantee that not only would the Bros. not get in your hair but on the contrary would lay out a good number in velvet carpets for you.

If you betray the least interest and are free in about three weeks I will dispatch the script to you by the fastest courier in the land. Steve Morehouse Avery is polishing it up now and of course all of us concerned would bend over backwards to do anything you wanted to it.

Any soap ?

Yours,

Errol Flynn.

*With Nora and Deirdre around the pool
at the Mulholland house - Summer*

July 26, 1945

Dear Errol,

I have been rather backward about replying to your note of June 21st, since I have been in the throes of starting a picture at Paramount and moving from one house into another. Today I am home with a cold and at last am able to answer your letter.

I believe I read in the papers that your plans are already under way for you to make the film you mentioned, "Never Say Goodbye", with Eleanor Parker, so your problem there has probably been settled. But even if we had been able to get together to discuss your idea and script and had been able to come to some agreement, I should most likely have been unable to go into production as soon as you would have liked, since I don't expect to finish this picture for another seven weeks and at the end of that time must take about three months off for a rest. I do wish you lots of luck, however, and please pass on my good wishes to Stephen Morehouse Avery.

All the best,

be used in his next scheduled film, *Don't Ever Leave Me*, whose title will be changed to NEVER SAY GOODBYE.

Tue July 10
Photos taken with Nora and Deirdre at Mulholland.

Wed July 11
Don Page to Tenny Wright: *"On Saturday, July 7th, our tailor from the Wardrobe Department and our wardrobe man went to Errol Flynn's home at 1:30P.M. and took some samples, and our tailor took measurements of Mr. Flynn. Mr. Flynn selected 2 samples to be made into suits, which said suits are being made for Mr. Flynn. Mr. Flynn agreed to bring 4 or 5 of his own suits to be tested for the production."*

Thu July 12
Filming sound and wardrobe tests for NEVER SAY GOODBYE.

Fri July 13
Continues doing sound and wardrobe test; with Nora at the Trocadero.

Mon July 16 through Wed July 18
Starts work on NEVER SAY GOODBYE, filming in the department store and (on 7/18) in Phil's apartment.

Mon July 23 and Tue July 24
Filming on the bridle path and outside Phil's (Flynn) apartment; Flynn to Warner Bros (on 7/24): *"Gentlemen: Since the theme song that goes through our picture now in production is titled "Remember Me", I am of the opinion having discussed it with Mr. Kern, the director, that this would make a much more saleable [film] title than the present one, 'Don't Ever Leave Me.' On polling co-workers, the latter title gives a slight impression of sadness, even to some people as if it were another war subject...'Remember Me' has had a very good reaction and would look great on a marquee. And I strongly believe that its simplicity is much to be preferred."*

Wed July 25 and Thu July 26
Filming in Phil's apartment; Olivia de Havilland's responds (on July 26) to Flynn's letter of June 21st *(bottom left)*.

Fri July 27
Steve Trilling responds to Flynn that, although the film's title has been changed to NEVER SAY GOODBYE, "Remember Me" *"might fit the picture better."*

Mon July 30 and Tue July 31
Continues filming in Phil's apartment and (on 7/31) in the drug store.

**Thu August 2 through
Sat August 4**
Filming in Luigi's Restaurant.

Mon August 6
Continues filming in Luigi's Restaurant; attends Louella Parsons' birthday party.

Tue August 7
Continues filming in Luigi's Restaurant; at a birthday party for Kay Williams at her home, also attended by Mervyn LeRoy, Keenan Wynn, Sonja Henie, Walter Pigeon, and others.

**Wed August 8 through
Sat August 11**
Continues filming in Luigi's Restaurant; at a gathering at John Decker's art gallery (on 8/10) in celebration of the artist's completion of two paintings for the WB film *The Two Mrs. Carrolls*; in attendance are Ethel and Lionel Barrymore, Cole Porter, Clark Gable, Anita Loos, Gene Fowler, and others.

With Craig Stevens, Robert Alda, and Ida Lupino who are on a neighboring set filming The Man I Love*;
at background left is the film's director, Raoul Walsh*

Mon August 13 and Tue August 14
Filming in the Central Park snow on a sound stage *(top right)*.

Wed August 15
No work: a national holiday is declared to celebrate the end of WWII.

Thu August 16
Filming in the lower floor of the Hamilton home; (8/20) Warners announces Flynn will star in *Stallion Road* by Stephen Longstreet; he never ultimately does.

Tue August 21 through Thu August 23
Filming in the upper floor of the Hamilton home, and (on 8/23) on the lower floor, and in Phil's apartment.

Fri August 24
Filming in Luigi's Restaurant.

Sat August 25
Filming in the upper floor of the Hamilton home.

Tue August 28
Ill; does not work.

Wed August 29 through Fri August 31, Sat September 1, and Tue September 4 through Thu September 6
Filming in the lower floor of the Hamilton home.

Fri September 7 and Sat September 8
Filming in the police station; on 9/8 attends a Victory Ball with Nora at the Mocambo *(center right)*; other attendees include Mr. and Mrs. James Roosevelt, and Mr. and Mrs. Elliot Roosevelt (Mrs. is the former Faye Emerson).

Mon Sept 10 and Tue September 11
Filming in Luigi's Restaurant and at the Hamilton home on Brownstone Street on the WB backlot, and (on 9/11) in the department store and in Phil's apartment.

Wed September 12
Ill; does not work; assistant director Don Page to Tenny Wright: *"Today, Wednesday, Sept. 12th, Errol Flynn was given a 9:00AM shooting call. About 8:30 this morning Alex, his house man, phoned to inform us that Mr. Flynn was unable to report to the studio for work on account of a very bad sore throat. Due to Mr. Flynn's absence, we had to rearrange our shooting schedule and it has cost us a considerable loss of shooting time today."*

Thu September 13
Filming in the upper floor of the Hamilton home; Robert Lueking, a disgruntled, AWOL private, sneaks onto the set and throws a cup of water in Flynn's face in revenge for an alleged altercation he'd had with Flynn at the actor's home; the man is arrested and turned over to military MPs.

Fri September 14
Continues filming in the upper floor of the Hamilton home (the mirror routine); letter from Roy Obringer to Jack Warner: *"When Flynn finishes 'NEVER SAY GOODBYE', which is the 2nd Thomson picture, we are entitled to have him commence, on 2 weeks notice, his services in the 7th picture. As of September 12th, Flynn has received 9 installments of $7000 each, or $63,000 [$921,902 in 2021 value], and we owe him an additional $27,000. As of October 4th, Flynn will have received 12 installments, or $84,000 [$1,229,203 in 2021 value], and there will remain only the 13th installment of $6000 to be paid him...."*

Sat September 15 and Mon September 17
Continues filming in the upper floor of the Hamilton home and (on 9/17) the lower floor; attends a birthday celebration (on 9/17) for Earl Carroll at the theater owner's estate, along with W. C. Fields, Jack Benny, Wallace Beery, Walter Pidgeon, Jack Benny, Jack Oakie, and 500 other invited guests.

Wed September 19 and Thu September 20
Filming in Luigi's Restaurant and (on 9/20) on the lower floor of the Hamilton home.

Fri September 21
Continues filming in Luigi's Restaurant; OBJECTIVE, BURMA! opens in London to heavy criticism by reviewers who demand the film be banned for its supposed misleading impression that the campaign was an exclusively

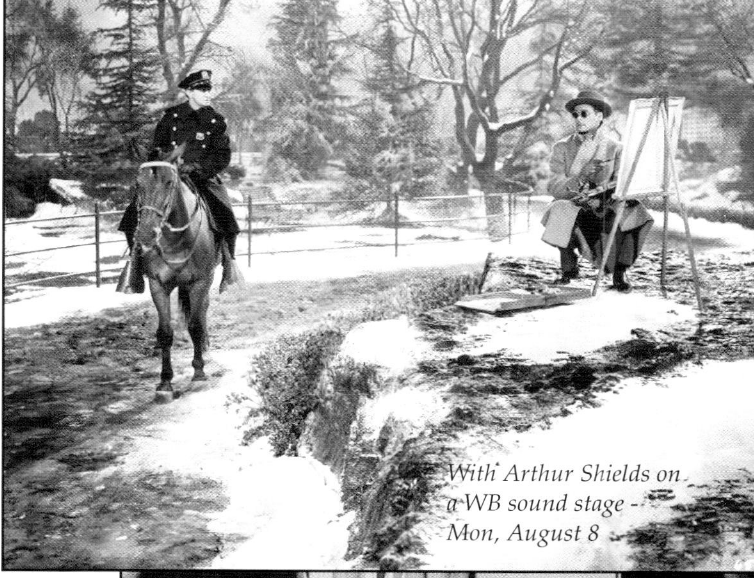

With Arthur Shields on a WB sound stage - Mon, August 8

With Nora at a Mocambo Victory Ball - Sat, September 8

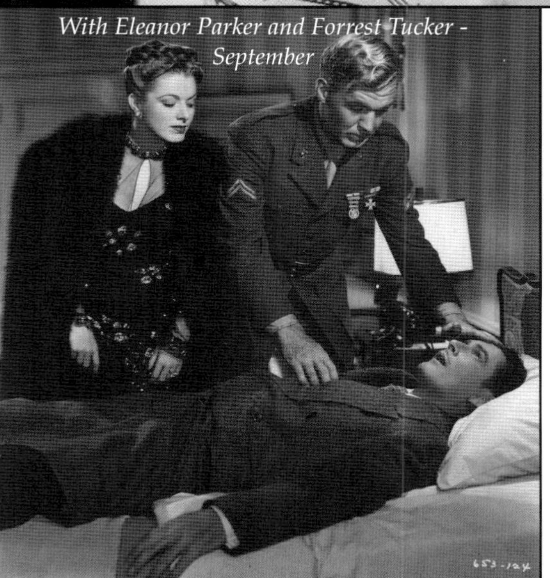

With Eleanor Parker and Forrest Tucker - September

Despite British criticisms—

500 cinemas to show 'Objective Burma'

Express Staff Reporter

MR. MAX MILDER, the American managing director in London of Warner Brothers and director of Associated British Cinemas, stated last night that despite criticisms of "Objective, Burma," because it ignores the feats of the 14th Army, he proposes to book the film for all the 500 cinemas he controls.

Criticisms of "Objective, Burma" — which features Errol Flynn as the leader of the American paratroopers— in the Sunday newspapers included phrases such as these:—

Why should we pour dollars into America... the 14... here?

Fury over Flynn

THREE battles for Burma have now been fought, one real, one celluloid, and one on paper. In the first, men shed their blood. Then came Errol Flynn, dripping glycerine sweat. Final victory fell to the film critics through the copious sacrifice of ink. Crafty in strategy, furious in tactics, their cohort has advanced on Leicester-square, dealt Flynn a solid blow, sentenced his image to temporary banishment from the West End, and permanently deprived the wives and sweethearts of suburbia of such diversion as may be derived from the spectacle of screen heroes acting in a jungle

---

WARNER BROS. PICTURES. LTD.

Telephone GERRARD 5600 (15 lines)

Telegram WABROPIC R A T H LONDON

WARNER HOUSE - WARDOUR STREET - LONDON - W.I.

All communications to be addressed to the Firm and not to individuals

24th September, 1945.

GENERAL RELEASE OF 'OBJECTIVE, BURMA' SUSPENDED.

The general release of 'Objective, Burma' will be suspended after the picture completes its engagement at Warner Theatre on Thursday night.

In announcing this decision, Mr. Max Milder, managing director of Warner Bros. Pictures Ltd., stated: "Criticism levelled against the production has accused Warner Bros. of deliberately ignoring the major part played by the 14th Army in the Burma campaign. Without any foundation in fact, the protests have exaggerated what we intended solely as a piece of screen entertainment into some sinister move against the friendship of our two nations. The absurdity of these charges is realised by everybody who knows Warner Bros.' record as the only American or British film producing company to attack the Nazi menace before the war, and the only American company to champion the Allied cause

---

24th September 1945

The Managing Director,
Messrs. Warner Bros. Pictures Ltd.,
135, Wardour Street,
London, W.1.

Dear Sir,

I have already received complaints about the proposed showing of your film OBJECTIVE BURMA. I would ask you to be wise enough to withdraw this film, since it is an insult to the British Forces who sacrificed so much in this Campaign. The cause of Anglo-American unity, which was never more vital than it is today, will definitely be adversely affected by this travesty of a film. The American Soldier has done sufficient in this War to establish his valour without phoney films, designed apparently to put money in the pockets of the producers, regardless of the harm they may do to the national interests of both countries.

If this film is shown generally, I propose to press for the establishment of an organisation which will prevent a repetition, and this would involve the film industry in additional restriction. I hope that the good sense and self discipline of the industry will prevent this step being necessary.

Yours sincerely,

W. S. Shepherd, M.P.
Lieut. Royal Sussex Regiment.

"Objective, Burma."

In view of the distortion of true facts, may I humbly suggest that you stuff this film down the lavatory pan, along with some of the other American rubbish you flood our market with. What tripe you people make, and what a wicked waste of good film.

" *advance BRITISH FILMS.*"

American one.

Sat September 22

Filming in the Hamilton kitchen and breakfast room.

Mon September 24

Filming in Phil's studio, the black velvet shots, and in the department store; Warner Bros. London managing director Mike Milder announces that OBJECTIVE, BURMA! will be distributed to all 500 theaters in England as originally planned.

Tue September 25

Finishes work on NEVER SAY GOODBYE filming straight and process shots with Eleanor Parker in the Pullman car *(below right)*.

Wed September 26

Warners announces that the studio will not open OBJECTIVE, BURMA! in England after all until further notice; it also announces that Flynn and Ida Lupino will star in ESCAPE ME NEVER, soon to begin filming.

Fri October 5

The studio union strikers who have been picketing outside the front gate of Warner Bros. engage in a riot with protesters, resulting in the injury of over a dozen people.

(Left) Some of the numerous responses to OBJECTIVE, BURMA! Top left, The Daily Express - Mon, September 24; bottom left, The Evening Standard - Wed, September 26; top right, an inter-office memo from the Warner Bros. London office - Mon, September 24; center right, complaint from a British officer to the Warner Bros. London Office - Mon, September 24; bottom right, a letter sent to Warner Bros. from a correspondent using a pseudonym - Tue, September 25

Sat October 6

Arrives in San Francisco on a shopping excursion for a new boat; he stays at the Hotel Alameda.

Wed October 10

RKO releases the picture, *George White's Scandals*; a song written for but not used in the film was to have these lyrics as sung by Joan Davis and Jack Haley:

  "But I know when I wake up
  It won't be Errol Flynn
  Who'll bring my breakfast in."

Sun October 14

Purchases the *Zaca*, a 118' schooner, from Joseph Rosenberg for $40,000 ($585,335 in 2021 value); the boat, which had been built by Templeton Crocker in 1930, was recently been the employ of the U.S. military, where it served as a gun-boat patrolling the waters around the Golden Gate Bridge since June 12, 1942; while in San Francisco, Flynn orders $60,000 of renovations to the *Zaca* ($878,002 in 2021 value), and hires Howard Kingsley as skipper and overseer of the work.

Tue October 16

Returns to Los Angeles.

Sat October 20

In San Francisco with Nora to check on the renovations to the *Zaca*; they stay at the Hotel Alameda.

Wed October 24

Leaves with Nora and a crew of ten for Santa Monica on the maiden voyage of the *Zaca*.

Sat October 27

Arrives with the *Zaca* in Newport Beach after stormy seas that result in the need for repairs.

Wed October 31

At a Halloween costume party at Romanoff's; Flynn attends sans costume but is made an honorary prince.

November

Early this months Flynn sails the Zaca for a week to the California Channel Islands and the Baja Peninsula; Nora is not with him.

Tue November 20

Begins work on ESCAPE ME NEVER, filming in the bread shop on Dijon Street on the WB backlot.

Mon November 26

Filming at the gasthaus (inn) at the WB Calabasas Ranch.

Tue November 27 through Thu November 29

Filming in Sebastian's (Flynn) room; on 11/29 pays $2,500 for the addition of a new wing on the Mulholland house ($36,583 in 2021 value).

Fri November 30 and Sat December 1

Continues filming in Sebastian's room and (on 12/1) in the hall.

Sun December 2

Is at the Mocambo, where he runs into Nora, who is there with actor Paul Brooks.

Mon December 3

Filming in Gemma's (Ida Lupino) room.

Tue December 4 and Wed December 5

Filming a process shot on a mountain road.

Fri December 7

Ill and in hospital for his recurring malaria.

Sat December 8

Ill; does not work; a news item reports that Flynn has sold four of the nine and a half acres of his hillside estate.

Mon December 10 through Wed December 12

Filming more process shots on the mountain road.

Thu December 13

Filming in the gasthaus and in Sebastian's room.

Background photo, left: the Zaca

Fans waiting in the hall outside Flynn's room at the Hotel Alameda in San Francisco - Sat, October 20

(Left) Flynn in an ad for Resistol Hats - the January issue of Esquire *magazine*

With Ida Lupino and Gig Young - December

Fri December 14
Filming more process shots on the mountain road.

Sat December 15 and Mon December 17
Filming process shots at the mountain stream, and (on 12/17) on the bridge, and in the church.

Tue December 18
Filming in the hotel foyer.

Thu December 20
Filming outside the hotel.

Fri December 21
Filming process shots on a mountain road.

Sat December 22
Filming on the hotel terrace.

Mon December 24
SAN ANTONIO opens in Los Angeles at the city's three Warner theaters; director Sam Wood is said to have offered Flynn $85,000 ($1,243,837 in 2021 value) for the rights to the actor's book, *Showdown*.

Tue December 25
Spends Christmas at Mulholland with Nora and Deirdre, gifting his wife a 17th-century gold jewelry box filled with extravagant jewelry, including a bracelet of his own design.

Wed December 26 and Thu December 27
Continues filming on the hotel terrace and (on 12/27) in Sebastian's London rooms; memo from unit manager Al Alleborn (12/26): *"The call was given to Errol Flynn to be ready at 9:00 o'clock; he claimed he did not have transportation and we had to send a car to his home for him and he did not show up until 10:45 AM."*

Fri December 28
Filming process shots in the grassy lane and at the brook; SAN ANTONIO premieres in New York at the Strand Theater.

Sat December 29
Continues filming process shots in the grassy lane and process shots in the summer house.

Mon December 31
With Ida Lupino at a New Year's Eve party at the Masquers Club to honor servicemen; Nora attends as the date of Robert Hutton.

1946

Thu January 3 and Fri January 4
Filming in the hotel garden and (on 1/4) in the summer house, and straight and process shots in the grassy lane.

Sat January 5 and Mon January 7
Filming straight and process shots in the grassy lane, and (on 1/7) in Sebastian's London room.

Tue January 8
Filming in Sebastian's room.

Wed January 9
Filming in Fenella's (Eleanor Parker) London home.

Thu January 10 through Sat January 12
Flynn and Ida Lupino both ill; company is unable to shoot.

Mon January 14 and Tue January 15
Filming inside and (on 1/15) outside Fenella's London home.

Wed January 16
Filming in Sebastian's rooms; inter-office memo from unit manager, Al Alleborn: *"Flynn was 1 hour and 50 minutes late arriving at the studio."*

Thu January 17
Filming outside Fenella's London home; with Nora, attends an exhibit of sculpture at the Decker-Flynn Gallery (where a fight breaks out over one of Decker's *"sculptures"*).

Fri January 18
Continues filming outside Fenella's London home and in the theater.

Sat January 19 and Mon January 21
Filming in Sebastian's London rooms; (1/21) inter-office memo from unit manager, Al Alleborn: *"Miss Lupino & Mr. Flynn held up the company 35 minutes this morning."*

Tue January 22 through Sat January 26
Filming in the theater, and (on 1/22) process close-ups in the café.

Mon January 28
Filming in Sebastian's London rooms and on Shabby Street (Tenement Street on the WB backlot); inter-office memo from unit director, Al Alleborn: *"Errol Flynn was one hour late this morning, holding up the company."*

Tue January 29
Filming in the hospital and farmhouse.

Wed January 30
Filming on the theater gallery stairs on New York Street on the WB backlot.

Thu January 31
Filming at the coffee wagon, in the theater gallery, and recording post-synchronization in the WB music building.

Tue February 5
Performance of *Gentleman Jim* with Joan Lorring on the CBS program, *Theatre of Romance Radio (center right)*.

Thu February 7
Finishes work on ESCAPE ME NEVER, filming in the farmhouse.

With Eleanor Parker

Performing GENTLEMAN JIM with Joan Lorring at CBS Radio - Tue, February 5

Mon February 18
Flynn's second novel, *Showdown*, is published *(left)*.

Mon February 25
Throws a surprise birthday party for Nora at the Mulholland house.

Wed February 27
With Nora at the Mocambo.

Thu February 28
Flynn's MCA agent, Arthur Park, requests Alex Evelove (WB publicity director) to obtain clearance for Flynn to appear on the *Band Wagon Radio* show on 3/10 from 4:30 to 5pm; the request is later withdrawn.

Early March
Guests and press are invited to go sailing on the *Zaca*.

Thu March 7
Guests on the radio program, *Sealtest Village Store*, hosted by Jack Haley.

Sat March 9
"When Errol Flynn takes off for Brazil, he'll have an outline of the picture he's going to shoot there. So he'll probably return with the film Orson Welles hoped to get. Orson seems to have just shot everything at random with no story or exact idea of what he wanted. But the Flynn opus will have not only background but Errol in the foreground." Hedda Hopper in *The Los Angeles Times*.

Thu March 21
Telegram from Jack Warner to Steve Trilling about Flynn being loaned out to MGM: REFERENCE BUDGET LIFE WITH FATHER ADD DIFFERENCE OF FIFTY THOUSAND [$715,588 in 2021 value] WE PAY MGM AND MGM PAYS US FOR FLYNN MAKING IT AN EVEN THREE MILLION FIVE HUNDRED [$50,091,154 in 2021 value].

Fri March 22
Flies with John Decker to San Francisco to attend Decker's solo exhibit at the de Young Museum.

With Nora on the Zaca - March

Flynn's second book, published Mon, February 18

Sun March 24
Returns to Los Angeles.

Mon April 1
Warner Bros. enters into a deal with MGM to trade the *"services"* of Errol Flynn for William Powell, whom they wanted for *Life With Father*; Flynn, in the exchange, did THAT FORSYTE WOMAN.

Wed April 17
It is reported that Flynn's dog Moody has been struck by a car and killed in Newport Beach while Flynn was there having the *Zaca* retrofitted.

Sat April 20
Is in Phoenix, which he leaves on this day, arriving in Wichita, KS, the next day and staying at the Lassen Hotel.

Errol Flynn is heart-broken. His dog, Moody, a schnauzer like his Arno which was lost at sea, was run over and killed by a car at Newport Beach.

The Bradford (PA) Era - *Wed, April 17*

Wed April 24 and Fri May 3
Makeup and wardrobe tests for CRY WOLF.

Thu May 9
Flynn is offered a new contract with Warner Bros. to commence on November 11, 1946, guaranteeing two pictures per year at $10,714.28 per week ($153,340.19 in 2021 value) for not less than fourteen weeks per film. *"Whereas, differences which have arisen in connection with the production by* [Flynn's production company] *Thomson Productions of above referred to motion pictures* [UNCERTAIN GLORY and NEVER SAY GOODBYE] *have caused all parties concerned to conclude that it is mutually advisable to discontinue further production under said agreement upon the completion of production by* [Thomson Productions] *of the third (3rd) of the aforesaid seven (7) motion pictures, which said third (3rd) motion picture is to be produced by* [Thomson Productions] *and based upon the novel 'Cry Wolf,' by Marjorie Carlton."*

Fri May 10
Attends the horse races at Pimlico Race Course in Baltimore, MD.

Mid May
With Nora and Deirdre sailing the *Zaca* for a few days to Santa Catalina and Santa Barbara.

Wed May 22
Flies to San Francisco.

Thu May 23
The Philadelphia Inquirer reports that Flynn has been in a *"slight argument"* with a U.S. Marine after being *"heckled"* at the Finocchio Club in San Francisco.

Fri May 24
Wins the Hollywood junior doubles match with Ralph Godsey, defeating the team of Tom Cleary and John Delantoni at the Berkeley (CA) Tennis Club *(top left)*.

Sun May 25
Loses a semifinal junior veteran's doubles tennis match at the Berkley Tennis Club with Ralph Godsey against Herschell Hyde and Warren Sisson.

Fri May 31
Begins work on CRY WOLF, filming on the bridle path at Providencia Ranch *(bottom left)*.

Mon June 3
Filming in the cemetery.

Wed June 5
Filming in the Caldwell home and (on 6/6-8, and 6/10-12) on the lower floor of the Caldwell home.

Thu June 13
Filming on the upper floor of the Caldwell home.

Mon June 17
Attends the American Society of Cinematographers' 25th Anniversary Banquet Ball with Nora at the Ambassador Hotel; attendees include Katharine Hepburn, Shirley Temple, Ronald Reagan, Alan Hale, Greer Garson, Maureen O'Hara, Douglas Fairbanks Jr., Red Skelton, and others; Flynn is *"cleverly satirized"* as a Western hero during the proceedings.

With Ralph Godsey at the Berkley (CA) Tennis Club - Fri, May 24

With Barbara Stanwyck and Geraldine Brooks at Providencia Ranch - Fri, May 31

Wed June 19, Thu June 20 (Flynn's 37th birthday), **Mon June 24, and Tue June 25**
Filming on the lower floor of the Caldwell home.

Fri June 28 and Sat June 29
Filming on the upper and (on 6/29) lower floor of the Caldwell home.

Sun June 30
Sells stock and corporate interests in his Thomson Productions to Warner Bros. for $125,000 ($1,788,970 in 2021 value).

Early July
Photo shoot by Fred Morgan on the *Zaca*, the yacht never leaving the dock *(bottom right)*.

Mon July 1
Inter-office memo from unit manager Don Page: *"Company unable to shoot today…because of the strike."*

Tue July 2 and Wed July 3
Filming on the lower floor of the Caldwell home; a letter is received by Warner Bros. (on 7/3) from attorneys, Loeb and Loeb, regarding liquidation of Thomson Productions; Standard Capital and Domestic Finance Corporation of Maryland are the buyers, paying $800,000 ($111,449,407 in 2021 value).

Fri July 5, Sat July 6, Mon July 8, and Tue July 9
Filming on the upper floor of the Caldwell home; (7/9) agrees to take part without pay in the advertising and publicity surrounding the Twentieth Anniversary of Talking Pictures; inter-office letter from Nathan Levinson to Steve Trilling (7/9): *"Errol Flynn has selected the following feature pictures which he would like to borrow for his trip: Action In the North Atlantic; Arsenic and Old Lace; Christmas In Connecticut; Gentleman Jim; Hollywood Canteen; Jezebel; Kings Row; Man Who Came To Dinner; Mildred Pierce; Now, Voyager; Princess O'Rourke; Rhapsody In Blue; Roughly Speaking; Saratoga Trunk; Yankee Doodle Dandy....He has also requested some short subjects....Flynn did tell me that the first opportunity he would have to return any of the films with safety would not present itself until after he reached Panama....Mr. Flynn has purchased a special generator for his boat without having asked us what to do in order that he might be able to operate the new RCA projector which he is expecting to receive shortly...."*

Thu July 11, Fri July 12, Sat July 13, and Mon July 15
Filming on the lower and (on 7/12 and 7/15) upper floor of the Caldwell home, and on (7/13) in the laboratory.

Tue July 16
Continues filming on the lower floor of the Caldwell home; Robert Ford (Flynn's attorney) to Roy Obringer: *"I am informed that yesterday afternoon Jack Warner agreed with Lew Wasserman that in order to equalize Errol Flynn's income tax for the year 1946, he would advance a portion of his salary on Flynn's next picture....Flynn is to receive the sum of $125,000 [$1,788,970 in 2021 value] on or before February 15, 1947."*

Wed July 17
Continues filming on the lower floor of the Caldwell home; Roy Obringer to Ralph Lewis (of Freston & Files): *"…Inasmuch as Flynn contemplates making a voyage by boat when he finishes 'Cry Wolf' and apparently needs some money, Mr. Warner has agreed to advance him $100,000 [$1,431,176 in 2021 value] against the compensation payable to him for [his next] picture."*

Thu July 18
Continues filming on the lower floor of the Caldwell home; signs a contract allowing the use of his image on the Motion Picture Relief Fund stamps, to be issued in 1947.

Fri July 19
Signs a contract with Columbia Records to record an audio play of *The Three Musketeers*; Steve Trilling to Roy Obringer: *"J.L. has approved our loaning Errol Flynn some 16-mm prints to be taken on his proposed ocean trip, all of which are to be returned prior to or on Flynn's return to the studio in November, and Flynn warrants that if any or all are damaged or lost, he will pay for the cost of replacement...It is distinctly understood these films are for his private use only, not to be shown publicly, will be screened only aboard the boat for Flynn and perhaps one or two people traveling with him, and we want a letter covering this entire agreement executed by Flynn...Attached is Levinson's memo indicating the prints being supplied. As soon as you have the letter of agreement drawn, will you turn it over to me and I will have Flynn properly sign it, as it is a confidential matter between Flynn and ourselves and not even his agent knows about it. Of course, we want this whole matter kept confidential for reasons we all know."*

Sat July 20
Continues filming on the lower floor of the Caldwell home and on the terrace; Professor Flynn arrives in New

With Barbara Stanwyck on the set of CRY WOLF

On the Zaca - Early July

York from Ireland on the *S.S. Washington*, docking at Pier 62 North.

Sun July 21

Signs the letter of agreement with Warner Bros. for the loan of 16-mm films for his *Zaca* voyage.

Tue July 23

Filming at the airport in Long Beach, CA and post-synchronization recording in the WB music building.

Wed July 24

Letter to producer Henry Blanke: *"....I'd like to specially point up a little matter here and now that I'd find too difficult to tell you to your face - it's not so simple to throw a bouquet at a guy while he's looking, is it? What I'm getting at is, I think you're wonderful. You are a man of taste, judgement, good manners, and all these in a community prone to discount such qualities as of little account providing you stay a winner....My last two pictures with you as 'driver' have been a relief and a real pleasure....I am your sincere and respectful admirer...."*

Sun July 28

Signs a contract with Columbia Records to record a performance of *The Three Musketeers*; Prof. Flynn arrives in Los Angeles.

Fri August 2

Prepares for the upcoming science trip on the *Zaca* by receiving, with Nora, typhus and smallpox inoculations at Mulholland; Flynn's assistant, Jim Fleming, co-signs the acceptance form for Flynn for the loan of the 16mm prints for the *Zaca* voyage.

Sat August 3

Finishes work on CRY WOLF, filming on the terrace, in the hall, and in Sandra's bedroom; sends a letter to Professor Carl Hubbs of the Scripps Institute in La Jolla, CA: *"Dear Professor Hubbs: I hardly think I need tell you how delighted I am you are coming with us [on the marine life expedition on the Zaca]...I should warn you that our expedition is not only of interest to the scientific world, but also to the press. There will be a press reception, therefore, aboard the Zaca at Santa Monica on the 8th of August - the eve of our departure...Personally, I would have preferred to have left without any fan-fare from the press, but I have found after much experience, that it is better to round them up, give them all a clear cut story of the facts, and get rid of them sooner than have one here, one there, ten there, bothering us when we are engaged in important work...please make arrangements to be there on Thursday the 8th of August - the Fourth Estate would like to get a crack at you and dad for an interview...See you soon...Errol."*

Thu August 8

Photo shoot on the *Zaca*, moored off the Santa Monica pier, prior to embarking on the scientific expedition down the coast of Mexico and to the Caribbean (*photos this page*).

Mon August 12

Sets sail on the expedition to film THE CRUISE OF THE ZACA with Nora, Prof. Flynn, John Decker, archer Howard Hill, Prof. Carl Hubbs of the Scripps Institute of Oceanography, cameraman Jerry Courneya, his movie stand-in Jim Fleming, and a crew of ten.

The Zaca, moored off the Santa Monica Pier - Thu, August 8; on it with Flynn are (top) Howard Hill, Prof. Flynn, and Dr. Carl Hubbs; (center) Prof. Flynn and John Decker; and (right) Nora

Tue August 13

In La Jolla to gather scientific equipment from the Scripps Institute.

Fri August 16

At Guadalupe Island collecting marine specimens.

Wed August 21

The *Zaca* stops at the Isles of San Benito off the Baja California coast, and then on to Cedros Island.

Thu August 29

17-year-old crew member, Wallace Berry, Jr., incurs an injury by accidentally harpooning his foot while inspecting the *Zaca's* rudder underwater *(top right)*; he is taken care of (utilizing ether stored on board) by Flynn, Prof. Flynn, and Carl Hubbs, and is later transported to a hospital upon arrival in Acapulco on September 8th.

Sun September 8

The *Zaca* arrives in Acapulco; John Decker mutinies, leaving the ship and not returning.

Fri September 20

Travels to Mexico City with Nora and Prof. Flynn; the professor flies back to Burbank, with Errol and Nora remaining in the capital for a few days.

Mon September 23

Letter to Carl Schroeder, editorial director of *Screen Guide* magazine: *"....Scientifically speaking the expedition has been an enormous success. Professor Hubbs of Scripps Oceanographical [sic] Institute told me this morning that he has definitely identified twelve different species of fish entirely new to science. We had hoped that we might be lucky enough to find perhaps three!....The deck of the ZACA looks like the backyard of an aquarium; nets, deep sea dredges, sounding devices, five gallon jars of anchovie-like fish, crabs, seaweed, bizarre looking octopus...."*

October

Is included in the release of the 13-minute Warner Bros. short, BLOW-UPS OF 1946; while in Acapulco, agrees to lease the Zaca to Columbia Pictures for four weeks to be used in the filming of Orson Welles' picture *The Lady From Shanghai*.

Wed October 2

Letter to Prof. Carl Hubbs at the Scripps Oceanographical Institute: *"....Last night in a very fine dip net we caught a small two inch specimen that looked all the world like one of the eel family. The fish was the most thoroughly transparent I have ever seen, almost transluscent, just two small black dots for eyes, and a fin structure most unusual...."*

Sun October 13

Letter from Acapulco to his accountant Al Blum: *"That was a shock to learn ZACA is not covered by insurance.... Please advise immediately if we are recovered. If you can't get it there I'll try in Mexico City because I have too much personal property, cash too, to leave for Tahiti uncovered...I haven't yet received the charts etc. and am waiting for them anxiously....I guess you might as well forget the navigator - I can pick up a good man here much cheaper. I thought you might have been able to get someone who liked the idea of a trip to Tahiti more than the dough... Re. the colored pictures of my paintings; I wanted to hang them on board ship, so the enlargements should be as big as poss[ible]...."*

Thu October 17

In Acapulco celebrating Rita Hayworth's birthday on the Zaca *(bottom right)* while the yacht was being used in her husband Orson Welles' film, *The Lady From Shanghai*.

Sat October 26

Travels with Nora to Mexico City for her flight back to Los Angeles, where she arrived on the 28th.

Sat November 2

The L.A. Times reports that Flynn has spent $10,000 for a freighter ($143,118 in 2021 value), the *Lottie Bennett*, which was used in filming *Mutiny On the Bounty* and will be converted into a floating cabaret off the coast of Acapulco, with bandleader Teddy Stauffer in charge of operations.

Mon November 4

The *Zaca* is filmed in scenes for *The Lady From Shanghai*; NEVER SAY GOODBYE begins opening across the United States, on this date at the Fox Theater in St. Louis, MO.

Fri November 8

The *Zaca* is returned to Flynn; writes to Nora from the *Zaca* in Acapulco (and dated incorrectly as "Friday 7th – 1946," which was probably a combination of late Thursday when the long letter was

With Prof. Flynn and Howard Hill attending to the injured Wallace Berry - Thu, August 29

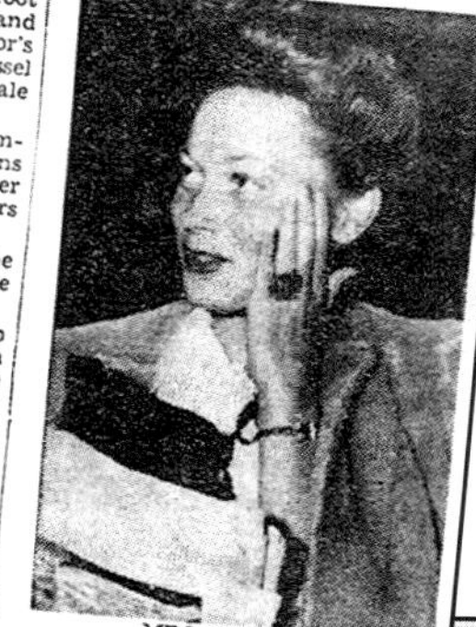

A Herring's Named for Nora; to Crew, She's Capt. Bligh

By United Press

HOLLYWOOD, Sept. 9—Crew trouble crabbed Errol Flynn's venture into the field of marine science today.

Artist John Decker, a member of the volunteer crew on Errol's 118-foot yacht, the "Zaca," jumped ship and turned up muttering that the actor's wife, Nora, had taken over the vessel and turned out to be a sort of "female Captain Bligh."

Decker and several other crew members parted company with the Flynns at Acapulco, Mexico, Decker said, after three weeks of cruising Mexican waters in search of new varieties of fish.

"After Nora got her sea legs, she kind of took over things, sort of like Captain Bligh," Decker said.

"She decided the cruise should keep right on going—finally winding up in Europe. And it's getting to be the hurricane season off the Mexican coast.

"After all, we were only guest crew members. So a bunch of us just upped and left for home. A kind of mutiny against our lovely 'ca tain,' we called it."

The cruise was a success, considered from a scientific standpoint, and found "lots of fish," Decker said.

He said that one of the new ones, a "sort of herring," was named for Nora.

MRS. FLYNN
She took over.

The United Press - Mon, September 9

With Nora, Rita Hayworth, Orson Welles, and Teddy Stauffer celebrating Rita's birthday on the Zaca - Thu, October 17

With Rita Hayworth on the Zaca *- October*

begun and Friday after midnight when it continued): *"....Well, first the Columbia [Pictures] crowd wound up with the boat day before yesterday....[Orson] Welles + [associate producer, Richard] Wilson had dinner aboard last night to go over the bill....I had put on the bill a lot of junky items I felt would make him holler. He did. So we threw those out and he okayed the important ones...The ones he squawked about went like this: Chula (dog) 5 days @ $50 - $250 Cat 2 " " $25 - 50 Monkey 1 " " $25 - 25 His eyes came out so far I thought he was going to have a seizure. 'Christ man!' he yelled 'Didn't a trainer go with any of them? I can't go for this!'...'Orson' I said in a hurt tone 'How do you know what hardships these animals went thru' to become actors? But if you want them to play bit parts for nothing, okay.' I took a pencil and scratched thru the items and he deflated, signing the rest with no beef...Oh yes, the monkey. He weighs about half a pound + is a riot. In love with Chula and tries to do fantastic sex things to her. She likes it.... With luck we should sail about the 12th so you have plenty of time to write me more, and sweetie please do because I love your letters...Address in Tahiti is just Yacht Zaca care Post Master, Papeete, Tahiti....Give Diedre a great big hug for me and for you un muy fuerte abrazoi de mi carason [sic] – don't know how to spell it but darling I mean it?...XXXXXX Errol."* Flynn appears not to have actually sailed to Tahiti.

Sat November 9

Continues filming with Howard Hill on the returned *Zaca*; the two add to footage that will be turned into the short documentaries CRUISE OF THE ZACA and DEEP SEA FISHING, neither released or seen until 1952.

Tue November 12

Written to Nora on *Zaca* stationery: *"....We should sail in a few days now, the work being nearly complete. Pepe de la Vega can't come, leaving me in a spot for a celestial navigator.... Columbia is nearly thru' – the studio is yanking the company back, saying the film is lousy and would have looked better if shot at Catalina! I saw some of the rushes – never let me hear of Orson [Welles] being called genius. My God it was a disappointment. In more ways than one – I hate to be let down about a guy's talent and was hoping for good things from the Wonder Boy. He should stick to those soap operas on the air where he knows what's cooking. Personally we hit it off fine though...I hope you're looking after yourself instead of injuncting Old Dad [Errol] to be careful. Which incidentally I have been sweetheart so don't worry about me...How is it Hill never dropped me a line to report on the film? Will you call him + tell him he's a louse?...Sweetest – all my love and remember I'm thinking of you all the time...."*

Thu November 21

Letter to Nora on Hotel Majestic stationery of Mexico City: *"....leaving 7 a.m. tomorrow morning for the water – ZACA – Acapulco – and setting sail for blue water soon as I get there: deep water that is! Blue + deep!...I just wanted you to know you have to separate from a dame to appreciate her integrity. Remember our beefs, our fights, when we're together? I wonder how I could possibly tell you how superior, how far you outrate in dignity, your sisters [other women]? Those Broads, Tomatoes, Twiddgetts, Dolls, Women, Girls, Crows, whose limited, circumscribed, fungoid minds, disgust and discourage – you shine, kid! SHINE...Oh, well. So you're superior, wonderful little human female – and my dame, the one I know + love and sometimes tremble with fear at the thought of being without – Always remember that, Nora – Old Dad... Ni, ni, sweetheart! A kiss to you and oh yes – kiss that odd little Deirdre thing, who came from some strange tremulous region, on the butt, please?...I LOVE YOU! There! In writing! God, woman, what a case for your lawyers!"*

Fri November 22

Leaves Acapulco for the Panama Canal.

Mon December 9

Travels through the Panama Canal, then on to the San Blas Islands where he and the crew will spend 10 days; Warner Bros. announces Flynn will star in the comedy, *One Last Fling*; he never does.

Mon December 16

Letter to Nora written on Zaca stationery: *"....Going thru' the Panama Canal, and the whole of last week in the San Blas Islands where we have been dodging a storm centre, has been an experience I wish you could have shared with me. What a fantastic place! A group of 16,000 Indians, living on these thousands of tiny, coconut-covered atolls in a condition that they have hardly changed since the days of Columbus. The women all wear gold rings thru' their noses, are frighteningly ugly, and both men and women hate all whites. They speak no English or Spanish and their own language reminds me of Esquimaux [Eskimo]...We dodged the storm and are now at sea, Lat: 8°23' South, on our way to Cartagena, where, barring more disturbances, we should berth tomorrow at noon. I'll wire you on arrival. I sent you 7 more reels of color film, some of San Blas. Please, will you go over to Blum's house, run it, and write me what kind of stuff I'm getting? Under or over exposed or what? You should have received 15 or 16 reels in all by now....Chula and Señor Soto the monkey are great, but resent the newest guest, by name of Hedda, a lady parrot who only speaks (and laughs) in San Blas Indian....After leaving Cartagena may head north to Haiti, thence to Bermuda where there are facilities to haul out and recondition next May for a Summer crossing of the Atlantic, following the Great Circle route. Much safer, better sailing. Down this way even the trades blow sometimes strength 4, which means anything up to 50 miles an hour. No fun....I got your letter in Colon but was being hurried thru' the Canal....Very happy darling girl you're feeling well. Remember these things – this time you will have a much easier delivery, not to compare with the first. Secondly, all kidding apart, I'd just as soon a girl as a boy, especially since we both know its gender was decided many months ago and we can't do anything about it even if we wanted to. So don't worry, you nut! Oh yes – don't forget to tell the doc you want those extra couple of stitches; one will do but two – well, that's talking...."*

Fri December 20
Telegram to Nora from Cartagena: BAD TIME AT SEA TWO SAILS LOST IN STORM BUT EVERYTHING OKAY LEAVING AFTER TOMORROW FOR PORT AU PRINCE HAITI WRITE ME THERE LOVE AND MISS YOU INCREDIBLY.

1947

Wed January 1
Arrives in Kingston, Jamaica, with damage to the *Zaca's* storm and foresails; stays at the Myrtle Bank Hotel; guests that have come aboard along the way include Miss Kelly Foster of Panama, and Dr. Otto Roehr, Wolf Schoenborn, Jose de la Voga, and Apolonio Diaz, all of Mexico; states in an interview that he *"retired from motion pictures five months ago."*

Thu January 2
Is a guest of hotelier Abe Issa at the St. Andrew Club, and later goes to the Colony Club.

Fri January 3
Works on repairing the *Zaca.*

Sat January 4
Sails north for dinner at the Dunlookin Inn near Ocho Rios.

Tue January 7
Wire from Lou Espinosa to Roy Obringer: WHILE IN KINGSTON JAMAICA FLYNN PULLED IN FOR YACHT REPAIRS HIS PLANS LAST FRIDAY WERE TO REMAIN KINGSTON CARE OF MYRTLE BANK HOTEL UNTIL TO-DAY OR TOMORROW THEN PROCEED PORT AU PRINCE HAITI FOR INDEFINITE STAY. HAVE CONTACTED PRESIDENT HAITI ASSURE FLYNN PROTECTION AND USUAL COURTESIES

Fri January 10
The *Zaca* is robbed by five men in two canoes; they escape, but most of the loot falls into the sea as the police close in; only one of the robbers is caught.

Sat January 11
Visits the north shore village of Port Maria.

Sun January 12
Flies to Port-au-Prince by invitation of the Haitian president Dumarsais Estime, accompanied by Dr. Roehr and Mr. Schoenborn.

Wed January 15
Returns to Kingston, Jamaica.

Thu January 16
Wire from Jack Warner to Steve Trilling: ATLANTIC OVERSEAS EDITION TIME JANUARY 13 HAS STATEMENT SUPPOSEDLY GIVEN BY FLYNN AT KINGSTON JAMAICA DECLARING HE RETIRING FROM CINEMA ETC. GET VERIFICATION THIS; is interviewed by the *Daily Gleaner* aboard the *Zaca*, opining on the subject of the "feudal" Jamaican economic system (causing some controversy) and about his plans to move the *Zaca* to Port Antonio.

Sat January 18
Sails to Port Antonio with a Mr. Castille and Miss Dawn Calder, registering at the Titchfield Hotel.

Sun January 19
Fishing in the Port Antonio harbor and Boston Bay, later returning to Kingston.

Tue January 28
Travels to Sedge Pond to visit friends and attend a revival meeting at nearby Sandy Gully.

Errol Flynn Cruise Brings Damage Suit

Errol Flynn's trouble-laden sea voyage in his $200,000 yacht Zaca shipped another cargo of woe yesterday when a $35,000 damage suit was filed in Superior Court by a former seaman on the vessel.

The action was instituted here by Wallace Berry Jr., 17, San Francisco, son of an Army major stationed in Korea, who said he was struck in the leg by a harpoon while he was swimming alongside the craft in Mexican waters Aug. 29. The harpoon was thrown from the yacht, he said.

Flynn was "so busily engaged in other pursuits," Berry said, that he failed to provide adequate care and as a result Berry said he suffered a bone infection which will permanently cripple him.

Flynn left Acapulco Nov. 22 with his yacht en route to Cannes, France.

The Los Angeles Times
Sun, December 1

Errol Flynn Busy
on Isle Purchase

KINGSTON (Jamaica) Feb. 1. (P)—Errol Flynn is completing negotiations to buy a 60-acre coconut-fringed island off Jamaica, for a holiday resort. Known as Navy Island, the island has a large mansion, fresh water springs and white sand beaches.

The price reported agreed on is $80,000.

The Los Angeles Times
Sun, February 2

Greetings from Jamaica, B. W. I.

Errol Flynn's Navy Island — Port Antonio

A postcard from the 1940s

Thu January 30

Attends the International Tennis matches at St. Andrew Club in Kingston with Dawn Calder.

Fri January 31

Travels by flying boat to the Titchfield pier in Port Antonio with Robert Howe, the owner of Navy Island, the property in Port Antonio harbor which Flynn is interested in purchasing; later the two return to Kingston.

Sat February 1

Embarks on a 10-day cruise on the *Zaca* around Jamaica.

Sun February 2

Arrives at Port Antonio, suffering from a sprained ankle received while playing a tennis match in Kingston.

Mon February 3

Negotiates for the purchase of the 60-acre Navy Island.

Tue February 4

Flynn's ankle sprain worsens and a medical consultation in Kingston concludes he has broken a bone in his foot; a cast is applied.

Wed February 5

Returns by flying boat to Port Antonio, piloting the Stramaer Flying Boat much of the way.

Fri February 7

Closes the deal for the purchase of Navy Island; he plans to keep the island as a private resort for family and friends.

February

Letter to Nora about this time: *"....they are a piratical bunch of waterfront rats around here. Did you read by any chance of the raid they made on the ship? Pedro was on watch and naturally asleep. Suddenly over the rail came six big black bastards. Pedro woke up to find one of them standing over him with an upraised iron bar, offering to crack his skull if he made an outcry. Meanwhile the others started looting the ship. They piled a whole lot of stuff (the only thing of value being a case of champagne presented to me that day by a pal) into canoes and took off. Pedro raised the alarm and we sent off the launch after them. Then Appollonio got the Higgins [landing craft] after them too. When the launch drew near they threw most of the stuff overboard + and jumped into the water themselves. Then a dreadful thing happened! There was a most unholy scream as the speedboat propeller ran over one of them. His leg was amputated day before yesterday. In spite of everything my champagne was being sold on shore yesterday – for ¼ its value. I've therefore been seeing nothing but cops ever since and have let the whole waterfront know there are four loaded guns ready + waiting for the next gentlemen with filibuster notions...Before I go further: Please ask Jack to give the enclosed note to Bill Tilden – what a dreadful thing [presumably Tilden's arrest and conviction on morals charges]. I only just heard of it + still don't know the details...Now for the news of the month! I have bought an island off the north coast of Jamaica. Navy Island, right near Port Antonio – get a map + look it up. It's near 100 acres, perfectly, absolutely perfectly beautiful – am leaving on ZACA to take over tomorrow. It runs sheep, some cattle, and the rest is cocoanuts – am taking plenty of film of it so will show you more eulogies of its loveliness. To me it's the perfect place for Dad and that bitchy old mother of mine to retire. I wrote + told them about [it] + they are naturally thrilled. The overseers house is quaint + lovely too + and there is on one end the remains of a Spanish fortification. Apollo + I went spear fishing off its shores last week + got 4 snapper in as many minutes....Ask [Al] Blum honey please to see my car is working okay + the house is cleaned up + ready to get going. Ask him please to have a valet, butler for me lined up. What's Alex [Pavlenko, his former butler] doing? If he's fired by now, and he should be, maybe he needs a job?....Honeychild I'll be seeing you soon – am just about beginning to get nervous about our next [child] and have a whole list of possible names on hand, of both sexes...."*

Sat February 8

Throws a party aboard the *Zaca* which is moored at Navy Island; music is by the Andrew Hamilton Orchestra with a floor show by Tony Walters.

Sun February 9

Sails to Kingston.

Thu February 13

Sails back to Port Antonio.

Fri February 14

Is sued by an American butcher for an unpaid bill of $842 ($10,201 in 2021 value) for meat delivered to the Zaca the previous August; Flynn denies receipt of the delivery.

Sat February 15

Returns to Kingston, the *Zaca* remaining in Port Antonio until Flynn's next visit to Jamaica.

Tue February 18

Flynn flies to Miami en route to Hollywood; he is accompanied by Dawn Calder.

Wed February 19

Arrives in Hollywood, foot in a cast.

Sun February 23

Makes arrangements at St. Joseph's Hospital in Burbank for Nora and her due baby.

Mon February 24

Written to Nora on "Mulholland Farm" stationery: *"The night before your birthday. Nora I am thinking of you – and coming events! I know you have found so many deficiencies in me, so many faults to bear with. Thank you. Thank you so very much –Me."*

Tue February 25

Takes Nora out to dinner at The King's Restaurant in (now) West Hollywood.

Thu February 27

Attends a stable auction at Santa Anita Park hosted by Louis B. Mayer.

Sat March 8

Receives the script for SILVER RIVER; a $6,000 writ ($72,690 in 2021 value) is issued against Flynn for salvage assistance when the *Zaca* was in Colombian waters; unless and until paid the boat will remain in Port Antonio.

Mon March 10

Writer Owen Crump to Jack Warner: *"....This afternoon I called Flynn on the phone for his reaction* [to the SILVER RIVER script]. *Here is the text of Flynn's phone conversation relevant to the script: 'I have read most of the script. As a Western, I think it's damned good. I wish it would have been given me for one of the five other Westerns they had me do....I'm not going to be the Gene Autry of the future....' I told Flynn I would convey his decision to the front office. He said, 'By all means -- they might as well know what the score is.'"* Later, Crump again writes to Warner: *"In my note re Errol Flynn this afternoon, a paragraph was inadvertently left out. Flynn made it quite clear that, under no circumstances would he do any western: 'A month ago I told the studio I would not come back and do a Western, but they didn't believe me—Just went to a lot of trouble anyway.'"*

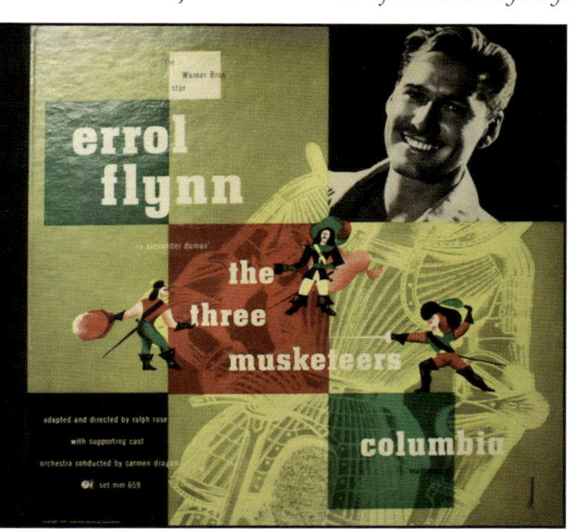

The Columbia 4-disc, 78 RPM record album

Wed March 12

Errol's and Nora's daughter is born at St. Joseph's Hospital in Burbank, weighing 8lbs. 2oz.; two days later Errol publicly announces her name as Rory; makes out a check for $20,000 ($242,301 in 2021 value) to the First National Bank of Pasadena; is sent a memo from Roy Obringer that, according to Flynn's contract, Flynn must be available to commence his next picture—a Western—on March 28th.

Week of March 17

Flynn's recording of *The Three Musketeers* (he in the role of D'Artagnan) is released in a 4-disc, 78 rpm record album *(left)*.

Thu March 20

The Domestic Finance Company sells its share of Thomson Productions to Fannie L. and A. N. Pritzker of Chicago; they now own ½ interest.

CLASS OF SERVICE

This is a full-rate Telegram or Cablegram unless its deferred character is indicated by a suitable symbol above or preceding the address.

WESTERN UNION (19)

JOSEPH L. EGAN
PRESIDENT

SYMBOLS

DL=Day Letter
NL=Night Letter
LC=Deferred Cable
NLT=Cable Night Letter
Ship Radiogram

The filing time shown in the date line on telegrams and day letters is STANDARD TIME at point of origin. Time of receipt is STANDARD TIME at point of destination

SJ37 SER PD=WB HOLLYWOOD CALIF 13 1011A   1947 MAR 13 AM 10 45

ERROL FLYNN=

:7740 MULHOLLAND HIGHWAY HOLLYWOOD CALIF=

DEAR ERROL: YOU HAVE DONE IT AGAIN. CONGRATULATIONS TO

BOTH YOU AND YOUR DEAR WIFE=

ANN AND JACK WARNER.

CLASS OF SERVICE

This is a full-rate Telegram or Cablegram unless its deferred character is indicated by a suitable symbol above or preceding the address.

WESTERN UNION (28)

JOSEPH L. EGAN
PRESIDENT

SYMBOLS

DL=Day Letter
NL=Night Letter
LC=Deferred Cable
NLT=Cable Night Letter
Ship Radiogram

The filing time shown in the date line on telegrams and day letters is STANDARD TIME at point of origin. Time of receipt is STANDARD TIME at point of destination

S108   SER PD=WB HOLLYWOOD CALIF 13 1223P   1947 MAR 13 PM 12 33

MR AND MRS ERROL FLYNN=

:STJOSEPHS HOSPITAL 501 S BUENAVISTA BURBANK CALIF=

HEARTIEST CONGRATULATIONS ON THE ADDITION TO YOUR EVER

GROWING FAMILY=

JERRY WALD.

Tue March 25
Has a meeting with Jack Warner from 1 to 2pm, then with Roy Obringer from 2:45 to 4pm discussing wardrobe and makeup.

Late March
A 990 sq. ft. addition to Flynn's Mulholland house is begun, complete with an attic room (reached by outdoor stairs) that includes a view to the bedroom below via a two-way mirror.

Tue April 1
Renews the contract with the Columbia Recording Corporation, the company for which he recorded the audio play of *The Three Musketeers*.

Thu April 3
Makeup tests for SILVER RIVER; memo from production manager Chuck Hansen to Tenny Wright: *"Today, Thursday, we tested Errol Flynn in the #1 Makeup, which is the Gettysburg sequence, using improvised wardrobe. There was no wardrobe actually ready—it was ready for fitting only....I gave Errol a call for 9:00 AM Wednesday, April 9th, to come in and test his first 5 outfits...Understand from [Perc] Westmore that Flynn returns from his trip on Monday that he will be in the studio on Tuesday morning, April 8th, to see Westmore."* Memo from production manager Chuck Hanson to Tenny Wright: *"When we scheduled 'Silver River,' we laid it out in such a manner as to keep away from [using] Ann Sheridan for the first 3-1/2 weeks...The script covers four different periods; this meant jumping out of continuity and also putting cast on salary ahead of time in order to keep the company shooting...Today, Thursday, while we were shooting makeup tests of Errol Flynn, he told me in the presence of [asst. director] Russ Saunders that he would not jump out of period continuity after this picture started shooting; he did not mind jumping from one sequence to another in the same period, but he absolutely refused to jump from one period to another...In order to keep away from [using] Ann Sheridan prior to May 7th, it is necessary that we follow the above mentioned schedule, which means jumping from one period to another."*

Sat April 5
Travels with Nora to Palm Springs for a few days, during which time he plays several matches with world tennis champion Donald Budge; the *Harvard Lampoon* votes Flynn and Faye Emerson the *"most welcome retirements"* (relative Flynn's recent announcement of leaving filmmaking).

Mon April 7
Roy Obringer receives a memo from writer Ben Cohn requesting a release for Flynn to record a greeting for the opening of the re-release on a double bill of THE SEA HAWK and THE SEA WOLF, and the opening of ESCAPE ME NEVER; memo from producer Collier Young to Steve Trilling: *"…I have suggested to Jerry Wald that he contact Flynn later in the week and perhaps arrange a meeting with Flynn and all concerned, so that Mr. Flynn feels like he is a part of this project from the beginning. In this way we can largely forestall, I think, the usual crisis."*

Thu April 10
Screen tests with actor Jim Davis.

Fri April 11
Wardrobe tests for SILVER RIVER.

Wed April 16
More wardrobe tests; Alexis Smith is being considered for the role of the Queen in the upcoming ADVENTURES OF DON JUAN.

Mon April 21
Begins work on SILVER RIVER, filming the wagon train sequence at Providencia Ranch; memo from producer Owen Crump to Steve Trilling: *"Errol Flynn called me at five o'clock this afternoon and was extremely nice; said he was sorry if he had caused me any trouble; etc., etc. I assured him we would get a script in good shape...It was a nice gesture and, I hope, constitutes a happy omen."*

Tue April 22 through Thu April 24
Continues filming the wagon train sequence; memo from Jerry Wald to Jack Warner (4/24): *"[Director Jean] Negulesco, [screenwriter George] Oppenheimer and myself had lunch with Flynn today to discuss 'DON JUAN.' Flynn's reaction to the new script was as we anticipated—tremendous. He thought the new concept of the character was excellent, and the entire story line to his liking...We expect to have the first draft of the script finished in ten days or two weeks, at which time we will let him see a copy. Of course we will make sure that you and Trilling see it first."*

At Providencia Ranch - April

Fri April 25
Continues filming the wagon train; memo from Owen Crump to Steve Trilling: "[Scenarist] *Harriet Frank and I had lunch with Errol Flynn today—went over the re-write pages. He approved—he even liked them surprisingly enough… God is Love!*"

Sat April 26
Filming process shots in the wagon, and the court-martial; THE SEA HAWK is re-released (with 10 minutes edited out) on a double billing with "The Sea Wolf"; memo from Steve Trilling to Owen Crump: "*You were present when I spoke to Errol Flynn whose suggestion it was that John Ridgely might be a good Stanley Moore…We of course planned for Forrest Tucker and if it works out, I feel that he might be the best choice…Bear this in mind if I should be away when the casting is being done and by all means somebody should talk with Flynn later on so that he knows we gave his suggestions consideration…I don't want to dampen his enthusiasm on this project.*"

Mon April 28
Continues filming process shots in the wagon, and the wagon train battle at Providencia Ranch; memo from editor Alan Crosland, Jr. to Tenny Wright: "*….[It is understood] from the Unit Manager that Flynn will not work out [of] continuity in the barroom sequence so far in advance…*"

Tue April 29
Filming in the gambling tent.

Wed April 30 through Fri May 2
Filming in the Union encampment; (5/1) Flynn's sister Rosemary, recently divorced in Las Vegas from her fist husband, marries Maj. Charles Warner (no relation to the movie family) in Washington, D.C. Warner is currently doing historical research in the capital; newspapers report that Flynn did not attend on account of his shooting schedule on SILVER RIVER.

Sat May 3
Filming the court-martial and battle scene at Providencia Ranch.

Mon May 5
Filming at the WB Calabasas Ranch, the freight yards, and the siding at the Union encampment.

Tue May 6 and Wed May 7
Filming in McComb's (Flynn) place.

Thu May 8
Filming in Beck's (Thomas Mitchell) office.

Fri May 9
Filming in McComb's place.

Sat May 10 and Mon May 12
Filming in the ship's card room, and (on 5/12) in McComb's office and home.

Tue May 13
Filming in the bank office; columnist Harrison Carrol reports that Flynn was so upset over losing his St. Christopher medal while filming last month that "*the crew got a land-mine detector and found the tiny souvenir--under several inches of pulverized soil*"; the medal had been given to him by a priest in Rabaul, New Guinea, sixteen years earlier.

Wed May 14 and Thu May 15
Ann Sheridan starts work on the picture (5/14); filming in the ship's card room and corridor and (on 5/15) in McComb's office and home.

With Jonathan Hale at the WB Calabasas Ranch

Fri May 16
Continues filming in McComb's office and home; Tenny Wright to Roy Obringer: "*The enclosed note is regarding a tooth that Errol Flynn broke in a scene in our picture 'Silver River.' I suppose we are stuck for it—what do you think?*" Attached note from Wright's secretary: "*Dr. William D. Wallace, dentist, Beverly Hills, phoned. Said Errol Flynn had told him to contact you regarding the bill. It amounts to $250 [$3,029 in 2021 value]. Wallace said he will send you an itemized statement.*"

Sat May 17
Continues filming at McComb's place.

Mon May 19 through Wed May 21
Filming in the ballroom and trophy room; Nora, Deirdre, and Rory move into Mulholland sometime this week.

Tue May 20

Letter to Jack Warner: *"Dear Jack: I have been thinking a great deal lately about the possibility of your making the 'White Rajah', the story of the Brooks family of Sarawak…I think in view of the fact that the Brooks have, so to speak, abdicated from Borneo, the picture might be easier to make today. The plot the original Rajah Brooks played in history in Queen Victoria's time would certainly make this a far more interesting yarn than 'Anna and The King of Siam', and also today it is now possible as I understand it to show Queen Victoria on the screen, which when I first wrote the story was not permitted, King Edward not having then abdicated…I re-read the original you bought from me a few days ago [meaning he read it a few days ago], and I can only repeat that there is a natural equally as find [sic] as 'Captain from Castille' in excitement and actual, factual happenings…What do you think? Very best to you, dear boy…."*

Thu May 22

Continues filming in the ballroom and trophy room, and at the campsite; Flynn's friend Freddie McEvoy is a guest at the Mulholland house until May 24th.

Fri May 23 and Sat May 24

Continues filming at the campsite.

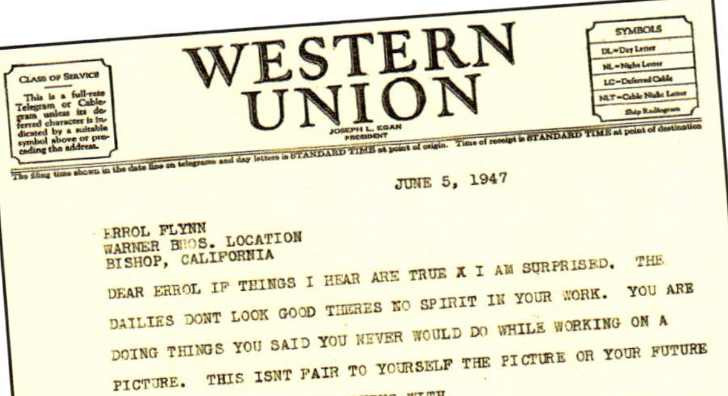

With Thomas Mitchell at Swall Meadows in the California Sierras - Thu, June 5

Mon May 26

Filming in the trophy room.

Tue May 27 and Wed May 28

Filming at the campsite and campfire.

Thu May 29

Filming in McComb's office and home.

Fri May 30

Filming process shots on the boat deck and straight shots at McComb's place.

Sun June 1

Leaves WB Studios at 8am, arriving in Bishop, CA, at 3pm.

Mon June 2

Filming in the mine region, 15 miles outside Bishop.

Tue June 3

Filming at the campsite, on the road, and at the stagecoach.

Wed June 4

Filming at the wagon train and on the road.

Thu June 5 and Fri June 6

Filming at the vista, 20 miles outside Bishop *(top left)*, and (on 6/6) on the road to the mine.

Sat June 7

Filming the wagon train and the posse chase; Nora and Sean visit Errol on location.

Sun June 8

Flynn's artist friend, John Decker, dies; Flynn leaves Bishop at 8am, arriving at WB Studios at 2:30pm; in a tennis exhibition at the Beverly Wilshire Hotel, playing with pro Pauline Betz against pro Sarah Palfrey and Mickey Rooney.

Mon June 9

Filming in McComb's place; inter-office memo from Jack Warner: *"Called Errol Flynn after receiving his wire from Bishop dated June 7, as he did not receive wire he claimed he sent in answer to mine dated June 5th (left)…He started saying something reference his contract and if I was not satisfied with his work. Told him this was ridiculous and that my telegram said nothing about his contract…I told Flynn there was no spirit in his work. He said you could not show much spirit in long shots and I told him those very words proves [sic] that he has no spirit…Finally got him to admit that he drinks every night but not on the set…."*

WESTERN UNION

JOSEPH L. EGAN
PRESIDENT

CLASS OF SERVICE

This is a full-rate Telegram or Cablegram unless its deferred character is indicated by a suitable symbol above or preceding the address.

SYMBOLS

DL = Day Letter
NL = Night Letter
LC = Deferred Cable
NLT = Cable Night Letter
Ship Radiogram

The filing time shown in the date line on telegrams and day letters is STANDARD TIME at point of origin. Time of receipt is STANDARD TIME at point of destination

JUNE 5, 1947

ERROL FLYNN
WARNER BROS. LOCATION
BISHOP, CALIFORNIA

DEAR ERROL IF THINGS I HEAR ARE TRUE X I AM SURPRISED. THE DAILIES DONT LOOK GOOD THERES NO SPIRIT IN YOUR WORK. YOU ARE DOING THINGS YOU SAID YOU NEVER WOULD DO WHILE WORKING ON A PICTURE. THIS ISNT FAIR TO YOURSELF THE PICTURE OR YOUR FUTURE AND THE PEOPLE YOU ARE WORKING WITH.

JACK WARNER

With his stand-in Jim Fleming and his son Sean outside Bishop, CA - June

Tue June 10

At the memorial gathering for John Decker at the artist's 1215 Alta Loma Rd. home in Hollywood, and later to the service at Inglewood Cemetery *(top right)*; filming at the Silver City Mine (Bronson Canyon in Hollywood); inter-office memo from unit manager Chuck Hansen: *"Mr. Flynn returned to set at 3:25 P.M., not in wardrobe or makeup. Miss Sheridan had to leave set at 4:00 P.M. for hair appointment. Unable to shoot scenes without cast."*

Wed June 11

Continues filming at the mine, in the mine office, and in a montage of the mine *(bottom right)*.

Thu June 12 and Fri June 13

Filming in the Silver City Bank and office and (on 6/13) office retakes and process shots of the stagecoach.

Sat June 14

Filming process shots in the studio of the Bishop, CA, vista.

Mon June 16 through Wed June 18

Filming at St. Joseph's dock and street at the WB Calabasas Ranch.

Thu June 19

Filming in the Silver City streets (including on Main Street) at the WB Calabasas Ranch; memo from assistant director Russ Saunders to Tenny Wright: *"At 4:00PM Mr. Flynn was called on set to shoot an added scene between 'Banjo's'* [Barton MacLane] *Henchmen and Mr. Flynn—the scene was put in his dressing room at 1:30PM. Mr. Flynn refused to work, claiming he had not received the scene. It was the opinion of the staff around the camera that Mr. Flynn had been drinking; however, he was in his wardrobe and makeup."* Memo from Jerry Wald to Jack Warner: *"Just a reminder about our talk regarding Curtiz and DON JUAN. Mike told me yesterday that he had no picture lined up for October and would be interested in the project."*

Fri June 20

Flynn's 38th birthday; continues filming in the Silver City streets at the WB Calabasas Ranch until fog prevents further work, then later in the mine office at the studio; summary of a telephone conversation between Flynn and Jack Warner at 3:30pm. Flynn initiated the call: <u>Flynn</u>-*Jack, I'm so upset I cannot work and would like to have a private conversation with you to get this straightened out.* <u>Warner</u>-*I don't see why we have to talk about it, all I am trying to do is get the picture finished.* <u>Flynn</u>-*I'm trying to be humble and kind but I do not like to be asked to please go to work and I am not going to stand down here and be bawled out publicly and listen to a lot of shit. My record is absolutely clear. Nobody is ready to work yet. You and I can always do business together but I can't do business with any in-between-man.* <u>Warner</u>-*I've forgotten about the things that happened a week ago and also the telegram you sent.* <u>Flynn</u>-*I will not work until the set is cleared of the stool pigeons. You should come down to the set to see what is going on. The sooner I get out of here the happier I will be. You have too many stool pigeons around.* <u>Warner</u>-*Let's not waste a lot of time talking about this and forget it.* <u>Flynn</u>-*The cop on the door is taking notes of every move I make. I know because I saw his notebook. Put* [head of security] *Blayney Matthews in the film with his cops and have a Max Sennett comedy. Would be great! If I can't see the person I work for, fine!* <u>Warner</u>-*There is nothing to see you about. We just had a tough break in the weather.* <u>Flynn</u>-*I just want to see everybody concerned with this whole thing as I am too nervous to work. Get the agents and lawyers for both sides and let's have a talk.* <u>Warner</u>-*If you don't want to work the only thing I can do is to close the picture and hold you responsible.* <u>Flynn</u>-*That would be the best thing to do. You clear this air or I am not going to work. Will call my doctor and lawyer.* <u>Warner</u>-*What do you need your doctor for?* <u>Flynn</u>-*You made me too nervous. I need a doctor.* [Ann] *Sheridan is here listening to me and she is nervous herself. Said she is so nervous she can't hold a paper. I must see you before I can do any more work. Let me know when I can come up. I will be waiting for a message from you.* <u>Warner</u>-*If you have any fair play you would go ahead and make the picture. I have a lot of responsibility and can't be stopping for everything. What else can I see you about?* <u>Flynn</u>-*I want everybody there. I want Tenny Wright, the director, the assistant director on the picture and everybody.* <u>Warner</u>-*There is nothing to see you about. Just go to work.* <u>Flynn</u>-*Listen, I am here ready to work and am legally within my rights. You know that.* At this point Flynn hangs up. A further summary of the call stated: ....*Company had been called in from location at noon time as weather was no good, fog was obscuring the sun. While Mr. Warner was talking to* [producer Owen] *Crump, Flynn walked on the set, just as Crump said the Company was waiting for Flynn. Crump suggested that Flynn speak to Mr. Warner. Mr. Warner asked Flynn why he was so long getting to the set* [from the WB Calabasas Ranch] *when company had dismissed at noon at location. Flynn said he could not get a driver to bring him in from location. After a few more words Flynn started to swear and stated if Mr. Warner would get the policemen off the set there would be better work done, that Mr. Warner should come down and get in front of the camera instead of sitting in his office, etc. Mr. Warner told Flynn he hoped that he (Flynn) was not trying to pull the same stunt Spencer Tracy did to get out of his Fox contract and also stated that Flynn would be held responsible for every*

With Georgia and Red Skelton, composer Jimmy McHugh, and Edward G. Robinson at John Decker's funeral service, Inglewood (CA) Cemetery - Tue, June 10

At Bronson Canyon in Los Angeles

With Chico and Ann Sheridan - July

*Rehearsing with Ann Sheridan
on the McComb bedroom set -
second week of July*

hour he had held the company up since the picture started. Conversation terminated when Flynn hung up." Inter-office memo from Chuck Hansen: *"Company delayed because of Mr. Flynn's phone discussion 3:30 to 4:15 P.M."* Memo to Jack Warner: *"Errol Flynn has requested Bob Ford, his attorney, and Dr. Nolan* [permission] *to drive on the lot today."* This was approved.

Sat June 21

Filming in McComb's home; a surprise belated birthday party is thrown for Flynn by Ann Sheridan and Flynn's son Sean; Sean presents his father with a pet monkey which Flynn names Chico; the monkey is eventually given to the Griffith Park (now Los Angeles) Zoo in December of 1950.

Mon June 23

Continues filming in McComb's home, dining room, and at the banquet.

Tue June 24

Filming retakes in McComb's office, and in Chevigee's (Monte Blue) office; memo to Jack Warner from his secretary Bill Schaefer: *"Attached wire is a report we finally got from Western Union on the wire Flynn is supposed to have sent you from Bishop:* OUR BISHOP OFFICE ADVISED THEY HAD NO RECORD OF A PREVIOUS MESSAGE TO JLWARNER SIGNED FLYNN JUNE 5 6 OR 7...*Would be good for Roy* [Obringer] *to have this in his files just in case."*

Wed June 25 and Thu June 26

Filming in McComb's home foyer and dining room.

Fri June 27, Sat June 28, and Mon June 30

Filming in the Silver City streets at the WB Calabasas Ranch and (on 6/28 and 30) at McComb's place.

Tue July 1

Continues filming in the Silver City streets, in the saloon, and at the graveyard.

Thu July 3

Continues filming in the Silver City streets and outside the Silver City Hotel; Flynn receives a letter acknowledging his agreement to appear in a small bit in *Always Together*; he never does the bit.

Sat July 5

Continues filming in the Silver City streets and outside the Silver City Hotel.

Sun July 6

Throws a birthday party for Los Angeles journalist Sara Hamilton.

Mon July 7

Continues filming in the Silver City streets, on the road, and on the wagon train; Jack Warner to Collier Young: *"….You can advise* [Errol Flynn] *that anytime he wants a print to run at his home, we will be happy to supply him with one free so he will not have to buy one. We would prefer that he only ask for prints on Saturday and Sunday, not during the week...Also, tell Flynn that he owes us approximately $1,200* [$14,538 in 2021 value] *for 16mm prints that were not returned to us from his last cruise."*

Tue July 8

Filming in McComb's home.

Wed July 9 and Thu July 10

Ill; does not work; Roy Obringer receives a subpoena (on 6/9) to appear in court on July 29th to testify in a case of Liliane Carre Flynn [Lili Damita] against Flynn.

Fri July 11

Filming in the foyer of McComb's home.

Sat July 12

Ill; does not work; with Nora at the Mocambo.

Mon July 14

Filming in McComb's home; memo from Owen Crump to Steve Trilling: *"On Page 131 there is an extra little scene* [which] *Raoul Walsh suggested. He and Flynn discussed it on the set this morning. I also agree that it is a good idea because it gives us a little more 'time' where we need it in the story."*

Tue July 15 and Wed July 16

Continues filming in McComb's home and (on 7/16) bedroom; memo from Jerry Wald to Steve Trilling (on 7/16) concerning ADVENTURES OF DON JUAN: *"Arthur Park* [Flynn's agent] *advised me that Pat Neale* [Patricia Neal] *was not interested in doing any pictures this summer...I think we should write in Viveca Lindfors, tentatively, for the role of the Queen. She is perfect for it."*

Thu July 17 and Fri July 18
Continues filming in Mike's bedroom; CRY WOLF premieres at The Strand in New York City on 7/18.

Sat July 19
Filming in McComb's home.

Mon July 21
Filming process shots on the buckboard and carriage.

Tue July 22
Filming at the Silver City Mine in Bronson Canyon.

Thu July 24
Filming on the hilltop at Providencia Ranch, and a retake of the process shots of the wagon train (on a treadmill).

Fri July 25
Filming process shots of the carriage and funeral carriage; inter-office memo from Flynn to Jack Warner: *"Thanks for your note of yesterday, or the day before, concerning a conference to determine the commencment [sic] date of DON JUAN....My agent at M.C.A., Mr. Park, tells me he has already contacted your office for an appointment but that you've not been well. Hoping that you're feeling better by now...."*

Sat July 26
Filming at the mine in Bronson Canyon.

Mon July 28
Continues filming at the mine in Bronson Canyon.

Tue July 29
Does not work; appears in court with Lili to defend against charges of back alimony and child support payments; the court rules in favor of Lili, the amount totaling $6,000 ($72,690 in 2021 value) plus an additional $12,000 ($145,381 in 2021 value) for Lili's taxes, this added to his regular monthly payment of $1,500 a month to her ($18,173 in 2021 value).

Thu July 31
Filming in the Silver City streets at the WB Calabasas Ranch; memo from Owen Crump to Tenny Wright: *"Col. Warner requested two additional shots of Flynn:...1. A full figure leaning against the bunkhouse, and...2. A closeup at the same location...As you know, we can pick these shots up at the stage while we are shooting the interior of the bunkhouse."*

August
Is offered a new contract commencing on January 2, 1948, that guarantees him three pictures over two years at $14,285.72 per week ($173,072 in 2021 value) at not less than fourteen consecutive weeks per picture.

Fri August 1
Continues filming in the Silver City streets.

Sat August 2
Filming in the bunkhouse and dubbing dialogue in Projection Room 14; memo from Owen Crump to Steve Trilling: *"This morning on the set both Flynn and Sheridan wanted to know what the plans were re the 'Love Montage.'...I told them you and Col. Warner wanted us to get the film completely cut before deciding on the montage...."*

Fri August 8
Filming solo close-up retakes on a horse, on Midwest Street, and in the bunkhouse; with Nora at a tribute for Walter Winchell and his Damon Runyon Cancer Fund held at the Mocambo *(bottom right)*; attendees include Frank and Nancy Sinatra, Dorothy Lamour, Jimmy Durante, Dinah Shore, George Montgomery, Al Jolson, Eddie Cantor, and others.

Sat August 9
Completes work on SILVER RIVER with process shots of the vista and in the bunkhouse and on the hotel porch.

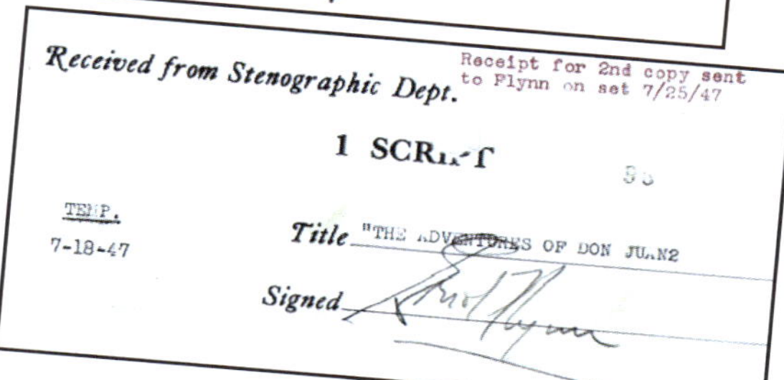

July 22nd, 1947.

Dear Errol:

Would like to set up an appointment with you, Vince Sherman, Jerry Wald, Steve Trilling and myself to discuss the commencement date of DON JUAN as I want to state now that there is a serious problem confronting us with respect to our next Technicolor camera commitment.

Any day after you have finished work or whenever you say, I will be happy to get the boys together as it will only take ten to fifteen minutes to discuss our problems and decide where we are going.

Please phone my office and let them know when you can make it.

Best wishes.

Jack

Mr. E. Flynn
Studio

Received from Stenographic Dept. Receipt for 2nd copy sent to Flynn on set 7/25/47

1 SCRIPT

TEMP.
7-18-47

Title "THE ADVENTURES OF DON JUAN2

Signed Errol Flynn

With Nora and Frank Sinatra, and (behind) columnists Walter Winchell and Leonard Lyons at the Mocambo - Fri, August 8

Mon August 11

Photo shoot at the studio.

Wed August 13

Errol and Nora leave for Kingston, Jamaica, via Miami for a three-week vacation, arriving the next day, staying at the Myrtle Bank Hotel, and visiting the American consul; CRY WOLF begins opening in theaters around the United States, on this date at the Indianapolis Theater in Indianapolis, IN; the Fox Theater in St. Louis, MO; and the Strand in Hartford, CT.

Fri August 15

Errol and Nora move on to Port Antonio, staying at the Titchfield Hotel and checking on the *Zaca* which is still moored there; Bill Ferguson is the yacht's chief engineer.

Thu August 21

Jack Warner agrees in writing to furnish Flynn with a 16mm print of every film Flynn has made to date at Warner Bros., from CAPTAIN BLOOD to ADVENTURES OF DON JUAN; Flynn enters into a twelve-year contract with Warner Bros. at one picture per year (half of which are to be in color) at $200,000 per picture ($2,404,712 in 2021 value); note by Flynn written to Nora on Titchfield Hotel stationery in Jamaica: *"Honey – I've fixed up – for you – a very quiet but very special treat for tonight...Errol."*

Sat August 23

Errol and Nora attend a party at the Titchfield in advance of the next day's rafting races, which Flynn has helped organize *(top left)*; music is provided by the Titchfield Minstrels.

Sun August 24

The Errol Flynn Stakes, the first annual river rafting races on the Rio Grande River, take place, with Nora shooting the starting pistol *(bottom left),* and Errol providing the 1st, 2nd, and 3rd place cash prizes; there are 24 contestants, with 1,500 spectators at the starting line.

Memo from Jack Warner to himself (from around this time) regarding notes to bring up in a meeting with Flynn's agent, Lew Wasserman: *1. Apparently Flynn does not want to answer my letter or I would have heard from him...Therefore, so there will be no misunderstanding, you convey to Flynn that we expect him to report approximately Sept. 26th, the date of commencement of photography on his next picture...2. So there will be no further misunderstanding, our company is reserving the right to keep track of the things that transpire during each day the picture is in production...If Flynn is late, if liquor is being used so that from the middle of the afternoon on it is impossible for the director to make anymore scenes with Flynn, if liquor is brought on the set or into the Studio---we must hold Flynn legally and financially responsible for any delay in the making of this picture...We may go so far as to abrogate the entire contract and sue him for damages...3. When Flynn returns from abroad, there shall be a meeting with Flynn, his agents, Steve Trilling and Obringer...We want to lay this on the line cold as to just what we plan and Flynn must live up to the production rules of this company...4. We will never again make pictures where Flynn or any other artist becomes incoherent due to liquor or whatever it may be. When a director informs Production that it is impossible to shoot further because the actor or actress cannot properly handle their assignment we may as well quit. This has happened repeatedly during the last pictures we have made in which Flynn has appeared and we cannot permit it any longer."*

Thu August 28

According to the *Jamaica Daily Gleaner*, the Flynns' parrot Polly fell overboard on this day, inducing Errol to dive fully clothed into the Port Antonio sea to save the bird.

Wed September 3

Travels to Kingston, staying at the Myrtle Bank Hotel.

Thu September 4

Lunch at the Myrtle Bank Hotel with Nora and Sir Anthony Jenkinson, 13th Baronet of Walcot, England.

Sun September 7

Errol, Nora, and Apolonio Diaz visit Montego Bay, bathing and visiting the Doctor's Cave Bathing Club and Montego Bay Yacht Club.

Fri September 12

Gives a party aboard the *Zaca* with the Titchfield Orchestra providing entertainment.

Sat and Sun September 13 and 14

Closes a deal for 2,000 acres of land known as Castle Comfort, along with a number of head of cattle, in the Boston Bay area of Port Antonio.

Dancing with Nora at a party at the Titchfield Hotel in Port Antonio, Jamaica - Sat, August 23

With Nora as she shoots the starting pistol for the Errol Flynn Stakes rafting races in Port Antonio - Sun, August 24

Wed September 17
Travels to Kingston with Nora to prepare for the return home to Los Angeles.

Thu September 18
Errol and Nora fly from Jamaica to Miami.

Fri September 19
After delays due to stormy weather, Errol and Nora arrive in Los Angeles *(top right)*; Steve Trilling to Roy Obringer: *"Errol Flynn did not report yesterday, and I understand from MCA that his departure was delayed and all planes grounded account of Florida hurricane...You might want to take some legal position so we are not forced to commence salary payments until he actually arrives."*

Mon September 22
Memo from Steve Trilling to Roy Obringer: *"Errol Flynn reported Saturday, September 20th, to commence services, preparation, etc. for his role in 'The Adventures of Don Juan.'"*

Tue September 23
Dick Maybery to Tenny Wright: *"I spoke to Errol Flynn today and asked him to come in for Fencing Rehearsal tomorrow, Wednesday, 9/24, but he said that he could not do it, as he was working on the script, but would possibly start Thursday, 9/25 on the Rehearsal."*

Wed September 24
Inter-office memo from Jerry Wald to Steve Trilling: *"....Mr. Flynn has now decided he does not want to wear any of the costumes made for him in [ADVENTURES OF DON JUAN], and wants to go back to the type of costumes that Barrymore wore...This, I'm sure you realize, is an impossibility, because we have all our costumes made. If we were to change Mr. Flynn's costumes, we would have to change the wardrobe of all the other people around him....Inasmuch as Flynn did okay the original costume sketches, there is little else for us to do but to proceed with the costumes we have.... Flynn did approach me the other day regarding Bill Travilla's doing a couple of new outfits for him, which I agreed to do.... from what I gather from the grape-vine, Mr. Flynn is planning to have Mr. Travilla make all his costumes...."*

Thu September 25
Work on ADVENTURES OF DON JUAN finally resumes with sound and photo tests with Viveca Lindfors.

Fri September 26
Fencing rehearsals from 10am to noon at Flynn's Mulholland house; sound rehearsals later at the studio.

Mon September 29
Inter-office memo from unit manager, Frank Mattison: *"Mr. Flynn was given call for fencing rehearsal but did not report."*

Tue September 30
Inter-office memo from unit manager, Frank Mattison: *"Mr. Flynn came on lot at 10:45am, discussed fencing routine with [director Vincent] Sherman and Fred Cavens [fencing instructor], also looked at models for fencing routine. Did not rehearse fencing. Left lot at 1:15pm."*

Wed October 1
Memo from Dick Mayberry to Steve Trilling and Roy Obringer: *"Errol Flynn came in at 10:45AM yesterday, Tuesday, and after looking at Technicolor Tests he discussed the Fencing Routine with Fred Cavens and Vincent Sherman on Stage 21, the set in which the first duel takes place. From there Flynn went to the Model Room, in the Art Department, and discussed the Fencing Routine that takes place at the finish of the picture. He then went to lunch, and left the lot at 1:15PM and did not return."* Memo from Dick Maybery to Tenny Wright: *"Errol Flynn started Fencing Rehearsals at 11:15AM today, Wednesday, and rehearsed until 12:45PM, at which time he went to Wardrobe Department for fittings. He did not rehearse the remainder of the day."*

Thu October 2
Wardrobe and makeup tests.

Fri October 3
Inter-office memo from unit manager, Frank Mattison: *"Don Turner [Flynn's double] and Fred Cavens in Studio at 8:00 A.M. Dressed in fencing clothes. Left in car to go to Errol Flynn's home. Fenced from 9 to 10:30 A.M. with Errol Flynn...."*

Sat October 4 through Sat October 11
Fencing rehearsals at home.

*Arriving with Nora in Los Angeles -
Fri, September 19*

Mon October 13

Begins filming ADVENTURES OF DON JUAN with scenes on Catherine's balcony and wall *(top left)*

Tue October 14

Continues filming on Catherine's (Mary Stuart) balcony and wall; Frank Mattison to Tenny Wright: *"Regarding the matter of which I spoke to you concerning treatment for Flynn's face, I discussed it with [Steve] Trilling and am going to talk to the doctor today…as to the price etc. Understand the charge will not be more than $20-$25 a visit [$242.30 and $302.88, respectively, in 2021 value]."*

Wed October 15

Continues filming on Catherine's balcony and wall, and in Catherine's bedroom; inter-office memo from Frank Mattison: *"This picture is moving along very slowly, but I attribute it to Sherman getting acquainted and understanding how to work with Flynn. I believe this will be a good combination once they get fairly co-ordinated. That's why Mr. Flynn seems to be co-operating and knows his lines."*

Thu October 16

Continues filming on Catherine's balcony; inter-office memo from Frank Mattison: *"Flynn has had a great deal of dialogue and is doing very well with it."* Memo from Frank Mattison to Tenny Wright: *For your information, I have not seen Dr. Case since I first spoke to you regarding a treatment for Errol Flynn. However, I talked with Flynn and he informs me that the visits to the doctor's office will be at the rate of $10.00; he did not think the charge would be over $20 or $25 at the most for visits to the studio…I am waiting for the doctor to come in either today or tomorrow, Friday, and will inform you accordingly."*

Fri October 17 and Sat October 18

Filming in Catherine's bedroom.

Sun October 19

Performs with Dorothy Malone in the radio play "Night Operator" on the *Hollywood Star Preview* program.

Mon October 20

Continues filming in Catherine's bedroom and on her balcony and wall.

Tue October 21

Filming in Diana's (Helen Westcott) apartment.

Wed October 22

Filming on a country road at Providencia Ranch *(bottom right)*.

Thu October 23 to Sat October 25

Filming in the London apartment and on Dijon Street on the WB backlot.

Mon October 27

Filming in Diana's apartment and balcony.

Tue October 28

Continues filming in Diana's apartment; inter-office memo from Frank Mattison: *"Sherman and Flynn talked to me yesterday afternoon and they were greatly perturbed about going out of continuity for 22 pages, in order that we may jump the first scenes with the 'Queen.'"*

Wed October 29 and Thu October 30

Continues filming in Diana's apartment; Freddie McEvoy arrives (10/29) to stay at Mulholland, announcing plans for a radio series with Flynn about big game hunting, which will take them to Africa after the completion of Flynn's current film.

With Mary Stuart - Mon, October 13

With director Vincent Sherman in Catherine's (Mary Stuart) bedroom - third week of October

A production photo taken at Providencia Ranch, Flynn on the left and Alan Hale to his right - Wed, October 22

Fri October 31

Filming in the English cell and in the Spanish Embassy in London; attends a Halloween costume party with Nora at the Westside Tennis Club.

Sat November 1 and Mon November 3 through Thu November 6

Continues filming in the Spanish Embassy and also (on 11/4-6) in the Spanish inn; (11/3) with Ann Sothern and Jack Carson recording spot announcements for the Friendship Train, a one-time charity event that collected foodstuffs from citizens on a junket across America that were then delivered to the people of France and Italy who were in desperate need of assistance after the war.

Fri November 7

Continues filming in the Spanish inn; memo from Steve Trilling to Jack Warner: *"My sources have already advised that Errol Flynn has passed the word along that he will 'absolutely refuse to have Doug Kennedy play the part* [of Don Rodrigo in ADVENTURES OF DON JUAN].'" ESCAPE ME NEVER opens at the Strand in New York City.

Sat November 8

Filming the fight sequence against six soldiers in the Spanish inn; memo from Steve Trilling to Frank Mattison: *"Under the circumstances, I would pay the attached bill from Frank Nolan who administered the injections to Errol Flynn, thereby saving the time he would absent himself from the set to go down to Nolan's office. Have Tenny Wright put it through Production, charge to Adventures of Don Juan, and if there is going to be any continuance of this, I think there should be some understanding either with Flynn or his agent who should continue to pay. It should not be carried on indefinitely."*

Mon November 10

Continues filming in the Spanish inn.

Tue November 11 to Thu November 13

Filming in the Madrid street and inn.

Wed November 19

Filming outside the Spanish inn and in the king's study.

Tue November 25

Continues filming in the king's study and in the throne room; costume test for the throne room scene; Paramount Pictures requests permission from Warner Bros. to use Flynn's name in lyrics to be recorded for use in the film, *A Foreign Affair*: *"Two G.I.s are riding thru Berlin on Tandem with the Heroine (Jean Arthur) sitting between them. They are singing to the tune of 'Daisy, Daisy, give me your answer, do.'*

Joe: 'Fraulein, Fraulein, wilst du ein Candy Bar
Schoen, fein, Fraulein, you like G.I.s nicht wahr?
At home, though you won't believe us
The girls could take or leave us,
But in Berlin, we're Errol Flynn
Ach, du Wunderbar Candy Bar!'"

Wed November 26

Continues filming in the throne room, the first day filming with Viveca Lindfors.

Fri November 28, Sat November 29, Mon December 1, and Tue December 2

Continues filming in the throne room; (12/1) Paramount Pictures' request to use Errol Flynn's name in their picture *A Foreign Affair* is turned down; (12/2) Warner Bros. announces that Flynn will next star as a 17th-century soldier of fortune in a film called *General Crack*; he never does.

Wed December 3

Ill; does not work; memo from Frank Mattison to Tenny Wright: *"Around Midnight yesterday, Tuesday, December 2nd, Errol Flynn phoned Dick Mayberry, the assistant director on this show, and stated he was suffering from the flu and a cold and would unable to work today, Wednesday, December 3rd...."*

Thu December 4

Ill; does not work; inter-office memo from Frank Mattison: *"Errol Flynn was unable to work yesterday owing to illness, and I was informed by (Flynn's assistant) James Fleming yesterday afternoon that Flynn would be unable to come in today. However, he felt quite sure that Flynn would be*

Filming in the Spanish inn on a WB soundstage - November

With Barbara Bates and Alan Hale on the Spanish inn set - November

With Robert Douglas (standing, center), Romney Brent, Viveca Lindfors, and Jeanne Shepherd

With Alan Hale - second week of December

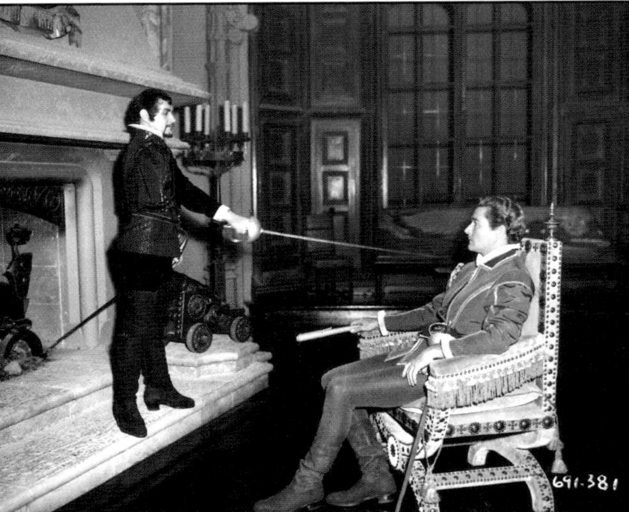

With Robert Douglas - Thu, December 11

in tomorrow. This unexpected illness of Flynn worked hardships on us today, inasmuch as we are rushing a set through so that we may, if necessary, continue tomorrow by working in the torture chamber." Guests on the Campbell Soup radio show with Jack Carson.

Fri December 5
Ill; does not work; Frank Mattison to Tenny Wright: *"Yesterday, Thursday, Dec 4th, I talked with Errol Flynn and he stated he did not believe he would be able to work today, Friday….I talked to Flynn again this afternoon, Friday, at 4:00PM and he tells me he is ready to come to work tomorrow, Saturday."*

Sat December 6
Ill; does not work; Frank Mattison to Tenny Wright: *"At 11:15AM today, Saturday, when we phoned Errol Flynn to come in this afternoon to be ready at 2:00PM, he informed Dick Maybery he was still feeling very badly; fever blisters were bothering him and he did not feel he could come in this afternoon."*

Mon December 8
Filming in Don Juan's house; Warners announces Flynn to star in *The Turquoise*, by Anya Seton, and with Ann Sheridan in *One Last Fling*; he never films either.

Tue December 9
Continues filming in Don Juan's house and in Lorca's (Robert Douglas) chamber.

Wed December 10
Continues filming in Lorca's chamber.

Thu December 11
Continues filming in Lorca's chamber, with Lorca slicing Juan's epaulet *(center left)*, and in the trophy room with the Queen; inter-office memo from Frank Mattison: *"Flynn was off the lot and got into a packed eatery place with the result he came back late to the set."* It is announced that Flynn will be filming *Lucky Baldwin* for MGM, though he never does; Flynn's letter to his old friend Dr. Hermann Erben: *"…a friend is to me one of the rare treasures we can find in this world; and if I can lay claim to any kind of virtue I like to think it is a talent for lifelong loyalty to those very few humans I care for in the world. I now have so many children my house is like a fucking zoo….Surprisingly I find I like children very much - the only trouble with them, of course, is that they grow up to become people. People I do not like at all…."*

Fri December 12, Sat December 13, and Mon December 15
Continues filming in the trophy room; inter-office memo from Frank Mattison (12/12): *"We had to wait again for Flynn to return from lunch. I am going to talk to him today and see if he will not stay on the lot for lunch."*

Tue December 16 to Sat December 20
Filming in the Queen's (Viveca Lindfors) study and (on 12/19 and 20) in the palace corridor.

Mon December 22
Continues filming in the palace corridor.

Tue December 23
Filming in the Spanish inn at the WB Calabasas Ranch with Raymond Burr.

Wed December 24 and Sat December 27
Filming in the palace corridor.

Thu December 25
Christmas at Mulholland with Nora and their daughters; Deirdre receives her first bicycle.

Sun December 28
Drives with Nora and the girls to Idyllwild in the mountains above Los Angeles so the girls can experience their first snow.

Mon December 29 and Tue December 30
Filming in the Queen's study and (on 12/30) close-ups with Raymond Burr outside the Spanish inn.

Wed December 31
Filming in the dungeon with Raymond Burr and Monte Blue; receives a five-week salary prepayment, personally approved by Jack Warner; attends a New Year's Eve party with Nora

Celebrating Viveca Lindfors' birthday with Vincent Sherman, Romney Brent, and Lindfors' current beau, Don Siegel - Mon, December 29

hosted by producer Sam Spiegel; guests include Shelley Winters, Robert Stack, Ida Lupino, Edward G. Robinson, Cornel Wilde, and others.

1948

Fri January 2
Continues filming in the dungeon corridor.

Sat January 3 and Mon January 5
Filming in the dungeon.

Tue January 6
Filming in the cell and dungeon corridor.

Wed January 7 and Thu January 8
Filming in the torture chamber; inter-office memo from Frank Mattison (1/8): *"Mr. Flynn went home ill at 12:30 P.M."*

Fri January 9
Ill; does not work; Frank Mattison to Tenny Wright: *"Shortly after lunch yesterday, Thursday, Errol Flynn complained of being bothered by his hemorrhoids; they were bothering him to such an extent that it was necessary for him to go home. We were able to continue working without him until 6:00PM...Late last night, we were informed that the doctor had advised Errol Flynn to stay in bed today, Friday; therefore, he will not be in to work today. We hope he will be in tomorrow, Saturday."*

Sat January 10
Filming in the torture chamber.

Mon January 12
Ill; does not work; memo from Frank Mattison to Tenny Wright: *"As you know, Errol Flynn was unable to work Thursday and Friday, as he was bothered with his hemorrhoids. He reported on Saturday and worked although he suffered considerably...."* Memo from Tenny Wright to Jack Warner: *"....Flynn is at the Monte Sano Hospital....Flynn does have hemorrhoids, and [Dr.] Nolan is having a consultation with a proctologist tonight, but does not have any intention of operating...However, Flynn does have a temperature of 102°, is vomiting, and has symptoms of malaria. Nolan has made blood and smear tests and is awaiting the results of these tests. As far as we can tell right now, Flynn either has a recurrence of malaria or possibly the so-called Virus X [an influenza]. Nolan has also called in Dr. Louis Chandler, a chest specialist, for consultation...I asked Dr. Nolan how long he thought Flynn would be out, and he could not tell me definitely at this time. His guess, however, pending a more definite prognosis, is that Flynn will be out for about a week. He assured me that he would do everything possible to get Mr. Flynn back to work just as soon as possible. He will keep in touch with me, and as soon as he knows for sure what is wrong, will let me know when we can expect Mr. Flynn to return to work."*

Tue January 13
Production closed down indefinitely on account of Flynn's illness; memo from Tenny Wright to Jack Warner: *"....according to Dr. Nolan, [Flynn] has Virus X, and very nearly pneumonia, which they are trying to prevent. Dr. Nolan expects that Flynn will be out at least from seven to ten days...Also, he was examined by a proctologist, and Flynn has a bad case of protruding hemorrhoids....If [the proctologist] doesn't operate, Flynn will have quite a lot of trouble doing the duels, where he has to jump around a lot...."*

Fri January 16
Letter from Flynn's attorney Robert Ford to Dr. C. D. Dickey: *"My client, Errol Flynn, reports that on Monday, January 12, and on several succeeding days, you made scurrilous and insulting remarks to his physician concerning Mr. Flynn. Your conduct, as reported, was very slanderous, wholly unjustifiable, and caused Mr. Flynn much anxiety which was a serious deterrent in his recovering from his illness...Mr. Flynn has instructed me to take legal action against you....However, I shall hold the matter in abeyance for several days to afford you an opportunity to apologize and to retract your slanderous remarks...."*

Mon January 19
Returns home from the hospital.

Fri January 23
Photographing gray whales off the coast of San Diego with helicopter pilot Bob Williams.

Filming in the dungeon hallway - January

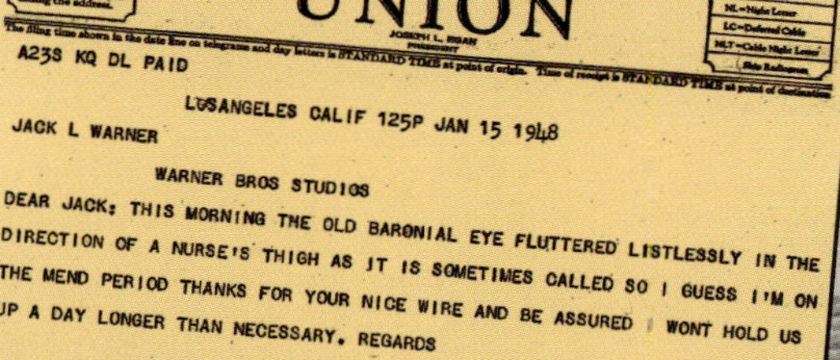
JANUARY 14TH 1948

ERROL FLYNN
MONTE SANO HOSPITAL
2834 GLENDALE BLVD
LOS ANGELES

DEAR ERROL: TRIED TO CALL YOU. H VING NO PHONE COULD NOT TALK TO YOU, BUT MOST IMPORTANT THING IS TO REGAIN YOUR HEALTH AND BE YOUR OLD SELF AGAIN REAL SOON. WITH EVERY GOOD WISH.

JACK WARNER

WESTERN UNION

A23S KQ DL PAID

LOSANGELES CALIF 125P JAN 15 1948

JACK L WARNER

WARNER BROS STUDIOS

DEAR JACK: THIS MORNING THE OLD BARONIAL EYE FLUTTERED LISTLESSLY IN THE DIRECTION OF A NURSE'S THIGH AS IT IS SOMETIMES CALLED SO I GUESS I'M ON THE MEND PERIOD THANKS FOR YOUR NICE WIRE AND BE ASSURED I WONT HOLD US UP A DAY LONGER THAN NECESSARY. REGARDS

ERROL

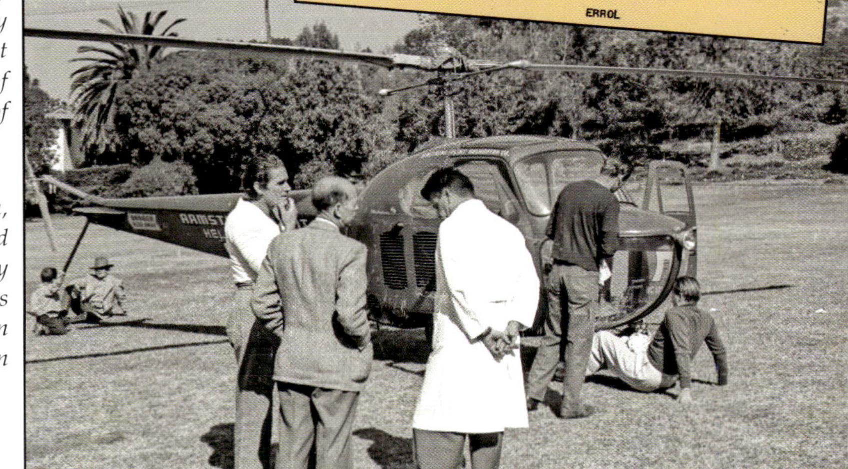
At the Scripps Institute in San Diego with the institute's head, Harald Sverdrup, and Dr. Carl Hubbs - January

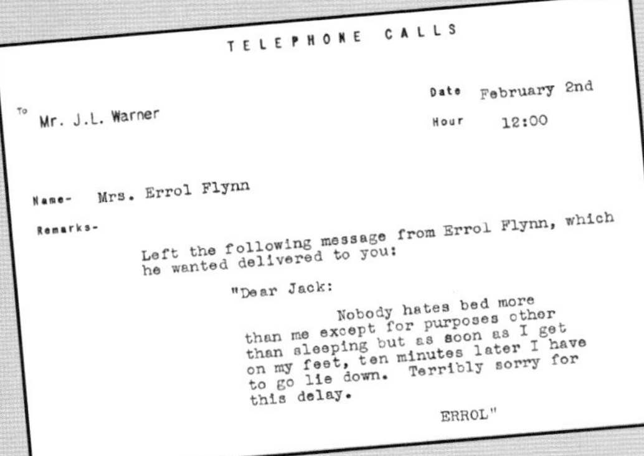

With Jerry Austin - Thu, January 29

TELEPHONE CALLS

To Mr. J.L. Warner
Date February 2nd
Hour 12:00

Name- Mrs. Errol Flynn

Remarks-

Left the following message from Errol Flynn, which he wanted delivered to you:

"Dear Jack:

Nobody hates bed more than me except for purposes other than sleeping but as soon as I get on my feet, ten minutes later I have to go lie down. Terribly sorry for this delay.

ERROL"

Sat January 24

Tenny Wright to Frank Mattison: *"Yesterday I heard from Jim Fleming who said that Flynn would definitely report for work Wednesday, 1/28/48...Will you kindly contact Flynn on Tuesday, before you call any crews and see if it is definite that he is coming in?...."*

Mon January 26

Dr. Nolan to assistant director Dick Maybery: *"I am going to give [Flynn] a shot of penicillin in about an hour; he's bothered with the sniffles. It looks like Wednesday—don't see any reason why he shouldn't be able to work on Wednesday."*

Wed January 28

Finally returns to work, filming alone with Jerry Austin in the hallway and on the Grand Staircase.

Thu January 29

Continues filming in the hallway *(top left)* and on the Grand Staircase; inter-office memo from Frank Mattison: *"Errol Flynn arrived at Makeup at 8:40 am and was perspiring excessively, which made it impossible to put any makeup on him. We phoned his doctor, Dr. Nolan, who came to the Studio to see Flynn and ordered him home around 11:00am. We did not work with Flynn.....but used his double [Don Turner]."* Charlie Greenlaw to Jack Warner and Steve Trilling: *"Dr. Nolan just called me and gave me the following information regarding Flynn:...Flynn is at home in bed with symptoms of another cold; however, Dr. Nolan is a little worried because Flynn is running a sub-normal temperature. He told me that he would be happier if Flynn were running a fever. He suggests that Flynn stay at home in bed until about Monday, unless there are complications...Dr. Nolan will see Flynn again this evening and will call me tomorrow about 8:30."*

Fri January 30

Ill; does not work; production manager Charlie Greenlaw to Jack Warner and Steve Trilling: *"Dr. Nolan called me up at 8:30 this morning to tell me he saw Errol Flynn last night and that Flynn's condition was about the same; however, he suspected a slight congestion in the chest and gave Flynn a shot of penicillin. He is still worried about Flynn's sub-normal temperature which he says indicates lack of resistance, and he intends to give him a shot today to induce a slight fever to combat the cold which Flynn has caught."*

Sat January 31

Ill; does not work; Tenny Wright to Jack Warner: *"Dr. Nolan called me at 3:00PM today to tell me that Flynn was feeling considerably better and that if we had nothing strenuous scheduled for him he could undoubtedly come in on Monday."*

Mon February 2

Ill; does not work; inter-office memo from Charlie Greenlaw to Jack Warner: *"....Dr. Nolan telephoned me at home yesterday afternoon about 2:30 and told me that FLYNN had awakened with a temperature and was feeling badly and would not be able to come to work today...."*

Tue February 3

Ill; does not work; inter-office memo from Frank Mattison: *"Production closed until further notice due to Flynn's illness....I know Warner's doctors were at Flynn's house last night, and no doubt they will make a report to Warner and Trilling today and we will proceed accordingly."* Roy Obringer to Jack Warner: *"I talked to Dr. Schiff this morning. Dr. Culley examined Errol Flynn about 10:30 this morning. Culley's report is that Flynn's sinuses are greatly congested with pus formation and that this is also affecting Flynn's left ear drum. Culley at the present time is administering medicated and hot packs to Flynn and intends to see him sometime tomorrow to wash out his sinuses...Also, Culley indicated to Schiff that in order to clear up the sinus condition it may be necessary for Culley to hospitalize Flynn for three or four days so that Culley would have adequate equipment, nurse services, etc. Dr. Schiff has talked to Dr. Nolan and Nolan is very cooperative and is quite willing that Flynn be hospitalized, if necessary, under Culley's or Schiff's observation. Schiff will report to me again tomorrow following Dr. Culley's further visit with Flynn, and at which time I presume Culley will determine whether or not to hospitalize Flynn for the three or four days involved."*

Wed February 4

Suffering from acute ear infection; inter-office memo from Frank Mattison: *"Errol Flynn through his agent, Art Parks, wanted to take care of his wardrobe man, but inasmuch as we have no work for him, and I informed Parks it did not seem possible for us to pay him money, even though it came from Flynn, while the picture is closed down. I have suggested to Parks, and I believe he will follow it through, that Flynn reimburse the wardrobe man if he so desires, with a direct check."* *"Résumé of Disposition of Artists Charged to 'The Adventures Of Don Juan', Prod. #691, during its shut-down period due to Mr. Flynn's Illness commencing Wednesday, Feb. 4, 1948: Errol Flynn-By special agreement with him, W.B. will get free time during his period of illness which will be added to his terms for this production (18 days), Viveca Lindfors, Robt.*

Douglas, Alan Hale-Laid off effective 2/4."

Thu February 5

Memo from Tenny Wright to Jack Warner: *"....[Dr. Culley] stated Flynn's sinus condition was practically cleared up and that he was giving him one additional treatment tomorrow morning; that Flynn was having cold sweats and he thought that Flynn could stand an eight or ten day period of recuperation and....understood that Flynn made arrangements to go to Phoenix tomorrow...."*

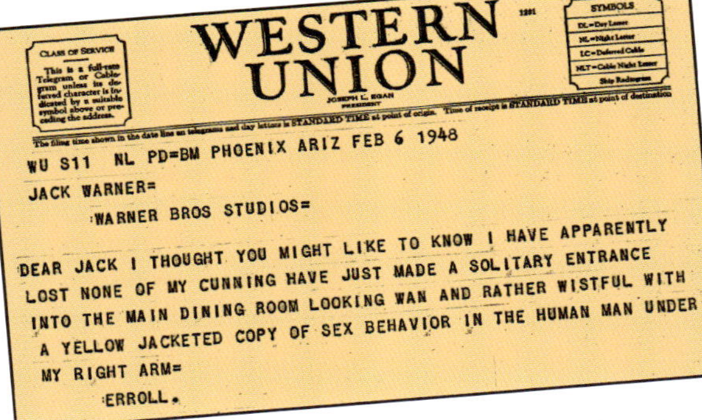

Fri February 6

Charlie Greenlaw to Jack Warner: *"Dr. Frank Nolan just telephoned me and said that Errol Flynn has left for Arizona. Dr. Nolan said that he had talked to Dr. Kully [sic] and that they both expected Mr. Flynn to come back the week-end of February 15th and be able to work beginning Monday Feb. 16th."*

Tue February 10

Travels with Nora to Chandler, Arizona, staying at the San Marcos Hotel.

Thu February 19

With Nora dancing at the Racquet Club in Palm Springs.

Fri February 20

Inter-office memo from Frank Mattison: *"All we need is to keep Flynn on his feet for about 4-1/2 or 5 weeks and this thing will be wrapped up. With good luck we might do it in less time."*

Sat February 21

Returns to Los Angeles with Nora.

Tue February 24

Memo from Frank Mattison to Tenny Wright: *....Dr. Kelly [reported] that Flynn's ear had not responded to treatment, and that Mr. Flynn would not be able to work tomorrow, Wednesday, and possibly not before Monday of next week...."*

Thu February 26

Roy Obringer to Steve Trilling: *"....Dr. Hiatt....was advised by [Dr.] Culley that Errol's ear, while it did not hurt, was still very bad and was running pus continuously. Culley, upon being question [sic] by Hiatt as to whether or not Flynn could work, stated very definitely no, that he didn't want to take the chance on mastoids developing...Therefore, Culley feels that it will take a week or 10 days before Flynn is able to work, and Hiatt figured that we should figure on a week from Monday, or March 8th, as Flynn's possible return date."*

Sat February 28

Frank Mattison to Tenny Wright: *"....Dr. Hiatt phoned me and stated that Errol Flynn would not be able to report for work until probably one week from next Monday, March 8th...Dr. Hiatt intimated that Flynn wanted to return to work sooner but that he, Dr. Hiatt, felt it would be to our advantage to have Flynn stay out a couple of days more until he was in better health and better able to work...Dr. Hiatt stated that Flynn should be able to report for work on Monday, March 8th [corrected in pencil to the 15th]."*

Thu March 4

Frank Mattison to Tenny Wright: *"[Dr. Culley] informed me that Errol Flynn's ear is still running. It has not responded to the sulpha drug treatment or the penicillin treatment. They have given him a blood test and are going to make an analysis of his blood to see if they can find out what particular germ is causing his trouble...[He] was very emphatic about Flynn not being able to return within one week, which means he would not be in before the 11th or 12th of March... My recommendation is that we close as many people [on the picture] as possible....and get them off salary until we have assurance that Flynn will be able to return to work."*

Sat March 6

At Romanoff's.

Mon March 8

Frank Mattison to Tenny Wright: *"....I spoke to Doctor Hyatt and Kulley [sic] and they informed me that Errol Flynn's ear has stopped running and has dried up, but that Flynn has had a great deal of penicillin, etc. in his system, and that on the advice of our doctor they are asking Flynn not to report for work before Monday, March 15th, one week from today."*

Tue March 9

Travels with Nora to the Palm Springs Racquet Club *(next page, top left)*.

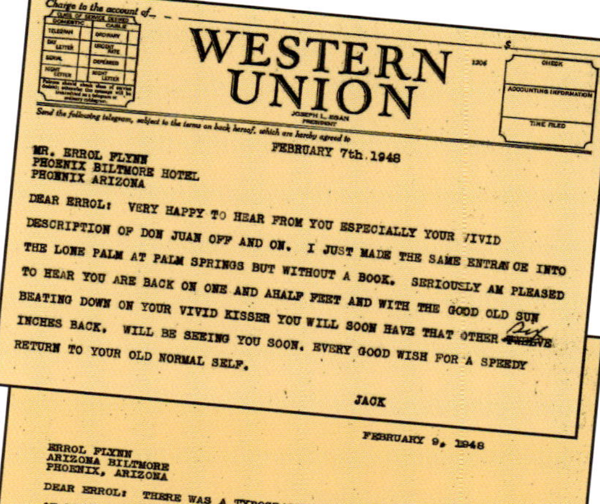

At the Palm Springs Racquet Club - Tue, March 9

With Vincent Sherman and Ann Rutherford - Wed, March 24

Fri March 12

Inter-office memo from Frank Mattison: *"I will contact Errol Flynn himself, as I must talk to him regarding the re-dying of his hair before we shoot with him on Monday. Will arrange to have him come in early on Monday as it will only take about 45 minutes to fix his hair. We are all keeping our fingers and legs crossed in the hopes that he does get in here and we do get started with this thing at last."*

Mon March 15

Filming the fencing academy drill without sound; rehearsing the fencing academy drill.

Tue March 16

Continues filming the fencing academy drill.

Wed March 17 through Sat March 20

Filming in the fencing academy (with Ann Rutherford on 3/18); Frank Mattison to Tenny Wright (3/19): *"In accordance with the discussion between Art Klein and yourself regarding cars for Flynn, I spoke to Flynn with the result we are sending him a station wagon, taking he [sic] and his dogs from the studio to his house and return as usual."* Records a 4 ½-minute publicity interview transcription (on 3/20) in connection with SILVER RIVER; memo from Roy Obringer to Jack Warner (3/18): *"We have received notice from MGM designating April 20, 1948 as the date they will require Flynn to work out our commitment with them. As you know, under the deal whereby we obtain the services of William Powell, we agreed they could have Flynn for 16 weeks for $150,000 [$1,669,705 in 2021 value]....If Flynn finishes* [ADVENTURES OF DON JUAN on] *April 18th, then it is problematical whether or not he would be willing to start two days later for MGM without some rest...."* Flynn ultimately doesn't begin work for MGM until January of 1949.

Mon March 22 and Tue March 23

Continues filming in the fencing academy.

Wed March 24

Filming in the garden with Ann Rutherford *(bottom left)* and David Bruce; agrees to his appearance (a scene from THE ADVENTURES OF ROBIN HOOD) in a Bugs Bunny cartoon.

Thu March 25 through Sat March 27

Continues filming in the garden; Frank Mattison to Tenny Wright (3/26): *"Confidentially, I have heard that Flynn has protested the taking of* [cameraman Woody] *Bredell off this picture. He has complained to his agent, Art Park, and no doubt the front office will hear from him today."* Frank Mattison to Tenny Wright (3/27): *"Flynn called me to his dressing room and told me he was 'pooped' and that the only way we could get the close-ups was to do them today. Also, that I would have to get someone to fence for him with David Bruce in addition to the double. I got Fred Cavens and we are fitting him up to step in this morning to get the sequence finished. Flynn said he was unable to cope with either the double or Bruce. I told Errol that no matter what he threw at Cavens with his sword that Cavens would take it and that it would make Errol look good."* Frank Mattison to Tenny Wright (3/27): *"....Errol Flynn refused to work after 4:00 o'clock. Talked to him and told him we had only 2 more shots to finish him in the sequence but he told me 'Matty, my legs are tired and I'm going home.' We discussed the matter for a few minutes but he was really tired. He is still very weak and the duel is very strenuous for him. I am convinced Flynn is going to be very difficult through this* [climactic Grand Staircase] *duel sequence, and I impressed it on Sherman that we will have to use a double whenever it is possible. Flynn is aware he is not back in good health and that he simply can't take it."*

Mon March 29 and Tue March 30

Filming in the corridor of the Queen's chapel; (on 3/30) Roy Obringer indicates that Flynn has asked for a $150,000 loan ($1,669,705 in 2021 value).

Wed March 31 to Fri April 2

Filming in the palace corridor.

Early April

"BLOW-UPS OF 1947" is released, with Flynn in several segments.

Sat April 3

Continues filming in the palace corridor; Frank Mattison to Tenny Wright: *"We got the* [drapery] *Fire Shot the last thing on Saturday afternoon and it worked perfectly. This time Sherman listened to the others concerned, with the result we got a wonderful shot. Don Turner* [Flynn's double] *deserves a lot of credit because he handled the burning drapes and his timing was perfect."*

Mon April 5 to Thu April 8

Filming on the Grand Staircase.

Fri April 9

Continues filming on the Grand Staircase; Frank Mattison to Tenny Wright: *"The reason for getting so few shots was due to the fact that we were using Robert Douglas duel with Errol Flynn. As you know, Douglas has a very bad leg…..due to the war and is not as agile as he should be for this picture….Sherman wanted a shot with Flynn. Flynn was somewhat delayed in getting ready and about 5:00 P.M. Sherman insisted on going home; he was sick and could not wait any longer for Flynn. I spoke to Flynn and he told me he had great difficulty getting the tights, etc. and getting dressed, as he had been completely unwardrobed without makeup when called back for the Shot."*

Sat April 10 and Mon April 12 through Thu April 15

Continues filming on the Grand Staircase (director Raoul Walsh fills in for an ailing Vincent Sherman on 4/10).

Fri April 16

Filming in Don Juan's apartment with Alan Hale and Viveca Lindfors.

Sat April 17

Continues filming in Juan's apartment, and also in the torture chamber.

Mon April 19

Filming the film's final scene, on the road at Lasky Mesa from 10:50am to 4:50pm with Alan Hale and Nora *(bottom right three)*; returns to the studio soundstage to film with Hale on horseback against a blue backdrop with foliage, shooting from 7:20pm through 9pm without dinner; these close-up shots, Flynn's last ever with Alan Hale, will be dropped into the first reel of the film; finishes work on ADVENTURES OF DON JUAN.

Sat April 24

Signs a deal with the J. Arthur Rank organization in England to do one picture a year.

Mon April 26

With Nora at the wedding reception of Lana Turner and Bob Topping at the Bel Air home of publisher William K. Wilkerson; on this day Flynn sues *Movie Stars Parade* magazine for $300,000 ($3,339,410 in 2021 value) because of their article titled "My First Kiss" in the May (current) issue, falsely claiming Flynn wrote it; Roy Obringer to Monroe Rubinger: *"The Publicity Department wishes to bring Errol Flynn & Nora Flynn into the photographic galleries and/or other location for necessary photography at 9a.m. o'clock on April 27. Is it okay for us to proceed?"* Monroe Rubinger to Obringer: *"If both artists agree to come in, without compensation, it will be okey provided they agree to sign a salary waiver (waivers were sent to you earlier today for their execution)."*

Tue April 27

Roy Obringer to Cy Wilder: *"Will you please prepare a check in the sum of $1500 [$16,697 in 2021 value], made payable to Mr. Errol Flynn, which sum is to reimburse him* [in advance] *for all transportation, hotel and other expenses incurred by him and Mrs. Flynn in connection with their appearance at the world premiere of our picture 'Silver River' in Denver, Colorado, on May 18, 1948…May I have this check as soon as possible."* Telegram from head of publicity Mort Blumenstock to Alex Evelove: OK $1500 FLYNN. PLEASE WIRE ME MOMENT PAPERS ARE SIGNED AS ENTIRE PROMOTION IS AT STANDSTILL UNTIL WE CAN GUARANTEE FLYNN APPEARANCE

Wed April 28

Is interviewed at his home for a four-minute spot in connection with ADVENTURES OF DON JUAN (by and for whom is not made clear in the WB Archives); Roy Obringer to Eddie Selzer: *"….In attempting to get clearance from Flynn on the Bugs Bunny picture, Flynn's agent advised that Flynn wanted $1000 [$11,131 in 2021 value] for this. Therefore, unless I can get this straightened out, you had better forget the idea of cutting the clip of Flynn into the picture."*

With Robert Douglas, Viveca Lindfors, Romney Brent, and Jerry Austin - April

Above with Alan Hale and Nora Eddington Flynn (also left) at Lasky Mesa - Mon, April 19; below, the same location today

At the Point Mugu Naval Station luau with LCdr. Holt and the luau hostess - Fri, April 30

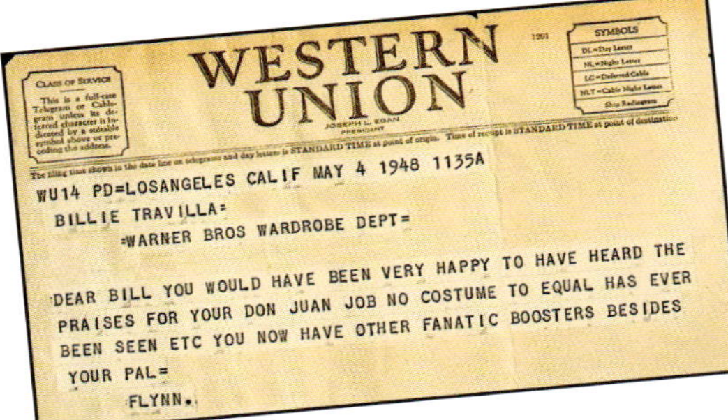

With Nora at the Pump Room of the Ambassador East Hotel in Chicago - Thu, May 20

Fri April 30

Attends a luau at the Point Mugu Naval Station just north of Malibu, CA *(top left)*.

Thu May 6

Leaves for New York via St. Louis with *Life* magazine photographer Peter Stackpole (news sources report Flynn has finally had his long hair from ADVENTURES OF DON JUAN shorn); they travel to Columbia, MO, checking in to the Daniel Boone Hotel, and later visit the Kappa Gamma Sorority House on the campus of the University of Missouri.

Fri May 7

Nora arrives in St. Louis and is greeted by Errol *(top right)* and Peter Stackpole; handwritten note by Steve Trilling for a telegram: *"Dr. [Conrad Walles, St. Louis, MO] anxious to get hold Flynn—account prescription—Rectal problems—15% cocaine suppositories w/ hydrochloric."*

Sat May 8

Arrives in New York with Nora and Peter Stackpole, the Flynns staying at the Hampshire House.

Mon May 10

At the El Morocco with Nora.

Mon May 17

Flies with Nora to Denver to promote SILVER RIVER; on that day Flynn appears at a hospital fund-raiser with Colorado governor William Lee Knous and Denver mayor J. Quigg Newton on the steps of the capitol building *(center right)*; receives the keys to the city; throws a silver dollar "across" Cherry Creek; and ends the day at a fund-raising dinner, also attended by Al Jolson.

Tue May 18

Continues the promotional tour with a visit to Mayor Newton in the mayor's office, the *Denver Post* newspaper with editor Palmer Hoyt, and the radio station KFEL for an interview with deejay Ray Perkins; after a banquet held for Errol and Nora, SILVER RIVER premieres at three theaters in the city; over 1,000 fans are on hand outside the Webber Theater where Errol and Nora appear in person.

Wed May 19

Flies with Nora to Chicago, staying at the *Ambassador East Hotel*; cable from Lynn Brown in Denver to Lew Wasserman: WILL YOU MCA AND WARNERS PLEASE GET TOGETHER AND CUT OUT ANY FURTHER PROCRASTINATION/DOES FLYNN NOT GET A FAST HUNDRED AND FIFTY GRAND OR IN JACK'S OWN WORDS 'A YARD AND A HALF' OR WHAT DOES FLYNN GET/JUST GIVE ME INSTANT REPLY IN MOST SIMPLE OF WORDS.

Thu May 20

SILVER RIVER is given a special premiere at the Strand in New York; with Nora at the Pump Room *(bottom left)*.

Fri May 21

Leaves Chicago for Miami with Nora, arriving in Kingston, Jamaica, the next day; later they go on to Port Antonio, staying at the Titchfield Hotel.

Sun May 23

On the *Zaca* with Nora; is interviewed by the *Daily Gleaner*.

Tue May 25

SILVER RIVER begins opening around the United States, on this day at the Fox Theater in St. Louis, MO.

With Nora at the airport in St. Louis - Fri, May 7

On the steps of the Denver Capitol building with mayor J. Quigg Newton and Governor William Lee Knous - Mon, May 17

Mon May 31

To Kingston with Nora for business meetings concerning their upcoming self-produced film *The Zaca Jamaican Adventure* (which is never completed), and staying at the Myrtle Bank Hotel.

Tue June 1

Gives another interview to the *Daily Gleaner.*

Wed June 2

In Kingston interviewing prospective actors for the film.

Fri June 4

Returns to Port Antonio to do some initial location shooting for the film.

Thu June 10

Attends the opening of the Grand Carnival with Nora; the event is held at the Anglican Church at Fort Lawn; later they attend the inaugural picnic races of the "Flynn Stakes."

Mon June 14

Back in Kingston with Nora for more business, dinner at the Myrtle Bank Hotel, and a U.S. Naval party at the Glass Bucket Club.

Tue June 15

Location shooting for the film takes place today and over several days.

Sat June 19

With Nora at the Morgan's Cove nightclub shooting footage of singers and dancers for the film.

Sun June 20

Flynn's 39th birthday.

Tue June 22

With Nora at the Capitol Theatre, where outgoing minister of communications, William Bustamante, gives a valedictory speech.

Thu June 24

The *Zaca* is finally released from withholding by the courts for the salvage arrears and given over to Flynn; it is reported to him that all the film so far shot is unusable due to a damaged camera.

Sun June 27

Leaves Port Antonio on the *Zaca* with Nora and Jerry Courneya, heading for Guantanamo Bay, Cuba.

Tue July 6

Back in Port Antonio, where a repaired camera is ready for continued shooting of the Flynns' Jamaican film.

Mon July 12

Shooting location work on Navy Island with actor Ranny Williams, today and for the next few days.

Tue July 20

Roy Obringer to Arthur Park: *"On July 2, 1948 I wrote you regarding certain hotel bills and other expenses incurred by Errol Flynn in connection with his attending the premiere of 'Silver River.' These hotels are annoying our New York office for payment of these bills and I would, therefore, appreciate your having Al Blum arrange to make out the checks to the respective hotels referred to in my letter and either mail them direct and let me know about it or send them on to me for mailing."*

Wed July 21

Flynn's parents arrive in Kingston, prepared to settle on one of Errol's properties.

Wed July 28

Flynn and Jerry Courneya fly to the Cayman Islands to film sharks and spearfish; Nora left for Los Angeles the day before.

Thu July 29

Flynn and Courneya return to Port Antonio, unsuccessful in their hunt for sharks to film.

Tue August 3

Flynn sails the Zaca into Montego Bay for a few days in search of sharks to film.

Fri August 6

Films alligators in captivity at Doctor's Cove Bathing Club.

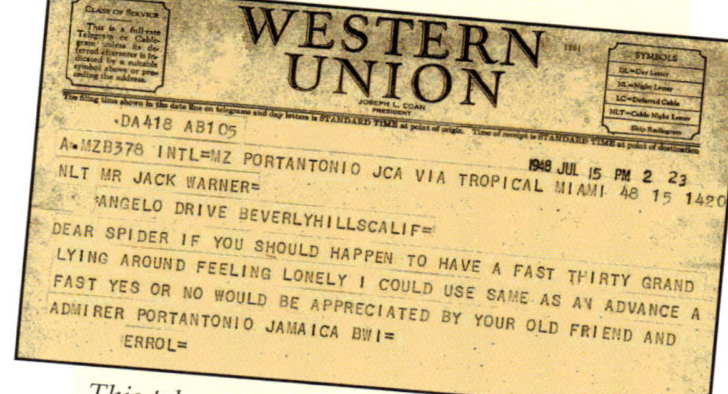

This telegram never reached Jack Warner, as he was traveling through Europe

Filming at the WB New Ranch - Mon, August 30

A production still of WB New Ranch, just west of their Calabasas Ranch - Mon, August 30

With Jimmy Stewart, Cobina Wright, and Nora at Wright's birthday party held at her home - Sat, September 11

Sat August 7
The Zaca returns to Navy Island at Port Antonio.

Thu August 12
Leaves Jamaica for Los Angeles via Miami.

Tue August 17
Memo from producer William Jacobs to Steve Trilling: *"Errol Flynn would like to put Stewart Jerome on this picture. He insists that he will be a lot of help and will contribute something…Confidentially, I know the boy is not much of a writer. He has been a kind of junior writer around here at some studio. I have read one or two things that he has done and never thought that he has much promise. However, Flynn made this very urgent. I told him that I did not have the Authority to put him on and that I would have to talk to you about it. Advise me what to do."*

Wed August 18
Memo from Lou Baum to Tenny Wright: *"Errol Flynn was in today, Thursday, for a fitting of his wardrobe."*

Wed August 25
Letter from Roy Obringer to Flynn: *"Thanks for your letter of August 23, 1948, authorizing us to deduct from your salary the amount of [$1500 for] your purchase from W.&J. Sloan Furniture Company…. Our Purchasing Department who issued the purchase order is advised that the amount of your purchase was $2,059.50 [$22,925.05 in 2021 value]….[which] includes a $600 sofa which, I understand, you may return….it will be wise for you to let us know if you have or propose to return the sofa…."*

Fri August 27
Memo from William Jacobs to Steve Trilling: *"Ray Heindorf has two songs he submitted to Ray Enright and myself. Both of the titles escape me for the moment. But one is a sultry torch song—very modern—and the other is a kind of cowboy song that Flynn could do very well to guitar accompaniment."*

Sat August 28
Filming wardrobe tests for MONTANA.

Mon August 30 and Tue August 31
Begins work on MONTANA, filming on the prairie at what is called the "WB New Ranch" (in Calabasas, *top left*); letter from Flynn's accountant Albert Blum to Roy Obringer (8/31): *"Last week I talked with you about the bill of [costumer] Don Loper's addressed to Mrs. Errol Flynn in the sum of $259.59 [$2,889.59 in 2021 value]…Errol steadfastly refuses to pay this bill on the grounds that this wardrobe was used by Mrs. Flynn in the picture [ADVENTURES OF DON JUAN] for which she received only enough to pay her Screen Actors Guild dues….I wish you would advise me as soon as possible…."*

September (no specified date)
Unidentified inter-office memo: *"Mr. Chuck Ross called—said Flynn is having a man come out tomorrow from Sloans to see about having the sofa recovered….he will then take the sofa @$600 plus….and until some decision is reached Sloans will not bill us….the sofa has been returned to Sloans for the time being…."*
Sometime this month Flynn purchases a 1948 Custom Super 8 Packard Victoria convertible from Albertson Bros. in Culver City, CA.

Wed September 1 and Thu September 2
Continues filming on the prairie; letter from Roy Obringer to Albert Blum (9/1): *"With reference to your letter of August 31, 1948, relative [costumer] Don Roper's billing Mrs. Errol Flynn in the sum of $259.59 for wardrobe….Mrs. Flynn, at that time expressed a desire to purchase a Don Loper dress, which….was a modern dress and was not used by her in the 'Don Juan' picture….Therefore….I see no reason why we have to pay the entire cost of the dress…."* Inter-office memo from Lou Baum (9/2): *"Errol Flynn seems to be happy."*

Fri September 3 and Sat September 4
Filming at the campfire at the new WB Ranch.

Tue September 7 through Sat September 11, Mon September 13 through Fri September 17
Continues filming at the campfire, and also on Fort Humboldt Street at the WB Calabasas Ranch.

September 11
Attends a birthday party with Nora for columnist Cobina Wright in Wright's home at 1700 Coldwater Cyn., Beverly Hills *(bottom left)*; attendees include Louella Parsons, Joan Fontaine, Jimmy Stewart, and Danny Kaye.

Tue September 21 through Thu September 23

Filming on the Ackroyd Ranch at the WB Calabasas Ranch; (on 9/21) with Nora at the Ice Follies at the Pan Pacific Auditorium in Los Angeles.

Fri September 24 and Sat September 25

Filming in the hotel room with Alexis Smith and Paul E. Burns *(top right)*.

Tue September 28 to Fri October 1

Filming in the Little Big Horn Saloon.

Sat October 2

Continues filming in the Little Big Horn Saloon, and also in the Ackroyd home; inter-office memo from production manager Lou Baum to Tenny Wright: *"Errol Flynn was given a 10:00 A.M. call this morning, Saturday. He showed up a little late, claiming he had his piles operated on last evening. I am inclined to believe his story—he had to sit on a cushion all day....Flynn showed a lot of evidence of having had too much liquor...."*

Mon October 4 and Tue October 5

Filming on Fort Humboldt Street and (on 10/4) at the WB Calabasas Ranch with 1,600 sheep *(center right)*; inter-office memo from Tenny Wright to Roy Obringer (10/4): *"....we had trouble on the set Saturday again with Errol Flynn. Apparently he had been drinking and was in such a condition we could not photograph the scene, and the company was dismissed at 4:40 PM...Col. Warner would like to have you find out how much money it cost the company, for which Flynn was directly responsible, because he was not in a condition to render his services....Also, Col. Warner wanted me to let you know that on September 23rd, Flynn had his mother-in-law call in and say that....he would not be in that day....A couple of days later an item appeared in the papers stating that there had been a terrific quarrel at the Flynn house...."*

Wed October 6

Filming in the cemetery at the new WB Ranch.

Fri October 8

Filming in the Ackroyd living room and recording the film's song, *Reckon I'm In Love*; unit manager Frank Mattison to Tenny Wright: *"We received a verbal OK yesterday for Errol Flynn's commitment for this picture [IT'S A GREAT FEELING], but the Legal Dept. told me not to have him sign the release as his agent would handle this."*

Sat October 9

Filming at the campfire.

Mon October 11

Inter-office memo from Frank Mattison: *"I might say, for your information, there was no evidence of drinking on our set as far as Flynn was concerned."* Lou Baum to Tenny Wright: *"....Please be advised that Flynn called [asst. director] Oren Haglund this morning to tell him that he was waiting for the doctor to cauterize his piles, and that he would get to the studio just as quick as possible; although he says he is coming in contrary to the doctor's orders. He got here about 11:20AM and is working now...I will talk to him regarding working later tonight to make up some of the time lost this morning."* Continues filming at the campfire; begins and finishes work on IT'S A GREAT FEELING, filming the wedding in Judy's (Doris Day) home from 5:50 to 6:20pm *(bottom right)*.

Tue October 12

Continues filming at the campfire; is voted most popular actor in France according to *Cinemonde* magazine (Ingrid Bergman is the most popular actress).

Wed October 13

Filming in the Ackroyd home; Lou Baum to Tenny Wright: *"He was all right until about 3:30PM. After a lengthy rehearsal and after going into a take, they decided there was no use going any further—he was too intoxicated. He was dismissed at 5:30PM."*

Thu October 14

Continues filming in the Ackroyd home; Errol and Nora are formally separated when she moves out of the Mulholland house.

Fri October 15

Ill; does not work; Lou Baum to Tenny Wright: *"I went to the Burbank Hospital today about 2:30PM and inquired about Flynn's condition. I talked to the Nurse and she told me that he was in a lot of pain and would not permit me to see Errol."* Letter from Jack Warner to Roy Obringer: *"....we are closing MONTANA....on*

With Paul E. Burns - Fri, September 24

With Paul E. Burns and Nacho Galindo at the WB Calabasas Ranch - Mon, October 4

With Doris Day filming his scene for IT'S A GREAT FEELING - Mon, October 11

Reading a letter from Capt. Alexandre de Manzierly, French Consul of Los Angeles, announcing that Flynn has been voted most popular actor in France by readers of Cinemonde *and* La Cinematographie Francais, *and will be presented an award in Paris - October*

Saturday, October 18th....Dr. Hiatt explained it will be at least a week or ten days before Flynn can walk, sit on a horse and the type of physical action necessary to finish the picture...."

Sat October 16

Ill; does not work; inter-office memo from Lou Baum: *"Picture closed until further notice, due to illness of Errol Flynn."*

Week of October 25

Is presented the *Cinemonde* magazine Best Actor award by French consul Sascha de Manziarly.

Tue October 26

Filming in the Forsythe ranch house; Tenny Wright to Steve Trilling and Roy Obringer: *"....We got the shot and then the company went to lunch; just in the nick of time, as Flynn was showing definite evidence of too much liquor. We needed him for one more shot after lunch....However, even for that shot he returned one half hour late from lunch."*

Thu October 28 to Sat October 30 and Mon November 1

Continues filming in the Forsythe ranch house.

Tue November 2 and Wed November 3

Filming in the Ackroyd home; Roy Obringer to Arthur Park (11/3: *"You will recall in November, 1947 we billed Mr. Errol Flynn for a considerable amount of wardrobe which he claims was returned, and we subsequently wrote off the bill, except, however, Mr. Flynn did acknowledge that he kept two silk shirts that were made up for him and which were included in the bill. The cost of the two shirts was $48.69. Also, when Mr. Flynn was in New York City in May, 1948, he requested we secure for him some theatre tickets, which we did, at a cost of $105.00....I would appreciate receiving Mr. Flynn's check payable to Warner Bros. Pictures, Inc. in the sum of $153.69 [$1,710.78 in 2021 value]...."*

Thu November 4

Filming straight and process shots on Humboldt Street, and process shots of a bucking horse; Arthur Park to Roy Obringer: *"....I have discussed the items of shirt and theatre tickets with Errol Flynn. He has advised me to instruct his business manager, Al Blum, to make payment for them...."*

Fri November 5 and Sat November 6

Filming outside the Forsythe home; prior to going to the WB Calabasas Ranch for work, Flynn meets at his home at about 9am with Sam Kress (head of MGM Wardrobe) and an associate for a conference about THAT FORSYTE WOMAN; books passage (11/6) to Europe for November 26th aboard the *Queen Elizabeth* but ultimately does not go.

Mon November 8

Continues filming outside the Forsythe home, and also in the countryside (on a WB soundstage).

Tue November 9

Filming process shots in the countryside with Smith and S. Z. Sakall; records a 4 ½-minute transcription for MONTANA publicity; lunches at Romanoff's with THAT FORSYTE WOMAN producer, Leon Gordon, then goes with him to MGM for wardrobe selection and fittings; memo from Tenny Wright to Roy Obringer: *"Kindly have Dr. Hiatt contact Dr. John Costello and find out from him how long he thinks it will be before Errol Flynn will be able to work on a horse. I heard from Jim Fleming last night that Dr. Costello had instructed Flynn not to get on any live or mechanical horse for sometime."*

Wed November 10

Tenny Wright to Steve Trilling and Roy Obringer: *"....[On Tuesday, November 9th, director Ray] Enright told Lou Baum he was still dissatisfied with the setup for the stampede sequence, and that he told Flynn about it. Flynn then called Baum over to him and told him he was giving legal notice that he was not [okaying] any work to be done for him with a double. He said that, 'according to his contract he had the right to ok or turn down the use of a double and that he was turning it down'....We are going ahead and finishing up the sequence of the stampede the way we laid it out. This is the only thing we can do, as we can't wait around for Mr. Flynn to get well so he can sit on a horse, since we are not sure of when that might be...."*

Fri November 12

More wardrobe fittings at MGM.

Sat November 13

Filming process shots of the stampede.

With Alexis Smith - November

Mon November 15

News reports announce that Flynn has transferred a half share of his Navy Island in Port Antonio, Jamaica, to Stephen F. Raphael for £2,200 ($115,862 in 2021 value).

Thu November 18

Roy Obringer to F. E. Witt: *"Please prepare a check for $1,000 payable to Errol Flynn which is to partially defray his expenses in connection with his proposed trip to Paris, France, to receive an award…."* Is briefly reunited with Nora and is seen out with her at a Sunset Strip nightclub.

Leaving Pasadena with Nora for New York - Sat, November 20

Sat November 20

From the *Associated Press*: *"Film star Errol Flynn and his wife Nora boarded a train together here [Pasadena, top right] for New York….as they have patched up their recent differences. Flynn, earlier scheduled to fly east alone, was said to have agreed to make the trip with his wife at her request. He planned to tour France and Italy and be present at the mid-January New York opening of his latest picture 'The Adventures of Don Juan' [sic] but he was not sure whether his wife will go with him to Europe."* While in New York he and Nora stay at the Savoy Hilton.

Sat December 4

With Nora at the El Morocco in New York *(top left)*.

Tue December 7

Arrested in New York for kicking a police officer.

Wed December 8

A Warner Bros. stenographer notes for the record: *"Flynn arrived in Mid-Manhattan Magistrate Court 153 E. 57th Street, New York City (arrest part), with his lawyer to face a male judge (Schwobe). The lawyer (Mr. Green) asked for a reduction of the charges. The judge agreed and reduced the charges from third degree assault to disorderly conduct and gave Flynn and his lawyer a recess in which to prepare the necessary papers. About ten minutes later they re-appeared in court. The lawyer said that his client (Flynn) wished to plead guilty to a disorderly conduct charge but before doing so wanted to make a public apology to the arresting officer. Flynn made the apology and then the judge sentenced him to $50.00 fine [$556.57 in 2021 value] or 30 days. Flynn paid the $50.00 fine. As he left the court room he was photographed by dozens of newspaper photographers and worked his way through a crowd of bobby-soxers to a waiting cab in which he and his lawyer departed."*

With Nora and Olive Hamilton (Mrs. William B. Leeds Jr) at El Morocco in New York - Sat, December 4

With his attorney Morris Green (left) leaving the Mid-Manhattan Magistrates court - Wed, December 8

Fri December 10

Is seen off by Nora at Idlewild Airport on his way to Havana and Jamaica.

Tue December 14

Wire from Mort Blumenstock to Jack Warner: RE FLYNN. HE IN HAVANA HARBOR FOR NEXT FOUR DAYS AND WILL THEN FLY TO KINGSTON. PLANS TO BE IN L.A. BY DECEMBER 31ST.

Wed December 15

ADVENTURES OF DON JUAN has a fund-raising premiere at the Warner Theater in Pittsburgh, PA; telegram from Flynn to Arthur Park: PLEASE TELL WARNERS ACCEPT JANUARY THIRD COMMENCEMENT MY SERVICES FORSYTHE SACA [SIC] INSTEAD DECEMBER FIFTEENTH STOP INSIST NO CHANGES OF SCRIPT I READ AND AGREED TO PLAY--FLYNN.

Sat December 18

Roy Obringer writes to MGM of Flynn's expecting a 16mm print of THAT FORSYTE WOMAN without cost to him, no later than six months after the film's release.

Fri December 31

ADVENTURES OF DON JUAN opens widely across the United States.

Judge waits 30 minutes for Errol Flynn

New York (AAP)

A judge waited 30 minutes for the actor Errol Flynn to appear in Court on a charge of having kicked a policeman on the shin.

Then he confiscated Flynn's $500 bail, and issued an arrest warrant.

Three hours after he was due to appear in Court Flynn was found at the Savoy Plaza Hotel. He told the police: "I didn't sleep until 9am because of this trouble."

When he arrived at the Court Flynn told the Press: "This is the worst public appearance I have ever made."

When Flynn was brought before Magistrate Doris Byrne, she accepted his apologies for having failed to appear earlier. She also restored his $500 bail which had been confiscated.

Directing Flynn to appear in Court tomorrow, she looked Flynn sternly in the eye and said: "Be here."

New York newspapers described Flynn as an Irish-born film star, although he was born at Hobart.

The Melbourne Argus
Tue, December 7

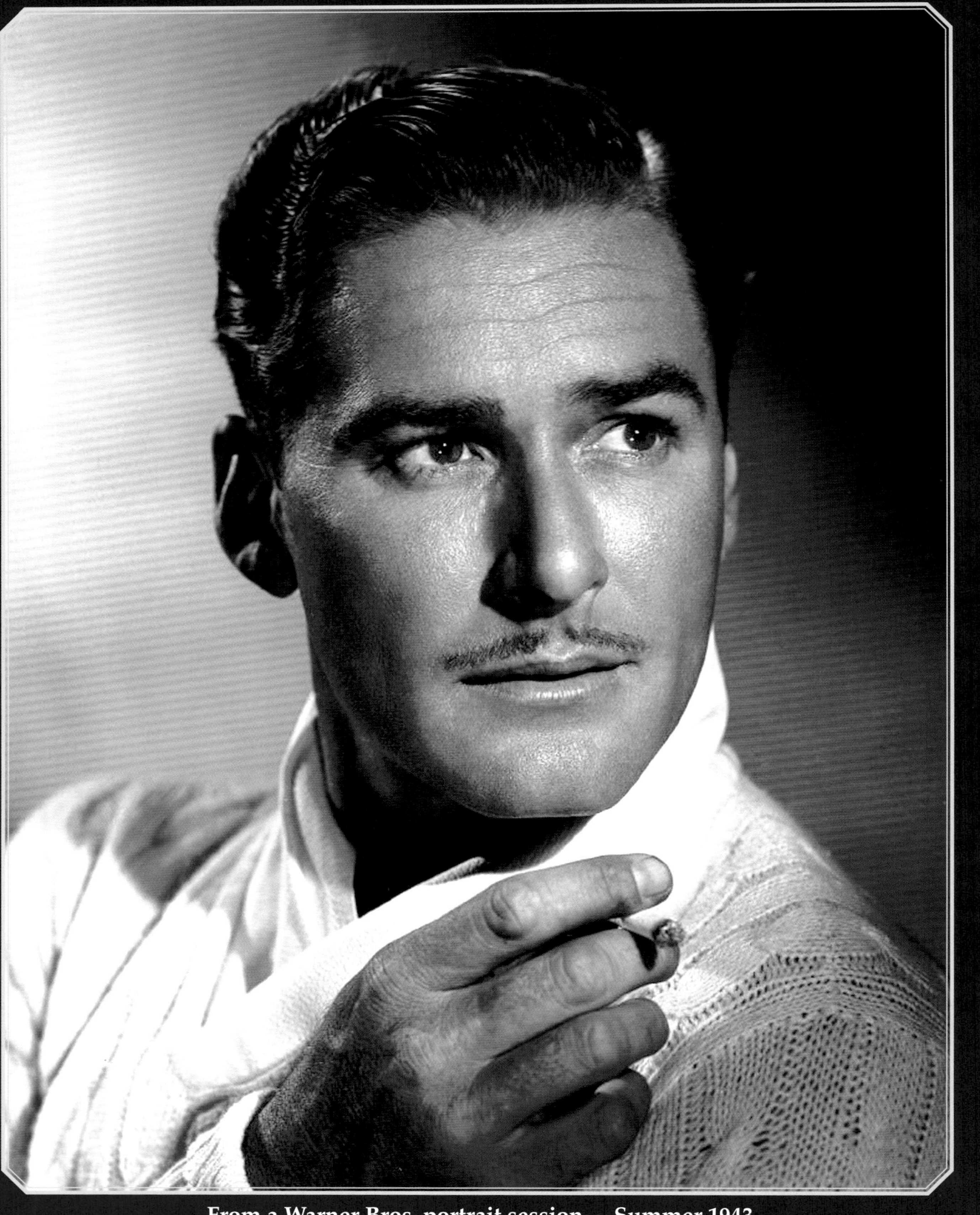

From a Warner Bros. portrait session ~ Summer 1943

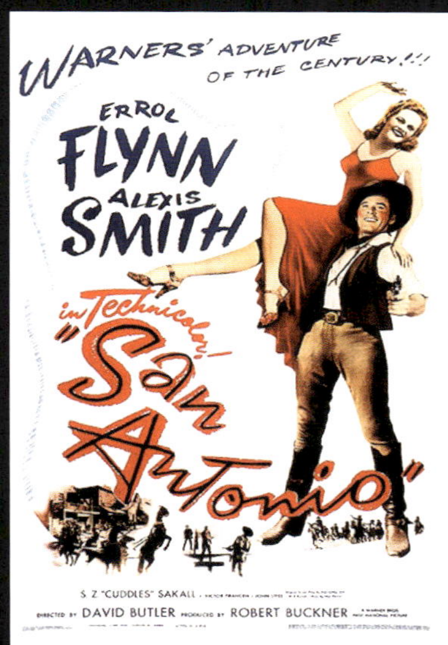

The films of 1943~1948

As the 1940s crossed into a new decade, Errol Flynn found himself in uncertain straits. He had long complained that Warner Bros. hadn't given him enough opportunity to work in films other than the heroic costume adventures for which he was primarily known. But that complaint wasn't quite accurate. In the fifteen years since shooting to stardom in CAPTAIN BLOOD, Flynn made six dramas (GREEN LIGHT, ANOTHER DAWN, THE SISTERS, UNCERTAIN GLORY, CRY WOLF, and ESCAPE ME NEVER) and four comedies (THE PERFECT SPECIMEN, FOUR'S A CROWD, FOOTSTEPS IN THE DARK, and NEVER SAY GOODBYE). But during his prime years the public lined up at the box office more often for Flynn's heroics than for his humor or other acting talents.

Now the realities of world war had a transforming effect on the public's tastes, and the popularity of adventure and fantasy gave way to postwar social realism and a new genre called "film noir." This all landed Flynn in a curious middle ground: his films of old-world gallantry became passé to current audiences, while at the same time these audiences couldn't fully accept Robin Hood in modern street clothes. He was enthused that his studio agreed to loan him out to MGM for two films, but neither film—THAT FORSYTE WOMAN or KIM—did much to enhance his waning popularity.

What seemed a possible solution was to make films in Europe where his image of old was still somewhat in public favor. The year 1950 saw him in the south of France marrying for a third time (to actress Patrice Wymore), shooting a film (THE ADVENTURES OF CAPTAIN FABIAN), and setting up residence there on his yacht, the *Zaca*, a move which would soon become semi-permanent. In 1952 he filmed CROSSED SWORDS in Italy, during which time he was stricken with a serious liver infection and almost died. His doctors' dire warnings to desist from consuming alcohol if he wanted to survive were only briefly heeded, and soon enough he was again drinking...in increasing amounts as the years wore on.

At this point, no longer under exclusive contract to any studio, Flynn dove headlong into a project that consumed his interest and eventually his savings. He believed that WILLIAM TELL, on which he was also producer, would return him to cinema prominence, and so he invested $430,000 of his own money in the venture with the promise from Italian investors that they would match the amount. An entire stone village was built as a set in the Italian Alps, the new technology of wide-screen photography was utilized, and noted Oscar-winning cinematographer Jack Cardiff had already shot about thirty minutes of film when it was discovered that the Italian investors had reneged on their promise. Flynn was crushed. As 1953 came to an end, his third daughter Arnella was born, a wondrous event for him in any other circumstances, but the star's attention was focused on raising the money to keep his film afloat. Despite his desperate pleas to every outlet and individual he approached, none came through with the necessary funds, and WILLIAM TELL faded into legend as much as the story upon which it was based.

1949

January
Begins filming THAT FORSYTE WOMAN at MGM (the daily production files were destroyed by MGM in the 1970s).

Fri January 7
Recalled by Warner Bros. to film added scenes for MONTANA with Alexis Smith on Fort Humboldt Street at the WB Calabasas Ranch; completes work on the picture.

Sun January 9
Deirdre's fourth birthday is celebrated a day early at Mulholland; she receives a pony named Brownie from her father.

Mon January 17
The rare, heavy Los Angeles snowfall requires plowing around Flynn's home, resulting in him being late to work at the MGM studio.

Fri January 21
Attends a party at the home of *Photoplay* magazine reporter Sarah Hamilton; Anne Baxter and John Hodiak are also in attendance.

Fri January 28
Warner Bros. announces Flynn's next film will be *The Candy Kid*; it does not come to fruition.

With Janet Leigh, Robert Young, and Greer Garson in a scene from THAT FORSYTE WOMAN

The MGM 25th anniversary group portrait; Flynn is in the second row, fifth from the left - Thu, February 10

With Dorothy Lamour at his Mulholland house party - Sat, February 12

Thu February 10
Poses for MGM's 25th Anniversary portrait *(above)* and later attends its luncheon; the event boasts 58 stars and an 18-piece orchestra.

Sat February 12
Hosts a party at his Mulholland house *(bottom right)*, attended by Clark Gable, Shirley Temple, Dorothy Lamour,

Alexis Smith, Bruce Cabot, Jennifer Jones, Van Johnson, Joan Fontaine, Robert Stack, Shelley Winters, Loretta Young,, and many others; a sketch artist is available to draw the stars, while Georgie Jessel acts as announcer for the white mouse races in the circular building on the grounds; the affair lasts from 8:00pm to 6:00am.

Tue February 22
Attends the opening of the Palm Room at the Beverly Hills Hilton; guests include Rosalind Russell, Gloria Swanson, Van Johnson, Walter Pidgeon, Irene Dunne, and others.

Sat March 5
Warner Bros. prepares a check for $88,095.19 ($952,137.20 in 2021 value) in compensation to Flynn for 6½ weeks of work.

Mon March 7
Warner Bros. approves of the release to Flynn of 16mm prints of SILVER RIVER and ADVENTURES OF DON JUAN.

Sat March 12
Celebrates Rory's second birthday at Nora's house.

Sun March 13
According to Harrison Carroll in the *Evening Herald Express*, Flynn hosts a small dinner party at his Mulholland home with Greer Garson in attendance.

Mon March 14
Warner Bros. previews MONTANA at their theater in Huntington Park, CA.

Fri March 18
Completes work on THAT FORSYTE WOMAN.

Mon March 21
Has dinner out with Greer Garson.

Tue March 22
Flies to New York.

Wed March 23
Arrives at LaGuardia Field and is greeted by London stage actress Eve Ashley *(left)* and her husband, Flynn's friend Stephen Raphael.

Thu March 31
Wallace Berry, the young sailor who was accidentally harpooned during the August 1946 *Zaca* expedition while off the coast of Acapulco, wins $3,000 ($32,424 in 2021 value) in a settlement against Flynn; he originally sued for $35,000.

Fri April 1
The IRS asks Warner Bros. to verify Flynn's yearly salary as $270,000 for 1945 ($3,951,010 in 2021 value), and $405,356.92 for 1947 ($4,910,927 in 2021 value). *"In August 1946 Mr. Flynn's records show $100,000.00 received as an advance. No picture is designated."* Thomson Productions is listed as having earned $96,619.81 for UNCERTAIN GLORY in 1945 ($1,413,874 in 2021 value), and another $10,105.27 up to July 30, 1946 ($144,624 in 2021 value).

Sat April 2
At the El Morocco with Mary Maxwell for a goodbye party for Freddie McEvoy who is moving to Europe.

Sun April 3
Leaves for Europe on the *Queen Mary* with Stephen Raphael and Eve Ashley.

Fri April 8
Arrives at Cherbourg, a day later than scheduled due to a storm at sea.

Sat April 9
Arrives in London on business with Stephen Raphael.

With Eve Ashley in New York - Wed, March 23

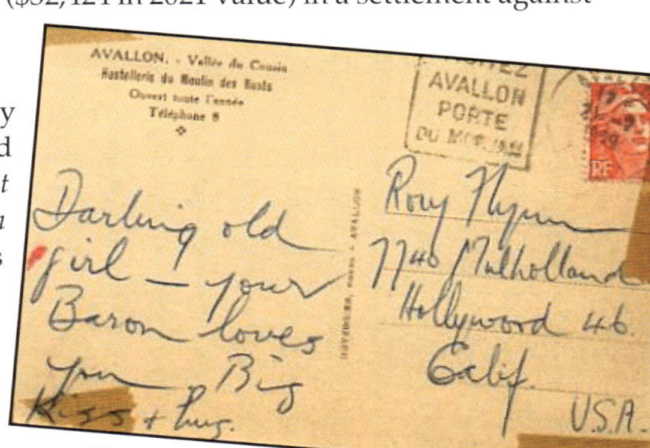

Flynn's postcard from Avallon in the Vallée du Couisin to his two-year-old daughter Rory, sometime during his driving tour this spring: "Darling old girl-your Baron loves you. Big Kiss + hug."

Sun May 1

Meets Romanian princess Irinia (Irene) Ghica while dining with Freddie McEvoy at La Tour d'Argent restaurant in Paris; shortly thereafter they take a week-long motoring tour around France.

Thu May 12

Roy Obringer receives a letter from Arthur Park indicating that Flynn is on an automobile trip around Europe at the present.

Fri May 20

Signs the hood of a yellow and black checkered Renault car during the "Night of Madness" at the Club Du Vieux Colombier, a theater in the District Saint Germain Des Pres in Paris *(top right)*.

Fri May 27

In Cannes with Irene for the wedding of Rita Hayworth and Prince Aly Khan.

Wed June 8

The *Zaca* (without Flynn) leaves Port Antonio, Jamaica, for the 5,000+ mile sea journey to Nice, France.

Sun June 12

Drives with Irene to Florence for several days.

Fri June 17

Is in the release of the MGM documentary short *Some Of The Best*.

Mon June 20

Flynn celebrates his 40th birthday in Rome at the Hotel Excelsior; the princess had given Errol a pre-birthday gift of Cartier cuff links; writes a letter from the hotel to Nora Eddington's stepmother, Marge *(center right)*: *"Marge – how's my One and only? Ah, sweetie, s'a funny thing how often, when I see something beautiful, lovely or inspiring, I wish to myself 'Gosh – if only Gammie could take a gander - - -Too - - - with me – us –'; or whoever, like your little sweet self, happens to be seeing the same thing, with the same eyes. Well –guess I just miss you – and all the good, nice things you stand for — hi, pal!...Irene has finally gone to sleep – having given me her own odd version – Roumanian – of a birthday party – for me – You – and probably only you – would have loved it! She had given me her present – cufflinks, (carefully ordered long ago from Cartier, Paris) a week ago. Natch, I forgot to wear them—you know me, and this cut her to her Slav quick! She smiled – on the outside. Inside, I dunno what cooked; until she began to damn the Russians to hell, perdition + back again. Then she toasted me – sitting up very straight – and hoped I would live to be a hundred. Upon my prompt assurance I would loathe any such fate; she glared at me balefully + demanded if I would still at a hundred forget to wear the 'gufflinks'? upon my quick assurance that I had no shirt back from the laundry fit to grace such 'gufflinks' she sneered (but with a tear in the eye) 'Errol –tu est un salud, un menteur, mais je t'aime-ba! Which is to say – 'you're a son of a bitch and a liar but I love you, you--! A good girl, Marge, really good – for me – Tough! Hates drinking (by me, natch!) Easily made happy – very, very grateful for the smallest kindness. Suspicious – can spot a crook or hustler a mile off. Wants to know everything – but especially America. Knows you already; Honey, Brownie, Rory and has a deep respect for everything you stand for. You're going to like this broad, I betcha: different – very. She's like Sam* [Deirdre]. *Tell Honey I have thought over very carefully the vitally important decision of bringing her back – have lived with mother and herself. No marriage – told 'em anyone who considered marriage in this modern day only had to observe myself and my failures to realize this. She's given me a lot of real happiness – guess that's all. And she's good --- you know?"*

Wed June 22

Letter written by Flynn to Burt Lancaster from the Hotel Excelsior in Rome: *"Dear Burt—(know you won't mind this informality—always figured 'Mister' should be reserved especially for people like Mr. Mayer or Mr. Warner—or even Mister Hakim.) However—many thanks indeed for your notes which I know full well as well-disposed & meant & now I want to thank you for it—The fact is tho', I'm not here to work or even try to; on the contrary—have been trying only to see if I couldn't slow down a tempo of living not only much too furious but one which seems to have somehow got out of control. Be sure that if Senors Bigazzi or Ferrara do me the favour of a phone call I'll most certainly want to tilt a glass with these gentlemen—and at the same time mention your high regard for them. Incidentally, chum, and very sincerely, hope you won't mind if I say this writer holds your work in high esteem too? Thanks again—and watch those fucking Warner Bros with the wary eye of an Egyptian surrounded in mid-desert by vengeful Israelites; certainly, tho', you must have the Fréres figured—just stare at 'em—they wilt! Best luck—Burt. Errol Flynn."*

Thu June 23

In Palermo, Sicily, with Irene.

Fri June 24

Travels to the island of Stromboli to meet with Ingrid Bergman and director Roberto Rossellini regarding

Signing a Renault car during "Night of Madness" in Paris - Fri, May 20

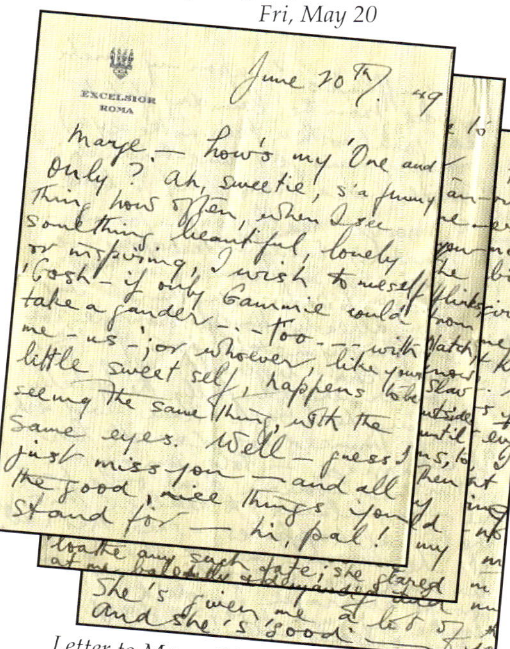

Letter to Marge Eddington from Rome - Mon, June 20

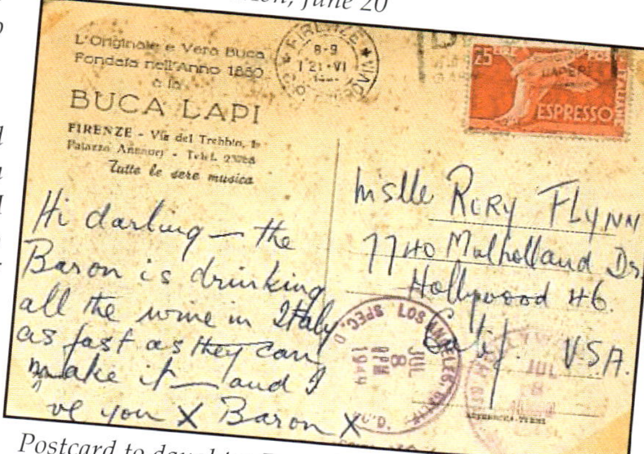

Postcard to daughter Rory during his driving tour, this from Florence (the July 8th postmark is evidently from after he had left Italy): "Hi darling-the Baron is drinking all the wine in Italy as fast as they can make it-and I love you X Baron X"

Handwritten text by Flynn for a telegram to Nora on the eve of her divorce appearance - Wed, July 6: "Hi ma very very sincerely but very sincerely don't let that personal appearance tomorrow get you too nervous stop stand up straight honey and remember I'm pulling for your happiness stop tell Sam [Deirdre] I love her...Baron"

Dear Errol:

A few weeks ago Lew Wasserman told me you would rather not do another Western picture for an indefinite period of time. Therefore, we have picked a very good melodrama for you, temporarily entitled THE MIAMI STORY, which we are making plans to start shooting around October 1st.

I am sure, Errol, that you fully appreciate and are aware of economic conditions in the world today, not only with respect to the picture business, but all other types of business, and consequently our company must make good pictures at a cost which will insure a profit. Therefore, Errol, and with all friendliness, I want to say that unless you personally feel you want to play a part in doing this and make this type of picture, I would rather have you say that you desire to terminate our association by now cancelling your contract with us.

We have been good friends for a long time and I desire it to continue that way. Therefore, I am leveling with you on this as we cannot have a repetition of the losses, trials and tribulations which we encountered in the making of some of your past pictures. Life is too short and there is too much to be gotten out of it while we are here to be finding fault with each other or have difficulties come up which are so unnecessary.

Please let me hear from you by return airmail as I would rather deal direct with you on this very important subject as this is a serious matter and we cannot risk anything and must adopt a very strict economic business procedure in the making of all our future productions if we are to survive.

Hope you are having a good vacation and would appreciate hearing from you immediately.

Sincerely,

Mr. Errol Flynn
Grand Hotel
Cannes, France

Copy of a letter from Jack Warner - Mon, August 8

a potential film project to be filmed on the island titled *Volcano*.

Sat June 25

Travels to the island of Isola Salina to meet with Anna Magnani regarding a different film project also titled *Volcano (top right)*; that film was later made with Magnani, but without Flynn.

Sun June 26

Returns to France from Salerno with Irene, staying in a rented villa in Nice.

Wed June 29

With Irene in Paris for several days, at one point meeting her mother.

First week of July

The *Zaca* arrives at Gibralter on its way to Nice and is held up by the authorities because the crew has firearms.

Sat July 2

Sued for divorce by Nora; travels with Irene from Paris to England; on his travel document he writes "sex" under occupation, and "occupation" under sex; the immigration officers are not amused.

Sun July 3

Flies alone to Los Angeles via New York, arriving the next day.

Tue July 5

Is recalled by MGM for retakes on THAT FORSYTE WOMAN.

Thu July 7

The divorce from Nora is final.

Tue July 12

Is recalled by MGM for one last day of retakes on THAT FORSYTE WOMAN.

Thu July 14

Throws a party at Mulholland for a few guests that include Lana Turner, Greer Garson, Ann Sheridan, and Bob Topping.

Fri July 15

At MGM studios doing looping (overdubs) for THAT FORSYTE WOMAN; leaves on an overnight flight to New York.

Sat July 16

Continues on TWA from New York to Paris, ultimately heading to Cannes and Nice.

Sun July 17

Nora marries Dick Haymes in the garden of his Canon Drive house in Beverly Hills.

Thu July 21

With Irene and El Morocco owner John Perona dining at Cap D'Antibes Beach Hotel.

Late July and August

Traveling and cruising the Mediterranean with Irene: sails from Cannes to Genoa before returning to Nice; flies to Paris for a few days, attending the Folies Bergére (where Josephine Baker is performing), shopping, and visiting Irene's mother; sails from Nice to Cannes for a short visit, staying at Le Grand Hôtel; they are at times seen dining at the Chez Gegene and Dede restaurants; attends the Bal des Petits Lits Blanc (8/11), a charity affair to aid children with tuberculosis which is held at the Casino du Palm Beach des Cannes (also in attendance are Daryl Zanuck, Merle Oberon, and the Duchess of Windsor); flies to Rome to bring the Countess Dorothy di Frasso to Venice for the 10th Venice Film Festival; sails to Juan-les-Pins, a village in Antibes, staying at the Hotel

In Palermo with Anna Magnani and Prince Raimondo Lanza - Sat, June 25

With Rory at Mulholland in front of the Gauguin-July

du Ca-Eden-Roc for a few days; sails to St. Tropez and back to Cannes.

Mon August 1
IT'S A GREAT FEELING opens.

Wed August 31
Jack Warner to Roy Obringer and publicity director Alex Evelove: *"I gave a script of 'THE CLEANUP' today to Lew Wasserman to send to Errol Flynn."*

Fri September 2
Attends the opening ceremonies of the Third Cannes Film Festival *(top right)*.

Wed September 14
At Da Bouttea's Restaurant in Cannes with actress Danièle Parola, Tyrone Power, and Linda Christian *(center right)*.

Fri September 23
Flynn's attorney Robert Ford is in the Los Angeles District Court to protest taxes on alimony payments.

Late September
Travels to Paris with Irene.

October
Wire from Roy Obringer to Mort Blumenstock: METRO IS DISTRIBUTING HUNDREDS OF POSTERS ALL KEY CITIES ANNOUNCING MGM RETURNS TO GERMANY LISTING MGM STARS INCLUDING ERROL FLYNN. DOES ONE OR TWO PICTURE DEAL GIVE RIGHT TO CALL HIM A METRO STAR. EVEN IF DOESN'T SHOULDN'T THERE BE LEGAL COMPLAINT AS MATTER OF FORM?

Mon October 10
Flynn's Warner Bros. contract expires; wire from Roy Obringer to Mort Blumenstock: MGM HAS NO RIGHT IN GENERAL ADVERTISING OR PUBLICITY TO INDICATE FLYNN ONE OF ITS STAR ARTISTS. USE OF FLYNN'S NAME TO BE MADE ONLY IN CONNECTION WITH PICTURE FLYNN APPEARED IN AND IT MADE CLEAR IN ADVERTISING THAT FLYNN APPEARED IN PICTURE. WILL PROTEST TO MGM RE GERMAN POSTERS BUT ONLY AFTER CONCLUSION DEAL NOW PENDING INVOLVING MGM USE FLYNN FOR ADDITIONAL PICTURE.

Tue October 25
Arrives in Paris, staying at the George V Hotel; is at Carrol's nightclub with model Annabelle Schaub, where he gets into a tussle with photographers trying to take his picture; the photo is printed in the magazine *Samedi Soir*.

Thu November 3
THAT FORSYTE WOMAN opens at the Loews in Pittsburgh, PA.

Sat November 12
Letter from Jack Warner to Flynn's agent, Lew Wasserman: *"Am sorry I did not get to see you before you went abroad as I wanted to talk to you about Errol Flynn giving us a complete release from his contract....I had hoped to talk to you about getting this release from Flynn while you were in England. If Errol is not there, you could contact him by phone wherever he is, for I feel we do not want to make any more pictures with him...It is needless to go into the story about Flynn as you know it as well as I do....We just do not want to make any more pictures with him. We have more than a year before we are committed to* [contract] *him again...."*

Tue November 15
Flynn announces his engagement to Princess Irene, who has flown in from Paris to be with him; she gifts him a box of garlic-flavored snails *(bottom left)*, his favorite on the Tour Argent menu in Paris; the Associated Press reports the engagement *"between Errol Flynn, famous American film star, and Rumanian-*

Meeting Argentinian actress Tilda Thamar at Cannes - Fri, September 2

At Da Bouttea's Restaurant in Cannes with: Danièle Parola, Tyrone Power, and Linda Christian - Wed, September 14

In London with Romanian Princess Irene Ghica, opening her engagement gift to him of garlic-garnished snails - Wed, November 15

With Princess Irene Ghica at the Marble Arch Odeon in London for the premiere of THAT FORSYTE WOMAN - Thu, November 17

born Princess Irena Ghica, aged twenty, who lives in Paris with her mother. The Princess is the daughter of the late Prince Jean Ghica, who was killed in an air crash 12 years ago, and Princess Ebi Ghica, now re-married under the name of Donescu. They met in Paris 6 months ago and plan to be married there or in London in Spring, 1950. Today, Princess Irene Ghica flew from Paris in a specially chartered plane to join Errol Flynn who is at present in London to appear at the Royal Command Film Performance at the Odeon, Marble Arch, tomorrow."

Thu November 17

Attends the Royal Command Performance of THAT FORSYTE WOMAN with Princess Irene *(top left)* at the Marble Arch Odeon Theatre in London along with 2,200 attendees; there, along with Greer Garson, he is formally greeted by Queen Elizabeth the Queen Mother.

Tue November 22

Writes a letter to Nora's mother, Marge, whom he nicknamed Gammie *(top right)*: "Darling Gammie – now what in God's name do you mean? What've I done now, girl?...I just got your wire yesterday and all day Sunday Irene + I hung around London phones (which are not a bit like ours in the States) because I guessed my two broads might be spending the day with you and I did so terribly want to hear all your voices. When Steve, Eve, Irene + I couldn't get thru – the wire phones just weren't (and still are not) working...Now come on Gammie – how many times do I have to tell you that you're the woman I trust + have my real, true faith in, above all others? Please sweetie, don't get sore at me for some imaginary wrong -- + forgive me my many oversights for I love you   Baron." Added to the top of the letter, presumably by Marge: "We sent snapshots – waiting for oversea's late telephone call. Deirdre came to spend weekend waiting for promised telephone call."

Fri November 25

"Rory – my very darling girl – will you please think of me? As I do of you? Your old boy the Baron" *(center right)*.

Sun November 27

Flynn's letter to his 2½ year-old daughter, Rory, from the Savoy Hotel in London *(bottom right)*: "Rory Darling...I am going to see you soon – just as soon as I finish work in India. And, my golly, am I excited! I mean, when I give you your great big hug when I get off the plane! Oh boy!...XXXXXXXX Baron." From the same time period, Flynn writes to his family: "Am waiting word from MGM when I go to India. Meanwhile am having so many anti-plague, anti this and that my fanny looks like a dart board."

Fri December 2

Arrives in Bombay (now Mumbai), India.

Early December

Leaves for Delhi, India, from where the production company will travel to Lucknow to begin filming KIM at St. Xavier's Christian School; goes on a leopard hunt in the Lucknow area hosted by the Maharajah of Bundi; in the following days he is in Mysore to visit the sacred Chamudi Hills and the zoo, and is gifted with a rare mouse dear by the Rajah; filming of flora and fauna in the area takes place; in the end, only about three shots of Flynn actually in India will

ERROL FLYNN IN BOMBAY

Welcome By Fans

Bombay film fans gave a great welcome to Errol Flynn as he alighted at Santa Cruz airport on Friday afternoon.

Dressed in a fawn tweed suit, the tall film celebrity looked fresh and elegant, his short beard adding to his masculine charm.

Large crowds, which had awaited his arrival at Santa Cruz airport since morning, literally mobbed him, men and women vying with one another for his autograph. Mr. Flynn smilingly obliged as many as he could.

Mr. Flynn told press representatives that for the first time in the history of the American film industry, Metro Goldwyn Mayer were spending a colossal sum in India. It would be on the production of Rudyard Kipling's "Kim". The expenditure was necessary to give the picture a realistic touch.

When asked how he accounted for his glamour, Mr. Flynn said with a smile: "That's because I am a good liar." To another question, he replied that "Kim" was one of his favourite books which he had read repeatedly for the last ten years.

After a day's halt in Bombay, Mr. Flynn will proceed to Delhi and thence to Lucknow. He was met at the airport by Mr. L. Kamern, Managing Director of Metro Goldwyn Mayer in India, Burma and Ceylon.

The Times of India
Sat, December 3

A letter to Marge Eddington - Tue, November 22

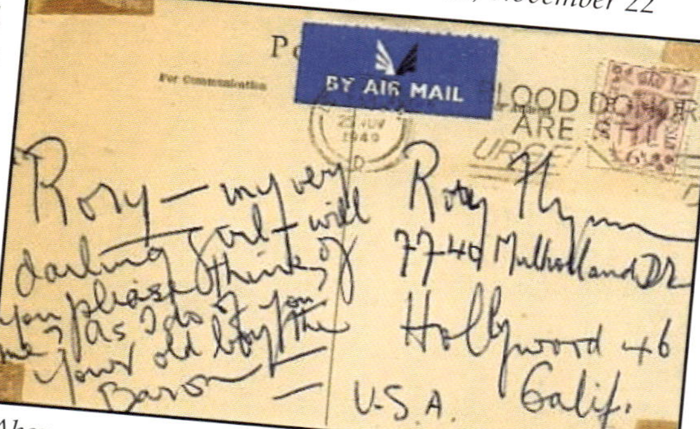

Above, a postcard to his daughter Rory - Fri, November 25; below, a letter to her - Sun, November 27

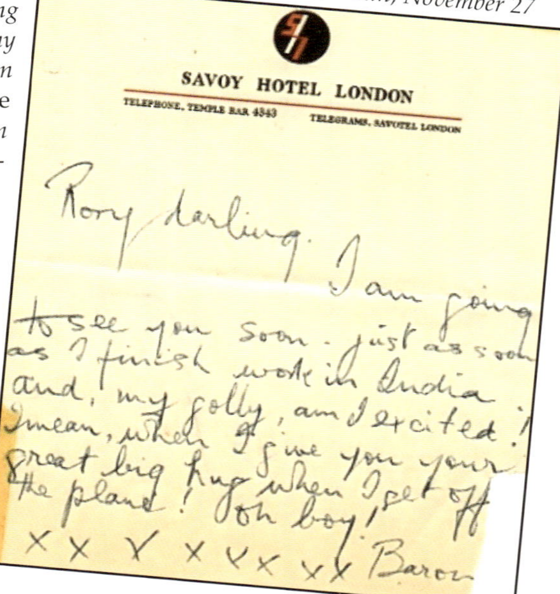

be used in KIM, comprising less than a minute of screen time; writes to his daughters from India on MGM India stationery: *"Rory and Sam [Deirdre] darlings and this is for Rory too, please explain to her will you Sam? I am trying so hard to get you a wonderful thing for Christmas – a little animal, named Samree [top left]…Maybe I can or can't…love you your Baron."*

Sat December 24

Warner Bros. releases the Bugs Bunny cartoon "Rabbit Hood," which includes a live action clip from THE ADVENTURES OF ROBIN HOOD.

1950

THE FIFTIES

Sun January 1

MONTANA has a one-day preview at the Earle Theater in Philadelphia.

Fri January 6

Announces plans to do a film co-written with William Marshall and to be shot in France; they changed the title several times ("The Last Buccaneer," "Bloodline," "The Towers of New Orleans," "The Bargain") before deciding upon THE ADVENTURES OF CAPTAIN FABIAN.

Sat January 7

Leaves Bombay, India, for Paris; the flight shortly returns to Bombay because of mechanical problems but resumes soon after; unfortunately, the mouse deer dies when the cabin pressure in cargo fails; the flight eventually stops in Egypt before heading on to Paris.

Sun January 8

"Errol Flynn, star of 'Montana,' sent a cablegram from Bombay, India, expressing his regret at being unable to attend [the Helena premiere]. *He is busy making a picture of Rudyard Kipling's 'Kim.'"* The Helena Independent Record.

Mon June 9

Arrives in Paris and is met by Irene; sometime while in Paris, does a walk-on cameo in the Merle Oberon-Paul Henreid film, *Pardon My French*, though it is difficult if not impossible to identify him in any scenes.

Tue January 10

Travels alone to Cannes to oversee the *Zaca*, on which he will now live; MONTANA premieres in Helena, Montana, at which Alexis Smith, Ruth Roman, Alan Hale, and James Brown are in attendance.

Wed January 11

Flynn's new 12-year Warner Bros. contract guarantees him $200,000 per picture ($2,207,407 in 2021 value) and allows for one picture per year with another studio; MONTANA begins opening in theaters nationwide.

Mon January 16

The Hollywood Reporter announces that Fawcett Publishing will print 1,500,000 copies of a comic book version of MONTANA.

Fri January 20

Is met by Irene upon his arrival in Paris.

Sat January 21

In Cannes.

Tue January 24

Letter to director Lewis Milestone: *"Dear Milly Many thanks of yours, and of course I must have missed the fucking script by not more than an hour, as I got your letter just as I got out of town in a hot hurry, an angry mother hard at heels. As usual, I was entirely innocent of ill-doing….I need hardly tell you I'm more than delighted at any prospect of an interesting story I could do with you. Am going to do a Niven Busch yarn in France when I finish MGM's KIM and am quite frankly fed up with working in Hollywood and allways [sic] being harassed by tax gatherers, ex-wives, or mistresses-to-be….Let us therefore' get-together, as the quaint saying goes, and see if we can't contrive some original device to fuck those who fuck us--d'accord?"* To which Milestone sometime later wrote at the top: *"…I too am returning to Hollywood for one picture with Twentieth--I'm flying Sunday. Will see you there…."*

Posing with the rare Indian mouse deer presented to him by the Maharajah of Mysore - December

At the Chogan Gate in Bundi, the only scene in KIM in which Flynn is clearly shown in India - December

Postcard to Rory from Egypt on a stopover from India to France; "Hello sweetheart - won't be long before I see you XXXXXX Baron" - probably sent on Sat, January 8

With Princess Irene and Flynn's manager Sonny Vaughn in Kitzbühel, Austria - last week of January

Wed January 25
Leaves for a few days of skiing in Kitzbühel, Austria, with Irene *(top left)*, staying at the Grand Hotel.

Tue Jan 31
Returns with Irene to Paris from Kitzbühel; they stay at the George V Hotel.

Thu February 2
Departs alone from Le Havre, bound for New York aboard the *Ile de France*; Irene remains in Paris to work on her U.S. travel visa.

Thu February 9
Arrives in New York where he will stay for the next few days.

Fri February 10
The press reports seeing Flynn on the town with society denizen and future columnist Carol Bjorkman (Yorke).

Tue February 14
Flies to Los Angeles and is met at the airport by Nora's stepmother, Marge Eddington, who has become secretary and housekeeper at Mulholland; with him is a 10-month-old puppy from Lhasa, Tibet that he has brought home for his daughters for their belated Christmas celebration.

During this time period the bulk of filming on KIM takes place at Lone Pine, CA, and MGM Studios (the daily production files for the film were destroyed by MGM in the 1970s).

With Dean Stockwell in the Alabama Hills of Lone Pine, CA - February

A belated Christmas with Deirdre and Rory at Mulholland - February

Above left, dressing for a scene at Lone Pine, CA, the edge of Flynn's close-cropped, red wig clearly visible - February; above right with Robert Douglas - March

Wed February 15
According to *Variety* magazine, Flynn and William Marshall enter into a contract on this day to film HELLO GOD; sometime during the subsequent period Flynn probably films his scenes for the movie in Santa Barbara.

Wed March 1
Filming at Mahbub Ali's (Flynn) door.

Sun March 5
Dean Stockwell's 14th birthday is celebrated on set.

Mon March 6
Filming in Mahbub Ali's abode.

Thu March 9
Filming the campfire/killing scene.

Wed March 15
After arriving in Los Angeles a few days earlier, Flynn's mother Marelle has a mild heart attack on this day and is hospitalized.

Thu March 16
Errol's father arrives from Jamaica along with Errol's aunt Betty Glover to tend to Marelle.

Fri March 17
Filming with Dean Stockwell in Father Victor's (Reginald Owen) bungalow and on the veranda.

Sat March 18 and Mon March 20
Filming at Creighton's (Robert Douglas) bungalow.

Thu March 23
The custody case of Errol and Nora's daughters is finalized; Flynn's attorney Jerry Giesler announces that Errol and Nora will have shared custody, with physical custody of Rory going to Errol; Flynn will pay $300 a month support for Deirdre, and $550 a month [$ 3,311 and $6,070 in 2021 value] to Nora when the girls are not with him, along with a $3,500 lump sum [$38,630 in 2021 value] to cover expenses.

Wed April 19
Jack Warner to all department heads: *"The Picture heretofore known as GHOST MOUNTAIN will now be called ROCKY MOUNTAIN."*

Above right with Sherry Jackson, and above with Armando Formica and Joe Mazzuca in Santa Barbara, CA - probably February

With Broderick Crawford, Van Johnson, and (in front) Harpo Marx - Sat, April 22

With Princess Irene on Navy Island in Port Antonio, Jamaica - Spring

Thu April 20
Filming in the camp tent.

Sat April 22
With his son Sean at the Shrine Auditorium in Los Angeles for the Friars Club Frolic of 1950, where they are masters of ceremonies *(top left)*; also in attendance are Jimmy Stewart, Edward Arnold, Phil Silvers, George Jessel, and others.

Fri April 28
Flies out of Los Angeles on his way to Jamaica.

Sat April 29
Arrives in Kingston, Jamaica, and is met there by Irene; they stay at the Myrtle Bank Hotel.

Sun April 30
Errol and Irene travel to Port Antonio, staying at the Titchfield Hotel and checking in on the *Zaca* at Navy Island.

Thu May 4
Dinner with Irene at Knutsford Park in Kingston as guests of the governor's wife, Lady Molly Higgens.

Fri May 5
Lauren Bacall is announced as Flynn's costar in ROCKY MOUNTAIN; she is ultimately not cast.

Sat May 6
Errol and Irene are special guests at the Titchfield for a celebration of the rafting races scheduled for the morrow.

Sun May 7
Attends the Errol Flynn Challenge Cup rafting races on the Rio Grande River, with Irene a passenger on one of the rafts.

Mon May 8
Flynn leaves alone for Los Angeles to appear in court concerning Lili Damita's request for back alimony payments.

Tue May 9
Appears in Los Angeles Superior Court to petition Lili's claim for back alimony; he protests that Lili has *"traveled extensively throughout the United States and abroad and has lived in an extravagant manner without making an attempt to live conservatively or earn a livelihood, although she is capable of doing so."*

Wed May 10
Flies back to Kingston, Jamaica; an article in the *Sydney Morning Herald* reports that Flynn is asking the Los Angeles courts to reduce his alimony payments to Lili; he is currently paying $23,200 a year ($256,059 in 2021 value) for support of her and their son Sean, as well as $550 a month ($6,070 in 2021 value) to Nora for her and their two daughters; this, along with $150,000 ($1,655,555 in 2021 value) in back federal taxes is *"causing him financial embarrassment."*

Sun May 14
Drives with Irene from Port Antonio to Kingston, staying at the Myrtle Bank Hotel.

Mon May 15
Misses a flight with Irene from Jamaica to Los Angeles, instead flying into New Orleans.

Tue May 16
Flies from New Orleans with Irene to Los Angeles, meeting his mother, father, and Marge Eddington at the airport in the evening *(bottom right)*.
Sometime after arriving in Hollywood, Flynn is called to MGM for retakes on KIM; Flynn's phone number at the Mulholland house is HE-9791.

With Prof. Flynn, Marge Eddington, Princess Irene, and Marelle at Los Angeles International Airport - Tue, May 16

Thu May 18

Patrice Wymore and Phyllis Thaxter are given sound and photo tests for ROCKY MOUNTAIN; Patrice wins the part.

Sat May 20

Flies to New York to discuss with businesspeople his upcoming, self-produced films with William Marshall.

Tue May 23

A subpoena from Lili Damita is delivered to Warner Bros. legal counsel Roy Obringer to appear in court on May 25th to testify as a witness in her alimony and support case against Flynn, her former husband; the court date is changed to August 1st.

Thu June 1

Filming wardrobe and makeup tests for ROCKY MOUNTAIN.

Tue June 6

Leaves studio at 1pm for Gallup, New Mexico.

Wed June 7

Arrives in Gallup at 7:30am; stays at the Hotel El Rancho.

Thu June 8 through Sat June 10, and Mon June 12 through Fri June 16

Begins filming ROCKY MOUNTAIN in the Broken Desert; Patrice is on location (6/8) and begins filming with Flynn (until dark) on 6/12.

Sat June 17

Continues filming in the Broken Desert, and also at the waterhole.

Mon June 19 and Tue June 20

Flynn's 41st birthday; continues filming in the Broken Desert and at the waterhole.

Wed June 21

Continues filming in the Broken Desert; Irene and Marge Eddington have arrived on location.

Thu June 22 through Sat June 24

Continues filming in the Broken Desert.

Mon June 26 through Wed June 28

Filming in Box Canyon; letter from Flynn to William Marshall, written on stationery from the Hotel El Rancho in Gallup, regarding their upcoming production of ADVENTURES OF CAPTAIN FABIAN (6/27): *"I will not go into our personal disagreements upon the fundamental relationship between us. I understand a corporation is formed and our separate functions clearly defined. Without having seen the draft of any such papers, I am much relieved. Differences such as these must be settled at the earliest possible time, or a bad picture – or no picture – will be the inevitable result. Another thing – when Mr. Florey has read these yellow pages, I do wish you would request him to write me at length and in detail any objections, suggestions, or improvements. Don't you think it's a little abnormal, since I am to produce this picture, that the Director has never even so much as discussed it with me? I regard Mr. Florey as a fundamentally sound, technically [indecipherable] director. You will recall the objections made in his selection by you at first, which I withdrew. Please assure Mr. Florey that he can expect from me only the warmest and most comprehensive cooperation. I personally propose to leave him alone to do his job, which, as a man of much expertise, he will best achieve with the least amount of interference. That's a hint, Son. I do hope I may have the pleasure of hearing from you soon...My very best regards to yourself, Julie, [costume designer] Valles, [Vincent] Price, etc. Sincerely Errol Flynn."*

Wed June 28

Irene and Marge Eddington return to Los Angeles, with the princess leaving for Paris on the 6th; the Flynn/Ghica engagement is soon announced as broken.

With Princess Irene at Warner Bros. looking over costume designs for ROCKY MOUNTAIN - last week of May

With Guinn "Big Boy" Williams, Rush Williams, Slim Pickens (with rifle), Dickie Jones, and Sheb Wooley (right rear) on location in New Mexico

With Patrice Wymore at McGaffey Lake, NM - Tue, July 4

Thu June 29 seven days a week through Sat July 15
Filming at the Top of the Rock (the Kit Carson Springs area northeast of Red Rock Park); goes fishing with Patrice at McGaffey Lake in the Cibola Forest (7/4); Patrice gifts Flynn with an Alsatian puppy which he names Cold Nose (7/5).

Mon July 17 through Thu July 20
Continues filming at the Top of the Rock with Patrice, and (on 7/20) in the Broken Desert and on the highway; leaves the location by train with Patrice at 7:30pm on 7/20.

Fri July 21
Arrives with Patrice in Los Angeles at 9:12am.

Mon July 24
Meets with his attorneys, Jerry Giesler and Robert Ford, to discuss the upcoming divorce decree court appearance.

Wed July 26
With Patrice post-recording dialogue for ROCKY MOUNTAIN in Projection Room #14 at the Warner Bros. studio.

Thu July 27
With Patrice at the wedding eve party thrown by Betty Hutton for Louis Sobol and Peggy Strohl at the Crystal Room of the Beverly Hills Hotel.

With director William Keighley (in beret), northeast of Gallup, NM - July

With Patrice on location, northeast of Gallup, NM - July

At Mulholland with Deirdre, Brownie, and Sean (above left), and with Rory, Patrice, and Onyx (above right) - weekend of July 28th

Weekend of July 28th

With Patrice, Marge Eddington, Sean, Deirdre, Rory, and some of the children's friends at Mulholland riding horses *(previous page, two bottom photos)*; Flynn's horse Onyx is reported to have recently been retired from films.

Mon July 31

Receives a 16mm print of MONTANA from Warner Bros.

Tue August 1

In court with Lili over back alimony *(top right)*.

Sat August 5

Flies to Catalina Island with his son Sean to bring the boy to summer camp; along for the ride are Patrice and Marge Eddington; after a night on the island, the adults return to Mulholland.

Tue August 8

Finishes work on ROCKY MOUNTAIN, filming process *("stereo")* shots outside the camp area and mountaintop, and close-ups in a stagecoach and camp area.

Wed August 9

Flies to Witchita, KS, to meet Patrice's parents Winnie and James and her brother Jim.

Fri August 11

Leaves for New York with Patrice and then on to Paris without her to begin filming ADVENTURES OF CAPTAIN FABIAN.

Sat August 12

Arrives in Paris.

Week of August 14

Flynn's business manager Al Blum flies to Paris to help sort out problems concerning ADVENTURES OF CAPTAIN FABIAN: French authorities require both English and French versions of the film, labor permits are required for all workers on the film, Warner Bros. is unhappy he's making a film for a minor studio, and 20th Century Fox is unhappy that their contracted star, Micheline Presle, is in the film.

Sun August 20

Takes a train from Paris to Nice, staying at the Negresco Hotel.

In a Los Angeles court with Lili and his attorneys Jerry Giesler and Robert Ford - Tue, August 1

With Patrice at Wichita Municipal Airport, KS - Fri, August 11

Mon August 21

Begins filming THE ADVENTURES OF CAPTAIN FABIAN (the daily production notes have not been located); exteriors are filmed in Nizza and Villefranche in the Cote d'Azur until the second week of September; though living on the *Zaca*, Flynn retains a room at the Hotel Negresco in Nice.

Tue August 29

Letter from Flynn's longtime double Don Turner outlining expected salary for work on THE ADVENTURES OF CAPTAIN FABIAN (at this point titled *The Bargain*), co-signed by Flynn and producer William Marshall: *"It is agreed I am to receive $350 per week* [$3,863 in 2021 value] *beginning August 25 payable weekly at the end of each week for services in the Bargain week to week. Travelling expenses Holliwood* [sic] *to location and return. Living expenses at the rate of highest favored technician. Beginning August 25. My services are to double for Errol Flynn to do the personal services attendant done for him in the States. I am to be paid either in francs or dollars at employers convenience but place of payment is Nice, France of $50 per week plus $300 per week in Hollywood."*

Fri September 1

Is in New York on a short break from filming in France and attends the opening of *Tea For Two* at the Strand *(bottom right)*; Patrice, along with starring in the film, is also appearing live onstage between showings.

As Capt. Michael Fabian in
THE ADVENTURES OF
CAPTAIN FABIAN

In New York for the premiere of Patrice's film
Tea For Two - Fri, September 1

With Héléna Manson in a scene from THE ADVENTURES OF CAPTAIN FABIAN

Mon September 4

Is back in France filming THE ADVENTURES OF CAPTAIN FABIAN.

Sat September 23

Patrice arrives in Paris with her parents to meet up with Errol at the Hotel Prince de Galles; she gifts Flynn with a black poodle which he names Fubar.

Mon September 25 and Wed September 27

Filming underwater scenes in Paris with Vincent Price, which on 9/27 runs until 3am the following morning.

Thu September 28

Errol gives Patrice a six-carat sapphire engagement ring *(top right)*.

Sun Oct 1

Patrice is fitted for her wedding gown at Balmain of Paris.

Tue October 3

In Paris, announces upcoming wedding to Patrice.

Thu October 5

ROCKY MOUNTAIN opens at the Fox Theater in San Francisco.

Sat October 21

Travels by train to Monte Carlo, where he is greeted by Patrice; they share lunch with her parents on Freddie McEvoy's boat; later Errol and Patrice relax on the Zaca before heading to the casino in the evening.

Sun October 22

With Patrice at the French Lutheran Church of the Transfiguration in Nice, rehearsing for the wedding the following day; Patrice receives a puppy from Claude McEvoy (Freddie's wife), which she names Greno.

Mon October 23

Errol and Patrice are first married in a civil ceremony at 11:00am at the Monaco Town Hall *(bottom three)*, officiated by Mayor Charles Palmaro (the ceremony is broadcast over local radio); over 3,000 people are waiting outside the building when the couple exits; Errol and Patrice briefly separate, she having lunch with her parents, he with Freddie McEvoy on the *Zaca*; at 4pm the couple is wed in the Lutheran Church of the Transfiguration in Nice, the ceremony performed by the Reverend Franck Gueuthal; best man is McEvoy, while his wife Claude is matron of honor; the couple exchange plain platinum rings, and are then escorted back to Monte Carlo by French police to the Hotel de Paris for the 6pm reception *(next page, top center and right)*; Errol and Patrice leave the reception two hours later for their honeymoon aboard the *Zaca*;

With Patrice who is displaying her engagement ring in Paris - Thu, September 28

Below, the crowd outside the Monaco Town Hall surrounding Errol and Patrice's limo

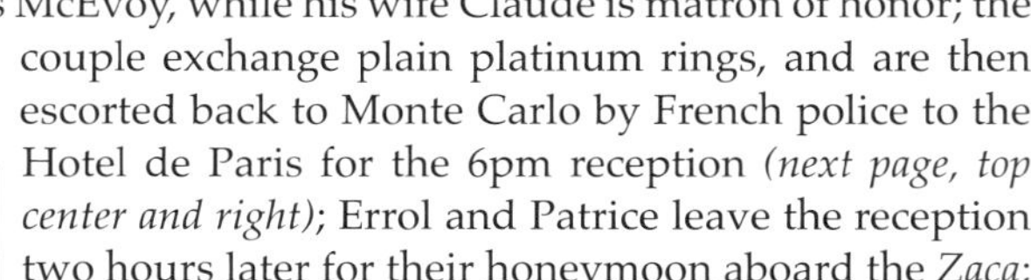

The Detroit Free Press - Fri, October 6

Below, with Patrice and Monaco mayor Charles Palmaro during the wedding ceremony in the Monaco Town Hall - Mon, October 23

Disembarking the Zaca in Monaco for the civil wedding - Mon, October 23

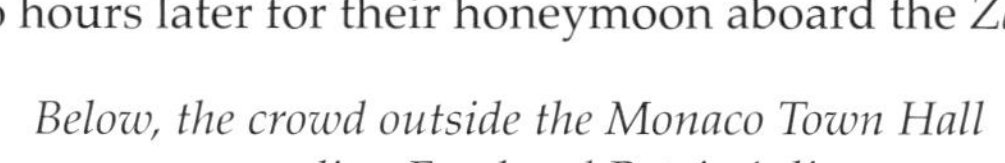

Disembarking the Zaca in Monaco for the church wedding - Mon, October 23

Leaving the Church of the Transfiguration in Nice with Patrice after their wedding; behind her are her parents, and behind him is his best man, Freddie McEvoy

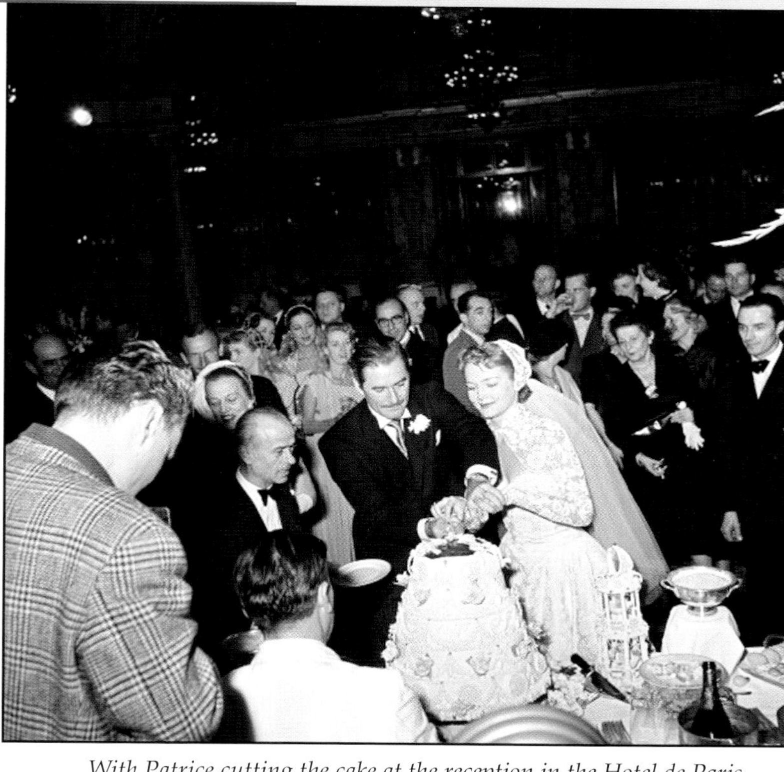

With Patrice cutting the cake at the reception in the Hotel de Paris

during breakfast earlier in the day Flynn is served with a summons concerning another charge of rape.

Tue October 24

Sometime during this day Flynn slips on a wet dock in Nice while getting into a speedboat and seriously damages his lumbar and ilium; a U.S. Naval doctor does an examination and prescribes a week of bed rest.

Mon October 30

Meets with William Marshall on the *Zaca* to discuss the continuation of filming on THE ADVENTURES OF CAPTAIN FABIAN.

Wed November 1

Appears in a Monte Carlo court to face charges of the rape of 16-year-old Danielle Dervin (variously listed as Duvivier), who accused Flynn of committing the act on the *Zaca* the year before; her parents are seeking £100,000 ($4,965,020 in 2021 value).

Fri November 3

Note on telegram paper from the *Zaca* presented to the press by Flynn's French lawyer about the rape issue: *"ZACA 3rd Nov. 1950 Having had attempted blackmail tried upon me by experts I have to have a pretty darn good memory. But I must confess this lady has the advantage of me because apparently after 18 months she has just remembered something that never happened...Errol Flynn."*

Wed November 8

Letter to William Marshall, director of ADVENTURES OF CAPTAIN FABIAN: *"I do not understand your 'self-serving' letter of November 5, 1950, so I have sent it to my legal advisors... You write: 'I received your letter through Charles Gross in which you advised myself and Sacha Kamenka, Director of Production of our picture, that you did not agree to the transparencies for back projection and that you have taken the decision of having the company return to Nice in 20 days and/or when you are able to work.'...I never wrote you any letter to this effect."* He then adds by hand: *"The rest of the statements in your letter are equally ridiculous and untrue."*

With Patrice, honeymooning on the Zaca - Tue, October 24

Letter to his daughters Deirdre and Rory

FLYNN GOES BEFORE JUDGE

Accused of assault

MONACO, Saturday.—Errol Flynn and Danielle Dervin, the 16-year-old French girl who has accused him of assault, appeared before Judge Biasset in his chambers here to-day.

Flynn was questioned alone for 20 minutes before the girl arrived.

Under Monaco's laws they both told their stories to the judge, who has to decide whether there are grounds for a court trial.

No one—not even the two lawyers—was admitted to the court building. Ten policemen barred the entrance.

Flynn's wife of a month, Patricia Wymore, and his lawyer, Jacques Cotta waited in a café across the street.—Agency messages.

Agency Messages - Sat, November 25

Mon November 20

Sails into Cannes with Patrice; writes a letter from there to his daughters, Deirdre and Rory *(top left)*: *"Cannes, France 20th / Darling Sam + Rory How are my two sweethearts? Golly, how I miss you both and what a great enormous hug + kiss I'm going to have for you when I get back! I hear mummy is in the east around New York + I'll bet you miss her too and boy! will she be happy to see you both again! The old baron has been a bit sick lately – nothing bad, of course but I slipped + hurt my back! Ouch! I had to wait around with a crutch and now a walking stick! Isn't that a bit silly, slipping in the rain? And I didn't have too much cooking sherry either or I wouldn't have minded so much! In a couple of days the ZACA sails for Gibraltar via the Balearic Islands – look on the map + you'll see -- Cowpoke...[Patrice] says to tell you she loves you both enormously and she hopes you'll keep your fingers crossed for her so she won't get seasick. She has two wonderful French poodles, one named Yuki (a girl) and the boy named Zut, both black. Aren't they funny names? Cowpoke gets the strangest idea for names; she has a cat onboard named Merde, a Siamese who instead of meowing like an ordinary cat says 'merde, merde…' so that's what she calls him. Gammie [Grandma Eddington] writes she hasn't seen much of you because you've been in Palm Springs but you're both very good + very pretty + very polite and you love me. I'm bringing you back some lovely presents. You must wait: I won't tell you what they are."*

Wed November 22

Sails to Villefranche for lunch with Patrice, and then back to Cannes.

Sat November 25

Is at the Monte Carlo Palais de Justice before magistrate André Biasset on charges of statutory rape of 16-year-old Danielle Dervin.

Tue November 28

Returns to work on THE ADVENTURES OF CAPTAIN FABIAN.

Wed December 6

Sails with Patrice to the French Island of Ile de Porquerolles for three days; KIM begins opening around the United States, on this date at the Strand Theater in New York City.

Saturday December 9 to Monday December 11

With Patrice on the Mediterranean during bad seas, arriving in Palma de Mallorca on the 11th and staying at the Hotel Maricel while the *Zaca* undergoes repairs.

Tue December 12

Letter from Patrice to her family: *"Dearest Gang, Well we finally arrived in Palma and received your two letters. They had been forwarded from Cannes. We had three days of very bad seas before arriving on the island of Majorica or Mallorica [Mallorca]. It's spelled many different ways however it's off the coast of Spain. The trip was wonderful even though very rough. We stopped on a group of islands off the coast of France for two days they were called Porcololles [Porquerolles]. In the summer the entire island is a nudist colony but not during the winter. Can't say I blame them. It was ---cold. Errol was furious. He didn't see one tit. We stopped in a couple villages and talked with the natives or rather Errol did. My pigeon French is getting better. From there we crossed the Mediterranean to Majorica...."* Errol adds a note of his own to the parents: *Jim --- how come you didn't get on to this Roulette? That oil racket is the bunk, pal --- Pat + I have a steady annuity, which pays off every night! Minnie – don't let the press worry you – no two people could be happier or have more trust in each other ---Love to you both Errol"*

Wed December 13

With Patrice in Port of Gibraltar.

Sat December 16

Arrives in Paris with Patrice.

Week of December 18

Completes filming of THE ADVENTURES OF CAPTAIN FABIAN.

Mon December 18

Files a suit over distribution of HELLO, GOD; the suit complains that the picture should not be released since his contract stipulates that his one yearly alloted film outside Warner Bros. must be a *"major release by major studio"*; the film would satisfy neither requirement.

Wed December 20

Returns with Patrice to Mallorca.

Mon December 25

Celebrates Christmas with Patrice in Mallorca; sometime this week the couple sets sail on the Mediterranean;

Woman Held for Tearing Up Errol Flynn's Patio

A misdemeanor complaint charging malicious mischief or disturbing the peace will be sought today against the woman who raised a ruckus at Actor Errol Flynn's home Christmas night, Hollywood police said yesterday.

Originally booked as a Jane Doe, the woman subsequently was identified as Mrs. Ruth Heberle, 35, of 1068 Pittsfield Lane, Ventura.

Held in City Jail

She is being held in City Jail on suspicion of burglary. But Sgt. G. C. Schlotzhauer of the Hollywood burglary squad was skeptical yesterday about the District Attorney issuing a burglary complaint as a result of the woman's strange behavior at Flynn's hilltop home at 7740 Mulholland Drive. The actor is in Europe.

It was indicated, however, that the case might be turned over to the Police Department's psychopathic detail.

Wrecked Patio

After pushing past a maid, Mrs. Julie Miller, Mrs. Heberle proceeded to take Flynn's place apart, particularly the patio where she hurled barbecue equipment into the swimming pool, smashed pots and sent a wheelbarrow crashing down a hillside.

Arresting officers said her only explanation was: "Flynn has been bothering me and my daughter for three years."

NAMED — Mrs. Ruth Heberle, who assertedly caused damage in Errol Flynn home while he was away.

The Los Angeles Times
Wed, December 27

---

a storm damages the *Zaca* and it pulls into Saccone, Gibraltar for repairs; Errol and Patrice celebrate New Year's Eve there.

Sat December 30
The Danielle Dervin rape case is dismissed by the court for lack of evidence.

1951

Mon January 15
Errol travels with Patrice from Paris to Los Angeles via New York (arriving on the 16th, *top right*) for treatment at Burbank Hospital for his ruptured vertebra.

Wed January 17
Checks into Burbank Hospital where Dr. Nolan recommends a stay of a few days after determining Flynn's spinal injury is worse than suspected.

Sat February 10
The Superior Court of Los Angeles finally dismisses the 1943 Shirley Hassau Evans paternity suit against Flynn.

Wed February 28
Flies alone to the Bahamas via Miami, staying at the Windsor Hotel in Nassau.

Mon March 5
At the Windsor Hotel bar, Flynn has an altercation with Canadian mining tycoon Duncan McMartin, who violently slaps him, severely aggravating Flynn's already injured back, which is still in a brace.

Wed March 7
Flies to Kingston, Jamaica, checking in to the Titchfield Hotel; while there he begins therapy for his injured vertebrae (and now also ribs); the continued use of a back brace is recommended.

The week of March 8
The *Zaca* arrives in Port Antonio after a month's sailing from the Mediterranean; it berths at Navy Island.

Thu March 8
Letter from Navy Island in Jamaica to Nora concerning footage of her in CRUISE OF THE ZACA (*bottom right*): *Hail the morn!...Nora dear pal, mother of my progeny, you who are charged with the sacred task of ensuring the fierce Flynn blood to Posterity. Good morning! I am sitting in the early dawn, my wicked little red-rimmed eyes gazing o're [sic] the vast ocean at The Titchfield Hotel, where I got drunk as a fiddler's bitch last night, seeking what sad escape from reality I – shit, this is my only sheet of paper so I'll quickly to the point. Al [accountant Blum] + Art [manager Park] have asked me to reassure you about you + the Jamaican footage [for CRUISE OF THE ZACA] I sold Warners. Don't be afraid sweetie. W.B. actually were the first to bring up the question of 'bad taste' and the necessity for extreme care in presenting the shorts to the public. But just in case their idea of good taste should differ from ours, ours will prevail. Because under the terms of the sale (horribly small by the way) I must narrate each one. Natch – if I see anything I am the least bit doubtful about, I don't narrate. My lips, (dry at this moment from my hangover) shall be sealed – unmentionable torture, the rack itself, could never force one single…oops! Hold 'em, Joe. But you can of* course check this with Art Park and you'll see we are in no danger because of that clause. If you want to, when I see what sort of cutting job they do, you + I and Dick [Haymes, Nora's husband] can give it a gander together, but in any case you can rest assured I'd never let anything by that wasn't right, and can advise you to sign the release without doubts. Since I've just got enough room left may I tell you that this moment holds some bitter sweet nostalgia for this always-devoted ex? I mean it's hard to look in any direction, at any tree or flower or some remembered fragrance in the air without a pang and a sigh, a laugh and even a tear – for the might-have-been-but-wasn't – Aha! Well! My piercing

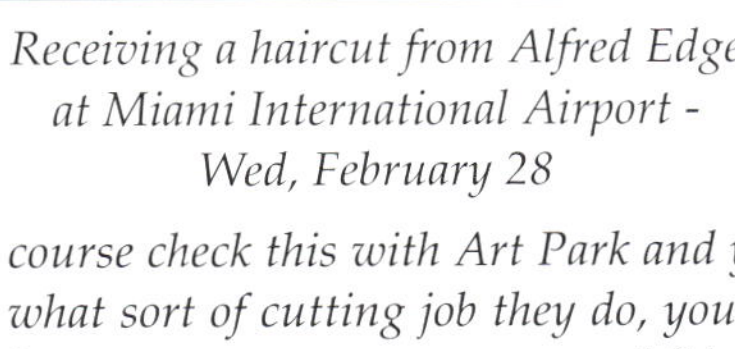

Receiving a haircut from Alfred Edge at Miami International Airport -
Wed, February 28

With Patrice at LaGuardia Airport -
Tue, January 16

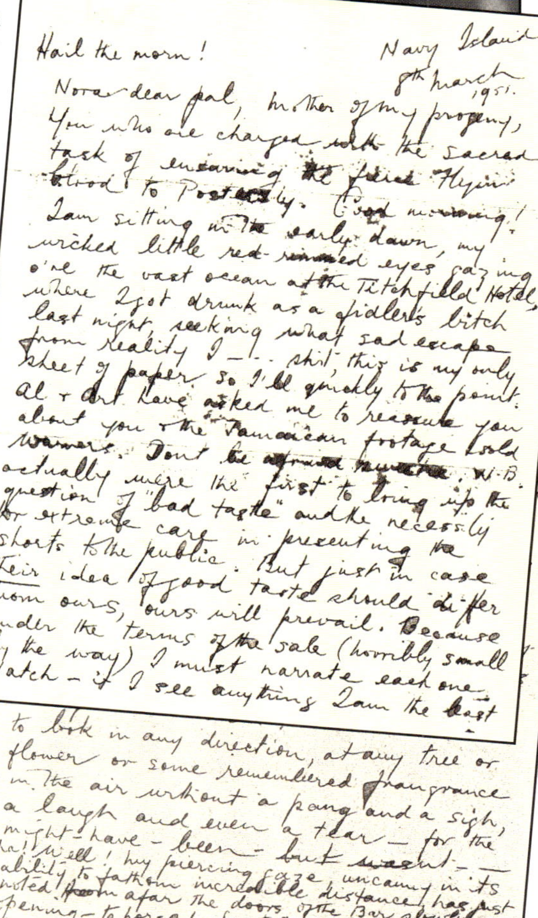

Letter to Nora from Port Antonio, Jamaica -
Thu, March 8

With Patrice at the San Souci Resort in Ocho Rios, Jamaica - Sun, March 25

With Patrice at the Ice Capades in Los Angeles - Thu, March 10

gaze, uncanny in its ability to fathom incredible distance has just noted from afar the doors of the Bar slowly opening – to horse! Love to Sam [Deirdre] Rory + always your Baron."

Wed March 14

Patrice arrives in Port Antonio for several weeks' stay.

Fri March 16

THE ADVENTURES OF CAPTAIN FABIAN premieres in France with the title of *The Tavern of New Orleans*; on a fishing trip with Captain and Mrs. Tom Gifford on the captain's boat, *The Stormy Petrel*.

Sat March 17

Visits a doctor for his increasing back pain.

Sat March 24

The Flynns attend the start of the Easter Regatta at the Royal Jamaica Yacht Club, later having dinner at and attending the Regatta Ball at the Titchfield Hotel.

Sun March 25

Spends Easter night with Patrice at the Sans Souci Resort in Ocho Rios on the outskirts of Port Antonio *(top left)*.

Mon March 26

Attends the close of the regatta races, where Patrice hands out the awards at the Titchfield Hotel.

Tue March 27

Noel Coward visits the Flynns in Port Antonio. Coward's diary page for that day says, *"Dined with Errol Flynn and his wife Pat. Drinks on his yacht, which is beautiful, then barbecue dinner on his island – palm trees – lit by torches. Both of them extremely nice; a real lovely evening."*

April

Flynn purchases his friend Stephen Raphael's Jamaica holdings for $67,000 ($698,070 in 2021 value), bringing Flynn's total land ownership to 200 acres; travels with Patrice to Miami, shopping and looking into maritime equipment for the *Zaca*.

Thu May 10

Attends the Ice Capades with Patrice at the Pan Pacific Auditorium in Los Angeles *(bottom left)*.

Tue May 15

$1.00 contract for *Voyage of the Zaca* is signed and dated; the finished film is to be purchased for $15,000 ($156,284 in 2021 value).

Thu May 31

Throws a 10th birthday party for Sean at the Mulholland house; Dierdre and Rory attend—along with ex-wives Lili and Nora; Prof. Theodore Flynn wrote about this occasion in an article in January of 1960 (three months after his son's death): *"In the middle of the party my eyes nearly popped out of my head in disbelief when I saw Errol nonchalantly take the lovely redhead Nora on his knee while his present wife, Pat Wymore, looked on...This was too much for me. I strode forward and said sharply to my ex-daughter-in-law, 'This is no way to act. Get off at once and behave yourself.'...The guests watched with interest. What would Nora do? What would Pat do? The atmosphere was electric... Nora looked at me. She must have sensed I was in earnest. She climbed off Errol's knee rather shame-facedly and went to another corner of the room. Everybody breathed again and the party chit-chat was resumed."*

Thu June 14

Fails to appear in Long Beach Municipal Court on a five-week-old traffic ticket for running a red light at Pacific Coast Highway and American Avenue; an arrest warrant is issued.

Wed June 20

Flynn's 42nd birthday.

Thu June 21

Flynn's attorney Robert Ford pays for the Long Beach traffic ticket to prevent Flynn doing jail time.

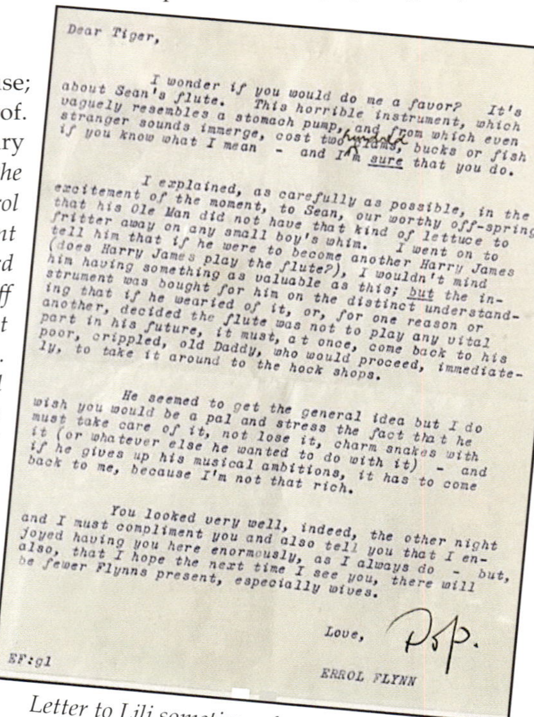

Dear Tiger,

I wonder if you would do me a favor? It's about Sean's flute. This horrible instrument, which vaguely resembles a stomach pump, and from which even stranger sounds immerge, cost two hundred bucks or fish – if you know what I mean – and I'm <u>sure</u> that you do.

I explained, as carefully as possible, in the excitement of the moment, to Sean, our worthy off-spring, that his Ole Man did not have that kind of lettuce to fritter away on any small boy's whim. I went on to tell him that if he were to become another Harry James (does Harry James play the flute?), I wouldn't mind him having something as valuable as this; <u>but</u> the instrument was bought for him on the distinct understanding that if he wearied of it, or, for one reason or another, decided the flute was not to play any vital part in his future, it must, at once, come back to his poor, crippled, old Daddy, who would proceed, immediately, to take it around to the hock shops.

He seemed to get the general idea but I do wish you would be a pal and stress the fact that he must take care of it, not lose it, charm snakes with it (or whatever else he wanted to do with it) – and if he gives up his musical ambitions, it has to come back to me, because I'm not that rich.

You looked very well, indeed, the other night and I must compliment you and also tell you that I enjoyed having you here enormously, as I always do – but, also, that I hope the next time I see you, there will be fewer Flynns present, especially wives.

Love,

ERROL FLYNN

EF:gl

Letter to Lili sometime after their son's birthday party on May 31

With Sean at the Flamingo Hotel in Las Vegas - June

With Sean on Lake Mead - Sat, June 23

Fri June 22

Takes his son Sean on a trip to Las Vegas, staying at the Flamingo Hotel *(top left)*.

Sat June 23

Fishing at Lake Mead with Sean *(top right)*.

Sun June 24

Returns with Sean to Hollywood.

Tue June 26

Leaves on a five-week USO tour to Korea with Jack Benny, actresses Benay Venuta, Marjorie Reynolds, and Dolores Gray, mentalist Harry Kahne, pianist June Bruner, and guitarist Frankie Remley *(bottom right)*; two performances are given at their first stop at Travis Air Force Base near San Francisco.

Wed June 27

The USO tour leaves Travis for a stopover in Honolulu, arriving at 10am, and leaving for Wake Island in the evening.

Thu June 28

Arrives at Wake Island with the USO tour, giving two shows for the troops; the tour then continues on to Japan.

Fri June 29

Arrives in Tokyo with the USO Tour, which is greeted by over 1,000 fans; Flynn visits a sick bay for his back pain.

Sat June 30

Along with Jack Benny and 100 government officials is the guest for a reception and cocktail party at the home of General Matthew Ridgway, Supreme Commander of the Allied Powers.

Mon July 2

Leaves Tokyo with the USO tour arriving in Seoul, South Korea, later that day.

Wed July 4

Two USO shows are performed for over 10,000 troops at a base near Taegu (today Daegu).

Fri July 6

Inter-office memo from Roy Obringer: *"In connection with 'The Voyage* [Cruise] *Of The Zaca' film purchased from Errol Flynn, keep in mind that under the agreement we have agreed that we will not make any picture of greater length than 3,000 ft. in which scenes showing Errol Flynn and Nora Eddington appear. We can use the film in other pictures regardless of the length provided scenes of Flynn and Eddington do not appear therein. Also, with respect to Nora Eddington, we have agreed that we will not utilize scenes in any picture which involve Nora Eddington in the so-called 'swimming pool kissing scene' or 'the sun bathing scene while lying in the grass'. Also, we are not allowed to use Nora Eddington's name on the main title or in any advertising. The only reference to Nora Eddington's name can be in Flynn's narration, at which time he is to refer to her by her first name and in any other manner as may be consistent with the subject matter of the scene."*

Tue July 17

Is sued by screenwriter Charles Gross for $8,930 ($93,041 in 2021 value) in back payments due on Gross' adaptation of the novel *Fabulous Ann Madlock* for the film THE ADVENTURES OF CAPTAIN FABIAN.

Fri July 20

Travels back to Tokyo with the USO tour; he decides to leave the tour and heads back home, arriving in Honolulu the next day, the 21st.

Tue July 24

Arrives in San Francisco.

Sat July 28

Travels to Reno to file Nevada state papers in preparation for a film he plans to make there about Admiral Matthew Perry; staying at the Riverside Hotel, he attends the

In Los Angeles leaving for the USO tour with (foreground) actress Marjorie Reynolds, Jack Benny, and actress Benay Venuta; (background) pianist June Bruner, tap dancer Dolores Gray, guitarist Frank Remley, and mentalist Harry Kahne - Tue, June 26

With Col. Muncie and Jack Benny in Korea - July

Arriving back in Los Angeles after the Korea USO tour - Tue, July 31

In a cricket outfit at Griffith Park in Los Angeles - Sun, August 12

With Patrice at the premiere of A Streetcar Named Desire *- Tue, September 18*

Dennis Day show there in the evening, Day inviting him up on stage.

Sun July 29
Meets with his friend and attorney Melvin Belli at the Cal-Neva Lodge in Lake Tahoe, discussing the financing of a film he plans to do in Japan.

Tue July 31
Returns to Los Angeles *(top left)*.

Second Week of August
Errol and Patrice attend a baseball game between the Hollywood Stars and the Los Angeles Angels at Pote Field in Griffith Park; later at the event he dons a British cricket outfit and stands at home plate inviting a pitch *(center left)*.

Wed August 15
Signs a contract with Universal Pictures to film AGAINST ALL FLAGS; at Ciro's with Patrice.

Fri August 17
Leaves Los Angeles for Port Antonio with Sean, but the plane is forced to land in New Orleans due to a hurricane in Jamaica.

Sun August 19
Flies with Sean from New Orleans to Havana, staying at the Hotel Nacional.

Mon August 20
Dines with Mississippi travelers Mr. and Mrs. N. B. Gillis Jr. and J. B. Day.

Tue August 21
Treats Mr. and Mrs. N. B. Gillis Jr. and J. B. Day to an evening at the Tropicana nightclub.

Sat August 25
Leaves Havana for Kingston, Jamaica, with Sean, greeted there by Flynn's parents, and moving on to Port Antonio, checking into the Titchfield Hotel.

Thu August 30
THE ADVENTURES OF CAPTAIN FABIAN premieres at two theaters in Paris and begins opening around the United States, on this date at the Fox Theater in Detroit, MI.

Sat September 1
With Sean at the Titchfield Hotel ball celebrating the Errol Flynn Cup river races to be held the following day.

Sun September 2
With Sean in Berrydale for the start of the races down the Rio Grande River.

Tue September 4
Acts as master of ceremonies at the Carib Theatre in Kingston in a charity event to raise money for victims of the recent hurricane.

Fri September 7
Leaves Kingston for Los Angeles with Sean.

Tue September 18
Warners announce Flynn will star in MARA MARU; attends the premiere of *A Streetcar Named Desire* with Patrice at the Warner Bros. Beverly Hills Theater *(bottom left)*.

Thu September 20
Is again charged in a Monaco court with the rape of Danielle Dervin; he is ordered to appear in court in January.

Mon September 24
Letter to fencing master Aldo Nadi sometime after the news of Universal's signing of Flynn to do AGAINST ALL FLAGS: *"Dear Aldo – Production of 'AGAINST ALL FLAGS' is so far off, it is hard to make plans, at this time. I don't think it will go this year but you can be sure I will be looking out for you when we start preparing the action stuff...."*

Tue September 25
Files suit in a Los Angeles court to dissolve his business partnership with William Marshall.

Fri September 28
Two dental surgeries are performed on Flynn to remove a cyst from his jaw.

Thu October 4
Filming sound and wardrobe tests for MARA MARU.

Sun October 7

Letter to Nora from Mulholland *(right)*: *Hello sugar-puss – and was I happy to get your sweet Ottawa letter! Like after I talked to you on the phone – such a glow – such a rich warm surge of feelings you'll never believe! Ma darling – it's very apparent to me now that you alone have the capacity to inspire and touch such depths as remain to be deeply moved in this old heart...You know it was funny the other day – up came a brave citizen from Texas, a lawyer and doubtless richer even than Mrs. John Ireland, who wanted to buy this house; and having felt for some time that perhaps a change of environ might be for the best I was seriously considering his proposal....Suddenly I was not listening to this joker....In my mind's eye, a handy little device I generally reserve for the seduction of young girls, I seemed to see sidling across the living room a slender graceful young animal dressed in black. Crabwise she slithered towards me, blue eyes downcast from nerves and girlish fear of a terrain never to be anything but fearful, and she was skinny and her hair shone the right way and she was so beautiful yet somehow wistful that my heart gave the same great leap it always did when she said I'm terribly sorry to be late....You know this could easily become a love letter, if it isn't already....And now for the spot news – especially the gossip –absence of which I am well aware can drive you to a nervous decline...1. Sean has a teen-age Praying Mantis, captured in Palm Springs, which he has been forced to domocile [sic] up here in a bottle, due to the unreasonable prejudice of certain of his household to bugs...2. Steve Raphael's wife has been delivered of a baby, a man child who resembles no one we know, and Freddie MvEvoy's wife is expecting. The latter are sailing on their hot yacht from Gibraltar to Nassau...3. Shirley Names, from whom I haven't heard in years, paid a drop-in surprise visit here, -- fortunately during my absence at the studio. She met Pat. Phew! That's when shit hit the fan! She's 'separated.' Now what?...4. You have more people, worthwhile, who love you than you know. I mean it, Fatso!...5. I am a bit worried about Rory and if it could be done without offending Sam [Deirdre] I'd like to have her come down + hang around with me for a while....6. I loved Moulin Rouge [the Hollywood nightclub] – thanks Ma. Aren't you the nice one to think I'd like it. Thanks...7. Stay off airplanes...8. Are we at long last getting over our mutual shyness?...9. My best meant regards and a really cordial hello to your old man Richard [Haymes], and after the last time I met him and got a bit of chance to know him I can readily perceive why you, amongst others, go all out for this guy – the bastard! Disconcerting as hell, this sort of thing. You dedicate yourself to an undying hatred, even on dark nights an Olympian revenge worthy of the soul searing cries. Prometheus (nuts, I've run out of lead. And no cracks about 'lead' – Fatso!) anyway, as I was saying – that wife-stealing sonofabitchin' husband of yours has such a deprecating 'niceness' about him you get drawn involuntarily to the pig. He has it – especially that best kind of humour – whimsy, a sort of self-deprecating bewilderment. No pretentions [sic], no self aggrandizement about your boy. (Couldn't like him more, Ma; if it means anything Hope it does – really.) But tell him, will you, just warn him! NOT TO GO TOO FAR! We Flynns, vain, hot-blooded Tasmanian mountain men tho' we be, may only be wrought upon to a limit! Just let him steal one more wife of mine and God's blood I'll __ well anyway a hint, a word of caution, Richard! Beware! I mean it! It's not for nothing, my friend, Joanne [Dru, Haymes' previous wife] and I can almost pay Jerry Giesler's bill. Nay! Scoff if you will Sir... And to you little Nora all my devotion my dear, very dear, girl. Errol."*

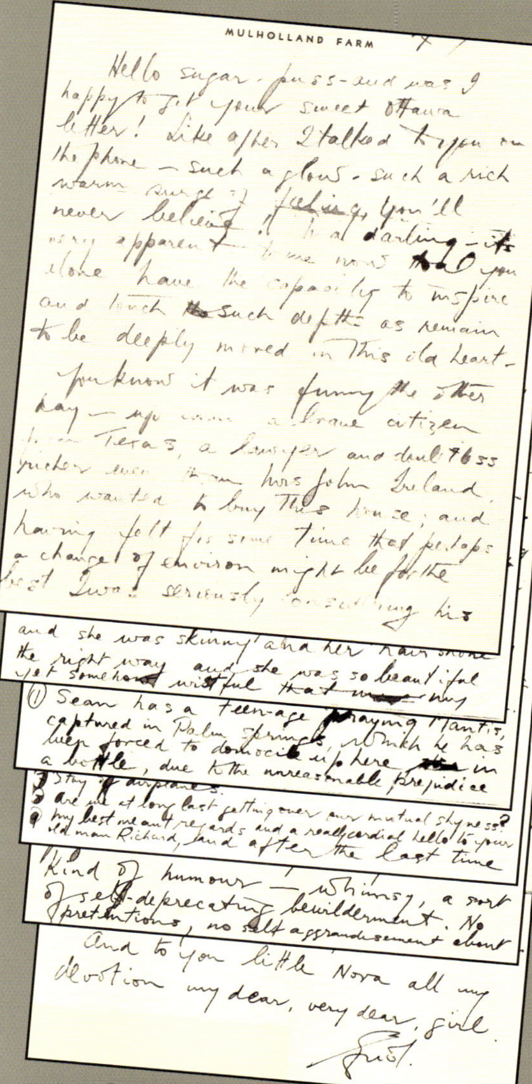

Letter to Nora - Sun, October 7

ERROL FLYNN SLAPPED DOWN IN NIGHT CLUB

Express Staff Reporter: New York, Friday

ERROL FLYNN, the 42-year-old swashbuckler who hands out the punches in all his films, was slapped down hard this morning in a New York night club.

And the man who slapped him down, a 41 year old Canadian goldmine millionaire and playboy named Duncan McMartin, had done it before.

That first blow – to the side of the head—was struck in a bar at Nassau, Bahamas, one night in March and Flynn sued for £80,000 damages.

This morning, with the case still to be heard, McMartin approached Flynn's table in the lush El Morocco.

He asked Flynn : "Why did you sue me?"

Flynn said : "I've been a defendant so many times I want to know how it feels to be a plaintiff for a change. There aren't many people I can sue. You're a rarity. You're a guy I can sue."

McMartin asked about a report that Flynn had sold a friend a 20 per cent interest in his claim for damages.

Flynn asked how McMartin dared suggest such a thing and said : "I ought to break you in two."

And then recalling some film or other, Flynn said they could go downstairs, lock the doors, and settle their argument man to man.

But there and then—crack went McMartin's palm against Flynn's face, and McMartin walked out.

Flynn stormed : "If I was anywhere else but El Morocco I'd go after him but the owner is too good a friend of mine for me to fight here."

It was nothing like an Errol Flynn film.

The (U.K.) Daily Express
Fri, October 20

Fri October 12 and Tue October 16

Filming wardrobe and makeup tests for MARA MARU.

Thu October 18

Flies alone to New York.

Fri October 19

Runs into Duncan McMartin again at the El Morocco and gets into another fracas resulting in McMartin again hitting Flynn *(bottom left)*; in respect for the restaurant's owner, his friend John Perona, Flynn does not hit back; instead he informs his lawyer to add $100,000 to the pending lawsuit ($1,041,896 in 2021 value); he later tries to confront McMartin at the man's hotel, but the hotel clerk calls the police, who bring Flynn to the station house; he is released in the early morning.

Sat October 20

Returns to the El Morocco where McMartin is also staying; the two men vow to kill each other.

Sun October 21

Arrives back in Los Angeles.

On location for MARA MARU at Wilmington, CA - October

With George Revanent - November

With Patrice at the Mocambo - Sat, November 17

Mon October 22

Begins work on MARA MARU, filming on the salvage boat and freighter (on location at Donohugh's Boat Service docks, Berth 117 in Wilmington, CA, *top left*).

Tue October 23

Continues filming on the salvage boat, and also on the dock; celebrates with Patrice their first wedding anniversary, she gifting him with a mounted globe, and he gifting her with a diamond brooch.

Thu October 25 and Fri October 26

Filming in Mason's (Flynn) bungalow and on the dock, all at the studio, and (on 10/26) in the yard behind WB Stage 19.

Sat October 27

Filming night shots at the salvage shack and yard behind Stage 19.

Mon October 29

Filming process shots on the salvage boat and salvage yard.

Tue October 30

Filming in Andy's (Richard Webb) apartment and Mason's bungalow on Dijon Street on the WB backlot.

Wed October 31

Continues filming in Andy's apartment, and also outside the Venus Bar on the soundstage; inter-office memo: *"Mr. Flynn sick and sent home at 5:10."*

Thu November 1

Ill with undulant fever; company is shut down due to Flynn's illness; "Voyage of the Zaca" title changed to CRUISE OF THE ZACA.

Fri November 2

Company remains shut down due to Flynn's illness.

Sat November 3 and Mon November 5

Filming at the studio in the salvage yard and shack and (on 11/5) in Andy's apartment and in the bungalow.

Tue November 6

Filming in the hotel and bar.

Wed November 7 through Fri November 9

Filming in the detective's office and corridor; two of Flynn's closest longtime friends, Freddie and Claude McEvoy, are lost at sea off the coast of Morocco; Flynn offers to adopt the McEvoy's five-year-old step-daughter Romaine; her natural father eventually takes her in.

Sat November 10 and Mon November 12

Filming outside the church at the WB Calabasas Ranch and (on 11/12) on a street at the Ranch.

Tue November 13

Filming inside the San Fernando (CA) Mission.

Wed November 14 through Sat November 17

Filming in the catacombs at the studio (*center left*); signs a contract with MGM (on 11/15) for a series of radio programs titled *Modern Adventures of Casanova*, to be broadcast throughout 1952; with Patrice to the Mocambo (on 11/17) for a party for London nightclub owner John Mills (*bottom left*).

Sun November 18 and Mon November 19

Travels to the Balboa, CA, location and (on 11/19) films on the *Mara Maru* and the dock at Balboa.

Tue November 20

Filming on the set in the catacombs, the church vestibule, and in Benedict's (Raymond Burr) apartment.

Wed November 21 through Sat November 24

Continues filming in Benedict's apartment and (on 11/23 and 24) straight and process shots on the MARA MARU set.

Mon November 26

Continues filming straight and process shots on the *Mara Maru*, also in the dining salon, all on the set.

Tue November 27

Filming on the set in Benedict's apartment, and straight and process shots on the *Mara Maru*.

Wed November 28
Filming on the set in a diving suit on the *Mara Maru* deck in a storm.

Thu November 29 and Sat November 30
Filming straight and process shots on the *Mara Maru* deck in a storm, and (11/30) in the pilot house and the cabin in a storm, all on the set.

Sat December 1
The company is unable to shoot today due to Ruth Roman's sprained shoulder and the illness of Robert Cabal.

Mon December 3 through Wed December 5
Filming in the jungle on the WB backlot and in and outside the hut on the set; at Ciro's (possibly on 12/5) with Patrice, Bruce Cabot, and Francesca De Scaffa (Mrs. Bruce Cabot).

Thu December 6 and Fri December 7
Filming process shots of the *Mara Maru* bow, and (on 12/7) process shots in a diving suit at the *Mara Maru* bow, and in Stella's (Ruth Roman) cabin, all on a soundstage.

Mon December 10 through Wed December 12
Filming on the *Mara Maru* deck and (on 12/12) in a storm, all on a soundstage.

Thu December 13
Filming pickup shots in the catacombs, the detective's office, hut, and close-ups underwater, all on a soundstage.

Fri December 14
Filming retakes in and outside the salvage shacks (on the WB backlot), underwater on the set, and post-recording of dialogue.

Mon December 17
Celebrates Patrice's birthday at Romanoff's; his gifts to her are a white lace cocktail dress (which she wears for the occasion), and a gold medallion engraved with musical notation from "their" song, "Dearie"; Nora and her husband Dick Haymes are in attendance.

Tue December 18
Continues post-recording of dialogue.

Wed December 19
Signs off on the final script for CRUISE OF THE ZACA.

Fri December 21
With Patrice at the annual Christmas party hosted by columnist Edith Gwynne at her Hillcrest home in Beverly Hills; guests include Bruce Cabot, Lewis Milestone, and Van Johnson.

Sat December 22
Travels with Patrice to Acapulco to look over the Club Sirocco for the first time; it is a restaurant in which he invested and is operated by his friend Apolonio Diaz.

Mon December 24
Errol and Patrice return to Los Angeles.

Tue December 25
Spends Christmas at Mulholland with Patrice and his three children.

Wed December 26
At WB Studios recording narration for THE CRUISE OF THE ZACA.

Fri December 28
Travels to the Hotel del Coronado with Patrice.

Sun December 30
The Danielle Dervin rape case is finally dismissed after fourteen months.

Mon December 31
Spends New Year's Eve with Patrice at the Beverly Hills Club.

1952

Thu January 3
The first episode of *The Modern Adventures of Casanova* is broadcast; there will be 39 half-hour radio episodes in all, aired on most Thursdays and finishing on January 8, 1953.

With Patrice who is filming "She's Working Her Way Through College" on another soundstage - November

With Paul Picerni and Raymond Burr - November

With Ruth Roman

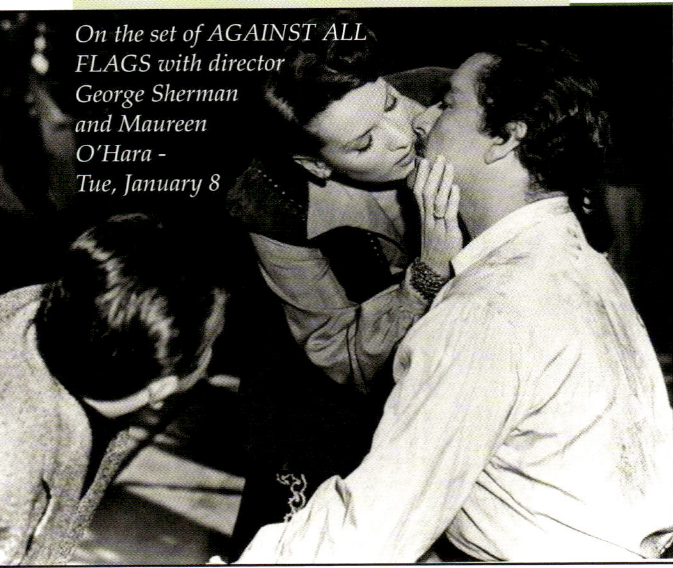

On the set of AGAINST ALL FLAGS with director George Sherman and Maureen O'Hara - Tue, January 8

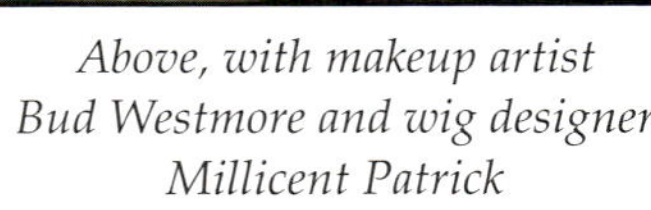

Above, with makeup artist Bud Westmore and wig designer Millicent Patrick

Mon January 7

Is given an insurance physical for the Universal film AGAINST ALL FLAGS; begins shooting with a scene of Hawke (Flynn) meeting Spitfire (Maureen O'Hara); Flynn's secretary is listed in paperwork for AGAINST ALL FLAGS as Miss Gloria La Touf.

Tue January 8

Films the shaving scene with O'Hara.

Wed January 9

Filming scenes of Hawke and Spitfire bidding for Princess Patma (Alice Kelley); a letter to WB from Cecil Tennant, agent for Laurence Olivier and Vivien Leigh (Mrs. Olivier), to Harry Mayer at Warner Bros. indicates that the two stars would probably not be interested in appearing in THE MASTER OF BALLANTRAE.

Thu January 10

Radio broadcast of *The Phony Count*, episode #2 of *The Modern Adventures of Casanova*; more episodes are broadcast on subsequent Thursday nights: *Family Vendetta* on 1/17; *Adventures in Switzerland* on 1/24; episode #5 on 1/31; episode #6 on 2/7; *A St. Valentine's Day Adventure* on 2/14; episode #8 on 2/21; episode #9 on 2/28; episode #10 on 3/6; episode #11 on 3/13 about an attractive divorcée of independent means; episode #12 on 3/20 about an adventure in Mexico; episode #13 on 3/27 about an escapade in a Parisian nightclub; *The Bride of the Rain God* on 4/3; episode #15 on 4/10, which takes place on the French Riviera; episode #16 on 4/17 about the smashing of a smuggling syndicate; *The Back Dowry Pearls* on 4/24; episode #18 on 5/1 with Patrice in the cast; episode #19 on 5/8; episode #20 on 5/15 about an Egyptian adventure; *Marble Arms*, on 5/22; episode #22 on 5/29; episode #23 on 6/5 about stolen jewels from a Kashmir casino; episode #24 on 6/12 about a search for an Egyptian tomb; episode #25 on 6/19 about an adventure surrounding a jade bracelet; episode #26 on 6/26 concerning the solving of a murder (conclusion of the first season).

Fri January 11

At Bluff Cove in Palos Verdes, CA *(below)*, filming Hawke's boat entering the harbor, him and his men being taken prisoner on landing, and being tied to stakes on the beach.

Below left with Maureen O'Hara at Bluff Cove in Palos Verdes, CA - Fri, January 11; below right, the same location today

Most Thursdays from January 3, 1952 through January 8, 1953

With Lou Costello and Bud Abbott on the set of their picture, Lost In Alaska *- January*

Sat January 12

Filming of Hawke and his men fixing a cannon and fighting with Gow (Harry Cording).

Sun January 13

Makes his television debut on the Colgate Comedy Hour with Abbott and Costello, performing in two skits: one as a lowly cowboy and another as a Mexican bandido named Black Pedro; also on the program are Rhonda Fleming, George Raft, and Bruce Cabot.

Mon January 14

Is sent home from the studio with a cold.

Tue January 15

Filming the rescue of Princess Patma.

Wed January 16

Filming Hawke taking over the wheel and discovering Patma is a princess.

Thu January 17

His home on Mulholland is isolated because of severe rains; is picked up by Jeep and is 55 minutes late; filming the rescue of Princess Patma.

Fri January 18

Filming the acquisition of a map from Harris (John Alderson); filming Spitfire's request for a kiss; it is reported that the winter storm has caused much damage to his Mulholland house.

Sat January 19

Filming Hawke's fight with Roc (Anthony Quinn).

Tue January 22

Filming Hawke's trial and the pike fight with Swaine (Michael Ross).

With Patrice, Janet Leigh, and Tony Curtis at the Club Del Mar in Santa Monica - Sat, January 26

Thu January 24

Complains of a sore tongue; Dr. Morton is sent for and treats Flynn for an ulcerated tongue caused by a rough edge on some dental bridge work; Flynn's personal dentist Dr. Sweeney is sent for and he repairs the bridge, causing a twenty minute delay on the set; Flynn is also treated by a Dr. Gourson.

Fri January 25

Records a voice track at WB for the United Jewish Appeal.

Sat January 26

Filming Hawke and his men boarding the *Scorpion*, and the killing of Roc; attends the Hollywood Foreign Press Awards with Patrice at the Club Del Mar in Santa Monica *(bottom left)*; Patrice is a nominee for a special award.

Tue January 29

Filming Roc and his pirates capturing Hawke.

Wed January 30

Filming Hawke buying a pistol and sword, and Spitfire asking to speak privately with Hawke.

Thu January 31

Filming the map found on Hawke, Spitfire's anger at Hawke, and Hawke telling MacGregor (Mildred Natwick) to trust him.

Fri February 1

Hurts his foot during an action scene: it is a medium shot of him climbing over the side of the ship, jumping down to the deck, taking a belaying pin, crossing over to a pirate at the mast in the foreground, knocking him

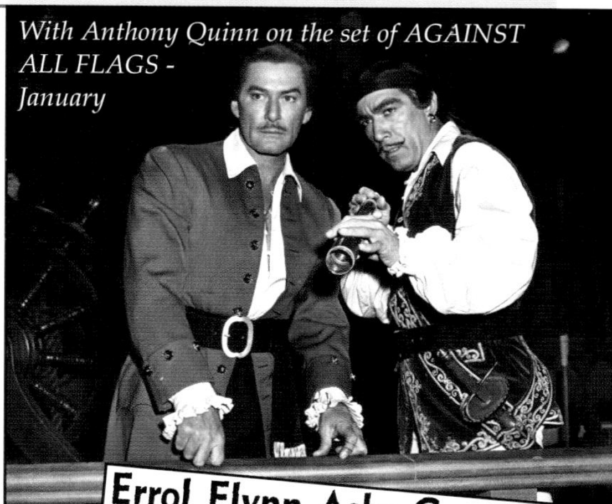

With Anthony Quinn on the set of AGAINST ALL FLAGS - January

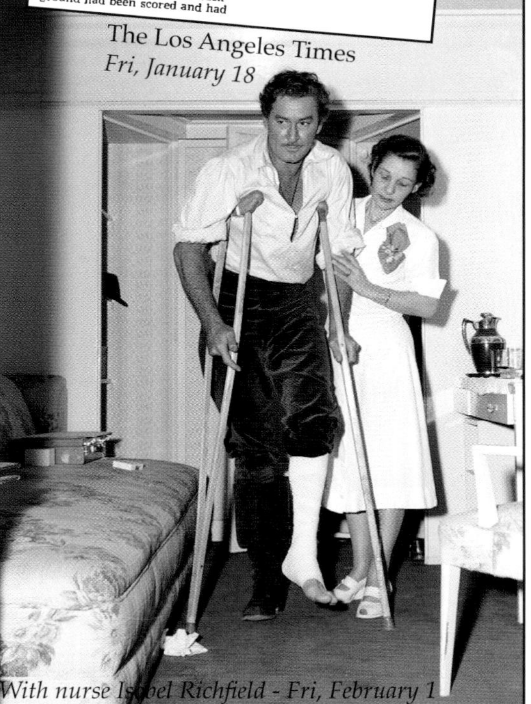

Errol Flynn Asks Court to End Film Partnership

Errol Flynn, screen actor, charged yesterday that he was deceived into participation in a film venture to cancel a partnership agreement and a $25,000 promissory note.

The actor took the legal step by filing a cross complaint against William Marshall, motion picture producer who brought suit against Flynn a month ago for collection on the note.

Title Changed

Flynn said that he did not know when he entered into the agreement that the subject of the film would be detrimental to the public welfare in that it was of pacifist nature and contrary to the foreign policy of the United States and of other nations opposed to Communist aggression.

When he first signed the note in payment for half interest in the film, originally entitled "Before You Sleep Tonight" and later changed to "Hello, God," he was not aware of these circumstances.' Flynn said that Marshall fraudulently represented that he had spent more than $50,000 on the production already, that the musical background had been scored and had

been written by a European conductor of distinction and that it could be extended from a strictly documentary nature to a feature-length production.

Worked 10 Days

The actor also said that under the agreement he was promised $2700 a day and actually worked 10 days as an actor and narrator. He contends that the film is of inferior quality and cannot be improved because of the poor film used and the poor sound recording. He asserts that under his contract with Warner Bros. Pictures, Inc., he is allowed to make outside pictures but these must be first-class productions.

Flynn's cross complaint was prepared by Attys. Jerry Giesler and Robert E. Ford.

The Los Angeles Times
Fri, January 18

With nurse Isabel Richfield - Fri, February 1

*With Maureen O'Hara - the above photo
and below, Mon, February 4*

*With Marion Davies at the Mocambo -
Fri, March 7*

out, and taking his sword; is taken to a doctor's office and found to have fractured a small bone in his foot; returns to the set at 2pm, ready for work *(previous page, bottom right)*; inter-office memo from unit manager Percy Ikerd: *"At approximately 11:30am during the shooting of a fencing scene on the deck of the boat between Mr. Flynn and a double for Mr. Quinn, Mr. Flynn complained of hurting his foot. A nurse was called to the stage as Mr. Flynn's foot started to darken in the area he complained was hurting. Mr. Flynn was put in a studio car and sent to Dr. Hearn's office in North Hollywood where X-rays were made. Dr. Hearn reported at 1:05pm there was a fractured metatarsal in Mr. Flynn's foot and felt he would be unable to work for six weeks. However, at 2pm Dr. Hearn called Parker Harris of our (WB) insurance department and reported after consulting, Mr. Flynn insisted it would not be necessary to place the foot in a cast and it was the doctor's opinion he would be able to continue work, provided there was no strenuous action involved. Mr. Flynn returned to the stage at 2:05pm after having his foot bandaged. Although uncomfortable he worked in one scene and was dismissed at 3:25pm and given a 9am call for Saturday which he accepted."*

Sat February 2

Inter-office memo from unit manager Percy Ikerd: *"Mr. Flynn was scheduled to report to makeup at 9:15am but he called Mr. [director, George] Sherman at 8:30am to say he would be unable to come in due to his foot he injured on Friday. He reported he was in considerable pain and unable to put his foot down to stand up. Company was dismissed at 10:20am as they were unable to shoot any longer without Flynn. Crew went to stage #12 boat set to prepare it....for Monday."*

Sun February 3

Inter-office memo from unit manager Percy Ikerd: *"Mr. Flynn was unable to work this date [on] account [of] being in hospital having cast put on his injured foot, making it necessary for company to work around him."* A claim of $18,520 is made against Flynn's Cast Insurance ($182,037 in 2021 value).

Mon February 4

Filming of Hawke alerting MacGregor, Spitfire revealing her name, Hawke asking her trust and exiting garden *(top left)*, Patma refusing to go without Hawke, and being flogged *(center left)*.

Tue February 5

Filming of Hawke asking Cloudsley (Lester Matthews) to forget Spitfire, of discussing his venture with Hornsby (James Craven), and of being flogged; inter-office memo from Percy Ikerd; *"Company worked around Mr. Flynn - he reported to stage approximately 3pm having had a cast put on injured foot. Discussion was held with him and it was determined he would be unable to do any strenuous action scenes until cast was removed. It was decided to use him in the scenes that did not require a lot of physical action and his dueling scenes would be held in abeyance with the fracture which would be approximately March, 25, 1952."*

Wed February 6

Filming Hawke and men grabbing the anchor.

Thu February 7

Filming of fight in the rigging and Hawke sliding down the sail (a double for Flynn).

Mon February 18

In a radio performance of "Kim" with Dean Stockwell.

Thu February 21

Signs a re-conformation of his 1950 contract extension (of 1947), indicating he has completed two years of the contracted twelve with the filming of ROCKY MOUNTAIN and MARA MARU.

Late February

Travels with Patrice to Apple Valley, CA, for a few days and while there decides to purchase three acres of land.

March

Sometime this month Flynn purchases a Ryan Aeronautical Super 260 Navion; the four-seat, double-engined plane will be kept in Kingston, Jamaica, until a private landing strip can be built on his property in Port Antonio.

Tue March 4

Completes filming of MARA MARU with a closeup in the pilot house.

Fri March 7

At a cocktail party at the Mocambo; his old friend Marion Davies is also there *(bottom left)*.

Wed March 12

Sometime before the McMartin court case (probably on this day), Flynn writes to Nora: *"Wednesday Darling Ma – The [cuff]links go with me, so do the ties + so does Egbert the Elephant! And I know that if your hopes + good wishes for me prevail – I'll be back from Nassau with a bankroll so high a giraffe won't be able to look over it without getting a crick...I shall pat the ZACA very quietly on her rump + whisper confidentially that you send her a very kind thought – And that you've not forgotten her...I don't have to say more about the gifts do I – they came from a heart as warm as the sun itself...I'll take care – and be goddamned sure you do the same! Hear me? Baron."*

Thu March 13

Leaves for Miami with Patrice on an overnight stopover to Nassau, Bahamas; they stay at the Nautilus Hotel in Miami Beach; telegram to Flynn from the Marcus Loew Booking Agency: PLEASE ACCEPT THIS TELEGRAM REGARDING THE POINT RAISED BY YOU LAST NIGHT THAT IF WITH YOUR FULL COOPERATION AND SERVICES WE ARE UNABLE TO COMPLETE RECORDING OF TWENTY-ONE ADVENTURES OF CASANOVA PROGRAMS DURING THIS PERIOD OF YOUR RETURN TO LOS ANGELES STARTING APRIL 10, 1952, WE WILL ARRANGE TO RECORD THE REMAINDER OF THE TWENTY-ONE PROGRAMS OUTSIDE THE UNITED STATES AT TIMES AND PLACES WE DESIGNATE....Flynn's response: MANY THANKS....YOUR WIRE REMOVES ALL MY WORRIES STOP WILL CHECK IN 8TH OR 10TH OF APRIL....REACH ME AT NAUTILUS HOTEL MIAMI BEACH OR TOMORROW HOTEL WINDSOR NASSAU. KINDEST REGARDS.

Fri March 14

Arrives in Nassau with Patrice and the Dr. Nolans; after discovering their hotel is co-owned by Duncan McMartin, the foursome moves to the Fort Montagu Hotel.

Mon March 17

Errol and Patrice attend the opening of the court case against Duncan McMartin in Nassau; Flynn testifies and is cross-examined.

Tue March 18 through Thu March 20

Cross-examination of Flynn continues, and then (on 3/18 and 19) of witnesses.

Fri March 21

Flynn's witness, Dr. Nolan, testifies as to the severity of Flynn's injuries.

Sat March 22

The trial continues, Flynn's attorneys resting their case.

Mon March 24

The trial continues, with the defense insisting that McMartin's "slap" could not have caused the extent of injury claimed by Flynn.

Tue March 25

Duncan McMartin takes the stand, describing his accused acts as merely a "good-bye slap" and a "friendly tap on the cheek as a goodbye gesture."

Thu March 27

The defense in the trial rests their case.

Fri March 28

After three hours of deliberation, the jury in the McMartin case returns a decision in favor of Flynn; the judge awards him $14,000 ($137,609 in 2021 value) plus court costs; McMartin promises to appeal.

Tue April 1

Travels with Patrice to Kingston, Jamaica, checking in to the Myrtle Bank Hotel.

Wed April 2

Flynn finalizes the purchase of the Titchfield Hotel (the amount is not disclosed); sails with Patrice on the *Zaca* to Port Antonio.

Sun April 6

Warners announces Flynn will star in *The Sea Rogue* in England in the summer; he never does.

Mon April 7

At the Titchfield, greets Lord Munster, Under-Secretary for the Colonies; Mr. E. M. West, Director of Agriculture; and others dignitaries who are touring Port Antonio.

Thu April 10

It is agreed that Flynn will receive $160,000 ($1,572,673 in 2021 value) for 14 weeks of work on THE MASTER OF BALLANTRAE, with $11,428.57 prorated thereafter ($112,333.79 in 2021 value).

Sat April 12

Letter from Warner Bros. U.K. producer Gerry Blattner to director William Keighley: *"We feel now this* [new

With Patrice in the Nassau, Bahamas courthouse - Mon, March 31

Flynn buys Titchfield Hotel

To change name

MOVIE STAR Errol Flynn concluded negotiations yesterday for the purchase of Titchfield Hotel, Port Antonio.

Neither the actor nor his solicitor would reveal anything about the price.

At the Myrtle Bank Hotel yesterday, shortly before he left for Port Antonio, Flynn said he had been negotiating to buy the hotel for some time.

"It is my intention to change its name, make certain extensions for the time being. Of course, all this is separate from the Folly hotel project which my wife plans to carry out shortly."

Titchfield, which is one of the oldest hotels in Jamaica, has a capacity of 50 beds.

Last December it was reported that Mr. Alfred Shaouy, industrial engineer and businessman of New York, and brother of Mrs. Abe Issa, was negotiating to acquire the hotel for the current tourist season.

Since then, there have been reports of other negotiations pending now in the Flynn purchase.

The Daily Gleaner of Jamaica - Thu, April 3

rewrite direction of the story] *falls more into the class of a swashbuckling romantic action packed yarn with rooting interest in the leading man, and less emphasis on the sprawly moody character studies of the original BALLANTRAE. With Errol Flynn playing 'James,' you will better visualize the character of this adventuresome spirited scoundrel – likable withal…"*

Tue April 15
Leaves Jamaica for Hollywood.

Thu April 17
Fencing rehearsal for return to filming of AGAINST ALL FLAGS.

Filming his final work in AGAINST ALL FLAGS - Sat, April 19

Fri April 18
Inter-office memo from unit manager, Percy Ikerd: *"Mr. Flynn complains that his injured foot was bothering him and he was examined and bandaged by his personal physician, Dr. Nolan, at 12:30pm. At 3:50pm it was decided that routine was too difficult for Mr. Flynn with his foot in this condition, and set up was changed to an easier one. Ready to shoot at 4:10pm, total loss of time, 20 minutes."*

Sat April 19
Completes work on AGAINST ALL FLAGS, filming Hawke running a pirate through, crossing to the edge of the crow's nest and climbing over it *(top left)*.

Wed April 23
MARA MARU premieres at the Warner Theater in New York City.

Thu April 24
MARA MARU begins opening around the United States, on this day in Philadelphia.

Wed April 30
Memo from Steve Trilling to a Lou Espinosa: *"Flynn preference suite two people* [London Hotel] *Claridge."*

Fri May 2
Cable from Gerry Blattner to Steve Trilling: *"Have reserved double suites Savoy for Flynn June 9th, Keighley May 19th, as no accommodations Claridges Berkley these dates."*

Mon May 5
Flies in his new Navion aircraft from Los Angeles to Shreveport, LA, with business partner Barry Mahon, who is instructing student-pilot Flynn; after a fueling stop, they continue on to Miami.

Tue May 6
Arrives in Miami, checking in to the Nautilus Hotel, and spends the next few days shopping for a new fishing boat.

Wed May 7
Attends the boxing matches at the Miami Beach Auditorium with Barry Mahon and actor John Loder.

Thu May 8
Letter from Gerry Blattner to Warner Bros. executive producer Steve Trilling: *"Had a talk yesterday with Arthur Abeles* [WB distribution head] *concerning Errol Flynn's arrival. Both Arthur and I feel that we should, if possible, avoid a Press Reception as we think that Flynn is unfortunately not too tactful or diplomatic in his treatment of the Press—which does not go down very well in this country* [England]. *However, if you or Flynn have other definite ideas on this we will of course be glad to hear from you further."*

Sun May 11
Appears on Ed Sullivan's *Toast of the Town*, performing with Paulette Goddard in a spoof of TV detective shows *(bottom left)*; his take for this appearance is $5,000 ($49,146 in 2021 value).

Mon May 12
Returns to Miami with Barry Mahon, checking in to the Nautilus Hotel, and purchases a 40'-long fishing boat, which is scheduled to be delivered to Port Antonio; letter from Gerry Blattner to Steve Trilling: *"This*

With Paulette Goddard on Toast Of The Town - Sun, May 11

will confirm my telephone conversation with you today regarding the necessity of engaging Mr. [Al] Wyatt to double for Flynn in England. Flynn called me from New York to emphasize this fact. Flynn definitely realizes the difficulty in regard to [double] Wayne Coulter and the others he mentioned to you in his telephone conversation of last week. However, he insists that arrangements be made for the one person. He was quite pleased about your engaging [fencing choreographer] Mr. Crean. Errol would like to know when he can receive a script."

Tue May 13

Patrice arrives in Miami; she and Errol name the new fishing boat the *Nautilus* and sail it around the Miami area for a few days; during their stay they accept an offer to model new clothes for a fashion spread in the Miami Daily News, which appears in the June 4th issue of the paper, along with a spot on a local news broadcast that day; they are gifted with the clothes *(top right)*.

Wed May 14

Letter from Steve Trilling to Gerry Blattner: *"Errol Flynn is scheduled to sail on the Liberte out of New York June 11th arriving Plymouth the 17th…"*

Fri May 16

Flies to New York to appear on Ed Sullivan's *Toast of the Town* show; a devastating fire on the Warner Bros. backlot destroys Sound Stage 21, the largest in the world, originally built for THE SEA HAWK.

Mid-May

Flynn's parents are, at this point, active in retirement in Port Antonio: his mother Marelle is manager of the Titchfield Hotel, and his father, Prof. Flynn, is a local school teacher who also works part-time at the hotel.

Sat May 17

Letter from Steve Trilling to Gerry Blattner: *"…To protect ourselves on Errol Flynn's arrangements….besides the 11th June Liberte reservation we also booked passage for Flynn on the Ile de France out of New York 4 June…. in the event we decide to move up sailing dates. Am pretty sure by now you are resolved to adhere to Flynn's original arrival date 17 June – and we could therefore give the 4th sailing date to [production manager, Frank] Mattison….or have him fly so he is there while the sets are being constructed and locations selected…"*

Sun May 18

Acts with Paulette Goddard in another private eye skit on Ed Sullivan's *Toast Of The Town* TV show.

Tue May 20

With Mr. and Mrs. Thompson Andrews at the Stork Club.

Wed May 21

Flies back to Miami.

Thu May 22

Flies in his private plane with Barry Mahon to Kingston, Jamaica, staying at the Myrtle Bank Hotel.

Fri May 23

Flies his plane to his Boston estates property in Port Antonio, Jamaica, landing on his new airstrip.

Sun May 25

Letter from Flynn in Port Antonio, Jamaica, to Steve Trilling: *Hello dear boy! Can you give me an answer to a couple of questions? First, the script – so far I haven't even seen a draft, so if it's available would you airmail me one down here? No. 2. In making personal living arrangements in England Pat + I don't know how to proceed in the absense [sic] of any future activity you may have in mind for her. In other words I've been thinking of living as near the actual shooting as possible. But if Pat's going to work + I'm along alone, any old humble abode, a bed of straw and a jug of ale or mead for a pillow, will do. If Pat's going to have some time I guess we'll live in London at the Savoy. Quite unofficially could you give me some clue as to when she's likely to be needed? So I can make plans accordingly? And please, dear boy, don't suggest a suspension*

Modeling Mal Marshall clothes with Patrice for the Miami Daily News - May; he could be seen wearing this shirt on occasion for several years

because the dear girl wants to work – odd tho' it strikes me...Yours — Errol"

Thu May 29

Letter from William Keighley to Steve Trilling: *"…You will be most enthusiastic about the following. As we have planned it, Flynn will never be in kilts. The first scene where he rides the horse it would be incorrect to have the kilts; the same thing is true when he leaves for the battle of Culloden; he returns in the same costume; for the pirate sequence, apparently he would not wear kilts; and when he returns as an English gentleman; so you have no worries kilt-wise with Flynn..."*

Fri May 30

Flies commercially to New York via stopover in Miami.

Sat May 31

Letter from Steve Trilling to Gerry Blattner: *"…Flynn's hair has become somewhat darker in recent years – therefore Max Factor is making the wigs the same color as the wig used by Flynn in his most recent Technicolor picture AGAINST TWO FLAGS [sic] completed at Universal about six months ago. If you and Keighley want to lighten the color…this of course can be handled in England – you probably will be making some preliminary advance makeup and wardrobe tests anyway…"* Letter from Steve Trilling to Gerry Blattner: *"…please be sure that the hotels are put on record in this respect [not to allow cast and crew to withdraw funds directly from hotels] especially with Errol Flynn coming into England. As I advised you before (confidentially) Flynn is notorious here for leaving unpaid personal balances to be picked up later by Warner Bros.…"*

Sun June 1

Appears in the audience of *Toast of the Town* with Paulette Goddard and Basil Rathbone.

Mon June 2

Flies to Miami; while there he purchases another plane, a Republic RC-3 amphibian aircraft from the Roberts Flying School, which will be delivered to Kingston; letter from Steve Trilling to Steve Blattner: *"…Am attaching copy of a note received from Errol Flynn – which is for your information. We have plans for Pat Wymore….therefore she is not now scheduled to go to England with Errol. Flynn has by now received the first 44 pages of BALLANTRAE dated 6/10/52 – Whatever additional pages are received prior his leaving for England, will see he also gets a copy. Please note his comment about living arrangements….you will just have to use your good judgment when Flynn arrives and make accommodations fit the best requirements, because it is impossible to finalize anything until he actually arrives and you are able to determine what you want to furnish him and what will satisfy him. I would keep the Savoy reservations for the time being….am sure you can always dispose of them if he doesn't like or want them – but again you will just have to take it in stride when Flynn arrives. It is quite possible there could be a change of plans and Wymore would still go along…so protect yourself until Flynn arrives in Merrie old London…."*

Wed June 4

Flies to Jamaica; the *Miami Daily News* features an article in its women's section with Errol and Patrice posing in Mal Marshall wardrobe.

Thu June 5

Cable from Gerry Blattner to Steve Trilling: *"Suggest Flynn bring his normal Technicolor makeup matching hair coloring he chooses."*

Fri June 6

Flynn calls Steve Trilling from Port Antonio to inform him of a travel itinerary that includes flying to New York June 10th and arriving in England the morning of the 12th.

Sun June 8

$14,000 ($137,609 in 2021 value) in damages is awarded to Flynn in the McMartin case, but court costs are reduced from f5,712 to fl,478; DEEP SEA FISHING is first shown, on this date on American television over WFIL, Philadelphis, PA.

Mon June 9

In a memo from Steve Trilling to Mr. Espinosa, Flynn's tentative itinerary is given as leaving Kingston, Jamaica, via KLM Airlines on June 9th at 2:45, arriving in Miami at 6:55pm; leaving Miami at 11:59pm on Eastern flight #636W, arriving in New York on June 10th at 6:10am. Trilling continues: *"Please arrange met airport and delivered Hampshire House per our prior arrangements."* Leaving New York on June 11th; Flynn's valet is Yves Malise, sometimes referred to as Malvisi. *"Flynn's excess*

Errol and Patrice in an advertisement for Robert Burns Cigarillos - June

baggage is to accompany Malvisi on Liberte." Flynn's reservation is changed to a BOAC flight #BA510, leaving Idlewild Airport at 5pm on June 11th.

Tue June 10

Is in New York; dines at El Morocco; telegram to Steve Trilling: THINK BALLANTRYE [sic] SCRIPT FIRST CLASS FLYING TOMORROW EVERYTHING FINE; telegram from Steve Trilling to Flynn: DEAR BARON HAPPY HAVE YOUR REACTION TO SCRIPT. KEIGHLEY TOLD ME ON PHONE FEW DAYS AGO BALANCE [of script] WILL MATCH IT SO WE SHOULD HAVE EXCITING PICTURE. HAVE PLEASANT TRIP KEEP PUNCHING FOR YOUR DEAR ALMA MATER. BEST STEVE. Letter from Gerry Blattner to W. Hoffin, Esq., manager of the Savoy Hotel in London: *"As we are now about to start production on our next Picture, I would like to take this opportunity of formally, and confidentially, bringing to your notice a point of policy this Company has had to consider, which is to ask you to be good enough not to make any cash advances to any persons who are employed by, or connected with, this Company, and may be staying in your Hotel, unless previously authorized by myself in writing....Reference Errol Flynn, who will be arriving in this country on Thursday next, the 12th June, and for whom you have reserved a suite at our request, I would point out that, in this particular case, we have an arrangement by which Mr. Flynn will be responsible for his own Hotel account, which will you kindly render to him weekly for his personal payment."* Telegram from Mr. Mayer to Steve Trilling: FLYNN REQUESTING SUBSTANTIAL ADVANCE. ARE YOU AVAILABLE PHONE CALL; telegram from Gerry Blattner to Steve Trilling: AFTER PRESSURE PUBLICITY DEPARTMENT [Arthur] ABELES SELF FEEL WISE HAVE SMALL RECEPTION FLYNNS ARRIVAL. ASSUME MRS. FLYNN NOT COMING.

Wed June 11

Telegram from Steve Trilling to Gerry Blattner: FLYNN FORCED CHANGE PAN AMERICAN FLIGHT 100 LEAVING NEW YORK 4 PM ELEVENTH.

Thu June 12

Arrives in London to begin shooting THE MASTER OF BALLANTRAE and is met by his valet, Yves Malvisi; checks into the Savoy Hotel.

Fri June 13

Is honored at a dinner reception at the Savoy *(top right)*.

At London's Savoy Hotel - Fri, June 13

Sat June 14

Travels to Northampton to open the Northampton Repertory Theatre's Garden Party at Broughton Hall, the home of Mrs. Helen Panther, the theater's chairman of the directors; over 2,500 guests attend *(bottom three)*

Errol Flynn's return to Northampton - Sat, June 14: Above left, speaking to 2,500 fans at Broughton Hall; above center, backstage at the repertory with actress Margaret Denyer; above right, on the repertory stage again after 18 years

Tue June 17

At the races at Ascot; Steve Trilling sends a note to Gerry Blattner informing him that the knee boots sent over to be used by Flynn were custom-made for Flynn for ADVENTURES OF DON JUAN, at a cost of *"$100 per*

With Diana Dors at Morden Hall in Surrey, England - Sat, June 21

pair, total value $700 [$6,880 in 2021 value]…*and are a permanent part of Flynn's period costume wardrobe."* The seven pairs sent were: two black suedes, two brown suedes, two red kids, and one black kid.

Fri June 20
Flynn's 43rd birthday.

Sat June 21
Attends the Film Stars Garden Party at Morden Hall in Surrey, where he meets with British actress Diana Dors *(top left)* and Indian actress Nimmi *(top right)*; in an interview for the North American Newspaper Alliance, Nimmi said that Flynn *"admire my little feet. He ask permission to tickle my toes. I say no."*

Mon June 23
The New York Times reports that Flynn's *"recently published novel 'Showdown' was banned in Ireland today on the ground that it is indecent and obscene."*

Tue June 24
His measurements for the wardrobe department on this day are: 43" chest, 34½ waist, 33½ inseam, 16" collar, 35" sleeve, 7⅜ (or 23½") hat, 10½ shoe U.S., and 6'2" height.

Wed June 25
Has dinner with starlet June Thorburn.

Fri June 27
With Roger Livesey, begins his first day of filming THE MASTER OF BALLANTRAE at Fistral Bay in Newquay, Cornwall *(left and below)*; telegram from the studio to Gerry Blattner: REQUESTED

With Indian film actress, Nimmi at Morden Hall in Surrey England - Sat, June 21

Above and right, speaking with director William Keighley at Newquay, Cornwall - Tue, June 27

LOCAL MCA OFFICE THEY SHOULD ADVISE FLYNN WE WOULD CONSIDER REFUSAL TO WORK SUNDAYS A BREACH OF CONTRACT. IF NECESSARY YOU CAN ALSO SO ADVISE FLYNN.

Sat June 28

Continues filming with Roger Livesey at Fistral Bay.

Mon June 30

Begins filming the courtyard sequence.

Tue July 1

Letter from William Keighley to Steve Trilling: *"…Start of the duel. Erroll [sic; Keighley repeatedly misspells Flynn's name] looked wonderful and did well though it did take about eleven starts to get one of the scenes. The scene is played mostly in close shots as it is the first opportunity we have of knowing these two brothers and their feelings towards each other…Fight well rehearsed and should be cleaned up [finished] tomorrow."*

Wed July 2

Letter from William Keighley to Steve Trilling: *"Finished the Jamie-Henry [Flynn—Anthony Steele] scene and went into the duel…Erroll misses [fencing master] Fred Caven[s] but has been very co-operative being on time for all shots."* A second unit crew in Glencoe, Scotland, films a double for Flynn marching away from the camera.

Thu July 3

Cable from Gerry Blattner to Steve Trilling: YOU SHOULD HAVE INFORMED FLYNN REGARDING SUNDAY SINCE IN FIFTEEN YEARS HAS ONLY WORKED TWO SUNDAYS BOTH LOCATION. Letter from Flynn to his accountant Al Blum: *"….I have large cash expenditures for which it is impossible to get receipts….At the present moment I am trying to rent a house and will have to dish out £200 or £300 [$12,523 in 2021 value] to the lady owner to get her to let me move in earlier. She will give no receipt for this as she wants it in cash and apparently doesn't want anyone to know about it….Warners in their usual charming manner, have pulled a fast one on me….THEY WANT ME TO WORK ON SUNDAYS."* Letter from William Keighley to Steve Trilling: *"Our usual poor start, this time the fault of Tony Steele who is supposed to have misunderstood the call [time] and arrived at nine – the consequence first shot after ten. It was a dueling shot and had to be practiced by him and Erroll. The latter continues to be wonderful, always on time and works hard on the duel. It has been difficult for him as Steele is left handed and Crean while an excellent Coach uses a style entirely different from that of Caven[s]. It would spare time and money, I feel certain, if you would send Caven[s] over for the sword play in Palermo where work permits are not a problem…Our most difficult scene is behind us, that between Erroll and Henry [Steele], including the duel…"*

Fri July 4

Letter from William Keighley to Steve Trilling: *"[Anthony] Steele threw his knee out running from the spot where he thinks he's killed Jamie….I don't think it will be noticed…"*

Sun July 6

Filming scenes of the scaffold being built and Jessie (Yvonne Furneaux) seeing it.

Mon July 7

Moves into a house at 15 Church Row, in the Hampstead area of London, where he will live while filming at the Elstree Studios; letter from William Keighley to Steve Trilling: *"Finished Jessie getting into the house and the gallows shots also the redcoats trying to enter the house."* Letter from Frank Mattison to Steve Trilling: *"Rejoined the [second] unit at Ballachulish for the Glencoe sequence [using a double for Flynn]…When [the soldiers] lined up…it was the saddest excuse for men I have seen – not but one man the size of Flynn – the rest young school boys and small men."*

Tue July 8

Filming the dance sequence (without Beatrice Campbell); more second unit filming of troops in Scotland; postcard from Genevieve (Mrs. William) Keighley to the Trillings: *"This you will never believe – but it's true. Last nite Errol called to say he had moved + was afraid Bill + studio did not have his new number + wanted to be sure to get his 'call' [to report]! P.S. He said to tell Bill he loved him + not to make the 'call' too early!!"*

Wed July 9

Rain prevents second unit filming in Scotland; letter from William Keighley to Steve Trilling: *"…Erroll refused to work after six but we had other work to do without him…This studio is fine for an average [size] production…When you need the head of wardrobe for Erroll she's fifteen miles away in London working with Beatrice Campbell."* Letter from Gerry Blattner to Walter L. Jacks of Warner Bros. Paris: *"I have this morning had another talk with Mr. Robin Fox, of M.C.A. London, and he advises me that Errol Flynn considers that the total [limousine] hire charge amounting to Fr. 44,000 Warners should pay 50% of this as a publicity expense. I would add that Mr. Flynn did not go to Paris at my request,*

With Sam Kydd and Anthony Steele; the photo is signed by Flynn to his daughters: "Sam [Deirdre] + Rory! Like this horse darling girls? Tony [Steele] on [my] left plays my younger brother. Baron"

With Felix Aylmer, Beatrice Campbell, Anthony Steele, and Mervyn Johns - July

With Beatrice Campbell - Wed, July 16

and would suggest, therefore, that you refer to New York the question of recoupment."

Thu July 10

Finishes filming in the courtyard; William Keighley to Steve Trilling: *"…Errol broke a tooth which was put back on a temporary basis. He's having it attended to tonight…"* Rain again prevents second unit filming in Scotland.

Fri July 11

Filming in the castle; Beatrice Campbell begins work on the film; rain again prevents second unit filming in Scotland.

Sat July 12

Letter from William Keighley to Steve Trilling: *"Back to work in the morning [Sunday] with or without Erroll…"* Rain prevents second unit filming in Scotland for a third straight day.

Sun July 13

Because of rain in Scotland, the second unit can only get a shot of a herald on a horse.

Mon July 14

Letter from William Keighley to Steve Trilling: *"Tomorrow we shoot the third section dancing sequence."*

Wed July 16

Filming dance sequences *(top left)*; letter from Gerry Blattner to Jack Warner at Villa Aujourd'hui, Cap d' Antibes: *"…The Picture is now proceeding smoothly – Keighley has settled in very well: Flynn is on top of his form, and at the moment has given us no trouble at all. "*

Thu July 17

Letter from William Keighley to Steve Trilling: *"Tomorrow we start the blow-up of Erroll at the party and then into the fight."*

Fri July 18

Letter from William Keighley to Steve Trilling: *"Flynn knew his dialogue and the scene was very well played. [This coming] Sunday I had hoped to start the fight but as Erroll will probably not appear I'll be obliged to jump into the middle of it and pick up various cuts without him and use a double whenever possible. This takes more time but probably saves an explosion. Erroll continues to work well insofar as his role is concerned, likes the script and is happy generally. I started on a close up of him this A.M. and he was right on time…"*

Sun July 20

Letter from William Keighley to Steve Trilling: *"…Erroll was finally called for Sunday though I had advised it being done weeks ago simply to clear the air and not postpone the inevitable crisis. He arrived on time but after my first shot a close up of Tony Steele backed up by a crowd it took one hour and thirty minutes to get the next shot – one of Erroll – Now he was ill and cannot work tomorrow and it's really costing oodles of money – today, alone with all those extras and laborers on double time. I'm sure a deal should be made with Erroll. In principal [sic] he must report on Sunday but if he holds up production and it would be difficult to prove he did it purposely wouldn't it be wiser to pay him extra which I believe he would make a deal on. I know legally you are right – but –He played the big scene which I made in long shots starting the big fight. It was so late when I got them that I made a shot of Tony throwing him the sword and that was the end 5:50 P.M. Erroll played the scene excellently and knew the long speech perfectly. I got it the second take…I am shooting portions of the fight tomorrow without Erroll and no time will be lost."*

As Jamie Dury in
THE MASTER OF BALLANTRAE

Mon July 21

Ill; does not work on *"a really hot day"* (William Keighley to Steve Trilling); telegram from Gerry Blattner to Steve Trilling: HAD WARNERS DOCTOR VISIT FLYNN TONIGHT AWAITING THEIR REPORT. FLYNNS DOCTOR PHONED STATING FLYNN SHOULD NOT WORK TWENTYSECOND BUT FLYNN REPORTING FOR WORK AGAINST HIS DOCTORS ADVICE / SUGGEST REQUEST NEW YORK OFFICE IMMEDIATELY DISPATCH FLYNN PARCELS SAME CONTENTS YOU SENT ME DURING ILLNESS. Flynn's medical report is signed off by Dr. Ian M. Hall; his salary for that day is deducted; around this time, Jack Warner is insisting on cutting down costs on the picture; he had earmarked $1,250,000, but it is now being predicted to end up costing $1,400,000 ($13,760,891 in 2021 value); telegram from Steve Trilling to Gerry Blattner: CONFIDENTIALLY PREFER WE NOT SEND FLYNN PACKAGES YOU SUGGESTED YOUR CABLE, FLYNN SALARY AND EXPENSES FOR THIS PURPOSE. IF YOU DID NOT PROMISE TRY AVOID DOING SO.

Tue July 22

Letter from William Keighley to Steve Trilling: *"Tomorrow we pretty much finish the fight with little running over to*

Thursday." Letter from Frank Mattison to Steve Trilling: *"…We also ran into Flynn trouble – in working on Sunday….on Friday he told me –and others interested – that the hay fever – or cold – or both –was affecting his sinus and he had a doctor treating him. Having worked with Erroll for the past 15 years I have suffered through several illnesses with him. Almost know what the result will be – an advance – so in talking I mentioned the call. He resented [him] and his agents being threatened but said, 'I'll come in for the call on Sunday even if I have to get out of a sick bed to do it.'….Sunday when I came to the studio Mr. K[eighley] was prepared to shoot all day without Erroll if need be but Erroll was in the studio ready to work and did. You know the story – it has happened in Burbank – Flynn's doctor appears, tells us Flynn should stay home, rest, etc….Yesterday – Monday – we got a very good days work without him. Today Flynn was in and we had 12 set-ups so this is the second good day in a row. Having made many Flynn pictures I have found we keep him working best when there are no arguments, or threats, or retaliations, or bickerings. The main idea being to keep him in front of the camera and get the picture finished which I hope we can do from now on. Incidentally, we are having the usual dames troubles. It seems as if there are always pimps around with dames, trying to get in with Flynn…."*

Wed July 23

Letter from Frank Mattison to Steve Trilling: *"Yesterday, Tues: July 22, 13 set-ups. One of the best days yet. Today, Wed, seven set-ups. But there is a reason Errol gave us a good day Tuesday and today. Right after the first shot with him, someone handed him a bill for close to 200£ [$ 8,341.59 in 2021 value] for his auto transportation. You must know what happened…."* Letter from William Keighley to Steve Trilling: *"…At ten thirty we were again ready when Erroll blew the top of the stage off. He'd been given a bill at this inopportune moment for his car. What his arrangements are concerning this matter I don't know but it was an hour before he calmed down. Once on the set he really works and he is doing the duels very well indeed – working really like mad. This was not enough – so in a short rehearsal after the shooting the fencing instructor slipped on the stairs. It is feared he cracked a bone and will not be able to fence tomorrow. Someone else has been secured but as it was all layed out by Crean it's likely to be a serious blow."*

Thu July 24

Letter from William Keighley to Steve Trilling: *"The accident to the fencing instructor last evening proved to be a chipped bone so he was unable to do more than hobble around with the aid of a cane. As I was using his back in all fights with Erroll doubling for all the English officers it meant that some other expert fencer had to be found. One was located last evening and fortunately Erroll had enough confidence in him to duel against him and that proved really lucky as frankly I rather expected him to refuse as he is rightly very careful about his opponent's ability…We did much better than hoped for. Erroll worked like mad and by six twenty he was completely pooped – asked me, jokingly, if I was trying to kill him. You will be amazed at him in this fight – nothing like it for Erroll since Captain Blood. We'll finish it tomorrow thank goodness… Erroll's knuckles have been pretty well battered by some of his less experienced fencers. [When] I see he is worried I change them before he has time to ask. He's been deeply appreciative of this and it shows in his performance."* Telegram from publicist Jerry Deming to Steve Trilling: WILL SERIOUSLY HAMPER RELATIONSHIP FLYNN IF PRESS CAR ACCOUNT AS WEDNESDAY HE WALKED OFF SET / THIS REASON HOLDING UP SHOOTING THIRTY MINUTES / THREATENING PHONE JL [Warner] / SUGGEST YOU ENDEAVOR DEDUCT IT FINAL SETTLEMENT.

Fri July 25

Filming of montage sequences; telegram from Steve Trilling to Jerry Deming: THOROUGHLY UNDERSTAND YOUR PROBLEMS BUT WE MUST TAKE STAND SOMEWHERE OR FLYNN WILL OVERRIDE YOU RIGHT DOWN LINE. WE HAD PRIOR EXPERIENCE SO YOU PROFIT BY IT. UNLESS YOU DEEM COMPLETELY INADVISABLE RELAY FOLLOWING CABLE TO FLYNN. Letter from William Keighley to Steve Trilling: *"…Erroll's next picture will be with Mike Frankovitch and Monty Marks, 'Fire Over Africa' with Jack Cardiff directing or at least so Cardiff told me today. It is supposed to follow immediately the closing of our film. Aside from waiting several times for Erroll today it was normal."* Telegram from Gerry Blattner to Steve Trilling: THANKS YOUR CABLE 25TH / HOWEVER NOT USED AS HAD LONG CORDIAL TALK FLYNN TONIGHT / HE PROMISED EVERY COOPERATION THEREFORE WILL HOLD YOUR MESSAGE FOR IMMEDIATE USE IF OCCASION ARISES.

Sun July 27

Flynn does not work; letter from Frank Mattison to Steve Trilling: *"Mr. Blattner tells me that he and Flynn had a few drinks –or was it A drink? And Flynn has promised to help us get through with this picture as soon as possible…I suppose you have heard that Errol plans to make a picture over here as soon as this one is finished. It is no secret – Jack Cardiff our 1st cameraman tells me he is to direct it."*

Filming the duel at Elstree Studios, northwest of London -July

Filming the prison scene - Thu, July 31

Gable And Flynn
At French Resorts

BEAUVILLE, France (UP) — Clark Gable, shooing off photographers, and Errol Flynn, shuttling between golf and the casino, Tuesday led an American "invasion" of channel coast resorts traditionally filled by the British. "We've never seen so many Americans," hotel owners reported.

*The Corvallis Gazette-Times of Texas
Tue, August 5*

With Yvonne Furneaux - Thu, August 7

Mon July 28

Filming of Col. Banks condemning Flynn and Livesey; letter from William Keighley to Steve Trilling: *"…The latest on Erroll   He is to do a story* [a film, CROSSED SWORDS] *in Italy for Milton Krims before the African one -- or – so 'tis said. I've read it and it's awful."*

Tue July 29

Letter from William Keighley to Steve Trilling: *"…Start tomorrow on the scene in Alison's room with Jessie. We moved over to the set late this afternoon and the girls know their dialogue…Then into the spiral staircase outside the cell door.* [I'm] *asking that Carl Coombs be sent to Palermo rather than an English publicity man. Some of them are a bad influence on Erroll but Coombs is not…"*

Wed July 30

Letter from William Keighley to Steve Trilling: *"…Shot the complete* [Yvonne] *Furneaux scene today… also shots of the prison escape, which we continue tomorrow…"*

Thu July 31

Filming the prison scene *(top left)*; letter from William Keighley to Steve Trilling: *"…We have one complication. Erroll is screaming for a hot love scene in the pirate sequence* [later in Palermo]. *He wants Marianne* [Gillian Lynne] *to make a furious play for him he of course rejecting her for love of Alison. What to do?…"* At a surprise birthday party for Beatrice Campbell.

Fri August 1

Letter from Frank Mattison to Steve Trilling: *"Flynn continues to ask for* [Al] *Wyatt, dresser, and stand-in and double, being handy with a sword…Pat Crean pleases Errol and makes him look good as a fencer, with Wyatt taking the beating on the knuckles 'as' Errol fencing the actor who plays 'Arnaud.' It will work out Okeh."*

Sat August 2 and Sun August 3

With Clark Gable on the French Riviera, playing golf and visiting the casinos (8/2), and fishing together off the coast (8/3).

Tue August 5

Letter from William Keighley to Steve Trilling: *"At breakfast 4:15 A.M. the telephone rang and the message was as follows Erroll Flynn has a broken tooth and Tony Steele injured his knee again and is confined to his bed. What next? We shot around Flynn who finally appeared on the set close to form and did a fair amount of work…"* Letter from Frank Mattison to Steve Trilling: *"Errol's tooth had to be attached and set again – which sent him to the dentist. And being the day after a* [Summer Bank] *holiday, it was noon before dentist showed up, with Errol waiting in his office and did not get him until after lunch."*

Wed August 6

Filming on the prison set and Flynn riding into the castle.

Thu August 7

Filming the castle sequence, Jessie's death *(bottom left)*, and *"Flynn and Burke through the flames into the tunnel whence they will be pursued tomorrow by the soldiers."* William Keighley to Steve Trilling

Fri August 8

Finishes filming the castle sequences; letter from William Keighley to Steve Trilling: *"…Regarding Erroll. It is not a question of acceding to his whims. You are saddled with him, let's face it, and our desire is to get the maximum amount of work from the young man. After all these years you know you have a problem child on your hands. He'll never do anything to break the contract but it is so easy to find that a make-up is ruined, a wig has gone wrong and needs redoing, an old back injury etc. etc…Handling makes a director a neurologist who would like to effect a cure. Finding that impossible he tries the only remedies he knows to keep the malady in check. I have never had the slightest difficulty with him on the set. He does whatever I ask him without question. That in itself is an achievement but they do have difficulty getting him on the set and dressed."* Letter from Frank Mattison to Steve Trilling: *"Other problems Errol Flynn's passport has expired. I am going to the American Embassy Saturday morning (tomorrow) at 11 a.m. with him – he must appear in person. I only learned about it when transportation man told me that Errol wanted to vacation this week and in Ireland. But passport was N/G: he can't even go to Italy until he gets a new one – will advise you later if there is any trouble..Saw some rushes of Errol Sunday – he is fighting, handling the sword – like he did ten years ago –and he looks better than I have seen him for some years past."*

Sat August 9

With Frank Mattison at the American Embassy in London to renew his passport.

Sun August 10

Filming Jessie's cottage, a night sequence; letter from Frank Mattison to Steve Trilling: *"To-day was another good day, shooting wise. Tony Steele and Errol both in and working; our best Sunday."*

Mon August 11

Frank Mattison accompanies Flynn to the passport office, reporting to Steve Trilling that it went *"without any trouble or incident."* Filming a night sequence in the exterior village street; William Keighley writes to Steve Trilling that he hopes *"to finish the street tomorrow then move inside for the exit from the tunnel sequence."*

Tue August 12

Letter from William Keighley to Steve Trilling: *"We had good weather today and finished the Ballantrae village shots [on the back lot]."*

Wed August 13

Telegram from Gerry Blattner to Steve Trilling: FLYNN REQUESTING WE CONTINUE HIS ENGLISH WEEKLY EXPENSES ALLOWANCE. HE UNDERTAKING PAY ALL HIS LIRE HOTEL LIVING EXPENSES OTHER THAN TRANSPORTATION TO AND FROM ITALY / I THINK MEETING HIS REQUEST MIGHT SAVE ARGUMENT LATER AS TO WHAT WERE LEGITIMATE ITALIAN EXPENSES. Cable from Steve Trilling to Gerry Blattner: OKAY TO CONTINUE FLYNN WEEKLY EXPENSE ALLOWANCE WHILE HE ON LOCATION IN ITALY. ONLY HOWEVER BE SURE HAVE LETTER AGREEMENT THIS EFFECT SIGNED BY FLYNN THAT HE PERSONALLY RESPONSIBLE FOR ALL ASSUMES ANY AND ALL LIVING EXPENSES HE INCURS ITALY LOCATION. PROTECT YOURSELF ACCORDINGLY WITH LOCAL HOTELS RESTAURANTS. Letter from William Keighley to Steve Trilling: *"You know what Erroll is – wonderful with me personally but the assistants find it most difficult to produce [deliver him] on the set."* Telegram from Gerry Blattner to Steve Trilling: FLYNN STATES HIS CONTRACT CALLS FOR PUBLICITY WHILST LOCATION / REQUESTING ENGLISH PUBLICITY MAN GO PALERMO.

Thu August 14

Filming the exit from the tunnel *(top right)*, though the circuits blew out at some point during the day; William Keighley to Steve Trilling: *"…Errol very co-operative today. Sat on set all day…"* Telegram from Steve Trilling to Gerry Blattner: NO PROVISION FLYNN CONTRACT SEND PUBLICITY MAN ITALY OR ANYWHERE INCUR NO UNNECESSARY EXPENSE.

Filming the tunnel exit with Roger Livesy - Thu, August 14

Fri August 15

Leaves London for Paris.

Mon August 18

Reports to the location at Palermo, Italy; he is staying at the Villa Igiea Hotel.

Thu August 21

Letter from Frank Mattison to Steve Trilling: *"Still yelling for ship to shore service…production dept. claimed impossible to secure. Yet when Mr. Flynn had to wait and ride in a tub-boat, Errol himself went to telephone and 1 hour later Cris-Craft speed boat came out – Prince Lanza's Craft but this was no good for the Company, as operator would only take orders from Flynn. We did some shooting but less than half a day's work."*

Fri August 22

Ill; does not work; heavy seas result in limited filming.

Sat August 23

Calm seas but trouble getting boat service, which delayed filming.

Sun August 24

No filming; letter from William Keighley in Palermo to Steve Trilling: *"…We lost Monday and part of Tuesday and more than half of Thursday…I'm up to my knees in the tea being handed around and I trip over the sandwiches – Eat, eat eat all day long and when they're not eating they're drinking – the crew works but they're too damn many of them."*

Wed August 27

Is unable to work until 4:30pm.

Thu August 28

Letter from Frank Mattison to Steve Trilling: *"Yesterday Errol was sick and I couldn't get him out to the boats before 3 P.M. and Mr. Keighley had to shoot around him up until that time. Sickness has been quite common, nearly everyone has had some bit of it…Tomorrow Friday we hope to finish the 'Sea Nettle' [ship] so it can be converted to the 'galleon' – we will also finish the sloop tomorrow."*

Filming in Palermo, Italy - August

With Charles Goldner and Gillian Lynne at Tonnara Florio in the Arenella area of Palermo - September

In Palermo with Jacques Berthier and his wife Lily Baron, and (behind) Roger Livesy and cinematographer Jack Cardiff

Fri August 29 and Sat August 30

Filming on the small ship and (on 8/30) on the large ship.

Mon September 1

First day of work on the ramp; Flynn's "lawyer," Barry Mahon, is on the set, informing Frank Mattison of Flynn's invitation to the Venice Film Festival.

Wed September 3

Work on the ramp continues; asks permission of Frank Mattison to attend the Venice Film Festival; letter from Gerry Blattner to Flynn: *"Dear Errol, I understand you have been invited to attend the Venice Film Festival during the coming week-end, I must however point out to you that if you leave Palermo for the Festival your absence will very seriously interfere with the shooting schedule and result in serious financial loss to the Company. Under these circumstances it is with regret that I must ask you to decline the invitation. With kindest personal regards, Sincerely, G. Blattner."* Gerry Blattner withdraws this note to Flynn and refers the matter to Steve Trilling; a wire arrives from Warner to Errol, presumably saying no to his request to go to Venice.

Thu September 4

Delays filming by half an hour; writer-director Milton Krims visits the set; letter from Flynn in Palermo to Jack Warner: *"....Jack I am sure you will be the first to appreciate production problems over here. The more time available for pre-production, the better the picture....I am making this a personal request, Jack, and while I don't think it is good taste to remind you of past requests you have put up to me I recall our talk in London when you told me how important it was that I gave 'Ballantrae' my fullest cooperation. I promised you I would....I don't know what reports you've had, but I know myself that I have kept my word to you and have given 'Ballantrae' all I could... Incidentally 'Fire Over Africa'* [Flynn's independent potential film] *will be in Technicolor, a good gutty action story with a first class cast, and if you are interested in releasing same I have made no deal as yet and would be happy to talk business..."* (the film was eventually made as *Malaga* without Flynn); letter from Steve Trilling to John J. Glynn, Warner Bros. New York: *"Have turned over to Roy Obringer your correspondence of 26 August concerning the Paris car rental by Errol Flynn; Roy will try to effect collection from Flynn's last salary check for this picture – this, of course, confidential. However, so that we may be protected legally….you please instruct Paris (Jack or Westreich) to immediately send Flynn a letter along the following lines so that there can be no assumption of Warner Bros. responsibility for this charge...'Dear Mr. Flynn: The bill for the rental of a limousine for your personal services while you visited Paris on – (date) has been presented to us. It amounts to Francs 44,000 which at the rate of Francs 372.5 is the American dollar equivalent of $118.39* [$1,163.68 in 2021 value]. *As a convenience to you we are making payment, but shall expect reimbursement from you. Our Messrs. Jacks and Redon specifically pointed out to you at the time that our company had no cars in Paris, and that any car rental would be at your own expense, to which you consented; they also advised you the approximate cost of the various kinds of cars available for rental.'...Prior to Flynn's arrival in Europe we requested Blattner to warn everybody concerned not to indebt themselves in any manner for Flynn, as we had made arrangements to pay Flynn a fixed sum of money covering all personal expenses. Although this is a small amount it does create unnecessary work to effect collection….and would appreciate your again advising these people to have Flynn pay as he goes along and not force us into the position of paying a bill and then trying to collect from Flynn, as in this instance."*

Off the coast of Palermo, manning a speedboat rented from Prince Raimondo Lanza - September

Fri September 5 and Sat September 6

More filming, and (on 9/6) a slow day of filming due to the *"trick"* fireworks on Mendoza's (Charles Goldner) hat (note from William

Keighley); OBJECTIVE, BURMA! reopens at the Warner cinema in London, the film now including a new prologue clarifying the British involvement in that theater of the war.

Sun September 7

Filming begins of the galleon sequences.

Tue September 9

Letter from Gerry Blattner to Steve Trilling: *"…Flynn has been loaned a speed craft by a local prince [Raimondo Lanza] on the strict understanding that although the Company paid a very good hire for the launch and for the petrol consumed, nobody but Flynn was allowed to use it unless expressly invited by Flynn. The latter point appears to have irritated Keighley as I understand he refused to go with Flynn and demanded another launch for his own personal use, which left us with a shortage of launches for moving the company and materials which became more irritating as some of the launches proved to be unreliable…I have had several talks with Errol Flynn which have been most cordial – he is enthralled with the location and went out of his way to tell me that he felt the whole location had been very well managed. In fact he is thoroughly enjoying himself, has no beefs at all so far as the Company is concerned, except I regret to say he indicated that there is a very definite lack of sympathy between himself and Keighley which wants close watching."*

Sun September 14

Telegram from Gerry Blattner to Steve Trilling: FLYNN STARTED AGITATION FOR [Al] WYATT, AS ENGLISH DOUBLE HAS FRACTURED ANKLE. KEIGHLEY ARRANGED SUITABLE SUBSTITUTE BUT HE BELIEVE FLYNN WILL BE DIFFICULT STATING ACCORDING TO CONTRACT HE HAS RIGHT APPROVAL OF DOUBLE.

Mon September 15

Ill; does not work; telegram from Steve Trilling to Gerry Blattner: ADVISE FLYNN PLEASE READ CONTRACT. NO APPROVAL DOUBLE. YOU HOLD FIRM YOUR POSITION AND IF FLYNN CREATES DIFFICULTY HAVE ATTORNEYS SERVE LEGAL NOTICE ON HIM. WILL HOLD HIM RESPONSIBLE AND EXERCISE RIGHTS UNDER CONTRACT. Telegram from Gerry Blattner to Steve Trilling: FLYNN IN BED ALL TODAY STATES DUE TO STOMACH TROUBLE. AM DUBIOUS. Cable from Jack Warner to Flynn: SORRY TO HEAR YOU NOT FEELING WELL BUT THESE TURBULENT TIMES THINGS JUST TOUGH FOR US AS THEY ARE FOR YOU. AM SORRY. COUNTING ON YOU TO FINISH PICTURE QUICKLY POSSIBLE. REGARDS. Telegram from Steve Trilling to Flynn: THANKS YOUR LETTER MOST HUMOROUS AND REALIZE SERIOUSNESS THIS ONE TIME. HAPPY NOT WITH YOU. PAT EXCELLENT IN PICTURE. HOPE YOU NOW FEELING BETTER. BESTEST STEVE.

Tue September 16

Telegram from Gerry Blattner to Steve Trilling: FLYNN OKAY TODAY. COMPANY PHYSICIAN EXAMINED FLYNN YESTERDAY NO TEMPERATURE COMPLAINED STOMACH PAINS SIMILAR THOSE EXPERIENCED PREVIOUSLY BY SOME MEMBERS COMPANY. THEY MOSTLY TOOK PILLS AND CARRIED ON WORK.

Sat September 20

Telegram from Gerry Blattner to Steve Trilling: FLYNN RAISING DIFFICULTIES ABOUT FLYING MONDAY VIA AIRCRAFT ROME PANAMERICAN ROME PARIS VIA PARIS LONDON / WANTS GO BY TRAIN / IF INSISTS WOULD DELAY SHOOTING TWO DAYS / PROPOSE IF NECESSARY SERVING WRITTEN NOTICE INSTRUCTING HIM TO FLY. Telegram from Steve Trilling to Gerry Blattner: PROCEED MAKE WRITTEN DEMAND FLYNN FLY PALERMO LONDON EMPHASIZE FLYNNS INSISTENCE TRAVEL BY TRAIN WILL RESULT IN LOSS TWO DAYS PRODUCTION AND UNNECESSARY EXPENSE.

Sun September 21

Cable from Gerry Blattner to Steve Trilling: SERVED WRITTEN NOTICE FLYNN HOLDING HIM RESPONSIBLE FOR DAMAGES EVENT HIS NOT CONFORMING OUR TRANSPORT ARRANGEMENT.

Mon September 22

Upon leaving for London, Flynn's flight on Pan Am has engine trouble 1½ hours out of Rome and returns; it takes off again after repairs are done but 1½ hours out it has more engine trouble and returns again to Rome; he eventually succeeds in making it to Paris at 3:30am, necessitating an overnight stay before continuing on to London.

Tue September 23

Arrives back in London, checking into the Savoy Hotel.

Wed September 24

Ill, does not work; Western Union Wire from Jack Warner to Errol Flynn at the Savoy Hotel in London, England: HAPPY YOU WERE AIRBOURNE ALL WAY AND GLAD SOON BE THROUGH WITH PICTURE. ABOUT REPLY TO YOUR LETTER WE JUST CANNOT MAKE SNAP ANSWER ON YOUR DEAL. WHEN WE MADE DEAL ORIGINALLY

Filming the galleon fight - September

With Jacques Berthier - September

FOR YOU REMAIN ABROAD WE DID SO IN GOOD FAITH AND WE WANT TIME ARRANGE OUR OWN PROGRAM IN EUROPE. THEREFORE GIVE ME CHANCE TO WORK OUT SOMETHING AND SEE IF CAN BE OF ASSISTANCE TO YOU PERSONALLY. IN ANY EVENT EXPECT YOUR COOPERATION TO COMPLETE PICTURE AS SOON AS POSSIBLE. AS OF COURSE YOUR DOING SO HAS NOTHING TO DO YOUR OTHER PROBLEMS.

Thu September 25

Telegram from Gerry Blattner to Steve Trilling: FLYNN WORKED TODAY / HE EXTREMELY HAPPY / THANKS TO JLS [Warner] CABLE EVERYTHING APPEARS ALL SERENE. A bill in the amount of $118.39 is sent to Flynn from Henri Descombes, Secrétaire Général, for the Paris limousine rental.

Tue September 30

Telegram from Gerry Blattner to Steve Trilling: FLYNN CLAIMS CONTRACT [for MASTER OF BALLANTRAE] EXPIRES 27TH SEPTEMBER.

Thu October 2

Telegram from Gerry Blattner to Steve Trilling: FLYNN NOW AGREES CONTRACT FINISHES 30TH SEPTEMBER. REGRETS ANY INCONVENIENCE. Telegram from Steve Trilling to Gerry Blattner: FORGET PORTRAIT SITTING FLYNN…DEFINITELY LIMIT POST SYNCING TO TWO DAYS. FLYNNS CONTRACT EXPRESSLY PROVIDES FOR COMPENSATION OF SERVICES BEYOND FOURTEEN WEEK PERIOD AND NO LETTER NECESSARY. TELL FLYNN J.L. SAID HE SHOULD STOP BEING A BARRISTER, SOLICITOR, K.C. [King's Counsel]; *The Modern Adventures of Casanova* radio show continues in season two with episode #27; more episodes are broadcast on subsequent Thursday nights: *The Sumatra Adventure* on 10/9; episode #29 on 10/16 about the saving of a girl from a murderous spouse; episode #30 on 10/23 about an African adventure; *The Gold Brick Swindle* on 10/30; episode #32 on 11/6 wherein a war criminal plots blackmail; episode #33 on 11/13 about an Alaskan adventure; episode #34 on 11/20 about a purloined Tibetan mask; episode #35 on 11/27; episode #36 on 12/4 wherein our hero tracks down counterfeiters; episode #37 on 12/11 wherein a murder in France leads to intrigue in Mexico. episode #38 on 12/18 about a mummy in France.

Sun October 5

Letter from director William Keighley to Steve Trilling: *"….please understand that anything that follows is in no way a personal attack on any individual but a purely business observation on the filming of the picture…Now for our boy friend Flynn. Never in the film has he been any trouble once he is before the camera.*

Outside the Elstree soundstage with his new blue Targa Florio from Frazer-Nash of Isleworth, England; it was the first in a production of 200 made - October

He takes directions and has given no worry to the director – but – he's been an expensive baby for you. Whether the time sheets show it accurately or not he has in the opinion of the director added conservatively a week to ten days to the picture. If ever he is permitted to make another picture away from the control of the studio WB will be deserving of all they get and they'll get it. He is utterly inconsiderate of the studio and J.L [Warner] and loses no opportunity to advertise the fact to cast and crew. It's an abominable attitude and an intolerable one for others who have the interests of the studio in mind. The one instance in which he was of great help was in learning the fencing routines so quickly and well."

Mon October 6 through Wed October 8

Continues filming, and (on 10/8) completes the filming portion of MASTER OF BALLANTRAE; letter from Frank Mattison to Steve Trilling (10/8): *"Keighley was going to spend the day with Flynn on post-sync [voice overdubs] but I guess the W.B. Farewell Party or Gerry's [party] was too much for Errol as he did not come into the studio to-day. W.B. doctor says so, I apologize to G.B. [Gerry Blattner] for the above remark made in his office this A.M. as Flynn really looked bad yesterday – and the day before when a doctor had to come in and give him a shot to ease the pain in his back – So Errol has promised to meet Keighley tomorrow at 9:15 am. There are about 60 loops [dubs] to do."* Letter from William Keighley to Steve Trilling: *"In between disgruntled actors [was] your star who refused to work [Sundays] and when he did was conveniently ill Monday. Don't let anyone tell you that time was not lost when Errol failed to appear such as when he came back from Italy. 'Shooting around actors is always expensive.'"*

Thu October 9

Does two hours of post-syncing before having to leave because of illness; cable from Gerry Blattner to Jack Warner: FLYNN FAILED REPORT WORK DUE SICKNESS CAUSING SHOOT AROUND HIM FOLLOWING DATES JULY 21 AUGUST 22 SEPTEMBER 15 SEPTEMBER 24 / UNAVAILABLE STUDIO UNTIL LUNCHTIME AUGUST 5 DUE BROKEN TOOTH / UNAVAILABLE UNTIL THREE AUGUST 21 PALERMO DUE SICKNESS ALSO AUGUST 27 UNTIL 430 SICKNESS / SCRIPT CLERK DIARY SHOWED ADDITIONAL EIGHTEEN HOURS THIRTYFIVE MINUTES LOST OVER PRODUCTION PERIOD WAITING FOR FLYNN / UNABLE ATTEND POST SYNCING OCTOBER 8 TWO DOCTORS ADVISED DAYS REST WAS WILLING TRY COME IN AFTERNOON / POST SYNCED TODAY LEAVING TWO HOURS / POST SYNCING TOMORROW. REGARDS.

Fri October 10

Does post-syncing for MASTER OF BALLANTRAE; telegram from Gerry Blattner to Steve Trilling: HOSPITAL SPECIALIST RECOMMEND JAMIE [Flynn] WEARS SPINAL BRACE FOR SIX TO TWELVE MONTHS / MEDICAL REPORT FOLLOWING / ALL POST SYNCING COMPLETED TENTH.

Mon October 13

Letter from Frank Mattison (aboard the *S.S. United States*) to Steve Trilling: *"This is about Errol Flynn. As you know, I have worked with him since he started at W.B. Many times I have talked to him as a father and sometimes I have been able to influence him to do what was right. But I have been very successful in getting him on the set to work. When I came back to London, from Scotland, there were difficulties. After finding a second assistant being bartender and mixing drinks in Errol's room, I took over. It worked very well. In the course of time, he became quite frank and outspoken regarding his independent ventures. I think he said he was getting $60,000 [$589,752 in 2021 value] against (or with) a percentage of the producer's share (not in the distributors). We talked of the picture he made a year ago. I think [Herbert] Yates and Republic got it. Errol also told me about his lawyer (Mahon) coming over to London and Italy to set up a deal with Milton Krims and of further production by a Mr. Marks (related to Technicolor) in conjunction with Mike Frankovitch, and intimated that if he gave him his signature on a contract they could get the money to make the picture with frozen funds of some company in the United States (it might have been Standard Oil?). I told him: 'Errol, you are making a big mistake, the only people you have ever made any money with is W.B., and every time you make a picture and it goes through some other releasing company, you hurt Errol Flynn more than anyone else. W.B. suffer when they try to hold up the price for a Flynn picture, because it stands to reason no one will pay Republic what they pay W.B. Other exhibitors will want to cut their deals also when the word gets around that we spend a million and a half dollars on a picture and some "shoe string" promoter gets a Flynn picture for $60,000 or less to Flynn and can get the cost below $800,000 [$7,863,366 in 2021 value]. All you have to do Errol, is make one or two "stinkers" and you are through. I don't know whether W.B. have to take or make any more Flynn epics, but for your sake, if you do make outside releases, why don't you protect yourself, if you can not get a large release and a good one, by putting them through W.B. under their guidance?' I think I hurt his ego, but he respects me a great deal more for telling him the truth. Now, back to 'Master of Ballantrae.' When I went on ahead to Italy, I did not see Errol for four days. In Palermo, George Maynard and Alligan, the publicity man, were the 'elbow-lifting' companions, until they ribbed Errol to 'phone me at two in the morning about getting a quiet room away from the noise.' I did. The next day, I moved the production manager out of his quiet room and put Errol in there. This did not break up their joint party, but they carried on a few nights longer, until Maynard put Errol to bed at 2:00 A.M., and at Errol's insistence spent an hour trying to get a Doctor off the battleship in the harbor. Needless to say, no Doctor. But Flynn went to sleep, while Maynard was trying to get the Doctor, and was ready to work at 9:00 A.M. next morning, while Maynard was sick for two days. When GB [Gerry Blattner] arrived, he joined in the festivities with Errol. Some of this I shall have to tell you in person; like Flynn getting 120,000 liras for the rent of Prince Lanza's Criss Craft before GB knew he had the money. Since that time, I find GB has been covering up for Errol in Rome and in London. I think I wrote you that GB gave a party Wednesday, for the crew at W.B.'s expense and Errol was there. He couldn't come into work Thursday, so it delayed the finish one more day."*

Fri October 17

Flies to Miami where he meets up with Patrice and gives her a white poodle as an anniversary gift; she names it Joy Boy.

Sun October 19

Flies with Patrice to Nassau in the Bahamas for a short vacation.

Tue October 21

Flies with Patrice on BOAC to Montego Bay, Jamaica; letter from Gerry Blattner to Steve Trilling referencing complaint Flynn made in newspaper interview about how stuntmen got such a lousy deal: *"Am passing this on to Roy Obringer for his Flynn file; it might have a value later."* Blattner added that *"the particular stuntmen he refers to were perfectly satisfied with the weekly salaries agreed with before production, in addition to which I granted them a bonus…each whilst on the actual location because they had done such a good job. They were highly delighted with this bonus, and Errol's comments were quite unnecessary."*

Wed October 22

The couple continues on to Kingston, checking in to the Myrtle Bank Hotel.

Thu October 23

Drives with Patrice to Port Antonio, checking in to the Titchfield Hotel.

Fri October 24

Flynn writes a $10,000 check for repairs on the Titchfield Hotel ($98,292 in 2021 value).

Court Orders Flynn To Pay

HOLLYWOOD, Oct. 28. (U.P)— Errol Flynn owes his frist wife $105,712.80 in alimony and tax payments, a judge has ruled.

Superior Judge Clarence L. Kincaid yesterday ordered the screen star to pay Lili Damita $40,500 in back alimony, $61,260.71 in taxes on alimony Flynn previously was ordered to pay, and $3,952.09 for the education of their 11-year-old son, Sean.

Miss Damita had charged in a civil suit that Flynn had not paid her alimony for more than a year. They were divorced in 1942.

The Idaho Times-News
Tue, October 28

Mon November 3

Errol, Patrice, and a crew of eight sail the *Zaca* out of Port Antonio on a trip to Cuba.

Tue November 4

The *Zaca* arrives at the U.S. Naval Station at Guantanamo Bay, Cuba.

Wed November 12

Flies with Patrice and their poodle Joy Boy from Kingston to London *(top left)*.

Thu November 13

Costume fittings for CROSSED SWORDS; at a party at the Roman villa of producer Vittorio Vassarotti to celebrate the creation of his new company, "Vi-Va Film-Mahon," and its first film, *The Master of Don Juan* (later titled CROSSED SWORDS), to star Errol Flynn.

Fri November 14 and Sat November 15

Makeup and wig tests, and (on 11/15) final costume fittings; later (on 11/14) at a cocktail party at the Hotel Excelsior given by Bud Ornstein of United Artists.

Sun November 16

Interviewed by the Italian press; leaves for Naples by car; dines at his hotel, the Vesuvio.

Mon November 17

Sightseeing in Naples; dinner with Patrice, Barry Mahon, and Milton Krims, the respective producer and director of CROSSED SWORDS.

Tue November 18

Begins filming CROSSED SWORDS (the daily production notes have not been found).

Wed November 19

Filming in the Royal Park of Capodimonte in Naples.

Thu November 20

Continues filming.

Fri November 21

With Patrice boating in a rented motor launch; AGAINST ALL FLAGS has a special premiere in Amsterdam.

Sat November 22 and Sun November 23

No filming in the Royal Park because of the weather; lunches at the home of a friend (11/23).

Mon November 24

Continues filming; American journalists visit the set.

Tue November 25

Visits the shipbuilding yards in the morning with Patrice; filming in the afternoon.

Wed November 26

Continues filming; the 20-minute short CRUISE OF THE ZACA opens at the Embassy Theater in New York; the 16mm film has been blown up to 35mm for theatrical release.

Thu November 27

Continues filming; attends a cocktail party with Patrice given in their honor at the home of Italian film producer Vittorio Vassarotti *(bottom right);* in attendance is Flynn's current co-star, Gina Lollobrigida.

With Patrice and Joy Boy in London - Wed, November 12

Above, having makeup applied for his first scenes in CROSSED SWORDS, and right, being coached by fencing instructor Enzo Musumeci in the Royal Park of Capodimonte in Naples - November

With Patrice and Gina Lollobrigida at a party in Naples - Thu, November 27

Fri November 28

Filming in the covered sets due to the weather.

Sun November 30

Visits Pompeii with Patrice, Barry Mahon, and associate producer Arthur Vilieside.

Tue December 2

Resumes filming; letter from Gerry Blattner to Steve Trilling: *"I have a small query concerning a man by the name of MALISE. He was, I understand, Flynn's valet, and Flynn states that as you paid his fare from Los Angeles to London he considers that you should pay Malise's fare from London to Cannes, via Paris, amounting to approximately £23.0.0 [$958.93 in 2021 value], in lieu of the cost of returning him to the U.S.A. Apparently Malise was called to the French Colours [drafted] and was prevented from continuing his employment as Flynn's valet. Should be glad to have your confirmation that it is okay to pay above sum."*

Thu December 4

Continues filming.

Fri December 5 and Sat December 6

Filming at Castello Lancellotti in Lauro outside Naples.

Mon December 8

Letter to Warner Bros.: *Gentlemen: Confirming my wire of December 7, I wish to inform you that I have signed a contract to do my outside picture for 1953 starting April 1st. This, of course, is subject to your pre-emption rights per our contract. As per our above-mentioned contract, it is my understanding that you will inform me as to your decision within five working days of receipt of such intention by me to do this by cable in care of the Hotel Vesuvio, Naples, where I will be until after Christmas. My best regards to all of you and my sincere hope that you will enjoy all the best for the coming New Year. Very sincerely yours, Errol Flynn."*

Tue December 9

Letter to Nora from Naples *(bottom right): "Dear Nora Astonishingly I have just learned that the girls have been living up at the* [Mulholland] *farm for the last couple of weeks. I say astonishingly not because I have the least objection but merely that common courtesy or even civility should have prompted you to acquaint me with the fact. I also understand they have not been going to school. Apparently their education, so piously put forward by you as the reason for your refusal to let them see me in Jamaica, is dependent upon your whim and convenience...Nora, I truly hope you are not going to let your personal feelings whatever they are interfere with my right to see as much as possible of the girls. This would be a pity. Would you please let me know if you are agreeable to their spending their next Easter vacation with me? At this time I do not know for sure where I will be but it will most probably be in Italy. This address will reach me for the next couple of weeks. Yours Errol."*

Thu December 11

Continues filming; out for a drive to Sorrento with Patrice in their Chrysler; letter from John J. Glynn (Warner Bros. New York) to Steve Trilling: *"….we call to your attention just a few of the rather unusual items* [cash disbursements] *we have noticed in connection with 'Master of Ballantrae'…..2. A number of payments explained as 'E. Flynn Bar Bill.' 3. Disbursement of lire 377,110 explained as 'hire of Chris Craft for E. Flynn,' and another item for Lire 200,000 'advance to E. Flynn for payment of hire on Chris Craft.' 4. A number of advances made to and for account of E. Flynn."*

Fri December 12

Hosts a party at the Bar Vesuvietta in their hotel and gives Patrice a ruby ring for her birthday (her birthday being on the 17th).

Sun December 14

Continues filming, this on a Sunday due to the picture being behind schedule.

Wed December 17

Continues filming; rain over the next several days prevents filming.

Bottom right, letter to Nora from Naples

At Castello Lancellotti in Lauro, Italy - first week of December

With Gina Lollobrigida

Mon December 22 through Wed December 24

Continues filming; takes part in a pizza-tasting contest on 12/22 in Naples, helping to determine the best pizza made by chefs from New York and Italy; AGAINST ALL FLAGS opens at the Midwest Theater in Oklahoma City, OK, on 12/23.

Thu December 25

Throws a Christmas party for the cast and crew.

Sat December 27

Letter from WB editor James Moore to film editor Jack Harris concerning MASTER OF BALLANTRAE: *"Let me quote Mr. J.L. Warner: 'Close shots of Flynn in cell not good. Stay in master long shot as Flynn leans against wall with Allison talking to him through cell door....Understand that there is no criticism whatever of anything* [Harris' editing work] *except Flynn's personal appearance."*

Sun December 28

Comes down with a fever and liver infection and is admitted to the International Hospital in Naples (until January 10th); filming continues around him.

1953

Sun January 4

Letter to Al Blum: *"Re Mulholland servants, I agree they should go back on the same deal as before when I was absent for an extended time....I think it* [$2,887 a month in 2020 value] *was reduced in half. But I would appreciate very much if you would assume your old Simon Legre* [sic] *role and be the heavy. I don't want to lose them....You have not replied at all to many leading questions I asked you weeks ago....Re cash position, things couldn't be worse and, in the near future, they are not going to improve....Re the children, I am wondering what action their mothers could bring against me whilst I am out of the country....I don't see how I could ever be criticised if I could show that I have set this money* [$9,756 a month child support, in 2021 value] *up in a bank for the children on the premise it was going to the mothers instead of the youngsters. A marvellous illustration of this was when Nora rushed into your office on the eve of her flying jaunt to Europe and got from you a month's advance...."*

Tue January 6

Telegram from Gerry Blattner to Steve Trilling: LONDON PAPERS REPORT FLYNN HAD JAUNDICE NAPLES.

Thu January 8

Filming of CROSSED SWORDS moves to Cinecitta Studios; the final pre-recorded radio episode of *The Adventures of Casanova* is broadcast.

Sun January 18

Is released from the hospital in Naples and travels to St. Moritz in his blue Targa roadster the next day.

Mon January 26

In a bobsled race at St. Moritz; leaves for Rome.

Wed January 28

Letter on personalized CROSSED SWORDS stationery from Viva Film to Dr. Ellis Sturgo, a London psychiatrist: *"....I damn near kicked off with that damned hyppolysis* [sic] *– liver stopped functioning + I clearly heard the clatter of old Charon's oars as he readied his craft to ferry me across the Styx. Am still very feeble but, due to an aesthetic youth spirit in godliness and a mother as tough as a New York cop my constitution has made recovery remarkable...."*

February

Continues and completes filming CROSSED SWORDS; letter written to his accountant Al Blum around this time: *"Please cash in right away one of my U.S. Govt. bonds and send proceeds to Guaranty Trust, 5 th Ave. + 44th N.Y. I am going to try to hold the others until June + coupon time (or does this make any difference?)...Anyway, I ask you to sell the others as soon as possible and at best price possible and convert the proceeds into $5000 cashiers checks* [$48,778 in 2021 value]...."*

The Baltimore Sun - Sun, January 4

The Chicago Tribune - Sat, February 21

Letter written to his daughters around this time while living in Rome *(top left)*: *"My darling Sam [Deirdre] and Rory. Thanks so much for the letter you both wrote me. I do wish you'd write more often. I love getting a letter from you because you have no idea how much I miss you two tomatoes and just wish I could give you the biggest hugs & kisses. Tons of love from your Baron."* Letter written to Dr. Ellis Sturgo around this time: *"....Chum – when you have my sinus stuff made up will you please leave out more bicarbonate? Will explain when I see you. There's so much bi-carb it somehow solidifies and doesn't look good + doesn't help...."*

Letter written to his daughters around this time while living in Rome

Wed March 4

Enters into a verbal contract with Barry Mahon (his producer/partner), Tony Roma (producer with Roma Films), and landowner Count Adolfo Fossataro for the purposes of filming WILLIAM TELL.

Sat March 7

A written contract is drawn up for the agreement made on March 4th to film WILLIAM TELL.

Tue March 10

Letter to Nora from Rome *(top right)*: *Nora my dear – your letter of the 3rd has just reached me but you didn't answer the very important request I made – that you would agree to the girls spending 4 or 5 months with me here – it's the only way in the foreseeable future I can figure that will give the girls a chance to remember their old man or even know they've got one. Besides they could learn a foreign language – in my own experience a very vital factor in any human's education. Obligations here prevent me coming to the U.S. for some time – I'm up to my neck casting and preparing my second of three productions in Italy, William Tell, and don't dare leave because my basic contract with bankers and others stress that I personally be on the spot for all decisions and even every check issued must be co-signed by me. I'm spending their money lavishly but am personally responsible for every lira that goes out so I don't dare turn my back or I'd come visit the kids in the U.S....So please Ma let me know if you'll agree to them coming over and spending more than the usual few days or weeks – since I can pay their expenses of the journey in lira I can manage it...[Accountant, Al] Blum at last informs me he is behind in his payments to you but doesn't say how much. I'm sorry – I just ain't got no dollars right now but in a couple of weeks I should touch some loot upon delivery of my present film to New York – will then catch up with you. Sorry."*

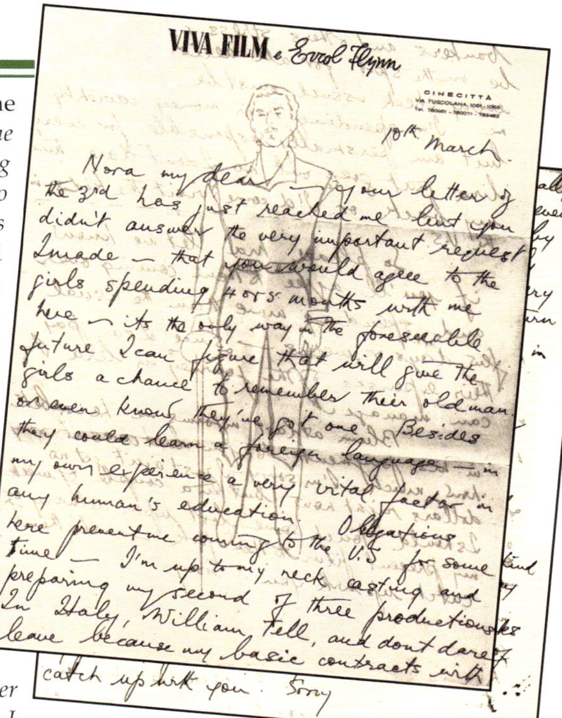

Letter to Nora from Rome - Tue, March 10

Thu March 26

Liens totaling $820,572.89 ($8,005,165 in 2021 value) are filed against Errol and Nora by the U.S. government for back taxes from 1946 to 47 during the time they were married; Nora is later relieved of responsibility as per their divorce arrangement.

Mon March 30

Lunches at Rome's Ristorante Pasetto *(bottom left)*.

March-April

Sometime during this stay in Rome, he writes an essay in his diary *(bottom right)*: *"Faith? Some say we shall never know God's purpose, that there is no God nor any purpose, that we humans are like the ants crushed under a boy's foot for the fun of it...But then there are those who will tell you with firm conviction that never a flea jumped from a dog's back that God didn't know of...What is Faith? And why are you born with or without it? For certainly from what I have observed in this life, Faith is not a thing you develop. On the contrary, if I have developed anything definite it is a dull smoldering anger at the abysmal mystery of my presence of this earth, with not the least clue to any reason for it; a mystery that probably not even death will solve for me. Why am I alive?...What, then, is Faith? In what? Today, in my early forties I find myself in a state of tortured confusion where my every past action or experience, my daily movements are measured and appraised by one who does not seem to be myself....Faith? Why does it elude me? Why cannot I find peace of mind like those I envy? Those who have listened and heard and felt, and having done so, contritely let fall all other barriers and started to believe wholeheartedly in God?....Faith—I wish I had it."*

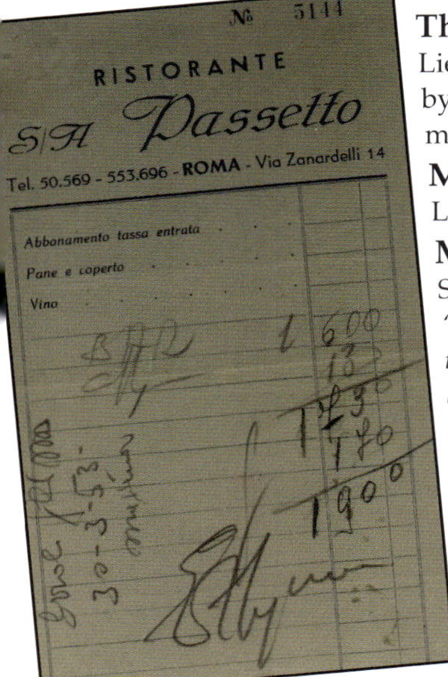

Check from Flynn's lunch at Ristorante Passetto - Mon, March 30

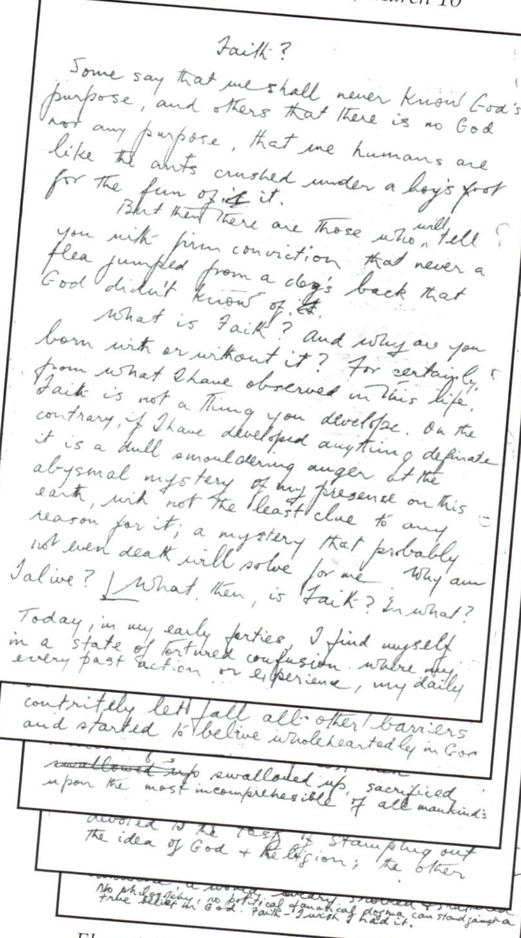

Flynn's Rome essay on faith - Spring 1953

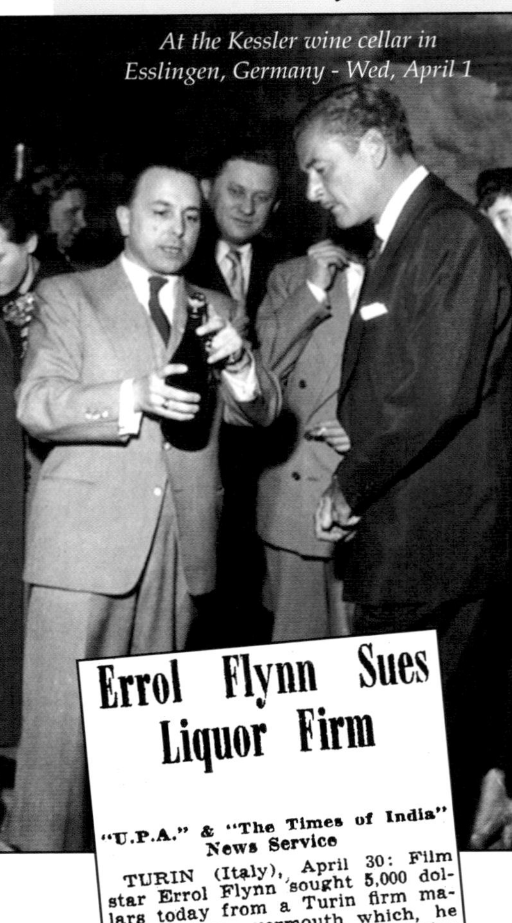

At the Kessler wine cellar in Esslingen, Germany - Wed, April 1

At the Mercedes plant in Stuttgart - Thu, April 2

At a restaurant in Garmisch-Partenkirchen, Germany - Wed, April 8

In Oslo with Miss Norway - Fri, June 5

Wed April 1

Arrives at Stuttgart Airport where he is welcomed by the mayor, local dignitaries, and several German movie stars; later he is given a tour of the Kessler sparkling wine cellars (Germany's oldest) in Esslingen *(top left)*.

Thu April 2

Is given a tour of the Mercedes Benz plant in Stuttgart *(top right)*; the company gives him a green 1953 300S cabriolet for his use while in the area.

Fri April 3

At the Circus Krone in Stuttgart.

Sat April 4

Attends the premiere of AGAINST ALL FLAGS at the Metropol-Palast in Stuttgart; buys a black 1953 Mercedes-Benz 300 for 50,000 marks ($116,091 in 2021 value).

Sun April 5

Travels from Stuttgart to Munich, checking in to the Bayerischer Hof Hotel; sometime in the early part of this month Flynn visits his sister Rosemary, who is now living in the Rhineland.

Wed April 8

In Garmisch-Partenkirchen, staying at the Hotel Alpen-Hof (now gone), in part to search for a yodeling instructor for the William Tell film *(center right)*.

Tue April 14

Flies back to Rome from Germany.

Mon April 20

Flies back to Munich around this date to interview prospective cast and crew for WILLIAM TELL.

Wed April 22

Meets with Tony Roma and Count Fossataro to discuss problems over the financing of WILLIAM TELL.

Fri April 24

Is interviewed in his hotel room by international reporters.

Tue April 28

Attends the Cannes Film Festival with Patrice.

Sat May 2

With Patrice celebrating Bing Crosby's 50th birthday (the crooner was claiming only 49) a day in advance at the Bonne Auberge Restaurant in Cannes *(bottom left)*; also attending are Gary and Rocky (Mrs.) Cooper.

Sun May 3

Flynn's accountant, Al Blum, dies; Flynn will claim in his autobiography that Blum embezzled much of Flynn's money.

Tue May 12

With Patrice in Monte Carlo for a few days; Nora tells the press that while the Flynns are in Europe she is moving into the Mulholland house because of back child support payments.

Mon May 18

Enters into deal to have Barry Mahon serve as his attorney.

Thu May 21

Returns to Rome with Patrice.

Fri June 5

In Oslo to attend the Miss Norway contest *(bottom right)*, later personally greeting the winner, 22-year-old

Errol Flynn Sues Liquor Firm

"U.P.A." & "The Times of India" News Service

TURIN (Italy), April 30: Film star Errol Flynn sought 5,000 dollars today from a Turin firm manufacturing vermouth which, he said, had damaged his reputation as a movie hero by depicting him as a drinker.

Flynn objected to the publication of an advertisement showing him and his wife, Patricia Wymore, sipping the firm's brand of vermouth in a Naples restaurant.

The Times of India - Thu, April 30

With Bing Crosby, Patrice, and actress Simone Delamare, celebrating Bing's birthday in Cannes - Sat, May 2

Synnove Gulbrandsen, with a kiss on the hand

Thu June 11
Pays $200,000 ($1,951,116 in 2021 value) to the IRS toward his tax lien.

Sun June 14
Filming of WILLIAM TELL begins; an entire stone village has been built in Courmayeur, Italy, in a location now occupied by Club du Sport.

Fri June 19
With Eve Ashley, Bruce Cabot, and Patrice at George's American Bar in Rome (top right).

Sat June 20
Flynn's 44th birthday; arrives in Courmayeur in his blue Frazer Nash Targa Florio.

With Eve Ashley, Bruce Cabot, and Patrice at George's American Bar in Rome - Fri, June 19

With Antonella Lualdi and Guido Martufi

With Guido Martufi at Lago Blu, Italy

With director Jack Cardiff

Sun June 21
Flynn's first scenes for WILLIAM TELL are filmed in Courmayeur, Italy *(surrounding photos)*.

With Waltraut Haas

With Guido Martufi

Errol Flynn, 2 Others File Tax Appeals

[Chicago Tribune Press Service]

Washington, Aug. 5 — Errol Flynn, the actor, Arthur J. Rooney, professional football magnate, and Robert Lehman, Wall street banker, faced a common difficulty today—alleged income tax deficiencies of substantial size.

In petitions appealing the rulings of the commissioner of internal revenue, filed here in the United States Tax court, Flynn, Rooney, and Lehman denied owing any additional taxes.

The government holds that Flynn owes an additional $218,-628 in income taxes plus $114,-655 in fraud penalties for a total of $333,283 on unreported income from movie making in 1945-47.

A bureau of internal revenue notice attached to Flynn's tax court petition revealed the actor reported a net income of only $1,074.80 in 1946, a year in which the bureau claims his movie salary alone totaled $239,900.

Flynn Denies Charges

Flynn, in his petition drawn by Paul Ziffren, attorney and former Chicagoan, denies all of the bureau's allegations.

The Chicago Tribune
Wed, August 5

Sat June 27
Files suit with Gina Lollobrigida against the Carpano Vermouth company for unauthorized use of their names.

Sat July 11
Flynn's company, Junior Films, takes over as sole producer of WILLIAM TELL.

Thu July 16
Unit manager Federico "Fritz" Del Fauro leaves the film because of unpaid wages.

Tue July 21
In a memo to production supervisor Elvira D'Amico, Bruce Cabot threatens to leave the film if his wages are not paid.

Wed July 29
MASTER OF BALLANTRAE has a first showing at the Strand Theater in Hartford, CT.

Fri August 21
Bruce Cabot refuses to work on WILLIAM TELL and leaves the production.

Fri August 28
Filming of WILLIAM TELL comes to a halt when finances run out; only thirty-four pages of a 140-page script have been filmed, representing about 30 minutes of film: all that remain today are 119 12"-diameter cans of film, 3 16"-diameter cans of film, representing a total approximately 72,000 feet of film; all are said to be stored in the archives of Boston University.

Sun August 30
Attends the Venice Film Festival.

Mon August 31
At a party given by Countess Natalia Volpi at the Volpi Palace in Venice; also in attendance are Rex Harrison, Lilli Palmer, Farley Granger, Thilda Tamar, and others.

Wed September 2
After midnight during a party at the Lido Excelsior Hotel that began on Tuesday, Flynn slips while dancing with 19-year-old Jamine Leplat and displaces a vertebrum *(bottom center)*; the next morning (9/3) a Dr. Guido Cassone is called in who prescribes bed rest and a back brace *(bottom right)*.

With Brigitte Bardot on the Lido beach in Venice - Tue, September 1

Above, dancing with 19-year-old Parisian, Jamine Leplat, at the Hotel Excelsior - Wed, September 2; and right, wearing the brace prescribed by Dr. Cassone - Thu, September 3; Flynn inscribed the photo with "The New Look for the boys!"

Tue September 8

Mort Blumenstock, head of Warner Bros. publicity, receives an irate letter from a fan who had just seen THE MASTER OF BALLANTRAE, saying in part: *"My husband and I….go to few movies any more, because they just aren't as they should be, and after seeing this particular picture, we'll see even fewer…I've never written a letter of this kind before, but I just can't explain the contempt I feel in my heart for a company and a producer and for Mr. Wm. Keighley, whom I had highly respected till now, for allowing such filth to be put before the young people and children of this country. I'm refering [sic] to the girl that did the dance in the <u>sheer</u> blouse with <u>nothing</u> on under it!…How a member of the female race could stoop so low, and have so little decensy [sic] about herself as to permit her body to be placed in view of all the people, all races, of this country…The horrible thing is what this sort of thing is doing to the teenagers tho – and then we wonder why we have so much delinquency…I think you all belong in jail….I'm only 25 and I love a good time as much as the next person, but so far is <u>far enough</u>!…. I'd hate to be in your shoes on Judgement Day!…."* Blumenstock attached a note saying, *"Would not attempt to answer this and recommend you throw it in the basket…"*

Tue September 15

Appears with Bruce Cabot on a TV show in Milan.

Fri September 25

An Italian court order is issued to seize property owned by the production company making THE STORY OF WILLIAM TELL; approximately $16,000 ($156,089 in 2021 value) is owed to actors, bit players, crew, innkeepers, and a lumberyard.

Sat September 26

Authorities seize all outdoor sets, film equipment, and other properties at the Courmayeur location.

Tue September 29

More filming equipment, along with Flynn's Targa sports car is seized by the authorities representing his creditors; a mortgage listing of Flynn's property housed in the Beverly Hills Storage and Warehouse Co. includes the Van Gogh and Gauguin paintings.

Tue October 13

Count Fossataro ends his involvement as co-producer of WILLIAM TELL.

Mon October 19

Flynn meets Patrice at the airport in Rome upon her arrival from Kansas *(below)*; they will

With Patrice at Ciampino Airport in Rome, acting as her interpreter - Mon, October 19

Way Now Clear to Shoot Movie, Says Errol Flynn

ROME, Sept. 27 (U.P.)—Actor Errol Flynn said tonight the field is now clear to carry on with the shooting of his picture "William Tell" following a sort of overture by creditors at Aosta today.

A court in Aosta yesterday impounded all property including cameras and lighting equipment belonging to the Junior Films-Errol Flynn company on a demand of unpaid personnel and hotel keepers.

Creditors met today and decided to hold up their action and let the producers complete the film.

The Los Angeles Times
Fri, September 27

Bailiffs seize Errol's car

Rome, Wednesday

Film star Errol Flynn sat gloomily in his flat last night pondering on the avalanche that has hit his company,"Errol Flynn's Enterprises."

For yesterday bailiffs moved in on his big color film, "William Tell," now on location in the Valley D'Aosta, Italy.

They seized his sports car, and took over the three-quarters finished film, the costly camera equipment, costumes, and scenery.

The company, it is alleged, has not paid salaries, hotel bills, or tradesmen.

About £66,000 is needed to save the film, but after a day of emergency moves there was no sign last night of Errol Flynn getting it.

Producer Brian Mahon said last night that the trouble was caused by the failure of the Italian promoters to put up all the money they had promised.—"Argus" Service.

The Melbourne Argus - Thu, October 1

Creditors Are In Full Cry

ERROL FLYNN, at present being hotly pursued in Italy by hordes of actors and film folk demanding money, declares they are "worse than angry women," according to a report from Rome.

From A Staff Correspondent in London

FLYNN insists that he is not to blame for his "William Tell" film unit going unpaid.

"Certain Italians who are responsible for financing the film have run out on me," he says.

Meanwhile, however, truckloads of penniless actors and technicians are chasing Flynn all over Italy for their money. They have not been paid for six weeks —ever since finances went bust in an alpine village near Mont Blanc, Italy, where they were then on location.

Looking somewhat shattered, bedraggled and middle-aged, Flynn declares he will do all he can to get payment for all and also finish the picture, which experts say would have been a masterpiece. Jack Cardiff was directing, and Flynn was William Tell.

A magnificent £10,000 model town had been built on the slopes of Mont Blanc as background. It is now under snow.

The Sydney Sun Herald - Sun, October 11

live in that city in a rented home at Via Antonio Bosio 25.

Wed November 4
Arthur B. Krim, president of United Artists, views footage of THE STORY OF WILLIAM TELL but passes on becoming involved with its completion.

Wed November 11
Flies to London, checking in to the Bayswater Inn.

Thu November 12
Attends the premiere of *From Here To Eternity* at the Leicester Square Theatre in London *(left)*.

Sat November 14
Guests on the BBC radio show, *In Town Tonight (below right)* making a plea for financing to complete WILLIAM TELL.

Mon December 7
Rex Harrison and Lili Palmer lease the Mulholland house for ten weeks at $1,000 ($9,756 in 2021 value).

Sat December 12
Flynn is announced to be the producer and emcee of a TV variety show called *International Talent Hunt*; it doesn't transpire.

Tue December 15
Arrives in New York from London aboard Pan American Airways; while there, he is in discussions with United Artists about the release of CROSSED SWORDS.

Sat December 19
At the El Morocco with model Gita Hall.

Mon December 21
Makes a $15,000 tax payment ($146,334 in 2021 value); appears as a guest on the TV program *Masquerade Party*.

Thu December 24
Returns to Rome from New York.

Fri December 25
Daughter Arnella Roma is born (6.5 lbs) in Rome.

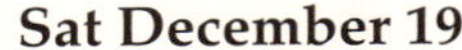

In London with actor (and Flynn lookalike) Paul Brooks and Brooks' wife Jeanne Crain at the premiere of "From Here To Eternity" - Thu, November 12

With Miss Sweden, Ulla Sandklef, at the London radio show In Town Tonight *- Sat, November 14*

Left, a telegram from Rome to Patrice's family in Kansas announcing the birth of her and Errol's daughter Arnella Roma - Fri, December 25

From a Bert Six portrait session ~ Spring 1950

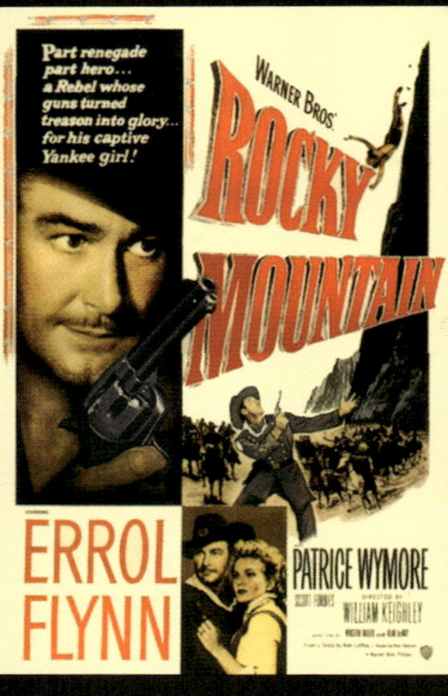

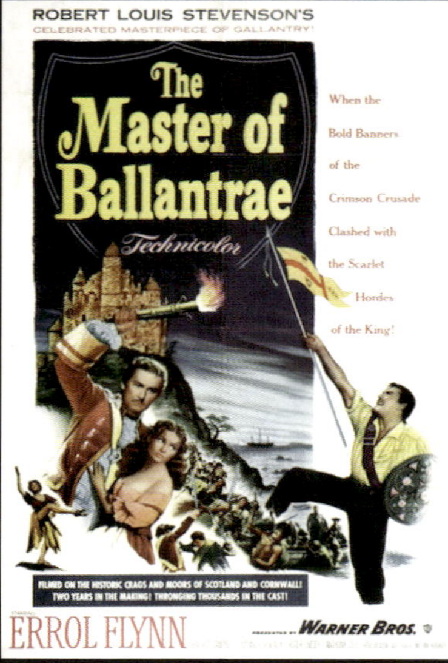

The films of 1949~1953

7
FALLING STAR
1954~1959

These final years could not have been joyful ones for Errol Flynn. Owing serious back taxes, expatriated in Europe, separated from three of his children by ocean and continent, and in declining health, Flynn nevertheless maintained his usual chin-up public facade and forged ahead. He helped whittle his tax burden by making two romantic films in England (LET'S MAKE UP and KING'S RHAPSODY), which were fairly successful there, owing in no small part to the national popularity of his co-star Anna Neagle. Flynn's portrayals are better than critics have acknowledged, especially when taking these performances on their own merit and not in comparison to the action-adventure hero he once was. In this latter persona he gave it one final theatrical stab while in England (THE WARRIORS) before heading back to the United States, by which time he himself was in agreement with his critics that he was past his swashbuckling prime.

A hardened, more weathered Flynn emerged in subsequent films. He was given the support of producers like Darryl F. Zanuck and Jack Warner through the opportunity to show this new, weathered side in roles like the drunkard in THE SUN ALSO RISES and his idol John Barrymore in TOO MUCH, TOO SOON. While his career seemed to be once again on the ascent, his marriage to Patrice was unraveling, with the teenager Beverly Aadland as her replacement. Beverly was his constant companion in the remaining two years of his life, sticking with him through a misguided and failed attempt at a stage play, a final major film shot in Africa (THE ROOTS OF HEAVEN), and ventures into Castro's revolutionary Cuba.

The remaining months of Flynn's life were devoted to producing what would be his swan song in films, an amateurish docu-drama made in Cuba (CUBAN REBEL GIRLS), which featured Miss Aadland, and putting the finishing touches on his autobiography with the book's ghostwriter, Earl Conrad. Though in obvious poor health, Flynn's exhausting regimen of constant travel never let up, with regular jaunts to Cuba, Jamaica, New York, and Los Angeles.

During his last trip to Hollywood in September of 1959, Flynn performed his final work as an actor: a made-for-TV Western and a guest spot on the *Red Skelton Show*. In desperate need of money, he reluctantly decided to part with his beloved *Zaca* and in October traveled with Beverly to Vancouver to discuss its sale with a prospective buyer. While there, Flynn suffered the heart attack that ended his abbreviated, fifty-year life. He had long voiced his desire to be buried on his cherished property in Jamaica instead of in Hollywood, which he'd come to loathe, but Patrice—still legally his wife—overruled and had the actor laid to rest at Forest Lawn, a stone's-throw from Hollywood.

Flynn had come into the world in a port city on one side of the Pacific, and left it in another port city across that same ocean. He would now find rest on a hill high enough to catch the Pacific breezes, a sailor home from the sea.

1954

With Shelley Winters at a party in Rome - Tue, January 19

With Bruce Cabot and Patrice at a circus in Rome - Sun, January 24

With Patrice arriving in Frankfurt, Germany -Thu, February 4

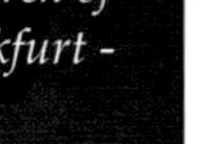

With Patrice at the March of Dimes benefit in Frankfurt - Thu, February 4

January
Sells his Acapulco establishment, Club Sirocco.

Fri January 8
The California Supreme Court rules against Flynn in his bid to reduce his $18,000 ($174,295 in 2021 value) per year alimony payments to Lili Damita.

Thu January 14
A Los Angeles court summons Flynn to appear regarding twelve months past due child support payments of $550 per month ($5,326 in 2021 value).

Tue January 19
A news report claims Flynn was in a tussle with stand-in Jack Easton on this night at a Rome cocktail party *(top left)*; Flynn's business partner Barry Mahon later states it was a mistaken report, and that Flynn and Easton were simply rehearsing a fight for an unidentified film scene; also there were Shelley Winters and Edmund O'Brien with his wife Olga San Juan.

Wed January 20
The Los Angeles court appearance is called off because of a promise by Flynn to pay the past due child support payments.

Sun January 24
With Patrice and Bruce Cabot attending a circus in Rome *(center left)*.

Thu January 28
Writes a letter to Barclays Bank in London: *"....I regret the confusion concerning the cheque my father handed to your Jamaican Agents...Without realizing that this check was still outstanding I transferred most of my funds from Barclays Bank of Gracechurch Street, to Switzerland, without leaving them any instructions as to a possible outstanding cheque... Please find enclosed a cheque for $468.00 [$4,532 in 2021 value], in payment of the interest and I regret the confusion...."*

Sat January 30
Letter to Justin Golenbock: *"....It is vital that I do not settle with the government* [Internal Revenue Service] *only to have my first wife especially step in with some terrifying claims and grab what has been saved out of the* [financial] *wreck....the amount of cash* [available] *for the immediate future does not seem adequate to meet obligations I have incurred due to a disastrous year imposed upon me by the Internal Revenue...."*

Thu February 4
Arrives in Frankfurt, Germany, from Rome for the March of Dimes benefit at the EUCOM Headquarters casino attended by nearly 300 guests; Flynn, as master of ceremonies, auctioned a *"surprise package"* from Lauren Bacall, refusing to divulge the contents because, as he said, *"Bogie forbids disclosure"*; the "surprise package" included a perfumed nightgown of Bacall's; he also reads passages from the book *The Sexual Behavior of the Human Female*, remarking that *"Sex isn't sex anymore, it's arithmetic!" (bottom left and center)*.

Tue February 9
Signs a contract with the French outfit Comet Television Films, Inc. to produce 26 half-hour television dramas on a show called *The International Talent Scout*; the series is not produced.

Sat February 20
Another request by a Los Angeles court to have Flynn appear on March 5th regarding back child support payments was called off because of a promised settlement.

March
Rex Harrison and his wife Lili Palmer complete their 10-week lease of the Mulholland house.

The South China Morning Post - Sat, February 13

Mon March 1
Leaves Rome for Brazil with Patrice and Arnella, arriving in Rio de Janeiro the next day.

Mon March 8
Arrives in Buenos Aires, Argentina, for the first Mar del Plata International Film Festival; an estimated 300 police were needed to guard the 230 stars arriving for the festival; over the course of the festival, from March 9th to 11th, Flynn is seen with Fred MacMurray, Edward G. Robinson, Mary Pickford, Walter Pidgeon, Joan Fontaine, and others, and meets with Argentine president Juan Peron, who offers Flynn a prize stud bull for the actor's Jamaica estates; the Jamaican government ultimately forbids the importation of the bull.

Sat March 13
Leaves Argentina for Kingston, Jamaica, arriving the next day, where the family is greeted by his parents; they move on directly to the Titchfield Hotel; it is reported that Flynn plans to film the famous Jamaican story "The White Witch of Rosehall," with shooting to begin in October; it is ultimately never made.

Fri March 19
Ends his 20-year relationship with Warner Bros. Pictures with an agreed financial settlement.

Late March
Approves a mural by artist Olga Lehmann for the lobby of the Titchfield Hotel *(left)*; the title of the painting is *The Landing of Captain Bligh on Navy Island in 1793*, the event the painting depicts.

Spring
Arnella is baptized in Port Antonio, with Flynn's parents in attendance.

Sat April 3
Sells the Titchfield Hotel to the McCormick Shipping Corporation for an undisclosed price.

Mon April 15
A private screening of CRUISE OF THE ZACA is held for Errol, Patrice, the elder Flynns, and select guests at the Capitol Theatre in Port Antonio.

Sat April 24
The lawsuit against Carpano Vermouth (see June 27, 1953) is judged in favor of Flynn, with the actor being awarded $414 ($4,009 in 2021 value).

Mon April 26
Leaves for New York via Miami.

Tue April 27
While in New York, he signs his will and (under the assumed name of Thomson) attempts to borrow money with his Van Gogh and Gauguin paintings as collateral.

Wed April 28
Arrives in London to prepare for the filming of LET'S MAKE UP (titled LILACS IN THE SPRING in the U.K.); greeting him at the airport are the film's director, Herbert Wilcox, and Wilcox's wife, the film's co-star, Anna Neagle *(bottom right)*.

Sat May 1
With Anna Neagle on the British TV show *In Town Tonigh*t, to talk about LET'S MAKE UP.

Sun May 2
Is interviewed and photographed at the Savoy Hotel.

Mon May 3
Dance rehearsals with Anna Neagle for LET'S MAKE UP begin this week at a local dance studio.

Fri May 7
Rehearses a dance number with Anna Neagle.

Mon May 17
First day of filming on LET'S MAKE UP (the daily production notes have not been located).

With artist Olga Lehmann and the mural she created for the Titchfield Hotel - March (see also page 299)

With director Herbert Wilcox and his wife, actress Anna Neagle, at London Airport - Wed, April 28

AN ERROL FLYNN MOB SCENE.

Crowds Carry Star on Shoulders in Argentina.

Mar Del Plata, Argentina, March 8. (Reuters)—Police rescued Errol Flynn from crowds who lifted him from his car and carried him shoulder-high on his arrival here today for Argentina's first motion picture festival.

The crowds repeatedly broke through 300 police guarding 230 screen stars and executives, who drove in a procession of 100 cars from the station to their hotel. The procession took one and a half hours to cover the 3-mile route.

The Kansas City Times
Tue, March 9

ERROL FLYNN and PATRICE WYMORE FLYNN

1953 INCOME TAX RETURN

SCHEDULE B

EXPENSES IN CONNECTION WITH PROFESSION AS ACTOR AND ACTRESS, RESPECTIVELY

Gifts and entertainment.	$1,000.00
Legal and accounting	22,975.00
Travel and automobile	4,430.00
Dues and periodicals	350.00
Agent	800.00
Secretary	2,500.00
Telephone and telegrams	2,682.74
Personal manager	6,000.00
Photographs	800.00
Publicity	1,000.00
Research	500.00
Office expense	5,750.00
Flowers	50.00
Broadcasting expenses	50.00
Bank charges	14.35
Theft by business manager	20,668.75
Interest paid to Government on deficiency	39,807.18
TOTAL EXPENSES	$109,378.03

May-June
Continues filming LET'S MAKE UP.

With Anna Neagle filming LET'S MAKE UP (titled LILACS IN THE SPRING in the U.K.)

Wed June 2
Attends the Derby horse race at Epsom Downs in Surrey, England.

*With Arnella and Patrice in England -
Tue, June 15*

Thu June 3
Attends with Anna Neagle the premiere of *Johnny Guitar* at the Leicester Square Theatre in London.

Tue June 15
Patrice and Arnella arrive in England from Rome *(bottom left)*.
Around this time he meets with the Chauvels for the first time since 1932 and, with Patrice, fêtes them at London's Savoy Hotel.

Sat June 19
Letter to Justin Golenbock: *"....I cannot understand the situation concerning my income tax settlement? I did not realise that this depended upon the filing of my last years income tax....it seems to me that I shall be older than Rip Van Winkle before this is finished...."*

Sun June 20
Flynn's 45th birthday.

Tue June 22
Writes a letter to his New York attorney, Justin Golenbock, regarding money which his former accountant, Al Blum, had *"cleverly applied to his own tax indebtedness,"* and which amounted to *"$20,000 in one year alone."* In fact, his 1953 tax form lists $20,668.75 in *"theft by business manager [$200,136.51 in 2021 value]."* He also mentions not being able to get a response from Apolonio Diaz, to whom he had lent $12,000 ($116,197 in 2021 value) toward opening a restaurant in Acapulco; writes a letter to his father in Jamaica: *"Dear Pop....Very distressed to hear about your loss in the death of J.P. Hill [Professor Flynn's biology colleague], and while we know that these things are inevitable certainly a deep gap seems to be felt at this moment....If you want to, we can contribute the amount of your passage to London return. I cannot possibly, as much as I would like to, include the price of fare for mother as well....Pat and Arnella are fine, and I've nearly finished the picture which has gone very well indeed. Production plans are afoot to make the White Witch of Rosehall in Jamaica, we hope before the end of this year...."*

Thu June 24
In a recording studio in Holborn recording songs for LET'S MAKE UP; they include "Lily of Laguna," "Gathering Lilacs," and "I'm All Alone"; in the evening with Patrice attending Night Of 100 Stars at the London Palladium,

a charity affair to benefit the Actor's Orphanage; among the attendees are Boris Karloff, Marlene Dietrich, Laurence Olivier, Vivien Leigh, John Mills, Douglas Fairbanks Jr., Noel Coward, and others.

Wed June 30
Writes a letter to Justin Golenbock, concerning his (Flynn's) secretary, Ada Klock: *"....P.P.S. I'd appreciate if you'd tactfully tell Ada Klock 116,197 ck that I cannot afford to pay $60 a week [$580.98 in 2021 value] for her services which, while valuable, are not necessary. If you don't care to do so I'll understand – but I feel it would come better from you than me – for obvious reasons. EF."*

Fri July 2
Attends a fête at Northampton in Franklin Gardens, hosted by the Northampton Theatre Guild to aid the guild's Little Theatre Fund.

Sat July 17
CROSSED SWORDS has a first showing in the United States at the Stardusk Drive-In in Sheboygan, WI.

Thu July 22
Allied Artists announces Flynn will star in *The Black Prince* (later to be retitled THE DARK AVENGER, and in the United States THE WARRIORS), production to begin on August 3rd; wires John Huston at the Metropole Hotel in Cork, Ireland: HALLO JOHNNIE SUGGEST YOU GET WARNERS SHOW YOU "CRUISE OF THE ZAVA [sic]" FOR WHALE SEQUENCES STOP IF ANY USE HAVE EXTRA FOTTAGE [sic] WHICH HAPPY GIVE YOU FOR FREE JUST BECAUSE YOU CAN'T FIGHT WORTH A DAMN STOP ALL BEST LUCK MOBY DICK   ERROL.

August and September
Filming THE WARRIORS at Tring in Hertfordshire and at Elstree Studios (the daily production notes have not been located).

With Laurence Olivier at the London Palladium for the Night of 100 Stars - Thu, June 24

Here and right, as Prince Edward in THE WARRIORS (titled THE DARK AVENGER in the U.K.)

With Joanne Dru and director Henry Levin

With Peter Finch, Alistair Hunter, and Henry Levin (second from right)

Opportunity for Dames Only: Wanna sleep in Errol Flynn's bedroom? Here's your chance. An ad reads: "Errol Flynn offers his famous Mulholland Farms for rent or lease, completely furnished. Projection and theatre room. Caretaker Pool. Tennis court Pony ring with pony. $950 a month." (Why the pony, Errol?)

From Walter Winchell's column of Sat, August 21

Receiving his raffle gift of perfume at the Petits Lits Blancs charity ball in Deauville, France - Sun, August 29

Wed August 11

Letter from John Huston's secretary: *"....Dear Mr. Flynn: The day after Mr. Huston received your telegraphed offer of the film CRUISE OF THE ZAVA [sic] he sent you the following telegram c/o Lee Katz, 8, Lower James Street: DEAR ERROL: THANKS FOR YOUR GENEROUS OFFER AND WILL DO EVERYTHING TO AVAIL MYSELF OF SAME STOP WHOM DO I CONTACT TO SEE THE FILM REGARDS, JOHN. I am sorry that the telegram did not reach you. Would you be kind enough to send your reply to Mr. Huston here c/o Fishguard Bay Hotel, Fishguard, Wales – or give Mr. Katz the answer so that he can arrange to obtain the film. Mr. Huston was in London for one day recently and tried to telephone you unsuccessfully. I understand he left a message for you and I do hope you received it. Sincerely, Lorraine Sherwood...Secretary to John."* An Elstree Studios inter-departmental communication to John Huston sometime shortly thereafter: *"Errol Flynn's Whaling Film: Mr. Flynn's whaling film is all in 16mm Kodachrome. It has been blown up to 35mm but apparently this copy is not available. Lee [Katz] would like you to ring Mr. Flynn at Kensington 5530 as he feels a direct request would settle the matter. Cecil F. Ford."*

Wed August 25

Letter to John Huston's secretary, Lorraine Sherwood, from Associated British Picture Corporation, LTD: *"Dear Lorry, Evidently Errol Flynn has copied Jack Benny in having vaults beneath his house, but in Errol's case I am reasonably sure there is no money in the vault. In any event, it seems that the whaling material he has mentioned to John is stored in these Mulholland Drive vaults and what Errol had in mind was that we would delegate someone in Hollywood to go up to the vaults, pick the whaling film out from among the mass of other film he apparently has stored there, view same and send on to us here anything of interest. Also it seems that Warners own all the whaling subjects that Flynn has edited and the only material he is offering us would be trims and cut-outs. In view of the foregoing, would you please ask John if he has anyone special in Hollywood to whom he would like to delegate the task of viewing the material, or whether we should write Walter Mirisch and ask him to send a cutter up to try and find the specific pieces of film having to do with whaling? After which, Walter might try to look over the material... Finally, is there any point in pushing the matter any further at all? I may be doing Errol an injustice, but I have a feeling that his offer was somewhat in the nature of a grand slam play and that the likelihood is that we are playing happy fun games. Then again perhaps I am wrong, I frequently am. Best, Lee Katz."*

Fri August 27

Flies with Patrice to Deauville, France.

Sun August 29

At the Petits Lits Blancs charity ball in Deauville, France *(bottom left).*

Vincent Price Sues on 'Bargain'
LOS ANGELES, Sept. 11 (AP) —Vincent Price, the actor, contends the role he played in "The Bargain" was too much of a bargain. He filed suit yesterday for $15,000 against William Marshall and Errol Flynn, producers of the picture, charging that they had promised him $35,000, but paid him only $20,000.

The Los Angeles Times, concerning THE ADVENTURES OF CAPTAIN FABIAN - Sat, September 11

Tue September 14

Society playboy Serge Rubenstein begins renting the Mulholland house for one month at $950 ($9,199 in 2021 value).

Wed September 15

Flynn's parents visit him on the set of THE WARRIORS.

Fri September 24

Travels to Tobermory Bay, Scotland, to go deep sea diving for sunken treasure with Ian Douglas Campbell, the 11th Duke of Argyll; the objective is a wooden galleon of one of the ships of the Spanish Armada; he returns to work on the 27th.

Sat October 9

Letter to Justin Golenbock: *"....Contact [Zaca captain] Stafford directly about his requirements and needs to get the [Zaca] over to Monte Carlo. The boat should outfit in this port....the departure of the vessel must not be delayed for want of money for outfitting etc....Otherwise she hits dirty weather in the Atlantic, and dirty weather can be costly by the time she arrives....[I] estimate cost of bringing Zaca from Jamaica to Monte Carlo, including cash obligation to Stafford, at about $15,000.00 [$145,246 in 2021 value]...."* Hedda Hopper reports that *"Lili Damita says if Flynn returns to Hollywood she'll put him in jail right away on a back alimony charge. Perhaps that's the reason he's staying in England to make another picture, 'King's Rhapsody,' opposite Anna Neagle."*

Wed October 13

Signs a three-year contract with producer Herbert Wilcox to make six films.

Late October

Moves with Patrice and Arnella to their new Rome apartment.

Mon October 25

Letter to Justin Golenbock: *"Nora's hearing in Santa Monica comes up on the 19th Nov. of this year. I feel she has been trying by her various cables to me asking for money, to set up a record that will impress the judge. I feel that I must....Convince the court (if Nora actually goes to court) that you have held [support] money for my children only awaiting for some indication from Nora that the money would be spent on the children and not her...Obviously, Nora's telegrams employ words and phrases such as: 'Children in dire need' etc, when asking for money 'Send Dollars pending settlement.' This terminology was never Nora's vocabulary range...."*

Fri November 5

Leaves for Tangier to scout locations for a possible television series, and as a residence to avoid heavy taxes (is back in Rome by the 11th).

Thu December 16

Travels to Monaco with his family, staying in Villefranche, returning to Rome on Friday the 10th.

Sun December 19

Fishing and duck hunting with Patrice at Lake Fogliano near Rome *(bottom right)*.

Tue December 21

LET'S MAKE UP premieres at the London Pavilion.

Thu December 23

Letter to Justin Golenbock: *"....I have had no word from the Zaca but presume she is still outfitting at Barbados. I think [Skipper Richard] Stafford would have cabled me if she had left...."*

Sat December 25

Spends Christmas in Rome with Patrice and Arnella.

1955

Mon January 3

Writes a letter to Justin Golenbock in which he mentions that *"some years ago I loaned a man called Appolonio Castillo Diaz, $12,000.00 to start a restaurant [in Acapulco]. I was to be repaid the $12,000.00 [$116,197 in 2021 value] and split any profits 50/50 there after. The fellow obviously intended to cheat me from the beginning as I have never seen a penny and he has consistently refused to answer any of my letters."* Flynn ends the letter with a P.S.: *"Is there anyway that Lili could get a judgment against me in Jamaica? This has me worried."*

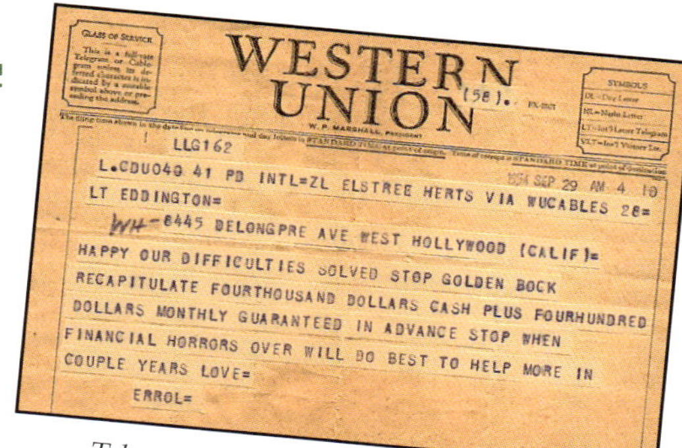

WESTERN UNION

LLG162

L.CDU040 41 PD INTL=ZL ELSTREE HERTS VIA WUCABLES 28= 1954 SEP 29 AM 4 10

LT EDDINGTON=

WH-8445 DELONGPRE AVE WEST HOLLYWOOD (CALIF)=

HAPPY OUR DIFFICULTIES SOLVED STOP GOLDEN BOCK RECAPITULATE FOURTHOUSAND DOLLARS CASH PLUS FOURHUNDRED DOLLARS MONTHLY GUARANTEED IN ADVANCE STOP WHEN FINANCIAL HORRORS OVER WILL DO BEST TO HELP MORE IN COUPLE YEARS LOVE=

ERROL=

Telegram to Nora - Wed, September 29

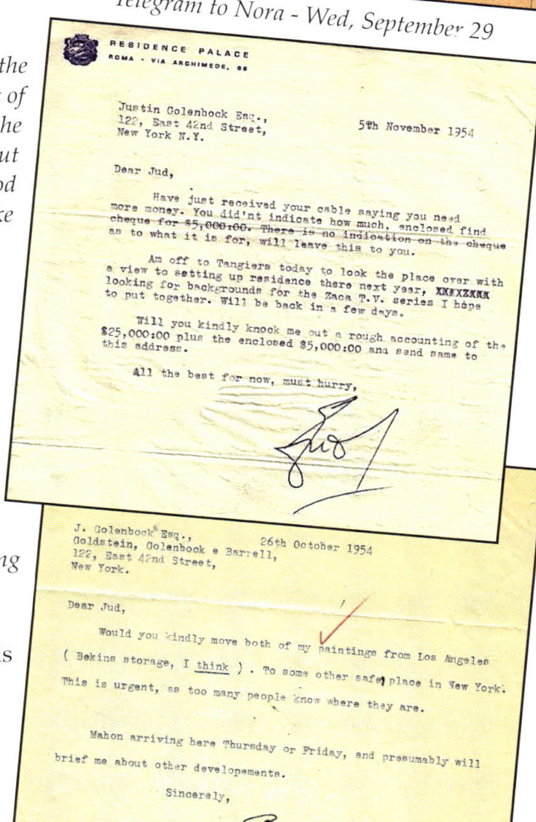

RESIDENCE PALACE
ROMA - VIA ARCHIMEDE, 88

Justin Golenbock Esq.,
122, East 42nd Street,   5th November 1954
New York N.Y.

Dear Jud,

Have just received your cable saying you need more money. You did'nt indicate how much, enclosed find cheque for $5,000:00. There is no indication on the cheque as to what it is for, will leave this to you.

Am off to Tangiers today to look the place over with a view to setting up residence there next year, XXXXZXXX looking for backgrounds for the Zaca T.V. series I hope to put together. Will be back in a few days.

Will you kindly knock me out a rough accounting of the $25,000:00 plus the enclosed $5,000:00 and send same to this address.

All the best for now, must hurry,

J. Golenbock Esq.,   26th October 1954
Goldstein, Golenbock e Barrell,
122, East 42nd Street,
New York.

Dear Jud,

Would you kindly move both of my paintings from Los Angeles (Bekins storage, I think). To some other safe place in New York. This is urgent, as too many people know where they are.

Mahon arriving here Thursday or Friday, and presumably will brief me about other developements.

Sincerely,

Duck hunting with Patrice at Lake Fogliano, Italy - Sun, December 19

With Anna Neagle and Herbert Wilcox on Montserrat above Barcelona, Spain - March

With KING'S RHAPSODY choreographer Jon Gregory, music arranger Jack Olsen, and Patrice in Barcelona - March

With Patrice and their daughter Arnella, who is seen briefly in KING'S RHAPSODY

Tue January 4

Arrives in London with Patrice and Arnella and stays at the Savoy Hotel; letter from his producer/partner, J. Barret (Barry) Mahon: *"Dear Errol=It is hereby agreed that you have my advance from 'King's Rhapsody' of $8,000.00 for part payment of my debt to you of $8,455.00 as accrued [$82,483 in 2021 value]. The remaining $455.00 plus $1,000.00 you have just advanced me will be paid $500.00 on my arrival in England and $-150.00 per week or more until all is paid. I thank you for all your help. Sincerely, J Mahon"*

Sun January 9

LILACS IN THE SPRING (American title, LET'S MAKE UP) opens at the Gaiety Theatre in Manchester, England.

Mon January 10

Begins filming KING'S RHAPSODY (the daily production notes have not been located).

Sat January 22

Billboard magazine reports that CBS TV is planning a new series titled *March Or Die* which will star Errol Flynn in his U.S. television debut; the series would be about the Foreign Legion and be filmed both in London and on location in French Morocco; it was ultimately never made.

Thu February 17

Flies from Paris on BEA to London, where on this day Bruce Cabot is suing Flynn for £17,300 ($657,608.25 in 2021 value) in back payments for work done on WILLIAM TELL.

Errol Flynns Plan TV Series

HOLLYWOOD (NEA) — Hollywood on TV: Fasten the seat belts on the living room easy chairs. A telefilm series titled "At Home With the Flynns," starring Errol Flynn and wife, Patrice Wymore, may be just what television needs.

I mean the homey, folksy, just-plain-mortals touch.

Like episodes about the beautiful blonde on the yacht next door. Or the problem of the missing caviar.

Errol, Patrice and small daughter, Arnella, face the cameras for the reported "intimate peek at their private lives" in Portugal next June. There will be 39 episodes in the series with many to be shot aboard Errol's luxury yacht, the Zaca. "Come with me to the porthole, honey, and let's look at the moon."

I already can visualize the opening show:

It's a domestic comedy aboard the Zaca. Patrice gets a cablegram saying Ava Gardner's stopping for lunch. But there's only one magnum of champagne left in the cooler. Pat signals Errol, who comes up in a diver's suit from a treasure ship he's exploring and dumps $8,000,000 worth of pieces of eight on deck.

"But there's only one bottle of champagne," wails Pat. Then .

Well, I guess you get the idea. But that blonde on the yacht next door is intriguing, at that.

The News Herald *of Franklin, PA - Fri, January 21*

March

Confidential magazine publishes a defamatory article claiming Flynn was with a prostitute on his wedding night in 1950 *(top right)*; it enrages him and he sues the publication; letter to Justin Golenbock this month: *"....My first reaction* [to Lili's lawyers, Loeb & Loeb] *however, is that an astronomical amount of money is being claimed and that I see very little merit in trying to meet these claims if the amount of money claimed is more than the* [Mulholland] *house and property are worth, so what's the point of trying to salvage it?....Yes, I read the article in 'Confidential' and I feel very strongly proceedings should be intended, and would like to go after them...I'm quite sure the article was not planted by Cabot, and it is such a mass of libel I do not want to let it go unchallenged...The opening statement should demonstrate alone how obviously untrue the whole article is. For instance: it seems to have overlooked the fact that Pat and I were married in Monte Carlo, and immediately left on board 'The Zaca' for Tanger* [sic], *so it is hard to imagine how we could have been disporting ourselves in the manner described in my house in Hollywood. Let's go after them, Jud....I will be leaving for Barcelona next Wednesday, the 9th of March to complete 'King's Rhapsody' which incidently* [sic] *is turning out very well with Pat doing quite the outstanding job...It is possible we may go right into 'William Tell' immediately after Spain, instead of Yugoslavia...."*

IT WAS SCARCELY A COUPLE OF HOURS since blonde and lovely Pat Wymore had walked down the aisle with Errol Flynn. The beautiful bride was in an upstairs bedroom of her new husband's home in Beverly Hills, shaking the rice from her hair when there came a soft knock at the door.

Blushing prettily, Pat danced over and threw it open to find her mate of some 120 minutes resplendent in white tie and tails, with a fresh boutonniere in his lapel.

Bowing low, the dashing Mr. Flynn kissed his wife's wrist and expressed the hope that she'd enjoy a good night's sleep. Before the wedding, Pat had dated Errol long enough to know she had an inspired nut on her hands, but this was too much for even her cast-iron aplomb.

"How do you mean, 'get a good night's sleep'?" she gasped. "And, if I'm not being too inquisitive, where are *you* going?"

The suave hero of a hundred melodramas attempted one more bow and nearly sprawled at her feet. Recovering hastily, he leered significantly at his spanking new spouse.

"I, my dear, am going out to keep a dinner date," he muttered thickly. With that, Flynn zig-zagged down the steps and out the front door of his mansion on Mulholland Drive. He was off to dine and spend the rest of the night—with a call girl.

The incident was novel, to be sure, but only to the new Mrs. Flynn. For in the years before Errol beat it to Europe to escape tax and alimony difficulties, he built up a legend about himself and the midnight frolics in his home that made his swashbuckling heroics on the screen seem like the antics of the Bobbsey Twins.

There was, for instance, the night some months after his marriage to Miss Wymore, when she kicked up her spirits at a party and started dancing for their guests. Pat is no slouch with her heels and toes and had the assembly hypnotized, which may have been too much for the ham in Flynn.

Scene Was Better Than a Minsky Finale

At any rate, Errol—better known to his friends as "the Baron"—suddenly ran out into the middle of the floor with fire in his eye and began to tear off his wife's clothes. Pat broke for safety, yelping in alarm, as Errol staggered after her. The scene was better than a Minsky finale.

Other nights, he turned producer and showed his guests movies of himself and former girlfriends in non-musical comedies that would make the entire Johnston office faint. One starred Errol and a willowy hoyden in nude romps through a tropical garden, and another was an underwater ballet in the seas off Jamaica which had the fish calling for an encore.

But Errol really scaled the heights with dinner parties that Emily Post could chew on for a lifetime. His favorite function of this type spotlighted pressed duck on the table and fresh squabs around it. The duck he presumably got from his butcher. The quails were invariably vice dollies, culled from long lists he kept in an assortment of little black books.

Flynn's weakness for the play-for-pay babes was well nigh incredible, even for Hollywood. He used to order them up not one, two or even three at a time but in coveys of 10, 15 and 20 at a brace.

Some were there to entertain him. Others, as it turned out, were present strictly to enjoy the fun when he staged such practical jokes as allowing his guests to watch through an elaborate peephole while a pal cut capers with one of the dally-for-dough dames.

The fact that he was presenting his buddies in such real-life one act plays might never have come to light had not one of the victims—in this case Bruce Cabot—gotten wise to the stunt.

Errol had a majestic bedroom which he seemed only too willing to loan out to tried and true associates at a moment's notice. Most of them jumped at *(Continued on page 51)*

From the March 1955 issue of Confidential Magazine

Wed March 9

Leaves for Barcelona to continue filming KING'S RHAPSODY, arriving the next day *(previous page, top two)*.

April

Sometime this month Flynn flies to Jamaica to prepare the *Zaca* for shipping to the Mediterranean (Patrice is not with him); he may have accompanied his crew on some portion of the Port Antonio-Miami-Bermuda leg of the trip; the *Zaca* will arrive in Mallorca in late May.

Tue April 5

Errol and Patrice stand in as best man and maid of honor for the wedding of (KING'S RHAPSODY choreographer) Jon Gregory and Helene Keller aboard the passenger-cargo ship *S.S. Exochorda*, docked at Barcelona.

Wed April 20

THE DARK AVENGER (THE WARRIORS in the United States) premieres at the Carlton Theatre in Westminster, London.

Fri April 29

Sends a long letter to Justin Golenbock outlining a number of issues of importance: his irritation with William Marshall for selling the television rights to THE ADVENTURES OF CAPTAIN FABIAN to Alexander Salkind (*"the worst kind of fraudulent dealing possible"*); his admitting to secreting away the negative of scenes from HELLO GOD in which he appears so as to prevent Marshall from selling it to TV (*"I want 50% of the proceeds but no under the table deals such as Marshall is an expert in conniving"*); his *"getting nervous"* about his passport expiring on August 1st; his concern over Golenbock's office supplying his son Sean with too much *"pocket money"* ($100, or $976 in 2021 value) for the trip to Europe to visit Errol and Patrice (*"He is liable to go showing it around and could easily get in trouble with that amount of money on him"*); his frustration with having spent over £4,000 ($152,277 in 2021 value) to have the *Zaca* delivered from Jamaica to Monte Carlo though the boat turned back while on the Atlantic because the skipper's wife *"got scared"*; his feeling of being *"in jeopardy"* over whether the corporate

As Richard, King of Laurentia in
KING'S RHAPSODY

setup of his properties should be Panamanian or Tangierian; his delight in announcing that a new script for WILLIAM TELL is now ready and that the completed film will *"take its place among those pictures that have been held as the 'best'"*; his opinion that *"it is idiotic to let 'Lilacs in the Spring' go out in America under that title"*; and his question about the location of his valuable Van Gogh and Gauguin paintings and to be sure that *"an expert examines them before storing in New York."*

Thu May 5

Is offered a starring role in a Hollywood WWII story called *The Good Shepherd*; he never does the film.

Tue May 24

In a London court of appeals, Flynn defends himself to Lord Justice Jenkins against Bruce Cabot's £17,300 lawsuit. The lord justice agrees with Flynn's appeal, that Cabot was not "employed" while working on WILLIAM TELL, but only given four-weeks work, and the case is dismissed.

Wed June 1

Flies from Barcelona to New York on Pan Am.

Tue June 7

Guests on TV's *The Martha Rae Show* along with boxing champion Rocky Graziano.

Wed June 8

With Patrice at a party thrown for him at the El Morocco restaurant by John Perona, the club's owner.

Sun June 12

Leaves for Los Angeles with Patrice, where they visit Rory and Deirdre.

Thu June 16

Leaves Los Angeles with Patrice for Mallorca via New York.

Sat June 18

Leaves with Patrice for Barcelona.

Sun June 19

Errol and Patrice travel back to Mallorca.

Mon June 20

Flynn's 46th birthday.

Wed June 22

At the Savoy Hotel in London.

Summer

At the Hotel Bonsol in Illetas, Mallorca; travels by car around Spain with Patrice in early July, revisiting locations from his 1937 visit to cover the Spanish Civil War.

Fri July 1

Writes a letter from the Maricel Hotel in Palma, Mallorca, to his business partner Barry Mahon in which he recounts a telegram he recently sent to director Herbert Wilcox indicating his readiness to restart the filming of WILLIAM TELL, presumably with Wilcox at the helm: AM READY WILLING AND ABLE TO PERFORM FIRST WEEK AUGUST ACCORDING AGREEMENT WITH YOU AND INTERNATIONAL IN WILLIAM TELL STOP YOU READ FINAL SCRIPT BEFORE ME AND ACCORDING YOUR WIRE YOU THOUGHT IT GREAT STOP REPEAT I AM READY PROCEED AUGUST AND AM CONFIDENT YOU WILL HAVE COMPLETED ALL FINANCIAL AGREEMENTS BY THEN; he goes on to relate that United Artists does not feel the film is *"good for me. I don't agree with this. I think a rewrite to clear up the problem is not difficult."* The filming didn't commence in August, nor was it ever made.

Sun July 3

The South China Morning Post reports that *"a superior court judge has approved an agreement between Errol Flynn and his former wife, Lily Damita, that their 14-year-old son, Sean Leslie Flynn, be permitted to visit his father in England this summer."*

Fri July 15

Letter to his attorney, Justin Golenbock: *"Would you also* [contact] *Abercrombie + Fitch for their catalogue? Thanks…. Would you be a sport and call Abercrombie + Fitch + have them send me airmail – but individually packed – 6 RES-Q-PAC. These are small packs for use with* [A]*Qualung Diving…."*

August

Sails the Mediterranean with Patrice, stopping in Minorca, Villefranche, Monte Carlo, and Sicily.

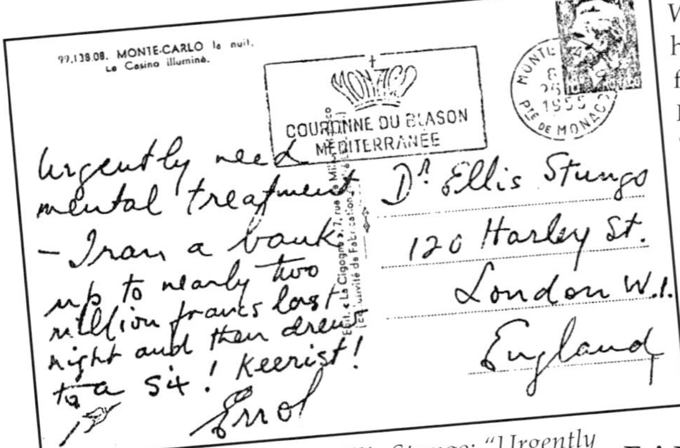

Postcard to his friend Dr. Ellis Stungo: "Urgently need mental treatment—I ran a bank up to nearly two million francs last night and then drew to a six. Keerist [Christ]!" Thu, August 25

Wed August 24

THE WARRIORS has its American opening at the Timonium Theater in Baltimore, MD.

Sat September 3

Letter to Justin Golenbock: *"....I am sending a large file which just recently arrived from Rome. They will give you a much clearer picture of the two matters: (1) The Blum fiasco (2) The one letter I can find from Appolonio Castillo Diaz of Mexico. Incidentally the promisary [sic] notes that I had from Appolonio were in the Blum files. I can only imagine they are with Ada Klock or Braunstein who must be holding them for some kind of ransom. When you have analyzed both these matters I would very much appreciate hearing from you. Especially in the Mexican matter because I have $12,000 [$117,067 in 2021 value] cash down ther [sic]....Re [Herbert] Wilcox I have an original of his letter regarding the $25,000 [$243,890 in 2021 value] that is owed to me....Re Paintings Van Gogh, Gauguin Would you kindly tell me exactly what is against these paintings i.e. Where are they? How are they stored? Have they had an expert to examine them for preservation purposes? This is terribly important, Are they properly insured/ How much is owed against them...Jud, I don't like to put you to this trouble but all of the materials that I ordered when I was in New York, for instance the Stove, Fridge, the record playing machine, and the Barbecue have come in here equiped [sic] with A.C. only instead of A.C.D.C. which I ordered. This will not permit me to operate these machines with the ships [sic] current unless I have a tremendous transformer....Did I write to you or just make notes about an air conditioning unit (A.C.-D.C. motor) for a room on the Zaca, area 35' x 30' x 7'.... Incidently [sic] the Seeburg phonograph arrived here pretty well smashed up....[it was] packed upside down with all of the delicate instruments suspended in mid air....I have just received a call from the Zaca Capt. to say the stove has just arrived and is broken up too. Apparently it arrived packed upside down too!....I have just received your cable advising me the Option was not picked up....I had better get to work pretty soon or I will be broke all over again...Producer finance self styled is coming to see me here in a few days concerning a picture in Mexico. Something to do with Hernan Cortez and the Conquest....If the deal is a good one I will consolidate it here and ask you to clear up the legal details under the terms we discussed in New York....In the files left you by the Blum office what did you come across concerning land that I own near Cedar City Utah. I bought this land years ago and have no idea what happened to it. Please advise....I haven't heard from Barry, I haven't heard from Wilcox, I haven't heard from anybody. However I send you all my best regards...."*

Mon October 3

Is reported to be in Mallorca suffering from malaria.

Wed October 26

KING'S RHAPSODY opens at the Warner Theatre in London; Flynn is visited in Mallorca by agent Sam Jaffe, who will soon officially represent him.

With Julie London and Bobby Troup at the Cameo Restaurant in New York – Thu, January 5

Thu October 27

Telegram to Flynn from director Herbert Wilcox: DEAR ERROL SURE YOU WILL BE GLAD TO KNOW THAT KING'S RHAPSODY WORLD PREMIERE LINKED TO TELEVISION OPENED LAST NIGHT WITH SCENES UNPRECEDENTED IN HISTORY OF INDUSTRY – HERBERT.

Wed November 9

Flynn's Mulholland house is auctioned on the steps of the Los Angeles Hall of Justice for $1,988.62 ($19,400 in 2021 value); Robert McIlwaine and George H. Thomas, the only bidders, won the property in exchange for $1,500 owed them by Flynn for publicity they had done on THE ADVENTURES OF CAPTAIN FABIAN; the house will soon be reclaimed by Flynn's first wife, Lili Damita.

1956

Tue January 3

Guest on TV's *The Martha Rae Show* performing in a scouting skit.

Thu January 5

At the opening of the Julie London and Bobby Troup show at the Cameo Restaurant in New York (*bottom left*).

Sat January 14

Takes Deirdre and Rory out shopping in Los Angeles.

Thu January 19

Writes a letter to Marcel Leduc of Inter TV Films concerning advance

Errol Flynn's Estate Auctioned for $1,988

LOS ANGELES, Nov. 9 (AP)— The Hollywood Hills mansion and estate of actor Errol Flynn —estimated to be worth $350,000 —was auctioned for only $1,-988.62 today to satisfy a court judgment against the actor.

However, Flynn, who is now in Spain, will have a year in which to pay the $1,988.62 and recover the property.

The seven-acre estate has a 30-room house, servants quarters, riding ring, stables and a large swimming pool.

The auction was conducted on the steps of the Hall of Justice and Deputy County Marshal Dan Johnson said only one bid was received. The property was acquired, at least temporarily, by J. N. Benson of La Jolla, Calif., on his telegraphed bid.

Robert, George H. and Thomas McElwaine Jr. obtained the judgment on their claim that Flynn owed them $1,500 for publicity work they did for a film he made in Nice, France, in 1950.

The Hartford Courant
Wed, November 9

*In Santa Monica Superior Court -
Thu, February 2*

*With Arnella, Patrice, Deirdre, and Rory at the
Garden of Allah Hotel in Hollywood - February*

*As Francois Villon in
SWORD OF VILLON - February*

payment for the *Errol Flynn Theater*, adding in pen: *"The remainder of said £10,000 Sterling* [$362,170 in 2021 value] *shall be deposited in my account in Credit Suisse, Geneva."*

Sat January 28

Flynn signs over his Mulholland house to Lili to cover back alimony and child support payments

Thu February 2

"Front row feminine spectators gaze intently at film star Errol Flynn who appeared in [Santa Monica] *Superior Court to answer charges that he is some $5,500* [$53,455 in 2021 value] *in arrears on support payments to ex-wife, Mrs. Nora Eddington Flynn Haymes for their two children."* International News *(top left).*

Mon February 6

From 10:30am to 2:45pm Flynn rehearses the duel for THE SWORD OF VILLON, his final swashbuckler, which will be presented by Screen Gems for their Screen Directors Playhouse TV series; meets Patrice and Arnella, who are arriving at Los Angeles International Airport from Spain; sometime this week he throws a belated birthday party for Deirdre at the Garden of Allah Hotel where he, Patrice, and Arnella are staying; 30 of Deirdre's friends along with her sister Rory attend the festivity *(bottom left).*

Tue February 7

Begins filming THE SWORD OF VILLON on stages #3 and #4 at Hal Roach Studios, working from 8am to 4:50pm; at some point during filming, his daughters Deirdre and Rory visit him on the set.

Wed February 8 through Fri February 10

Films and completes work on THE SWORD OF VILLON (from 8am to 4:55pm on 2/8, 8am to 6:15pm on 2/9, and 8am to 7pm on 2/10); Flynn receives $10,000 for the work ($97,192 in 2021 value); the contempt case against him by Nora is dismissed in Santa Monica Superior Court after her attorney admitted that more than the demanded back child payments had been received.

Mon February 13

Signs a contract with Universal International to film ISTANBUL.

Tue February 14

Wardrobe tests for ISTANBUL with Cornell Borchers and John Bentley at Universal from 7:30am to 2:30pm.

Mon February 20

Begins work on ISTANBUL with an examination for insurance; first scenes shot are in Nural's (John Bentley) office, with Flynn's first shot being his entering the office.

Tue February 21

Filming outside Stephanie's (Cornell Borchers) apartment and on the street (European Street on the Universal backlot).

Wed February 22

Attempts at filming at the airport (Los Angeles International) and outside the hangar are unsuccessful due to an overcast sky; memo from unit manager Lew Leary: *"Mr. Flynn was late due to court appearance in Santa Monica";* filming in the curio shop back at Universal Studios.

Thu February 23

Filming in Jim's (Flynn) hotel room and corridor; attends the Golden Globe Awards ceremony with Patrice at the Coconut Grove *(bottom right).*

With Patrice at the Golden Globes in the Coconut Grove Hotel - Thu, February 23

Fri February 24
Signs the contract with Universal for ISTANBUL (four days *after* starting work on the picture); filming in the hotel lobby and cocktail lounge.

Mon February 27
Filming at the roadblock and outside the hotel fire *(top right, on European Street)*.

Tue February 28
Filming outside the freight yard and at the hangar (at Los Angeles International Airport); radio performance of "The Magnificent Rogue," a sound biography of W. C. Fields, with guests sharing anecdotes about the comedian.

Wed February 29
Filming in the hotel lobby, the cocktail lounge, and the corridor.

Thu March 1
Filming in the curator's shop and the priest's study.

Fri March 2
Filming in and outside Stephanie's apartment and on the street; stills are shot between 12:10 and 12:18.

Mon March 5
Filming in the rug shop, corridor, and weaving room.

Tue March 6
Filming in the rug shop, the alley, and outside Stephanie's apartment (master fuses blow out on European Street as Flynn enters in the background with the thug standing on the corner); dinner with Patrice at the Coconut Grove.

Wed March 7
Filming in Stephanie's apartment.

Thu March 8
Filming in the rug shop; attends a birthday party for Gene Fowler at Chasen's restaurant.

Fri March 9
Filming in the police office and in the curator's office.

Mon March 12
"Errol Flynn tossed his first Hollywood party this week—featuring cake and ice cream. The party, held on the set of 'Istanbul' at Universal International, was in honor of the ninth birthday of his daughter, Rory....The huge chocolate cake with white icing bore the inscription: 'Happy birthday to Rory from The Baron'...'I don't particularly like the nickname,' Errol said, 'but my daughters prefer it to "Daddy."' A Universal Studios press release *(center right)*.

Tue March 13
Filming in Jim's room and in the corridor *(bottom left)*.

Wed March 14
Filming in the cocktail lounge.

Thu March 15
Filming at the airport on Universal stage 17 (company loses two hours due to a technical problem with the rear screen projection); stills are shot at 10:00am; writes a letter to Justin Golenbock mentioning the ongoing issue of Richard Stafford, the *Zaca* skipper who failed to deliver the boat to Monte Carlo and cost Flynn a fortune (*"Let him sue. I have the whole record and so have you...."*); he also asks advice on what to do with his (Flynn's) surplus of 35mm CROSSED SWORDS prints, musing that *"I can't think of any black-market outlets,"* and wondering if *"the Russians might be interested"*; Flynn references land he owns on Sunset Plaza Drive in Los Angeles, wondering *"who holds the deed?"*; he also writes a letter to the producers of his upcoming British TV series, alarmed over what he considers to be *"trite and corny"* episode scripts: *"I would be ashamed to show these stories to the teenage daughter of the policeman at the*

Filming the fire scene in ISTANBUL - Mon, February 27

Celebrating Rory's birthday on the set of ISTANBUL; (back row) John Bentley, Cornell Borchers, producer Albert J. Cohen, Flynn, Patrice, and director Joseph Pevney; (front row) Rory's friend Eileen (daughter of Mulholland farm's caretaker), John Bentley's son Roger, Rory's friend Bill Hendricks, Arnella (on the table), Rory, Deirdre, Pevney's daughter Jan, and Rory's classmate and best friend, Mary Ellen Hendricks - Mon, March 12

Filming in Jim's (Flynn) hotel room - Tue, March 13

With Nat "King" Cole filming in the lounge in ISTANBUL - Thu, March 22

With Cornell Borchers - Wed, March 28

front gate here at Universal International. He might get my pass cancelled for contributing to the delinquency of the public."

Fri March 16

Filming in the airport (on a soundstage), in Nural's office, and in the hotel lobby.

Mon March 19

Filming in Fielding's (Torin Thatcher) bedroom and living room.

Tue March 20

Filming at Fielding's villa.

Wed March 21

Does not work; *"I'm determined to finish this film* [WILLIAM TELL]. *I'm a stubborn fellow,"* Flynn states in a quote released by Universal; in another press release Flynn claims he will begin filming WILLIAM TELL all over again after finishing ISTANBUL.

Thu March 22

Filming outside Aziz's (Vladimir Sokoloff) place and in the cocktail lounge; Nat "King" Cole begins filming on this date, entering the lounge, sitting at the piano, and playing the introduction to a song; he then joins Flynn and Borchers to talk about music, girls, etc., later he is filmed singing the complete song, "When I Fall In Love."

Fri March 23

Filming in the cocktail lounge and in the bar making a telephone call; Nat "King" Cole finishes filming, singing "I Was a Little Too Lonely."

Sat March 24

Letter to Justin Golenbock concerning producer Charles Deane and a potential film: *"....I have set the deal at $140,000* [$1,360,685 in 2021 value] *plus a percentage we mentioned for me to do the picture....what I said to him was I wanted $25,000 put up for the commitment. I don't mind where it's put, just so it is put up...."* The film, which was to be shot in Portugal from September through December, was never made.

Mon March 26

Filming in Karen's (also Borchers) bedroom, Jim's room, Boyle's (Leif Erickson) room, and outside at a fence.

Tue March 27

Filming in the plane, in the taxi, a process shot on the street, and outside the hangar; attends the Academy Awards at the Pantages Theater with Patrice.

Wed March 28

Filming in the cocktail lounge, in Stephanie's apartment, on the street, on the balcony, in the water taxi, and at the airport (on a soundstage); attends the premiere of *Alexander the Great* at the Fox Wilshire Theater.

Thu March 29

Company does not work due to Flynn's court appearances: in the morning he appears in Los Angeles Superior Court to face a judgment against him for $13,560 in agents fees ($131,792 in 2021 value) to MCA Artists, Inc., from 1955 (the suit against him was discharged); in the afternoon he appears as a witness in federal court concerning an F.B.I. investigation of a Beverly Hills doctor and the doctor's overprescribing of drugs which Flynn was suspected of receiving.

In Los Angeles Superior Court - Thu morning, March 29

Fri March 30

Filming on the hotel balcony, in the water taxi, and outside the airport (on a soundstage); according to a Universal press release, Flynn spent a recent day off shopping for Easter gifts for his daughters in a department store's junior miss section.

Sun April 1

Attends the Thalians event at the Beverly Hilton Hotel *(top left)*.

Wed April 4

Completes work on ISTANBUL filming scenes in the cargo ship, in Nural's office, in the bar, on Stephanie's terrace, and at the Istanbul airport; his salary for the film is $150,000 ($1,457,877 in 2021 value); THE SWORD OF VILLON for Screen Directors Playhouse is broadcast on United States TV.

Mon April 9

Arrives in London *(bottom left)*.

Thu April 19

Letter to his attorney Justin Golenbock *(top right)*: *"Encls: my last check stubs Dear Jud. Sean, my boy, gets out of school May 13. Enclosed here is check for $500 [$4,860 in 2020 value] to cover plane fare plus particular expenses (I understand the fare is about $430?). I hope there's not going to be another one of those last minute disappointmen [sic] Lili habit[u]ally pulls. I wish she'd make his trip definite this time, as I'm making many plans + so is he. I've had no word from you about my immigration-passport problem + I'm really beginning to worry. Did you receive [Zaca Cpt.] Stafford's accounting? He said he'd sent it to you weeks ago. Yours, Errol Please let me hear from you."*

With Tony Curtis at the Thalians event - Sun, April 1

Thu April 26

In a letter to Justin Golenbock Flynn expresses concern about contracts for THE BIG BOODLE not having yet arrived, especially *"since I have made all plans to leave here [England] on the 13th, for Cuba [where the film is to be shot]. Naturally I'm anxious to know if there [are] any hitches in the deal...."* He also asks Golenbock to *"please ask Lakeside Golf Club [in Burbank, CA] to send you the monthly bill for my membership...."*

Tue May 1 and Thu May 10

Writes letters to Jud Golenbock; the May 10th letter concerns, among other things, the continuing hope for the resurrection of the William Tell project: *"If 'TELL' can be made this year, I'll be happy, in fact I am holding off on the other two offers, that is, 'LORD JOHNNY' and the one here called 'THE BRIGAND', until we have a definite YES or NO on 'TELL'."*

With Patrice and Arnella in London - Mon, April 9

He continues that *"Lord Johnny"* *"is a good story but I do not want any percentage of the profit... any cash payment of less than $100,000 is out [$971,918 in 2021 value]."* He finishes the letter still wondering *"what ever happened to the buyer for the Gauguin?"* Letter to Marge Eddington (5/10): *"....Am pleased to hear the girls [Deirdre and Rory] have finally got a home they can call their own....I am very disappointed I haven't heard from them while I have been in England...."*

Meeting Cuban president Batista at the Presidential Palace in Havana, with Rossana Rory and Gia Scala - May

*Letter to Justin Golenbock-
Thu, April 19*

Sun May 13

Flies on Pan Am from London to New York, arriving in Havana the next day; he joins the Cuban actors' union (ACAT) for $60 ($583.15 in 2021 value) on Tuesday the 15th.

At some point this month meets with Cuban president Fulgencio Batista in the Presidential Palace *(bottom right)*.

Fri May 18

Begins filming THE BIG BOODLE in Havana (the daily production notes have not been located).

Filming THE BIG BOODLE in Havana: *above left, in the casino with Rossana Rory (on the left); above center, at Morro Castle; and above right, with Pedro Armendáriz, Rossana Rory, and Gia Scala (on the ground)*

With Patrice and Arnella upon their arrival in Havana - Wed, June 20

Letter to Justin Golenbock - Wed, June 27

Sun May 27

On the casino set of THE BIG BOODLE.

June

Letter from ISTANBUL producer Albert J. Cohen, sent to Flynn sometime early this month in Havana: *"....In making some changes in the picture, and also not wanting to offend Turkey or any of its Government Officials, I find that we will need three new lines of dialogue from you to replace those that we have in [ISTANBUL]. They are as follows: 1. In the scene between you and Cornell, where you have just thrown out of your hotel room the sneak thief character, and say to Cornell, 'Oh, darling, they have robberies like this all the time here'…The reason for changing this line is obvious, as it does make the Turkish Police Department look inefficient. The new line I would like to get from you is, 'Why get the poor fellow in trouble?...He's just a petty thief.' 2. The next new one needed for cutting purposes is one to replace the present line when you and Cornell come down the hotel hallway, approaching your room and, as you unlock your door, the original line was, 'Not in Turkey. Here they wrap up the bridal bed in red tape.' The new line should be, "I forgot about the posting of the banns for three weeks.' or 'I should have known about posting the banns and waiting three weeks.'...3. The third line is near the end of the picture where you say goodbye to Nural at the airport. You now say goodbye using the Turkish expression 'Alla Marladik [sic].' Because of the fact that we have cut out a piece of the scene where we explained what we meant, now this expression will confuse the audience and very few people will know what it means. I want to replace it with simply, 'So long, Nural.' All of these lines should be spoken and recorded with volume used as if you were speaking to someone not more than two or three feet away from you. In other words, in a normal tone, not too low or too high. May I suggest that when you do these you do several versions of each line so that we may have a choice....We all miss you around the lot...."*

Wed June 20

Flynn's 47th birthday; Patrice and Arnella join Errol in Havana *(center left)*, Patrice throwing a party for him at the Nacional Hotel; a telegram is sent to production manager Henry Spitz from producer George Golitzen at Universal: ANXIOUSLY AWAITING ANY NEWS ABOUT WILD LINES [overdubs] WE REQUESTED YOU GET FROM FLYNN IF ANY PROBLEM CALL ME COLLECT TOMORROW

Thu June 21

Cable from Henry Spitz to George Golitzen in reply to previous day's cable: WILL DO TRACKS TUESDAY ON INTERIOR STUDIO IN MEXICO CITY.

Wed June 27

Letter to Justin Golenbock *(bottom left)*: *"....Re [Errol Flynn Theatre producer Marcel] Le Duc - Think I can get back to England by 15 July - <u>must</u> have Rossana Rory tell him -- where are scripts?...Have I been paid? By [production company of THE BIG BOODLE] Monteflor? Will Le Duc provide plane ticket for me - only me - to London? Will pay rest myself...."*

July

With Patrice and Arnella in Jamaica.

Filming THE ERROL FLYNN THEATRE: *Top left, "The Duel" with Edmund Willard and Yvonne Savage; top center, "A Wife for the Czar" with Patrice Wymore; and top right, "Strange Auction" with Sean Flynn*

Mon July 2

Telegram from George Golitzen to Henry Spitz at the Hotel Bamer in Mexico City: WHAT'S LATEST ON FLYNN'S LINES / VERY ANXIOUS TO HEAR / DUBBING PICTURE NOW / THANKS

Mid-July

Returns to London with Patrice and Arnella.

Sat July 7

Sails from Miami to Jamaica with Patrice, Arnella, and Sean on the *S.S. Evangeline*, arriving the next day.

Wed July 18

Flies with Patrice, Arnella, and Sean to London via Miami, arriving the next day.

Thu July 19

Resumes work on *The Errol Flynn Theatre*.

Tue July 24

Slips in his hotel (the Bray in Windsor) and is taken to the hospital with back and arm pain, though no serious injury.

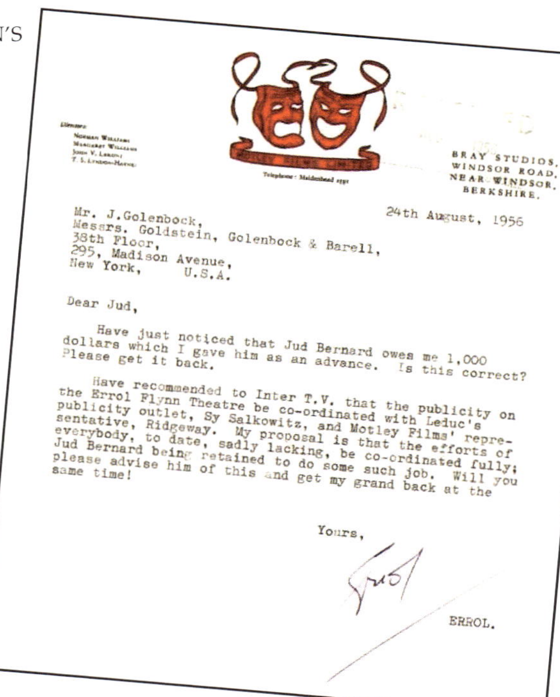

Directors:
Norman Williams
Margaret Williams
John V. Lemon;
T. S. Lyndon-Haynes

BRAY STUDIOS,
WINDSOR ROAD,
NEAR WINDSOR,
BERKSHIRE.

Telephone: Maidenhead 2391

24th August, 1956

Mr. J. Golenbock,
Messrs. Goldstein, Golenbock & Barell,
38th Floor,
295, Madison Avenue,
New York,   U.S.A.

Dear Jud,

Have just noticed that Jud Bernard owes me 1,000 dollars which I gave him as an advance. Is this correct? Please get it back.

Have recommended to Inter T.V. that the publicity on the Errol Flynn Theatre be co-ordinated with Leduc's publicity outlet, Sy Salkowitz, and Motley Films' representative, Ridgeway. My proposal is that the efforts of everybody, to date, sadly lacking, be co-ordinated fully; Jud Bernard being retained to do some such job. Will you please advise him of this and get my grand back at the same time!

Yours,

ERROL.

Tue August 7

Writes a letter to Justin Golenbock in which he laments the fact that the press exaggerates his every ailment: *"....All that happened was, in a film fight in Cuba, I busted a piece off my elbow and it was giving a bit of trouble. It seems every time I cut my finger, everybody credits me with a broken back...."* He expresses worry over the $25,000 still owed ($242,979 in 2021 value) him by producer / director Herbert Wilcox for KING'S RHAPSODY and whether Golenbock thinks Wilcox even *"wants to pay me"*; he reports that he has added to his Jamaica ranch by purchasing Red Poll cattle for something *"in the vicinity of $7,000 dollars [$68,034 in 2021 value]"*; continuing, he admits that *"I have always wanted to do a [TV] series around the Zaca,"* something recently proposed by Marcel Leduc, the producer of *The Errol Flynn Theatre*; the *Zaca*, he adds, has recently been rented by Mary Pickford; he concludes that the William Tell project is now financially cleared to begin (even at this late date), and wonders what has happened with the lawsuit against *Confidential* magazine.

Tue August 14

A letter to Justin Golenbock contains more frustration over the poor quality of the episodes for *The Errol Flynn Theatre*: *"....Half of the stories they have shot stinks [sic]. Unless [the producer] Leduc gets some more money and re-shoots a lot of it with top material, top directors, and cast, the project is doomed to failure....I have a feeling he is hiding from me..."*

British TV ad for "The Errol Flynn Theatre"

Presenting the Bathing Beauty cup to Joyce Lewis, with Patrice and an unidentified girl at the Leicester Theatre in London - Tue, August 28

Thu August 16

In a letter to producer Marcel Leduc, Flynn complains about aspects of *The Errol Flynn Theatre*: *"....We have sadly been lacking in* [promotional ideas]. *Even if the Errol Flynn Theatre is saleable (a dubious matter at this time, because in my opinion we have too many poor 'Episodes' to balance against the few <u>good</u> ones.) I have been amazed what little effort has been spent on Stills* [photos]....*Why not even a Stills man, or an American expert told to follow me. Paulette Goddard? my son? Patrice Wymore et al during filming? With the Queen's swans on the river Thames?....Flynn, son, girls, bikinis, etc., etc., etc., ???...."*

Fri August 17

Writes a letter to his Jamaican estate manager which mentions his plan to purchase more heifers and *"some pure bred pedigreed pigs which I wish to establish on Navy Island...."* A letter is also written to CROSSED SWORDS producer Nato De Angeles, indicating that Flynn is STILL expecting to film WILLIAM TELL: *"Now, at long last, I can see daylight. There is no possibility of* [previous backer] *Fossataro or anyone else appealing* [the decision of the Italian courts in his favor] *or being in a position to sue any new Company that would be formed to make 'WILLIAM TELL'. Even your friend* [Bruce] *Cabot has no chance, having been defeated in the English Courts and having got lost in the Italian Courts....As soon as the Court of Appeals in Italy turns down Fossataro's lawyer's submission, which is certain, I can get financed immediately by UNIVERSAL INTERNATIONAL or WARNERS....I could start this new venture any time after March (perhaps before)....Like many others who heard the Italian Courts' decision, 'WILLIAM TELL' has again become a most inviting plum, from all kinds of sources - you have no idea...."* In a letter to Vincent Grossett at Flynn's Boston Estates in Jamaica, he mentions that his father, Prof. Flynn, has *"relinquished his position there"* as general manager of the estate.

Tue August 28

With Patrice and Sean attending the premiere of *It's a Wonderful World* at the Leicester Theatre in London; in a ceremony there, Flynn presents the Bathing Beauty of Great Britain award cup to Joyce Lewis (*bottom left*).

Sun September 2

The Flynns fly to Barcelona from Mallorca, where they have been spending several days on the Zaca; Sean returns home.

Sat September 8

Films the introduction to *The Errol Flynn Theatre*.

Sat September 15

The Errol Flynn Theater TV series debuts in the U.K. *(top left)* with *The Mirror* starring Patrice; filling out the year on Saturday nights, more episodes are broadcast in the U.K.: *The Fortunes of War* with Flynn and Christopher Lee on 9/22; *The Girl In the Blue Jeans* with Glynis Johns and Herbert Lom on 9/29; *The Red Geranium* on 10/6; *All In The Family* with Mai Zetterling on 10/13; *A Wife For The Czar* with Errol and Patrice on 10/20; *Farewell Appearance* on 10/27; *The Sealed Room* with Glynis John and Herbert Lom on 11/3; *The Model* with Patrice and Christopher Lee on 11/10; *The Duel* with Flynn on 11/17; *Madamoiselle Fifi* with Paulette Goddard on 11/24; *The Ordeal of Carol Kennedy* with Patrice and Derek Bond on 12/1; *The Transfer* with Brian Aherne on 12/8; *The Kinsman* on 12/15; *Evil Thoughts*, a pilot for a projected 1953 TV series on 12/22; and *1,000th Night of Don Juan* with Errol Flynn on 12/29.

Thu September 20

Arrives in Ibiza for surgery, presumably for the back injury he incurred on July 24th.

On the Zaca with Captain Patrick Cother, Eduardo Sala, and Arnella off the coast of Tangier; Flynn's arm is bandaged from an injury received in a fight with a photographer - November

Sat December 1

The Errol Flynn Theatre debuts in the United States and continues on subsequent Saturday nights until March 22, 1957.

Wed December 26

Writes a letter to Justin Golenbock covering a number of concerns: *"What has been done with the cash remaining from the sale of the Gauguin after all obligations were paid? And has the Van Gogh been properly preserved and stored out of New York State?....Please remind me when I arrive [in New York] that I wish to make a few changes in my will.... My life story is, as you know, worth anywhere from $100,000 on up [$971,918 in 2021 value]. It would be ridiculous to pay a writer fifty percent of its earnings, especially since I shall necessarily have to do a great deal of the work myself....I have read several recent autobiographies, including those of Ava Gardner and Gary Cooper, and I would definitely not want mine to be written in the glib and syrupy manner of the usual autobiography, which read like a story from Silver Screen...A man named George Frazer, or Frazier....once did an excellent candid story on me at which everyone but myself was aghast (my father wanted me to sue him). I want someone of this caliber to to do the story...."*

Thu December 27

ISTANBUL opens at the Liberty Theater in Eunice, LA.

1957

Thu January 3

Flies from London to New York aboard Pan Am; Patrice welcomes him upon his arrival *(above right)*.

Sat January 5

The Errol Flynn Theater episode *The Cellini Cup* with Mai Zetterling is broadcast in the U.K.; more episodes are broadcast on subsequent Saturday nights: *Love Token* with Rosanna Rory and Christopher Lee on 1/12; *My Infallible Uncle* with June Havoc on 1/19; *Strange Auction* with Errol, Patrice, and Flynn's son Sean on 1/26; *Rustle of Silk* on 2/2; *First Come, First Loved* with Jean-Pierre Aumont on 2/9; *Take the High Road* with June Havoc on 2/16; *Rescued* with Errol Flynn on 2/23; *Declasse* on 3/2; *Out of the Blue* on 3/9; a rerun of *The Sealed Room* was broadcast on 3/16.

Sun January 6

Guests on TV's *The Steve Allen Show* (Flynn was at the January 4th rehearsal).

Mon January 14

Appears as a contestant on the TV game show *The Big Surprise*; this weekly show is broadcast on Mondays.

Thu January 17

Attends the funeral for Humphrey Bogart at All Saints' Episcopal Church in Beverly Hills.

Mon January 21

Appears again as a contestant on the TV game show *The Big Surprise*.

Wed January 23

At a test screening for the public before THE BIG BOODLE was released, cards were distributed for viewers to write their opinions; some of the comments included: *"Don't bother to see it." "If you once enjoyed Errol Flynn—don't see it." "Good to see Errol Flynn again." "I think William Holden should have played Errol Flynn's part." "Anything with Flynn is corny." "Flynn looks too old." "Errol Flynn—why doesn't he act his age." "....most completely spoiled by the presence of Errol Flynn—bad casting." "....starring a swashbuckler who has lost his swash." "Errol Flynn should never have returned to movies. He's just about had it." "Errol Flynn's smile frequently looked forced." "....my prejudice against [Flynn] for the reputation he has in moral issues spoiled the picture for me." "Errol Flynn is so old!"* Asked *"Which scenes did you like least?"* one viewer wrote, *"Mr. Flynn's love scenes,"* and another incredibly admitted, *"Where Stephanie [Cornell Borchers] touched Nat Cole's hand."* Arrives in Jamaica with his father and attorney Justin Golenbock, staying until Saturday, 1/26.

Fri January 25

THE BIG BOODLE opens with a special screening in San Antonio, TX.

Mon January 28

Wins $20,000 ($188,749 in 2021 value) on the TV game show, *The Big Surprise*.

Wed January 30

Signs a contract for $10,000 ($94,375 in 2021 value) with CBS TV to star in the television Western film WITHOUT INCIDENT.

Patrice welcoming Errol in New York on his return from London - Thu, January 3

With Mike Wallace on The Big Surprise *game show -January*

The Daily News - *Tue, February 12*

Flynn's note confirming 16-year-old Ron Shedlo as his personal secretary: "To whom it may concern. Would you please give Ronnie Shedlo permission to pick up my fan mail still photographs and anything dealing with me of this nature. This applies to Universal International-Warner Bros.-KTLA United Artists-M.G.M. Allied Artists-and the newspapers." - Sun, March 3

February
In Salina, KS, with Patrice and Arnella; discusses with Huntington Hartford (2/3) the idea of doing a play.

Mon February 4
Wins $30,000 ($283,124 in 2021 value) as a contestant on the TV game show *The Big Surprise*, answering questions on ships and the sea.

Sat February 9
Letter to Deirdre and Rory: *"....My darlings – Sweet Sam and Rockin' Rory (otherwise known as hoodat) Thank you both so much for your letters – when you write to me it gives me a wonderful feeling – I feel I'd like to catch the first magic flying carpet from Bhagdad [sic] to L.A. so I could grab you in my arms and smother you with hugs + kisses, mmmm! Oh well – won't be long before I can do it. I'll be in Garden of Allah about the 21st. Hey, listen (or rather have a look) next Tuesday T.V. when I talk about you both some more! I'll try to make it funny just for your special fun – sort of a secret message to you both that only we know about. Every time I talk about you the BIG SHOTS on the Network get mad but I don't care about them. 'This is against regulations of N.B.C. Mr. Flynn,' They snarl 'Please desist!'...'Of course, gentlemen' I smile. 'I'll never mention my daughters on your Network again, be assured.' So just see, darlings –So be assured I will! I'm going to read some imaginary messages from you to me but please keep it secret – it's all fun – for you both....Darling girls – I love you – guess now we can all make Jamaica (if I don't lose next Tuesday) wish me luck!!! Your Baron."*

Mon February 11
Returns to the TV show *The Big Surprise* and turns down the opportunity to go on to the $100,000 jackpot ($943,746 in 2021 value).

Wed February 13
Arrives in Miami for a two-week vacation and a Heart Fund Charity Ball at the Palm Beach Towers on the 14th.

March
Sometime this month Flynn makes 16-year-old fan Ronnie Shedlo his personal secretary *(bottom left)*; Shedlo will remain in this capacity until the end of Flynn's life.

Fri March 1
Letter written to a Mr. Goldstein who is working for Justin Golenbock: *"....Has any word been received from the State Department to my two requests for extension of the expiring date of my passport from October 1957 to around February 1958?....I've written to them several times, and now I'm getting nervous....I ordered four kinescopes from the producers of the 'Big Surprise.'* [the TV game show on which he recently appeared] *Would you please check on the cost of these?...."*

Sat March 2
After having a polyp removed from his tongue, Flynn leaves for Tucson for ten days to work on the *Playhouse 90* TV episode *Without Incident (below two)*, which films during this month; locations include Box Canyon until March 6th, and then the Old Tucson Studio, finishing up in the Twin Buttes area on the weekend of the 8th.

On the set of "Without Incident" at the Old Tucson Studios in Arizona - March

In Tucson with Rodolfo Acosta and John Ireland (behind Acosta) - March

The Los Angeles
Times
Fri, March 29

Fri March 8

Appears at a press conference for the Tucson Press Club.

Thu March 14

Vincent Price wins a default judgment against Flynn for $15,000 ($141,562 in 2021 value) in unpaid salary for THE ADVENTURES OF CAPTAIN FABIAN.

Tue March 19

Back in Los Angeles at this point, Flynn agrees to a contract with 20th Century Fox to star in THE SUN ALSO RISES for a total sum of $81,000 ($764,435 in 2021 value).

Fri March 22

Signs a letter of intent to purchase the rights to Beth Day's book *Sky Pilot* (probably the original title of her book, *Glacier Pilot*): *"I hereby agree that Errol Flynn shall have the exclusive option to purchase Beth Day's 'Sky Pilot' to be published by Henry Holt & Co. and The Readers Digest, for the sum of $25,000 [$235,937 in 2021 value]....Carlton Cole, agent Dated March 22, 1957."* Flynn never made a film of the book.

April and May

In Morelia, Mexico, and Mexico City to film THE SUN ALSO RISES until May 10 (*surrounding photos; the daily production notes have not been located*); stays at the Hotel Alameda.

With Tyrone Power in Morelia - April

With Mel Ferrer, Ava Gardner, and Eddie Albert at Churubusco Studios in Mexico City - May

Above, in Mexico dictating his autobiography - April

Below, with Eddie Albert in Plaza Monumental, Morelia - April

A letter written from Mexico to his daughter Rory - April

In front of the Hotel Virrey in Morelia, Mexico - Mon, April 8

Thu April 4

Official starting day for Flynn's employment on THE SUN ALSO RISES.

Sat April 6

Films the Pamplona Plaza scenes and the Café Iruña exterior scenes.

Mon April 8

Films in front of the Hotel Virrey de Mendoza; letter to his daughters: *"Darlings It hurts so much and I am so disappointed that we won't be able to see each other this summer...I must go to Spain to try to make some money and besides the Jamaica house is not yet finished...But whatever happens I am definitely going to pick you up and take you to Jamaica for the Christmas vacation. And you can help me get this new house fixed up and all feminine and stuff. All the things I don't know anything about...and we'll have horses and boats and maybe I can even fix you up with some dates, although I guess I'm going to be a little jealous when all those nice looking guys come around...I love you so very, very much. Your Baron"*

A letter written from Mexico around this time to his daughter *(top left): "Rory darling – I'm terribly sorry but way down here in Mexico I've just heard by phone that our plans won't come off for you to come here and be with me + put some weight on you and you fix my breakfast + learn Spanish and all the other things we planned. The Laws of the State of California and your mother say you can't come maybe your mother can tell you why not. I can't. I'm terribly sorry if you're disappointed, my moppet. I am too. I had everything arranged here for you. You were going to be the "Governess" of Tyrone Power's two childred [sic] – they're about 5 and 6 I think – and arriving tomorrow. You also had to take care of seeing Audrey Hepburn's miniature dog got a nice piece of fresh grass to do his business on. There were so many other jobs for you to take care of you would have to have been The Sorcerer's apprentice!!! or anyway Mother Hubbard! I love you sweetheart and I'll be seeing you about June 1st Your Baron."*

Mon April 15

Is sued for $44,000 ($415,248 in 2021 value) by his attorney Robert E. Ford over unpaid legal fees between 1948 and 1956.

Mon April 22

Letter to his attorney Justin Golenbock while on location in Morelia, Mexico: *"....Please send a check for $25 to the Larry Edmund's Bookstore....The bills to be paid are for the Hertz Agency, the Lakeside Golf Club and a pharmacy....One of the enclosed papers is a note from [Barry] Mahon and Nato de Angeles renouncing all claims to 'William Tell.'...what about [attorney Robert] Ford's statement that International Films was formed 'to defraud creditors'?...As I told you on the phone, Ford offered to settle for $10,000 [$94,375 in 2020 value] of which he would 'kick me back' $3000 (which I would naturally declare). I accepted this deal the second time he offered it, but I'm still afraid of a double-cross. He might obtain a default judgment. Let's keep a jump ahead of him on this...As of this late date I still haven't received a letter from you....I'll ask you again for an accounting of monies you sent to Switzerland for me. And I haven't the least notion of what monies I've been paid by Fox or where they are...Your silence is more baffling every day...."*

Early May

In a letter to Justin Golenbock, Flynn voices concern about not having received full payment for his work on THE BIG BOODLE: *"I don't get it. $12,750 a week for 6 weeks amounts to $76,500. What happened to the rest? The deal was for 100,000 dollars [$943,746 in 2021 value]. Will talk to you about this when I see you at the Airport, Monday."*

Errol Flynn Quits Fight to Carry Son to Mexico

HOLLYWOOD (UP)— Actor Errol Flynn has given up an attempt to gain court permission to bring his 10-year-old daughter, Rory, to Mexico City where he is making a picture.

Attorney Jerry Giesler, Flynn's lawyer, announced Friday in Santa Monica Superior Court that the actor had decided not to battle with his ex-wife, Mrs. Nora Eddington Flynn Haymes, over the issue.

Mrs. Haymes, Rory's mother, opposed Flynn's petition on the ground that if granted Rory would be taken out of the jurisdiction of California courts.

The Alabama Journal— with a mistaken headline - Sat, April 13

Mon May 13

Now in Mexico City, Flynn writes a letter from the Hotel Bamer to Justin Golenbock, complaining about the attorney's non-response to him (Flynn): *"....Since coming to Mexico I have sent you no fewer than seven letters.... and several cables...."* He adds in pencil at the end of the typed letter, *"I'm hurt, pal; 'specially from a friendship viewpoint -- as well as being neglected from the business viewpoint. What's up?"* To Cuba the next day.

Sat May 18

Travels to Miami from Cuba; in Ciudad Trujillo (now Santo Domingo), Dominican Republic, sometime this week.

Thu May 23

Flies from Santo Domingo to Idlewild Airport, New York *(top right)*.

Sun May 26

Is the best man at the wedding of Teddy Stauffer to Ute Weller in Shrewsbury, NJ; later he is a guest panelist on TV's *What's My Line?*

Tue May 28

At the New York premiere of *A Face In the Crowd*, afterward attending a party at the Eden Roc Club.

Thu June 6

Is in Paris at this point; *Without Incident*, an episode of *Playhouse 90*, is broadcast on United States TV.

Wed June 19

In Palma de Mallorca, agrees to a deal with screenwriter James Edward Grant (*Sands of Iwo Jima*, *Hondo*, *The Alamo*, etc.) for $15,000 ($141,562 in 2021 value) for Grant to write the screenplay for Flynn's planned film of *The White Witch of Rosehall*; the film is never made.

Thu June 20

Flynn's 48th birthday; arrives with Patrice at Berlin's Tempelhof Airport for the Berlinale film festival; about 500 fans greet him there, with a brass band providing a welcoming performance; after loudly complaining about the small size of his booked rooms at the Hotel Kempski, the festival's director, Alfred Bauer, vacates his own apartment at the Hotel Gehrhus for the Flynns.

Fri June 21

Attends the opening of the Berlinale film festival at the Zoopalast *(below left and center)*.

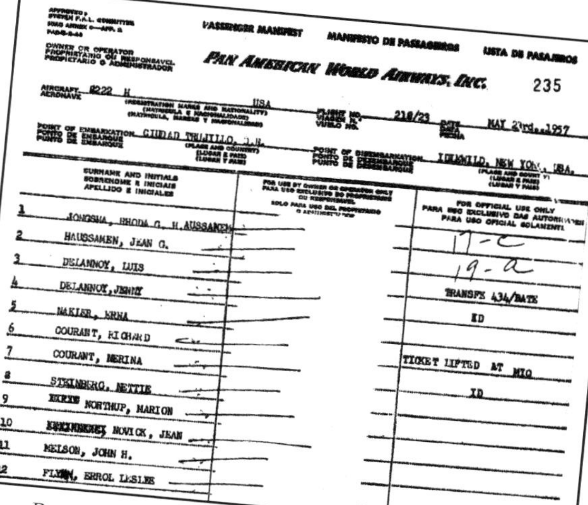

Pan Am passenger list from Ciudad Trujillo (now Santo Domingo), Dominican Republic, to Idlewild Airport in New York - Thu, Mat 23

Arriving at the Berlinale with German actor Wolfgang Lukschy (Flynn's German dubbing voice) and Patrice - Sat, June 22

Meeting Romy Schneider at the Berlinale

With Trevor Howard, Nadia Gray, and Patrice at a cocktail party at the Hotel Gehrhus during the Berlinale

Sat June 22

At the Berlinale, Philip Ridgeway of Pan American Public Relations Ltd. announces that *"Flynn has just concluded negotiations with the government of the Dominican Republic to inaugurate their new film industry with his own production*

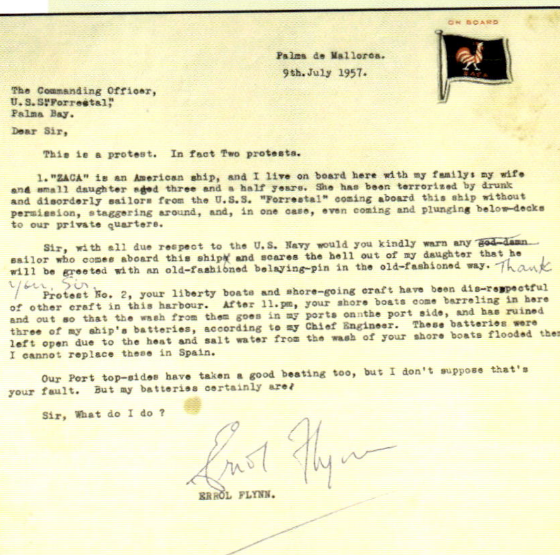

*At Idlewild Airport in New York -
Wed, August 14*

of 'The White Witch of the Indies'. Mr. Flynn will produce and star in the film, a project he has been developing for several years....Mr. Flynn and his party....have decided to advance their production date to September in order to complete the film in time to enter it in next year's Berlin Festival...." The film is never made.

Wed July 10

Writes from Palma de Mallorca to MGM executive Ben Thaw concerning Ava Gardner and the possibility of getting her for *The White Witch of the Indies* (as it has now evidently been retitled): *"I went with [screenwriter James Edward] Grant to Madrid a few days ago to see Ava Gardner, who told me that her contract with M.G.M. would finish in a little over a year, and Ava appeared extremely interested in this property, and doing it with me....As a personal favour, I would like to ask you personally and without, of course, any kind of reflection on Ava, if it is true that she will be free to make any deals outside of Metro in one year's time? THE WHITE WITCH is perfect for her as a vehicle...."*

Thu July 11

A response from the commanding officer of the *U.S.S. Forrestal* to Flynn's letter of July 9th: *"....All instances of annoyance to you and your family by U.S. Navy personnel are....deeply regretted....I certainly agree with you, sir, that an old-fashioned belaying pin is the proper weapon and most appropriate. However, immediate action will be taken to keep the sailors well clear of the area in which the ZACA is moored. I am sure you have long recognized, though the natural curiosity of [people] to congregate in the vicinity of and observe a person of your fame and importance....I met you once, sir, in the Vesuvio Hotel, Naples, when you were demonstrating how to toss off straight shots of vodka while rolling the glass from ear to ear. Mighty impressive, I must say....R.L. Kibbe."* Patrice's initial response to the commanding officer: *"Dear Captain ~Many thanks for your note. Unfortunately Errol had gone to bed and was fast asleep when it arrived so I have taken the liberty of answering it....our Captain advises me that all is well so I want to convey our profound thanks for your generosity and consideration....Best Regards....P.S. Speaking for myself who ever those handsome men were send them back anytime – with batteries or without."*

Wed August 14

Arrives in New York from Spain *(bottom left)*, checking into Roosevelt Hospital to take care of knee and rib injuries suffered ten days earlier *"in a speedboat accident off Palma, Majorca."* The South China Morning Post, 8/15.

Fri August 16

Flies to the Dominican Republic at the invitation of President Trujillo and stays until the 20th to continue discussions about various film projects that the president would finance.

Wed August 21

Inter-office memo from Jo and Art Napoleon (screenwriter and director of TOO MUCH, TOO SOON) to executive producer Steve Trilling: *"A combination of events causes us to write this: 1. Henry Blanke ran the test of John Emery as John Barrymore for us. 2. He told us you were not enthusiastic about Errol Flynn in the part. As far as Emory is concerned, we understand why at first glance he seems a good choice. His physical resemblance to Barrymore in his later years is striking, and his imitation, though very broad, is good. However, we feel Emery's conception of Barrymore is much too superficial. He has the idea that celebrities behave in private in the same manner as when they are on public display. He seems to think that to snort, to arch his eyebrows and to roll his r's is to play Barrymore....This leads us to Flynn and the reasons we feel he would be ideal in the part. 1. He has to convince no one that he once was a big star in a grand manner. 2. Both on and off screen, he has much the same exuberance and vitality as Barrymore – even the same problems with women and alcohol – and like Barrymore, is aging and falling on leaner days. 3. He has the chemistry of a star – the inexplicable ability to charm, excite and move human beings – something that Emery does not have and never will have. 4. Physically his features resemble Barrymore's closely enough, but more important, he has the same kind of athletic vitality and the same authoritative, yet devil-may-care attitude that people associate with Barrymore. This is particularly important in that we plan to do his introduction aboard [Barrymore's yacht] the Infanta – before he has started downhill. The whole reason for the scene is to give the audience a memory of what Barrymore was so they can contrast it ironically with what he becomes. The scene would be impossible with Emery, and perfect with Flynn. 5. Another reason, that you may or may not think is material, is that we feel that the casting of Flynn as Barrymore – especially as an aging Barrymore -- can give the picture a big boost in terms of publicity and exploitation. 6. We've heard that he's superb in 'THE SUN ALSO RISES' and might well get very hot again as a big character actor. True or not, he will also be infinitely more help at the box office than Emery...."*

Fri August 23

Attends the world premiere of THE SUN ALSO RISES at the Roxy Theater in New York City.

Thu September 26

Telegram from Harry Mayer to Steve Trilling: FLYNN DEAL OKAY FOUR WEEKS PLUS TWO. NINETY THOUSAND

[$849,372 in 2021 value] WITH UNDERSTANDING HE RECEIVE EQUAL STAR BILLING.

Fri September 27
Warners announces Flynn's return to the studio to film TOO MUCH, TOO SOON.

Tue October 1
Telegram to Flynn from Jack Warner: ....RETURNED TO STUDIO VERY LATE THIS AFTERNOON AND FOUND YOU HAD CALLED....WANT YOU TO KNOW AM VERY HAPPY YOU ARE RETURNING TO THE FOLD AND HOPE THIS WILL BE BEGINNING OF A WONDERFUL NEW ASSOCIATION OR SHALL I SAY A CONTINUATION OF A WONDERFUL ASSOCIATION....

Monday October 7
Telegram from Flynn to Steve Trilling: ....JUST PHONED GRAHAM WAHN ASKING WHEN I MUST REPORT COAST HE DOESN'T KNOW STOP PLEASE ADVISE ME DIRECTLY HERE 1 BEEKMAN PLACE OR GOLENBOCK AS I AM FRESH OUT OF THEATRICAL AGENTS STOP VERY HAPPY STEVE TO BE RETURNING TO ALMA MATER
Telegram from Steve Trilling to Flynn: ....WE TOO HAPPY HAVE YOU ABOARD....

As John Barrymore in
TOO MUCH, TOO SOON

Sun October 13
Arrives in Hollywood from New York, staying at Huntington Hartford's Hollywood Hills home, the Pines.

Mon October 14
Signs a contract with Warner Bros. for TOO MUCH, TOO SOON at $22,500 per week ($212,343 in 2021 value), with a minimum of six weeks; *"Errol Flynn American Airlined in from London yesterday for role of John Barrymore in Warners' 'Too Much, Too Soon.'" Variety* magazine.

Tue October 15
Filming b&w makeup and wardrobe tests for TOO MUCH, TOO SOON, arriving at 1:40pm—40 minutes late.

Thu October 17
Begins work on TOO MUCH, TOO SOON, filming in the Barrymore living room and in Diana's bedroom.

Fri October 18
Continues filming in the Barrymore living room and on the stairs; a report on Flynn from the set: *"Apparently drinking—dismissed at 4:45PM."* Note to Flynn from Jack Warner: *Have been so tied up this week it has just been impossible for me to get away from the office but I promise to come down to the set on Monday to say hello to you...Know that everything has been going along fine, I think the script is excellent, and am sure we will get a swell picture....Your old pal...."*

With Arthur Loew Jr. and his fiancée Joan Collins at a party at her Hollywood home - October

Bottom left, with Diana Barrymore, the autobiographical author of Too Much, Too Soon; *bottom center to right, on the set of* TOO MUCH, TOO SOON *with Dorothy Malone and director Art Napoleon, and far right with Dorothy Malone - October*

Attends the opening of "My Man Godfrey" at Grauman's Chinese Theatre with daughters, Rory and Deirdre *(top right)*; *"Errol Flynn looked his best with a daughter on each arm - 10-year-old Rory, and Deirdre, 12. These girls from his Nora Eddington marriage, clung to Mr. Flynn, and I thought how nice it would be if he saw them more often."* Sheilah Graham's Hollywood Today.

Sat October 19

Attends the Publicists Association's annual Ballyhoo Ball at the Riviera Country Club in Pacific Palisades *(top left)* and is arrested (with actress Maura FitzGibbon) for taking a policeman's badge, booked on a charge of drunkenness *(bottom left)*, and released on $20 bail ($188.75 in 2021 value) early the next morning.

Mon October 21

Continues filming in the living room; a report on Flynn from the set: *"Mr. Flynn delayed 20 minutes (5:25-5:45pm) from Makeup by lawyers discussing legal action* [re the Riviera Country Club arrest]." Assistant director George Vieira: *"...apparently had been drinking – unable to remember dialogue & coordinate with action. Made 6 takes of scene 6:35 to 7:30 – although unsatisfactory, 2 takes were printed...While placing eagle on chandelier, eagle hurt trainer's arm & tore claw from toe...."*

Mon October 21

In municipal court, Flynn's attorney Robert E. Ford pleads innocent to charges of drunkenness on behalf of Flynn; Sirpuhe E. Philibosian closes a deal to buy the Mulholland house for $125,000 ($1,179,683 in 2021 value).

Tue October 22

Continues filming in the living room; report on Flynn from the set: *"Drinking – unsatisfactory performance and dismissed at 4:10PM."*

Wed October 23

Continues filming in the living room, on the stairs; report on Flynn from the set: *"Again drinking. Repeated rehearsals 5:45 to 6:15PM— could not remember dial. and action."*

Thu October 24

Continues filming in the living room, on the stairs, and in the foyer; report on Flynn from the set: *"Co. waited 2:35 to 2:50PM for Flynn's return from lunch. Quite drunk in afternoon and dismissed at 5:15PM."* Telegram from Cye Martin to Steve Trilling: DEAR STEVE I THOUGHT I WOULD SEND YOU THIS WIRE AFTER READING IN NEW YORK THE UNDESIRABLE FRONT PAGE PUBLICITY ABOUT ERROL FLYNN YOU STILL MAY SERIOUSLY RECONSIDER GENE WESSON FOR THE PART.

Undated handwritten letter from Flynn to Steve Trilling from about this time: *"Friday   Hello sport! This is to thank you – for your understanding + help, Steve—for both of which, ever since I've known you, you have in abundance. To 'God for Harry, England and Saint George!' I would add 'and for God's sake give us more Trillings!' Your friend, Errol."*

Fri October 25

Continues filming in the living room; report on Flynn from the set: *"After return from lunch at 1:45PM, Flynn had great difficulty with dial.—had received 'flu' shot and claimed it made his tongue thick. Left set to change shirt—gone 10 minutes. Started at 2:25PM for 1 ½ pages dial. By rehearsing each speech individually between pickups and running up to 2 ½ minutes each take, dialogue was covered by 3:15PM. Director read each line so that actor* [Flynn] *could repeat same. Dismissed at 5PM and short time later left stage in middle of* [Dorothy] *Malone take, making considerable noise."* Is the special guest of honor at the Motion Picture Costumers Ball at the Beverly Hilton Hotel; it was at this event that he met Olivia de Havilland again after many years, and the last time they would ever see each other.

Mon October 28

Continues filming in the living room and in Diana's bedroom; report on Flynn from the set: *"Flynn there all day*

With Rory and Deirdre at the opening of My Man Godfrey - Fri, October 18

With Maura FitzGibbon and Clint Walker at the Riviera Country Club in Pacific Palisades, CA - Sat, October 19

At West Los Angeles Police Station - Sat, October 19

Errol Flynn Pleads Not Guilty; Trial Set Nov. 15

Errol Flynn, who started a game of 'hide-the-badge' during the Screen Publicists' Ball early Sunday morning and wound up being arrested as a drunk when the policeman didn't get his badge back, yesterday pleaded innocent to the drunkenness charge.

Atty. Robert Ford appeared for Flynn and Municipal Judge Leo Freund set a jury trial for Nov. 25. Miss Maura FitzGibbon, 21, an actress companion of a friend of Flynn's who was booked with the 48-year-old actor, is due in court today to plead to the drunk charge against her. Both are free on $20 bail each.

Meanwhile, Officer William Friedman, who made the arrest after Flynn started passing Friedman's badge around, still is hunting for the badge.

Miss FitzGibbon said she tucked it in a glove and promptly lost the glove. Yesterday Officer Friedman filed a lost report on his badge with the Police Department.

The Los Angeles Times-Tue, October 22

but Co. waited 15 minutes for him to return from lunch. Another wait from 5 to 5:30PM. Unsatisfactory performance, and was dismissed at 5:55PM." Memo from Flynn to Steve Trilling: "Suggestion, if you don't mind. In the tag of our story when Diana finds happiness, it is extremely important to insure its believability and heighten the dramatic impact _without being maudlin_. I feel very strongly that Diana should either play the scene in front of the profile of her father - (OR) - perhaps, turn to his portrait on the wall behind her and whisper: ....'Is this what you wanted, Daddy?'....Both portrait or photograph and especially Diana should be smiling....If her father had such an influence on his daughter, in my opinion the audience will really like this....Do you think it's wise to just lose her father entirely at the end?" Dorothy Manners writing for Louella Parsons in _The Los Angeles Examiner_: "Following his arrest at the Ballyhoo Ball, Errol Flynn received a cable from his wife, Pat Wymore, in Majorca; 'So upset, darling. I've never asked you to do anything before but please do take the Barrymore role seriously. Acting has always been a game to you. But please, please make this role important.' One thing Errol has discovered is the mob of friends he has. I can't tell you how many of the press agents, who were hosts at the Ballyhoo Ball, have called to tell me they are going to testify in Errol's favor that he was not drunk nor disorderly. Just to make sure such unfortunate publicity is not repeated, Errol says, 'I'm going to lock myself in when I'm not on the set of Too Much, Too Soon. I cabled Pat that I've never taken any part as seriously as playing John Barrymore. She won't have to worry.'"

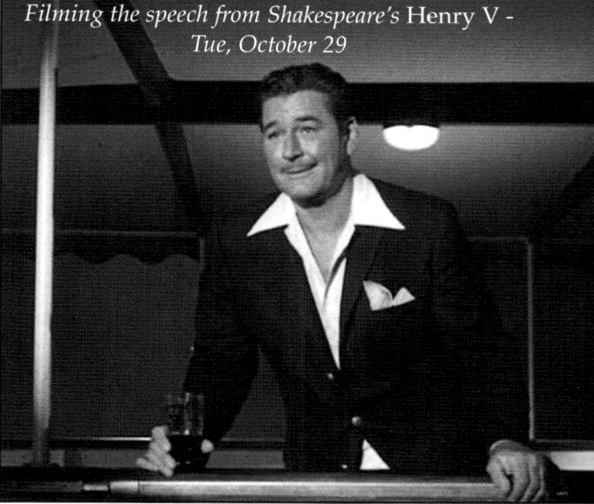

Filming the speech from Shakespeare's **Henry V** _-_
Tue, October 29

Tue October 29
Filming process shots at sea and in the motor launch, and on the deck of the _Infanta_ (Barrymore's yacht) and at the railing _(top right)_; report on Flynn from the set: "_Flynn there all day. Only one 5 min. holdup._"

Wed October 30
Filming on the _Infanta_'s fantail; report on Flynn from the set: "_Only one 5 min. wait and remained with Director after Co. dismissed at 5:55 until 6:15PM discussing next day's shooting._" KING'S RHAPSODY has its first American showing—on TV in Wausau, WI.

Thu October 31
Continues filming on the _Infanta_'s fantail and in the water _(bottom right)_; report on Flynn from the set: "_Flynn had 9:15AM call. Co. waited from 10 to 10:05AM for him. He made one take of long speech—refused to make 2nd take—and lost the Co. 5 minutes in discussion with Napoleon. Another wait for Flynn from 11:55 to 12:25PM. Flynn dismissed at 6:15PM at which time the Co. went to dinner and made shots with Malone._" The press reports that Flynn has filed a $250,000 ($2,359,366 in 2021 value) false-arrest lawsuit against William Friedman, the 39-year-old police officer who arrested him at the October 19th Screen Publicists Ball; meets 15-year-old Beverly Aadland on this date on the Warner Bros. lot, invites her to dinner at the Cock and Bull restaurant in (now) West Hollywood, and later to the Huntington Hartford house in the Hollywood hills where he has been staying; he soon has her added as an extra on TOO MUCH, TOO SOON, though she is not listed in the daily production sheets.

On the WB soundstage - Thu, October 31

Fri November 1
Filming in the _Infanta_'s shower and in the Barrymore bedroom and kitchen; shooting publicity stills with Dorothy Malone from 1 to 1:10pm; report on Flynn from the set: "_Late call because of working late Thurs. Altho Flynn was to report on set at 9:15AM, he did not arrive until 9:40AM. Co. finished the shower seq. at 10:15AM at which time he was told he had 25 minutes to go to Makeup to have nose and hair touched up. However, Flynn did not leave the stage to go to Makeup until 11:20AM and arrived back on the stage at 11:40AM. The camera actually waited 20 minutes for him to appear._" Director Art Napoleon to Steve Trilling: "_....When I talked to you_ [Saturday morning], _I was only half awake and still low about those last two murderous days with Flynn....every time we move the camera or change a light, Flynn disappears into his dressing room, and it never takes less than fifteen minutes to get him out again—each time a little more loaded....the reason I have constantly gone for closeups is that it is apparent to me that Flynn has no timing and the only way I can control this to any degree is in clean closeups which will allow me to shorten or lengthen the beats whenever necessary in the cutting....invariably Flynn was unable to go through a master_ [long take] _and/or hit marks, etc. Frequently he would just stop and demand that I break it up. Sometimes I would convince him to go on, and sometimes I couldn't....I want to repeat how important I feel it is to reshoot the set-up of Barrymore on the bed talking to Michael..._ [because of] _his abominally_ [sic] _unconvincing performance in a key scene._"

Sat November 2
Lunch with Beverly at the Lakeside Country Club across from WB Studios; invites her again up to the Huntington Hartford house and, according to her, first gives her the nickname "Woodsie," short for wood nymph.

Sun November 3
Invites Beverly and her mother to visit him at the Huntington Hartford house, probably on this date; later they travel to watch Deirdre in a riding program at the Los Angeles Equestrian Center.

Beverly Aadland's walk-on in TOO MUCH, TOO SOON - Tue, November 5

Tue November 5

Filming the soundstage party; Beverly appears in this scene *(top left)*; report on Flynn from the set: *"At 5:45P assistant Director [George Vieira] was called to Mr. Flynn's Dressing Room and worried that Mr. F would not work after 6:00P. Impossible to get shot in time left. Discussion lasted to 6:05P—Setup broken and new lineup."* Report on Flynn from the set: *"Flynn ready for 1st shot. Kept company waiting from 12:40 to 12:50PM. Co. decided to work into the night after having dinner but Flynn refused to work after 6PM. Therefore, this [day's] seq. is not finished and will have to be done later."*

Wed November 6

Filming on location at Union Station in Los Angeles.

Thu November 7

Filming in the Barrymore living room and kitchen; report on Flynn from the set: *"Flynn was on set at 9:15AM. He was 10 minutes late from lunch. Big discussion with Napoleon 3:10 to 3:40PM—holding up the Co. Also held up the Co. while on the phone 5:05 to 5:10PM. Flynn dismissed at 5:30."*

Fri November 8

Continues filming the soundstage party.

Sat November 9

Attends the World Adoption International Fund (WAIF) Ball with his daughter Rory at the grand ballroom of the Beverly Hilton Hotel *(center left)*.

Mon November 11

Records overdubs of dialogue from 10am to 12:30pm.

Tue November 12

Continues filming in the Barrymore living room; in the *Los Angeles Herald Express*, Harrison Carroll reports: *"Errol Flynn's wife, Patrice Wymore, flew in from Majorca without daughter Arnella, but the youngster will follow as soon as her new nurse can get a passport. Patrice will stay in this country as long as Errol, [and] plans a night club tour with European dancer Pedro De Cordoba. 'Pedro will do flamenco numbers and I will do American jive,' she says. This will be her first time back before the bright lights in almost two years. Much excitement when Flynn's 10-year-old daughter, Rory (Nora Haymes is her mama) came out to watch dad work in 'Too Much, Too Soon,' and got lost. Studio policemen found her 45 minutes later. 'She's a true Flynn,' proclaimed Errol, 'One hour on the lot and she gets arrested.'"*

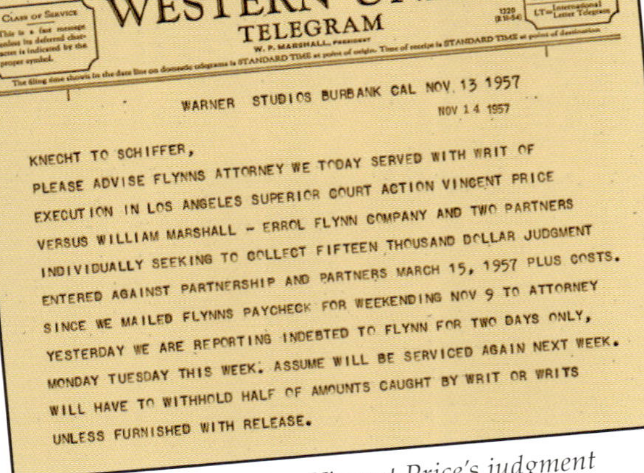

With Rory and Esther Williams at the WAIF Ball at the Beverly Hilton Hotel - Sat, November 9

WESTERN UNION
TELEGRAM

WARNER STUDIOS BURBANK CAL NOV. 13 1957
NOV 14 1957

KNECHT TO SCHIFFER,

PLEASE ADVISE FLYNNS ATTORNEY WE TODAY SERVED WITH WRIT OF EXECUTION IN LOS ANGELES SUPERIOR COURT ACTION VINCENT PRICE VERSUS WILLIAM MARSHALL — ERROL FLYNN COMPANY AND TWO PARTNERS INDIVIDUALLY SEEKING TO COLLECT FIFTEEN THOUSAND DOLLAR JUDGMENT ENTERED AGAINST PARTNERSHIP AND PARTNERS MARCH 15, 1957 PLUS COSTS. SINCE WE MAILED FLYNNS PAYCHECK FOR WEEKENDING NOV 9 TO ATTORNEY YESTERDAY WE ARE REPORTING INDEBTED TO FLYNN FOR TWO DAYS ONLY, MONDAY TUESDAY THIS WEEK. ASSUME WILL BE SERVICED AGAIN NEXT WEEK. WILL HAVE TO WITHHOLD HALF OF AMOUNTS CAUGHT BY WRIT OR WRITS UNLESS FURNISHED WITH RELEASE.

Telegram concerning Vincent Price's judgment against Flynn for unpaid salary from work on THE ADVENTURES OF CAPTAIN FABIAN

Wed November 13

Overdub recording from 10 to 10:30am at the WB Los Feliz studio in Room 14-98; filming at the Hillside Road and gates, and outside the Barrymore home—Flynn's final scene in a Warner Bros. film *(right)*.

Fri November 15

Note from Jack Warner to Flynn: *"I like the title 'Sporting Blood' as that's exactly what I am...Want you to know I appreciate your very lovely letter and am very happy with your part in the picture. everything I have seen has been excellent and I have a hunch we will have a hit [and that] it will come off as well as that 'sleeper' you were in called CAPTAIN BLOOD. If you are at the studio next week, please drop in and say 'hello'....P.S. I can hardly believe that CAPTAIN BLOOD was made over 22 years ago. It seems just like yesterday."*

With Dorothy Malone, Flynn's final filmed scene in a Warner Bros. movie - Wed, November 13

Tue November 19

"And Errol Flynn is going domestic with a vengeance. He and dotter Rory were a twosome shopping at Ralph's supermarket on Sunset Blvd. He said he'd never seen anything like it in Europe. And no one in Hollywood's ever seen anything like Flynn at a supermarket!" Army Archerd in *Daily Variety*.

On the set of TOO MUCH, TOO SOON, showing a visiting Alexis Smith the Phoenician antique vessels he found while skin diving off the coast of Spain - Thu, November 21

Wed November 20

"The Errol Flynns brought Pat's Spanish [dancer Pedro] *De Cordoba along* [to Hedda Hopper's house], *Errol telling Hugh O'Brien, Charlie Brackett, Bill Frye of the time when he and Lili Damita lived across the street from me. I didn't have to move from my bed to hear them battling. He neglected to say, however, he got up at dawn, came across the street in his dressing gown to beg me not to write about it. Like an idiot, I didn't. But I remember the dialogue, and brother, was it racy."* Hedda Hopper in *The Los Angeles Times*.

Thu November 21

Alexis Smith visits Flynn for lunch on the set of TOO MUCH, TOO SOON *(top left)*.

Fri November 22

Continues post-recording, dubbing the telephone conversation with Michael Strange (Neva Patterson); Municipal Judge Gerald C. Kepple dismisses the drunk charge against Flynn and actress Maura FitzGibbon on the recommendation of the city attorney's office; *"The Errol Flynns' four-year-old daughter, Arnella, (she arrives over the weekend) will have a problem when she enters an American kindergarten in February. She speaks only French. Besides 'mama' and 'papa,' the only English word she knows is 'look.'"* Harrison Carroll in *The Los Angeles Herald Express*.

Below with Arnella and Patrice on the Huntington Hartford estate in Hollywood - late fall; top right, the family on the Hartford estate grounds and, bottom right, the same location today

From his last portrait sitting for Warner Bros. - Fall

The Jeruselem Post
Mon, December 28

Tue November 26

Director Art Napoleon to editor Rudi Fehr: *"Last night Owen* [Marks, editor] *put the wild track* [dubbing] *which Mr. Flynn recorded for the telephone sequence with Michael…in the dailies. Unfortunately this wild track should be rerecorded because Mr. Flynn doesn't sound drunk enough, and unless he sounds drunk there is no motivation for Michael's hanging up or for Diana's subsequent anger with him over getting loaded…."* Completes work on TOO MUCH, TOO SOON with more post-recording—Flynn's final day ever of work for Warner Bros. *(top right).*

WARNER BROS. PICTURES, INC.
FINISH WORK NOTICE

NAME ERROL FLYNN   DATE Tues, 11/26/57   HOUR 5:15PM

PICTURE #843 "TOO MUCH, TOO SOON"   PART "John Barrymore"

REMARKS:

Post-recorded and finished as of this date.

cc: RJO: HB: BH: BO:

rm

APPROVED

THIS NOTICE IS INTENDED AS A RECORD AND IS NOT TO BE CONFUSED WITH A PAYROLL NOTICE

Work notice for Flynn's dubbing on TOO MUCH, TOO SOON, his final work for the studio that made him a star

Wed November 27

Flies to New York; sometime in the last few days of the month (possibly on this day) he appears at a Friars Club Roast for comedian Joe E. Lewis, hosted by Jack E. Leonard.

Sun December 1

Guests on *The Steve Allen Show* in a parody of the game show *To Tell The Truth*, broadcast live on NBC from 8:00 to 9:00PM; he then appears as a mystery guest on the CBS show *What's My Line?*; returns to Los Angeles sometime in the next few days.

Thu December 5

Beverly Aadland guests on TV's *You Bet Your Life* with Groucho Marx.

Mon December 9

Screenwriter Jo Napoleon to Steve Trilling: *"Everyone at the studio who knew anything about scheduling seemed to agree that the picture could not be shot in under 40 days – [even] if everything went well. What with Flynn, [cinematographer Nicholas] Musuraca, Dorothy's [Malone] continual tardiness, etc. everything did not go like clockwork."*

December 13

Attorneys for Errol and Nora announce that he will set up a trust fund for Deirdre and Rory, depositing $6,600 ($62,287 in 2021 value) the 1st of each year.

Wed December 18

Signs a contract with Famous Artists Associates talent agency to manage him; around this time Sean comes to spend the holidays with his father.

Mon December 30

A portion of a letter from attorney Melvin Belli: *"Dear Errol and Pat: Thanks very, very much for the lovely party which I missed but which I heard about and wished I hadn't missed so I could have heard about it first hand…I've got my new book just about in manuscript, the one I want you to do the introduction on…."*

Late December

Telegram from John Huston to Darryl Zanuck concerning casting in Huston's upcoming film, ROOTS OF HEAVEN: DEAR DARRYL RE FORSYTHE WHAT ABOUT RIVER KWAI DOCTOR OR NIVEN OR PREFERABLY FLYNN.

1958

Wed January 1

Travels to New York, checking in to the Park Lane Hotel; telegram from Darryl Zanuck to John Huston at the Kyoto Hotel in Japan: NIGEL PATRICK NOT AVAILABLE BUT THERE IS STILL OUTSIDE CHANCE WE MAY GET ERROL FLYNN FOR FORSYTHE STOP SINCE FORSYTHE AND MINNA START ON TREK WITH SECOND UNIT IT IS ESSENTIAL THAT WE MAKE DECISION ON FORSYTHE SOON AS POSSIBLE.

Sat January 18

Attends the New York Film Critics reception at Sardi's.

Sun January 19

Telegram from Darryl Zanuck to John Huston: …STILL HOPEFUL OF GETTING FLYNN FOR FORSYTHE… WE FIGURE ON STARTING SECOND UNIT TREK WITH MINNA AND FORSYTHE APPROXIMATELY FEBRUARY FIFTEENTH.

Fri January 24

Is involved in a fracas in a New York bar that results in his being accused of stealing an expensive ring.

With Jan Brooks in
The Master of Thornfield -
Sun, January 26

Sun February 2
Arrives in Detroit; interviewed on WCKR Miami.

Wed February 5
"If Errol Flynn's contract for the Huntington Hartford play 'The Master of Thornfield' comes even close to meeting the rumors circulating in Sardi's, it makes some kind of show business history: envious fellow-thespians are murmuring wildly about a rehearsal fee 'for keeping himself available,' an impressive salary set for the run of the play and a percentage of the profits...." Dorothy Kilgallen.

Sun February 9
Film historian Tony Thomas records an interview with Flynn backstage during rehearsals, probably on this date; Patrice is also there, having arrived the day before; she returns to Los Angeles three days later.

Mon February 10
Debuts in *The Master of Thornfield* at the Shubert Theater in Detroit *(top right)*; the show continues until February 15th

Mon February 17
The Master of Thornfield opens in Cincinnati.

Advertisement for the Detroit run of
The Master of Thornfield

Tue February 18
Tells reporters in a news conference in Cincinnati that he will leave *The Master of Thornfield* by the weekend; *"Errol Flynn's performance in the play 'The Master of Thornfield' is giving the rest of the cast an acute case of jitters. He still doesn't know all his lines and is ad libbing a la John Barrymore in 'My Dear Children' when his memory fails him, leaving the other actors in a state of frenzy because they just don't know what's going to happen next."* Dorothy Kilgallen.

Thu February 20
According to *The New York Times*, Flynn complained that the play was "no more fit for Broadway than 'Jack and the Beanstalk'" and that he couldn't do much with what is written. Huntington Hartford, the play's author, countered that, "I have yet to hear my play, from Mr. Flynn, as I have written it."

Fri February 21
Signs the contract with 20th Century Fox to film THE ROOTS OF HEAVEN.

Sat February 22
Bows out of the play *The Master of Thornfield* after this evening's performance.

Sun February 23
Leaves for New York where he meets up with Beverly.

Mon February 24
Sends a note from the Park Lane Hotel in New York to Jack Warner, who is also in the city: *"....Am off to Africa in a couple of days - to do the Zanuck picture with Johnny Huston -- very exciting Africa--! In line with the new Administration Policy of Integration would you like me to bring Warners back a black starlet? Might be great for the new Warnercolor, huh?"*

Thu February 27
Arrives in Paris on a 36-hour layover before leaving for Africa; on the flight he composes a letter to Beverly, saying, *"I guess I'm halfway across the Atlantic. I seem to be the only one awake—perhaps because I keep thinking of a very strange young soul, whose image is before my eyes as I write this....I know, and so do you, that you have to face some facts, some situations when you get back to Los Angeles* [from new York] *that are going to be far from easy for you...."*

Sat March 1
Leaves from Bourget Airport in Paris for Fort Lamy (now N'Djamena) in French Equatorial Africa *(bottom right)*, and then on to Fort Archambault, Chad; films the THE ROOTS OF HEAVEN in Chad throughout March and April (the daily production notes have not been located).

Mon March 3
"Errol Flynn's off-the-cuff comments about his recently abandoned role in 'The Master of Thornfield' are entertaining in an inflammable way. He's blasting everyone connected with the production." Dorothy Kilgallen.

Sat March 8
Telegram from Fort Archambault (now Sarh), Chad, to Beverly at the San Carlos Hotel in New York: WHY

With Trevor Howard leaving Paris for French Equatorial Africa to film
THE ROOTS OF HEAVEN - Sat, March 1

Filming THE ROOTS OF HEAVEN in French Equatorial Africa (now the Republic of Chad);
top left with Juliette Gréco; top right with Juliette Gréco, Darryl F. Zanuck, and John Huston

NO LETTERS VERY LONELY; *"Errol Flynn's hasty departure from Huntington Hartford's 'The Master of Thornfield' prompted his wife, Pat Wymore, to do a bit of fast moving, too. Soon after Errol exited from the star role in the play, Mrs. Flynn and her young daughter vacated the guest house at the Hartford California estate."* Dorothy Kilgallen.

Wed March 12

"Huntington Hartford is—quite understandably—steaming over Errol Flynn's unexpected exit from the star role in 'The Master of Thornfield.' The unpleasantness may wind up in a legal fight..." Dorothy Kilgallen.

Tue March 18

Letter to Beverly: *"What a funny, adorable idiot you are. Do you really think that I can just pick up a telephone and call you?....But I do know one thing for sure—that my heart, my real heart, goes out to you as I write this....I have so much to say to you, but this hurricane lamp is fouling up my prose. Dear, very dear, little girl, I think of you constantly...."*

Wed March 19

Mentions in a letter to Beverly that he's finally received two letters from her dated February 23rd and March 3rd.

Thu March 20

According to a letter sent from Africa by Flynn to Beverly, she has already met his sister, Rosemary; his address for Beverly to write him is Boite Postal 83, Maroua, French Cameroon.

Wed March 26

Letter to Beverly from Cameroon: *"My God, woman, what will you do next? (But keep doing it--I love it)....You addressed your letter to Zanuck. He had a ball. Opened, it was presented to me with a roll of African drums at lunch just now. He carefully pretended to let the enclosures drop, picked them up and opened and said in a mincing voice, 'Oh Errol—here's a little itsy-bitsy weter for you'....It was no use to look dignified or aloof—or just offhand. You are the very soul of discretion, you dope. But I'm alone now and laughing, shoulders shaking and happy for a while, because your letter is very much you...."*

Wed April 2

In a letter to Beverly, Flynn asks her to remember to bring 12 cartons of English Oval cigarettes, yellow nitrate "poppsies" (ampules), a copy of Emerson's *Essays*, and quail eggs, before she leaves to join him in Africa.

Fri April 4

In a letter from Sean to his mother, Lili, whom he calls *"the best mother I could ever want,"* he writes from the Lawrenceville School: *"I'll be back in 10 weeks and I hope to get a job with some construction company…It pays about $50 [$458.58 in 2021 value] a week which is very good for this type of work…This is all I want to be happy and I know it will work. If father and M.G.M. want me to do a picture, they can all go to hell—I just want to be with my family."*

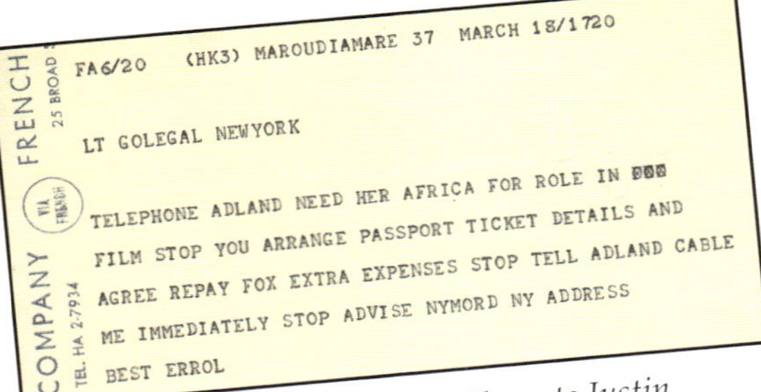

FRENCH COMPANY
25 BROAD
(VIA FRENCH)
TEL. HA 2-7934

FA6/20   (HK3) MAROUDIAMARE 37   MARCH 18/1720

LT GOLEGAL NEWYORK

TELEPHONE ADLAND NEED HER AFRICA FOR ROLE IN DDD
FILM STOP YOU ARRANGE PASSPORT TICKET DETAILS AND
AGREE REPAY FOX EXTRA EXPENSES STOP TELL ADLAND CABLE
ME IMMEDIATELY STOP ADVISE NYMORD NY ADDRESS

BEST ERROL

Above, telegram from Flynn to Justin Golenbock requesting he arrange for Beverly Aadland to come to Africa; and below, Golenbock's response

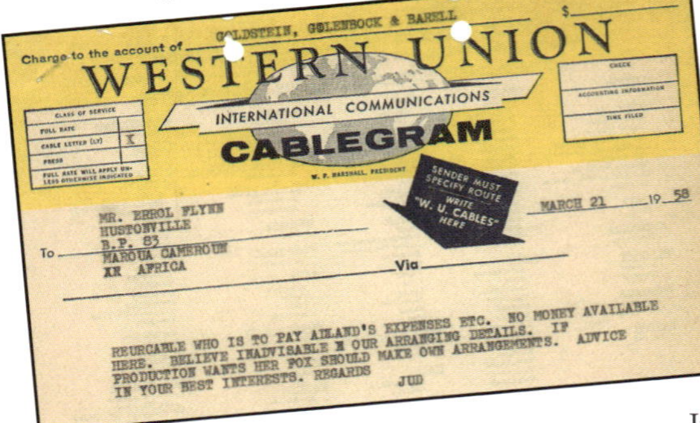

Charge to the account of GOLDSTEIN, GOLENBOCK & BARELL $____

WESTERN UNION
INTERNATIONAL COMMUNICATIONS
CABLEGRAM

W. P. MARSHALL, PRESIDENT

CLASS OF SERVICE
FULL RATE
CABLE LETTER (LT)   X
PRESS
FULL RATE WILL APPLY UNLESS OTHERWISE INDICATED

CHECK
ACCOUNTING INFORMATION
TIME FILED

SENDER MUST SPECIFY ROUTE WRITE "W. U. CABLES" HERE

MARCH 21 19 58

To MR. ERROL FLYNN
HUSTONVILLE
B.P. 83
MAROUA CAMEROUN
XR AFRICA   Via ____

REURCABLE WHO IS TO PAY AILAND'S EXPENSES ETC. NO MONEY AVAILABLE
HERE. BELIEVE INADVISABLE M OUR ARRANGING DETAILS. IF
PRODUCTION WANTS HER FOX SHOULD MAKE OWN ARRANGEMENTS. ADVICE
IN YOUR BEST INTERESTS. REGARDS   JUD

Wed April 9
Beverly travels to French Equatorial Africa to join Flynn on location.

Mon April 14
Sean writes to his mother, Lili, that he would be quite happy in a job *"loading cement."*

Mid-April
Letter to his friend Teddy Stauffer: *"....How goes it with you my boy? In about two more weeks (have been here a month and I think a sentence at Gayenne or Devils Island would have been preferable) will be back in Paris - staying the Hotel Napoleon....Will be there sometime finishing the picture....I have a wonderful [offbeat] role -- I make love to a teen age elephant and neither of us talk of it....I did the most unforgivable awful thing last week in French Equitorial Africa - shot an elephant. Honestly I didn't want to--but you know how it is in such cases, when the pressure's on you don't want to say 'No-- I don't want to' and you don't say it and shoot? I still feel like an assassin. At least to my amazement I hit the poor bastard right where they told me, so he didn't even let a fart. Do you want a couple of iv-ery tusks? I don't....Our leading lady Juliette Greco is a doll - a real doll...."*

Fri April 18
Travels with Beverly to Brazzaville in the (now) Republic of Congo for a few days; letter from Flynn's father in London to his son's attorney, Justin Golenbock, in New York: *"....Marelle is much worried over the possibility that one of Errol's wives or children may be able to dispossess us in the event of his dying before we do. I know nothing, of course, about his will but I am sure there will be many claimants to his estates and other property...Errol was to be in Paris at this time but I have heard nothing. Perhaps the picture is not yet finished...."*

May
Travels with Beverly from Africa to Marseilles (where he shows her the *Zaca*) and then to Paris; continues filming THE ROOTS OF HEAVEN at the Studios de Boulogne-Billancourt, west of Paris *(center right)*; Beverly is given a small part in the film and two short lines: *"Good evening. Who's that?"* Attends a party with Beverly for Charles de Gaulle; during this period they travel to England, where he and Beverly dine with Professor Flynn.

Fri May 9
TOO MUCH, TOO SOON premieres at New York City's Odeon and Sutton theaters.

Sat May 17
Arrives in Paris with Beverly, checking in to the Hotel Napoleon.

Wed June 4
Arrives in London with Beverly, staying at the Old Bell Country Inn in Hurley outside London.

Thu June 5
With Beverly at the Lido Club in London.

Tue June 17
Travels with Beverly to the Brussels World's Fair.

Fri June 20
Flynn's 49th birthday.

Sun June 22
About this date he slips and falls at a friend's home in Paris, injuring his back; admits himself to the American Hospital on the 25th, remaining for a few days.

Sun July 6
With THE ROOTS OF HEAVEN complete, travels with Beverly on the *Ile de France* from Marseilles to New York, arriving on 7/11 *(bottom right)* and checking in to the Park Lane Hotel.

Tue July 8
It is reported that *Confidential* magazine has settled Flynn's one-million-dollar libel suit against them for an undisclosed sum.

Thu August 7
Flies to Jamaica with Beverly to begin writing the autobiography; Earl Conrad will act as ghostwriter for Flynn.

Sat September 27 and Sun October 5
Sends telegrams from Port Antonio addressed to Beverly at 5425 Santa Monica Blvd. in Los Angeles.

On location in Africa - April

With Darryl F. Zanuck on the Paris soundstage - May

On the Ile de France *in New York - Fri, July 11*

With Trevor Howard, Juliette Gréco, Darryl F. Zanuck, and unidentified at the premiere of THE ROOTS OF HEAVEN in New York - Wed, October 15

The first page of a letter from Flynn's mother Marelle to his autobiography ghostwriter, Earl Conrad - Fri, November 14

Mon October 6

Sends a telegram from Jamaica to Beverly informing her he is leaving for New York; letter from attorney Melvin Belli to Flynn: *"I've got another good book on the law....on which I'd like to have you to do the introduction.... had lunch at the Chateau Madrid above Nice - - they now feature the peasants' special, a strawberry omelete, but the owner tells me you are trying to take credit for inventing it!"*

Fri October 10

Letter from Flynn's mother, Marelle, to Earl Conrad: *"Dear Mr. Conrad...you can tell Errol when you see him that he can count on me to co-operate with the memoirs. I will get copies made of some of the early photographs + will write at length + try to answer all your questions. I would be afraid to send the original photographs, as you can imagine they are precious to me + I would [not] like to risk their loss...Yours ever, Marelle Flynn."*

Wed October 15

THE ROOTS OF HEAVEN premieres at the Palace Theatre in New York City *(top left)*.

Thu October 16

Beverly arrives in New York to be with Flynn.

Fri October 17

The South China Morning Post reports that an Italian court of appeals has ruled in favor of Flynn in his lawsuit against the Italian film company that was financing his film WILLIAM TELL but went bankrupt, leaving the film unfinished; the amount of damages *"will be fixed by another court."*

Wed October 22

"The eight-year marriage of Errol Flynn and actress Patrice Wymore today was reported 'coming apart at the seams.'...New York Journal-American columnist Louis Sobol said Flynn told him as much but declined to say if the couple were headed to the divorce courts...'I think all statements of this kind should emanate from the lady,' Flynn was quoted...However, in Phoenix Miss Wymore said, 'I haven't heard anything about it. I'm shocked. I don't know what to think...I can only assume that an Irishman with a couple of drinks under his belt is liable to say anything.'...However, the 49-year-old Flynn admitted that he and Patrice, 28, had not lived together for some time....'It isn't because there is any other woman in my life or, as far as I know, any man in hers.' Flynn was quoted...." The Los Angeles Times.

Mon October 27

Broadcast of Flynn's guest appearance on *The Arthur Murray Party* TV show.

Fri November 14

The Atlanta Constitution reports that *"Flynn will fight the upcoming lawsuit of millionaire Huntington Hartford, who is suing Flynn for half a million dollars, claiming breach of contract over Hartford's stage adaptation of 'Jane Eyre.'"* First page of a letter from Marelle to Earl Conrad *(bottom left)*: *"....By this mail I am sending you some of the photographs, + then I shall try to answer your questions. As a child, as a baby even, Errol always loved to dress up, + act the part, - actually living the part as, one day, when staying with my parents, I had taken him for a walk, + he was playing trains, when we met an old friend of the family, to whom I was glad to proudly show my little son. To my surprise Errol would not speak, - he who usually had everything in the world to say. Later, when the man had passed, I asked him why he would not speak, + he answered, 'Doesn't he know that trains cannot speak?' I said "of course but he doesn't know that you were a train. 'Well then,' said Errol, 'he is very stupid'—he was then only about 2 ½ years old. That was a remarkable thing about Errol, the extraordinary long words he used + his little grown up manner of speaking — which was extremely funny, + used to make me die of laughter. On another occasion, we were invited to a tea party on a Japanese warship, and I decided to take him too, knowing how he would like to see the warship. The headmaster of his preparatory school was there — Errol was about six at the time. I said to Errol, 'Aren't you going to speak to Mr. So + So (I've forgotten the man's name)' + Errol replied, 'No, mummy as a matter of fact I'm avoiding him.' I, highly amused at such a reply, asked why, and was told, 'Well, if I speak to him he is sure to enter into a long conversation with me.' This sort of speech made me sure he was going to be a great writer — and I still am of that opinion — had he only applied himself to writing seriously...."*

Sat November 15, Fri November 21, and Sat November 22

At the "21" club in New York on 11/15, at El Morocco on 11/21, and at Chandos on 11/22.

Tue November 25

Travels to Cuba (Beverly having returned to California), staying at the Hotel Nacional in Havana.

Fri November 28

"Patrice Wymore, who hasn't seen husband Errol Flynn since February, is plunging into a career of her own....She has asked Flynn to fly from New York for her night club opening [at the Coconut Grove on 12/4] *and expects him to be here. Whether or not he'll make it is another matter. He is notably unpredictable and has told reporters that their marriage is 'coming apart at the seams.'...It's news to her...'I don't know a thing about it,' says the third Mrs. Flynn. 'As far as I know, nothing has changed. I have no idea what is going to happen.'..."* Bob Thomas in the *Austin American Statesman*.

Sat November 29

Beverly joins Flynn in Cuba; sometime while at staying the Hotel Nacional, Flynn writes a will bequeathing ⅓ of his estate to Beverly.

November-December

Sometime during this period Flynn is with Ernest Hemingway at the Floridita Bar in Havana.

Mon December 22

With Cuban sugar baron Pedro Rodriguez playing at the Nacional Hotel casino.

Tue December 23

Receives word that he will meet Fidel Castro.

Wed December 24

"Flynn's new screen career is not alone responsible for the revitalized state of his fortunes...'Property I have in Jamaica, after lying valueless for years, has suddenly come good, and must now be worth about three million dollars,' the ex-broke Mr. Flynn says happily....His marriage (to Patrice Wymore) is about to be dissolved, and teenage actress Beverly Aadland is spoken of as the fourth Mrs. Flynn." The *Australian Women's Weekly*.

Thu December 25

Flies with Beverly and producer Victor Pahlen to Camagüey, Cuba, checking in to the Gran Hotel.

Fri December 26

Flies deeper into rebel territory and completes the trip to meet Castro by Jeep.

Sat December 27

In the early evening meets Castro at the revolutionary's headquarters in a sugar mill in Oriente Province *(top right)*; stays (and bathes) at the El Cobre Monastery.

Mon December 29

With rebels in a clash at a sugar mill in Central Palma; he claims to have been slightly wounded by a bullet.

Wed December 31

Traveling by Jeep with Fidel Castro, Castro's brother Raoul, and their band of rebels to the port city of Santiago.

1959

Thu January 1

Hears that Santiago has fallen and Batista has fled Cuba; follows Castro to Santiago and claims to have been slightly wounded on the shin by gunfire along the way.

Fri January 2

Hunkered down in the Santiago outskirts while skirmishes take place.

Sat January 3

More skirmishes; claims he left Castro on this night.

Sun January 4

Secures a room at the Casa Granda Hotel in Santiago; from Flynn's personal notes: *"Must quit—things getting a bit too hot. I'm behind a marble pillar on hotel porch but being only one around here feel lonely—bullets—too many coming too close make me feel that way. Going to make a dash for it inside hotel. Here goes."*

Mon January 5

Flies back to Havana; Ron Shedlo writes to Flynn immediately after seeing the Harrison Carrol article *(bottom right)* in the *Los Angeles Herald*: *"I tried my best to keep* [the interview] *as discreet as possible but* [Harrison Carrol] *ran away with himself. First of all, I didn't want my name in it. However, he said that the article wouldn't be effective unless he could tell the source. Second, I called Mrs. Eddington who got in contact with him, and she gave my age as being 18 I guess. I hope that you are not angry...."*

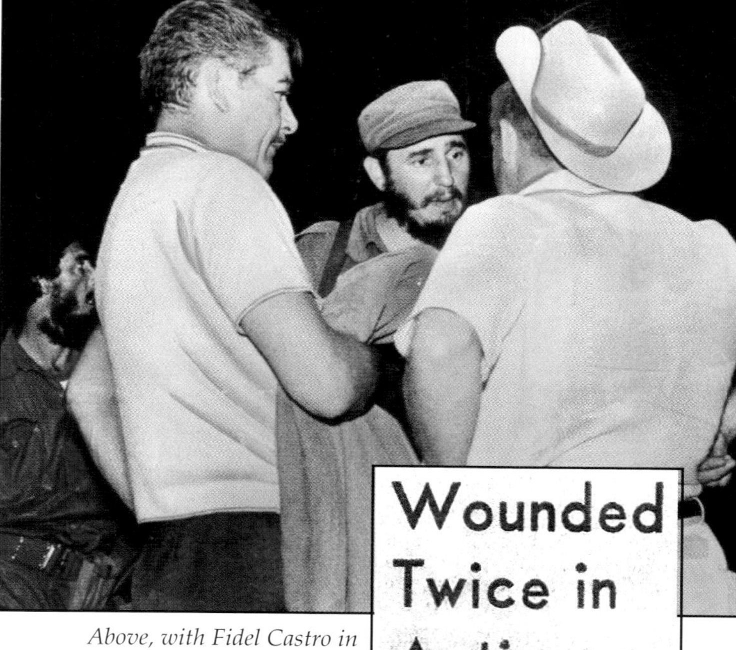

Above, with Fidel Castro in Oriente Province, Cuba - December

Wounded Twice in Action

(Martial law declared in Havana as rebel forces moving in. Story on A-5.)

By HARRISON CARROLL

Just as in one of his swashbuckling movies Errol Flynn not only has turned up safe in Havana but telephoned a friend here today that he has spent part of the last two weeks with rebel leader Fidel Castro and his men.

He has a personal, exclusive story, a real "scoop" to tell, declared the star, and pictures to go with it.

The friend who received the call from the actor is 18-year-old Ronnie Shedlo, who works as Flynn's secretary when the star is in town.

According to Shedlo, Errol called him this morning from the Hotel Nacionale in Havana.

"We could only talk a few minutes," said Shedlo. "He said that Castro's bearded soldiers were sleeping all around him.

"He said he had spent part of two weeks with the general and had received two slight wounds in the arm and in the leg. That's all he was able to tell me."

The Los Angeles Herald Express - *Mon, January 5*

Wed January 7
"The rebel publication Revolution scoffed today at Errol Flynn's report he was wounded while operating with Fidel Castro...'That one (Flynn) never saw Castro,' said Violeta Casals, a woman broadcaster for the rebel radio...." The Los Angeles Times.

Thu January 8
Arrives from Cuba at Idlewild Airport in New York *(top left)* sporting a black bandana that Castro gave to him, emblazoned with the emblem of "the new Cuba"; appears in New York on the Jack Paar television show *(near left)*.

Tue January 13
Guests on TV's *Front Page Challenge* in Toronto; is suspended from Actor's Equity on charges of "conduct unbecoming a member of the union" for withdrawing from the play *The Master Of Thornfield*; Flynn had called the play unfit for Broadway.

Fri January 16
Letter from Ronnie Shedlo: *"....I am enclosing a clipping on you by Time Magazine [see 1/17]. It is very un-complimentary which is usual for Time...I caught you on the Jack Paar Show, and thought you were great...Deirdre wants you to call her. She is very anxious to speak to you. It was her birthday last Saturday and she was disappointed not hearing from you...."*

Sat January 17
"Agog with glory after the fast tour as a 'freelance newsman' trailing Fidel Castro's rebels in bar-bereft Cuba, where his trained eye zeroed in on the local frails [ladies], thirsted mightily for a stiffer mode of life ('Water to me is undrinkable'), and scribbled notebooks full of tidbits for a biography of Hero Fidel ('We're on a first-name basis'), paunchy Cinemactor Errol Flynn, 49, swashbuckled into Manhattan to praise his friend. 'I've admired this man for at least two years,' said Flynn, leaning heavily on the Disneylandish bar (fuchsia with pink lights) in his apartment. 'There aren't many idealists left.' But back in Havana, thoughts of 'Reporter' Flynn, author of two barely remembered novels, seemed less idealistic. Morals-minded Castro followers joked at the memory of his roistering coverage, and dark-eyed rebelista murmured: 'We are more than happy to meet newspapermen we respect, but as to Mr. Flynn, we had the feeling he was not a real journalist." Time magazine.

Thu January 22
Hearst Newspapers officially certifies that Flynn is *"accredited as a special representative of the Hearst Headline Service,"* and that he *"is accompanied by Mr. Barry Mahon, his photographer."*

Fri January 23
Returns to Cuba *(bottom left)*.

Sat January 31
Escapes a fire in his apartment at the Havana Hilton, probably started by one of his cigarettes igniting a curtain *(bottom right)*.

Mon February 2
Moves to Havana's Hotel Comodoro.

Fri February 13
Writes a portentous sixteen-page essay titled "How to Die": *"Please listen pals. The only point I want to dwell upon in this report, is how the hell to quit this life when you know—I mean when you know you've got to go. To make a dignified exit, if possible, from our world as we know it and live upon...When death is inevitable and you know you've got it coming, would you settle for, for example, disease? Old age? Cancer? Who knows, perhaps a plane disaster will get rid of you? Or your liver will?....At any event, it all adds up to the way you go out....When it comes time, how? Shall we go screaming to the gas chamber? The Chair? Or walk bravely to the noose, or get carted in to the Emergency Ward on a stretcher, or in hand cuffs?....*

"*Sporting a rather exotic shirt, movie actor Errol Flynn gestures to firemen after they extinguished a blaze that nearly wrecked his apartment in the Havana Hilton....Officials said Flynn had been asleep during the fire, which had started when a curtain touched a lighted cigarette.*"
United Press International - *Sat, January 31*

Above, arriving at Idlewild Airport from Cuba; Beverly is with him under a fictitious name: Mrs. Barbara Evans, a model; right, later that day as a guest on the Jack Paar Show *- Thu, January 8*

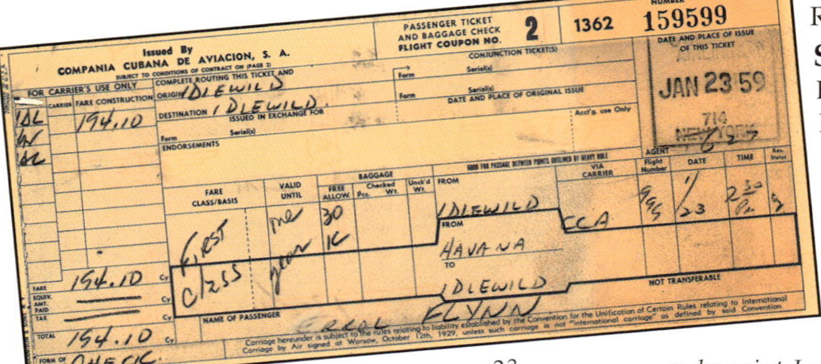

Flynn's ticket to Havana - Fri, January 23

Some men have to die tonight. One, two, three of them. And I have to watch it—because I have a job to do [reporting] *and I hate the idea....I have witnessed many gruesome sights in my life, but none more so than a human being facing the firing squad. I don't care how much he deserves it, it made me vomit—and I couldn't give a damn when I saw the expressions of faint amusement on the faces watching the hero of a thousand screen battles, Flynn, go white and heave his brave guts up...."*

Tue February 17
Is in a Havana court to face charges in connection with the fire in his Hilton Hotel room on January 31st; hotel security officers contend that the fire was caused by Flynn's carelessness with his cigarettes, and the hotel is seeking $6,024 in damages ($54,294 in 2021 value).

Sun March 1
Letter from Havana to his daughters, Deirdre and Rory, misdated as February 29 *(center right)* *"My Darlings: It's really terrible to be out of contact with you for so long now, but there has not been much alternative, because, as perhaps you have been reading in the papers, I managed to get involved in a bit of war down in this part of the world. Did you read my articles in the Hearst Press? Hope you liked them. Now I am going to start making a picture next week called 'The Rebel Girls'. Too bad you are not a bit older, you could both play parts. Actually, of course, some of the young rebel girls who were fighting in the mountains were not much older than both of you. Of course you would have had to dye your hair black, because there are very few blond rebel girls, that I came across, anyway, so as you can both imagine, I had a pretty quiet time of it, except for the shooting, because your Baron is, as you no doubt suspect, pretty much of a blond man at heart. Of course that was a lot of newspaper nonsense about me getting a wound in the leg. Actually, I think what happened was that a bullet knocked off a piece of marble from one of the thick pillows* [pillars] *I was hiding behind and it hit me, I really don't know. Anyway, something did. It could have been a bottle of rum for that matter, because it was pretty dark, so maybe even a dog bit me and I would not have known the difference. In the next few days I will be going back into the same mountains where all the fighting took place to get ready for making the picture, and will probably be gone for several weeks, but you can write to me c/o Hotel Comodoro, Havana, Cuba, and it will be forwarded on or held here for me until I get back. Didre* [sic], *sweetheart, your two sweet letters finally caught up with me and thank you very much. I love them and I am glad you like your present I sent from the Isle of Pines. As for you, Rory, my love, I am going to give you a kick on the bottom and then a kiss on it, because I did not hear from you. But maybe you wrote and I didn't get it. Write and let me know all the news. Give many a hug for me. Love you both! Your Baron P.S.- Oh, yeah—the enclosed check for $100.00* [$901 in 2021 value] *you can split between you and buy something you need. Please try not to go out and get drunk on it."*

Tue March 10
Is offered a role in a planned film called *Angel of Acapulco*, to be filmed in that city; the producers will pay $10,000 ($90,129 in 2021 value) per week with a two-week minimum; the film was never made.

Second Week of March to Late April
Beverly back in Cuba; CUBAN REBEL GIRLS begins filming (the daily production logs have not been located).

At Least He Remembered, Pat

Patrice Wymore opens a night club act in San Francisco today but hubby Errol Flynn can't be present.

So he sent her an olinga, a small Cuban animal.

"How appropriate," exclaimed Patrice. "It's nocturnal, a night prowler. Nothing could remind me more of Errol."

WYMORE Present

FLYNN Prowler

The Miami News - *Tue, February 24*

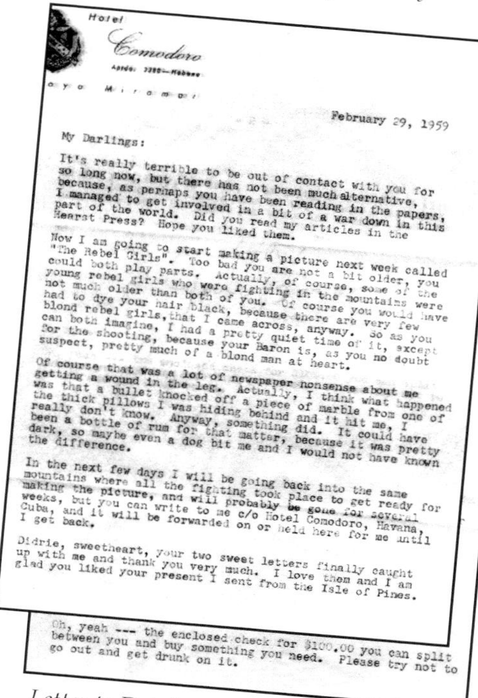

Letter to Deirdre and Rory from Havana

In Cuba shooting CUBAN REBEL GIRLS with (left and center) Beverly and (far right) a Cuban extra

Hotel **Comodoro**
P O BOX 3380
HAVANA · CUBA

March 14, 1959

For a title

Dear Earl:

Still think "Your Wicked, Wicked Ways" is not bad. Or perhaps "Our Wicked, Wicked Ways". Enclosed is copy of verse by unknown poet. (perhaps myself).

Your appraisal of the Damita-Flynn relationship is to the point. I will enlarge on it and try to clarify the psychological self at that age.

At that age, whilst I went around with an eager, hard phalic symbol between my legs, a steel-blue prick, like a geiger counter hungrily seeking molten, pliant metal to probe! This same instrument also needed, at that time of my life, intellectual nourishment — to force blood into the cells to feed upon. In this department, Lily was woefully inadequate. Any dispute in the objective sense was impossible. I mean the dialectic. She could never be objective, only subjective. Those highly emotional spontaneous Latin Minute brain cells that comprised her metabolism --- in plain words, she was bored stiff by any obtruse thoughts that didn't directly affect her day-to-day life. Mentally, she was no sponge. She was quite incapable of following any consecutive ling of thought, or mental process that had anything further to do than the shape of her hair, the color of her shoes, and did her bag match her dress, and was JOY the sexiest French perfume or not? She knew full well, and I would be a cad to refute it, that she was the greatest lay in the world, bar none and no holds barred.

importunities and when I found myself staring into that dark, dank cavern (in argot, a Cunt) plus a quite unfamiliar and pronounced odor --- well, old boy, it left a scar which took some years to heal I recovered, however, with the

IN LIKE ME ?
WHO'S IN? ME?
WITH, WHEN, WHERE?

Letter to Earl Conrad

Sat March 14

Letter to his autobiography ghostwriter Earl Conrad from the Hotel Comodoro in Havana *(top left):* "*Still think 'Your Wicked, Wicked Ways' is not bad* [for the title]. *Or perhaps 'Our Wicked, Wicked Ways'....Your appraisal of the Damita-Flynn relationship is to the point....At that age, whilst I went around with an eager, hard phallic symbol between my legs, a steel-blue prick like a geiger counter hungrily seeking molten, pliant metal to probe This same instrument also needed, at that time of my life, intellectual nourishment—to force blood into the cells to feed upon. In this department, Lily was woefully inadequate....She was quite incapable of following any consecutive line of thought, or mental process that had anything further to do than the shape of her hair, the color of her shoes, and did her bag match her dress, and was JOY the sexiest French perfume or not? She knew full well, and I would be a cad to refute it, that she was the greatest lay in the world, bar none and no holds barred... Very well, but the pure animal ferocious woman-tiger begins to pall on you after a certain time, no matter what physical shape you are in. You get tired and bewildered, because after the bang, there was nothing to talk about....We were poles apart, except in bed or on the floor or a park bench. Another facet of my relationship with Lily. It is, perhaps, a bit too intimate for the book. You see, what I regarded as errotic* [sic] *love-making in those days came as natural* [to me] *as a duck takes to water. She was what you might term an all-around-the-worlder. However, when she one day took me rather gruffly by the ears and proposed a certain position for the sex-exercise I was shocked and horrified. It should be bourne* [sic] *in mind that at this time of my life, I had never even seen a snatch, let alone go down on one, and the thought of such an exercise filled me with horror. It was to me like dredging the murky depths, the very dregs of the barrel of the bottom of depravity. But she was by no means as put out about it as I was. She would fondle and handle my nuts as much as monkies* [sic] *handle coconuts. I really had no idea of how much a square I was, how God-awful normal....Once, it is true, I yielded to her importunities and when I found myself staring into that dark, dank cavern (in argot, a cunt) plus a quite unfamiliar and pronounced odor....well, old boy, it left a scar which took some years to heal. I recovered, however....Lily was so violently jealous and I did nothing to help her overcome it with my wandering eye. Although it is true that after I had a few plates, dishes of radishes etc etc broken over my head, I quickly learned to keep my gaze as fixed and glassy as one of those guards outside Buckingham Palace....You did not tell me what you thought of the alternating* [sic] *idea 'IN LIKE ME?' With a big question mark at the end.... Who's in? Me? With, when, where?*"

Mon March 23

Letter from Ronnie Shedlo: "*....*[Patrice's] *picture opened this week* [The Sad Horse]. *She has gotten good notices....Maura Fitzgibbons* [sic] *got married and I think is now living in Florida. I guess the $2,500* [$22,532 in 2021 value] *got her a husband....As you know, Otto* [Reichow] *still has your things and would like to know if you want him to send them somewhere....*"

Below left, with John McKay and Jackie Jackler in a scene from CUBAN REBEL GIRLS - Spring

Below right, with an unenthusiastic Beverly at a cockfight in Cuba during filming of CUBAN REBEL GIRLS

Tue March 24

Letter to Earl Conrad *(top right):* *"....Yes, Erben spoke English with a German accent; although his vocabulary was excellent, there was always a German intonation. It was not quite as thick as 'Darlink, I luf you; if you know vot is gut for you, let us fock now'. There was a slight intonation to his articulation. For example, when he said in disgust 'Ahh, shits!' you could not read into this 'Ah, shitz!'....Erben was highly articulate, coherent, with a choice vocabulary; slow delivery, knowing what he had to say, or wanted to say, before he said it, and regardless of the slight nuances of delivery, whatever Erben said, you understood it....NOW—I want to take you back to the time when I left New Guinea in haste and for that country's good. You recall that I had bought some hot diamonds from a IDB (Illicit Diamond Buyer) in order to beat the exchange difference in money from the Australian pound to the English....having worked and striven in New Guinea for four years, made one or two fortunes and almost a third, I was certainly not going to let any kind of deal, hot or cold, stand between me and the money I now wound up with, to try and start a new life. If you remember, I had fifty ounces of gold that I got, plus the uncut diamonds I bought from a gentleman, believe it or not, by the name of Flato. Flato had that extraordinary comodity [sic] in New Guinea at that time---a beautiful, lovely creature by the name of Clara, half Samoan, half German, and I oggled [sic] her with the hungry eyes of a young man who had not been layed, who had a hard on like a donkey, and nothing to do with it...Flato had everything I didn't. Cultured, suave, smoothe [sic], an athletic 35 years, had been around the world and seen it, and knew how to handle it---a type I had never met before....The coincidence was this. Not so much that his name was Flato, but that he should have been selling illicit diamonds, stolen, or bought, or acquired, from the Kimberly Mines in Africa, and that he should have them in his possession and be selling them in New Guinea. Of course, I should have realized that this was the best place to peddle IDB Diamonds...His first name was John, and the other day I read of another Flato, Paul Flato, now a resident in Mexico, with the police hot on his ass, a society jeweler from New York who disappeared South of the Border with a couple hundred grand worth, if not more, of diamonds from his famous New York diamond jewelry establishment....Is there some strange connection?....I never got to first base with that beautiful German-Samoan girl he had with him in New Guinea. She was far and beyond bums like me and the New Guinea Flato obviously had her well under control, mentally and physically. But I thought she was the most glorious vision I had ever seen in my life, with her dark, freckled skin, dark luminous, laughing eyes and a figure that you could never surpass in a PLAYBOY Magazine...Flato, diamonds, New Guinea, New York, Mexico, beautiful girls, same name---I wonder?"* Letter from Flynn's father to Flynn's attorney, Justin Golenbock: *"....I am much worried by a paragraph which I saw in an American paper to the effect that Errol must have surgery to his back otherwise he must expect to remain partially paralyzed. Is this true? Please let me know by return [mail]. I had arranged with one of our best (one of the best in England) surgeons who is an old + esteemed friend of mine to look at Errol's back and Errol agreed to this but unfortunately everything was put out of joint through the trouble over his girl friend...."*

Sun March 29

"Pat Wymore is considering flying to Cuba to catch up with Errol Flynn and attempt some kind of decision about their rather nebulous matrimonial situation. Friends expect her to ask for a legal separation as a starter." Dorothy Kilgallen in the *Washington Post.*

Mon March 30

Writes a letter from the Hotel Comodoro in Havana to Ron Shedlo concerning the personal property that need to be shipped to Jamaica: *"....I do want to get the stuff out of California to Jamaica as soon as possible....I certainly want Otto [Reichow] to give you my stuff to send out to Jamaica also....apply to me directly for the costs....Merle [Stolz] also has a lot of my stuff....She is a very dear friend of both Pat and me. I would like you, and you can show her this letter if necessary, to get this stuff crated and put on the same boat. Give those two nice [Stoltzes] my best love...As an out-of-work actor, I am opening a new Barbecured Pig Pit and Emporium in Jamaica and need the furniture. I don't know what to do about the pieces stored in Pat's name [whom he says he "cannot correspond with"], but the two pieces I am concerned mostly about is the large antique family boufett that used to be in the dining room at Mulholland. The other is my desk and chairs....At this writing, it looks now as if in a couple of months I will be in Germany, to make a picture....Munich...."* Shipping is to take place on the *Yawato Maru,* leaving from Miami on January 4, 1960; he also mentions that Benny Marks at Warner Bros. has all his films and projectors.

Wed April 8

Letter from Ronnie Shedlo: *"....you had better cross off the Stoltz's as friends of yours. Mr. Stoltz told me....his wife had given everything back to Pat. Now I have found out that on the Saturday that I was to go over there, he was seen by a friend who lives across the street from Pat, taking a bunch of boxes up to her bungalow...As far as the furniture in National Van is concerned, it is impossible to touch it. Everything there is in Pat's name and they will not give out any information what-so-ever...However, I do have some good news....I can have the furniture that is in Lyon Van and Storage (the buffet table, desk, etc.) shipped within the next two weeks...About the movie projectors and film. Benny Marks has told me that you cannot*

Hotel Comodoro letter reproduced at right:

Dear Earl:

March 24, 1959

I will get the letter off to Professor Glover about Mike and send you a copy.

Yes, Erben spoke English with a German accent; although his vocabulary was excellent, there was always a German intonation. It was not quite as thick as "Darlink, I luf you; if you know vot is gut for you, let us fock now". There was a slight American intonation to his articulation. For example, when he said in disgust "Ahh, shits!", you could not read into this "Ah, shitz!". There was a fine line of pronunciation and I suppose you could have taken him for any naturalized American, Scandinavian, or German.

Erben was highly articulate, coherent, with a choice vocabulary; slow delivery, knowing what he had to say, or wanted to say, before he said it, and regardless of the slight naunces of delivery, whatever Erben said, you understood it. Even when he spoke horrible Spanish, bastardly Italian, abominable French, you were left with no doubt as to his meaning. That answer you?

NOW --- I want to take you back to the time when I left New Guinea in haste and for that country's good. You recall that I had bought some hot diamonds from a IDB (Illicit Diamond Buyer) in order to beat the exchange difference in money from the Australian pound to the English. If I recall, there was about a 15 to 20% difference in the exchange rate, and having worked and striven in New Guinea for four years, made one or two fortunes and almost a third, I was certainly not going to let any kind of deal, hot or cold, stand between me and the money I now wound up with, to try and start a new life. If you remember, I had fifty ounces of gold that I got, plus the uncut diamonds I bought from a gentlemen, believe it or not, by the name of Flato. Flato had that extraordinary comodity in New Guinea at that time --- a beautiful, lovely creature by the name of Clara, half Samoan, half German, and I oggled her with the hungry eyes of a young man who had not been layed, who had a hard on like a donkey, and nothing to do with it.

Flato had everything I didn't. Cultured, suave, smoothe, an athletic 35 years, had been around the world and seen it, and knew how to handle it --- a type I had never met before. Not only was he very good looking, but he changed his tropical clothes -shirts, shorts, shoes --- so often that they were immaculate. He should have realized that this was the best place to peddle IDB Diamonds.

His first name was John, and the other day I read of another Flato, Paul Flato, now a resident in Mexico, with the police hot on his ass, a society jeweler from New York who disappeared South of the Border with about a couple hundred grand worth, if not more, of diamonds from his famous New York diamond jewelry establishment. The cops would dearly love to get Paul Flato for a brief talk. Paul Flato wanted to sell me some diamonds in the 40's for one of my wifes or associates', shall we call it.

Is there some strange connection? Here is a John Flato and a Paul Flato, both in the diamond business, hot or cold. It is an unusual name. Does it run in the blood of the Flatos --- I mean diamonds. Could there be a connection between these two gentlemen with odd names and a singular activity of selling hot diamonds?

I never got to first base with that beautiful German-Samoan girl he had with him in New Guinea. She was far and beyond bums like me and the New Guinea Flato obviously had her well under control, mentally and physically. But I thought that she was the most glorious vision I had ever seen in my life, with her dark, freckled skin, dark luminous, laughing eyes and a figure that you could never surpass in PLAYBOY Magazine.

Plato, diamonds, New Guinea, New York, Mexico, beautiful girls, same name --- I wonder?

All the best,

Errol Flynn

EF/mp
Earl Conrad
707 W. 171st Street
New York 32, New York

Letter to Earl Conrad

INVENTORY OF FILM

```
2 movie projectors
2 speakers
1 blank reel
12 thousand foot cans--nitrate film
8 two thousand foot cans--nitrate film
1 tin box--3 cans--51 reels (cut outs)
1 cardboard box--31 cans (cut outs)


1 600 ft. can      Road to Damacus
1 can              Cruise of the Zaca
1 double can       Rocky Mountain
1 double can       Montana
2 cans             Against All Flags
2 cans             Green Light
2 cans             Another Dawn
2 cans             They Died With Their Boots On.
4 cans             Burma Road
4 cans             Thank Your Lucky Stars
4 cans


3 cans             Mara Maru
"                  San Antonio
"                  Kim
"                  Dawn Patrol
"                  Sea Hawk
"                  Dive Bomber
"                  Charge of the Light Brigade
"                  Don Juan
"                  Dodge City
"                  Never Say Goodbye
"                  Gentleman Jim
"                  Uncertain Glory
"                  Robin Hood
"                  Desperate Journey
"                  Escape Me Never
"                  Prince and the Pauper
"                  Edge of Darkness
"                  That Forsythe Woman
"                  Santa Fe Trail
"                  Perfect Specimen
"                  Cry Wolf
"                  Captain Blood
"                  Elizabeth and Essex
"                  Silver River
"                  Virginia City
```

Above left, inventory of Flynn's film collection in National Van Storage, and above right, the cover of the May issue of Cavalier Magazine

ship these things out of the country. So if you like I will send them to the New York Apt...I will try to check for you what happened to the Ford. I can't understand it. The car was fully paid for, and if you had owed money to anyone I would think they would contact you before taking the car. Something is fishy...."

Sat April 11

Letter to Earl Conrad: *"Earl: Please let me know how much you have trimmed down or got on Bud Ernst. After Erben, he was my first and long-time friend in Hollywood, although it was this Benedict Arnold who practically forced me into my first marriage. I can elaborate on Bud quite a bit and we certainly had memorable times together in my early days behind the fog, smog, and grog curtain of Hollywood. How many words would you like on the shock a man gets when his dear friend, a roistering, Falstaffian ruffian, suddenly goes out, buys himself a 16 double-guage [sic] shotgun, some cartridges, and blows the top of his head off, when married to a beauty such as Betty Furness?....[G. P. Putnam's Sons, publishing] are all enthused about the use of the title 'MY WICKED WAY?', countered with the suggestion 'MY WICKED, WICKED WAYS' or 'MY WICKED WAYS?', which would be O.K. with me if they agree. Any way, they seem very hot."*

Thu April 23

Letter from Cuba to Justin Golenbock: *"Dear Jud...We are getting close to the finish on location, and as I told you I am really very pleased with what we've got, and anticipate no problems when we move to Miami, and wind up the finish in New York. Mahon has done a very good job and so have all the rest of the bunch. Barry may not be a Lubitsch, but he has a really impressive talent for getting a picture made. He wants me to exchange checks with him for some extra dough we need down here and which he will collect from Pathe. I agreed. Hope the John Martin deal is finalized? The script 'The Wake of the Drunken Sailor' is good. The Middle needs work, but all togeter [sic] it is suspenseful and a nice way to approach a semi-serio comedy. The tag needs work also. I will do it. Let me know about the terms and who, if anyone has been resolved upon, such as cast, director, location, etc. I would also like to know the production starting date of 'Thunder Above'...."*

Sat April 25

Justin Golenbock sends a letter to National Van Lines in Glendale, CA, informing them that *"....all of the property held by you under the name of Mrs. Errol Flynn is the property of Mr. Errol Flynn...."* Letter from Flynn to Earl Conrad: *"....I would like to do a column. I have always wanted to....I know I could write on controversial subjects, and adapt an aggressive attitude. I wish I could write as well as Ring Lardner in Newsweek....Down here in Cuba, for instance, there is an easy column available twice a day, so many things happen, especially on our motion picture set....I like your suggestion of 'Flynnanigans', but what do you say to 'What a World!'....I could think of plenty, starting with 'MY GOD!' or 'FUNNY LIFE, AIN'T IT?'"*

May

Poses for Bacardi Cuban Rum advertisement photos in Havana in the first week of the month, taken by Jessie Fernandez *(following page, top left)*; the ads are never used as the plant was shut down; sometime during this period he travels to Jamaica with Beverly and sees his parents and sister for possibly the last time.

Fri May 1

Ron Shedlo sends a letter to Flynn at the Hotel Comodoro in Havana informing him of the itemized costs of shipping the storage items to Jamaica: $632.60 ($5,701.59 in 2021 value) plus $356 for $20,000 insurance coverage; he adds that *"Deirdre had a temperature of 102 for about two weeks but is feeling better now. She is going to school on Monday. Rory's cat just had kittens....Nora is probably going crazy now...."*

Sun May 3

Is brought to police headquarters and lodges a complaint over what he claims was an unauthorized search of his apartment *(bottom left)*; in notes taken at the time he writes: *"I have just been invaded by the Cuban Secret Police and as of this dispatch feel a bit nervous but prefer not to display same....it appears that I am on my way to jail..... Nobody could tell me why I had to go....To me this looks more and more like a police state, shades of 1943 Germany.... Is this the new Cuba? Oh, Castro, what friends you are making. I never thought this would happen to me. But it has.... Under house arrest with no charges against me...."* It appears he and Barry Mahon are accused of failing to submit to the government a script and filmed scenes of CUBAN REBEL GIRLS for approval before shooting.

With journalists in Havana after he lodged a protest against the Cuban rebel secret police - Sun, May 3

*Posing for photographer Jessie Fernandez
in Havana for an unused
Bacardi Rum ad - first week of May*

Landing of Captain Bligh on Navy Island in 1793.

*Front and back of card from Beverly in Port Antonio to her mother in Los Angeles: "Momma,
This painting is now in the Hotel, but we are
going to put it in the new House. It's the story of
bringing Bread fruit to Jamaica from Haiti.
Love you   Woodsie.*

Tue May 5

Flynn's Los Angeles belongings are shipped to Jamaica via the *S.S. Taiten* out of Miami; his collection of his own films (plus *Road to Damascus*) are sent to his New York apartment; the shipment includes two 16mm projectors and 35 films *(list on previous page, top left)*.

Thu May 7

Flies to Miami to have his arthritic knees examined at Jackson Memorial Hospital; he and Beverly leave for Jamaica the next day.

Sun May 24

Letter to Earl Conrad from Port Antonio: *"....what do you think of this? On the first page to quote that jingle of mine (I don't know where it came from and it could easily have been from me) which goes like this: Come, all you young men, With your wicked wicked ways, Sow your wild wild oats in your younger days; So that we may be happy When we grow old--Ah, yes, happy and happy When we grow old. For the day's getting cold, The night's growing long. Well, darling, give me your arm And we'll joggle along - Yes, we'll joggle and joggle and joggle along...Earl, this will explain the title.... It seems to give me a feeling of ultimate happiness: two people somewhat like the gay editions of Maggie and Jiggs or that classic I can't remember which typifies two people gracefully growing old...."* He goes on to describe some of the people in his life: *"There is no subject upon which* [my mother] *is not an authority, and my father had better look out for himself if perchance a cross word every now and then escapes his loose jaw in a moment of convivial happiness. He is likely to crack out with terrible words like 'damn' or 'the hell with you', at which one of them my mother who has ears like an owl at night just bends one frightening stare on the old professor and he sinks into the obscurity from which he should never have emerged.... it is a funny thing that when you meet somebody who you fall in love with - and, of course, you never recognize the signals - The Small Companion* [Beverly] *who I will describe in due course did* <u>not</u> *glide in sylph-like in a dark shimmering gown which looked like she had it sprayed on her. On the contrary, when she came into my life I watched her for about four days and she looked like a drum majorette. She didn't glide, she pranced. You were reminded of a high-stepping filly - I was, anyway. I did my best to ignore her and she did her best to see that I didn't. Now, this Small Companion, just described, has matured a little bit, and I think she is crowding the age of 17, and this is after a 2-year association of being my secretary....I never believed that I personally could spend day after day, hour after hour, with any person, male or female, and be content; and this comes as a bit of a shock to me at my age, and I must confess I couldn't be enjoying it more. And she has been trying desperately to get pregnant, and I like the idea myself....it is a charming idea to wind up* [as] *two misanthropes living on a high spot in sin in a beautiful part of the world...."*

Wed June 10

Letter from Ron Shedlo to Flynn at the Titchfield in Port Antonio regarding Flynn's car in Los Angeles: *"As you probably know, the car was attached....some private detective who you owe the some* [sic] *of $1,300* [$11,717 in 2021 value]. *There is also a charge of $157* [$1,415 in 2021 value] *for the expense of storing it etc. I think it would be wise for you to pay these bills and get the car out of attachment....it is almost brand new; it has only 10,000 miles on it....Unless you send a letter* [with a check to cover the bill] *they will return the car to Pat instead of to me. (By the way she is back in town)...."*

Sat June 20

Flynn's 50th birthday, celebrated with Beverly at the El Morocco in New York.
Around this time he meets with Patrice at Romeo Salta's Italian Restaurant to discuss their separation, possible divorce, and why he has not lived up to his agreement of support for her and Arnella.

Fri June 26

With Beverly at Yankee Stadium for the heavyweight championship fight between Floyd Patterson and Ingemar Johansson (Johansson won).

Wed July 8

Notes to himself on a notepad: *"....Little, if anything, due Pat....Strange after seeing Harlow last nite with Cary* [Grant] *and* [Franchot] *Tone—Late Show* [in the film *Suzy*], *Woodsie* [Beverly] *better than Harlow....*[to Nora] *Darling please explain girls impossible take them Jamaica now and am terribly dejected because hate to have welch*[ed] *on a deal will they take a rain check...."*

*With Beverly at the Stork Club
in New York - June*

Flynn's comments to Earl Conrad about Jack Warner, **Sat, August 1**: *"Outside his office Jack Warner has an endearing sense of humor and can outcomic most of the comedians I know. I stress, outside, because inside his office you are confronted with all the lousy hostility and beastiality [sic] in Hollywood. That's Jack....Sometimes he's almost knocked me off my chair laughing especially the time there was an important luncheon for Madam Chaing Kai Chek [sic]. This distinguished lady rose to her feet and spoke of the troubles of Nationalist China. At one point she paused and in the silence Jack's voice came over loudly saying to someone, 'Jeezez, that reminds me. I've got to send my laundry out'. I doubt if the lady from China caught the idea, but I almost had a seizure."*

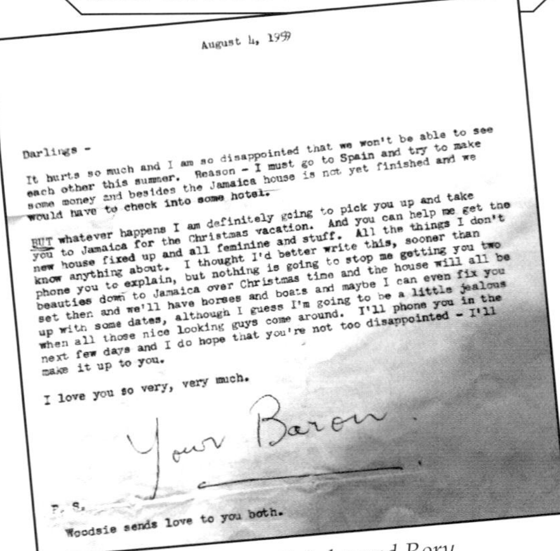

August 4, 1959

Darlings -

It hurts so much and I am so disappointed that we won't be able to see each other this summer. Reason - I must go to Spain and try to make some money and besides the Jamaica house is not yet finished and we would have to check into some hotel.

BUT whatever happens I am definitely going to pick you up and take you to Jamaica for the Christmas vacation. And you can help me get the new house fixed up and all feminine and stuff. All the things I don't know anything about. I thought I'd better write this, sooner than phone you to explain, but nothing is going to stop me getting you two beauties down to Jamaica over Christmas time and the house will all be set then and we'll have horses and boats and maybe I can even fix you up with some dates, although I guess I'm going to be a little jealous when all those nice looking guys come around. I'll phone you in the next few days and I do hope that you're not too disappointed - I'll make it up to you.

I love you so very, very much.

Your Baron

P. S,

Woodsie sends love to you both.

Letter to Deirdre and Rory

With Deirdre, Rory, and Nora at Los Angeles International Airport - Fri, August 28

Wed July 15

Ron Shedlo writes to Justin Golenbock informing him that he (Ron) will be driving Flynn's 1957 Ford Skyliner to Miami for shipment to Jamaica, thereby saving about $300 ($2,704 in 2021 value) in total shipping charges.

Mon July 20

With a race named in his honor, Flynn participates in ceremonies at Monmouth Park racetrack in Ocean Port, NJ.

Wed July 22

Is a guest on the television quiz show *Keep Talking*; the host is Vincent Price who is filling in for Carl Reiner; the next day he is offered a role in the play *The Woman with Red Hair*; nothing comes of it.

Sat July 25

Letter from Ron Shedlo to Flynn in New York: *"....As I explained on the phone I had an idea to get the silver elephant from Pat. [I'd have] Deirdre call her and state that you promised the elephant to Deirdre for her graduation. Well, she called Pat who told her that she needed money and had sold the elephant and didn't know where it was. I am sure this is against the law and she has no right selling something that does not belong to her, even if you are still married...."*

Mon July 27

Letter from Prof. Flynn in London to Justin Golenbock: *"....I hear that Errol is ill in hospital in New York and I am exceedingly surprised and hurt that I have received no news from you in answer to my last letter. Errol of course, will not write. I am depending on you for news. Please let me have some and please also give me full details as to his illness and other matters...."* Ron Shedlo writes to Vincent Grosett, the manager of Flynn's estate in Port Antonio, that he will be driving Flynn's car to Miami and meeting up with Flynn there on August 7th, after which they will together transport the car to Jamaica.

Thu July 30

Letter to Flynn from Vincent Grosett: *"....I have received a request from [shoemaker, Noel Brown] for payment of £12 [$404.38 in 2021 value]....I have also received a Bill from Dr. B.A. Shoucair for £5.5/ [$185.31 in 2021 value]-against you for treatment on June 10th, and £10.10/ [$340 in 2021 value]-for treatment of Miss Beverly Wood [Aadland] in August 1958, from Dr. McNeill...Please advise, as these bills are just piling up....and, of course, if you go on owing Doctors like this in Jamaica, when you are seriously ill you will find it exceedingly difficult to get one who will attend to you. It is a small Country, and these people talk a lot...."* Flynn writes humorously to Justin Golenbock about his (Flynn's) supposed will: *"RE: my kids: 1. Sean? --Ok, taken care of. 2. Deidre? --Ok, taken care of. 3. Rory? --Ok, taken care of. 4. Arnella -Not yet, properly. RE: Mothers of kids. They're God damn well taken care of, aren't they Jud? They saw to that themselves, didn't they. RE: Mother and Father. In good shape, no worries there, but the old bitch still annoys the hell out of me. FOR MY "SMALL COMPANION", WOODSIE: (If the little bitch is still around when I kick off) A half million bucks. She has been nice and kind to me, Jud, we have to take good care of her, get it, I'm not being apologetic. As for what's left the hell with it, anyone can have it who needs it....The pretty secretary typing this just observed she could use some, so why don't we give her some? Especially as I just noticed her outspoken attractive tits lean over the typewriter at an engaging angle, but that's beside the point. Or points....P.S. Anyone who comes to my funeral is automatically cut out of my will...."*

Sat August 1

Writes to Earl Conrad about Hermann Erben: *"Thanks to Erben and his lusty, practical outlook on men and mice, sex, morals and morons I was seldom ever trapped again in this world between the Skylla of good clean living and the wicked Charybadis [sic] of a good solid hard on (erection). Ladies and Gentlemen may I offer this suggestion that we should have more Erbens in our younger days."*

Fri August 7

Is offered the lead role in the upcoming Broadway play, *Edge of the Jungle*; nothing comes of it.

Mon August 17

Flynn's documentary, CUBAN STORY (THE TRUTH ABOUT FIDEL CASTRO REVOLUTION), premieres in Moscow (it is not seen in the west until 2001).

Fri August 21

Flynn's mother Marelle writes from England to Justin Golenbock to inform him that Flynn's father, Professor Theodore, has had a stroke the night before; she goes on to say that she does not know where Errol is and that *"he has not written to us for months...."*

Fri August 28

Arrives in Los Angeles *(bottom left)* with Beverly staying at the Beverly Crest Hotel (now the Mosaic Hotel); by September 15th they have moved on to the Hollywood Landmark Hotel on Franklin Avenue (now the Highland Gardens), room 127, his final address in Hollywood.

Filming The Golden Shanty *the first week of September; above left, with director Arthur Hiller; above center, with Deirdre, Rory, and Nora visiting the set; above right, with Patricia Barry*

First Week of September

Films a TV movie, THE GOLDEN SHANTY (*above three*), for Goodyear Theater on a three-day schedule (the daily production logs have not been located); the project had originally been announced in June of 1957.

Mon September 7

Flynn's mother Marelle writes to him from England (*bottom right*): "My dear Errol, In my cable to you [center right] *I told you that your father was better, but he had another bad turn this morning + the doctor gave me a solemn warning + said his family should be told, + other dreadful things. I am just desperate with anxiety, I'm terrified he might soon leave me. Please come if you can, not if you can -- come. Your mother with love P.S. Your cable has given him + me the greatest joy.*"

Tue September 8

Letter to George Caldough in Vancouver: "*Regarding the sale of the Zaca. 1. Yes, I have no objection to having my name associated with the ship. 2. As I outlined today, the price is $100,000 [$901,294 in 2021 value]....5. For the down payment on the vessel, 50,000 must be paid into a Swiss bank which I designate....7. Two small craft will go with the sale, my launch, double-ender and skiff. The speed boat is excluded but if you wish a separate deal can be arrange*[d]. *8. I have tentatively a T.V. series arranged in which the Zaca would figure. Of course, if you buy the vessel and the T.V. group want to charter it, that would be up to you to give a yes or no....I appreciate your offer to invite me to use Zaca a month out of the year, and I will certainly avail myself of it. Possessions are not much but Zaca has played a great part in my life and I can only hope she will in yours....*" Letter to *Zaca* captain Rick Allord in Mallorca: "*....take the gold bar* [from the Zaca] *and my other possessions and put them in a safe place and get a receipt for them including the gold bar....*" During this week Flynn visits Arnella without Patrice in attendance—it is probably the last time he ever sees her; a few days later he meets with Patrice, who notes he "*was not himself;*" it is probably the last time he ever sees her.

Wed September 9

Flynn's mother Marelle writes to a family friend about Prof. Flynn's stroke and says: "*....I wish you could get in touch with* [Errol] *and warn him and ask him to come to his father who wants to see him very badly....*[Errol] *may think I'm being hysterical but unfortunately I am not....*" The friend writes about this to Errol, saying: "*....Your mother would not write in such vein to me if she did not feel the matter is one of grave consequences...Errol—the decision is up to you whether to hasten to your dad's bedside....Don't take the chance of a lifetime of deep regret and self-reproach. You are needed, Errol, as never before. Don't let your loved ones down....*"

Thu September 10

Flynn writes to film distributor Joe Brenner in New York concerning CUBAN REBEL GIRLS: "*....I think we can get a very big place in the national press for the* [promotional] *party we agreed we should give, for very little money....As far as I can figure it will cost about $350 [$3,155 in 2021 value]....My job will be to tell everyone present that our picture was never meant to be pretentious, just an inside glimpse* [sic] *of what actually went on in Cuba during the Revolution. In light of current events, I am only happy that Senior Castro doesn't figure into the film. Aren't you?....*" Brenner responds on 9/14 that "*there is no doubt in my mind that we can do a very fine gross with CUBAN REBEL GIRLS....*"

Below, telegram from Flynn's mother, Marelle - Sat, September 5

WESTERN UNION TELEGRAM

OA182

O CDU566 39 PD INTL=CD STALBANS HERTS VIA MACKAY 5 1310=

LT ERROL FLYNN BEVERLY DREFT HOTEL=
125 SOUTH SPALDING BEVERLYHILLS (CALIF):

=VERY WELCOME CABLE ONLY JUST RECEIVED DADDY DISTINCTLY BETTER PLEASE USE STALBANS ADDRESS HOPE HEAR FROM YOU AGAIN SOON LOVE TO ALL LETTER FOLLOWING MOTHER 8 NEWHOUSE PARK STALBANS.

Letter from Flynn's mother, Marelle - Mon, September 7

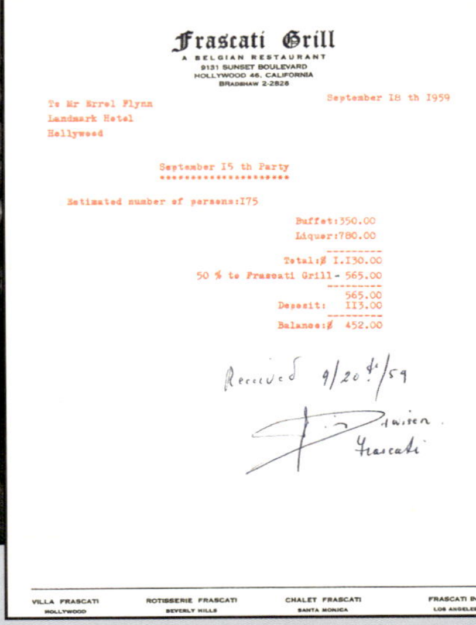

Frascati Grill
A BELGIAN RESTAURANT
9131 SUNSET BOULEVARD
HOLLYWOOD 46, CALIFORNIA
BRADSHAW 2-2828

September 18 th 1959

To Mr Errol Flynn
Landmark Hotel
Hollywood

September 15 th Party
****

Estimated number of persons:175

Buffet:350.00
Liquor:780.00

Total:$ 1.130.00
50 % to Frascati Grill - 565.00

565.00
Deposit: 113.00

Balance:$ 452.00

Received 9/20ᵗʰ/59

VILLA FRASCATI — ROTISSERIE FRASCATI BEVERLY HILLS — CHALET FRASCATI SANTA MONICA — FRASCATI INN LOS ANGELES

*The CUBAN REBEL GIRLS/Beverly Aadland birthday party at the Villa Frascati -
Tue, September 15; above left, with Beverly and her friend Linda Tartar;
above center, with Nora and Mickey Rooney;
above right, with Beverly, Rory, and (in the foreground) Deirdre*

*The bill for the Villa Frascati
party - Fri, September 18*

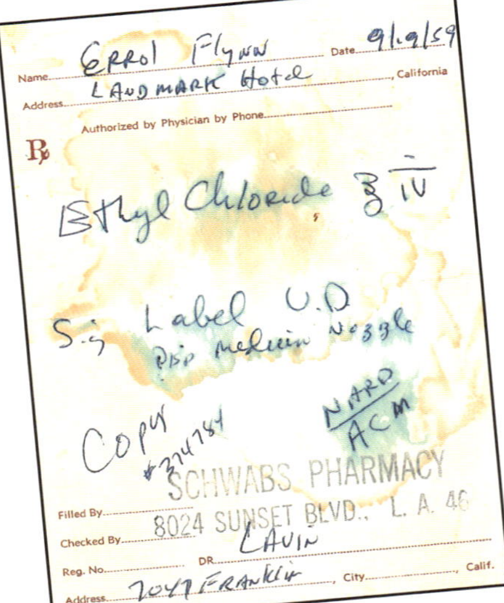

*Flynn's prescription for ethyl
chloride spray - Sat, September 19*

Tue September 15

A CUBAN REBEL GIRLS party, coinciding with Beverly's 17th birthday, is held at the Villa Frascati in Hollywood; writes a letter to Howard Cady at Putnam's: *"....What date do you think you will bring the book out?....Please be sure that the picture of me in the May 1958 issue of Esquire is used on the book cover...The only other two matters are: 1. The dedication - 'For a small companion.' 2. I still think that after the prologue the book should start out as I think I told you in my last letter, that - 'I detest autobiographies which start out something like, ah, there was joy and happiness in the humble abode of Professor and Mrs. Flynn when the first lusty yells of little Errol were heard. Etc Etc."* (his requested addition to the prologue, worded slightly differently, was included); receives a letter from Howard Cady, his editor at Putnam's: *"....I'm enclosing herewith the first 43 galleys of MY WICKED WICKED WAYS, which include everything in the first 203 manuscript pages....There is definitely a business risk in connection with references to your mother....even though we have toned down a couple of things rather delicately. Is there any chance of getting a release from her? Would she have the courage to sue? If she did take legal action, would it be at the risk of extreme poverty in her old age?....[With reference to the girl] Maura....Even though her name has been changed, could she be identified if she is the one high government official's wife who was half-Melenesian [sic], half-Polynesian? Should she be described as an Irish girl or otherwise identified to eliminate the risk of identification?....There is also some risk in connection with McDonald's sheep ranch [in Australia]. I have changed the name to McDermid and changed the name of the daughter. Is the whole thing sufficiently veiled to eliminate any risk?....I have an idea their libel laws are tougher than ours....There is also the problem of Erben....Is he alive today? Have you used his real name?....If he is alive, and there is no chance of getting a release, then there [is] a hell of a lot of things we will have to consider changing. Even though he may be a true friend, somebody could persuade him it would pay handsomely to sue...."*

Wed September 16

Letter to Joe Brenner: *"....It was hard to soft-sell [CUBAN REBEL GIRLS] because all my friends of the press wanted to build it up while I was trying to sell it down...However....all of the press seemed most impressed last night, and I'm sure we will get a very friendly coverage...I over extended myself for the press coverage, but I will pay the difference out of my own pocket and that hurts brother because many more people showed up than I expected. Free Loaders--no [sic] what I mean?...."*

Thu September 17

Letter to Howard Cady: *"....In regards to libel. I have no fears...Nor do I have any fears about Mike Curtiz. If you would like, I will try to get a clearance from Mike if you want, and I'm quite confident he will give it to me...Much more important is getting a clearance from my ex-wife Nora Eddington Haymes and I have been concerned about that page—namely because of my two daughters who might be humiliated....[But] the episode is too vital to my life to be lost....Concerning my business risk in connection with my mother....No, she would not have the courage to sue, she would be risking too much....Now, as far for the problem of (Erben) your remarks are well taken. Erben is alive today and nobody should be more surprised than he. But don't you think he comes out very well? Even if he wanted to, on what grounds could he be damaged by me. How could he possibl[y] resent my calling him one of the few friends in my life? But to be realistic I'll get a letter off to him in Germany and ask for a release, sight unseen and I know he will give it...."*

Weekend of Fri September 18

With Deirdre, Rory, Beverly, and Ronnie Shedlo spending the day at Pacific Ocean Park in Santa Monica.

Mon September 21

In San Francisco with Beverly and Ron Shedlo to visit Melvin Belli; while there is seen by Dr. Harry Elder and has medical lab work done.

Tue September 22

George Caldough writes to Ron Shedlo *"and/or Mr. Erroll Flynn"*: *"I spoke to Mr. Flynn a fortnight ago regarding the purchase of his schooner 'Zaca'. Since that time I have been in touch with [Zaca captain] Rick Allord once or twice and made a firm offer and to this date have heard nothing further...Would you be good enough to telephone me 'Collect' in Vancouver [Walnut 2-1352] regarding this matter and I believe we can make a deal which will be most agreeable to all parties concerned...."*

Fri September 25

Returns to Los Angeles from San Francisco with Beverly and Ron Shedlo.

Sun September 27

Sean writes a heartfelt letter to his father *(top right)*: *"Thanks for answering my letter at such prodigious speed—2 months. Well at least you did...I spent most my summer in Palm Beach, where I lived with mom and secured a job....I met and fell in love with a girl there. That's where the problem arises....Mom developed an animosity towards the girl and her parents because she thought that they were 'trying to marry her off to me' and she considered them below us in social stature....I did everything in my power to convince mom that marriage was in the distant future....But she went behind my back and the result was chaos....[The girl] wanted to write mother a letter to put her in her place but I restrained her - you and I know why....I would like to go down to Florida [from school in New Jersey] for Thanksgiving....and I haven't got the dough. I expect it will be about $100 [$901 in 2021 value] for the plane trip. I hope you can come to New York so I can talk to you - if you can't, I hope you can lend me the money...I really need your help - it seems I have nobody to talk to or ask advise [sic] from. I hope you will take this seriously - I really love the dame a lot. Here's hoping Love Sean."*

Mon September 28

Performs in the FREDDIE'S BEAT SHACK skit in a live preview of TV's *The Red Skelton Show*; is sent Dr. Elder's lab work, which indicates Flynn has *"Malaria Malariae ring forms"* and *"rare abnormal inclusion body in neutrophiles resembling leishmania Donovani"*; in layman's terms this translates to malaria still observed in his blood work, along with a tropical parasite which is fatal to thousands every year.

Guesting on The Red Skelton Show *(below three) - Mon, September 28; below center, with Skelton and Beverly*

*Letter from Flynn's son Sean -
Sun, September 27*

Audience ticket to The Red Skelton Show
on which Flynn was a guest

With Linda Tartar and Beverly at the circus - Thu, October 1

Above, with Beverly and Otto Reichow at Reichow's Hollywood home - Sun, October 4 (photo by Robert Bardey); below, the same spot today

Tue September 29

Performs live on *The Red Skelton Show*, his final professional work as an actor; letter from Howard Cady: *"....I would say that we are ready to start printing as soon as we have a word from you concerning these [edits], and the releases from Nora Eddington Haymes and Dr. Erben...."*

October

"When Flynn and young Aadland arrived in Los Angeles, she was wearing an engagement ring. He was determined to marry the teenager, but that was impossible, with Wymore blocking his way. She had yet to file for divorce, despite ongoing reminders of Hollywood's latest—and steamiest—May/December romance. One evening in early October 1959, a raging Errol Flynn stormed into the Marmont, demanding to see Patrice Wymore. He had been drinking....'He was in a terrible state,' Carmel Volti remembers....Carmel put in a call to Wymore in Bungalow C, more to alert her to the arrival of her drunken husband than to announce him. No one answered. 'She's not in,' Carmel told the staggering Flynn. He stared angrily at Carmel for an instant, then turned on unsteady legs and made his way towards the stairway leading to the garage. He hadn't been gone ten minutes when word reached the front desk that 'a bellowing lunatic' was trying to break into Bungalow C. He had tried to force his way through the front door, the caller reported, and was now attempting to get inside through a bathroom window. Two houseboys were sent to Wymore's bungalow. They found no one there. A few minutes later, Flynn reappeared in the lobby....'Oh, what a commotion he made! It was so sad to see him that way. To think that he was once a dashing matinee idol.'" From *Life at the Marmont: The Inside Story of Hollywood's Legendary Hotel of the Stars-Chateau Marmont*, by Raymond Sarlot and Fred E. Basten.

Thu October 1

With Beverly at the opening of Ringling Bros. and Barnum and Bailey Circus in Los Angeles; letter to Howard Cady: *"....I have several letters from Erben when I found him recently, and of course they are more than friendly....I am sure you will have no [repercussions] from this old friend, and of course I agree with you that it would be wise to get a clearance from him but I don't know how to go about getting it. To avoid legal complications I am concerned about nobody except Nora and Lilly...."*

Sun October 4

At the home of his friend Otto Reichow (*left*), Errol is interviewed and photographed with Beverly and Mrs. George Caldough, wife of the man interested in purchasing the *Zaca*, for a piece that is published in *Life* magazine on October 26th; letter to Vincent Grosett at Flynn's Jamaica estate: *"....I will be bringing my daughter down at Christmas time and I will appreciate Mr. Scott telling me how many horses and saddles there are....What has happened to the car I sent down?...."*

Mon October 5

Letter to Dr. Harry Elder in San Francisco: *"When I first met you with [Melvin] Belli I had you figured instantly as the finest example of American physician....[But] anyone who sends a patient a bill for only twenty-two dollars for all the attention you gave me has to see a 'head shrinker.'..."* Letter from Howard Cady at Putnam's, informing Flynn that the photo Flynn wants for the back cover of the book is *"absolutely out of the question....We are trying to....get permission to use the Esquire photo. Certainly it is better than this one, although the girls here in the office don't like it especially... Can you dig up anything else that might be suitable for the back of the jacket? Frankly, I think we would have greater success with an exciting, glamorous picture taken not too long after your arrival in Hollywood...."* Sends a response to Sean's letter of the previous week: *"Dear Sport...The enclosed check makes me convinced I am a soft touch, especially since I am short on ready cash, but in your case I can not let your 'pitch' go unheeded...Of course, it's not really my business, but I can only advise you that I believe in long engagements - say about five or ten years. Your girl sounds like a good guy from your description, which was practically nothing (you didn't even tell me her name), so the odds are if she really cares for you she won't mind waiting. How about sending me a picture of her? I want to see if your taste is as good as mine - and if it is I'm sorry for you....It is about time I heard from you, you slob. If you say you haven't had your Wicked Way with her, why not, pray tell? You can be no son of mine....Incidentally, this check is not a loan. Some day you can pay me back in my decreped [sic] old age....Best to both of you from your ever lovin' Pop...P.S. Deirdre and Rory keep asking about you and you should write them because for some unknown reason they seem to think very highly of you. I don't, you louse. * You needed $100 [$901 in 2021 value], I added an extra twenty-five for condoms and/or flowers."* Receives an airmail letter and round-trip tickets for him and Beverly to Vancouver from George Caldough: *"....This flight will see you in our fair city at 9:21 in the evening which shouldn't make it too tedious...I will pick you up at the airport and send out an 'all points' bulletin to*

Salmon, Sturgeon, Ling Cod, and Shadroe in the area that you are on your way...."

Wed October 7

Letter to Howard Cady at Putnam's: *"I agree that the black and white picture you sent me is not good...But on the other hand I'm not interested in the opinion of your girls in your office. I like the picture from Esquire and that's the one I want used...."* The *Esquire* magazine photo was ultimately used for the back jacket of *My Wicked, Wicked Ways* In a follow-up letter to Cady the same day he wrote: *"....I know that when you have to sell a book much depends upon the back cover. Perhaps you might arrange a composit[e] of me as a young man and what I am today as reproduced in the Esquire magazine. I disagree with this idea but please let me know your ideas too...My opinion is that the [Esquire] picture is moody - and that's what I wanted to get over to the readers...."*

The Cave Supper Club in Vancouver (now gone), the last place Flynn was seen in public

Fri October 9

Arrives in Vancouver, Canada, with Beverly Aadland to the discuss sale of the *Zaca* to George Caldough; interviewed at the airport by Vernon Scott; the couple first stays at the Sylvia Hotel and then moves to the Caldough home at 1026 Eyremount Drive (now gone) in the British Properties area of Vancouver.

Sun October 11

With Beverly at the Hotel Vancouver's Panorama Roof in the evening.

Mon October 12

With Beverly at the Cave Supper Club, 626 Hornby St. (now gone); Paul King of the *Vancouver Sun* quotes Flynn at the club: *"I love this town. The people, the mountains, the sea. I've traveled a lot, and I've lived and loved a lot—that's what I'm expected to say isn't it?—but I've seldom found a country as magnificent as this. It would be a wonderful place to die."* Flynn also mentions an upcoming appearance (Nov. 5th) on the *Big Party* television show.

Being interviewed by journalist John Arnett at Vancouver airport; the photos from this occasion are probably the last ever taken of Flynn -Fri, October 9

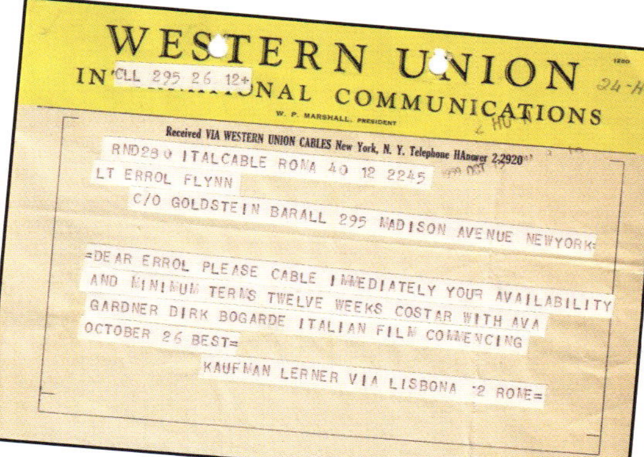

WESTERN UNION
INTERNATIONAL COMMUNICATIONS
W. P. MARSHALL, PRESIDENT

Received VIA WESTERN UNION CABLES New York, N. Y. Telephone HAnover 2-2920

RND280 ITALCABLE ROMA 40 12 2245

LT ERROL FLYNN
C/O GOLDSTEIN BARALL 295 MADISON AVENUE NEWYORK=

=DEAR ERROL PLEASE CABLE IMMEDIATELY YOUR AVAILABILITY AND MINIMUM TERMS TWELVE WEEKS COSTAR WITH AVA GARDNER DIRK BOGARDE ITALIAN FILM COMMENCING OCTOBER 26 BEST=

KAUFMAN LERNER VIA LISBONA 2 ROME=

Telegram from the Kaufman and Lerner Agency with an offer of a film for Flynn - Tue, October 13

Tue October 13

Flynn receives an offer to star in *The Angel Wore Red* (*center right*); the film was eventually made with Joseph Cotton in Flynn's would-be role; with Beverly and the Caldoughs for dinner at a seafood restaurant.

Wed October 14

The Caldoughs begin driving Errol and Beverly to the airport to return to Los Angeles when Flynn complains of severe pains in his back and left leg; George Caldough turns around at 10th Ave. and makes a call to his friend Dr. Grant Gould, who suggests they come directly to his penthouse apartment at 1310 Burnaby Street #201 (*right*) in the West End of Vancouver; after arriving Flynn is administered the pain killer demerol and initially feels better but then asks to lie down in the bedroom; some time later, Beverly looks in on him and discovers him to be unresponsive and turning blue; while CPR is being performed, one of Dr. Gould's guests, Art Cameron, manager of the Sylvia Hotel summons an ambulance; Flynn is rushed to Vancouver General Hospital, where, at 7:45 pm, he is pronounced dead; pulmonary embolism (not a heart attack) caused by a deep venous thrombosis in one or both of Mr. Flynn's legs is determined to be the cause; Beverly is brought back by the Caldoughs to their home.

Above, 1310 Burnaby Street in Vancouver, and right, #201, Dr. Grant Gould's penthouse in the building

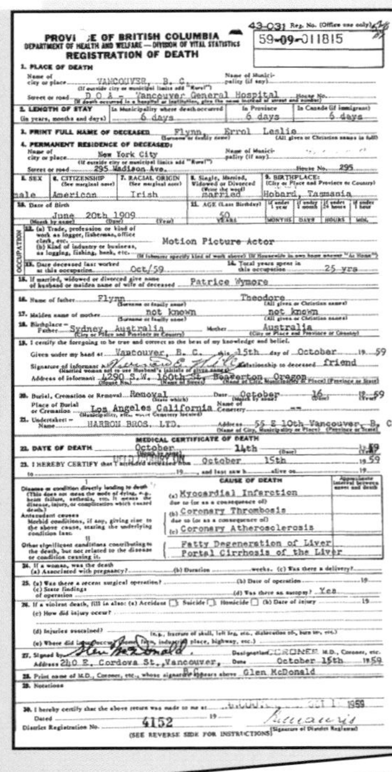

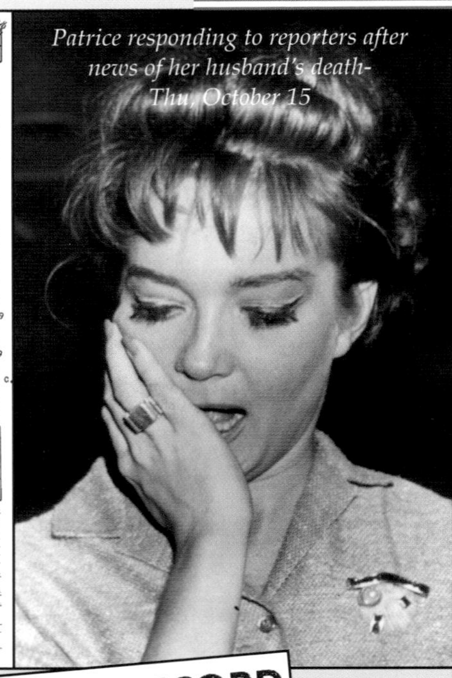

Patrice responding to reporters after news of her husband's death- Thu, October 15

Dr. Grant A. Gould
PHYSICIAN AND SURGEON

SUITE 1423, MEDICAL-DENTAL BUILDING
925 WEST GEORGIA STREET
VANCOUVER 1, B.C.

October 16th, 1959.

Commander Glen McDonald,
Coroner, City of Vancouver,
312 Main Street,
Vancouver, B. C.

Re: Errol Flynn, Deceased
October 14th, 1959.

Dear Sir:-

I received a telephone message from Mr. George Caldough of West Vancouver on the above date to the effect that his house guest Mr. Errol Flynn was leaving shortly for the airport, and before taking his flight desired sedation for acute low back and leg pain which had been bothering him for many months intermittently, but which had been particularly bad for the last two days. Owing to the fact that I had just finished my office appointments, I suggested that it would be more expedient for the patient to drop by my apartment en route to the airport and that I would examine him at this time.

Mr. Flynn arrived at my residence at approximately 3:45 p.m. accompanied by both Mr. Caldough and Miss Aadland. I assisted Mr. Caldough in helping Mr. Flynn negotiate the stairs as it was extremely difficult for him to flex his left leg. On arrival at my apartment examination disclosed that he was suffering from an acute intervertebral disc syndrome with sciatic radiation producing intense muscle spasm and pain down the left leg, as well as in the lower back. This condition rendered it impossible for him to sit down without an excruciating exacerbation of the pain. Accordingly, I administered 50 miligrams of demerol intravenously with the patient standing and supporting himself against a table. He obtained considerable relief almost immediately, but elected to remain standing with his back against the patio doorway which seemed to further ease the discomfort.

- 2 -

At no time did he complain of chest pains or dyspnea and he seemed in excellent spirits and reminisced at great length about his past experiences. He was offered a drink but refused. During this time Mr. Caldough was on the telephone attempting to delay the flight departure. I advised against the wisdom of making the flight at this time even though he was feeling considerably more comfortable. When he had relaxed sufficiently to be able to lie down without severe pain I manipulated his left leg while he was supine on the bedroom floor. This produced further relief and I suggested he remain on the floor in the lateral flexed position for several minutes before attempting to resume walking. He thanked me and said he felt "ever so much better". From time to time during the next twenty minutes one or other of the persons present would drop in and converse with him.

At approximately 6:45 p.m., his companion Miss Aadland came running to me saying that he had suddenly collapsed, that his colour was poor and that he had apparently stopped breathing. I immediately went to his aid and while commencing to examine him, Miss Aadland pulled a box of amyl nitrite ampoules from her purse and quickly broke one under his nose. This was the first indication of any previous cardiac involvement and it was confirmed subsequently by her that she had been instructed to carry this preparation as he had evidently suffered previous cardiac attacks. At this time only a faint heart beat was audible and I injected adrenalin directly into the heart, while instructing Miss Aadland to perform mouth to mouth respirations.

The Inhalator Squad was immediately summoned and administered oxygen and further resuscitation from 6:50 to 7:15 p.m. The patient did not respond and he was transferred to the Emergency Department of the Vancouver General Hospital where oxygen therapy was continued for a short time following intubation.

I finally pronounced Mr. Flynn dead at 7:45 p.m., although the exact time of expiry is possibly a matter of conjecture. In retrospect it is concluded that he died as the result of a sudden overwhelming myocardial infarction of such proportions as to produce death without premonitory symptoms.

I trust this summary will serve to elucidate a few points which may have been obscured by the press releases.

Yours very truly,

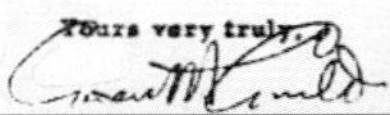

Above left, the death certificate; above right, Dr. Gould's summary of events of Flynn's death at his home

Thu October 15

Patrice, having just concluded a run of her nightclub act in Washington, D.C., flies to Los Angeles to make funeral arrangements.

Fri October 16

Beverly arrives back in Los Angeles, accompanied by Ron Shedlo, who had flown to Vancouver to escort her home; Flynn's body is shipped back to Los Angeles by train, accompanied by his longtime friend and double, Buster Wiles.

Sat October 17

Florence Aadland, Beverly's mother, releases Flynn's private letters to her daughter to the press.

Sun October 18

Flynn's body arrives in Los Angeles (*bottom right*).

Mon October 19

Flynn's funeral is held in the Church of the Intercessor at Forest Lawn in Glendale, CA, officiated by Episcopal minister Rev. Kermit Castellanos; Jack L. Warner delivers the eulogy and Dennis Morgan sings *Home Is the Sailor*; pallbearers are Mickey Rooney, Michael Romanoff, Guinn "Big Boy" Williams, Raoul Walsh, Otto Reichow, and Jack Oakie; among the approximately 500 mourners are Johnny Weissmuller, Betty Furness, Alexis Smith, Craig Stevens, Ida Lupino, and Howard Duff; not in attendance are Lili Damita, Nora Eddington, and Beverly Aadland, who is in San Francisco at the home of Melvin Belli; Flynn is buried in the Court of Everlasting Peace.

Buster Wiles (in hat and light tie) accompanying Flynn's body as it arrives at Union Station in Los Angeles - Sun, October 18

Deirdre and Rory being escorted to the funeral at Forest Lawn, Glendale - Mon, October 19

Patrice and Sean exiting the Church of the Intercessor after the funeral service

The memorial program

A Service of Memory

for

Errol Flynn

at the

Church of the Recessional

Now abideth Faith, Hope, Love these three; and the greatest of these is Love.
—inspired by I Corinthians 13:13

In the belief that a heart filled with Love knows no separation from those who live on in memory, these words are inscribed above the chancel of The Church of the Recessional, a faithful re-creation within Forest Lawn Memorial-Park of the church at Rottingdean, England, where Rudyard Kipling worshipped and found inspiration for his immortal poem "The Recessional."

Born	June 20, 1909 Hobart, Tasmania
Passed away	October 14, 1959 Vancouver, B.C., Canada
Services held	October 19, 1959 10:00 a.m.
Services conducted by	The Reverend Kermit Castellanos All Saints Episcopal Church Beverly Hills, California
Eulogy Delivered by	Mr. Jack Warner
Soloist	Mr. Dennis Morgan 'Requiem' - by Homer
Organist	Mr. C. Harold Dick 'Ah, Sweet Mystery of Life' 'I Believe' 'Yours Is My Heart Alone' 'Ich Liebe Dich' (I Love You)
Funeral Director	Forest Lawn Mortuary
Interment	Forest Lawn Memorial-Park Glendale, California

Wed October 21

Flynn's 1954 last will and testament is filed for probate in Surrogate Court, most of his estate going to Patrice; a legal battle begins over the will, with Patrice and Nora both making a claim for the estate; ultimately, the Jamaica property and personal effects go to Patrice, with his parents, Deirdre, and Rory receiving $10,000 each, and Sean $5,000 ($90,129 and $45,065, respectively, in 2021 value); Beverly receives nothing.

Mon October 26

A second, handwritten, unsigned, unwitnessed last will and testament written on Hotel Nacional note paper in Cuba, and naming Beverly as a one-third benefactor, is filed with the New York Surrogate Court; the other two benefactors are said to be Deirdre and Rory; this will is eventually deemed nil; *Life* magazine publishes an article titled "Finis For the Fabulous Flynn" which includes photos from the October 4th photo shoot.

Mon November 9

THE GOLDEN SHANTY, Flynn's final dramatic performance, is broadcast on United States TV.

Thu November 12

Letter from Flynn's mother Marelle to Ron Shedlo: *"I [had] been extremely worried over my poor boy for a long time, and I wrote to him several times telling him this, asking him what was making him so unhappy, as I know he was....I know now why he was so unhappy, he <u>knew</u> he had not long to live...."*

Thu November 19

Letter from Flynn's mother Marelle to Nora (*next page, top left*): *"My dear, It is hard for me to write letters yet, with the ache in my heart. I weep every time I start, but I do want to answer your sweet letter. We have suffered a terrible sorrow, made more hard to bear as we were expecting him home in two weeks time. When the telephone rang so early that fateful morning, in the dark of a winter's morning I rushed happily from my bed thinking it was to announce his arrival, to be told the awful news. I had to break the news to the professor who was still ill. I cannot still believe that I will never see him again. Another awful thing is that he knew he had not long to live, he had known for some time, but he bravely kept it to himself,*

Above, pallbearers (l-r) Michael Romanoff, Mickey Rooney, Jack Oakie, Raoul Walsh, and Guinn "Big Boy" Williams (Otto Reichow is obscured by Williams) carry Flynn's casket from the chapel on its way to the gravesite; below, the same spot today

Marelle's letter to Nora – Thu, November 19

carrying on in the bitter end. This we learn now from his doctors, and what he must have suffered mentally knowing he was doomed, only God himself would know, anyone with the zest of life he had + everything to live for, my poor poor boy. This has made my grief greater still. I can't bear to think of it. It explains in a way, the unhappy change in him these last years, when I thought he was deliberately destroying himself. I could not bear to see it. If I had only known the truth! A doctor friend from Jamaica over here on a visit home this summer tried to warn us, but as the Professor was seriously ill better not to tell him the truth. Errol was so concerned + worried over his father, sent cables, + telephoned. It was then he told me he was coming home in two weeks time. He was so sweet, just his voice is a happy memory for me. He had been angry with us for not receiving Beverly Aadland when they were in London. After all he was still married to Pat, we owed our loyalty to her, + had he been married to Beverly Aadland, she would have expected the same loyalty to herself from us. We could not understand how that girl could flaunt herself so brazenly in London with him, + how Errol could break all the conventions with a girl like that, before all our friends, + offend all good taste. He would never have done that in the past. However all that was cleared up when we spoke over the phone such a short time before he went...think that Pat did the right thing perhaps about the funeral. After all it's not certain that the properties in Jamaica will not be sold + in that case he would be there alone. Whereas in Forest Lawn he is amongst some of his family. I could not think she would decide on Forest Lawn just to spite Beverly Aadland, who after all is not important...Although she was the last of his girls, she was only one of a number, + we have heard that he tried to get rid of her in Jamaica....The professor is slowly getting better, but I am advised to get him away from London, with the fogs, for the winter. A friend has invited us for a time to her villa in Italy. I am afraid I cannot write much more my dear. There is so much to discuss + think about. It was very nice to speak to the girls that night. Deirdre sounds quite grown up, + Rory has a sweet little voice....I have written to the doctors in Jamaica to ask what actually what [sic] Errol was suffering from, for I feel, that had I known I am sure I could have saved him, or at least done a lot more for him. Do encourage the girls to write to us, we would like to know them better. They are growing up in complete ignorance of us, who are, after all, their very near relations...I seem to have lost all interest in life for the moment, but I hope I will buck up later on. We have been fortunate in having Rosemary + Charles nearby in London. They have been a great standby in our common sorrow. Rosemary was lately with him in Jamaica, but she did not foresee the great grief in store for us. My love to you all my dear, Marelle."

December

My Wicked, Wicked Ways (below) is published posthumously.

Flynn's final film, at a Times Square theater in New York City

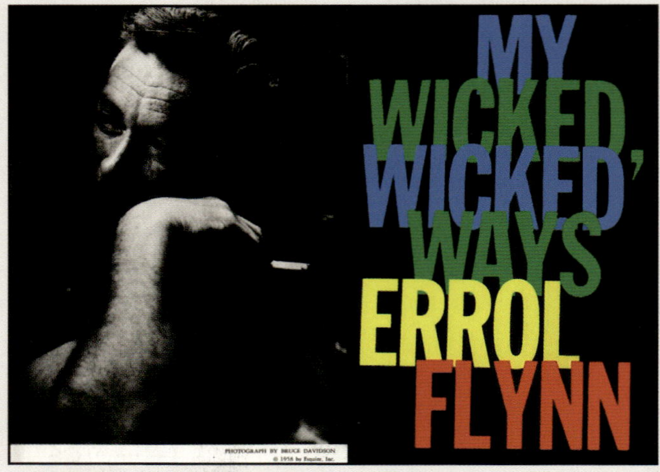

Wed December 23

Flynn's final film, CUBAN REBEL GIRLS, opens at the Roxy in Detroit, MI.

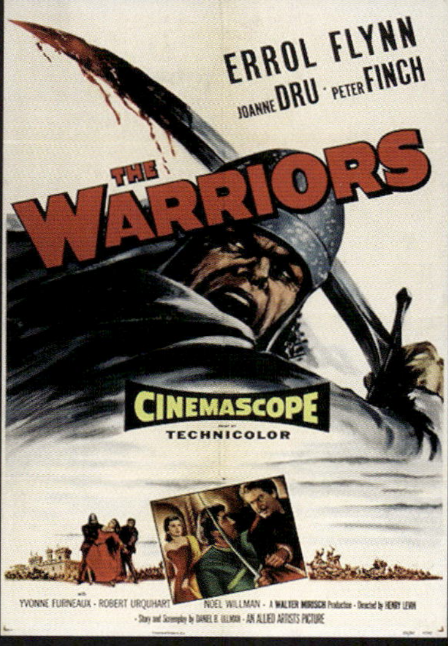

The films of 1954~1959

<u>Epilogue</u>

The controversies that surrounded Errol Flynn's life seemed to spill over into the years following his death. Beverly Aadland, still a teenager, was involved in the accidental fatal shooting of her boyfriend and became a ward of the court. Flynn's son Sean, by the late 1960s a freelance photographer, was captured by the Vietcong at the Cambodian border in 1970, was never seen again, and is presumed to have been executed by the Khmer Rouge; Sean's mother Lili finally had him legally declared dead in 1984. And Flynn's daughter Arnella died in 1998 from a drug overdose at the age of 44.

But what of Errol Flynn's legacy? He was, in his prime, one of the most successful and popular actors in Hollywood history and one of the most famous men of his day, yet today he is curiously almost forgotten. A casual visit to any of the myriad tourist shops that line Hollywood Boulevard will reveal quantities of memorabilia of Flynn's contemporaries like Humphrey Bogart, James Cagney, or John Wayne, but little if anything of Flynn himself. Why is that? There is, I believe, a key cultural reason.

Errol Flynn's grave at Forest Lawn Cemetery, Glendale, CA

The Second World War (and later the Vietnam War) had a hardening effect on audiences, who became ever more resistant to traditional sentiment in favor of the anti-hero. While pre-World War II audiences could be solidly unified behind Flynn's all-for-Queen-and-country portrayals, modern audiences, with their deep cynicism, find Flynn's style of heroism outdated if not downright farcical. Action films today can never embody the purity of patriotism they formerly exhibited, whether in adventure films or films depicting contemporary war, but must inevitably be reduced to an anti-establishment stance or, worse, parody (think *Star Wars* or the Indiana Jones films). Bogart, for instance, with his sullen bad-boy persona, managed to transcend the generations and be perfectly at home with modern audiences who comfortably welcome his go-to-hell on-screen attitude.

Bogart, Cagney, and Wayne have thus retained a certain relevance, while Flynn unfortunately has not. Rather than for the artistic idealism found in films of the past, today's audiences have a hunger for stark realism, even within the realm of fantasy (does any of the dialogue in *The Lord of the Rings* films have the poetry of THE ADVENTURES OF ROBIN HOOD?). Flynn's private life may have been anti-heroic and even decadent, but cinematic image is everything, and people's image of him today—if they have any image of him at all—is largely one of a swashbuckling hero, and that genre (as with traditional Westerns) seems unlikely to make a comeback.

But the problem goes further. It is not only audiences who reject the genre of swashbuckler, but film buffs and film schools themselves. There is a type of imprimatur afforded certain films and actors of the past, and while familiarity with the likes of *Citizen Kane* and Robert Mitchum is almost dogma, cinephiles and academia seem to outright ignore swashbucklers and, by association, Flynn.

Still, somehow the echoes of Errol Flynn's colorful life reverberate to this day because of a continual presence of a core of devoted fans eager to devour each book and film about him that seems to be produced for them alone. And the advent of the internet added extra assurance that his name and legacy will carry on and find new fans along the way who will be smitten by his uniqueness. The more you know about Errol Flynn, the more you want to know.

Appendix I - The 1933 New Guinea Diary (*text in boldface italics added by this author*)

Fri January 13

Saddleberg [Sattelberg] Mission 13th Jan 1933 Arrived here at 5 PM after leaving Finchafen [Finschafen] this morning at 10 PM. Broke journey half way at Yermen to give my boys time to cook some rice. Carriers would not carry beyond Yermen so paid them off and sent to Yehu for new lot. Cost of carrying very high in this district--they all know what money is. Saddleberg is 3650 above sea level but commands wonderful outlook over the sea – I can see Umboi Island from here – it must be 80 miles away.

Queer lot these Lutheran missionaries. For the main part they are German but there is a small sprinkling of Austrians of German parentage.

Father Holbig met me and gave me this room--very comfortable and I'm weary and a bit footsore as is usual on the first day out. Coloured prints of Christ are regarding me dolefully from every angle of the room. He is portrayed in a large variety of postures. Rebuking (or confusing) the Elders who have the longest & whitest beards I've ever seen; conferring blessings etc; Why is it that Christ is never shown smiling? He must have laughed sometimes. The prints are old though, probably done some 20 or 30 years ago when gaiety of any sort was still regarded as sinful.

Saddleberg Mission is the health resort for run-down and enervated missionaries. They're sent up here for a month every year to get the benefit of the excellent climate. I spotted a pretty girl when I came in today so I'll have to shave tonight. Three days' growth is no good even for a recruiter to wear. She's the little Dutch sister, I suppose—hope she comes to the table tonight. These missionaries treat their womenfolk like dirt. I stood up last night when Karcher's wife came into the room at Finchafen [Finschafen] and only succeeded in embarrassing everyone present!! It was a quite unprecedented occurrence for the entrance of a woman to be more than curtly acknowledged by a sort of grunt. The idea is for all the men to sit down and eat what the women bring in at odd intervals. When in Rome do as the Dagoes do.

They sing grace in German before every meal. I very nearly laughed aloud last night at a young Bavarian, newly arrived in the country, who was making the bravest effort to lower the tone of his naturally high falsetto voice. He had fully a dozen hairs in his beard....there are three lady helpers at the mission, all unmarried: Clara Holbig, Jutta Keysser, and Marie Uke…

Long day's march tomorrow—hope to make the Hube country in four days from here. If the rain holds off may make it in three. If it doesn't I won't be able to cross the WARIA River, perhaps for a week. Thank God I brought 2 bottles of O.P. Rum and the Bible and will thus have both drink and something to read. Have often wanted to read the Bible -- I believe it's very entertaining & instructive. There goes the Kai-Kai [dinner] bell. Hungry lot these missionaries so I'd better get along or the board will be cleaned.

Sat January 14

Stayed at Sattelberg today and rearranged my equipment for cheaper carrying. The paramount Luluai [territorial chief] of the District (Selembé) came up to see me this evening. We had a long discussion with WASANGE and TUTU MAN, the two TULTULs [native village interpreter] being present. The old man is a very distinct personality, quite a superior type. He has agreed to help me recruit, after no doubt making extensive inquiries about...He has agreed to send out three tultuls in different directions—Tutman to go to the Waria River, Inge to go to Mape, and Sambar to the beginning of the Hube country. They will meet me at Fior [Fio] Village in four days time (Saturday).

Sun January 15

Left Sattelberg after lunch at 2 P.M. and arrived at Fior [probably Fio] at 4:30. The track is about the best I have found inland and very beautiful besides. Crossed three mountain streams, each one dammed up at the crossing into crystal-clear pools. Bathed in the last one; first bath in three days. These pellucid pools were typical of New Guinea's specious beauty. They were fed by a sparkling stream flowing over bright limestone and fringed by capiac palms and coconuts. Several varieties of orchids were flowering among the surrounding undergrowth.

I sent carriers on ahead and shedding singlet and shorts leapt joyously into the cold water and lay there, lazily enjoying the rare sensation of a plunge bath and admiring my surroundings. As I lay there floating I noticed what I took to be innumerable black twigs attaching themselves one by one to my body, but took little notice of them. Then horrible thoughts occurred to me. I jumped up hurriedly and found my fears realized. I was covered in leeches who obviously hadn't had a square meal in months. Luckily I had matches with me so spent an hour burning them off, a proceeding which was watched with keen interest by some Fio boys who had come back along the track to find me. If leeches are removed by any other method except burning their tails to make them release their hold, a tropical ulcer will almost invariably form on the spot. I now look like a leopard, after dabbing myself with iodine on the bites.

Mon January 16

Fio village The mission has obviously benefited these people greatly in a number of ways. They have good roads, 20 odd head of cattle bought from the mission and bred up from an original three or four head. I know of no other natives who own a herd of cattle. They also grow English potatoes, kohlrabi, tomatoes. This morning I bought 24 green corn cobs, a dozen or so taroes for 1/-; a pineapple & half a dozen cucumbers were thrown into the bargain.

I think Wasange will get me a recruit here.

There is a little stream running right through this village and the rest house is situated a hundred yards or so from the village. Consequently I have no giant & irrepressible native pigs & dogs to annoy me. I thought at first I might get a little privacy too, but that is expecting too much. My every action has been keenly observed by at least 50 pairs of eyes ever since I arrived. But I'm very comfortable here and waiting until Saturday is not going to be so bad as I thought, particularly as corn, eggs, & fruit bare plentiful & of course very cheap.

Was very amused last night. My three Aitape boys, being in a strange country and having been used to finding enemies if they strayed a yard beyond their own hunting grounds in Wapi, have been scared stiff ever since they left the coast. An old woman brought them taro last night. Although very hungry they examined it dubiously and then asked Wasange, who was sitting down outside their house. 'Are you sure this food is not poisoned?' Wasange couldn't understand what they were asking at first & they had to repeat the question several times. When he did, he and the entire gathering burst out laughing at my 'bushmen.' With good cause, of course, as I suppose this village has been peaceful for 10 years or so. But it was not a ridiculous question. After all, only two days march further in, in the Hube, they would not stop at a small thing like poison if they thought there was something to be gained from it.

I hear there is trouble in Hube over a woman. Two villages are about to fight, so the talk goes. If it's right, things couldn't be better for me. Am bound to get recruits, probably from both villages if there's a fight as they'll want to get away to escape reprisals later.

Tue January 17

First boy this morning—good stamp of native, too. He'll look well leading an axe about although he doesn't suspect it yet. He thinks he's going to be my cook. This is a very good omen—to get a boy from the chief's village means that I'll almost certainly get as many as I want from other villages.

Big 'talk-talk' last night. The chief and his two tultuls came along and we discussed everything under the sun, including the late war, which appears to cause much amusement and astonishment. That all white men should indulge in extensive fighting among themselves after having given them, the black men, the very strictest injunctions against fighting, with prompt and severe punishment for disobedience, must, I suppose, appear to them somewhat paradoxical. It must have chaffed them a bit when they heard details about the Great War and were themselves prevented from carrying out those periodical raids and sorties against the neighbouring villages, which used to be their favorite occupation and hobby before we came along and told them they had to be friends.

Wed January 18

18th Fio Two more boys making three now. Excellent going. Went down to the BŪN River yesterday -- very peculiar formation, mainly a sort of limestone bottom with no wash in the river bed to speak of at all. Good looking wash on both banks though with no overburden more than 2 or 3 feet at any part. Will wash a few dishes down there [pan for gold] tomorrow although it's very unlikely if there's even colours. I believe all these rivers were well prospected years ago by the German missionaries + others. Have just finished reading 'The Good Companions'. Wonderful. Can Priestly ask for anything more from life than that gift of expression? I felt I knew personally every one of those characters at the end. Especially Micham Moreton [Morton Mitcham]—if he had been drawn from old Simpson, ex-actor-manager, now sandalwood king of Papua, he couldn't have been described more faithfully.

Three more boys today.

Thu January 19

19th Fio The rush has set in properly. Tutuman came back with 7 boys which makes 13 and I'll have two more tomorrow.

As all my boys come from the purlieus of this district all the old men of Fior [Fio] decided to read me an address. It was rather amusing. The entire village gathered round me while I sat in the middle of the circle on a tucker box. One old grey beard then got to his feet and began to harangue me in forcible but quite incomprehensible terms as he spoke in his own language.

I however nodded solemnly at each pause and later had his speech interpreted. He said in effect that Fior [Fio] had given me all their young men and I must not sell any of them & when their time had finished must bring them back myself and then I would be given new boys to take their place. He then wound up by stating that although he was talking to me in strong words I must not think he was 'cross'—and when I came would I bring him a dog? He then asked me, through the interpreter, if I would shake hands with him and I did.

Fri January 20

Broke camp this morning having recruited 16 boys (with my 3 Aitapes makes 19) and proceeded.

His running diary ends here but contains other undated entries. First, writing down—but misquoting--John Masefield's poem "Sea Fever":

I must go down to the sea again

To the rolling sea & sky

And all I ask is a tall ship

And a star to steer her by

And the wheels kick & the brown spume & the white sails shaking

And a grey mist on the sea's face & a grey dawn breaking

I must go down to the sea again.
To the gulls way & the whales way
Where the winds like a whetted knife
And a merry tale from laughing fellow rover
& quiet sleep & a sweet dream when the long trick's over.
This is followed by a list (upside down on the page) of native recruits and the goods they are being issued:
SELEMBE Valet razor. cane suit case
   Firworks   Paint (Blue & red)
INGE Serge laplap & singlet
Black Mission Shoot lamp [flashlight] serge lap lap
   Trousers singlet Clothes Mary
A native song or poem comes next:
Before me boy belong Companee
He grease im along fuse
Now me catchim big fella trouble
Now me stop calaboose
Fashion belong me e good fella fashion
Me no savvy laze
By'm by me loose in calaboose
My Christ me go quick a long place!
O calaboose e no 1 place.
This is followed by a continuation of the recruit list:
BASAGE Shootlamp [flashlight] [indecipherable] TANGAMA
   lap lap
   Singlet
   Basket suit case
KARBU Glitter blouse
TIAMBONG
NINGIO } lap lap & Singlet
DOME
HOMÉ (Tul-Tul) Striped costume – Serge lap lap
   Mary's [meri is a native woman] blouse Salt
HILO. Striped Short pants costume Mary's Blouse
   Trousers – serge lap – lap
BONIEVE laplap
SAMBAR Singlet Umbrella 2. Blouses 1 small
BELA 1 Serge laplap
     } 2 Singlets
BAU-U " "
MANSE SASANG INGRO
  lap lap singlets
KANE Beads
BUAMENG Singlet. Serge la lap & red pants
Then come random subjects:
The time I passed Dusty Miller on a lorry in Madang with 11 dogs for a recruiting trip. He saw me when I waved, turned around and went into his house.
Bill Stower and the egg trick on L. Bennet's mary's [native girl] head.
Grease
Potatoes
Onions
Syrup or jam
or honey
Salt
Marco Polo always recorded his surprise when he found no olives in the strange places he visited. The Chinese also betrayed astonishment when they learned the West had no bamboo--a lack which seemed to them incredible. So also of all the wonders of our modern civilisation nothing astounds News Guinea natives more than the fact that there are no coconuts growing in the lands whence we white men come. They cannot imagine a coconutless existence for to them the tree is the mainstay of life and supplies them with all their major necessities, food, clothing, house material, as well as countless other uses.
Essay on Several 'Don'ts' in The Art & Niceties of Seduction (without trousers) Compromising positions to avoid—Avenues of escape must be arranged first. Avoid betraying astonishment at credulity of victim—even in the dark. Draw analogy between the mention of word 'marriage' & and he who uses dynamite in exasperation after having failed with dry fly. Use of alcohol is to be deprecated except as last resort.
Here Flynn offers a bold personal declaration:
I am going to China because I wish to live deliberately… New Guinea offers me, it is true, satisfaction for the tastes I have acquired which only leisure can satisfy + I am leaving economic security and I am leaving it deliberately. By going off to China with a paltry few pounds + no knowledge of what life has in store for me there I believe that I am going to front the essentials of life, to see if I can learn what it has to teach and above all not to discover, when I come to die, that I have not lived. We fritter our lives away in detail but I am not going to do this. I am going to live deeply, to acknowledge not one of the so called social forces which hold our lives in thrall + reduce us to economic dependency. The best part of life is spent in earning money in order to enjoy a questionable liberty during the least valuable part of it. To hell with money! Pursuit of it is not going to mould my life for me. I am going to live sturdily + Spartan-like; to drive life into a corner + reduce it to its lowest terms and if I find it mean, then I'll know its meanness, and if I find it sublime I shall know it by experience—and not make wistful conjectures about it conjured up by illustrated magazines… I refuse to accept the ideology of a business world which believes that man at hard labour is the noblest work of God. Leisure to use as I see fit...To learn what is worth one's while...
Finally, a bit of philosophy:
One can never become a skillful reader, or acquire the ability to appreciate books, unless one first cultivates a keen sense of the relative value of things; for this sense is the quintessence of true education + culture. To learn what is worth one's while is the largest part of the Art of Life.
Time, for example, just one hour of time is far more important than money for time is life. Whenever you waste your time over printed words that neither enlighten or amuse you, you are in a sense committing suicide. The value, the intrinsic value of our actions, emotions, thoughts, possessions, occupations, of the manner in which we are living: this is the first thing to be determined; for unless we are satisfied that any of these things have a true value, even if only relative, our lives are futile, and there is no more hopeless realisation than this.

Sat March 26

"So! On train at last. Very nearly boarded the wrong one going in the opp direction due to the usual last minute frenzied rush always necessary when Damita is along. A lone photographer at station - don't know what paper - who made a number of pictures of self and Damita - then infuriated that lady by asking in French, "And what is the lady's name?"

Erben left last night (25') after having been refused all visas by U.S. consul. Yesterday afternoon we went to the Spanish Embassy to a reception given there for the U.S. Med Unit. The Ambassadoress, blonde timid and awkward but very nice.

Thought it would be very left[ist] so refused take Lili. Actually was held in one of embassy's best rooms, with liveried flunkey taking coats haughtily outside and obviously disdaining all and sundry, probably even himself. Introduced Erben to U.S. Consul Southard but found afterwards Erben was under [impression] he was talking to ambassador and panning the hell out of the U.S. Consulate.

Erben finally met my friend Xaviar who had treated me so well same afternoon earlier. Xaviar [Press Attaché at Embassy] gave him note to the Spanish Consul in Perpignon. We decided it was his best chance to get into Spain so he left last night.

I am to meet him in Perpignon tomorrow (27) and see if he has his papers - any sort of papers. I only hope he has not got to try to dive across border. Two men killed day before yesterday - shot as they crawled out of river near Cerbere. I know he'll get in - somehow. Any man who can travel thru Europe on a laundry slip, as I know he's done, will get in - passport or no passport. He must get a lot of nice big seals – these always impress the – French.

Sat March 27

Just arrived Perpignon. No Erben but a note from him with the Chef du Gare I, mysterious - everything has been arranged for him by telephone he says. He was told to leave yesterday and thinks he is going to get straight through to Barcelona. If not will meet me at Cerbere at the frontier. I just had time to rush after my luggage full of cameras etc. and get on the train again. Don't know that I like the sound of these strange telephone instructions but hope they're true.

Beautiful spring day warm sunshine, country beautiful. How can people fight a war in this lovely weather? Four hours train journey from here the most savage cruel fratricidal war is being waged.

Just passed some "houmous 40 Chevare 8" trucks Takes me back 14 years when I was 13 and the time I had to travel for 2 days slow train in one having busted my fare in Paris going on School holidays in England to Grenoble.

Erben is over! How, when or why I don't know. When, yes. He crossed last night at 8 p.m. so his note said. Naturally he couldn't say more.

Port-bou is a little fishing village. It has been shelled from the sea once - you can see the shell holes in the waterfront. Can't find out what happened to the large railway station but all the windows are broken and the doors - in the station stands a Vt class carriage that has been riddled by machine gun fire.

Everyone is armed –some with large knives plus revolver but all with revolver.

Altogether patronne 'e stop alone house lotu [pidgin for church], other fella something belong fight 'e stop onetime house lotu.

The train is stopped. Plane has been heard. All lights out - there weren't any before to speak of - all the bulbs had been painted with blue so that one can hardly see across the compartment. The stink is something! We are crowded with young Loyalists - all armed and with the oddest assortment of uniforms. Some have everyday suits, revolver, and just the cap of a uniform. Train stands absolutely still for at least an hour after the plane has been heard. No smoking allowed and it's cold. More soldiers, all kids, get in at every station. We are like sardines and smell like bad ones.

Two hours late getting to Barcelona. Fernandez, Warner's man, greets me although how he could see me I don't know - the station is almost pitch dark. Erben comes up, busting with good spirits. I haven't eaten for 24 hours so we find a Catalonian fish shop open. Bottle of wine some incredibly tough chops are the best money can buy. Afterwards go to Shanghai Rest, meet many people. Have to give short speech and am cheered when I finish up with clenched-fist Communist salute and the word "salute" - almost my only Spanish one. Great reception! Erben reminded me afterwards I said "God bless you all" - heresy here naturally as religion has been abolished. Lucky they didn't understand.

We ride around in a horse cab. No taxis after 8 p.m. and then only for a certain distance. This is to conserve gasoline - which is going to win or lose this war. There is a great shortage.

Fernandez implores me not to go to Madrid but am intrigued by the offer of those gov't party members to take us in an official car on Tuesday. May go - except for knowing that anyone caught on the Guadalajara road in the company of men with Loyalist cards are shot. Five newsmen have died like this.

I hear that Franco said last week that when & if he took Madrid he would shoot instantly all correspondents caught behind Loyalist lines! I tink'e long-long talk all same - no can do. [pidgin English]

Striking thing on Sundays, usually a day devoted to sport bull fights, football etc. by the unchurch-going Catalonian- now in wartime thousands of young people, men women, give up their one free day to go out & work in the munitions factories Catalonia makes almost all the munitions. Catalonians - intensely nationalistic, three and a half millions When the unions took over the big factories they could not meet the weekly wages payroll. The government therefore guaranteed the payroll - pay it each week, and the sums are credited to the government against eventual ownership when paid in full there will be true socialistic of all industry.

The government policy

If an employer has less than 100 laborers he can, at his option, he can withdraw the usual individual profits - but is government controlled. If over 100 he must come under complete government & union supervision, with the eventual object of complete socialization of industry.

There are no private autos in Catalonia or Red Spain. All have been commandeered for the use of govt. officials and the military. All fly flags of one sort or another. If I am ever allowed to write what I know & think back in America then the Propaganda Ministry will have made a bargain in supplying me with car. The Minister of Justice under whom the prison reforms are taking place spent 14 years in goal. Many officials seem to have served long sentences.

Two unions run a great textile factory - the manager is apparently elected by popular vote of the more numerous unions. He serves one year. If satisfactory then is up for election again.

20' July day after revolution not a policeman left in B[arcelona]. All hands left for front - no looting - complete order.   Money. Living extremely cheap. Bought 140 pesetas for 100 francs.

[Song of the] International Brigade. "We've got old Franco on the run, parlez vous We've met some tough sons of guns, arlez vous … inky pinky parlez vous. And when the boys went over the top, parlez vous And didn't we make those f[ascists] hop, parlez vous … inky pinky parlez vous.

They thought our boys were 'oh so green,' to be frightened by those fascist screams... Oh inky pinky parlez vous.

Franco said he'd take Madrid, parlez vous But now we'll say like hell he did, parlez vous... inky pinky parlez vous.

We'll put old Franco in the ditch, parlez vous And Mussolini the son of a bitch, parlez vous... inky pinky parlez vous. Franco Germany Italy Spain, parlez vous will never be able to do it again, parlez vous" Etc. War happenings.

Saw a tough guy in Chinatown dump doing pansy dance. He is a war hero - having captured a war ship almost singlehanded. An obvious pansy.

Ascaso (Francisco) G.N.T. (Anar[chists]) N (Confederacion National del Trabajo).

A regular army machine gun nest was place[d] in a tunnel sweeping a street. Anarchists had to pass this street. Ascaso said, "I'll fix that gun for you." He ran around the comer, clasped the gun to his entrails and died riddled. The gun was silenced long enough for his friends to shoot the gunners.

Direction - Making picture in Madridfor C.N. T. 4~

Met a little ex-nun in Madrid. Her story: she is now 18. Six months ago her convent was burnt, many of the nuns killed. She ran away to her father. Her father was afraid to let her stay with him & threw her out. She went to an aunt. The aunt threw her out too. She was afraid to go to the police. She went therefore to the nearest municipal committee - of which there is one every few yards in Madrid.

She had led a very cloistered life, knew nothing, had been in the sort of convent where it is forbidden to even look at a man. They tolerantly put her to work in the local kitchen. Then began to like her so asked her what she would like to do in the new life before her. She didn't know - then remembered having heard of the movies (had never seen one of course) Said she would like to be a movie star. "Ok," said the committee, "a movie star it is." They promptly took her to the man taking movies for the G.N.TG. With instructions to him to make her a movie star immediately.

A priest.

Hid for 2 months in a house. Felt himself going mad with the suspense. Decided to give himself up. Went to nearest committee, said "Do you shoot people here?" The man in charge scratched chin.

"Well-ll, sometimes."

"Then you'd better shoot me - I'm a priest."

"Oh," said m[an] in c[harge]. "A priest, eh? And you want to be shot. Well I'm afraid we aren't shooting here today - you might try at 21 San Bemado - I think they do it."

Priest went there.

"I hear you shoot people" - well - I'm a priest." Same puzzlement in officer.

"We've stopped shooting here" was the reply. 'The best we can do for you is to advise to go to the Casa de Gampo (originally former royal summer residence of King) at 8 in the evening. You must be there punctually."

8 p.m. The priest was there with his same request. "I must know what is to be done with me. I can't go on with this suspense!"

"Are you fascist?"

"No" said priest." "I'm a priest. But I've just been peacefully in my monastery. I know nothing of fascists communists or anything else. What am I to do?"

The young officer he met here was intelligent said, "What you want is a passport?

"Passport?" said priest. "What for?"

"To get out of the country" said officer.

Finally officer began to talk about the revolution. The p listened. "And you're really fighting this fascism in Spain? There are foreigners in Spain fighting us Spaniards?

"Sure" said officer.

"Then can I go fight?"

"Sure" said o[fficer].

I met him in the front line trenches - still fighting.

Of course the humour of this! The committee astounded when in came man wanting to be shot, asking "Why - but why do you want to be shot? Are you a fascist?

"No" said priest.

"Then why? You seem a nice fellow."

"Ah! But I'm a priest! Don't forget that!

Official in immediate agreement - "Yes, that's bad, a priest" - well I don't like to shoot you. So go somewhere else.

Country priest. Living with his servant in town.

Revolution comes. The people like priest - don't want to shoot him. So they go with gun pointed at his belly and make him marry the servant girl he's been living with for 6 years

Another priest.

Fat, fifty, not very popular. But the people don't dislike him quite enough to shoot him. So they decide to make him walk on top of a narrow ancient Roman aqueduct - certain that he'll fall & kill himself. Like a tightrope walker the fat old priest carefully picked his sweating way across. The crowd sees he might get across to their great surprise. Some want to shoot him before he gets across. But some latent sporting instinct makes others stop them. He makes the walk & escapes.

Bishop of Siguenza (where the battle is now raging) was with a handful of fascists in the town defending the cathedral. Finally the Bishop was captured with 10 fascists and all of them lined up against a wall for execution. The machine gun and rifles trained on them "Fire!" & of the 11 men only the Bishop falls. The other 10 absolutely unharmed. This shows the traditional hatred of the people for the priests. Every gun was trained on the Bishop. The firing squad did not stop laughing for hours - this being a joke which appeals greatly to the Spanish. Then someone suddenly remembered the other 10. "Come on don't let's keep them waiting, boys. Again the sporting instinct. The soldiers so grateful for the good laugh they let the other 10 off with prison.

American Hospital at Teracon. 14 wounded brought in Jarama.

Dr. Byrne (American) states emphatically that now the majority of wounds are explosive bullets. Most terrible wounds. Shattered faces. One English doctor was shot in the penis by stray bullet 2 klms behind Jarama front - went through scrotum. Another American boy - completely blinded. He told me, talking of America, he once saw the Califor hills & Golden Gate. Gave a faint terribly sad smile as said so. Am absolutely sick at the dishes of blood & puss everywhere. One little boy of about 6 leg amputated below knee after his town was bombed 3 weeks ago. They are dressing his stump. He is crying "Madre! Madre! Madre!" Erben took picture. Horrible.

Dr. Byrne standing about doing nothing. Shows us ward full of soldier wounded last night in fascist attack. Little Cockney from Shepherd's Bush asks me "What happened? Did they get over?" Asked him what happened. He said, "We was given the order to stand to & fire independent. 'And fired four or five rounds when was knocked on my face. Got up and saw kid behind me shaking [his gun]. I said, 'Wot in Christ 'ave you done you've shot me you bastard!' 'E began to cry. And 'e 'ad shot me right through the arse & tore through my testicles."

"Did it damage them?" I asked.

"Don't know yet" he sd. "But it wasn't kid's fault. 'E's been out there 51 days like I 'ave and 'is nerves is gone."   "Good luck," said I. Anything you want?"

He shook his head. Then "Yes! Some matches. 'Ave you got some? - They're bleedin' 'ard to get 'ere."

Dr. Byrne was doing nothing while these men brought in from Guadalajara. Might be dying. They looked it - horrible messes pus coming through their bloody bandages. I said, "Aren't you changing their dressings?" He shook head quizzically. "Can't. Not allowed to. They're not my patients."

"But they need it don't they?

He nodded. "Just not allowed to touch them. This young kid needs an amputation (pointing to a pale young Spaniard) but I can't do it. His arm's all shot away & gangrene setting in. This is professional etiquette or whatever it's called. I've tried touching the patients of other doctors and they just won't have it."

I couldn't get him to say any more but Erben did as one doctor to another.

"The Spanish doctors will," he says, "sacrifice life after life sooner than admit they can't do a certain bit of surgery. Each man is brought in with a slip on him reading what he needs - but if that slip says he needs a dose of salts and I know he needs surgery I am not allowed to touch him until the Spanish doc says so. When we do operate it's so cold the steam comes up out of his bowels and blinds me. No records whatsoever. No names on patients. If patient can't speak we don't know if he has had a dose of serum & if we give him one it may be the second & kill him

The Doc

The unions as I said control everything, including the movies. To work as an extra a girl must have signatures of U.G.T. and another. One girl lacked a signature. Erben took her card, looked at it, and with a gracious smile gave her his. Wonder if she's worked yet?

The boys of the l[nterational] B[rigade] insist on giving me a precious packet of woodbines. Opened, out comes a card of "Our King & Queen." All communists they still revere the king - not personally they care nothing for Alfonso but as a symbol. (Too many shell holes here to write.)

Amazing to suddenly come into a coffee house - all of which are invariably full to capacity with men - few women and those rarely young - and find an enormous roomful playing dominoes! You walk up the stairs and hear a loud staccato tapping - it might be a swarm of locusts or machine gun fire in the distance. Instead it just several hundred Catalonians playing dominoes very fiercely & drinking coffee. From the first week of the revolution the Govn't policy has been to continue normal life. Cinemas were opened, some musical comedies (& especially rifle ranges!). "Everything as normal" was the policy.

Sr. Carner (Ribalta) says the reason so many Spaniards came over (mutinied) outside Madrid in January after the leaflets were dropped on the fascist lines was because they suddenly woke up to the fact they were fighting against the Republic which is what they want to preserve. Naturally there are political factions Communist Anarchists Republicans but all these factions are united in the belief that they are defending Spain against an invader, i.e. Italians Germans with the figurehead of Franco taking his orders from German and Italian generals. They say the war has not been a civil war for many months. There are only conscripted Spaniards with Franco who would desert if the opp offered. They feel Spain is once more defending her soil as she did against Napoleon. He won every battle he fought in Spain but did he retain an inch of soil? Not one. Don't think the result will be any different in this case. The people here seem to hate fascism with all their heart. Add this hate to the natural one for a foreign invader and you have the spirit which makes volunteers flock to Madrid to defend it with the most amazing spirit ever seen. "They won't take Madrid while a man stands" is what three young fellows have told me. There is no conscription on this side. Franco has shot whole villages of those who refused conscription and it is a general order under him. With the Minister of Propaganda saw a French newsreel today which if released in England or America might lead to anything. It was strong stuff. Bodies of little children being dug out of bomb holes after an air raid dismembered corpses. screams and expressions of sheer horror on the faces of mothers. They can't release it in France either.

Thu April 1

International Brigade.

At last in Albacides [Albacete] - having food with the International Brigade - writing this on a long table of French food spirits - no one wears same uniform as another - hardly two types of headgear similar - many berets. Met little "ncashire" man upstairs. Many of the boys had been given 50 pesetas notes for 10 days pay, & couldn't change them into anything smaller. So had not dough for drink.

Pasablanca.

When l[ntemational] B[rigade] went in (the 13th & 14' English French Germans Poles Italians) they went in for commandeering food. gold crucifix over top of church door. Food was taken but gold cross wasn't touched.

The Church.

Carner: All the golden vessels turned out to be tin. When he took over the job of collecting the treasures of the Church thousands of truck loads of junk was burnt. The people had paid for gold ornaments - when examined it was found to be tin. Where was gold?

Narcissus Gernona.

Ancient saint worshipped for hundreds of years as a genuine body - simple people always had to leave money. When the glass top was taken off it was found to be wood stuffed with cotton. Where did the people's money go?

In the Revolution the money was squeezed out of the churches. No one knew what to do with it. They fought. Some said, "It belongs to the Gov." Others: "No, it belongs to the people." Finally they burnt it. Great piles of pesetas were made into a bonfire.

No monarchists. Ask any Spaniard how many sons Alfonso had - he can't tell you. All he knows about the royal family is that one son is a "bleeder" (hemophilia). No interest in royal family. Contempt for it generally.

Not a single Catalonian went to the defense of the Church when they were attacked. They despised it. The priests collected the people's money and gave it to the fascists. Outside many a church were trenches dug by the priests. The church knew for years this fascist uprising was coming. They handed everything to Franco, hoping to keep control of the people by siding with the prepared militarists.

In the convent of the "Little Sisters of the Poor" was found 300 million pesetas (in Madrid) in Barcelona (the Bishop) 7 million. The Bishop of Vich was found with 16 million. The Bishop of Gerona 14 million. The Little Sisters of the Poor had their money in Panama Canal bonds Argentina Ghade Elect. Hardly any Spanish stock. Some Imperial Russian Empire stock also which the Little Sisters had forgotten to unload.

Can't help reaction naturally there were atrocities. But Duratti f went to the Bishop of Barcelona said, "You must leave Sir." The Bishop walked safely through the line of Anarchists. They found 1 million cash! - he'd got rid of the rest!) in his house.

The pathetic result of piety of the peasants was that the money they gave or was coerced into giving was used by the Church to buy arms for the fascists to use against them.

Millions of pesetas - tens of millions lying in the coffers of the priests and nuns. Little of it spent in hospitals and for the poor. The poor when sick were told they must pay for some more candles to be lit for them, not spend a penny for a doctor. No wonder there was a reaction.

Transport. Port Bou.

The trucks were left in neutral territory, Over go the American . . . Transport[ation] Corps in civilian clothes, jump in trucks.

At border chains drop - over go trucks into Spain.

Most desperate poverty along Madrid road - as bad as Ireland - but these are not the people who are fighting - they are all working the fields young & old, men & women.

El Pedernoso

Here stands the windmill at which Don Quixote tilted - Erben took a picture of it - 140 kilometers from here is the Madrid front line.

We are staying the night at Quinta del Oro - outside supposedly forming section of Madrid front. I can hear desultory shells in distance.

This little hostel is full of soldiers. One is being taken into Valencia hospital, having been hit by dum-dum bullet. He scorns the idea that this side uses them too. Food terrible. No lights in town - the fascist planes come over every night. Am writing this by ancient lamp of oil in which floats a wick. Am still being told by young Spaniards that don't give a damn about politics - they are fighting for their country against an invader. And with what a spirit! One young lad in hospital - 3' time wounded - says he'll fight for Spain while he's alive. This pub - shithouse is impossible to enter so great a stink - shithouse poetry interesting - all antifascist. Water hard to get and of course hot water out of question - fuel too valuable. Am feverish with very sore throat and have only one thin blanket - lucky have flannel trousers & overcoat to sleep in. Desultory firing in distance - am getting used to it. Am sure Don Quixote stayed in this inn - it's so old. Rat holes in room corners - walls all crumbling away. Over one large wall hole - to hide it doubtless - is a very modern 3 ft. x 2 ft. mirror - wonder how got here.

New platoon has just arrived from Madrid - all Russians I think. Great big cheerful fellows & very hungry. They are bringing in their wounded for hot macaroni. Proceeding up to Madrid front tomorrow at 6 a.m. - have to pass very close fascist lines.

Had a minor war of my own tonight for possession of my bed. Six Russians wanted it finally won out by getting into it in middle of argument. Am sure 100 men have slept in it - very dirty.

International Brigade - in car, can't write!

One spy - everyone knew of him as spy except himself. He sent out his messages that an entire column was advancing across some sheep pasture. Next day the pasture was bombed. The boys went out & collected the mutton.

Esmond Giles Remillay [unintelligible] Winston Churchill, handsome sturdy very reserved English manner.

Gas stations all camouflaged for air attacks. Madrid depends on fuel to keep the many roads open. Erben wanted to take a snap of one - is rudely pushed back at point of rifle by two guards - hemp bagging is skillfully nailed over the gas station to give it as far as possible the appearance of a peasant's casafarm house.

From Albacedes the front line is 200 klms to nearest point. Scotchman named [unintelligible] - hopeless trying to write going 125 kms per hour while driver keeps looking back & taking his hands entirely off wheel to gesticulate.

Pedralles Palacio.

Present of the Barcelona rich to Alfonso. He never used it. A magnificent palace as long as Buckingham Palace. In the republic was used as girl's international school now these same girls are taking care of the Madrid evacuated children.

Beautiful furniture now badly frayed & worn being used as school seats. One once sumptuous guest suit[e] being used as carpenter's shop making aeroplane models. Look out any window you see the Imperial gardens, lily pools now badly fouled. Great trees in the park, many small children running among them.

Little plays given for the children in the midst of the war. The proceeds go to the war.

The children have their own little printing press. Paint their own posters. (The town is full of posters) - and the sculpture! Amazing! One boy of 15 showed his painting and one figure of a soldier in clay! A German - quite extraordinary.

Notice that all these activities take place in the spacious servants' quarters. The palace proper was a museum but all valuables have been removed & hidden in case of destruction by air raids. Went into the library of the palace proper. Beautiful rooms, only a few objects d'art left but these rare and lovely.

Fri April 2

Madrid Front Line.

We drive up to Madrid front lines (Barra de Arguelles) with 100 metres. Here city is a shambles. Tall houses absolutely demolished, the debris of which form the graves of hundreds of people. Here the guns cannon & machine are hard at - the echoes reverberating through the deserted streets.

We are silent knowing we are walking over the bodies of many. Walking through am missed narrowly by some falling debris. Some beautiful furniture being used in guard bivouacs. As we pass down what was once the Rosales, a great wide plaza with the rifle & machine guns right in my ears suddenly sound of piano comes from one great house. Go in - a soldier is playing a beautiful grand piano - the roof is off over his head - shell holes - he is quite alone playing to himself. This is weird - he is accompanied by the whine of shells. Can see the fascist trenches from over a park, one half mile or less away.

Pass courtyard of church some soldiers playing Pelota Basgra in it very happily while the bullets still echo through streets deserted. The echoes are amazingly clear.

We walk to the prison which a few weeks ago was in hands of fascists. Shrapnel everywhere like gravel. The yard is littered with fingerprint cards thrown out when the prisoners were released at beg of Rev. Many dead rats inside! Wonder why? Must have either been gassed or fumes of shells. Prison keys rusty now for hundreds of yards from the prison gates. As we come out of prison gates to Plaza Mongoloa, an officer suddenly rushes out so we are dragged behind sandbags. Apparently the snipers pick off visitors frequently here. It's true the fascists are in a ruined building plainly in sight 500 yards distant. The officer says they have a machine gun trained on it.

The boys wanting to go into trenches at night to relieve are merrily playing street football. An overturned tramcar with shell hole in it is the goal at one end. The shell hole in a wall is other goal. They are in great spirits. I notice 60 per cent of this platoon are carrying Italian rifles captured.

This part of city will need demolishing entirely to rebuild. It will take 10 years to 15 to rebuild simply to say nothing of priceless statue works of art, irreplaceable historic buildings ruined.

The trams still run up to the front. In the early days of fascist advance the trams were used to bring munitions to front line.

The system of barricades very interesting. Every street is barricaded by a brick rampart 6 ft. high but there is an opening overlapping thus

In order to allow cars to pass thru'.

Note: The Propaganda Dept keeps a wary eye open. On front of a bombed building I picked up a little virgin & child with heads blown off. Put it in pocket quietly. Two hours later, leaving, the officer asked me what I was going to do with it and what I was going to say about it in America. Had to talk for an hour to be allowed to keep it. Explained I would say if I did use it that it was symbolic of fascist bombing of Madrid otherwise it was just a personal souvenir. Erben picked up among the dead rats & filth of the prison a priest's gold braided habiliment & cassock. They had not been torn so perhaps he died in them. Erben wanted to put them in his pocket. Oh No! He argued & they got ugly. He pretended to put back and throw them where he'd found them. They followed him & wanted to put them back. But he had them in his pocket they found him with them Things looked ugly I made him throw them away

All night the guns are firing sporadically. On to Madrid - how much farther forward are we in the scale of civilization than the days of the Inquisition?

Madrid Streets at Night

Like a city of the dead. Get 50 yards & am accosted by guard of 3. Erben gives as excuse we are looking for whorehouse. Guard immediately softens. Everyone looks like ghosts. No traffic except occasional staff car which sheds light & tears thru' city at rate of 100 or 110 kilos per hr. The tall buildings rear up into sky against the stars. Dark & sombre. Accosted by guards every few blocks - tell same yarn [whorehouse]. Pass on with "Salut! Comrade." Erben in his fluent(?!) Spanish will insist on addressing everyone as "Senor" which is like greeting Schnelling with Howya, Londos!"

Suddenly right across street shot is fired in front our hotel. We slink into doorway after seeing the flash. Can't see a soul moving. Finally cross street to where it came from - not a soul in sight. Meal terrible tonight - not only do we have iced water in the hot water tap but the fried fish was also ice cold for dinner. So was the coffee.

Sent Damita a telegram tonight. Finished up with "need bath terribly also a romp." The sensor [sic] was most suspicious. I tried to explain "romp" was the word to play. Very rightly didn't believe me. Made me cut it out. Don't know if he allowed the former or not about the bath.

Annotated Bibliography

Books

Aadland, Mrs. Florence. *The Big Love,* as told to Ted Thomey, with an introduction by William Styron. New York: Warner Books, 1961. A somewhat retaliative book against the press on her daughter's behalf (though Beverly repudiated it), it does have a valuable amount of factual data concerning the where and when of events relating to the Flynn-Aadland relationship

Behlmer, Rudy. *The Adventures of Robin Hood.* Madison, WI: The University of Wisconsin Press, 1979. The making of the film, including the working script and the script from a deleted scene

_____. *The Sea Hawk*. Madison, WI: The University of Wisconsin Press, 1982. The making of the film, including the working script

_____. *Inside Warner Bros*. (1935-1951). New York: Simon & Schuster, Inc., 1985. The activities of the studio told through letters, notes, telegrams, and inter-office memos

_____. *Behind the Scenes: The Making of...* Hollywood-New York-London-Toronto: Samuel French, updated version, 1989. THE ADVENTURES OF ROBIN HOOD is one of the sixteen films given the "making of" treatment

Connelly, Gerry. *Errol Flynn in Northampton*. Corby UK: Domra Publications, updated edition, 1998. The only significant recounting of Flynn's year in Northampton's repertory company, and the truth about his first meetings with Lili Damita before their trip to America on the *S.S. Paris*

Conrad, Earl. *Errol Flynn: A Memoir*. New York: Dodd, Mead & Company, 1978. Conrad, who wasn't overly taken with Flynn, offers an impartial view of the man while the two worked on Flynn's autobiography, *My Wicked, Wicked Ways*, in 1958 and 1959

Eddington Flynn Haymes, Nora. *Errol and Me*, as told to Cy Rice. New York: Signet Books, 1960. Flynn's second wife gives what is probably the most up-close, intimate view of Flynn that has ever been written, including the detailed highs and lows of their six-year relationship

Fegerl, Joseph. *Errol Flynn, Dr. Hermann F. Erben: A Friendship of Two Adventurers 1933-1940*. Vienna: Joseph Fegerl, 1985. A compact book that fills in some of the gaps of Flynn's time in New Guinea, as well as Erben's time with Flynn at the front in the Spanish Civil War; indispensable in its listing of dates and events, as well as copious rare photos from the doctor's own camera

Flynn, Errol. *Beam Ends*. London, Toronto, Melbourne, Sydney: Cassell and Company Ltd., 1937. Flynn's first book, an accounting of his 1930 sailing trip with three friends up the east coast of Australia to New Guinea

_____. *Showdown*. New York: Sheridan House, 1946—Flynn's second book, a romantic adventure novel

_____. *My Wicked, Wicked Ways*. New York: G. P. Putnam, 1959. Flynn's posthumously published autobiography, one of the best of its genre, though many anecdotes are more the result of a vivid imagination than of fact

_____. *From a Life of Adventure: The Writings of Errol Flynn*, edited by Tony Thomas. Secaucus, NJ: Citadel Press, 1980. A selection of Flynn's own authorship, including excerpts from his books, newspaper and magazine articles, and journals

Flynn, Rory. *The Baron of Mulholland: A Daughter Remembers*. Rory Flynn, publisher, 2007. A collection of personal reminiscences, accompanied by family photos and letters

Matzen, Robert. *Errol & Olivia: Ego and Obsession in Golden Era Hollywood.* Pittsburgh, PA: GoodKnight Books, 2010. An in-depth look at the professional and personal relationship of one of Hollywood's classic romantic pairings

Matzen, Robert, and Michael Mazzone. *Errol Flynn Slept Here: The Flynns, the Hamblens, Rick Nelson, and the Most Notorious House in Hollywood*. Pittsburgh, PA: GoodKnight Books, 2009. The history of Flynn's Mulholland house, including an interview with this author about his tour through the house in 1983 while Rick Nelson was its owner

McAleer, Kevin. *Errol Flynn: An Epic Life*. Berlin: Palm Art Press, 2018. A unique and daring work that tells Flynn's story in rhymed verse through the use of Lord Byron's ottava-rima stanza from his epic "Don Juan"

McNulty, Thomas. *The Life and Career of Errol Flynn*. Jefferson, NC and London: McFarland & Company, 2004. By far the best straightforward biography on Flynn yet published

Moore, John Hammond. *The Young Errol: Flynn Before Hollywood*. U.S. and Canada: Trafford Publishing, updated version, 2011. One of the most indispensable of all books on Flynn, Moore thoroughly researched Flynn's comings and goings throughout the South Pacific in the years before the actor headed for England and Hollywood

Norman, Don. *Errol Flynn: The Tasmanian Story.* Hobart, TAS: W. N. Hurst and E. L. Metcalf, 1981. An interesting reminiscence by Flynn's boyhood friend in Tasmania, which includes some interesting events and dates

Thomas, Tony. *Errol Flynn: The Spy Who Never Was*. New York: Citadel, 1990. Thomas' informed retort to the unsubstantiated and malicious charge against Flynn having been a Nazi spy during WWII

Thomas, Tony, and Rudy Behlmer, and Clifford McCarty. *The Films of Errol Flynn*, with a foreword by Greer Garson. New York: Citadel Press, 1969. Along with *My Wicked, Wicked Ways* and McNulty's definitive biography, the third in a trilogy of the most essential books on Flynn; includes an in-depth biography by Thomas, reviews and production information of every film by Behlmer, and copious stills and candids from McCarty's collection

Thomey, Ted. *The Loves of Errol Flynn*. Derby, CT: Monarch Books, 1962. The best accounting of the 1943 statutory rape trial, gleaned from the official court notes that have now been lost; invaluable

Magazines

Archer, Steve. *An Untold Tale of William Tell*. FILMFAX, April/May 1993, pp. 50-59, 98. The only source of inside information on the filming of this failed project, the late Archer having been given entree to director Jack Cardiff's personal papers

"Finis for the Fabulous Flynn." *Life* magazine, October 26, 1959, pp. 133-136. The magazine's posthumous article on Flynn, with photos of him ten days before his death

"Movie of the Week: Robin Hood," and *"Errol Flynn, Glamour Boy, Seeks Adventure."* *Life* magazine, May 23, 1938, pp. 60-65. THE ADVENTURES OF ROBIN HOOD is given a splashy, photo-rich pre-promotion, while Flynn is covered in a separate article about his personal life and marriage to Lili Damita

Mumm, Jonathan. *A Return to Sherwood Forest*. FILMFAX, May/June 1989, pp. 70-72. An accounting of the filming of THE ADVENTURES OF ROBIN HOOD when on location in Chico, CA, in 1937

(Pages in **boldface** indicate the respective subject is presented in a photo, article, letter, etc.)

20th Century Fox 77, 185, 213, 219, 279
30 Acres (WB backlot) 90, **97**, 102
Aadland, Beverly 259, 285, **286**, 289, **290**, **291**, 292, 293, **295**, 298, **299**, 301, **302**, **303**, **304**, 305, 306, 307, **308**, 310
Abbott, Bud **231**
Abel, Walter 47
Abeles, Arthur (WB head of distribution) 234, 237
Academy Awards **42**, **100**, 272
Acosta, Rodolfo **278**
Adams, Trelawny 16, **17**, 18, 19
ADVENTURES OF CAPTAIN FABIAN, THE 206, 213, 217, **219**, **220**, 221, 222, 224, 225, 226, **258**, **264**, 267, 269, 279
ADVENTURES OF DON JUAN 142, 154, 159, 161, 162, 163, 164, 165, 166, **167**, 182, 185, 186, **187**, 188, 189, **190**, **191**, **192**, **193**, **194**, 195, **196**, **197**, 198, 200, 203, **205**, 208, 237
ADVENTURES OF ROBIN HOOD, THE 9, **7**, 31, 52, **60**, **62**, **63**, **64**, 65, **66**, **67**, **68**, **69**, **70**, 71, 72, 73, 74, 79, **83**, 213, 310
AGAINST ALL FLAGS 226, **230**, **231**, **232**, **234**, 235, 248, 250, 252, **258**
Albert, Eddie **279**
Alda, Robert **168**
Alexander, Ross 35, **36**, **39**
Alleborn, Al (WB unit manager) 49, 50, 60, 62, 64, 65, 67, 69, 74, 75, 166, 172, 173
Allied Artists 263
Allord, Rick (*Zaca* captain) 301, 303
Allyson, June **157**
American Red Cross Drive **147**
ANOTHER DAWN 46, 47, **48**, **49**, 50, 53, 59, **83**, 206
Archer, Claude "Charlie" (WB 2nd asst. director) 123, 129
Argentina: 105; Buenos Aires **104**
Arizona: Flagstaff 95, **96**; Phoenix 174; Sedona 7, **95**; Seligman 88; Tuba City 95; Winslow 88; Yuma **34**, **49**, 50
Armendáriz, Pedro **274**
Arnaz, Desi **94**
Arnold, Edward 216
Arnow, Max (WB casting director) 47
Arrowsmith, T. H. 16
Asher, Irving (head of WB England) 24, 28, 29, 30, 32, 35, 67
Ashley, Eve (Mrs. Stephen Raphael) **208**, 227, **253**
Astaire, Fred **166**
Astor, Mary **101**
Atwill, Lionel **36**
Austin, Jerry **194**, **197**
Australia: 11, 126; Ballina 17; Bondi 7, 19, 20; Bowen 17; Brisbane 17; Bundaberg 17; Cairns 17; Coff Harbor 17; Cooktown 17; Hinchinbrook Island 17; Gladstone 17; Hobart 11, **12**, 13, 14, 41, 42; Kings Cross (Sydney) 15, 20; Kyogle 16; Mareeba 17; Narrows, The 17; Port Alma 17; Port Stephens 16; Queensland 19; Sydney 7, 11, 14, 15, 16, 19, 20; Tasmania 9; Townsville 17, 20; Tuncurry 16
Autry, Gene 181
Aylmer, Felix **239**
B.C. Cricket Club, Vancouver 46
Bacall, Lauren 216, 260
Bacardi Cuban Rum 298, **299**
Bacon, Lloyd (WB director) 108, 110
Baggett, Lynn **147**
Baker, Josephine 210
Bardot, Brigitte **254**
Barrat, Robert **39**, 40
Barry, Patricia **301**
Barry, Phyllis 53
Barrymore, Diana **283**
Barrymore, Ethel 168
Barrymore, John 7, 110, 130, 131, 189, 259, 282, **283**, 285, 286, 289
Barrymore, Lionel 168
Bassermann, Albert 130
Bates, Barbara **191**
Batista, President Fulgencio **273**
Baum, Lou (WB production manager) 132, 133, 135, **136**, 148, 149, 150, 200, 201, 202
Baxter, Anne 207
Baxter, Warner **72**
Beam Ends 17, 49, 52, 54
Beery, Wallace 169
Bellamy, Ralph 45, **116**
Bella Vista (John Barrymore estate) 7
Belli, Melvin 288, 292, 303, 304, 306

Bennett, Joan 81, 100
Benny, Jack 163, 169, **225**, 264
Bentley, John 270, **271**
Bergen, Edgar (and Charlie McCarthy) 147
Bergman, Ingrid 201, 209
Berle, Milton 115, 164, 165
Berlin, Irving 77
Berlinale film festival **281**
Berry, Joe (WB location manager) 80
Berry, Wallace Jr. **177**, **179**, 208
Berthier, Jacques **244**, **245**
Best, William (Flynn's business manager) 54, 74, 77
Bickham, Marjorie **28**
BIG BOODLE, THE 273, **274**, 280, **309**
Bishop, Julie **147**, **149**
Blanke, Henry (WB producer) 10, 45, 46, 60, 62, 67, 98, 136, 137, 176, 282
Blattner, Gerry (WB UK producer) 233, 234, 235, 236, 237, 238, 239, 240, 241, 243, 244, 245, 246, 247, 249, 250
Bligh, Captain 12
Blondell, Joan 58, **59**, 85, **112**
BLOW-UPS OF 1946 (short) 177
BLOW-UPS OF 1947 (short) 196
Blue, Monte 143, 192
Blum, Albert (Flynn's business manager) 117, 125, 151, 159, 164, 177, 180, 199, 200, 219, 223, 239, 250, 251, 252, 262, 269
Blumenstock, Mort (head of WB publicity) 66, 147, 164, 197, 203, 211, 255
Bogart, Humphrey 58, **88**, 95, 96, 99, 260, 277, 310
Bohnen, Roman 36, **38**
Bond, Ward **134**, **154**
Borchers, Cornell 270, **271**, **272**, 277
Borge, Victor 102, 111
Borzage, Frank **46**
Boyd, Mrs. 28, 67
Boyd, William "Hopalong Cassidy" **101**
Brazil: 105, 173; Rio de Janeiro 103, **104**; Buenos Aires 261
BREAKDOWNS OF 1937 51
BREAKDOWNS OF 1939 86
Brent, George 33, 47
Brent, Romney **191**, **192**, **197**
British-American Hospital-Mexico City 164
British War Relief 118
Brooke, Michael (Earl of Warwick) 59, 67, **78**
Brooke, Sir James 43, 45, 184
Brooks, Geraldine **174**
Brooks, Jan **289**
Brooks, Paul 171, **256**
Brown, Harry Joe (WB producer) 32, 34, 35, 41, 42, 47, 48, 49, 51
Brown, James 158, 213
Bruce, David **101**, **105**, 196
Bruce, Nigel 45, 167
Bruner, June **225**
Bucknall, Nathalie **58**
Budge, Donald **61**, 182
Budlong, John "Jack" **120**, 121
Bugs Bunny 196, 197, 213
Burns, Paul E. **201**
Burr, Raymond 192, **229**
Burt, Charlie 16, **17**
BUSINESS AT WAR (short) 149
Butler, David (WB director) 143, 163, **166**
Byington, Spring **46**

Cabot, Bruce 33, 79, **81**, **85**, 86, **112**, 123, 125, **134**, 136, 139, 144, 160, 161, **166**, 167, 208, 229, 231, **253**, 254, 255, **260**, 266, **267**, 268, 276
Cady, Howard (Putnam publishing) 302, 304, 305
Cagney, James 47, 310
Caldicot, Richard 28
Caldough, George 301, 303, 304, 305
California: Algodones Dunes (Imperial Sand Dunes) **49**; Apple Valley 232; Balboa (rape trial) 145, (rape trial) 146, 228; Barstow 111; Beverly Hills 7; Bidwell Park-Chico 7, 62, **63**, **64**, **65**; Bishop **184**, 185, 186; Brentwood 110; Bronson Canyon **185**, 187; Busch Gardens-Pasadena, CA 58, **66**, **67**, 72, 73, **105**,**118**, **119**, 120; Catalina Island, CA 60, 62, 85, **94**, 102, 109, 118, 120, 125, 138, 146, 174, 178, 219; Channel Islands 79, 171 Chatsworth, CA 45, 106, **121**, 122; Chico 7, 62, 64, 66, 71; Elysian Park, Los Angeles **138**; Flintridge 59; Forest Lawn, Glendale 156; Fourth of July Cove-Catalina 120; Gofer Flats (at Providencia Ranch) 105, **158**; Hollywood 185; Iverson Ranch-Chatsworth 45, **121**, 122; Klamath River 47; L.A. County Arboretum (formerly the Lucky Baldwin Ranch)-Arcadia **133**, 134, **155**, 156, 157; Laguna Beach 7, **38**; La Jolla 177; Lake Arrowhead 144; Lake Sherwood 43, **44**, 46, 69, 70, 128; Lasky Mesa (Calaba-

sas) 43, **44**, 45, 46, 48, 49, 105, **106**, **122**, **123**, 162, **197**; Little River-Modesto 80; Lone Pine (Alabama Hills) **8**, **43**, 45, **214**, **215**; Long Beach 176; Melrose Ranch-Escondido **152**; Modesto **79**, **80**, (Orpheum Theater) **90**; Monterey **135**; Needles 111; Newport Beach 171, **174**; Norden **101**; Palm Canyon **40**, **51**; Palm Springs 79, 110, 156, 182; Palos Verdes **116**, **230**; Pamona 105; Pasadena **111**, 112, 116, **118**; Piru **127**; Point Loma-San Diego **115**; Point Mugu **102**, 127, **198**; Providencia Ranch (now Forest Lawn, Hollywood Hills) **47**, 59, 76, 105, 107, 116, **174**, **182**, 183, **190**; San Bernardino 138; San Diego 89, 121; San Fernando Valley **125**; San Francisco 79, 108, 114, 151, 167, **171**, 173, 174; San Pedro 77, 79, 108, 109, 120; Santa Barbara 33, 35, 120, 125, 174; Santa Cruz Island 85; Santa Monica **176**; Sherwood Forest 59, 128; Sierra Nevada Mountains **184**; Sky Valley Ranch (Chatsworth) 106; South Pasadena (property) 86, 123; Stockton 100; Sunset Plaza Drive, (now West) Hollywood 86; Swall Meadows **184**; Triunfo Canyon 90; Truckee 126; Victorville 96; Whites Landing-Catalina 118; Whittier Park 155, **156**, 157; Wilmington **228**
Callahan, Mushy 59, 131, 13
Campbell, Beatrice **239**, **240**, 242
Campbell, Ian Douglas, the 11th Duke of Argyll 265
"Candy Kid, The" 207
Cannes Film Festival **211**, 252
Cantor, Eddie 187
CAPTAIN BLOOD 7, 9, 31, 33, 35, **36**, **37**, **38**, **39**, **40**, 41, 79, **83**, 188, **206**, 241, 286
"Captain Hornblower" 94, 99
Cardiff, Jack 206, 241, **244**, **253**
Carpano Vermouth 254, 261
Carpenter, Byran **89**
Carrell, Ruth **153**
Carroll, Earl 163, 169
Carrol, Harrison 120, 183, 208
Carson, Jack 131, 191, 192
CASE OF THE CURIOUS BRIDE, THE **32**, 33
Cassini, Oleg 167
Castello Lancellotti-Lauro, Italy 249, **250**
Castro, Fidel 10, **293**, 294, 301, **302**,
Cavalier Magazine **298**
Cavalry Post Horse Show **86**
Cavens, Fred **51**, 163, 166, 167, 189, 239
Cedars of Lebanon Hospital (now Cedars-Sinai), Los Angeles **41**, 78
Chad 289
Chaplin, Charlie **129**, 132
CHARGE OF THE LIGHT BRIGADE **8**, 9, 38, 41, 42, **43**, **44**, 45, 46, 47, 49, 53, **83**
Chauval, Charles 11, 19, **20**, 262
Christian, Fletcher 12
Christian, Linda (b. Blanca Rosa Welter) 139, 143, 146, **211**
Churubusco Studios, Mexico City **279**
Cigarillos **236**
Cinecitta Studios-Rome, Italy 250
Cinemonde Magazine 201, **202**
Cinesound Studios 19, **20**
Circus Krone-Stuttgart, Germany 252
Clichy riots, Paris 54
Cohen, Albert J. (Universal producer) **271**, 274
Colbert, Claudette 33
Cole, Nat "King" **272**, 277
Coleman, Nancy **130**, **147**
Collins, Joan **283**
Colman, Ronald 167
Columbia Pictures 177, 178
Columbia Records 175, 176, **181**, 182
Confidential magazine **267**, 275, **288**, 291
Conrad, Earl 259, 291, **292**, **296**, **297**, 298, 299, 300
Cook, Clyde **49**
Cooper, Gary 57, **77**, 78, **166**, 252, 277
Cooper, Melville **78**
Cooper, Rocky (Mrs. Gary) **77**, **166**
Corbett, James J. 9, 84
Cording, Harry **36**, 101, 231
Costello, Lou **231**
Cother, Patrick (Zaca skipper) **276**
Courmayeur, Italy 7, **253**, 255
Courneya, Jerry 176, 199
Cowan, Shirley **129**
Coward, Noel 224, 263
Crain, Jeanne **256**
Crawford, Broderick **216**
Crean, Paddy (fencing choreographer) 235, 239, 241, 242
Crehan, Joseph 71, **132**, **134**
Crisp, Donald 44, **78**, 93
Crosby, Bing 102, 103, 111, **252**
Crosland, Alan Jr. (WB editor) 183

CROSSED SWORDS 206, 242, **248**, **249**, **250**. 256, 263, 271, 276, **309**
CRUISE OF THE ZACA, THE 176, 178, 223, 225, 229, 248, 261, 263, 264
Crump, Owen (WB producer) 181, 182, 183, 185, 186, 187
CRY WOLF **174**, **175**, 176, 187, 188, **205**, 206
Cuba: 10, 75, 226, 248, 275, 281, 292, **293**, **294**, **295**, 297, **298**, 307 Camagüey 293; Central Palma 293; Havana 273, **274**, **299**; Morro Castle **274**; Oriente Province **293**; Santiago 293
CUBAN REBEL GIRLS 259, **295**, 298, 301, **308**, **309**
CUBAN STORY 300
Cugat, Xavier **160**
Cukor, George 47
Curtis, Tony **231**, **273**,
Curtiz, Michael (WB director) 32, 33, 34, 35, 36, 37, 38, **39**, 42, 45, 67, **69**, 71, **72**, **73**, 79, 85, 90, **91**, 93, 97, **98**, 99, 100, 101, 104, 107, 185, 302
Custer, Gen. George Armstrong 9, 84
Daley, Cass **157**
Dalgety & Co., Ltd. 15
Damita, Lili (first wife) 24, **25**, 26, 2, 31, **32**, **33**, 34, **35**, **36**, 40, 41, 42, 44, 45, 47, 48, **50**, 51, **54**, 56, 57, 60, 61, 62, **65**, 70, **71**, **72**, **73**, **74**, 76, 77, 78, 79, **81**, 84, **85**, 86, 91, **93**, **94**, 98, 99, 102, 103, 109, 113, 118, 120, 123, 124, 130, 139, 152, **161**, **162**, 186, 187, 216, 217, **219**, **224**, 250, 260, 265, 267, 268, 269, 287, 290, 291, **296**, 303, 306, **308**, 310
Daniell, Henry 98
Daniels, Bebe 123, 167
Dantine, Helmut **149**, **166**
Darnell, Linda **157**,
Davenport, Harry **59**
Daves, Delmer **58**
Davies, Marion 46, 131, **232**,
Davis, Bette 33, **75**, 76, 77, 78, 89, 90, **91**, **92**, 93, 99, 147, 158
Davis, Joan 171
DAWN PATROL, THE **77**, **78**, **81**, **83**
Day, Dennis 226
Day, Doris **201**
Decker, John 110, **150**, 154, 155, 157, 159, 163, 166, 167, 168, 172, 173, **176**, **177**, 184, **185**
Decker and Flynn Galleries-West Hollywood **155**, 157, 159, 168, 172
DEEP SEA FISHING (short) 178, 236
De Gaulle, Charles 291
de Havilland, Olivia 33, **35**, **36**, **37**, 38, 39, **40**, 41, **44**, 45, 46, 49, 51, **58**, 64, **65**, **66**, 67, **70**, 71, **72**, **73**, **80**, **87**, **90**, **93**, 94, 104, **105**, **106**, 107, 108, **109**, **111**, 112, **118**, **119**, **121**, 123, **167**, **168**, 284
Delamare, Simone 252
Del Rio, Dolores 33, 34, 42, 44, 46, 57, 62, 78
DeMille, Cecil B. **58**, **71**
De Ruiz, Nick **69**
Dervin (sometimes called Duvivier), Danielle **221**, **222**, 223, 226, 229
DESPERATE JOURNEY **126**, **127**, **128**, 129, **130**, 131, 136, **141**
Denyer, Margaret **237**
Diaz, Apolonio 179, 180, 229, 262, 265, 269
Dibbs, Naomi (Flynn's fiancé) **15**, 17, 20
Dieterle, William (WB director) 48, 53
Dietrich, Marlene 32, **33**, 44, 57, **81**, 263
di Frasso, Countess 33, 40, 210
Diggins, Peggy **111**
Dill, Diana 117
DIVE BOMBER **114**, **115**, **116**, **117**, 121, **141**
Dodd, Claire **33**
Dodd, Jimmie **153**
DODGE CITY 9, 78, **79**, **80**, 81, **85**, **87**, (premiere) **90**, **141**; **junket**: **88**, **89**
Domergue, Faith 132
Dominican Republic **281**, 282
Donat, Robert 32
DON'T BET ON BLONDES 33, 35
Dora, Lorraine **161**
Doran, Ann **116**
Dors, Diana **238**
Douglas, Robert **191**, **192**, 195, **196**, **215**
Dru, Joanne 227, **264**
Duchess of Windsor 210
Duke, Doris 115, 120
Dumbrille, Douglas 96
Dunne, Irene 208
Durante, Jimmy 163, 187
Eason, B. Reeves "Breezy" (second unit director) 65
Eddington, Marge (Nora's stepmother) 160, 163, 164, **209**, **212**, 214, **216**, 217, 219, 222, 273
Eddington, Nora (second wife) **147**, 148, 149, 151, 153, **154**, 158, 159, 160, 163, **164**, (home at 9250 Cordell Dr.,

West Hollywood) *165*, (home at 3319 Hamilton Way, Hollywood) *166*, *167*, *168*, *169*, 171, 172, *173*, *176*, 177, 178, 179, 180, 181, 182, 183, 184, 186, 187, *188*, *189*, 191, 192, 195, *197*, *198*, *200*, 201, *203*, 209, *210*, 215, 216, *223*, 225, *227*, 229, 232, *249*, 250, *251*, 252, *260*, *265*, 270, *280*, 284, 286, 298, *300*, *301*, *302*, 304, 306, 308
EDGE OF DARKNESS *135*, *136*, *137*, 138, *139*, *141*, 147
Einfeld, Charles (WB director of publicity) 47, 66, 75, 96, 98, *111*, 124, 130, 164
Elizabeth, the Queen Mother 212
Elliot, James (husband of Rosemary Flynn) 110
Ellis, John *52*
Elstree Studios 239, 241, 246, 263, 264
Emerson, Faye *147*, 169, 182
Erben, Dr. Hermann Erben 11, 22, 23, 24, *25*, 26, 31, 46, 47, *48*, 53, *54*, 55, 56, *78*, 79, 109, 110, 192, *297*, 298, 300, 302, 304
Erdman, Richard *155*
Erickson, Leif 272
Ernst, Bud 34, 41, 60, *87*, 89, 109, 117 (rape trial) 145, 298
Errol and Me 159
ESCAPE ME NEVER 170, *171*, *172*, *173*, 182, 191, *205*, 206
Espinosa, Lou 165, 179, 234, 236
Esquire Magazine 304, 305
Evelove, Alex (WB publicity director) 173, 197, 211
Fairbanks, Douglas Jr. 28, 174, 263
"Faith" 251
Falkenberg, Jinx 44, *62*
Famous Artists Associates (Flynn's agents) 288
Farmer, Frances *58*
F.B.I. 100, 112, 132, *133*, 138, 147, 148, 151
Fellows, Robert (WB unit manager) 47, 59, 95, 97, 104, 105, 107, 117, 118, 122
Ferrer, Mel *279*
Fidler, Jimmy 67, 69, 74, 110, 123
Fields, W.C. *72*, 169, 271
Finch, Peter *264*
"Fire Over Africa" 244
Fitzgerald, Geraldine 103
FitzGibbon, Maura *284*, 296
Flaherty, Pat *131*
Flato, John 20, Paul *297*
Fleming, Jim (Flynn's double and assistant) 120, 137, 158, 176, *184*
Fleming, Rhonda 231
FLIRTATION WALK *30*
Florey, Robert (WB director) 161, 162, 163, 217
Flynn, Arnella (daughter) 206, *256*, 261, *262*, 265, *266*, *270*, *271*, *273*, *274*, 275, *276*, 278, 286, *287*, 300, 310
Flynn, Deirdre (daughter) 163, *164*, *165*, *168*, *172*, 174, 178, 183, 207, 209, 213, *214*, 215, *218*, 219, *222*, 224, 229, *239*, *249*, 250, *251*, 268, 269, *270*, *271*, 273, 278, *284*, 285, 294, *295*, 298, 300, *301*, *302*, 304, 307, *308*
FLYNN, ERROL: **alimony and child support:** 121, 123, 130, 152, *161*, *162*, 187, 216, 217, 218, *219*, *247*, 260, 265
airplanes Republic RC-3 amphibian 236; Ryan Aeronautical Super 260 Navion 232, 234, 235; **articles by:** *Hollywood Women, Heaven Preserve Them!* 60, *Hollywood's Not-So-Ancient Mariners* 69, *I'd Rather Play Tennis* 46, *Night On the Town, A* 57, *Seamy Side of Hollywood, The* 74, *What Really Happened To Me In Spain* 59, *Young Man About Town* 60 **birth:** *12* **boxing** 15 **cars** 124, 200 *160*, *246*, 250, *252*, 253, 255 **citizenship** 135; *death* 305, 306; **divorce:** 84, 152, 210, 215 **early homes:** *12*, *13*, *14*, 15, *25*, *26*, *28*, 29; **equities:** *122* **extortion of:** 151, Gelstrom, Jack 138 Seamster, Billy 138 Street, Robert 148, 149; **funeral** 306, *307*; **homes:** 8946 Appian Way, Hollywood *33*, *35*, *40*; 601 North Linden, Beverly Hills *61*, *78*, 91, 102, 123, 148; Castle Comfort-Port Antonio, Jamaica 188; Mulholland Farm (7740 Mulholland Highway, the Hollywood Hills) 7, 45, 84, 109, 110, 123, *125*, 132, 137, 143, 150, 151, 153, *166*,171, 172, 173, 181, 182, 183, 184, 189, 190, 192, 201, *207*, 208, *210*, *214*, *218*, 219, 227, 231, 249, 250, 252, 256, 264, 267, *269*, 284; 1709 Tropical Avenue, Beverly Hills 117 **illness & injuries:** 36, 37, *41*, *49*, 51, 79, 91, 93, 98, 99, 100, 102, 105, 107, 116, 120, 121, 125, 126, 127, 128, 129, 130, 131, 132, 133, 134, 135, 148, 149, 150, 156, 157, 158, 159, 161, 162, 165, 166, 169, 171, 172, 186, 190, 191, 192, 193, 194, 195, 196, 198, 201, 202, 206, *221*, 223, 224, 226, 228, **231**, 232, 234, 240, 241, 242, 243, 245, 246, *250*, *275*, *276*, 282, 291, *293*, 297, 299, 300 **measurements** 238; **immigration:** *42* **pets:** Arno (schnauzer) 37, 74, *76*, *78*, 85, 86, *97*, *103*, *109*, 111, 119, 123, *174* Chico (monkey) *186* Chula (dachshund) 178, 179 Cold Nose (Alsatian dog) 218, Fubar (poodle) 220 Greno (dachshund) 220 Joy Boy (poodle) 247, *248* Moody (schnauzer) 155, *158*, *174* Polly (parrot) 188, Señor Soto (monkey) 178, 179 Stella and Billy (Rhodesian Ridgeback dogs) 54, 57, 59, *103*,

125, **phone numbers:** 33, 125, 216 **salaries:** 25, 29, 30, 31, 40, 41, 43, 46, 47, 50, 53, 60, 69, 70, 77, 78, 84, 85, 93, 95, 97, 100, 108, 109, 117, 130, 131, 135,137, 169, 174, 175, 188, 208, 213, 233, 273, 279, 282, 283 **schools:** 13, *14*, 15 **taxes:** 116, 122, 152, 161, 175, 251, 253, 254, 256, 259, 261 **tennis** 15, 25, *32*, 33, 44, 45, 48, *58*, 60, 62, *76*, *85*, 94, 98, *108*, 158; 184 **marriage:** (first) 33, *34 (second)* 159, (third) *220* **yachts:** Bachelor, The (formerly the Cheerio II) *60*; Nautilus (Zaca's fishing boat) 235; Sirocco (the first, formerly Arop) *16*, 17, 20; Sirocco (the second, formerly the Karenita, Avenir, Simoon, and Watchettein) 31, *71*, 72, *73*, 77, 78, 81, 84, *85*, *86*, *94*, 102, 108, 109, 112, 115, *120*, 122, 145, 146, 147, 151; Zaca *171*, *173*, 174, *175*, *176*, *177*, *178*, *179*, 180, 181, 188, 198, 200, 206, 209, 210, 213, 219, *220*, *221*, 222, 223, 233, 248, 259, *265*, 269, 271, 273, 275, *276*, *282*, 291, 301
Flynn, Marelle (mother) *12*, 14, 23, *93*, *94*, 180, 215, *216*, 226, 235, 261, 265, *292*, 298, 300, *301*, 302, 307, *308*
Flynn, Rory (daughter) 181, 183, *208*, *209*, *210*, *212*, *213*, *214*, 215, *218*, 219, *222*, 224, 227, 229, *239*, *249*, 250, *251*, 268, 269, *270*, *271*, 273, 278, *279*, *280*, *284*, *286*, *295*, 298, *300*, *301*, *302*, 304, *307*, 308
Flynn, Rosemary (sister) 13, *14*, 23, *93*, *94*, 110, 183, 252, 290, 298, 308
Flynn, Sean (son) 84, 117, 118, 120, 139, 152, *184*, 186, 216, *218*, 219, *224*, *225*, 226, 227, 229, 250, 267, 268, *273*, *275*, 276, 277, 288, 290, 291, 300, *303*, 304, *307*, 310
Flynn, Prof. Theodore (father) *12*, 14, 16, 17, 18, 19, 23, 25, 54, *93*, *94*, 163, 175, *176*, *177*, 180, 215, *216*, 224, 226, 235, 261, 262, 265, 276, 291, 297, 298, 300, *301*, 302, 307, 308
Fontaine, Joan 104, 200, 208, 261
FOOTSTEPS IN THE DARK 99, 108, *109*, *110*, 111, 114, *141*, 206
Foran, Dick 58, 76
FOR AULD LANG SYNE 74
Ford, Robert E. (see also Rape trial) 147, 148, 152, 175, 186, 193, 211, 218, *219*, 224, 280, 284
Forest Lawn-Glendale, CA 259, 306, *307*
Formica, Armando *215*
Fossataro, Count Adolfo 251, 252, 255, 276
Foster, Art *133*, *143*,
FOUR'S A CROWD 71, *72*, *73*, 76, 77, *83*, 206
Fowler, Gene 157, *166*, 168, 271
Fowley, Douglas *85*
Francen, Victor 162
Francis, Kay 46, *48*, 49, 51, 53, *58*, 59, 81
French Cameroon 290
Friars Club (Hollywood) *216*, (New York) 288
FRISCO KID, THE *36*
FROM HERE TO ETERNITY *256*
Fryer, Elmer (WB photographer) *46*
Furneaux, Yvonne *242*,
Gable Clark 10, 168, *207*, *242*
Gabor, Zsa Zsa *114*
Gardiner, Reginald 167
Gardner, Ava 125, 132, 277, *279*, 281
Garfield, John *88*
Garson, Greer 174, *207*, 208, 210, 212
Gaudio, Tony (WB cinematographer) *65*
Gauguin, Paul ("Familie Tahitienne," painting) *152*, *152*, *210*, 255, 261, *265*, 268, 269, 273, 277
GENTLEMAN JIM 84, *131*, *132*, *133*, *134*, 135, 137, *141*, *167*, 175
George, Mr. (Flynn's Mulholland grounds keeper) 125, 164, 166
Ghica, Princess Irinia (Irene) 209, 210, *211*, *212*, 213, *214*, *216*, *217*
Gibbons, Cedric 42, 46, 62, *85*, 132
Gibson, Hoot *88*
Giesler, Jerry (see also Rape trial) 215, 218, *219*, 227, *280*
Girard, Bill *155*
Gilbert, Helen *96*
Gogh, Vincent Van ("Man Is At Sea, The," painting) *151*, *255*, 261, 265, 268, 269, 277
Goddard, Paulette 50, 81, 167, 234, 236, 276
GOLD DIGGERS OF 1935 30
Golden Globes *270*
Goldner, Charles *244*
Goddard, Paulette 50, 81, 167, *234*, 235, 236
Golenbock, Justin "Jud" (Flynn's business manager) 260, 262, 263, *265*, 267, 268, 269, 271, 272, *273*, *274*, 275, 277, 278, 280, 281, 283, *290*, 297, 298, 300
GONE WITH THE WIND *79*, *167*
Gordon, C. Henry *44*, 46
Gordon, Leon (MGM producer) 202
Gosta, Eric (Flynn's butler) 137
Gould, Dr. Grant *305*, **306**
Goulding, Edmund (WB director) 59, 67, *78*, 78, 79, 109, 119

Granger, Farley 254
Grant, Cary 94, 125, 132
Grapewin, Charlie *122*, *123*
Gray, Dolores 225
Gray, Eve *29*
Gray, Nadia *249*, *281*
Graziano, Rocky 268
Gréco, Juliette *290*, 291, *292*
GREEN LIGHT 41, 45, *46*, *47*, 48, 53, 54, *83*, 206
Green, Morris (Flynn attorney) 203
Greenlaw, Charlie (WB production manager) 194, 195
Gregory, Jon *266*, 267
Grimshaw, Miss Beatrice 20
Gulbrandsen, Synnove (Miss Oslo) *252*, 253
Gurney, Noll (Flynn's agent) 67, 74, 86, 91, 93, 94, 103
Haas, Waltraut 253
Hale, Alan 51, 53, 62, *63*, 69, *80*, *85*, 90, 93, *96*, *97*, *101*, *102*, *127*, *128*, 131, 174, *190*, *191*, *192*, 195, *197*, 213
Hale, Bobby *143*
Hale, Jonathan *183*
Haley, Jack 171, 173
Hal Roach Studios 270
Halvorsen, Lars 16, 17
Hamilton, Ward (WB makeup artist) 67
Hansen, Chuck (WB production manager) 182, 185, 186
Harrison, Rex 254, 256, 260
Hartford, Huntington 283, 285, *287*, 289, 290, 292
Haskin, Byron (WB second unit man) 108
Hassau, Marilyn *152*,
Hassau, Shirley Evans *152*, 153 , 223
Hawaii: 79, 112, 113; Hawaii, HI 113; Honolulu 108, 112, 113, 114; Huehue Ranch, Kona 113; Kalama Beach, Oahu 113; Kapaau, Hawaii 113; Kohala Coast, Hawaii 113; Kona 113; Pearl Harbor 113, 125
Haymes, Dick 210, 223, 227, 229
Hays, Roy 89, 90
Hays Office *167*
Haywood, George *105*
Hayward, Louis *29*
Hayworth, Rita 111, *177*, *178*, 209
Heacock, Frank (WB publicist) 79, 96
Hearst Headline Service 294, 295
Hearst, William Randolph 44, 57
Heindorf, Ray 200
Heinze, Walter "Wally" (Flynn's manager) 77, 108, *109*, 116, 118, 119, 124, 125, 126
Hellinger, Mark 166
HELLO GOD 215, 222, 267
Hemingway, Ernest 60, 293
Henie, Sonja 155, 168
Henreid, Paul 213
Hepburn, Audrey 280
Hepburn, Katherine 94, 174
Hill, Howard 60, 64, 78, 85, 86, 93, *176*, *177*, 178
Hill, Walter (Flynn's Mulholland farm groom) 110
Hiller, Arthur *301*
Hodiak, John *207*
Hollingshead, Gordon (WB assoc. producer) 37, 38, 40
Holloway, Sterling *157*
Homans, Robert *85*
Hoover, J. Edgar 132, 133, 138
Hope, Bob 103, 153
Hopper, Hedda 114, *147*, 173, 265, 287
Hopkins, Miriam *95*, 96
Horton, Edward Everett 58
Hotels: Alameda, San Francisco *171*; Alameda-Morelia, Mexico 279; Ambassador, Los Angeles *58*, *100*, 174; Australia-Sydney, 20; Bamer, Mexico City 275, 281; Bayerischer Hof, Munich 252; Berkeley, London 25; Beverly Crest 300; Beverly Hills *77*, *103*, 115, 184, 218; Beverly Hilton *96*, 97, 103, 208, 284; Biltmore, Los Angeles 42; Chateau Marmont, Hollywood 304; Chee's Jour Gnee-Rabaul, New Guinea 16; 103 Comodoro-Havana, Cuba 294, 295, 296, 297, 298; del Coronado-San Diego, CA 32, *76*,114, 229; El Rancho-.Gallup, NM 217; Excelsior, Rome 209, 248, *254*; Flamingo, Las Vegas *225*; Garden of Allah, Hollywood 32, *270*, 278; Alpen Hof-Garmisch-Partenkirchen, Germany 252; George V, Paris 211, 214; Havana Hilton, Cuba *294*, 295; Hollywood Landmark (now the Highland Gardens) 300; Hotel de Paris, Monte Carlo *221*; Knickerbocker, Hollywood 29, 33; Kona Inn, HI 113; Le Grand Hôtel, Cannes 210; Lido Excelsior-Venice Italy 254; Maricel, Palma de Mallorca, 222, 268; Myrtle Bank-Kingston, Jamaica 179, 188, 199, 216, 233, 235, 247; Nacional-Havana, Cuba 226, 274, 292, 293, 307; Napoleon, Paris 291; Nautilus-Miami, FL 233, 234; Park Lane, NYC 288, 289, 291; Portland Residential Hotel, London 25; Prince de Gaulles, Paris; Reforma-Mexico City 135, 159; Richard Springs-Chico,

CA 62, 71, 74; Ritz, Mexico City 139, 164; Ritz Towers, NYC 41, 123; Royal Hawaiian, Honolulu 108, 113; Santa Barbara Biltmore 20; Savoy, London 212, 235, 236, *237*, 245, 261, 262, 266, 268; Shoreham, NYC 300 St. Moritz, NYC 54; Sylvia-Vancouver, Canada 305; Titchfield-Port Antonio, Jamaica 179, 180, *188*, 198, 216, 223, 224, 226, *233*, 235, 247, 261, 299; Vesuvio-Naples, Italy 248, 249, 282; Villa Igiea-Palermo, Italy 243; Virrey de Mendoza-Morelia, Mexico *280*; Waldorf Astoria (and Towers), New York City 86, 94, 164
Howard, Trevor *281*, 289, *292*
Howe, James Wong (WB cinematographer) 125
"How To Die" 294
Hubbard, L. Ron 115
Hubbs, Dr. Carl *176*, 177, *193*
Hull, Henry *156*
Hughes, Howard *96*
Hunter, Alistair *264*
Hunter, Ian 35, 47, *48*, 49, 64, 76
Hunter-Kerr, Ken 15, 19
Huntley, G.P. 45, *122*
Hurrell, George *82*, *92*, 93
Huston, John *166*, 263, 264, 288, 289, *290*
Huston, Walter 136, *139*, 147, *166*
Hutton, Barbara 126
Hutton, Betty 218
Hyde, Mary Ann 125, 132
I ADORE YOU 25, 26, *27*
Ikerd, Percy (Universal unit manager) 232, 234
IN THE WAKE OF THE BOUNTY 19, *20*, 22, 25, 26
Inescourt, Frieda *48*, 50
International Brigade (Spain) 56
Ireland, John *278*
Irwin, Charles *101*, 102, *143*
ISTANBUL 270, *271*, *272*, *273*, 274, 277, *309*
IT'S A GREAT FEELING *201*, 210, *258*
Jackson, Sherry *215*
Jaffe, Sam 269
Jamaica: 142, 292, 293, 298, 308 Errol Flynn Stakes *188*; Kingston (St. Andrew Club and Colony Club) 179, (St. Andrew Club) 180, 181, 188, 189, (Glass Bucket Club) 199, 226, 232, 233, 235, 236, 247, 261; Montego Bay 188, 199, 247; Navy Island *180*, 203, 276; Ocho Rios 179, 224; Port Antonio (Boston Bay) 179, 188, 198, 199, 200, 209, *216*, 223, 224, 226, 233, 234, 235, 236, 247, 261, 267, 291, *299*; Port Maria 179; Rio Grande River 188; Sandy Gully 179; Sedge Pond 179
Japan 225
J. Arthur Rank 197
Jenkins, Allen 59, 115
Jerome, Stewart (screenwriter) 200
Jesperson, Mr. 23
Jessel, Georgie 208, 216
JEZEBEL 175
Jimmy Sharman Troupe 17
Johns, Mervyn 239
Johnson, Van 208, *216*, 229
Jolsen, Al 187, 198
Jones, Buck 88
Jones, Dickie 217
Jones, Jennifer 208
Jory, Victor *85*
Junior Films (Flynn's production company) 254
Kahanamoku, Duke 79, 113
Kahne, Harry 225
Karloff, Boris 263
Katz, Lee (asst. director) 60, 264
Kaye, Danny 167, 200
Keighley, William (WB director) 51, 60, 62, *63*, *65*, 67, *218*, 233, 236, 237, *238*, 239, 240, 241, 242, 243, 244, 245, 246
Kessler wine cellar-Esslingen, Germany *252*
Khan, Aly 209
Keil, William (skipper of the Sirocco) 109, 112
Kennedy, Arthur *119*, 126, *127*, *128*, *130*, 132
Kenny, Collin 90
Kerrigan, J.M. *101*
Kibbee, Guy 33
KIM 206, *212*, *213*, *214*, *215*, *216*, 222, *258*
King George V Coronation Ball *58*
King, Henry (Fox director) *280*
KING'S RHAPSODY 27, 259, 265, *266*, *267*, 269, 275, *309*
Klock, Ada (Flynn's secretary) 263, 269
Knowles, Patric *43*, 45, 46, 47, 62, *63*, 64, 66, 69, *70*, 71, *73*, 132
Koenig, William (WB producer) 34, 35, 36
Koets, Dr. Gerrit H. 11
Kraft Music Hall 102, 111
Krims, Milton 242, 244, 247, 248
Kydd, Sam *239*

LADY FROM SHANGHAI, THE 177
Lake Fogliano, Italy **265**
Lamour, Dorothy 187, **207**
Lancaster, Burt 209
Lane, Lola **88**,
Lane, Priscilla **88**
Lane, Rosemary **88**, **101**
Lanza, Prince Raimondo **210**, 243, 244, 245, 247
Larry Edmund's Bookstore, Hollywood 280
Lawford, Peter 166
Lawton, Frank 54
Leduc, Marcel 269, 274, 275, 276
Lee, Christopher 276, 277
Lehmann, Olga ("The Landing of Captain Bligh on Navy Island in 1793," painting) **261**
Leigh, Janet **207**, **231**,
Leigh, Vivian 81, 230, 263
Leplat, Jamine **254**
LeRoy, Mervyn (WB director) 33, 168
LET'S MAKE UP (LILACS IN THE SPRING in the U.K.) 259, 261, **262**, 265, 266, 268, **309**
Levin, Henry **264**,
Levinson, Nathan (WB sound engineer) 175
Lewis, Joyce **276**
Life Magazine 74, **75**, **120**, 138, 144, 198, 304
LIFE WITH FATHER 173, 174
"Lily of Laguna" 262
Lindfors, Viveca 186, 189, **191**, **192**, 194, **196**
Lindsay, Margaret **32**, **46**
Linkletter, Art 100
Litel, John **96**, **159**, **160**
Livesey, Roger 238, 239, 242, **243**, **244**
Lockhart, Gene **149**,
Loder. John 234
Loew, Arthur Jr. **283**
Lollobrigida, Gina **248**, **250**
Lombard, Carole **33**
London, Julie **269**,
Long Beach Municipal Court 224
Long-Innes, Rex 16, **17**
Lord, Robert (WB producer) 37, 41, 51, 53, 78, 79, 108, 110, 114
Lorring, Joan **173**
Los Angeles Angels (minor league baseball team) **226**
Los Angeles International Airport 270, 271
Los Angeles Superior Court 272
Louise, Anita 32, 33, 46, **47**, 48, 53
Lowry, Morton 78
Loy, Myrna 81
Lualdi, Antonella **253**
Lukas, Paul **152**, 158
Lukschy, Wolfgang **281**
Lundigan, William **105**, **106**
Lupino, Ida **166**, **168**, 171, **172**, 173, 193, 306
Lyles, Lee **88**
Lynch, Gloria 109, 110
Lynne, Gillian 242, **244**
Lyon, Ben 123, 167
Lyons, Enid **13**
Lyons, Leonard **187**
MacDonald, Jeanette 45
MacMurray, Fred 103, **116**, **117**, 261
Magnani, Anna **210**
Mahon, Barry 234, 235, 244, 248, 249, 251, 252, 260, 266, 268, 269, 280, 298
Malise (sometimes Malvisi), Yves (Flynn's valet) 236, 237, 249
Maley, Peggy **155**
Mal Marshall clothing **234**, 235
Malone, Dorothy 190, **283**, 284, 285, **286**, 288
Manet, Édouard ("Marguerite de Conflans Wearing a Hood," painting) 155
Manson, Héléna **220**
March, Frederic 47, **72**
March of Dimes **260**
"March Or Die" 266
Marshall, Brenda 94, **98**, **99**, 100, **102**, **108**, **109**
Marshall, William **105**, **106**, 217, 219, **231**
MASTER OF BALLANTRAE, THE 7, 230, 233, 234, 236, 237, **238**, **239**, **240**, **241**, **242**, **243**, **244**, 245, 246, 247, 249, 250, 254, **258**
MARA MARU 226, 227, **228**, **229**, 232, 234, **258**
Marble Arch Odeon, London **212**
Mar del Plata International Film Festival **261**
Marshall, William 213, 215, 221, 226
Martin, Mary 102, 111
Martufi, Guido **253**,
Marx, Groucho 288
Marx, Harpo **216**
Marx, Zeppo 33

Massey, Raymond 105, 107, 111, 127
Matthews, Blayney (head of WB security) 185
Mattison, Frank (WB unit manager) 43, 80, 85, 90, 91, 93, 95, 97, 98, 99, 102, 106, 107, 108, 117, 120, 122, 123, 131, 134, 135, 143, 155, 156, 157, 159, 160, 161, 162, 189, 190, 191, 192, 193, 194, 195, 196, 197, 201, 235, 241, 242, 243, 244, 246, 247
Mature, Victor 154
Mauch, Billy **53**, **57**
Mauch, Bobby **51**, **53**, **57**
Mawson Australian Antarctic Expedition 12
Maybery, Dick (WB asst. director) 33, 189, 192, 194
Mayer, Louis B. 181, 209
Mazzuca, Joe **215**
MCA 189, 198
McCord, Ted (WB cameraman) 34
McEvoy, Freddie 16, 136, 139, **143**, (rape trial 144, 145), 147, 155, 164, 184, 190, 208, 209, 220, **221**, 228
McEwan, Walter (asst. to Hal Wallis) 34, 47, 60
McHugh, Frank **88**
McHugh, Jimmy **185**
McLane, Barton 53
McMartin, Duncan 223, **227**, 232, 233, 236
McWilliams, Paul (WB studio doctor) 134
Menjou, Adolphe **72**
Mendoza, Harry **153**
Methot, Mayo **88**
Meyer, Johnny (WB publicist and Flynn assistant) 103, 108, 109, 110
Mexico 60, 123, 146, 147, 159, 163, 176, 179; Acapulco 147, 151, 164, 175, 178, 229; Asunción Bay 89; Baja 171; Cap (Cabo) San Lucas 77; Cedros Island 177; Cuernavaca 123, 159; Ensenada 62, 77; Guadalupe Island 177; Isles of San Benito 177; Mazatlan 86, 87 Mexico City 104, 123, 135, 139, 151, 159, 160, **164**, 177; Morelia **279**; Xochimilco 147
MGM **79**, 173, 174, 196, 203, 206, **207**, 210, 211, 212, 213, 216, 228, 282, 290
Michel, Willy **54**
Mid-Manhattan Magistrate Court **203**
Milestone, Lewis (WB director) 213, 229
Miller, Dusty 16
Mills, John 263
MIMI 28
Mirisch, Walter 264
Mitchell, Julien **101**, 102
Mitchell, Thomas **184**
Monaco **220**, **221**, 222, 226 (Monte Carlo) 252, 265, 267, 268, 271
Monmouth Park-Ocean Port, NJ 300
MONTANA **200**, **201**, **202**, 207, 208, 213, 219, **258**
Montgomery, George 187
Montgomery, Robert 41
Morden Hall-Surrey, England **238**
Morgan, Dennis 134, **147**, 306
Morris, Wayne **88**, **112**
Motion Picture Costumers Ball 284
Movie Stars Parade magazine 197
Mowbray, Alan 167
Muir, Jean 32, 33, 34 118
Mullen, J.G. (WB publicity agent) 104, 105
Mundin, Herbert 48, 63, 69
MURDER AT MONTE CARLO 28, **29**, 35, 36, 41, 67
Murray, Ken 100, 101
Musumeci, Enzo (fencing instructor) **248**
MUTINY ON THE BOUNTY (1935 film) 177
My Wicked, Wicked Ways 11, 18, **296**, 302, 304, 305, **308**
Nadi, Aldo 163, 226
Nagel, Conrad **125**
Napier, Diana 67
Napoleon, Art 282, **283**, 285, 286, 287,
Nassau 232, **233**
Nathan, Paul (secretary to Hal Wallis) 81, 125
Navarro, Ramon 78
Neal, Patricia 186
Neagle, Anna 259, **261**, **262**, 265, **266**,
Negulesco, Jean (WB director) 40, 182
NEVER SAY GOODBYE **167**, **168**, **169**, **170**, 177, **205**, 206
New Guinea 9, 11, Edie Creek 16, 19; Fincafen 21; Fio(r) 21; Kaparoko 18; Kavieng 15; Kenabot Plantation 15; Kikori 19; Kokopo 15; Laloki Plantation 18, **19**, 20; New Britain 22; Obamobu plantation 19; Port Moresby 17, 19, 20; Rabaul **15**, **16**, 22, 23; Rouna Falls 18; Saddleberg 21; Sepik River 16; Siassi Island Plantation 16; Taurama Point 17; Tavai 17; Umboi 16; Vitu Plantation 22
New Guinea Diary **21**, **22**, 312, 314
New Mexico: 10; Albuquerque **87**, **88**, 111; Fort Marey Park **111**; Gallup 88, 217, **218**; Hyde State Park **112**; McGaffey Lake **218**; Santa Fe **111**

Newquay (Fistral Bay), Cornwall 7, **238**, 239
Nightclubs and restaurants: 21, NYC 292; 400 Club, London 57; Ambassador East Hotel, Chicago **198**; Bonne Auberge-Cannes **252**; Brown Derby, Hollywood 51, 117, **129**, 165; Café LaMaze, Hollywood 42, 44, **50**, **81**; Cameo, NYC **269**; Cave Supper Club-Vancouver, Canada **305**; Chasen's, Hollywood 149, 271; Ching How, North Hollywood 125; Ciro's, Hollywood 102, 109, 123, **160**, 163, **165**, 226, 229; Club Del Mar-Santa Monica, CA **231**; Club Du Vieux Colombier, Paris **209**; Club Sirocco (owned by Flynn), Acapulco 229, 260; Cock and Bull, West Hollywood 285; Cocoanut Grove, Los Angeles 132, **270**, 271; Cotton Club-Culver City, CA 41; Da Bouttea's, Cannes **211**; Earl Carroll Theater, **81**, 163; Eagle's Nest Lodge-Catalina, CA 94; El Morocco, NYC 86, 198, **203**, 208, 227, 237, 256, 268, 292, 299; Finocchio Club, San Francisco 174; Florentine Gardens, Hollywood 117; George's American Bar, Rome **253**; Hawaiian Hut, Catalina 120; Hollywood Palladium 131; King's Club, Hollywood 32, 33; La Conga, NYC **94**; La Fonda restaurant-Santa Fe, NM **111**, 112; La Tour d'Argent, Paris 209, 211; Lido, London 291; Mayfair Club, Beverly Hills 44; Mermaid Club (now The Rainbow)- Hollywood 76; Mocambo, The-Hollywood **114**, **123**, 132, 134, 139, **151**, **155**, **169**, 173, 186, **187**, **228**, **232**; Panorama Roof-Vancouver, Canada 305; Pirates' Den, Hollywood 103; Ristorante Passetto, Rome **251**; Romanoff's, Beverly Hills **112**, 167, 171, 195, 202, 229; Sardi's, NYC **288**; Stork, NYC 235, 299; Trocadero, The-Hollywood 32, 35, 45, 78, **93**, **163**; Tropicana-Havana, Cuba 226; Usher's Bar-Sydney, Australia 16; Villa Frascati, Hollywood **302**
Night Of 100 Stars 262, **263**
Nimmi **238**
Niven, David **43**, 57, 58, **77**, **78**, 79, 81, 288
NORTHERN PURSUIT **148**, **149**, **150**, 151, 163, **205**
North Island Navy Base-San Diego, CA **114**
Oakie, Jack 78, 169, 306, **307**
Oberon, Merle 132, 210, 213
OBJECTIVE, BURMA! 142, **155**, **156**, **157**, **158**, 161, 164, **167**, 169, **170**, **205**, 244
O'Brien, Edmund 260
Obringer, Roy (WB legal counsel) 29, 30, 32, 41, 42, **43**, 46, 51, 53, 57, 66, 67, 69, 70, 71, 72, 73, **74**, 77, 87, 93, 95, 97, 98, 99, 103, 104, 106, 107, 114, 115, 116, 122, 125, 126, 127, 128, 130, 133, 135, 139, 148, 149, 150, 155, 160, **165**, 175, 179, 181, 182, 183, 186, 188, 189, 194, 196, 197, 199, 200, 201, 202, 203, 209, 211, 225, 244, 247
O'Connor, Una **99**, **102**
O'Driscoll, Martha **153**
O'Hara, Maureen 174, **230**, **232**
Olivier, Laurence 230, **263**,
Olsen, Jack **266**
Olsen, Moroni 96, **105**
O'Moore, Patrick **127**
O'Neill, Henry **106**, 107
Onyx (Flynn's horse) **190**, **218**, 219
Page, Don (WB production manager and asst. director) 167, 168, 169, 175
Pallette, Eugene 62, **63**, 69
Palmer, Lilli 254, 256, 260
Panama: 175; Canal 178, 179; Colon 179; San Blas Islands 178, 179
Pantages Theater, The 272
Panther, Helen 237
Paramount Pictures 163, **168**, 191
PARDON MY FRENCH 213
Park, Arthur (MCA agent) 173, 186, 187, 194, 196, 199, 202, 203, 209, 223
Parker, Eleanor 122, 132, **168**, **169**, **170**, 172, 173
Parker, Jean **88**,
Parks, Mrs. Madge 20
Parola, Danièle **211**
Parsons, Louella **57**, 95, 99, **100**, 168, 200
Patrick, Millicent **230**
Pavlenko, Alex (Flynn's butler) 125, 162, 169, 180
PEEKS AT HOLLYWOOD (short) 167
PERFECT SPECIMEN, THE 57, 58, **59**, 60, 64, **83**, 206
Peron, President Juan 261
Petits Lits Blancs charity ball-Deauville, France **264**
Pevney, Joseph (Universal director) 271,
Photoplay Magazine 59, 60, 69, 74, 114, 152, 207
Picerni, Paul **209**
Pickens, Slim **217**
Pickfair 45
Pickford, Mary **45**, **166**, 261, 275
Pigeon, Walter 168, 169, 208, 261
PIRATE PARTY ON CATALINA ISLAND 42
Polito, Sol **91**
Porter, Cole 168

Powell, William 46, 174, 196
Power, Tyrone 77, 132, 139, **211**, **279**
Presle, Micheline 219
Price, Vincent 217, 220, 264, 279, **286**
PRINCE AND THE PAUPER, THE 47, 50, **51**, **52**, 53, 56, 57, 58, **83**
Prince, William **156**
Prinz, Leroy 139
PRIVATE LIVES OF ELIZABETH AND ESSEX, THE 89, **90**, **91**, **92**, **93**, **94**, 95, 104, **141**
Puig, Eva **159**
Quinn, Anthony 154, **231**, 232
RABBIT HOOD 213
Radio shows: Armed Forces Radio System **157**; *As You Like It* (radio play, not performed) 60; Band Wagon radio 173; Campbell Soup radio show 192; Cavalcade Of America, The (They Died With Their Boots On) 124 Chase and Sanborn Hour 78, 109; Eddie Cantor Show, The 124; Gulf Screen Guild Theater (Mr. & Mrs Smith) 126; Hollywood Hotel (Captain Blood) 40, (Charge of the Light Brigade) 49, (Green Light) (The Prince and the Pauper) 53 and 57; Hollywood Star Preview (Night Operator) 190; In Town Tonight **256**; "Kim" 232; KNX radio (Holiday) 94; Lady Esther Guild Theater (Gentleman Jim) 154; Let Yourself Go 165; Lux Hour 51, 53, (Captain Blood) 54, (British Agent) 58, 64, (These Three) 67, (Green Light) **71**, (The Perfect Specimen) 85, 98, 99, (Trade Wind) 100, (Virginia City) 117; "Magnificent Rogue, The" 271; Modern Adventures of Casanova 228, 229, **230**, 231, 233, 246, 250; NBC Radio (For Richer, For Poorer) **125**; Phillip Morris Playhouse radio (The Lady Vanishes) 125; Screen Guide radio show 49, (Allergic To Ladies) 110; Sealtest Village Store 173; Silver Theater 122, 124; Standard Brands Rudy Vallee Radio Show (Captain Blood) 41; Theatre of Romance Radio (Gentleman Jim) **173**; Variety Review 90
Raft, George 231
Raine, Norman Reilly (WB screenwriter) 67
Rains, Claude 69, **102**
Ralph, Jesse 35, **36**
Rape trial 136, **137**, **138**, 42, 142, **143**; 321 St. Pierre Road, Bel Air **145**; ABCDEF **146**; Black, Morris "Morrie" **137**; Bolling, Police Lieutenant R. W. 136, 143, 144, 146; Boyer, Lynne 136, 137, 143, **145**; Brabon, Helga 144; Cathcart-Jones, Elizabeth (Mrs. Owen) 124; Cathcart-Jones, Captain Owen **144**, 146; Clemenshaw, Prof. C.M. **145**, 146; Cochran, Thomas W. (district attorney and prosecutor) **138**, 143, **144**, 145, **146**; Dell, Roland 136; Dockweiler, District Attorney John F. 146; Douglas H.W. 146; Eads, Lloyd 146; Faulconer, Municipal Judge Oda 137; Ford, Robert E. (Flynn's attorney) 136, **138**, 139, 143, **144**, 145, 146; Geraldi, Joseph **137**; Giesler, Jerry (Flynn's attorney) 137, **138**, 139, 143, **144**, **146**; Gray, Dr. Etta 138, 143, **144**; Green, Stella 145; Hanly, Philip N. 145; Griffith Park Observatory 146; HANSEN, BETTY (aka Bunnie Baker) 136, **137**, 143, **144**, 145, 146; Harvey, Patricia 145; Jones, Leland 146; Hopkins, John (prosecutor) 143, **144**, 146, 145; **jury:** Anderson, Ruby (jury forewoman) 143, **146**, Boehm, Lorene 143, **146**, Boyd, Charles 143, Chalfont, Mrs. A. (alternate juror) 143, 144, Curtis, Warren 143 Forbes, Elaine 143, Leahy, Mildred 143, **146**, Jacobsmeyer, Homer 143, Larson, Jennie 143, **146**, Minear, Nellie 143 Morgan, Lena 143, **146**, Welch, Georgette 143, Wood, Teresa 143, **146**; Knapp, Armand **137**; Jebbink, Joe and Sophie 145; Kingsley, Hayward (Sirocco skipper) 145; Longworth, Jean **145**, 146; Los Angeles District Attorney's Office 138; Los Angeles Federal Building (and Hall of Justice) 132, 133, **143**, **147**; Los Angeles Juvenile Control Division 84, 136, 145; Maurer, J.W. 144; McClure, Joe 146; Mervyn, Mona 145; Morgan, Virginia 144; Moss, Leonard V. 146; Moxom, Fred (bailiff) 143; "Mr. X" 146; Odell, Addie E. 145; Oliver, Corporal Hubert L. 144; Patterson, Elaine **145**; Pope, C. D. 146; Pulas, Dorothy (policewoman) **137**; Rooney, Henry 144; Ross, Private Martin E. 145; Ross, Mary 144; Satterlee, Florence 143, 144; Satterlee, Mickey June 143, 144, 145; SATTERLEE, PEGGY LARUE **120**, **137**, **138**, 143, **145**, 146; Still, Judge Leslie E. 143, **144**, 146; Sutton, Jay M. 144; Toupes, Agnes "Chi-Chi" 136, 137, 143, 145; Veitch, Deputy District Attorney Arthur 139; Walker, Police Sergeant Edward 136, 144; Walters, Judge Byron J. 137, 138; White, Eddie 136
Raphael, Stephen 136, 203, 208, 224, 227
Rathbone, Basil 7, 33, **38**, 42, 58, **62**, 64, 66, 67, **69**, 77, **78**, 90, 167, 236
Raymond, Gene 45
RCA **107**
Reagan, Ronald **105**, **106**, 126, **127**, **128**, **130**, 174
"Reckon I'm In Love" 201

Reeves, George 95
Regas, George 49
Reichow, Otto 296, 297, *304*, 306, *307*
Reinhardt, Max 42
Remley, Frankie *225*
Republic Pictures 247
Revanent, George *228*
Reynolds, Gene 106
Reynolds, Marjorie *225*
Ridgely, John 183
Roach, Hal 123
Roark, Aidan 80, *81*
Robinson, Edward G. *185*, 193, 261
Robinson, Frances *88*, *101*
Robson, Flora *98*, *99*, *108*, 125
Robson, May 58
Rockman, Michael *124*
Roma, Tony (producer) 251, 252
ROCKY MOUNTAIN 215, 216, *217*, 220, 221, 232, *258*
Roman, Ruth 213, *229*
Romanoff, Michael 132, 306, *307*
Rooney, Mickey 10, 125, 132, 184, *302*, 306, *307*
Roosevelt, Eleanor (Mrs. Franklin D.) *86*
Roosevelt, Elliot 169
Roosevelt, President Franklin D. *86*, 166
Roosevelt, Franklin, Jr. 111
Roosevelt, James, Jr. 86, 162, 169
ROOTS OF HEAVEN, THE 259, 288, *289*, *290*, *291*, *292*, *309*
Rory, Rossana *273*, *274*, 277
Rosenbloom, Maxie *88*
Ross, Bob (WB unit manager) 79
Rossellini, Roberto 209
Rubenstein, Serge 265
Royal Park of Capodimonte-Naples, Italy *248*
Royce, Mr. F.R. (WB Teddington) 30
Russell, Rosalind 71, *72*, *73*, 208
Rutherford, Ann *196*
Ryan, Jack 19
Sakal, S.Z. 202
Sala, Eduardo (Zaca helmsman) *276*
Salkind, Alexander 267
SAN ANTONIO *159*, *160*, *161*, *162*, *163*, *167*, 172, *205*
Sandklef, Ulla (Miss Sweden) *256*
San Fernando (CA) Mission 228
San Juan, Olga 260
SANTA FE TRAIL 104, 105, *106*, 107, 108, *109*; junket: *111*, *112*, *141*, Hatch, Carl (New Mexico senator) *111*, 112, Jinx (junket mascot) *109* Miles, John E. (Governor of New Mexico) *111*, Ortiz, Alfredo (mayor of Santa Fe, NM) 112, Seth Hall *112* Tio Coco *111*
Santa Monica Superior Court *270*
SARATOGA TRUNK 175
Sasha (photographer) *25*
Saunders, Russ (WB asst. director) 182, 185
Savage, Yvonne *275*
Sawyer, Joe *118*, *119*
Scala, Gia *273*, *274*
Schaefer, Bill (exec. secretary to Jack Warner) 108, 186
Schneider, Romy *281*
Scott, Randolph 95, 96
Screen Actors Guild 106, 200
Screen Gems 270
SCREEN SNAPSHOTS 47, 50, *58* (17th anniversary party), 78
Scripps Institute of Oceanography 176, 177, *193*
SEA HAWK, THE 9, 41, 45, 47, 89, 94, 97, *98*, *99*, *101*, *102*, 103, 105, 106, *108*, *132*, *141*; Albatross (prop ship) *98*, 101, 102, *108*, 182, 183, 235
"Sea Rogue, The" 233
SEA WOLF, THE 182
Seldes, George 55
Selzer, Ed (WB producer) 114, 197
Selznick, David O. *166*
Selznick, Myron (agent) 50, 81, (agency) 94, 103, (agency) 109, 122
Semels, Harry *76*
Sennett, Max 185
Shaw, George Bernard 28
Shayne, Robert *160*
Shedlo, Ronald *278*, 293, 294, 297, 299, 300, 303, 306, 307
Sheerer, Norma 46, 78
Shepherd, Jeanne *191*
Sheridan, Ann *89*, 99, *135*, *138*, 147, 182, 183, 185, *186*, 187, 192
Sherman, George (Universal director) *230*, 232
Sherman, Vincent (WB director) 116, *187*, 189, *190*, *192*, *196*, 197
SHE'S WORKING HER WAY THROUGH COLLEGE *229*

Shields, Arthur *169*
Shields, Frank 44
Ships: California Clipper *108*; D'Artagnan 23; HMS Queen Elizabeth 202; HMS Queen Mary *54*, *57*, 81, 208; Ile de France, 214, *291*; Lottie Bennett 177; Morinda 17; M.V. Macdhui 19; Nankin 22; SS Compiegne *23*; SS Friderun 22; SS Liberté ; 235, 237; SS Lurline 74, *79*, 113, *114*; SS Matsonia 79; SS Montoro *15*, 16 ; SS Paris 29; Tanda 23; SS Wahoo (submarine) 151; SS Washington 176; USS Enterprise 115; USS Forrestal 282
Shore, Dinah 187
Shourds, Sherry (WB asst. director) 91
Showdown 160, 163, 172, *173*, 238
Siegel, Bugsy 126
Siegel, Don *192*
SILVER RIVER 181, *182*, *183*, *184*, *185*, *186*, 187, 196, 197, *198*, 199, *205*, 208
Silvers, Phil 216
Sinatra, Frank *187*,
Sinclair, Ronald *127*, *128*
Sioux Indian Induction Ceremony *124*
SISTERS, THE 73, 75, *76*, 77, 78, 79, *83*, 206
Skelton, Red 174, *185*, *303*
Smith, Alexis *116*, 131, *132*, *134*, 147, 159, *161*, *162*, 182, 201, *202*, *207*, 208, 213, *287*, 306
Smith, C. Aubrey 71, *74*
Smith, Kate 97, 98, 122, *124*, *154*, 156
SOME OF THE BEST 209
Sophie (Flynn's Beverly Hills maid) 102
Sothern, Ann 191
South American tour 103, *104*
Spain: Barcelona 54, 55, *266*, 267, 268, 276; Guadalajara *56*; Madrid 56, 57; Mallorca 267, 268, 269, 276, 281, 282, 285, 301; Valencia 56
Spanish Civil War Diary *55*, *56*, 314, 315, 316
Spiegel, Sam 193
Stack, Robert 193, 208
Stackpole, Peter *120*, (rape trial 138, 143, 144, *145*, 146), 198
Stacy, Eric (WB asst. director) 117, 126, 127, 128, 129, 130
Stafford, Richard (Zaca skipper) 265, 271, 273
Stage work: *Master of Thornfield, The* 289, 290, 294; King's Theatre, Glasgow *Man's House, A* 28; Malvern Festival *Man's House, A* 28; *Marvellous History of Saint Bernard*, 28; *Moon And Yellow River, The* 28; *Mutiny 28, The, Tragical History Of Dr. Faustus, The* 28; New Theatre, London *Man's House, A* 28; Northampton Opera House *By Candle Light* 27 Northampton Repertory Company 24, 25, *27*, *237*, 263; *9:45* 27; *Crime At Blossoms, The* 26; *Bulldog Drummond* 26; *Conflict* 27; *Doll's House, A* 26; *Fake, The* 27; *Farmer's Wife, The* 27; *Grain Of Mustard Seed, The* 27; *Green Bay Tree, The* 27; *On The Spot* 26; *Othello* 27; *Paddy The Next Best Thing* 27; *Pygmalion* 26; *Seven Keys To Baldpate Inn* 27; *Sheppey* 27; *Soul Of Nicholas Snyders, The* 27; *Sweet Lavender* 26; *Thirteenth Chair, The* *26*; *Wind And The Rain, The* 27; *Yellow Sands* 26
Stanton, Will *143*
Stanwyck, Barbara *67*, *77*, *157*, *174*, *175*
Stark, Juanita 147
Stauffer, Teddy *177*, 281, 291
Steele, Anthony *239*, 240, 242
Steele, Freddie (Flynn's boxing double) 132
Stein, Jules (president of MCA) 130
Stephenson, Henry 44
Stevens, Craig 156, *168*, 306
Stewart, Jimmy *200*, 216
Stockwell, Dean *214*, 232
Stone, Lewis *72*
Strand Theater, New York City 33, 124, 164, 172, 187, 191, 198, 219, 222
STREETCAR NAMED DESIRE, A *226*
Stroheim, Erich von 157
Stuart, Mary *190*
Studios de Boulogne-Billancourt, Paris *291*,
Sturgo, Dr. Ellis 250, 251, *268*,
Sugar Bowl Ski Resort-Norden, CA 101, 125
Sullivan, Jean *152*
SUN ALSO RISES, THE 259, *279*, *280*, 282, *309*
Sutherland, Eddie (director) 167
Swanson, Gloria 208
Tailwaggers Foundation *77*
Tangier 265, 267, *276*,
Thiel's Plantation *22*
Tang, Frank *155*
Taplinger, Robert (WB director of publicity) 74, 75, 79, 81, 86, 87, 95, 124
Taylor, Robert 77
TEA FOR TWO *219*
Teddington Studios-Middlesex, England 24, 28

Television shows: Arthur Murray Party, The 292; Big Surprise, The *277*, *278*; Colgate Comedy Hour 231; Errol Flynn Theater, The 270, 274, *275*, *276*, 277; "Gold en Shanty, The" *301*, 307; Jack Paar Show, The *294*; Martha Rae Show, The 268, 269; Masquerade Party 256; In Town Tonight 261; Red Skelton Show, The 259, *303*; Steve Allen Show, The 277, 288; "Sword Of Villon" *270*, 273; Toast Of The Town *234*, 235, 236; What's My Line? 281, 288; "Without Incident" 277, *278*, 281
Temple, Shirley 174, 207
Tennis clubs and tournaments: Berkley (CA) TC *174*; Beverly Hills TC 59, *85*, 95; Film Players Tennis Tournament 91; Grossinger Canteen-by-Mail charity event, NYC 164; Lakeside CC, Burbank *33*, 49, 73, 273, 280, 285; Los Angeles TC *32*, 33, 45, *48*, 70, 91, 94, *108*; Midwick CC-Alhambra, Riviera Country CC-Pacific Palisades, CA *284*; 70; Motion Picture TT 158; Pacific Southwest Tennis Championships *108*; Palm Springs RC 98, 195, *196* Westside TC-Cheviot Hills, CA 44, 45, 48, *58*, *62*, 98, 143, 158, 191
Thalians event *273*
Thamar, Tilda *211*, 254
THANK YOUR LUCKY STARS *139*, *143*, 152
THAT FORSYTE WOMAN 174, 202, 203, 206, *207*, 208, 210, 211, *212*, *258*
That's What You Jolly Well Get 139, *143*
Thatcher, Torin 272
Thaxter, Phyllis 217
THEY DIED WITH THEIR BOOTS ON 117, *118*, *119*, 120, *121*, *122*, *123*, *124*, 125, 134, *141*
Thomas, Tony 289
Thomson Productions 135, 148, 152, 158, *167*, 169, 174, 175, 181, 208
Three Musketeers, The audio recording 175, 176, *181*
Tierney, Gene 154, 167
Tilden, Bill 136, 145, *164*, 180
TLA movie theater-Philadelphia, PA 7
Tobias, George *156*
Todd's Hollywood Clothes (ad) *220*
Tonnara Florio (castle)-Palermo, Italy *244*
TOO MUCH, TOO SOON 259, 282, *283*, 284, *285*, *286*, *287*, *288*, *309*
Topping, Dan 155
Toscanini, Arturo 104
Tracy, Spencer 185
Travilla, Bill 189, *198*
Treacher, Arthur 167
Trilling, Steve (asst. to Jack Warner) 104, 126, 148, 149, 159, 161, 162, 165, 166, 173, 175, 179, 182, 183, 186, *187*, 188, 189, 190, 191, 194, 198, 200, 202, 234, 235, 236, 237, 239, 240, 241, 242, 243, 245, 246, 247, 249, 250, 282, 283, 284, 285, 288
Troup, Bobby *269*
Trujillo, President Rafael 282
Tucker, Forrest *169*, 183
Turner, Don (Flynn's double) 189, 194, 196, 219
Turner, Lana 126, 197, 210
Tyne, George *155*, *156*
Ulman, William A. 43, 49
UNCERTAIN GLORY 142, *152*, 153, 154, 155, 174, *205*, 206, 208
Underwood, Agnes *147*
Union Air Terminal (now Bob Hope Airport)-Burbank, CA 114, *165*
Union Station, Los Angeles 87, *306*
United Artists 268
United Jewish Appeal, The 231
Universal (International) Pictures 226, 270, 271, 272, 276
University of Alabama football team *69*
USO 118, 119, 154; Victory Tour of Alaska: *153*, 154 Korea tour: *225*, 226
Vallee, Rudy 41, 103, *111*, *112*
Vancouver, Canada 301, 303, 304, *305*,
Vanderbilt, Gloria 125, 129
Van Pelt, Homer (WB photographer) 67
Vassaretti, Vittorio 248
Vaughn, Sonny (Flynn's manager) *214*
Velez, Lupe 109
Venice Film Festival 210, 244, 254
Venuta, Benay *225*
Villefranche, France 219, 222, 265, 268
VIRGINIA CITY 7, 94, *95*, *96*, *97*, 98, 99: junket: 100, *101*, *141*
Vitagraph Studios, Hollywood *37*, 40
Vi-Va Film-Mahon 248, 250
Volpi, Countess Natalia 254
Wald, Jerry (WB producer) 154, 155, 156, 164, 165, *181*, 182, 185, 186, *187*, 189
Walker, Clint *284*
Wallis, Hal (WB producer) 32, 33, 34, 36, 37, 38, 41, 42,

45, 46, 47, 48, 49, 50, 51, 53, 56, 57, 60, 62, 63, 64, 65, 66, 70, 71, 73, *74*, 79, 80, 81, 87, 89, 90, 94, 95, 98, 99, 100, 101, 102, 103, 104, 105, 107, 108, 110, 14, 117, 118, 119, 124, 125, 126, 127, 128, 129
Wallis, Minna (agent) 45
Walsh, Raoul 99, 119, 120, 122, 125, 126, 128, 132, 134, (rape trial 145, 146), 148, 149, *150*, 151, 157, 165, 166, *168*, 186, 197, 306, *307*
Warner, Ann (Mrs. Jack) 57, *81*, 132
Warner, Maj. Charles 183, 308
Warner, Jack L. 9, 24, 29, 30, 32, 35, 41, 45, 46, 50, 57, 60, 63, 64, 66, 67, 73, 74, 75, 78, *81*, *87*, *88*, 91, 93, 97, 98, 99, *100*, 103, 104, 105, 107, 108, *113*, *114*, 115, 116, 117, 118, 119, 121, 124, 126, 127, 130, 132, 133, 136, *138*, 139, 147, *148*, 154, 159, 160, 161, 163, (1801 Angelo Drive, Beverly Hills-home of 164), 165, *167*, 169, 173, 175, 179, *181*, 182, *184*, 185, 186, 187, 188, 191, 192, *193*, *194*, *195*, 196, 199, 201, 202, 203, 209, *210*, 211, 215, 240, 241, *244*, 245, 246, 250, 259, 283, 289, 300, 306
Warner Bros. Beverly Hills Theater 94, 172, *226*
Warner Bros. Calabasas Ranch 45, *70*, 77, *78*, 80, 81, 96, 97, 105, 106, 107, 120, 122, 123, *138*, 139, 157, 158, *160*, 162, *163*, 171, *183*, 185, 192, 200, *201*, 202, 207, 228
Warner Bros. Downtown Theater-Los Angeles 74, 101, 172
Warner Bros. Hollywood Theater 76, *81*, 105, 172
Warner Bros. New Ranch *200*
Warner Bros. New York Theater 234
WARRIORS, THE (THE DARK AVENGER in the U.K.) 259, *263*, *264*, 265, 267, 269, *309*
Warwick, John 19
Wasserman, Lou (MCA agent) 130, 139, 159, 160, 165, 175, 188, 198, 211
Wayne, John 104, 310
Welles, Orson 173, *177*, 178
Weismuller, Johnny 103, 306
Welbourne, Scotty (WB photographer) *61*
West Los Angeles Police Station *284*
Westmore, Bud (WB makeup man) 134, *230*
Westmore, Perc (WB head of makeup) 48, 50, 62, 95, 97, 117, 182
"When I Fall In Love" 272
White Rajah, The 42, 43, *45*, 47, 49, (*The Life of the First Rajah of Sarawak* 85), 99, 184
White Witch of Rosehall (variously titled *White Witch of the Indies*) 261, 262, 281, 282
Wilcox, Frank *105*
Wilcox, Herbert *261*, 265, *266*, 268, 269, 275
Wilde, Cornell 193
Wilder, Cy (WB treasurer) 32, 85, 99, 197
Wiles, Buster 123, 124, 131, 132, 135, 136, 137, 143, (rape trial 145,) 147, 151, 154, 158, *306*
Wilk, Jacob (story editor) 41, 57
Willes, Peter 77, *78*
William, Warren 46
William Tell 74
WILLIAM TELL 7, 206, 251, 252, *253*, 254, *255*, 267, 268, 272, 273, 275 , 276, 280
Williams, Esther *286*
Williams, Guinn "Big Boy" *88*, *96*, *97*, 109, *217*, 306, *307*
Williams, Rush *217*
Wilson, Lucy 17
Winchell, Walter 148, *187*
Windsor, Claire *88*
Winters, Shelley 193, 208, *260*
Wood, Sam 172
Wooley, Sheb *217*
Wright, Cobina 109, *200*
Wright, Tenny (production manager) 45, 47, 50, 51, 53, 57, 60, 62, 118, 66, 67, 69, 75, 80, 89, 91, 93, 97, 98, 99, 100, 102, 106, 107, 108, 117, 120, 121, 122, 123, 125, 127, 128, 129, 131, 133, 134, 135, *136*, 149, 150, 155, 156, 157, 163, 165, 166, 167, 168, 169, 182, 183, 185, 190, 192, 193, 194, 195, 196, 197, 200, 201, 202
Wyatt, Al (Flynn's double) 242, 245
Wymore, Patrice (third wife) 217, *218*, *219*, *220*, 222, *223*, *224*, *226*, *228*, *229*, *233*, 235, *236*, 245, 247, *252*, *253*, *274*, *255*, *256*, 259, *260*, *262*, *265*, *266*, *267*, 268, *270*, *271*, *273*, *274*, *275*, *276*, 277, 278, *281*, 282, 285, 286, *287*, 289, 290, 292, 293, 295, 296, 297, 299, 300, 304, *306*, *307*, 308
Wynn, Keenan 168
YANKEE DOODLE DANDY 147, 175
Yates, Herbert 247
Young, Collier (WB producer) 182, 186
Young, Edward *12*
Young, Gig *171*, *172*
Young, Loretta 208
Young, Robert *207*
"Zaca Jamaican Adventure, The" 199
Zanuck, Daryl F. 210, 259, 288, 289, *290*, *291*, *292*